EASTERN

COASTAL

ATLANTIC OCEAN

ALL ONE BODY:
The Story Of The
NORTH CAROLINA
LUTHERAN SYNOD
1803-1993

By
Raymond M. Bost
and
Jeff L. Norris

HISTORICAL COMMITTEE
North Carolina Synod
Evangelical Lutheran Church in America
1988 Lutheran Synod Drive
Salisbury, NC 28144

Published by North Carolina Synod, Evangelical Lutheran Church in America
1988 Lutheran Synod Dr.
Salisbury, North Carolina 28144

Printed in the United States of America

First Edition, 1994

Library of Congress Catalogue Card Number: 94-66008

By
Raymond M. Bost
and
Jeff L. Norris

ISBN 0-9641126-0-4

This book was printed by Delmar Printing Co.
Charlotte, North Carolina.

HISTORICAL COMMITTEE
North Carolina Synod
Evangelical Lutheran Church in America
1988 Lutheran Synod Drive
Salisbury, NC 28144
(704) 633-4861

TABLE OF CONTENTS

Preface   v

I.   The Scattering (1741)   1

II.   A Move Toward Unity (1709-1803) 13

III.   Division (1804-1837) 45

IV.   Slavery, Sectionalism (1838-1860) 69

V.   The Ordeal of War (1861-1865) 111

VI.   Surrender and Its Aftermath (1866-1869) 139

VII.   From Servant to Leader (1870-1902) 177

VIII.   Toward Union (1903-1920) 221

IX.   Reunited under ULCA (1921-1962) 243

X.   LCA in North Carolina (1963-1987) 281

XI.   Epilogue: ELCA in North Carolina (1988-1993) 321

Notes 335

Bibliography 385

Index 399

PREFACE

This book is a history of the North Carolina Synod through the formation of the Evangelical Lutheran Church in America in 1988 and its predecessor bodies. An important part of that history involves other Lutheran bodies in North Carolina with which the North Carolina Synod has interacted - the Tennessee and Missouri synods and the American Lutheran Church.

But the story, unfortunately, does not represent all Lutheran synods or congregations in the state. It does not, for example, encompass those congregations in North Carolina which represent other current Lutheran bodies: the Wisconsin Synod (with congregations in Charlotte, China Grove, Fayetteville, Greensboro, Hendersonville and Raleigh), the Church of the Lutheran Confessions (Hendersonville), the Old Apostolic Lutheran Church (under the Elders of Lapland in Wilmington), and the Apostolic Lutheran Church (High Point). Neither does it treat the role of those Lutheran congregations in the state which are not affiliated with a synod or association of churches. To those congregations and their members go our apologies if this story of the North Carolina Synod appears to speak for all Lutherans in the state. The appearance is not intentional.

The cover of this volume contains the names of two authors, but the project has many contributors.

Among the earliest contributors are the members of the Historical Committee of the North Carolina Synod, who began planning this volume in 1984, critiqued its drafts in later years and supervised its completion ten years later. Those serving on the committee during the decade included Martha W. Agner, Mary Anna Bader, Paul B. Beatty, John H. Bollinger, Robert M. Calhoon, James A. Chesky, Bernard Wm. Cruse, Jr., Mark J. Ericson, Gary R. Freeze, Ted W. Goins, Harry D. Hawthorne, Luther L. Knauff, Bob L. Mowery, Karl M. Park, Helen Peacock, Donald M. Phillips, George L. Rhyne, Catherine Safrit, Eleanor E. Sifford, Virginia Smith, M. Luther Stirewalt and Sarah Walker.

Michael C. D. McDaniel, bishop of the synod from 1982 to 1991, facilitated the project by promoting the employment of a synod historian, Raymond M. Bost, in 1986 to initiate the research and writing. Later, in the closing year of the project, he helped by recommending a second author, providing valuable insights into the synod's history during the period of his episcopate, and writing the section which closes the final chapter.

This work is the genius of Raymond M. Bost. Through his comprehensive and meticulous research, coupled with his distinctive approach to church history and his articulate writing, he has pieced together, especially in the first six chapters, a story of the synod unmatched in contextual analysis.

The fruits of his research also bring life to some of the later chapters, but, regrettably, he was unable to write those chapters because of the demands on his time when he became president of Newberry College.

This author is indebted to Bost for his inspiration, but also to many others who assisted in the completion of the final chapters during 1993-94.

Karl M. Park, the chairman of the Historical Committee, and George L. Rhyne, the bishop's representative to the committee, shepherded the project, providing both encouragement and logistical support. Park also assisted in the research and provided valuable guidance to archival resources.

Readers and evaluators of the draft of the book were Martha W. Agner, H. George Anderson, Robert M. Calhoon, Ray A. Cline, Bernard Wm. Cruse, Jr., Albert H. Keck, Karl M. Park, Michael C. D. McDaniel, Ernest L. Misenheimer, Catherine B. Norris and M. Luther Stirewalt.

Martha W. Agner, Robert M. Calhoon and M. Luther Stirewalt gave special skills to redirecting and fine-tuning some of the emphases, nuances and interpretations. Calhoon also contributed valuable historian and editorial insights, especially in Chapters I, III and VIII, and in the first two paragraphs of this preface. Assisting Calhoon in his contributions were Craig Fox and Lori Watson.

Bernard Wm. Cruse, Jr., volunteered long hours of his computer wizardry to formatting each page of the book, repairing the typesetting mistakes of the authors and compiling the index.

To my wife, Catherine B. Norris, goes a special word of thanks. She was not only gracious in forsaking social activities and handyman services for a period of nine months, but she helped generously and with no small measure of wisdom in all stages of the project, from research and writing to copyreading and proofreading. Without her valuable aid and encouragement, the project could not have been completed.

Raymond M. Bost joins me in expressing a debt to those individuals who in the past have written histories of the North Carolina Synod; we trust that this study will do justice to the foundations they laid. But we entertain no illusions that "All One Body" will be the final history of the church of our fathers. As Historian Clement Eaton has observed, "it will always be in the nature of historical writing that it is never finished or definitive." We only hope that this work will be as useful to future historians as the work of earlier historians has been to us. ✟

Jeff L. Norris
Hickory, North Carolina
March 3, 1994

CHAPTER I

migration from Germany to the New World in the eighteenth century was an adventure of staggering proportions. Henry Melchoir Muhlenberg, the patriarch of Lutheranism in colonial America, was one of seventy-five thousand Germans who made their way to the North American colonies before the American Revolution.[1] He left the University of Halle in the autumn of 1741. His teacher, the famous pietist scholar Gotthilf August Francke, advised him to seek the help of the Lutheran chaplain in the court of George II in securing appointment as a missionary in British North America.

Muhlenberg sailed for South Carolina on June 13, 1742, on a ship infested with rats and with steerage filled with cursing, angry English passengers. Calm seas and scant wind extended the voyage to more than three months; water ran low, and famished rats tried to lick sweat from sleeping passengers' faces.[2] Another German immigrant remembered the "awful misery, stink, smoke, horror, vomiting, seasickness of all kinds, fever, purgings, headaches, sweats, constipations . . . which do arise from stale and strongly-salted food and meat and from the exceeding badness and nastiness of the water."[3]

What circumstances led so many not simply to leave the Fatherland and seek domicile in a neighboring European country, but to risk their lives to colonize America? One of the major factors contributing to the removal of Germans from their homeland to the New World was warfare and the disruption of normal patterns of livelihood by the creation, sustaining and movements of military forces. The first Germans to come to Carolina were from the Palatinate, a portion of Germany bordering the Rhine River. Because of its proximity to France, a major power in seventeenth century Europe, the area was hard hit by a number of tragedies.

The Thirty Years' War (1618-48) "unveiled the barbarity of seventeenth-century warfare" in its initial phases in Austria and Bohemia, but when the battle scene shifted to the Palatinate "a new stage of atrocity was reached...."[4] The long-standing assumption that it was appropriate for a conquered people to provide housing for the army of occupation was expanded. Spanish conquerors demanded not only shelter for their soldiers, but services and provisions for the troops and enough revenues to cover the soldiers' pay.

Formerly, governments inclined toward militarism had been restrained by the drain imposed on their own national treasury by the maintenance of armies. The innovation of the Duke of Alva in requiring a conquered people to underwrite the total cost of one's military operation opened up the possibility of extensive military operations without the usual financial burdens associated with waging war. War became "an attractive business so long as cash or property could be forced from the populace."[5]

This new method of supporting military operations which was introduced in the Rhine valley brought with it other excesses. If the civilian population was to provide the army of occupation with shelter, services, provisions and even the taxes necessary to pay the soldiers, then the civilians must not simply be conquered -- they must be thoroughly intimidated. Terrorism should not only be tolerated but encouraged; violence perpetrated against civilians by soldiers became the order of the day.

Legions of camp followers came in the wake of the military battalions. Soldiers did not hesitate to extort from the local populace whatever they desired for the support of camp followers who were objects of their special interest. When, in desperation, the despoiled peasants banded together to relieve their distress and suffering, they simply provided their military foes with an excuse to demonstrate that arbitrary power and the sword had superseded law and justice.

Defying precise description, Germany suffered greater destruction during the Thirty Years' War than at any other time in its history. And the Rhenish Palatinate was one of the areas most devastated by the conflict, the population dropping to only one-third of the pre-war figure.[6]

After the Thirty Years' War, the struggle began in the Palatinate to rebuild the farms and reclaim the lands that had succumbed to weeds and underbrush. Under enlightened leadership, significant progress was being made, but it was interrupted by France's King Louis XIV.

"The situation of the Palatinate, the highway from France into the heart of Germany, together with its beauty and fertility, made it a Naboth's vineyard to Louis XIV, whose ambition was colossal, whose absolutism could ill brook denial, and whose rapacity recoiled from no extreme of cruelty."[7]

In 1670 he drove Duke Charles of Lorraine from his dukedom and claimed Lorraine as his own, and then launched the Dutch War of 1672. Next came movement into Alsace with the seizure of the ten Imperial towns and, in 1674, the overrunning of the Palatinate.[8]

Again, the Rhine valley became the highway for military movements. The French forces were brilliantly led, but carried out their military exploits with "a callous ruthlessness." Determined to prevent the use of the territory as a staging area for attacks, the French "systematically devastated" portions of the Palatinate.

"The people of the Palatinate watched the destruction of all that they had labored to build over the last thirty years. They were fortunate in not knowing that the future held even greater misery for them."[9]

The year 1685 witnessed the death of King Charles II in England and the accession of a Catholic, James II, to the throne. Later in the year Louis XIV, in the midst of vigorous efforts to stamp out Protestantism in France, renounced the Edict of Nantes and boldly announced French claims on the German Palatinate.

The War of the League of Augsburg (1688-97) followed, and featured Louis' cruelest and most destructive military venture into the Rhineland. Under Louvois, Louis' Minister of War, the Palatinate, Trier, Mainz and Cologne were quickly captured by the French.

In the military and political control which followed the invasion, the Palatinate was ravaged further. The area had provided refuge for many Huguenots when King Louis revoked the Edict of Nantes; neither the monarch nor his minions would forget that fact. Once again the policy of the conquerors was the exaltation of terrorism.

When a massing of German troops following the Magdeburg Concert finally forced the French armies to withdraw into France, the French forces were ordered "to devastate and burn the Palatinate to the ground so that it could not serve as the base for an offensive by the enemy."[10] While some French officers were repulsed by their destructive assignment, the common soldiers soon lost all semblance of discipline. Nearly a half million Palatines were driven from their farm lands and homes to become refugees.

The efforts of Louis XIV to win the crown of Spain for his grandson produced the War of the Spanish Succession, a decade of armed conflict starting in 1701. Once more military hostilities swept the territory that had already suffered so much from marching armies. In 1707 the French monarch invited his military forces to re-enact their devastation of the Rhineland in the War of the League of Augsburg twenty years earlier.

"With this", one historian observed," the cup of misery was full, and at once began that remarkable exodus, which in the next four decades brought so many thousands of the Palatinates to America."[11]

In the most recent study of German emigration to British North America, Professor A. G. Roeber writes evocatively about the society from which these people came and about the relationship of law to everyday life. These "towns and hamlets," he explains, were "guided by . . . four distinct sources of law: family and clan tradition, local custom, princely legal codes, and church prescription." These "threads," he continues, "wove a tight skein around the whole of life." Each of these kinds of authority came into play in local disputes over property, inheritance, land use, care for dependent children and elderly, and regulation of the economy.

Clergymen with their knowledge of moral codes played a key role in mediating disputes, as did merchants who were accustomed to moving between the local scene and distant market towns. Unlike the English-speaking world, where statute law and common law precedent defined legality, German law was a system of localized, ad hoc mediation. Even more than in Anglo-Saxon justice, property was the social glue which held society together because property was a family, more than it was an individual, possession and subject to local judicial regulation.[12]

The Protestant Reformation complicated this system of law and authority. The Palatinate had been Lutheran until 1563 when it came under the control of a Reformed (i.e., Calvinist) prince. In 1685 it became a Catholic principality whose ruler evicted Reformed pastors from more than one hundred parishes. Under pressure from Prussia, Holland, England and Sweden to accommodate Protestants, the Palatinate Catholics then agreed between 1705 to 1707 to a compromise in which five of every seven parishes should be Reformed and two of every seven Catholic. Lutherans shared with the Reformed in the income from land set aside for the support of religion, and Reformed pastors could charge Lutherans fees for performing pastoral acts.[13]

One of the pastors aggrieved by this turmoil and by Catholic takeover of his parish was Anthony Jacob Henckel, who graduated from Giessen University in 1688. At Giessen, Henckel must have encountered the Pietist movement.[14]

Pietism was a movement among German Protestants emphasizing devotionalism and moral and spiritual discipline over strict credal orthodoxy and liturgical exactitude. Pietism placed equal emphasis on knowing one's personal salvation - through intense devotionalism - and desiring to reform the world through generous acts of charity. While careful not to condemn property, Pietism placed Christian liberty on an equal footing with devotion to the well being of family and community.

How deeply Henckel imbibed Pietism during his studies at Giessen is not known, but his emigration to America and his ministry as the first ordained Lutheran pastor in Pennsylvania, from 1717 until his death in 1728, suggest that his Lutheranism detached him from Old World religious ways and gave him a mission to preach - characteristic Pietist values. Eventually, Henckel exercised a deep influence on Lutheranism in North Carolina, Virginia, Tennessee and Ohio; fifteen of his Henkel and Stirewalt descendants, including Paul Henkel, served as Lutheran pastors in North Carolina.[15]

For Anthony Henckel's neighbors, who from generation to generation knew nothing of life but their own small village, the seasonal planting and harvesting of crops, the paying of taxes, and encounters with disease and death which encouraged appreciation for the church's assurance of a better life hereafter, there was little incentive to indulge in dreams of acquiring great wealth.

But when marching armies trampled down the grain fields and gardens, those dependent on the soil for their livelihood and for the wellbeing of their families were understandably discouraged. When crops were lost or reduced in successive years, discouragement gave way to distress. Seeming pranks of nature could compound the distress into despair as in the fall of 1708 when, as the weeks progressed, "a winter, cruel beyond the precedent of a century, set in to blight the region. As early as the beginning of October the cold was intense, and by November 1st, it was said, firewood would not burn in the open air!"[16]

As if the economic disasters created by the War of Spanish Succession were not enough, German princes of this period often were bedazzled by the splendor of the court of Louis XIV. In the eyes of many, the French monarch provided a role model for the nobility of his age. Thus, princes of German states sometimes tried to imitate the luxury and excesses of the royal court in Paris, an undertaking that, for the common people, only expanded an already excessive tax burden.

Another economic factor promoting German emigration to the New World was the desire not simply to make a living but to acquire wealth. Speculation in land attracted many who hoped to acquire great tracts in the New World and sell it at a profit. The key to success lay in the expectation that "the extraordinary low ratio of people to arable land" would be changed by immigration-producing population growth and enhanced land values. Thus, having acquired an extensive tract of land, the next step was to foster the immigration that would populate it.

"From the start", according to one historian, "American land speculators looked to European sources of population for the settlers they needed and reached overseas to recruit them. Together with the shippers who profited by transporting the immigrants, they became thereby dynamic forces propelling forward the peopling of the land."[17]

To be successful in their undertaking, the speculators had to learn that their wisest move was not immediately to sell land to settlers or even rent it at a normal rate. More settlers could be attracted by unusually low rental rates. After their labor had cleared the land and turned its soil into productive fields, after communities were established, there would be time enough to sell the land or rent it at a handsome profit.

The first German settlement in what is now North Carolina was established by two Swiss, Louis Michel and Baron Christopher de Graffenried, who hoped to make their fortune by creating a colony in Carolina. As in other colonizing attempts, they sent out persons to recruit prospective settlers for the colony. Such recruiters, or "newlanders", were not above making extravagant claims because their compensation was based on the number of settlers they recruited.[18] Naturally, those responsible for the recruiting went to territories flooded with refugees from Europe's incessant warfare and religious strife. Thus, the Palatines were frequently the objects of recruiting efforts.

There was also some selective recruiting of persons with particular talents. De Graffenried hoped that the land between the Neuse and the Cape Fear rivers he had been awarded by the Lords Proprietors of Carolina would contain deposits of valuable ores and minerals. Therefore, he recruited a number of German iron workers from Nassau-Siegen to send to Carolina. But in 1714, de Graffenried released the twelve families to the Lieutenant-Governor of Virginia, Alexander Spotswood, who had discovered iron deposits on his lands on the Rappahannock. These immigrant iron workers at Germanna, who later established a new community at Germantown in Fauquier County, created the oldest German Reformed congregation in America.[19]

The desire to acquire wealth was often the inspiration for those who recruited Germans to people colonies in the New World. A Scotsman and a Swiss are representative of those who, even more baldly than de Graffenried and Michel, sought to use the misfortunes of groups like the Palatines to advance their own financial interests.

The story of the Scotsman took place in the Deep South where 169 German colonists received from the governor of Louisiana a land grant that created the German Coast twenty-five miles up the Mississippi from New Orleans.

Like the Germans who survived de Graffenried's colonization attempt in eastern North Carolina, the Louisiana settlers of the German Coast were abandoned by their purported leader and protector. Nearly eight thousand Rhinelanders and Palatines were duped by the extravagant tales of John Law, a Scottish financial speculator. Many of Law's victims died in port cities in France as they awaited transport. Of the three thousand who received transportation, only two thousand reached Louisiana, and nearly half of them died the first year since Law had made no preparation for their arrival and settlement. Law lost, rather than made, a fortune and ended up deserting the hearty survivors of his mismanagement who later formed the nucleus for an expanding German population in the area still known as German Coast.[20]

A Swiss associate of Law, Jean-Pierre Purry, was responsible for another ill-fated settlement for Germans, this time again in Carolina. Purry's primary interest in settling Germans in the New World coincided with the military interest of Governor Robert Johnson of South Carolina in protecting Charleston and the coastal plantations from Indian attacks. In 1732 Purry began a settlement on the east bank of the Savannah River twenty miles upstream from the city of Savannah.[21] Before the decade was over, Purrysburg contained more than one hundred houses and some six hundred settlers, but its promise was short lived. Neglect by government authorities and the unhealthy environs forced many of the Germans to move from the settlement inland to the South Carolina Piedmont as soon as they had fulfilled their three-year indenture.

In addition to wars and economic concerns, religion encouraged German emigration. In the era of the Reformation the elector of the Palatinate, Frederick III, had accepted the Calvinistic understanding of the Christian faith before becoming elector in 1557. Under his rule the Palatinate became a stronghold for the Reformed tradition and served as a base for Ursinus and his colleagues, with the explicit support of Frederick "the Pious", to produce the famed Heidelberg Catechism in 1562. But Frederick's successor as elector for the Palatinate, Louis VI, was a Lutheran, who began an alternation between Lutheran and Reformed electors for the Palatinate which continued for 130 years.[22] The cycle was disrupted during the War of the Spanish Succession when Elector John William became a Roman Catholic and tried to induce his subjects to follow a similar path.

Religion was also a factor, though intertwined with politics, in the Thirty Years' War. And again, in the second half of the seventeenth century, religious differences made difficult problems even more trying. Karl Ludwig, a Roman Catholic, became Elector of the Rhenish Palatinate through the Peace of Westphalia, but he went farther than most rulers of that day in extending toleration to those whose religious views differed from his own. His wise policies enabled the Palatinate to make real progress in recovering from the devastation of the Thirty Years' War. But with the death of Ludwig in 1680, a new group of Roman Catholic rulers with a different temperament exercised authority over the Palatinate.

"His successors", wrote one historian, "were fanatics, or ruled entirely under the influence of Jesuit advisers. The persecution of Protestants, the Lutheran and Reformed, was carried on systematically, their church property being confiscated to a very large extent, and the worshippers in many cases expelled from the country."[23]

When the War of the League of Augsburg ended with the Peace of Ryswick in 1697, the Peace itself insured that the Palatinate would continue to be the arena for religious strife. The treaty contained the infamous "Ryswick clause," a provision that the Catholic elector of the Palatinate hoped to use to eliminate Protestantism from the territory. It provided that, in all the territory which the French had conquered and were returning to the Germans, the current situation as related to Protestant-Catholic distinctions must prevail.

Since the French, in defiance of earlier agreements, had followed up their military conquests with attempts to displace Protestantism with Catholicism, the "Ryswick clause" represented a substantial setback for Protestant forces in the Palatinate. Responsible historians warn against assuming that the waves of immigrants who came to America from the Palatinate left their homes primarily for religious reasons.[24] But there were religious dimensions, a fact that made it easy for Germans to win sympathy and support by claiming to be "poor, persecuted Protestants," even when they did not come from sections of Germany where religious persecution existed.

The notion that religion prompted the movements of Germanic peoples cannot, of course, be laid solely at the feet of the immigrants themselves. Their contemporaries who spoke only English often heard of the religious persecution in the Palatinate in the closing decades of the seventeenth century. That, coupled with the large number of immigrant Palatines, encouraged others to assume that all those who spoke German were from "the Palatinate" and were fleeing religious persecution.[25] But the fact remains that the divisions in the church which were given institutional expression in the years following the Reformation added venom to the political and military struggles of the seventeenth century, and that was particularly the case in the Palatinate where there were significant numbers of Germans who followed the theological lead of either John

Calvin or Martin Luther. While the region's most conspicuous religious persecution came toward the end of the century, even the violence of the earlier Thirty Years' War was exacerbated by religion.

"The intention of punishing members of an unholy, alien faith was often given as an excuse for bestiality", according to one authority, "and governments often used this excuse to instigate it. While religion thus helped to unlock the forces of hell, passions could not be held in bounds."[26]

While religion was a factor, but not usually the dominant one, in encouraging emigration from the Palatinate, there were notable groups of German-speaking refugees set afloat in seventeenth century Europe whose primary reason for emigration was their commitment to their Protestant heritage. It was the struggle between Protestant and Roman Catholic understandings of Christian faith in Austria that produced these refugees, some of whom eventually established a German community on the Savannah River in Georgia.

Austria's population in the post-Reformation period was predominantly Roman Catholic, but particularly in sections like Salzburg, there were many who embraced Luther's understanding of the Gospel. On several occasions, Roman Catholic leaders in Austria made determined efforts to eradicate what had been declared by the Roman Church a damnable heresy.

One such attempt to purify the land of Protestant pollutants was launched by Leopold Anton of Firmian who became Archbishop of Austria in 1727. Protestants there had experienced persecution in 1588 and again in 1613-15 and 1685-86. In the ensuing four decades, they had recovered from those difficult times, but they remained keenly aware of their minority status. There were no "untoward demonstrations on their part. They had continued to attend church services, confession, and the Mass, and to have their children baptized by the priest. They even carried with them Rosaries so as to give every outward appearance of being good Catholics. Their evangelical services they held at night in their homes in such quiet manner as not to disturb their neighbors."[27]

As Protestants realized the seriousness of the new archbishop's attempts to cleanse his see of all traces of Protestantism, many made plans to emigrate. The Treaty of Westphalia, which marked the end of the Thirty Years' War, had given European princes extensive powers over their subjects, even to the regulation of public manifestations of religious life.

The treaty was not, however, devoid of concern for that freedom of conscience which emerged as Protestants and Roman Catholics found it necessary to live together. Among other things, the treaty provided that those who could not in conscience adopt the religion of their prince could at least enjoy their preferred forms of Christian worship within the confines of their own homes. Where this degree of freedom was deemed too restrictive, there was also assurance of the right to emigrate to the territory of a co-religionist and take along all of one's property.

When Austria's Lutherans sought permission to emigrate, they learned they did not enjoy the freedoms set forth in the Treaty of Westphalia. They were in Hapsburg territory, and Hapsburg lands had been placed "under a juridical regime distinct from the rest of the Empire."[28] Denied the freedom of movement that could insure the freedom of worship, Austria's Lutherans realized in 1731 that the archbishop was producing religious uniformity in the land. Should they capitulate or resist? They had read in their Bibles of covenants of salt such as the one God made with David in guaranteeing the kingdom to the Davidic line.

> Acting on that suggestion 300 men representing Lutherans in all parts of Salzburg met at Schwarzach, a little market village, on the 5th of August, 1731. The oldest members of the group gathered about a round table on which was a large vessel full of salt. The rest of the company crowded close to the elders. Then one of them with steady voice solemnly challenged the entire company to seal a covenant pledging themselves to abide by their Lutheran faith in life and in death. Thereupon each man came forward, bared his head, wet the forefinger of his left hand, dipped it into the dish, raised his right to heaven, swore by the Holy Trinity that he would remain true to his Lutheran faith and stand by his brothers in that faith, and then in token of that sacred promise swallowed a little salt as a kind of sacramental wafer.[29]

In the fall, the archbishop reversed his tactics. Instead of insisting that Austria's Protestants could not leave the country, he decreed that those who would not surrender their consciences to the church as manifested in the Roman Catholic hierarchy must leave Austria within three months. They were not permitted to take property with them, although they could dispose of their property before leaving. Because of this decree, thirty thousand religious refugees were added to eighteenth century Europe's moving masses. It was a small group of these Salzburgers who established themselves near the Savannah River in the Colony of Georgia.

While not every German immigrant to America necessarily came to these shores because of European wars, because of economic deprivation at home or lures abroad, because of religious strictures or persecution, or even because of a combination of just these factors, these were the issues that most often contributed to the migrations and movements that culminated in German settlements in the American colonies.

The compassionate concern in other countries in response to the deprivation and persecution of co-religionists helped to focus attention on the possibilities for a new beginning in the New World.

The plight of the Palatines, for example, excited sympathy and concern across the English Channel. There a Protestant, Queen Anne, had in 1702 succeeded her brother-in-law, William III, on the throne of England. The minutes of the British Board of Trade for 1708 record a communication from the Lords of Trade to the queen, "setting forth that certain 'distressed Palatines, who had been driven out of the Palatinate by the cruelties of the French,' forty in number, with one Joshua Kockerthal, a Lutheran minister, for their leader, had made application to the Board for transportation to America."[30]

The desired assistance was provided, the refugees were settled in what is now Newburgh, New York, before the end of summer, and Kockerthal was soon back in the Palatinate telling others of the generous aid provided by England for those interested in colonizing in the New World.

Thousands responded to the pastor's encouraging message. By the end of April 1709, five thousand arrived in London, and by October their number had grown to fifteen thousand. Housing and food for the refugees was a mounting problem. Warehouses, barns and army tents were used to shield the immigrants from the weather;

the government appropriated five pence per day per Palatine refugee for subsistence. It is estimated that in twenty-four months the British Government appropriated for the support of the refugees the sum of one hundred thirty-five thousand pounds.

After a while the British became restive under their burden of refugees. When the governor of New York suggested transporting the remaining Palatines to his colony to help manufacture naval stores, his proposal was readily accepted. Early in 1710, three thousand were dispatched for New York. The famed Robert Livingston, a man who is said always to have come out of business transactions with full, but rarely clean, hands, persuaded the governor to settle the Palatines on his lands on the Hudson River, a development the Palatines soon had cause to regret.

But the refugee problem in England was not easily resolved. Even as Britain sought to dispose of the problem by shipping folk overseas, the word was still spreading on the continent that Britain was hospitable to Palatinates who sought resettlement in overseas colonies. Thousands of Rhinelanders availed themselves of the opportunity to emigrate. Entire villages of German peasants in the Palatinate were suddenly on the move, hoping to find in England some means of egress to the New World and its promise of larger opportunities.

Not only western Europe's Palatinate fed the migration. In some areas of central Europe, the exodus was so substantial that authorities branded emigration a crime against the Fatherland. Pamphlets were published to counteract the claims of those promoting immigration to the American colonies. But the feverish desire to immigrate, dubbed "Rabies Carolina" by the Swiss, continued to spread, particularly in the Rhineland. Making their way to England, thousands found a way to secure passage across the Atlantic.   ✞

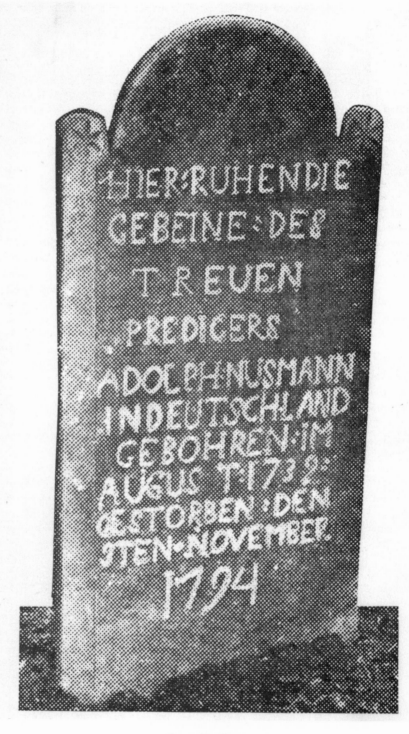

Grave Headstone
Adolph Nussman
First Lutheran Preacher in North Carolina
1773-1794

Bible Used by Adolph Nussman
(In Possession of Ellen Goodman Rives)

Gottfried Arends (Arndt) Home
(Near Lincolnton)
First President, North Carolina Synod
1803-04

CHAPTER II

The turbulent times that were the seventeenth century in western Europe pried tens of thousands of common folk loose from their ancestral moorings. Migrating from village to village and town to town in quest of opportunities for economic betterment or larger freedom, these moving masses little realized they were unravelling the fabric of a society long held together by attachment to particular parcels of land and enrollment in particular parish churches. This swarming population included tens of thousands of Germans who re-populated sections of Europe. A small portion of these mobile Palatines and Bavarians, Saxons and Hessians, Swabians and Swiss, found their ultimate place of settlement in one of the colonies in the New World.

Since European access to the colonies in the New World was by boat, early settlements in the Carolinas and Georgia were along the Atlantic Coast, the eastern border of the Coastal Plain. That Plain, a broad, flat expanse that once was the bottom of an ancient ocean, was attractive in many ways to those accustomed to producing their livelihood by tilling the soil.

As trappers and explorers moved inland in the Carolinas, it was soon noted that the colonies contained other distinct regions. Moving inland across the Coastal Plain in what is now North Carolina, one discovers that approximately 150 miles from the coast the Coastal Plain gives way to an area of rolling hills bisected by numerous fast-moving streams, an area later to be designated the Piedmont. The hills and streams of this area proved especially attractive to many German immigrants seeking a place to settle and raise a family.

And beyond the Piedmont is a third region, the mountains, a portion of the Appalachian chain which contains some forty peaks that soar more than six thousand feet above sea level. In sheltered but well-watered valleys amid these lofty sentinels, small clusters of German-speaking folk also developed their farms. The timing and nature of settlements united with the physical characteristics of North Carolina's internal regions to produce distinctive social, political, economic and cultural outlooks in each of its three regions.[1] Those distinctions had their impact on Lutherans no less than other North Carolinians.

Germans were not the dominant immigrant group in any southern colony or state. In North Carolina they never even achieved the quarter percentage of the total population which was characteristic of the nation as a whole. Yet the Germanic presence was, from early days, a part of the unfolding drama of the settlement of the South and of Carolina.[2]

There were, for example, Alsatians and Hessians among those Protestants who constituted Jean Ribault's sixteenth century Huguenot settlement at Port Royal, in what is now South Carolina. Ribault's Germans received no more pity than the French Calvinists when the Spanish destroyed Port Royal in 1566. To the north of Carolina, there quite possibly were some Germans among those original settlers at Jamestown in

Virginia in 1607.[3]

However, the really significant German settlements in the South were not a product of the sixteenth or seventeenth centuries. Rather, they began early in the eighteenth century after Germans had already created substantial communities in Pennsylvania and New York.

In 1709, after conferring with John Lawson who served as surveyor general for Carolina, Baron Christopher de Graffenried bought from the British government 17,500 acres of land in Carolina in order to establish a colony. De Graffenried and Franz Louis Michel formed a land company to foster settlement on the newly acquired land. While the colonization was launched as a Swiss enterprise, de Graffenried and Michel also agreed to settle some of the Palatines who were emigrating to England in great numbers. In January 1710, at the behest of de Graffenried, some 650 of the Germans accompanied Lawson as he set sail for Carolina. They did so with the assurance that, within ninety days of their arrival in Carolina, each family would receive 250 acres of land. Furthermore, the tracts of land provided these German families were to "be as contiguous as may be for the more mutual love and assistance of the said poor Palatines one to another, as well with respect to the exercise of their religion as the management of their temporal affairs."[4]

Unfortunately, not all who set sail claimed their tract of land. Poor food and crowding on board ship sealed the fate of many. Incautious eating and drinking after reaching the shore of what is now North Carolina reduced their ranks still further. Half of the fledgling colony of New Bern "died off before it was well settled."[5]

As if the distressingly high death rate were not bad enough, at least fifty of the survivors found conditions at New Bern so unpromising that they gave up and moved to Virginia. Of the German settlers who remained, it is not clear how many were Reformed and how many were Lutheran. Both traditions were represented in the Palatinate and in the waves of refugees generated there. However, de Graffenried clearly added to the Reformed population when he brought one hundred Swiss with him when, in September 1710, he came for a personal visit to the new settlement.

Morale was at a low ebb, and not even the helpful addition of fresh settlers from Switzerland could substantially alter that fact. It was not just that establishing farms and building homes in a wilderness was lonely, dangerous, and physically exhausting. There also were those who felt the absence of spiritual nurture. Christen Janzen wrote in April 1711: "But one thing lies heavy on us which I cannot write without weeping, namely the lack of a true and zealous pastor. For we have indeed cause to complain with Asaph, our sign we see no more, no prophet preaches to us any more, no teacher teaches us any more. We have, indeed, prayers in our houses every Sunday, but the zeal to cleanse away the canker of our old sins is so small that it is to be feared it [i.e., the canker] will consume everything to the foundation, if the pitying God does not come to our help."[6]

De Graffenried's colonists had been guided by Lawson to plant their colony in the territory of the Tuscarora Indians. While some contemporary observers believed relations between the Indians and the new colonists were quite satisfactory, the Tuscaroras were unhappy. In 1710 they sent a petition to the governor of Pennsylvania protesting the enslavement of their people and the appropriation of their lands. The kidnapping of Indians, especially women and children, and the selling of them into slavery, had become so extensive that the Pennsylvania legislature passed a law in 1705 against "the further importation of Indian slaves from Carolina."[7]

The Swiss and German settlers at New Bern may not have included any of the "Carolina traders" whose treatment of the Indians created hostility toward the white settlers. Nevertheless, the planting of the colony at New Bern in the heart of Tuscarora territory was a galling addition to a list of grievances that had been building for some time.

When Lawson and de Graffenried went out to explore the Neuse River valley in early September 1711 they were captured by the Tuscaroras. Lawson was executed and de Graffenried was kept a prisoner while some five hundred Indians attacked white settlements from the Neuse to the Pamlico. More than 130 persons were reported killed within two hours; more than eighty children were slaughtered. New Bern was one of the settlements that suffered the brunt of Indian fury. A two-year war between the colonists and the Tuscaroras and their allies ensued. It was only after assistance was received from Charles Town that the survivors at New Bern were freed of danger from Indian attack. The war ended "after orgies of atrocities on both sides, with the neighboring Tuscarora tribes decimated and driven off the land."[8]

Following the Tuscarora War, the surviving colonists began rebuilding their town. Under the leadership of Thomas Pollock, good progress was made, and by 1723 New Bern was sufficiently restored to be incorporated. But the progress was achieved at a price. The Palatines remembered him as a "Colonel" "who ruled both Governor and Country and acted ... as a General." Visiting the Palatine settlements, Pollock "took everything, even the Millstones and left us without any assistance intirely [sic] Naked to the Mercy of the Indians."[9] The colonists who survived began to disperse throughout what is now Craven County. With the passage of time and the abandonment of the colony by the discouraged de Graffenried, many were eager to move out on their own, especially since the Indian threat had been put to rest.

In September 1728, John Caspar Stoever, a widower from Frankenberg, Hessen, arrived in Philadelphia along with his son, John Caspar, Jr. The younger Stoever had completed a formal program of theological study, and when the father took the oath of allegiance to the British crown, he also signed himself as a "student of theology." The senior Stoever left his son in Pennsylvania, and went south to the Palatine settlement at New Bern. During his stay there, he married his second wife and fathered a second son.

Friction developed between Stoever and his wife and mother-in-law, and it presumably prompted Stoever's removal to a settlement in Virginia where some of de Graffenried's Palatines had initially found placement as iron workers. There Stoever gave evidence of his desire to become a Lutheran pastor and was called to that post. On April 8, 1733, he and the son whom he had left in Pennsylvania were both ordained by Rev. John Christian Schulze at Augustus Lutheran Church, Trappe, Pennsylvania.

It is not improbable that the senior Stoever provided religious services for the Germans at New Bern during his sojourn there, but no record of such a ministry has been discovered. He made a brief but important contribution to the development of the Lutheran church in Virginia. The Hebron parish secured a farm for him and equipped it with a parsonage. An entry in the Craven County, North Carolina, court records dated March 10, 1734, indicates that Stoever effected a reconciliation not only with his wife but also with his mother-in-law. Stoever promised "to love and honour his beloved wife, Mary Magdalena and to provide for her," while his spouse promised "to love and honour her husband in all things, and in love and faithfulness to obey his lawful commandments as a Christian wife ought to do." As for his mother-in-law, Stoever promised

> to maintain and clothe her and to show her all love and faithfulness due from a child; in consideration of which she promises as well to be careful of not giving offense herself, as [well as] to admonish her daughter to beware from offending and giving occasion of quarrel and strife, especially to leave off all evil speaking, backbiting and slandering which occasion offense, and truly to behave herself so in all things towards her child and son-in-law as becometh a loving and Christian mother, to the end the congregation may not be offended nor no new strife may be raised in the house.[10]

With the removal of Stoever to Virginia, the German settlers in eastern North Carolina were left without so much as a student of theology to provide religious leadership. That they continued to consider their own spiritual nurture a matter of importance is reflected in a contract entered into by builders Jacob Sheets, John Simons, John Kinsey and Peter Ramm in 1740. The contract dated August 2, 1740, notes a bequest of cattle had been "willed and given for the use of the Palatines or Germans." The twenty-three subscribers to the contract were committed to the building of "one house of worship or Chapel for the use of the High Germans of the Church of England." It was to be located "on the south side of Trent River between the ferry and John Kinsey's plantation."[11]

Although the Germans settling at New Bern had been promised 250 acres of land for each family, de Graffenried and Michel never got around to providing them with valid deeds to the property. Unfortunately, in the cold January of 1747, the Germans in Craven County found themselves evicted from the land.[12] Happily, the royal authorities recognized their plight and provided them with deeds to 250-acre tracts in other counties.

But since the new land grants were in Jones and adjoining counties, the "High Germans" who had united to build a place of worship on the south bank of the Trent were scattered among settlers from many backgrounds. The Koonces, Millers, Islers, Francks, Rheins, Nobles, Kornegays, Shelfers and the like ceased to be a small German enclave of the New Bern settlement and became instead families of German background who blended into the general population of eastern North Carolina. While these North Carolina colonists did not remain a close knit community clinging to the German language and culture and, admittedly, were not very numerous, to them goes the credit for establishing "the first permanent German settlement in the Southeast."[13]

The first quarter of the eighteenth century also saw German colonists establish themselves in the colony to the north of Carolina. German iron workers who had been recruited to create a mining industry in North Carolina ended up going to Virginia instead, and there creating a home for their families. These initial settlers from Nassau-Siegen were Reformed, but three years later German Lutherans became a part of the Virginia scene.   Like many of their fellow countrymen, the German Lutherans who ultimately settled in Virginia were, in their homeland, Palatines eager to escape the persistent trauma to which they were subjected. Attracted by the propaganda efforts of the agents of William Penn, they emigrated to Pennsylvania. They sailed down the Rhine for Holland, and there secured passage on a vessel bound for England and America. Disappointments and delays in England and an unusually rough crossing of the Atlantic presented many parallels to that of the first settlers of New Bern.

Having expended all their resources before leaving England, they arrived in the colonies as indentured servants who had to sell their labor for eight years to pay for their passage. The severity of the storms encountered in crossing the ocean resulted in their reaching land and selling their services not in Pennsylvania but in Virginia. There the services of these twenty German families were purchased by the lieutenant-governor who had imported some of their fellow countrymen three years earlier. Settled initially on lands along the Rapidan River which were owned by Spotswood, these settlers later received land grants at the foot of the mountains near the headwaters of the Rapidan when they completed their indentured servitude.

During their years of labor for Spotswood, the German Lutherans sought a pastor of their own tradition. As early as 1719, an emissary was dispatched to Europe where funds were sought to support a Lutheran pastor who would serve with the Reformed pastor already at work in Virginia. Efforts were also made to find funds for the building of a school and a place of worship. Regrettably, this effort produced nothing more than an offer from the Society for the Propagation of the Gospel in Foreign Parts to provide Virginia's German settlers with twenty-five copies of the *Book of Common Prayer* in their native tongue.[14] The refugees from the Palatinate had to be content with the ministrations provided by the Church of England through its German Parish of St. George in Germanna.

In 1725 the Lutherans who had labored for Spotswood earned their freedom to settle on tracts of their own. They did so, at the eastern base of the Blue Ridge mountains on the banks of White Oak Run and Robinson River in Spotsylvania County.

From this most westerly outpost of Virginia settlement, two members of the community were dispatched to Germany, once more to seek an ordained minister. A simple log structure was erected to provide their hoped-for pastor with a place for conducting worship.

Unfortunately, the second attempt to secure a resident Lutheran pastor for Virginia also failed. For a time worship services at "German Chapel" were conducted by the Reformed pastor or by laymen, providing a foundation for the historic Hebron Church of Madison County, Virginia. It was here that John Caspar Stoever, Sr., found his call to ordained ministry.

Farther to the south, on the western bank of the Savannah River a few miles upstream from Purrysburg, the colony of Georgia also had a notable German settlement. When the archbishop of Austria in 1731 attempted to drive all Protestants from the land, he set in motion a great tide of persons seeking a place to settle, where they would be free to worship God according to the understanding of the Gospel recovered in the Protestant Reformation.

Lithuania, Germany and Sweden were among the countries where large numbers of these Austrian refugees found shelter and an opportunity to make a new beginning.

In Austria, the expulsion of Protestants created a serious manpower shortage, and authorities had to intervene and slow down the tide. But in the winter of 1732, the gates were opened again, and large numbers of Salzburgers made their way to Holland.

At the end of the summer of 1733, a group of two hundred displaced Salzburgers made their way to Augsburg, Germany. There they established contact with the senior pastor at St. Ann's Church, Rev. Samuel Urlsperger, who was known for assisting Protestant refugees in finding a place to settle. Urlsperger was a contemporary and personal friend of the leader of German Pietism, Gotthilf August Francke, and, like Francke, was affiliated with England's Society de Propaganda Christi Cognitione, popularly known as the Society for the Promotion of Christian Knowledge (SPCK). Urlsperger had used his talents to organize support for foreign mission work in India, and he did not hesitate to employ the same skills to assist Protestants caught up in the shifting conflict between Europe's Protestant and Roman Catholic forces.[15]

In the fall of 1732, the SPCK persuaded the trustees of the Colony of Georgia to permit them to settle three hundred Salzburgers there. Urlsperger was aware of this, so when the Salzburgers arrived in Augsburg and contacted him in September 1733, he proposed that they authorize him to arrange for their resettlement in Georgia.

The response was not enthusiastic. The European's perception of America was not that of an exciting frontier which would be rolled back to make room for a new nation characterized by wealth, power and plenty. Rather, it was

> an uncivilized place on the distant margins of civilization--a place where the ordinary restraints of civility could be abandoned in pell-mell exploitation, a remote place where recognized enemies and pariahs of society--heretics, criminals, paupers--could safely be deposited, their contamination sealed off by three thousand miles of ocean, and where putative inferior specimens of humanity, blacks and Indians, could be reduced to subhuman statuses, worked like animals, and denied the most elemental benefits of law and religion....[16]

Reckless and lawless young men wanting to be free of the restraints of civilized society might be willing to undertake such a bold venture, but for mature, Christian men concerned about the welfare of wife and children, it was another matter. An idealistic clergyman with a Pietist's concern to evangelize the world might be eager to place Christian leaven in the dregs of society being shipped off to Oglethorpe's colony in Georgia. He might still succumb to glowing reports, like that penned by Kocherthal in 1706, of settlement opportunities in the New World.[17]

But Germans who survived the mismanaged colonization attempts by men like de Graffenried in Carolina and Law in Louisiana wrote letters to their relatives in Europe. The word spread of the hardship and danger involved in even the most carefully planned and diligently supported colonization programs. So when Urlsperger proposed to the refugees from the Salzburg that they become colonists in Georgia, they had to be persuaded. But persuaded they were, forty-two men finally agreeing to commit themselves and their families to the venture.

Thus it was that in late October, a group of seventy-eight Salzburgers left Augsburg for Rotterdam. Reaching the famed seaport in the Netherlands in late November, they were joined by two pastors from Halle, the great center of German Pietism. Two weeks later the Salzburgers and their pastors, John Martin Bolzius and Israel Christian Gronau, were on their way to Dover, and on January 8 they set sail for

Georgia. On March 7, 1734, they reached Georgia's port city, Savannah.

The site selected by the governor of the colony for the settlement of the Salzburgers was about twenty-five miles inland from Savannah in what is now Effingham County.[18] The community's population was boosted to a total of two hundred by additional groups of Salzburgers who arrived in 1735 and 1736.[19] In 1741 still another group arrived, this one numbering 162 persons. By this time, the village on the banks of the Savannah and the surrounding countryside could boast a total population of twelve hundred persons.

Under the leadership of their pastors, the Lutherans on the Savannah began a school for their children the same year they arrived in Georgia. The community suffered a high mortality rate in its first years, and in 1738 an orphanage was constructed, a building that also served as Ebenezer's hospital and place of worship until a separate church structure was erected in 1741-42. Classroom sessions, hours of worship, and even the time to go to, and return from, labor in the fields were soon being marked by a bell presented to the Salzburgers by the highly mobile evangelist, George Whitefield. Whitefield visited the Salzburger settlement in 1740, and he was much impressed with what he found there.

> The town is neatly built, the situation exceedingly pleasant; the people live in the greatest harmony with their ministers and with one another, as one family. They have no drunken, idle, or profligate people among them, but are industrious, and many have grown wealthy. Their industry has been blessed with remarkable and uncommon success, to the envy of their neighbors, having great plenty of all the necessary conveniences for life (except clothing) within themselves; and [they] supply this town (Savannah) with bread-kind, as also beef, veal, pork, poultry &c.[20]

Whitefield was not the only notable to be welcomed by the Salzburgers in their early years on the Savannah. On Saturday, October 2, 1742, Muhlenberg arrived in the city of Savannah to discharge his first official responsibility upon reaching the colonies, namely, visit the pastors at Ebenezer.[21] Arriving in the port city, he encountered Pastor Gronau who had come to Savannah to conduct Sunday worship for the city's German-speaking population. On Monday Muhlenberg reached the Salzburger settlement. He was impressed with the flour mill, "the first water [powered] mill in Georgia." He admired the new and "very well built" church.

After his trying experience in crossing the Atlantic, it was a special joy to join in worship with persons whose piety was akin to his own. "The dear Salzburgers sing accurately and beautifully, conduct themselves reverently during the hearing of God's Word, and behave courteously toward each other."[22] On the evening of October 11, the man who was to contribute so much to the unifying of scattered German Lutherans in America took his leave of the Salzburger settlement. But the brief visit had been a fruitful one. He always recalled with appreciation their industry and Christian faith. They, in turn, remembered him with respect, and turned to him in later years when serious difficulties beset Ebenezer.

Although the German settlement at Purrysburg did not long endure, it was not South Carolina's only site for German settlement in the early eighteenth century. When the colony at Purrysburg dispersed, some of its settlers may have made their way to neighboring Georgia, there to join the Ebenezer community or settle in the port city of Savannah. Some others possibly made their way to Charleston, but most of the inhabitants of the once promising Purrysburg apparently found a home in German settlements emerging in the interior of South Carolina.

Charleston itself, increasingly a port of entry, was an attractive place to establish residency for one possessing the educational or mechanical skills needed to work in a growing center of commerce and finance. On the other hand, those untutored folk whose roots were agrarian were likely to move from their port of entry to frontier townships such as Orangeburg, Amelia, Saxe-Gotha, New Windsor, or Hard Labor Creek. Charleston continued to serve as the port of entry for immigrants from Europe. For example, in July 1735, the *South Carolina Gazette* reported the arrival of two hundred Palatines most of whom were so poor they had to sell their labor and that of their children for a number of years in order to pay for their passage. The newspaper noted that while there were "some tradesmen" in the group, "most of them are farmers."[23]

Orangeburg and adjacent Amelia townships were sparsely populated, but the Germans who settled there provided important points of contact for other German-speaking folk moving on into the back country. German-speaking Swiss were settling in Saxe-Gotha northwest of present Columbia as early as 1737, and a settlement of "a few score German families" on the Salkehatchie in Barnwell County may have been begun even earlier. When Lutherans in North Carolina began to develop an umbrella organization for their scattered congregations, many were aware that there were a number of German-language congregations in South Carolina, congregations dating back to 1739 in Saxe-Gotha, 1743 in Orangeburg and 1755 in Charleston.

Unlike the developments in the interior of South Carolina, German settlements in the "midland" or Piedmont section of North Carolina were not produced by an expansion of earlier coastal settlements. Rather, they grew out of interior migrations, some passing southward from southwest Virginia and some passing northward from the interior of South Carolina. The convergence of the two streams of settlement was not unlike a military pincer movement, the two prongs of the pincer meeting near present day Charlotte.

The northern and far stronger prong of the pincer began in Pennsylvania on a peninsula on the west bank of the Delaware River where that southward bound stream swings slightly westward to encounter and absorb the Schuylkill River. Starting in 1682, the peninsula was the home of a dream of William Penn which he called "Philadelphia", a part of his larger dream that became the Commonwealth of Pennsylvania. Beginning with two square miles, the community on the Delaware expanded rapidly in territory, population and importance. Within eight years Philadelphia boasted eight merchants, twenty-nine shopkeepers, three brewers, three malters, nine master carpenters, seven master bricklayers, four brickmasters, "and an assortment of tailors, cobblers, chandlers, weavers, carters, sawyers and coopers."[24]

By 1740 the colony of Pennsylvania had already reached a population of one hundred thousand, and the three immigrant groups that would dominate the early history of the colony were clearly identifiable.

If one were to drive a stake in the bank of the Delaware in downtown Philadelphia, project a westward radius for twenty-five miles, and then strike an arc, the territory enclosed by that arc would be that largely settled during the years 1680 to 1710, the settlers being primarily of English background. If the radius were extended to seventy-five miles and a second arc struck, that second band of territory would be an area settled largely from 1710 to 1750. Embracing the counties from York in the south-central part of the colony to Northampton in the northeast, this second band roughly represents the "Dutch" country, settled largely by German-speaking immigrants.[25] Creating a third band of territory about seventy five miles wide just beyond the German settlements would incorporate the territory that proved to be a haven to many Scotch Irish from 1717 to the outbreak of the American Revolution.

Active recruiting on the part of William Penn, coupled with the unhappy experiences of early German immigrants in a number of other American colonies, led to steady growth in the number of Germans making Philadelphia their port of entry as they sought the opportunity to make a new beginning. Between six and seven thousand Germans arrived in Philadelphia in 1719 alone. As in the South, those who had the benefits of formal education or had learned a trade might opt for settlement in the port city. The vast majority of the immigrants, however, were the German settlers who quickly populated "the Dutch country" where their "thrift, diligence, and careful agricultural methods" soon made "the Dutch country" synonymous with "prosperous, well-kept farms which were as successful as any in America."[26]

But the influx of Germans did not stop when the farm lands in the German arc were all filled with settlers. Good farm land available for new settlers in eastern Pennsylvania was rapidly disappearing by the late 1720s, but between 1727 and 1740 eighty ships would unload fresh immigrants onto the docks in Philadelphia. In the next fifteen years, 159 ships brought new colonists to the City of Brotherly Love, the year 1749 alone seeing twenty-five ships deliver 7,049 Germans.[27]

In instances where these later German settlers possessed the means, they would often purchase a small tract of the increasingly expensive land in one of the counties in Pennsylvania's German arc. With growing family responsibilities, they would early begin planning for the day when they would sell their Pennsylvania property and move to the South where the same dollars would buy more land than in Pennsylvania. Families had begun moving southwestward from Pennsylvania into the Shenandoah Valley of Virginia by the mid-1720s. In 1727, Adam Mueller (Miller) moved from Lancaster County, Pennsylvania, to Page County, Virginia. Five years later, Joist Hite (Hans Jost Heydt), whose mill at the mouth of Pennsylvania's Perkiomen Creek had prospered, sold his property and led a caravan of sixteen families into the valley. By 1750 German settlers had moved as far into southwest Virginia as the New River.[28]

What began as a trickling overflow of immigrants from Pennsylvania's "Dutch Country" soon became an incredible stream of migration. It was not just that immigrants continued to pour into Philadelphia and add to the colony's swelling population. Settlement on the frontier of the colonies had been retarded by hostile Indians and the presence of the French who found it to their advantage to encourage Indian attacks on the frontier settlements of the English colonies. As the 1750s drew to a close, British forces were increasingly successful in defeating French troops and wresting key fortifications from their control.

> The British triumph over the French and the subsequent clearance of large areas through treaties forced upon the Indians, opened up large new portions of that potential territory, and, powered by intense speculations and an apparently insatiable

appetite for fresh land, the frontier of colonization was pushed forward in several major sectors. Thus the years after 1760 were a generally expansive and prosperous time, and despite considerable growth in urban areas and intensification of developments in some older regions, the most obvious geographic feature was a series of thrusts into new ground.[29]

The southern frontier was the scene of one of those significant thrusts, and it was especially attractive to those who had made temporary settlement in William Penn's colony. The main route followed by the moving masses became known as the Great Wagon Road. Starting from Philadelphia, it went westward to Lancaster and York in Pennsylvania, then swung south through western Maryland, and moved down into the Shenandoah Valley of Virginia.

Some left the valley early to pick up an Indian trail that would ultimately bring them into North Carolina near the present communities of Oxford and Hillsborough. The main stream of the southward movement proceeded through the valley into the southwestern portion of Virginia, where another parting of the ways took place. One branch moved southwestward into what is now east Tennessee, but the main branch moved more directly to the south to intersect the Dan River, whose valley reaches southwestward into Stokes County, North Carolina, and provides direct access to the upper reaches of the Yadkin. In North Carolina, the main route continued a southerly course into South Carolina where another parting of the ways took place, an eastern branch moving on to Camden and Charleston, while the westward branch moved off to the Great Wagon Road's southern terminus, Augusta, Georgia.

> Through this corridor passed thousands of heavily loaded covered wagons, some pulled by as many as six horses or oxen; homemade "carriages" whose heavy, clumsy wheels were cross-section segments of tree trunks; and, above all, trains of packhorses accompanied by family members on foot and by farm animals roped together or kept in small groups by snapping dogs or flicking whips. This migrant traffic, moving slowly south across the deeply rutted, tree-strewn, rocky road, was met, in the summer and early fall, by herds of livestock being driven to markets -- originally markets in Philadelphia, but by the 1770s also in a number of inland villages like Lancaster, Pennsylvania; Winchester, Virginia; Salisbury, North Carolina; and Camden, South Carolina.[30]

All along this increasingly traveled route, places emerged where the weary traveler might hope to find food and shelter. Isolated houses or cabins that provided no special facilities for travelers, but would provide some food and permit a transient to sleep under their roof (albeit, often on the floor) were called "ordinaries". There were also occasional taverns, facilities more accustomed to accommodating guests than the ordinaries but also more likely to be the meeting spot for local inebriates and rowdies. There were also along the route some inns, facilities erected precisely with the needs of the traveler in mind, but such places were few and far between, and, when available, too costly to attract a lot of the migrating German farmers.

It is estimated that by the late 1750s, two thousand settlers were making their way southward through the Shenandoah Valley each year, in addition to those who came into the valley and settled there. Where rivers were sufficiently wide or deep as to impede the southerly flow of population, flat-bottomed boats either pulled by ropes or poled across the most shallow part of the stream, served as ferries. The movement of the human tide continued, and by the 1760s the population in southwestern Virginia was growing at a rate of nine percent per year. In North Carolina the growth was even more dramatic.

> One observer noted that between January and October 1755, 5,000 migrants crossed the James River in southern Virginia heading for North Carolina, and that the numbers were increasing daily. In 1763 Benjamin Franklin estimated that in the previous three years 10,000 families had migrated to North Carolina from Pennsylvania alone -- a guess, to be sure, but roughly substantiated by the overall population figures and by the extent of new land opened to cultivation. In 1766 an observer in Salisbury, North Carolina, which like Fort Pitt was strategically located athwart major westward routes, reported that 1,000 wagons rumbled through the town en route to the west in the autumn and winter months alone. Between 1730 and 1750 the colony's population had doubled, from approximately 35,000 to approximately 70,000; by 1770 it more than doubled once again, reaching a figure between 175,000 and 185,000.[31]

The ethnic groups contributing most significantly to this phenomenal growth in North Carolina were the Germans and Scotch Irish.

While the precise dates for the founding of most of the early German settlements are not known, the pattern of dispersal as the newcomers reached North Carolina is clear. Those following the chief route into Piedmont North Carolina charted their course from southwestern Virginia south to the banks of the Yadkin River, settling the lands adjoining the river in what are today the counties of Forsyth, Stokes, Davie, Rowan, Cabarrus, and Davidson. The Moravian settlement in 1753 near the present Winston-Salem provided an increasingly attractive way-station for these migrants.

Those taking the more easterly route from southern Virginia into North Carolina turned westward on reaching Hillsborough, moving from Orange into what would become Alamance and Guilford counties. The Indian trail stretching eastward from the trading ford on the Yadkin through present Guilford and Alamance counties and thence northeastward into Virginia developed into an important connector between the Hillsborough area and the frontier settlements in the Yadkin Valley. It would serve as an avenue of communication between clusters of families with German roots who settled early near present day Gibsonville, Liberty, and Alamance, and the more numerous German settlers to the west, those located just east of the Yadkin near what became Lexington as well as those on the west bank of the Yadkin between Salisbury and present day Mt. Pleasant.

Apart from the Moravian settlements at Bethabara and Salem in what was then Rowan and later Stokes County, the largest concentrations of German settlers were in the area south of Salisbury and east of Concord in what is now eastern Rowan and Cabarrus counties. By 1750 clusters of German-speaking farmers were already sprinkled from Rowan and Cabarrus eastward to the Haw River near present day Burlington. By 1750 there were also German settlers joining the Scotch Irish in invading the territory west of the Catawba River in what are today Lincoln and Catawba counties. Henry Weidner (Whitener) had already settled on the stream that would bear his name (Henry River). Clearing out a home site for himself in the wilderness, he returned to Pennsylvania, married Mary Mull, and returned to North

Carolina with his wife and a young man whose family name became prominent in the area west of the Catawba, Conrad Yoder.[32]

For many of the families migrating from Pennsylvania to Carolina, the journey began in the early fall as soon as the crops were harvested. That meant they could arrive at their destination before the really cold weather set in, and with enough provisions to get them through the winter months.

On locating a site for settlement on the Carolina frontier, the first task was to clear some ground for crude log shelters for the family and the live stock. In a milder climate than that to which they had been accustomed, they could then turn their attention to the task of clearing additional ground for spring planting and for pasture. The industry, productivity and thrift of the German settlers was often noted. Governor Dobbs in 1755 observed, "They raise horses, cows, and hogs, with a few sheep; they raise Indian corn, wheat, barley, rye, and oats, make good butter and tolerable cheese, and they have gone into indigo with good success, which they sell at Charles Town, having a wagon road to it, tho' 200 miles distant...."[33]

The Germans in North Carolina did not have the clear, religious patrimony of the Salzburgers whose immigration to the New World was conspicuously related to their devotion to the evangelical faith. Nevertheless, they have been described as "fervently religious."

Later descendants of these early settlers inherited German Bibles, hymnals and devotional works like *True Christianity* by John Arndt. Devout they were, but they were divided in their religious loyalties. The Moravians, coming as a conscious and well-planned expansion of a base of operations in Pennsylvania, concentrated their settlements near Salem which early emerged as the center of Moravian operations in the South.[34]

Other German settlers, whether choosing to establish themselves in the valley of Virginia, the Dutch Fork of South Carolina or Piedmont North Carolina, were, denominationally speaking, usually a mixture of German Reformed and Lutherans. For a number of decades, they jointly supported a teacher to instruct their children, shared in common places of worship and selected their hymns of praise to God from the same hymnal. Unlike the Salzburgers in Georgia and the Moravians at Salem, these Reformed and Lutheran settlers in the interior of Virginia and the Carolinas did not bring clergy with them when they left Pennsylvania to move south. While the Reformed often seemed more efficient than their Lutheran neighbors in securing the service of an ordained pastor, there was such an acute and endemic shortage of clergy that both Lutheran and Reformed lay persons gratefully accepted the ministrations of an ordained pastor of either tradition.

But while almost always devoid of pastoral leadership, these settlers early began to make provision for their own spiritual nurture and that of their families. Devout lay persons were gathering their relatives and German-speaking neighbors for worship in at least informal congregations as early as 1745, even though for many years the best they could expect by way of worship leadership was the equivalent of a lay reader, an occasional visit from a Moravian missionary, or the services of some wandering German whose pastoral credentials might not withstand close scrutiny.[35] It seems probable that the congregations that later became known as Friedens, Gibsonville; St. John's and Zion (Organ), Salisbury; and St. John's, Concord, were already functioning congregations by 1750. In the next two decades Low's, Liberty; St. Paul's, Alamance; Reformation, Mocksville; Philadelphia, Dallas; Daniel's, Lincolnton; St. Paul's, Newton; Pilgrim, Lexington; and Cold Water, Concord, emerged as congregations.

Here in the gathered Christian community, the German settlers, weighted down with the knowledge that their eyes would never again behold the Fatherland, and, short of eternity, would never again see friends and relatives left behind in Germany, could at least find spiritual sustenance and nurture proffered in their native tongue. The bonds of fellowship forged by a common faith expressed in a common language carried over into the daily living of the German settlers, and those who, from the outside, observed their ready willingness to support one another were generous in their praise of the personal qualities that characterized most of the German settlers.

The fact that, outside the Moravian settlement, none of the congregations created by German settlers in Piedmont North Carolina in the 1740s and 1750s regularly enjoyed in its early years the services of a resident pastor, either Lutheran or Reformed, does not mean that pastors were never present in these congregations. Reformation, Mocksville, is a case in point. Established as Heidelberg Evangelical Lutheran Church, but popularly known as the Dutchman's Creek church, this congregation was functioning as early as 1766 and quite possibly went back to the beginning of that decade and the founding of the settlement. George Soelle, a Dane who was ordained as a Lutheran in his native land and entered the Unity of the Brethren in 1748, came to the American colonies in 1753. In 1770, he moved with several families to the Carolina settlement called Wachovia. During the years 1771-73, he conducted numerous missionary tours among Germans in Piedmont North Carolina.[36]

In 1772 while visiting in the home of Christoph Bube near Dutchman's Creek, Soelle encountered "an educated, ordained minister" from Hanover who was residing in the neighborhood, a minister whom he called "Wartmann". The reference is to Heinrich Burchard Gabriel Wortmann who was still residing in Rowan County as late as December 1773, when the county records list him as the witness to a will. Since John Caspar Stoever was not ordained when he was in North Carolina, Wortmann may well have been the first ordained Lutheran not a member of the Unity of Brethren to reside in North Carolina. Born at Mittelnkirchen bei Stade in Germany, he matriculated at the University of Gottingen in April 1738, and served a parish near Hamburg before moving to Pennsylvania in 1752.

In his first year in the colony, Wortmann served briefly at Alsace, Berks County; then at Trinity, Lancaster; and finally at Trinity, Reading, where he was "dismissed" in July 1753. In 1757-58, he served Upper Peaked Mountain, McGaheysville, Virginia, and possibly Rader's, Fort Run. The next report of his ministry is as pastor of St. John's, Charleston, South Carolina, following the death of Rev. John George Friedrichs in 1760. When Muhlenberg visited the Charleston congregation in 1774, he learned that Wortmann had gone "farther into the country," making it likely that he is the "Waterman" credited with serving Lutherans on Crim's Creek (now St. John's, Pomaria) following the pastorate of John G. Luft.[37]

When did Wortmann move to North Carolina? Was he on Dutchman's Creek for several years before his presence was noted by Soelle, or had he arrived only a few months earlier? Either is possible, but given the fact that the Heidelberg community was not a great distance from Salem, the latter seems more probable. When did the first settled Lutheran pastor in North Carolina take leave of Rowan County? Where did he go? No one is certain, but he apparently returned to Pennsylvania where a son, Laurentz, was born at Lancaster in 1775. The fragmentary record of the ministry of this pastor is typical of the surviving records of the service of the earliest pastors who served Lutherans in the valley of Virginia and in the Carolina.[38]

The fact that on occasion Lutherans on the southern frontier briefly had the services of a transient Lutheran pastor or someone posing as such should not obscure the fact that congregational life for the earliest Lutheran congregations in North Carolina grew out of the piety and concern of lay persons. It was their banding together to give tangible expression to their faith that enabled them to make the first beginnings at recovering their unity as people of God standing in a particular heritage recovered in the Protestant Reformation.

In addition to the passing visit of a transient pastor like Wortmann, the lay persons who created the first congregations of the North Carolina Synod had another occasional pastoral resource: the resident clergy in neighboring South Carolina.

The start of New Windsor, a settlement across the Savannah River from present day Augusta, Georgia, resulted in the advent of pastoral leadership of the Reformed persuasion for German-speaking folk in the interior. The first ordained minister to serve in the back country, Bartholomew Zouberbuehler, came with the New Windsor settlers, along with

> his son, Bartholomew, Junior, a student of theology; David Zubly [or Zubli], father of John Joachim Zubly then studying in Germany and later to become the most prominent minister in the Southern colonies; John Ulrich Giessendanner, the elder, ministering from 1737 in Orangeburg and Amelia; and his nephew, John Ulrich who succeeded his uncle. These five Swiss Reformed men, along with the Rev. Christian Theus, also Reformed, are the first and for many years...the only German Protestant pastors in the Colony.[39]

In North Carolina, the earliest religious ministrations by ordained German-speaking pastors in the Piedmont came at the hands of Reformed pastors. Christian Theus was ordained by the Charleston Presbytery in 1739, and apparently ministered among the Germans in the interior of South Carolina for five decades. Theus seems to have centered his ministry at St. John's Reformed Church, located a few miles below the junction of the Broad and Saluda rivers. But he is reported to have made occasional journeys into North Carolina in the days before either the Lutherans or the Reformed there could boast a resident pastor. According to a Reformed historian, Theus "fostered the weak German churches in North Carolina and held them together until permanent ministers came and located there."[40] Theus' missionary visits to North Carolina are believed to have occurred during the period 1745 to 1760.

Other German and Swiss Reformed clergy credited with service among the German settlers in Piedmont North Carolina include James Martin who was preaching at St. Paul's in what is now Catawba County as early as 1759. A Pastor Dupert of the Reformed Church is known to have visited St. Paul's in 1764, possibly in connection with a celebration of the long-awaited completion of "the Dutch meeting house."[41]

In addition to the services provided by Reformed pastors from South Carolina, North Carolina's early Reformed and Lutheran settlers could be grateful for the expanding Moravian settlement in Stokes County. The Moravian concern for mission outreach meant that German-speaking missionaries were taking leave of Salem from time to time to preach the Gospel on the southern frontier. While especially concerned about addressing those who knew not the love of God in Christ Jesus, they would also pause to bring the ministry of Word and Sacraments to German Christians who were serious enough about their faith to continue to meet together for worship. Lutherans often benefited from the missionary tours of George Soelle who could minister in both German and English. The missionary work undertaken by Soelle with its frequent crossings of the Yadkin was arduous indeed for one already in his sixties and in poor health.

> He was a poor horseman and preferred to walk but his doctor ordered him to travel by horseback. In his diary he wrote of getting dizzy riding across swollen streams and noted that sometimes friends swam his horse across a stream while he crawled across on a log or used a boat. Sometimes he lost his way, or his horse wandered off, and he had to borrow a mount until someone found his horse and returned it. On occasions he wrote of stopping at homes where there was little to eat for either him or his horse. Despite the hardships, he preached to congregations as far as sixty miles from Salem.[42]

In providing an occasional ministry to those of Lutheran and Reformed persuasion in Piedmont North Carolina, the Moravian missionaries like Soelle demonstrated their traditional commitment to evangelical witness coupled with an abhorrence of proselytizing from other Christian denominations.

But the ministries provided by Moravian missionaries and by Reformed pastors from South Carolina were clearly temporary and partial measures. German-speaking Christians outside the Salem community needed the same kind of settled, resident ministry enjoyed by the Moravians within the Salem community. The real beginning of such a continuing settled ministry among North Carolina's Germans outside Salem dates from the arrival of Samuel Suther in the Piedmont in June 1768.[43]

Settling in that portion of Mecklenburg County that became Cabarrus, Suther based his ministry in the Cold Water, Grace (Lower Stone) and Dutch Buffalo Creek congregations, just east of present-day Concord. His was, however, a ministry that stretched from Mecklenburg County in the west to Orange County in the east, with ministry documented at Pilgrim near present-day Lexington as well as Low's, Liberty. In October 1771, Suther responded to a call to serve Brick Church in Guilford County. From that more easterly base of operations, he also continued to provide the Reformed and Lutheran Christians in Alamance, Davidson, Rowan, Cabarrus and Stanly counties with occasional visits.

The decision of Suther to relocate in Guilford County forced the German settlers on Second Creek in southeastern Rowan County to confront several realities. Although Suther had been living in the area for over three years, the folk had grown to appreciate having a settled, German-speaking pastor in their midst. No doubt Suther would visit them from time to time, just as he would continue his occasional visits to Germans in the other counties. But the Germans in Rowan no longer had nearby an ordained pastor who spoke German when a funeral was to be conducted, a baby baptized, or a new Christian home established through Holy Matrimony. Such matters had to wait for months until Suther, a Moravian missionary, or a Reformed pastor from South Carolina, happened to come by. Older persons, in particular, were concerned that, should death claim them, they might be months in their grave before a real pastor came along to say a prayer over their final resting place.

But with all of their appreciation for the ministry that Suther had provided, there were those among the Germans on Second Creek who found in Suther one who forced them to recall the historic differences between the Swiss reformer, Huldrych Zwingli, and the father of their own tradition, Martin Luther. Intelligent, articulate and a true spiritual son of Zwingli, Suther accepted an appointment to serve as chaplain to the militia battalions from the area where he resided. Luther did not see fit to bestow on the fallen Zwingli the robe of a hero simply because he died on a battlefield, and Suther's acceptance of a military appointment probably did not elevate him in the esteem of many of the Lutherans he had been serving. But the critical issue was that Suther followed Zwingli in the thological perspective that had separated the Swiss reformer from the friar of Wittenberg from the time of their meeting at Marburg. Their differences in understanding the Lord's Supper led Luther to conclude that Zwingli was of a different spirit than the one that guided him. Years later in North Carolina, Samuel Suther would combine his delight in verbal battles with his Zwinglian understanding of the Sacrament of the Altar, launching "powerful and sarcastic attacks" on the Lutheran understanding of the Lord's Supper.[44] Clearly, if the Germans on Second Creek wanted the benefits of a Lutheran ministry in their midst, they would have to look to someone other than Samuel Suther.

Senior members of Lutheran families in eastern Rowan shared with one another their concern. Earnest conversations soon produced a plan. A resident German-speaking pastor of the Lutheran persuasion must be sought, and a school teacher for the youth. But how? Lutheran clergy were too few to meet the needs of their constituencies in the colonies to the north and to the south. It was decided that the best approach would be to seek help from the Fatherland, and a plan was developed to make application to the consistory of Hanover for assistance. Such an appeal might even merit the support of their monarch, King George III of England, the son of Princess Augusta of Saxe-Gotha. He was elector of Hanover and had taken as his wife Charlotte Sophia of Mecklenburg-Strelitz.

In 1771 approximately sixty German families listing themselves as adherents of the Augsburg Confession sought the assistance of the rector of St. Luke's parish, Rowan County.

Since they lived within the confines of his parish, a parish of the Church of England which was the established church in the colony of North Carolina, Rowan County Lutherans recognized they might appropriately ask his help in securing the special spiritual leadership needed by German Lutherans who had settled in Piedmont Carolina. The rector interceded on their behalf with the governor of the colony, securing his cooperation in urging the Bishop of London to look with favor on their project.

Two laymen, Christopher Rintelmann and Christopher Layrle, proposed to undertake the embassy for their fellow Lutherans at their own expense, an offer that was promptly accepted.[45] Before the end of 1772, Rintelmann and Layrle were heading south to Camden and Charleston on horseback. They went armed with an official commission from Governor Tryon and a letter of recommendation to the Society for the Propagation of the Gospel in Foreign Parts. In Charleston they sold their horses and bought passage on a ship sailing for England.

On arriving in England, Rintelmann and Layrle found an encouraging response. Rev. Johann Caspar Velthusen was serving as Lutheran Court Preacher when the visitors from the colonies arrived, and he assisted them in their undertaking. Moving on to Hanover, Germany, they found the key ecclesiastical group, the consistory, quite sympathetic to their plight, and quite willing to arrange for a pastor and teacher to serve overseas. Approximately $800 was raised as a fund to support a pastor and a teacher for the Germans in Carolina. Worship supplies including a silver host box donated in Holland, along with hymnals, catechisms and Bibles also were made available for the new ministry.

Rev. Adolph Nussmann was selected as the pastor to accompany Rintelmann and Layrle to Carolina. Nussmann was a native of Muenster in Westphalia. A devout Roman Catholic, he had entered the Franciscan order, but shortly before the arrival of the call to Carolina, he had converted to Lutheranism. The Consistory of Hanover supported the young man in his decision to become a Lutheran pastor, providing him with a scholarship to the University of Gottingen where he enrolled in April 1772. When Rintelmann and Layrle arrived in Hanover with their request for a pastor and a school teacher, the consistory was most enthusiastic in endorsing Nussmann for the pastoral post in North Carolina.

Velthusen was frankly concerned about the decision of the consistory. Was it wise to send a recent convert to Lutheranism on such a mission, a mission involving relative isolation from those structures and resources that could help a recent convert come to a deeper understanding of his newly embraced faith? As Nussmann made his way to America, he stopped off in London where he lived with Velthusen while awaiting a ship to Charleston. This contact completely won over the questioning Velthusen, who recognized the good judgment of the consistory in challenging Nussmann to undertake the mission. For twenty-two years, Nussmann provided pastoral leadership for Lutherans in Piedmont North Carolina.[46]

Johann Gottfried Arends was picked as the teacher to accompany Nussmann. A native of Gottingen, Arends attended the famed university there, and then enrolled in the school for prospective teachers in Hanover. The school had been created to prepare persons who were being called upon to provide religious instruction for youth. It may be that he also studied theology although no record of such studies seems to have survived.

Before the end of 1773, Arends and Nussmann arrived in Charleston, and made their way northward to the German settlement on Second Creek in Rowan County, North Carolina.

Nussmann entertained no illusions about the ministry to which he and Arends had been called. They, in the providence of God, had been placed in "remote forests" of a land on the "most distant border of the civilized world." The territory from Haw River to Henry River in Piedmont North Carolina was too vast and contained too many Germans to be properly cared for by Nussmann and Suther. By 1774, the parochial school teacher, Arends, was also visiting congregations such as Pine (Union) Church and Low's, although he was careful to respect the Lutheran understanding that in the life of the church, certain rites are reserved for those who are ordained.[47]

It appears that within a year after Nussmann's arrival at Organ Church, differences developed between some lay leaders in the congregation and the conscientious and committed pastor. Nussmann resigned from his post at Organ, and late in 1774 or early in 1775 entered upon a ministry at Dutch Buffalo Creek (St. John's, Concord), that he continued until his death in 1794. With Nussmann's resignation at Organ, steps were initiated to ordain Arends as his successor. Joachim Buelow, pastor of St. Paul's, Pomaria, South Carolina, conducted the examination and ordination in late August.[48]

Arends accepted his new appointment at Organ and made the Second Creek congregation the base for his ministry for the next decade. His ministry extended from Alamance and Guilford counties in the east to Catawba, Lincoln and Gaston counties in the west. There is no indication that Arends ventured into Mecklenburg, Cabarrus or Stanly counties, areas presumably understood to be the responsibility of Nussmann at Dutch Buffalo Creek. By the same token, although Nussmann paid occasional visits to congregations in Davidson, Guilford, Orange, Stokes and Forsyth counties, he did not intrude in the parishes that were the special responsibility of Arends. In 1785, Arends moved from Rowan to Lincoln County, making that his home parish for the remainder of his life.

The American Revolution disrupted the growth of Lutheranism in North Carolina. The colony itself was torn apart by internal conflict. Particularly after the British invaded North Carolina in 1780-81, the Tories could muster "hundreds of effectives who operated largely on an unsupervised basis with only nominal oversight from British officers."[49] In the Piedmont, where the strife between those favoring independence and the Tories was particularly severe, there had been rapid economic progress in the years just prior to the war, the settlers becoming largely self-sufficient in terms of providing themselves and their families with food, shelter and clothing. The war brought with it embargoes, shortages, wildly fluctuating prices, and inflation. Farm folk again and again found themselves victimized by marauding troops that confiscated their produce, either in the name of King George III or in the name of American independence.

> Many a plowshare rusted away in its unfinished furrow, many a field lay fallow for a long time, little improvement was made anywhere. The strength of manhood, which was needed at home for the development of the resources of the country, was more urgently required to fill up the rank and file of the army; and the women of that period were obliged to perform, to a certain extent, the hard labor that was needed to cultivate the soil, and to gather and prepare its production for home consumption, whilst the long winter evenings were spent in making articles of clothing for the family and for the relatives in the army.[50]

The conflict was no respecter of the church or its pastors. In Georgia, the Salzburgers found that one of their pastors sought to be a man of peace in the midst of conflict, while the other was a conspicuous Tory. When the British established themselves in Savannah, the Tory promptly headed to the port city, swore allegiance to the crown, and invited the occupation of Ebenezer by British troops, an invitation that was quickly accepted.

The Germans in South Carolina reflected significantly different attitudes, depending on where they lived, toward the issues that moved the colonies to rebel against the crown. Those in Charleston did not hesitate to embrace the cause of independence from England, even organizing a German Fusilier Company. On the other hand, Germans in the interior were aware that King George III was of the House of Hanover, a Lutheran and one who had befriended them. They had difficulty sympathizing with the agitation of Charlestonians and "by and large could not understand what all the fuss was about."[51] In southwestern Virginia the Germans won for themselves a reputation for devotion to the cause of independence, being a "God-fearing, liberty-loving people, who were ready to fight when their liberties or rights were encroached upon."[52]

In North Carolina, the German community in the Piedmont produced both conspicuous patriots as well as persons who could not take up arms against their monarch. Despite their being dispatched by the Consistory of Hanover, the home province of the king, North Carolina's two Lutheran missionaries were not sympathetic to the Tory cause. In Rowan Pastor Arends at Organ "was often harassed, persecuted, and at times in danger of his life," but he "took up the cause of American independence, defying both British soldiers and American Tories."[53]

The German settlement on Dutch Buffalo Creek in Cabarrus County was spared the invasion of a regular army, but did not escape harrassment by the Tories.

"Many settlers", a congregational historian reports," were robbed and some were killed, and others taken to prison. Prominent among the latter was John Paul Barringer, who, being too old for the regular service, was surprised and captured in his bed and taken to Camden and held as a prisoner of war...."[54]

Pastor Nussmann "joined his people in loyalty to the American cause and both suffered very much at the hands of the Tories."[55]

The outbreak of the American Revolution broke the lines of communication between the two Lutheran missionaries in North Carolina and the Consistory of Hanover which had sponsored their missionary effort. When the war ended, instead of renewing contacts with the church in Hanover, Nussmann turned to the former chaplain at the court in London, Velthusen. Velthusen had been appointed to the theological faculty at the Julius Charles University of Helmstaedt.

In May 1786, Nussmann dispatched the first in a series of letters in which he outlined for Velthusen the particular needs of the Lutherans whom he had been serving for more than a dozen years. Nussmann's overriding concern was the need for additional pastors, but he was also quick to point out the importance of Christian literature and instructional materials such as catechisms. He also tried to salvage funds that had been raised in Hanover for the benefit of Germans in Carolina. Did the fact that many of the Lutherans in North Carolina had been as ready as their Reformed neighbors to take up arms against King George III mean that the Carolinians had forfeited their claim to the funds solicited on their behalf?

At Helmstaedt a society was created to respond to the needs of the congregations in Carolina. Through Velthusen and the Helmstaedt Society, the funds collected by Rintelmann and Layrle were released and forwarded to Nussmann. Velthusen himself composed a catechism for North Carolina Lutherans which was known as the Helmstaedt Catechism.[56]

Some assistance was also made available to Nussmann and Arends, who struggled not only to serve their particular parishes, but also to expand their ministries to German-speaking communities that did not enjoy the services of a regular pastor. On June 27, 1788, there arrived in Baltimore Carl August Gottlieb Storch of Helmstaedt. Storch had been confirmed by Velthusen and later studied under him at the university. Completing his theological studies in 1785, Storch took a teaching position and was continuing to work as a teacher when Nussmann's plea for assistance came to the desk of Velthusen. Remembering young Storch whose career was a matter of special interest to him, Velthusen invited Storch to take up missionary work in North Carolina, and he agreed.

After spending some weeks in Baltimore, Storch caught a ship for Charleston. There he bought himself a horse, and set out for North Carolina and Nussmann's farm near present-day Mt. Pleasant. When attempts to settle Storch as the pastor at Friedens, Guilford County, did not work out, Nussmann arranged for his settlement in Rowan County. Initially serving the Lutherans in Salisbury, those at Pine (Union) Church and those at Organ (Zion), Storch soon added Irish Settlement (Lutheran Chapel) to his Rowan County parish.

He elected to make his home in Salisbury, a county seat that Governor Dobbs reported had only "seven or eight log houses erected" in 1755, but which by the time Storch arrived had already grown to fifty or sixty houses, ten of which housed German families like the Beards with whom Storch took up residence. From 1788 until his retirement because of ill health in 1823, Storch was an important participant in the struggle of North Carolina Lutherans to discover more fully the meaning of their unity in Christ.[57]

A second pastor dispatched to North Carolina by the Helmstaedt Society in response to Nussmann's entreaty was Arnold Roschen, a native of Bremen who had pursued theological studies at Gottingen and under Conon Nicolai in Bremen. Concluding his studies with Nicolai in 1788, Roschen was ordained for mission work in North Carolina and took unto himself a wife. In early fall he set sail for the New World, reaching Charleston in November. Early the next year he reached North Carolina where he purchased two hundred acres of land near Beck's, Lexington, and built a log cabin for his bride.

For twelve years Roschen provided a ministry of Word and Sacraments for the Lutherans comprising Beck's and St. Luke's, Davidson County; Dutchman's Creek (Reformation), Davie County; and Nazareth and Shiloh, Forsyth County. Roschen and his wife returned to Germany in 1800, and his experience may have contributed to the warning to prospective missionaries to North Carolina not to bring a European wife with them to the Carolina back country lest they encounter "a thousand sad experiences."[58] The theological outlook of these earliest North Carolina Lutheran pastors, was not that represented by either of the two most famous positions of the day, Pietism or Rationalism. As Lutherans in the seventeenth century attempted to expand, systematize and clarify Reformation insights, they produced an increasingly scholastic understanding of Christian faith. In so doing, a high premium was placed on assent to orthodox teaching. Such intellectualizing of the faith produced a reaction on the part of those who were convinced that true religion was a matter of the heart as well as the head. Seventeenth century leaders like Philip Spener and August Hermann Francke launched the movement called Pietism which was to find a home at the University of Halle. And what were the characteristics of this understanding of Christian faith?

"The Pietists", as their records show, "demanded a completely personalized religion which was gained by introspection and prayer. It found its source not in a body of rationalized doctrine but in the intensive reading of the Bible."[59]

When Pastor Muhlenberg visited the colony of Georgia, he sensed an immediate bond of kinship with the Salzburgers and their pastors because they shared this understanding of Christian faith and life that is called Pietism.

Another major theological development in this period was the growth of Rationalism. The origins of this movement are associated with the philosopher, Gottfried Wilhelm von Leibnitz, a man of Lutheran background with unusual breadth of learning. He charted brave new courses for philosophical thought. In so doing, he reflected an understanding of Christian faith significantly at odds with the heritage of the Reformation. Man's sinful nature was not something calling for radical change, a new birth. It was rather a minor flaw in human nature. God was perceived as the perennially friendly father, never as a wrathful judge intolerant of every trace of evil. The world was not a vale of hard work, suffering and tears that made one yearn to escape to the realms of blessedness; rather, it was a good world and one that human efforts could and should improve.

Others who contributed to the development of the Rationalistic mind set were Christian Freiherr von Wolff, a philosopher who in his early years was driven from his faculty position at Halle by the Pietists, and Christian Thomasius, a professor of law who also taught at Halle despite the fact that his "common-sense" philosophy undercut the Pietistic traditions of the University. These earlier thinkers laid the groundwork for the climactic philosophical work of Immanuel Kant. The work of these seminal thinkers that invaded theology decreed that educated reason should be the final norm and standard in all matters religious. Virtuous living here and now was seen as the purpose of all religion, and belief in God and the immortality of the soul were to be fostered since they aided man in striving for virtue.

Those who had nurtured Nussmann, Storch and Roschen in their theological studies were neither Pietists nor Rationalists, even though traces of these understandings of the Lutheran heritage may be found in their thought and practice. Instead, their theological mentors were a part of what has been described as the "Middle Group," theologians who sought to remain true to their Reformation heritage and avoid the extremes of both Pietism and Rationalism.[60] Key figures in this tradition were Johann Lorenz von Mosheim at the University of Helmstaedt and later, at the new University of Gottingen, Gabriel Wilhelm Goetten, who fathered the school for teachers in Hanover where Arends got his education and who also personally supervised the preparation of Nussmann for his work as a Lutheran pastor.

Velthusen, a German Chaplain at the Court of the King in England and subsequent professor on the theological faculty at Helmstaedt, seems to have had a similar theological outlook. During Nussmann's stay in London, he and Velthusen established a warm bond of friendship and mutual understanding. That personal relationship proved significant for the early development of the Lutheran church in North Carolina.

The growth in the number of pastors serving Lutherans in North Carolina no doubt hastened the day when Lutheran pastors and congregations in the state would bind themselves together in a synodical organization. The formal uniting of Lutheran congregations in North Carolina in 1803 actually had its beginnings more than ten years earlier.

Christian Eberhard Bernhardt had come to the colonies from Stuttgart, Germany, in 1786. He came to the Salzburger settlement in Georgia as a teacher and assistant to the pastor at Ebenezer, John Ernest Bergman.

Difficulties between Bergman, who had arrived the previous year, and the new teacher arose almost immediately, the difficulties attributed to Bernhardt's "levity of disposition and insubordination."[61] Bernhardt left Ebenezer and headed north. He made his way to what is now Cabarrus County, North Carolina, where in the summer of 1787 he began several months of assisting Nussmann of St. John's, Concord. Nussmann was impressed by the young man's innate ability, formal education acquired in Germany, and his personal religious commitment. Nussmann probably had a role in arranging for the young candidate for ordination to supply Union, Salisbury, and "several other churches besides."[62]

Another young man living in North Carolina in 1791, John Stanger from Wuerttemberg, was interested in securing ordination as a Lutheran pastor. Stanger, who had studied at the University of Tuebingen, spoke to Roschen of Davidson County about this matter. He had heard of a German settlement on the New River in southwestern Virginia, and asked Roschen, on his next missionary tour, to explore with the folk their possible interest in calling him as their pastor. By May 1790, Stanger apparently had received an official call from the New River settlement, and in that year he qualified at the Wythe County Court House to perform marriages "according to the Lutheran rite."[63]

Given the urgent need for more laborers in the fields "white unto the harvest" plus the availability of two persons with university training and a desire to serve as Lutheran pastors, the four ordained Lutheran ministers in North Carolina convened the first formal gathering of the Ministerium of the Lutheran Church in North Carolina in October 1791. No formal record of the meeting has come to light, but the journal of Arends indicates that this was not just an ad hoc gathering. On the contrary, the pastors resolved to meet semiannually "the first Sunday after Easter and the last Sunday in September." But in addition to organizing for semiannual meetings of Lutheran pastors in North Carolina, the October 1791 assembly ordained both Bernhardt and Stanger to the Gospel ministry.

The spring meeting in 1792 was scheduled for St. John's, Concord, where the "chairman" of the ministerium, Nussmann, resided. Bernhardt was designated as the preacher for the Sunday service in connection with the first meeting of the ministerium in 1792. In communications with friends in Germany, the good news was shared that the daughters and sons of the Reformation who lived in North Carolina now had their own ecclesiastical body. In 1792 that staunch friend of German immigrants in North Carolina, Velthusen, dispatched a package of books to the "six pastors now united in an evangelical synod" in North Carolina.[64] Records have not survived to indicate whether or not the Ministerium of North Carolina kept to its proposed meeting schedule or simply met on call. At any rate, five of the pastors identified with the ministerium met in May 1794, to ordain Robert Johnson Miller. Nussmann, who had been elected "chairman" at the first meeting in 1791, was still the "Senior" of the ministerium at that time, although death claimed him before the end of the year. His death and the growing infirmity of Arends no doubt contributed to a less active ministerium. The fact that two of the other members of the body left the state by 1800 and that the person ordained in 1794 was ordained to the Episcopal, rather than the Lutheran, ministry mitigated against strong organizational development of the body.

But if the Lutheran Ministerium of North Carolina was not an organization characterized by frequent meetings and extensive agendas, it was still sufficiently prominent in the thinking of North Carolina Lutherans that when Paul Henkel, who had moved into North Carolina in 1800, sought the following year to help his own son secure official endorsement for ministerial activity, he went not to the Ministerium of Pennsylvania of which he, the father, was a member, but to the North Carolina pastors "who had united themselves into something of a conference."[65] Pastors Storch and Arends complied with Henkel's request and, on behalf of the ministerium, authorized Philip Henkel to serve as a catechist. The continuing need for a body to help candidates for ordination achieve their credentials justified the perpetuation of an organization such as the ministerium in North Carolina.

Ministers properly prepared were needed to serve the twenty-seven Lutheran congregations existing in North Carolina at the turn of the century. In addition to twelve formed prior to 1774, there were: Union, Salisbury (organized in 1774); Morning Star, Matthews (1775); St. Luke's, Lincolnton (1776); Shiloh, Lewisville (1777); Nazareth, Rural Hall (1778); Lutheran Chapel, China Grove (1780); Cold Water, Concord (reorganized 1782); Emmanuel, Lincolnton (1785); St. Mark's, Cherryville (1786); Beck's, Lexington (1787); St. Luke's, Lexington (1788); Zion, Hickory (1790); Bethel, Lincolnton (1790); Salem, Lincolnton (1796); and Grace, Newton (1797).

But it was not just the need for an organization that could assist and certify candidates for ordination that encouraged the creation of the North Carolina Synod. Developments among the English-speaking Christians who surrounded the Lutheran congregations in North Carolina were confronting Lutheran pastors with a special challenge which demanded a response with one voice. The experience of the pastor who had recently moved from Virginia to Opossum Town just south of Salem was typical. The leaves were already turning yellow and red, brightening the October landscape, as this tall man mounted the saddle of his horse and headed eastward into the morning sunlight. The pastor, Paul Henkel, was off to Guilford County to visit his son, Philip, who had been licensed for the Lutheran ministry six weeks earlier.

The elder Henkel, who was guiding his son's theological studies, had dispatched young Philip to Friedens Lutheran Church to provide catechetical instruction for a number of the congregation's young people. Now he visited his son, concluded the instruction of the youth, confirmed them at a public service of worship, and had the satisfaction of admitting them to the Lord's Supper as the congregation joined in celebrating that sacred meal.

Henkel's visit to Friedens in the fall of 1801 was significant, far beyond the usual significance attached to a confirmation service and celebration of Holy Communion. For in carrying out these ministries, the pastor discovered that many who took part in the services "were deeply exercised."[66]

It was not difficult to discover the cause for the anxiousness and concern among the people. Each day that the pastor labored at Friedens brought him new reports of the impact being made by two young Presbyterian ministers who were preaching "here and there" in the area.[67] They had just returned from Cane Ridge, Kentucky, where on Saturday, August 6, Presbyterians had begun "a sacramental service," actually, a series of preaching services calling for conversion to the Christian faith and culminating in a celebration of the Lord's Supper.

The services at Cane Ridge that stimulated the Presbyterian pastors had been announced well in advance, and, since similar services at the Red River church had produced dramatic results the previous year, nearly 150 wagons discharged passengers at Cane Ridge to add to the teeming crowds that had come by foot and on horseback.[68] The little Presbyterian church at Cane Creek could hold only a tiny fraction of the assembled multitude, so while two Presbyterian ministers led Saturday's 11:00 o'clock service there, another Presbyterian pastor preached to a group assembled in the edge of the woods outside the church.

"Off in another direction", one account indicates, "a Methodist had an audience pressing close to him. Nearby was a knot of Negroes, one of them loudly exhorting the others. Besides the preachers, some of the worshipers, undistracted by the competition, were telling private gatherings of their experiences. One account said there were as many as 300 of these laymen 'testifying.'"[69]

To identify the persons who were converted and thus qualified for admittance to the climactic celebration of the Lord's Supper, a token made of lead was given to each convert. Over 750 tokens were distributed before the close of the Saturday morning services.

Those who came late to the gathering said that as they approached Cane Ridge they heard a sound like the "roar of Niagara." Preachers shouted to make themselves heard above the din, the converted filling the air with shouts of "Hallelujah!" and "Amen!" Those smitten by conscience and the proclamation of God's Law lay writhing on the ground emitting groans of desolation and pleas for mercy. Even the rumble of thunder and the drenching rain Saturday night had failed to dampen the emotions or quench the spirit at work in the multitude. A Methodist preacher reported that on Sunday morning hundreds fell prostrate on the ground before him in response to his preaching of God's Word.

Accordingly, the two youthful Presbyterian divines who made their way to Alamance County, North Carolina, the next week, were brimming over with excitement and anticipation. Confident they had witnessed a new Pentecost, they told their hearers at Cross Roads that the mighty works of God would soon be appearing in their midst. It was not long before the fiery preaching made an impact. "Women were driven into fear causing them to cry for mercy; others were aroused in their emotions causing them to express their sympathy and join in the shouting. The preachers took advantage of the opportunity by offering the assurance that this was but the beginning of the spiritual work...."[70]

An area preacher who initially opposed the emotion-laden services being conducted by the young Calvinists finally attended one of the events out of curiosity. He himself became convinced that this was a work of God and that the Millennium must be at hand. What had been Sunday worship services expanded from Friday to Monday and moved from indoors to outdoors.

"During this time there was constant preaching or exhortations were given", according to one account. "Anybody who wished could preach: men, women, young women or young men. The ordained preachers officiated at the beginning of the service during which time everything was quiet as they mostly preached in an orderly manner. After their sermons came the exhortations in which no order was observed but everyone said what came in his mind, and many intentionally uttered the severest things about death, the devil, judgment, and hell."[71]

Some were fearful, others confused, and still others became pale as death or fell to the earth unconscious. When a respected pastor who spoke the German language they so dearly loved visited their congregation, the elder members at Friedens were eager to discuss with him the strange religious happenings taking place among English-speaking folk in the area.

News of the revival in Alamance and Guilford counties spread quickly and roused interest and raised hopes in Rowan, Iredell and Lincoln counties, especially among the Presbyterians. Clergy acquaintances in North Carolina who supported what came to be known as the Great Revival, or Second Great Awakening, urged the senior Henkel to recognize that it was "a work of God," or, if he could not do that, to at least withhold judgment until he had personally attended a revival meeting and seen, heard and evaluated for himself this manifestation of religion. That Henkel agreed to do, and in February, he had his chance.

A Presbyterian and several Methodist preachers had announced that they would hold a revival near Dutchman's Creek southeast of the present town of Mocksville. Since Henkel was scheduled to spend the last week of January and the first week of February with the Heidelberg congregation in the same neighborhood, providing catechetical instruction for the young people, it would be convenient for him to learn first hand if the lurid stories he heard about revivals were really true.[72]

With the conclusion of the catechetical instruction, a service of confirmation with Holy Communion was held at Reformation on the second Sunday in February. Meanwhile, the revival near Dutchman's Creek, conducted camp-meeting style, was launched. This type of meeting was a novelty in what became Davie County and attracted a crowd of clergy as well as members of the laity. The Presbyterian who organized the affair was joined in his efforts by several Methodist preachers and by several Baptists as well. The Presbyterian saw that the site selected for the camp meeting "was placed in the densest woods where briers and brush were thickest. The pulpit or platform was built on a small elevation large enough to seat 10 men. At first several preached in due rotation but as the crowd could not be moved in this way, three or four preachers harangued at the same time with the most fearful expressions that they could invent until finally two young women rushed on the platform among the preachers, began to sink on the floor and to cry out with much agony and agitation."[73]

The Lutheran pastor and a Moravian counterpart were standing only five feet from the platform, so they had a clear view of what was transpiring on this second night of the revival. What they saw and heard left no doubt in their minds that it was in their judgment, "spiritual fanaticism" run wild.

A few days later at Friedens, Henkel carefully set forth for the congregation and his son what he was convinced was the true understanding of how God takes a corrupt human heart and makes it new in Christ Jesus. In an effort to still the storms of emotionalism, he visited a number of other congregations in the area, valiantly struggling to be pastoral and, at the same time, unwavering in setting forth the biblical understanding of baptism and regeneration as he addressed persons who were confused, questioning and divided in their reactions to the revival.

The first week in March, Henkel responded to a request from Pastor Storch of Rowan County that he join him in attending a massive camp meeting that had been announced for Shepherds Cross Roads just north of the present Mooresville in Iredell County.   Storch maintained cordial relations with several clergymen of other denominations, and through his contacts with Dr. Samuel E. McCorkle of the Presbyterian church he had received reports on the Great Revival. Could it not be that the revivals erupting in North Carolina were the work of God, His tool for uniting "the minds of the people of different religions" and bringing about "a universal conversion of mankind?"[74]   Storch's openness to the new approach to claiming souls for Christ was disturbing to some of his parishioners who urged Henkel to accompany their pastor to the Iredell County camp meeting.

When Henkel reached the camp meeting at sunset, he joined Pastor and Mrs. Storch for supper and a night's rest. The next morning the magnitude of the scene became apparent.

> The first thing that attracted my attention was the large assembly that had gathered. The report of the number of wagons was not exactly given, but there were no fewer than 300 besides other vehicles like carriages, chaises, etc. And there were just as many fires as wagons, and as many tents. The meeting began on Friday and continued through Tuesday. Almost all the wood was consumed for fires and for the erection of huts and platforms. An immense quantity was required for the fires as the exercises continued day and night without interruption. It was the coldest time of the year. The wagons and tents were placed in a regular circle.... In different directions a person could see small groups like little villages. On all sides were heard preaching, exhorting, weeping, lamenting, shouting, singing, praying, praising God, thanksgiving, etc. In many of the tents people were seen lying with covered faces, praying.... Some were lying in a trance.... On every platform there was unceasing preaching.[75]

From some of the "old Presbyterians" Henkel heard strains of "the Gospel as I love to hear it," but he could not understand the unwillingness of such respected colleagues to point out the defective understandings of regeneration advanced by many of the revivalists.

Henkel had come to the camp meeting expecting to play the role of observer. But when Storch's health prevented his fulfilling a commitment to preach, Henkel was prevailed upon to substitute for him, and one sermon led to another. Soon he was going from campfire to campfire accompanied by Storch and Robert Johnson Miller, setting forth what he believed to be a proper understanding of the work of God in the human heart. Between 2:00 p.m. and 2:00 a.m., the Rowan County native preached five sermons and delivered a number of other "exhortations." His attempts to calm the emotions of the groups he addressed and direct them toward a quiet confidence in the forgiveness of sins found in Christ Jesus were successful with a number of groups he addressed.

But his approach did not go unchallenged. "An old Presbyterian preacher," Dr.

James Hall, who had stimulated a group to great excitement, could hardly restrain himself until Henkel concluded his sermon to the same group. When Henkel sat down, Hall was on his feet at once, trying unsuccessfully to restore the group to the excited emotional state that characterized them prior to Henkel's calming sermon. Despite his determined resistance to excessive emotionalism, before that night was over, Henkel was invited to occupy the chief Presbyterian pulpit the following morning. However, he declined to do so. It was not just that his wife had accidentally overheard remarks that made her fear for her husband's safety; he doubted that his most valiant efforts in such an environment could really accomplish very much.

There were those who saw the revival as holding great potential for helping the church manifest its unity. Henkel noted that the Baptists early in 1802 began a revival only five miles from Pilgrim Lutheran Church, Lexington. They invited "the Presbyterians to hold their so-called Big Meeting with them with the offer of holding a union communion service together in order that at last the beginning be made for a general union of all denominations."[76] Before the date for the "Big Meeting" arrived, however, the Baptists had enlisted so many converts they no longer felt a need to use the Presbyterian event as an attraction, so they went ahead with their own celebration of the Lord's Supper, indicating that the idea of holding a joint celebration with the Presbyterians was "a misunderstanding."

Denominational success might in some instances cool enthusiasm for steps toward a manifest unity, but clearly revivalism and camp meetings made important contributions to the unity question. On the one hand, those who sponsored revivals generally felt a strong bond of kinship with others who believed in the efficacy of revivals, no matter what their denominational allegiance. At the same time, those who opposed revivals, if not driven into immediate cooperation, recognized themselves as having a kinship with each other in responding to one of the most conspicuous features of American religion.

But if revivals united some Christians across denominational lines in expectation of outpourings of the Holy Spirit, and united other Christians in the conviction that Christian worship should be conducted "decently and in order," it also proved a divisive force in religious life. It was not just that Christians in the United States were increasingly divided into two camps, revivalistic and anti-revivalistic. Revivalism spawned tension and divisions within historic denominations and even their individual congregations. Historic Thyatira Presbyterian Church in western Rowan County was so deeply divided over the issue of revivals

> that half the congregation and most of the elders pulled out of the church. A wagon with a measuring device attached to the wheels was used by adherents of the new school of worship to pace off exactly five miles at which spot a new church called Back Creek was erected.[77]

Paul Henkel visited his and his son's congregations in North Carolina with increasing frequency in an effort to stem the tide and prevent division within the congregations. In one of his own churches, the congregation attracted the largest attendance they had ever enjoyed when it was announced that on July 25, 1802, Henkel would preach on baptismal regeneration. Since the weather was threatening, the great crowd had to squeeze its way into the church building.

Church buildings were few and far between, and since pastors usually served a number of congregations, they could get around to a particular congregation only once a month or once every six weeks. Meanwhile, representatives of other denominations would visit and hold services in the same building. It was not unusual for persons to attend worship services whenever they were held, irrespective of the denominational affiliation of the pastor who happened to be officiating. Henkel recognized that not all in his audience that day held the Lutheran understanding he sought to expound, and he tried to present his theme as "tenderly" as he could. Nevertheless, some of the "immersionists" in the audience found his sermon very upsetting.

"One of their company who carried a large club in his hand stepped up to the pulpit and interrupted my sermon", he recalled. "He ordered me to be silent. I requested him to keep quiet until I was through, and then he might speak as much as he wished, but he continued to interrupt me until I had to stop. I left the pulpit and stepped before the table in order to speak with the fellow, but I was immediately surrounded by all his companions, men and women, and all seemed ready to attack me."[78]

Those who were so upset at Henkel's sermon spoke English; those who spoke German outnumbered them three to one. But the Germans were concerned that the house of God not be marred by a brawl, so they accepted the leadership of their pastor and the elders who led them out of the building.

Later Henkel, in joining Storch and other clergy for a series of services at Organ, Salisbury, observed, "We, the preachers, had different ideas about the revivals, and our disputations became very warm at times. . . ."[79] As the Second Great Awakening became domesticated in North Carolina, the Lutheran pastors recognized the need to maintain closer contact with each other and to develop a common understanding of revivalism and its implications for the Lutheran tradition. The need for closer contact and common understanding joined with the need for helping ordination candidates to call for united efforts by North Carolina's Lutheran pastors.

The two concerns also put Paul Henkel center stage. His preparation of his son Philip for ordination, as authorized earlier by the ministerium, had proceeded. The father was now concerned that his son be ordained by an established and recognized church, not just the loose association of pastors who had constituted the ministerium and ordained pastors in the past.

Yet he was not so much calling for the creation of something new as he was calling for the more formal structuring and the more efficient administering of an association Lutheran leaders in North Carolina had established in 1791. By adopting a formal constitution and, in the process deciding that ecclesiastical decisions in the Lutheran Church in North Carolina should involve laity as well as clergy, Lutheranism in North Carolina ceased to be simply a ministerium and became, in fact, what Velthusen had generously labeled the ministerium in 1792: a synod.

On March 20, 1803, Henkel visited Storch across the Yadkin to discuss the creation of "a Conference for the union of our Lutheran ministers in the state in order that we might further the education of young men who have ministry in view. Pastor Storch agreed to the plan. I next went to Pastor Miller in Lincoln County; he agreed to the plan, and then together we went to Pastor Arends, who although old and almost totally blind, agreed to attend."[80]

Thus it came about that, on the weekend of the Third Sunday after Easter, 1803, a series of worship services was held by the Lutherans at Pine (Union) Church a few miles southeast of Salisbury. Following these well-attended services, the pastors and lay delegates went into the town of Salisbury where, on Monday, they proceeded with the work of transforming a loose association of pastors, the North Carolina Ministerium, into a bond of unity for Lutherans, lay and ordained alike.

Through their efforts, Lutherans who had been torn loose from their familiar communal ties of church and family in Europe and scattered across the Piedmont section of North Carolina created at Lincolnton in the fall a continuing organization, the North Carolina Synod.

Muhlenberg led in the creation in 1748 of the first such Lutheran synod in the United States, the Ministerium of Pennsylvania. That body, by providing "oversight and giving direction to all its congregations, was a major step in fostering Lutheran identity and consciousness. . . ."[81] North Carolina's scattered Lutherans would discover that a synod could provide them also with a conscious identity as a part of the one, holy, catholic, and apostolic church. ✝

St. John's, Concord
Organized 1745

Organ, Salisbury (1794)
Organized 1745

Friedens, Gibsonville (1940)
Organized 1745

Paul Henkel
First Native North Carolinian Ordained
into Lutheran Ministry

St. John's, Salisbury (1927)
Organized 1747

CHAPTER III

DIVISION (1804-1837)

The day was hot, hot as a mid-summer Sunday in a Southern town; yet it was only the 28th of May. The afternoon sun was dropping and trees were already beginning to cast long shadows. But on the dusty wagon trails that were the main streets in Lincolnton, North Carolina, in 1820, the heat still weighed heavily on everyone who ventured forth. The one place in town where the early taste of summer apparently had not squelched all activity and movement seemed to be in front of a wooden structure which served as the town's church, a building only a block from the courthouse square. North Carolina's Lutherans were gathering for the annual convention of their synod; a number of men stood in front of the simple, wooden building that had recently had its walls and roof raised in order to make the building less oppressively hot on days like this one.[1] A cluster of delegates just outside the entrance to the building was approached by a solitary figure, quite probably the secretary of the synod, Gottlieb Schober, who launched a question in the direction of the clergy and lay delegates who had congregated near the entrance to the building. "Will you withdraw from the Synod?" Again he probed; "Will you submit to the decision of the majority of the ministers and lay-delegates, relative to the controversies and differences?"

After some verbal parrying and thrusting, the questions were answered quite explicitly:

> We will not withdraw from the Synod, nor will we be ruled by a majority, but are ready and willing to investigate everything according to the teachings of the Augsburg Confession and the Constitution of the Synod, but not otherwise.[2]

The response did not satisfy the interrogator. He pressed for a simple "yes" or "no" answer to his original questions, and was finally informed that the Henkel party would neither withdraw from the synod nor agree to be bound by whatever the majority of the pending convention decided. With that, the questioner withdrew only to return in a few minutes with a substantial delegation who had been awaiting his report. Again the questions were posed, and again the Henkel party insisted that the only appropriate way for Lutherans to resolve differences was on the basis of the Augsburg Confession and the constitution of the synod. The leader of the lately-arrived delegates insisted that the synod had no constitution in force by which the matters of difference could be adjudicated and that all must agree to settle the matter by a majority vote. To this the Henkel party again responded that matters of doctrine were involved in the dispute, and that doctrinal matters could only be decided by consulting the church's doctrinal standard, the Augsburg Confession which reflected the teachings of the Bible. Majority opinions should not be permitted to displace the synod's confessional position.

Neither group succeeded in persuading the other of the correctness of its position, so the two groups filed into the church building without resolving their differences. The president, C. A. G. Storch of Rowan County, delivered a lengthy address in German setting forth the position he sought to maintain amid the mounting differences disturbing the synod. The secretary, Gottlieb Schober of Salem, then delivered an even longer address in English, again contending that the constitution which appeared in his book *Luther* was not officially adopted by the synod as its governing document, but was merely a plan that might eventually be modified and adopted by the synod should it so see fit. The ensuing discussion revealed that the Henkel party understood the matter differently. The volume *Luther*, which Schober would describe as "by Dr. Luther," was actually prepared by Schober at the synod's request.[3] The book, including its constitution for the synod, was reviewed and endorsed by an official committee of the synod, and on the basis of the committee's recommendation, approved by the synod for publication and distribution. Subsequent attempts by Schober at the Lincolnton convention to depict the constitution in *Luther* as lacking official status failed to convince a significant portion of those present.

SYNOD PRESIDENTS
(prior to division)

1803-04	J. G. Arends	1813-15	C. A. G. Storch
1804-06	Paul Henkel	1815-16	Philip Henkel
1806-12	C. A. G. Storch	1816-21	C. A. G. Storch
1812-13	R. J. Miller		

The division between North Carolina Lutherans at Lincolnton in 1820 - in the vivid memory of everyone present - was a personal clash between the youthful, abrasive, brilliant David Henkel and the elderly, dignified Gottlieb Schober.

But simply personalizing the clash distorts the origins of the Tennessee Synod and its century-long separation from the North Carolina Synod. Beneath the clash of personalities was fundamental disagreement over sacramental theology and the primacy of Luther's teaching about baptism and the Eucharist. David Henkel and his supporters represented a confessional party in the dispute which defended traditional Lutheran sacramentalism; Schober and most of the North Carolina Synod pastors formed a denominational party willing to blend Lutheran, Episcopal, Moravian and German Reformed sacramental practices as a means of uniting people of those backgrounds into an American Lutheran denomination or - in the case of Robert Johnson Miller - an Episcopal-Lutheran denomination.

The Henkels had been a brooding presence in North Carolina Synod affairs. Miller, in 1816, called the family a "cloud in the north east corner of our little Synodical horizon," which he had "long seen it gathering," and which threatened to produce a "deluge," or worse yet an "explosion."[4] He meant that their insistence on the Augsburg Confession as the standard of Lutheran orthodoxy was bound to disrupt the fragile consensus among North Carolina Synod pastors and laity. The constitutional issues which the Henkels pressed in 1820 were just the explosion which Miller had long feared.

It reportedly was in the midst of the doctrinal debate that an officer of the North Carolina Synod exclaimed that whoever in the assembly was "a right Lutheran" should follow the officers of synod to John Harry's hotel where the synod convention would proceed with its business. The invitation provoked the retort, "Whoever is a real fanatic

(*Schwarmer*), let him follow; for you are no true Lutheran preachers; you are fanatics, and to such you belong."[5]

Thus, the young organization that united Lutheran congregations in the Carolinas, Tennessee and Virginia was fractured. Those gathering at the hotel continued the formal structure of the North Carolina Synod for the next one hundred years. Those who remained in the church decided to adjourn until July. At that time they met at Solomon's Church near Greeneville, Tennessee, and organized another Lutheran synod for the South, the Evangelical Lutheran Tennessee Synod. The two bodies would vie with one another for the commitment and loyalty of Lutherans in the Southeast, and each make its positive contribution to the development of future church bodies.

The division removed a number of congregations from the North Carolina Synod in the years that followed. Among them were churches near Lincolnton (Bethel, Daniels, Emmanuel, St. Luke's and Salem), Newton (Grace and St. Paul's), Cherryville (St. Mark's), Dallas (Philadelphia), Hickory (Zion), Lexington (Beck's), and Matthews (Morning Star).

CONVENTION SITES
(prior to division)

1803 St. John's, Salisbury; Emmanuel, Lincolnton
1804 Pilgrim, Lexington
1805 Union, Rowan County
1806 Organ, Rowan County
1807 Lincolnton
1808 Pilgrim, Lexington
1809 Lau's, Guilford County
1810 Organ, Rowan County
1811 St. John's, Catawba County
1812 Lincoln County; Lau's, Guilford County
1813 Pilgrim, Lexington
1814 Organ, Rowan County
1815 Emmanuel, Lincolnton
1816 Reformed Church, Guilford County
1817 Pilgrim, Lexington
1818 (no meeting)
1819 St. John's, Cabarrus County
1820 Lincolnton[6]

As new congregations formed, some elected to affiliate with the Tennessee Synod. They included: Coble, Julian (1812); St. Martin's, Albemarle (1820); Trinity, Vale (1822); Mt. Moriah, China Grove (1824); Lutheran Chapel, Gastonia (1828); Friendship, Taylorsville (1833); and St. Stephen's, Hickory (1837).

There were of course other congregations formed during the period which did affiliate with the North Carolina Synod: New Bethel, Richfield (1806); St. Martin's, Concord (1819); Luther's, Richfield (1830); St. Paul's, Salisbury (1830); St. Peter's, Salisbury (1832); St. Enoch, Kannapolis (1835); and St. Stephen's, Gold Hill (1837).

What were the factors that led to the confrontation and division at Lincolnton in

1820? A variety of issues were involved, some of which were theological, some organizational, some social and some quite personal. The search for Christian unity in North Carolina during the early nineteenth century raised difficult and divisive issues: the nature of the church, the sacraments, and, above all, the meaning of Christian unity. To what degree should one endeavor to put away the speech and thought patterns, the habits and the culture of "the old country?" Some, concerned to reflect the unity of God's people and the uniqueness of the bold new political experiment called America, urged Lutherans to identify with the main stream of American religious life. That main stream bore the designation "Puritan", but today a more helpful title would be "Evangelicalism". The rootage of the tradition was the Puritanism that so strongly shaped the life of early New England. As the noted church historian, Philip Schaff, observed when he arrived in the United States in 1844, "Puritan Protestantism forms properly the main trunk of our North American church," not Episcopal, Lutheran, nor German or Dutch Reformed.[7]

NORTH CAROLINA SYNOD PRESIDENTS

1821-23 Gottlieb Schober	1832-35 Henry Graeber
1823-24 C. A. G. Storch	1835-36 Jacob Scherer
1824-25 Jacob Scherer	1836-37 William Artz
1825-32 Gottlieb Schober	1837-38 Henry Graeber

Thus, at the birth of the United States, Congregationalism was the dominant religious denomination in New England, and Presbyterianism enjoyed that distinction in the East and in the South. From a theological point of view, these expressions of the Reformed faith were still the dominant traditions fifty years later.

A primary characteristic of the Puritan tradition and the Evangelicalism that emerged from it was the centrality of the Holy Scriptures. The Bible was perceived to be the one indispensable "means of grace" which must be made available for all to read and study. "It was the common ground of all evangelical denominations and provided the way of salvation apart from any denomination."[8]

In America this evangelical tradition came to emphasize a datable, personalized, conversion experience, preferably one "which came about suddenly and publicly and under excruciating emotional pressure."[9] Concern to exalt the grace of God revealed in Holy Baptism and the Lord's Supper receded as efforts were made to stress personal response to God's grace, especially the initial positive response of the believer. This stress on one's personal religious experience rather than God's astonishing initiatives and sustaining power was not as conspicuously dominant in the Great Awakening in the eighteenth century as it became in the Second Great Awakening.[10]

But as Lutherans began to identify themselves as Americans and not just displaced Germans, the datable, conversion experience had already joined belief in the Bible as a hallmark of the dominant forms of American Christianity, whether bearing the label Baptist, Methodist or Calvinistic.

The frontier revival blended together these traditions of the Bible as the universal sacrament and personal conversion producing holy living as the proof of participation in the redeemed community. In 1794 the Methodists in North Carolina began their official sponsorship of camp meetings, and the camp meeting quickly became a major vehicle for the revival in the Tar Heel State.[11] Conversion at a camp meeting did not always produce membership in a neighboring congregation, but reflections on the significance of the American Revolution and its mandate to assume responsibility for one's own destiny made it easier for many in the South as elsewhere "to participate in the only organization which sought them out, made them responsible for ordering a new holy community, and built the entire structure upon their own personal experience." Thus, the military success signaled by the surrender of Cornwallis at Yorktown and the necessary ecclesiastical adjustments mandated by the creation of a new nation produced "a political and social world view which was conducive to building a new religious community based on common participation in a holy life."[12] Using Methodist principles of organization, the revival movement in the early nineteenth century soon manifested itself in every section of the young nation, and the shared understandings that characterized the myriad congregations provided an important ingredient in the increasing sense of nationhood.

NORTH CAROLINA SYNOD CONVENTION SITES

1821	Lau's, Guilford County	1830 Lau's, Guilford County
1822	Pilgrim, Lexington	1831 Organ, Rowan County
1823	Organ, Rowan County	1832 St. Paul's, Lincolnton
1824	St. John's, Cabarrus County	1833 Friedens, Guilford County
1825	Brick Church, Guilford County	1834 St. Paul's, Wythe County, Virginia
1826	Zion, Botetourt County, Virginia	1835 St. John's, Salisbury
1827	St. Paul's, Lincoln County	1836 Pilgrim, Lexington
1828	Union, Rowan County	1837 St. John's, Cabarrus County[13]
1829	St. John's, Wythe County, Virginia	

What were the factors that prompted such a widespread response in the South to the calls for conversion? No doubt they were numerous and usually intertwined, but the relative isolation in which most frontier families lived out their days must have made an event like a camp meeting, in which hundreds and, on occasion, even thousands of persons came together for several days, events of great stimulation and excitement. But in reporting on conditions in the Carolinas and Georgia in May 1784, Pastor Nussmann pointed to another source of stimulus for response to revivals. "Thousands of families, with numerous children, scattered at wide intervals, are forgetting Christianity; their children know even less of it [than the parents], and their grandchildren are becoming genuine heathen."[14] It is likely that some memories and traditions of family identification with the Christian church in earlier times survived to stimulate both feelings of guilt and of longing. The population had grown so rapidly on the frontier that the church had not been able to keep up with either the growth or the dispersion.

The church had long relied upon the regular proclamation of the Gospel through Word and Sacraments plus religious instruction as the means for opening the human heart to conversion by the Holy Spirit. But with the vast hordes of unchurched persons who rarely had opportunity to hear a sermon, much less benefit from sacramental grace or religious instruction, it seemed to many some simpler, more direct approach must be taken to bring the good news of forgiveness of sins through Christ to the multitudes. When a noted Presbyterian divine proclaimed in 1829 that since God "had already done everything necessary for salvation," all that remained for "man's salvation depended on his own decision," he was but echoing a conclusion already reached by the vast majority who stood in that modified Puritan tradition of Evangelicalism.[15] For persons on the frontier, daily experience seemed to reinforce the idea of assuming responsibility for one's own fate. With such persons, a message placing the responsibility for one's religious success or failure on one's own shoulders struck a responsive chord.

TENNESSEE SYNOD CONVENTION SITES

1820 Solomon's, Greene County, Tennessee
1821 Zion, Sullivan County, Tennessee
1822 St. James, Greene County, Tennessee
1823 Sinking Spring, Greene County, Tennessee
1824 Koiner's, Augusta County, Virginia
1825 St. John's, Catawba County
1826 Buehler's, Sullivan County, Tennessee
1827 Zion, Sullivan County, Tennessee
1828 St. Paul's, Lincoln County
1829 Salem, Lincolnton
1830 Emmanuel, Greene County, Tennessee
1831 Buehler's, Sullivan County, Tennessee
1832 Phanuel's, Rowan County
1833 St. John's, Lincoln County
1834 (no meeting)
1835 Blue Spring, Greene County, Tennessee
1836 Philadelphia, Lincoln County
1837 Koiner's, Augusta County, Virginia[16]

It was not that the new understanding of Christian faith marked a complete departure from the faith known by earlier generations. Preaching, which enjoyed such prominence in those traditions that traced their roots to the Reformation, remained imperative since persons must be brought to a knowledge of their lost state, of God's offer of forgiveness, and of the necessity for a decision. Preaching was so urgently demanded that it might be undertaken even by persons devoid of formal education or theological study if they believed, and could convince at least some other persons, that they were "called" to do so. Decision in response to proclamation was the key; sacraments and catechetical instruction, along with theological education, were relegated to a subordinate status. They might help some persons, but many had been lured into formalism by rite and ritual, whether in worship or theological study. Some forms of Evangelicalism disparaged formal theological education and a sacramental understanding of Christianity. Others sought to combine traditional concern for educated clergy and the Gospel as communicated in Word and Sacraments with the chief features of Evangelicalism.

In the 1820s a new figure emerged on the American religious scene who breathed fresh life into Evangelicalism and stimulated much debate. Charles Grandison Finney, a lawyer turned evangelist, worked on the assumption that his predecessors in the Calvinistic tradition were mistaken in assuming that revivals were miraculous outpourings of the Spirit of God. On the contrary, he contended, by adopting the proper "means" or techniques and procedures, one could produce revivals of religion. His "new measures" designed to produce revivals were widely adopted and even more widely debated, provoking considerable debate even within the Lutheran community. Finney brought the revival thrust of the camp meeting to the town and city by introducing the protracted meeting. Unlike the camp meeting, the protracted meeting was held indoors, usually in a church but sometimes in a public hall or auditorium. "The main purpose of the protracted meeting was the conversion of sinners, but the promotion of vital piety among professing Christians was also recognized as an important objective."[17] Lutherans who would have been uncomfortable describing a series of their worship services as a camp meeting or revival could wax eloquent on the values of the "protracted meeting."

Finney's "new measures" included the "anxious bench," the practice of inviting to a front pew those made "anxious" by the preaching of the Law but not yet converted. Such persons then became the objects of special intercessions as well as exhortations. A South Carolina Lutheran pastor who was bold enough to sign himself "Revivalist" found this Finney technique to be useful:

> I am compelled to approve of the plan of calling up mourners to be prayed for; - my own experience teaches me that it is highly beneficial. I have seen sinners converted on the anxious seat.[18]

Other innovations associated with Finney include permitting women to give in worship services their testimony to God's workings in their lives, and preachers publicly praying for sinners by name, both those in attendance and those conspicuous by their absence, and for their conversion. More fundamentally, Finney introduced major changes in the theology historically associated with Reformed Christianity. At the same time he achieved national prominence and influence as a most "successful practitioner, almost the inventor, of the modern high-pressure revivalism which, as it spread, would have important consequences for the religious ethos of the nation as a whole."[19]

The ministry of Finney was associated primarily with the East and Northeast, but clergy in the South watched for outcroppings of the same enthusiasm that characterized the meetings conducted by Finney in Utica, Wilmington, Lancaster, Boston and New York City. From South Carolina, a Lutheran pastor reported on "four day meetings" conducted at St. Stephen's, Lexington, and at Bethlehem, Pomaria. At Lexington where a "commodious house of worship" had just been erected, the protracted meeting provided the occasion for an official consecration of the new facility.

> On Lord's day about one thousand persons attended, great effects were visible, hundreds were bathed in tears, a profound solemnity pervaded the whole assembly, more than one hundred individuals accepted the invitations given to those who desired to be personally conversed with on the subject of their soul's salvation.[20]

A week later, a similar meeting and well attended, was held in Bethlehem church, Newberry District, and with the same results. The writer was convinced Lutherans were "waking up from spiritual sleep, and fast abandoning their old prejudices on these subjects." To hasten that transition, the writer gave assurances on the one point at which he assumed Lutherans might, with some justification, take exception to protracted meetings. "These meetings were conducted in an orderly manner, attended with no unnecessary noise, every thing approaching to confusion was immediately checked."[21]

Since most Lutherans find revivalism, whether of the camp meeting or protracted meeting variety, foreign to what they understand Lutheranism to represent, one may ask how thousands of Lutherans in the South found it possible to embrace such an understanding of Christian faith. Pietism, of course, was one of the strands of Lutheran tradition that many German immigrants brought with them to the New World. Certain aspects of Pietism prepared the soil of many Lutheran hearts to accept a revivalistic approach to the spread of the Gospel. Bible study and prayer groups were conspicuous characteristics of classic Pietism. Evangelicalism's extolling of the authority of the Bible and the emergence of prayer meetings as accouterments to revivalism was looked upon by many Lutherans as proof enough of authentic ministry.

Again, it was characteristic of Pietism to stress a personalized, consciously appropriated and heart-felt piety. Early New England Puritanism endorsed similar concerns, but the shift from such legitimate concerns to the point where the crucial ingredient in Christian faith is a person's decision to accept Christ and not God's decision to redeem and reclaim the person is not difficult to make, especially when one's professions of faith are regularly punctuated with exclamations ostensibly giving God "the glory."

Once more, it should be noted that the Lutheran tradition has consistently professed its belief in "one, holy, catholic and apostolic" church, insisting on affirming the unity of God's people in Christ, even in the face of an astonishing array of diverse groups, each claiming to be a church. Pietism promoted a concern for recognition of sisters and brothers in the faith on the basis of their personal piety and holy living, rather than on the basis of denominational label. Like Pietism, revivals provided an opportunity to give tangible expression to one's underlying conviction that, in fact, the unity of men and women in Christ transcends denominational lines. That may not have been an influential factor in prompting initial Lutheran participation in this or that revival, but it was a significant factor for many as they reflected on the meaning of worship experiences in which they joined with large numbers of Presbyterians, Methodists, and Baptists in singing enthusiastic praise to God and in seeking his blessing.

R. B. Weiser, a Lutheran pastor in western Virginia, explained in detail why his German pietism led him to embrace revivalism. To be worthy of the name, he argued, religion must be not simply a matter of intellectual understanding and assent, a matter of the head; it must be "heart-felt", "experimental." No form of promoting the faith was better calculated, he believed, to produce "experimental Christianity" than revivalism.[22] In discussing the "origin" of revivals, Weiser parted company with the illustrious Finney. He was convinced that revivals have "their origin in heaven, in the mind of God." "We are not among those who believe, that genuine revivals can be got up at the pleasure of the preacher; although we do most firmly believe, that God is at all times, and in all places, willing to answer the prayers of his people, and to pour out his Spirit when we ask it in faith."[23]

Weiser had no difficulty reconciling revivalism with his Lutheran faith because he believed he saw in the Bible ample illustrations of revivals being used to promote God's kingdom. Ezra's expounding of the law of Moses to the people described in the eighth chapter of Nehemiah he saw as the prototype of later revivals.

> About fifty thousand people assembled early in the morning, on the Sabbath day. Ezra was the principal instrument in this glorious work. He took his stand on a temporary pulpit erected for the occasion. Ezra ascends the pulpit; he opens the book of the law; the whole congregation is in commotion; they stand upon their feet and look with deep anxiety upon the scribe, whose hands are clasped, and whose heart is directed to God! And what must have been the import of this holy man's prayer? The people had sinned against the Lord their God, they were generally backsliders; how appropriate then must not the prayer of Habakkuk have been: O! Lord, revive thy Work? He did not pray from a book, nor did he pray in a low tone, but he prayed from the heart, and must have prayed with a loud voice to be heard by fifty thousand souls; when he closed his prayer, the people all lifted up their hands, and said, amen! amen![24]

Ezra's preaching produced excitement, "a wonderful excitement, for the people all wept bitterly." Emotions began to run so high that by noon the governor, Nehemiah, "found it necessary to break up the meeting." The preaching of the Law had done its work; and when "the fountain of the great deep of their hearts" had been broken up producing "anguish, sorrow and remorse,"

> he poured the balm of consolation into their troubled hearts! How affecting must not this scene have been! To see fifty thousand souls, mourning and weeping, on account of their sins. O! this must have been a glorious revival of religion![25]

For Weiser, Pentecost was yet another instance of a biblical revival. It excited his imagination to reflect on that memorable scene. Three thousand souls saved? If that many were converted, there may well have been another ten thousand who were "awakened", and who can say how many were "alarmed"? Just picture the throng being addressed by Peter.

> Imagine this immense multitude, their hearts filled with the deepest sorrow, their consciences awakened into a painful and almost intolerable remorse, their fears alarmed, and their feelings excited to the highest pitch of intensity, and all exclaiming, in the bitterness and anguish of their troubled souls, what shall we do? Imagine all this, and you have a revival of religion.[26]

Given the magnitude of revivals Weiser saw in the pages of Holy Writ, his only concern was that contemporary revivals seemed puny by comparison.

Weiser readily admitted that revivals were controversial, as they had been in apostolic times, but "no one who had experienced a change of heart ever thought of opposing revivals." As for his contemporary opponents, he believed they could usually be categorized as "nominal Christians" or infidels, deists or heterodox of some sort. No doubt there were "some well-meaning and serious people" among the opponents of revivals, but for him the fact that "all the wicked and ungodly world" opposed revivals was "strong evidence that they must be of God."

Though Weiser also conceded that after the fourth century revivalism in the church declined, he exulted that, in the sixteenth century, the Lord "raised up another great Revival Preacher, in the person of Luther." Again the Holy Spirit was poured forth on the church. "Luther was a man, and but a man, but he was a man of God, a revival man, a man of revolutionary energy, and his preaching, like a peal of thunder in a calm summer's day, electrified the moral world!"[27] From Luther's time to his own day, Weiser was convinced that the Lutheran tradition had produced "some of the most devoted revival men in the world," men like John Arndt, Philip Spener and August Herman Franke. Abraham Reck of Winchester, Virginia, he considered among the first of the nineteenth century Lutheran revivalists, since his "measures" were considered new "and excited much opposition in the Synod." Happily, from Weiser's point of view, it was now possible to point to several prominent Lutheran pastors like J. G. Schmucker in Pennsylvania, Benjamin Kurtz in Maryland and George A. Lintner in New York who were reportedly revival men.

Weiser did not hesitate to confess his debt to Finney as he discussed the ways to promote revivals. Protracted meetings, "(or, as we call them in the Lutheran Church) conferences, are among the best means of promoting revivals." A pastor moving into a new parish might resolve to start out by preaching a series of sermons on topics such as human depravity, the consequences of sin, the nature of repentance, God's call to a new birth, and what it means to live a new life in Christ. Since most congregations had worship services only once a month, it would be half a year before the series could be completed. In a single protracted meeting or "conference" the entire range of topics could be set forth in three days!

The "anxious bench" also seemed to Weiser a valued tool. Clergy needed to confer directly with those "who profess to be awakened":

> The minister must give an invitation to those who are awakened to come forward to some particular place which he shall designate. Here then we have what are commonly called "anxious seats or benches." The minister calls for a separation in the congregation between the careless and the concerned. And is this contrary to the Bible? Did not Joshua do the same? And is not the very same thing done on every communion occasion?[28]

The fact that the anxious bench was prominently associated with the Methodist movement did not diminish Weiser's appreciation for it. That tradition "with her hundreds of thousands of active, intelligent and zealous members" and with "her apostolic energy, her wide spread and far-extended moral influence" should be proof enough of the value of the anxious bench.

Weiser recognized that most Lutheran opposition to revivals focused on overt expressions of emotion; "too much noise, too much weeping, too much groaning, too much sighing, too much praying!" He assured his readers that he was not an advocate "of noise and confusion, and especially not in the house of God." He would not think of opposing anyone's silent conversion.

> But man is a complex being consisting of soul and body. And these two are so interwoven with each other, that you cannot touch the one without affecting the other. When religious truth is communicated to the soul, it must be done through the channel of the body. When the body is in pain, the soul like a faithful companion

sympathizes with it.[29]

The Word of God can penetrate the human heart, but the one so wounded may use every ounce of self control to prevent those around him or her from knowing the true state of their soul. For months or even years the inner disquiet may be concealed from all human observers, and this very fact may be the reason the person never enjoys the peace God seeks to bestow. Weiser was convinced that many "have made themselves wretched and miserable through life, because they were too proud to make known the state of their minds!" On the other hand, persons with no less inner anguish may be "thrown into the greatest animal excitement, and may find relief sooner." Is it not the height of presumption to try to hold in check "the gush of feeling which flows from the awakened sinner's heart?" Who is to say "how much feeling those who are laboring under religious conviction are to have?"

The revivalism espoused by Weiser in Virginia, like that of Methodists, Baptists and Presbyterians in North and South Carolina, challenged Lutherans to join the Protestant main stream in the United States. Benjamin Kurtz, the editor of America's most widely circulated Lutheran periodical, the *Lutheran Observer*, was unremitting in his call to Lutherans to consider themselves a Protestant denomination. He wanted Lutherans to cooperate closely with all who placed appropriate stress on the sanctity of the Bible, the imperative nature of conversion and God's demand for holy living. At the same time he encouraged Lutherans to repudiate those portions of their heritage that made it difficult for them to embrace sisters and brothers in other Christian denominations, in "voluntary societies," and in that broad revivalistic tradition labeled Evangelicalism.

Not until 1843 was a significant attack launched on the increasingly dominant Evangelicalism. John Williamson Nevin, a professor of theology at the German Reformed theological seminary at Mercersburg, Pennsylvania, collected a series of articles he had written for a denominational publication and published them as *The Anxious Bench*, a work that the editor of the *Lutheran Observer* discredited. Nevin published his articles in an effort to discourage German language churches, Reformed and Lutheran in particular, from adopting Finney's "new measures." Nevin had no problem with classic Calvinistic revivals like those conducted by Jonathan Edwards at Northampton during the Great Awakening, revivals that were the result of the Holy Spirit's using solid, theological sermons to introduce persons to spiritual reality. But the contrived efforts of Finney and his followers were quite another matter. As Nevin developed his theological counterpoint to the revivalism of Finney and his followers, Nevin came to see that the real problem with the current revivalistic approach to church membership was its undercutting of a proper understanding of church and sacraments and the "system of the catechism" that rested thereon.[30] For Lutherans to join the American main stream on the grounds proposed by Kurtz would not be an advance, Nevin contended; rather, it would be a lamentable retreat from their Reformation roots and heritage.[31]

The waves of revivalism that were carrying the Methodists and Baptists to numerical dominance on the American scene were not interrupted by Nevin's publication. They continued to break unremittingly on the shores of American religious life on into the Civil War period. But a national debate was sparked by Nevin's attack on "new measures," a debate that consumed considerable space in publications like the *Lutheran Observer,* the Lutheran church paper most widely circulated in the South in the antebellum period. For Lutherans in the South, however, that was a debate that began long before the publication of *The Anxious Bench,* even before the rise of Finney to national prominence. It was a debate that first broke into the open at the convention of the North Carolina Synod at Lincolnton in 1820.

In North Carolina in 1803, it had been Paul Henkel's misgivings about revivalism which had prompted him to help transform the North Carolina Ministerium into the North Carolina Synod. Henkel's experience convinced him that these new developments were hostile to the understanding of Christian faith set forth in the Augsburg Confession. While the emotional excesses associated with the Second Great Awakening were the first thing to attract the attention of traditional Lutherans, it quickly became apparent that the real issue was not a question of liturgical propriety and having all things done "decently and in order." The preaching of Law and Gospel related to the personalizing of God's grace through the sacraments for persons like Henkel. Baptism lost all sacramental significance in the revival settings, and catechetical instruction and confirmation were robbed of their traditional role of leading the Christian to a more mature faith. Thus, Henkel traveled incessantly and preached and taught tirelessly in an effort to control "the fire" of revivalism breaking out around some Lutheran congregations, such as the one served by his son, Philip. The Rowan County pastor, Carl August Gottlieb Storch, on the other hand, was more sympathetic to the revival movement. In an enlightened age, the human mind was challenging new frontiers. Could it not be that God was pouring out His Spirit in new ways to inaugurate a new age in religion? Was it not the Spirit of God that enabled Methodists and Baptists, Presbyterians and Lutherans, to join each other in prayer and praise of God? Surely it was God's will that the people he had redeemed reflect their unity in Christian fellowship.

The other three pastors in the North Carolina Synod in its earliest years were Joseph Gottfried Arends, Philip Henkel and R. J. Miller. Arends was blind and would be claimed by death before the first decade of the nineteenth century had run its course. Philip Henkel could naturally be expected to reflect his father's resistance to the camp meeting and revival. Miller was ordained by the Lutheran Ministerium of North Carolina as an Episcopal priest. Paul Henkel observed that Miller "an English Lutheran Minister, preaches the gospel orderly, with effect, earnestness and due consideration."[32] Miller's move from Methodism to Episcopalianism suggests that he would have had little patience with the emotional excesses of the emerging camp meeting tradition or their deprecation of the sacramental.

In recognition of his seniority and years of service on the Carolina frontier, Arends was elected the synod's first president and Miller was named secretary. In 1804 and again in 1805, it was Paul Henkel who was selected for the post of president, with Miller continuing as secretary. With Miller and the two Henkels resistant to revivalism, Arends largely incapacitated, and only Storch inclined to see revivals in a positive light, anti-revivalistic forces were clearly in the ascendancy in the North Carolina Synod during the earliest years, even though the prevailing consensus was not unanimous.

It seems unlikely that that prevailing consensus was challenged by the addition to the ministerial ranks in 1806 of Christian E. Bernhardt. Ordained at the first meeting of the North Carolina Ministerium in 1791, Bernhardt's initial service had been in North Carolina, but in 1800 he responded to the call of Lutherans between the Broad and Saluda Rivers in South Carolina. The fact that, when he first immigrated to America, Bernhardt did not blend in well with the Pietistic culture of the Salzburger settlement in Georgia, but promptly won the respect and support of Pastor Nussmann in North Carolina, who represented a via media in relation to Pietism and Rationalism, suggests that Bernhardt would not have been among the supporters of revivals.[33] Another early addition to the ministerial roll was Ludwig Markert who was ordained in 1807, but like Bernhardt he would not long be available to influence the decisions of the North Carolina Synod. Bernhardt was claimed by death in 1809, and Markert served as the synod's first missionary to Ohio, Indiana and Illinois, where after 1816 he devoted himself to full-time ministry in that rapidly developing part of the nation.

But as early as 1810, the synod received into membership ministers whose years of service to the synod would be more numerous than those of Bernhardt and Markert, men who would play prominent roles in the shaping of Lutheranism in the Carolinas. Those men were Gottlieb Schober who requested and received ordination in 1810 and Godfrey Dreher who received a license the same year. Schober was already in his mid-fifties. The owner of slaves and some ten thousand acres of land, a lawyer, mercantilist, manufacturer, former postmaster and state legislator, Schober was never able to win acceptance into the inner circle of Moravian leadership at Salem. This fact may have contributed to the eagerness with which he embraced the honors Lutherans bestowed on him. Ignoring the New Testament admonition to "lay hands on no man suddenly" when it comes to selecting leadership, the North Carolina Synod immediately elected as secretary of the synod the man from Salem whom they had just ordained. Despite the fact that he elected to retain his status as a lay member of the Moravian church, Schober served as a Lutheran pastor for more than two decades.[34] As a Lutheran pastor, he was deeply committed to Christian unity, and may have been the first Lutheran leader in the nineteenth century to call for the creation of a common liturgy for Lutherans in the United States.[35]

Schober's concern for unity in Christ went beyond a mere concern for the Lutheran household of faith.   Applauding the Plan of Union which had brought Lutherans and Reformed together in Prussia, he hoped those traditions might experience a similar union in the United States. His ecumenical vision was even broader, however, since he would have been happy to see as one flock all who believed in the divinity of Christ and acknowledged him as the one mediator between God and man.[36]

The kind of difference Schober made in the life of the North Carolina Synod is reflected in the fact that the convention of 1810 authorized not only Lutherans but "members of Christian Churches" in general to meet together in private homes for hymn singing, prayer and the reading of sermons. These Pietistic assemblies were expected to take place without the presence of a pastor, although it was noted that the occasional presence of clergy could be helpful in assisting lay persons to arrive at the correct interpretation of more difficult and obscure Bible passages. The spirit of Schober is also reflected in the decision of the 1810 convention at Organ Church to direct clergy to conduct three day preaching events in which clergy from other denominations would be welcome to participate.[37]

Within the North Carolina Synod, there continued to be those pastors who adhered to Lutheranism's traditional insistence on the centrality of Word and Sacraments, with catechization as a necessary bridge to adult church membership. But under the leadership of Storch and Schober, the ranks of those who preferred the revival as a means of initiation into adult church membership were growing. In Schober's view, pastors who merely taught their parishioners to rely on the promises of God in Baptism and the Lord's Supper were inviting formalism, a reliance on externals; far better, he believed, to adopt the Pietistic approach and look for signs of true repentance and a genuine conversion.[38]

The swing of the synod toward revivalism moved rapidly until 1813 when David, a seventeen-year-old son of Paul Henkel, joined his brother, Philip, in serving under the aegis of the North Carolina Synod. David Henkel was a young man whose unusual gifts of mind and spirit emerged early.[39] Committed to the belief that continuation in true Lutheranism meant continuation in its confessional heritage, David argued that the synod over which Storch and Schober presided was not really Lutheran.

It was not that the North Carolina Synod consciously repudiated its Lutheran heritage. The constitution of the synod declared the first twenty-one articles of the Augsburg Confession to be "the point of union of our Church" to which every minister was pledged. The same document called on the clergy "to instruct all children of our members, from twelve years old and upwards, in the catechism; and to confirm them . . . when they are sufficiently enlightened."[40] But it seemed to David Henkel that the attempt of leaders of the synod to achieve closer union with other denominations through such measures as revivals undercut the Lutheran understanding of both the Augsburg Confession and the Sacraments, the foundation on which the catechetical approach to Christian faith and commitment rested.

David Henkel challenged the North Carolina Synod to compare its understanding of Baptism and the Lord's Supper with the views of Luther and the Lutheran confessional writings. In 1820 the synod was persuaded to declare itself with regard to the relation of baptism and regeneration. It affirmed "that baptism is beneficial, and ought to be attended to as a command of God: but we do not believe that all who are baptized with water are regenerated and born again unto God . . ." Henkel, on the other hand, insisted that the unique union of water and the Word of God in baptism is an instrument of the Holy Spirit, "a means of regeneration; because the word of God is the essence thereof."[41] With regard to the Lord's Supper, the synod said,

> We do not believe, nor teach, that the body and blood of our Lord Jesus Christ is corporeally received along with the bread and the wine . . . ; but that the true believer does spiritually receive and partake of the same through faith in Jesus Christ, and all the saving benefits of his death and passion.[42]

Henkel, on the other hand, was convinced that through eating the bread and drinking the wine, all communicants, not just those who had faith, actually received the body and blood of Christ, "inconceivable by human reason, and divinely mysterious."[43] For his efforts to restore true Lutheran teaching as he understood it, Henkel was challenged as one who taught that the mere rite of baptism was regeneration. His arguments for what he believed to be a Lutheran understanding of the real presence in the Holy Communion produced charges that he taught a Roman

Catholic view of that sacrament.

Unable to reconcile their differences within their synodical organization, Paul Henkel and his sons, David and Philip, led in the organization of a second synod for Lutherans in the South, the Tennessee Synod. For the next one hundred years, Southern Lutherans would have a choice between a synod that sought to embrace both the Lutheran heritage and American revivalism, and a synod that cast its lot with the Lutheran confessions and the "system of the catechism."

Six years after Schober and Storch, in 1812, had first written to the Pennsylvania Ministerium about closer cooperation, the ministerium responded by contacting all existing synods and inviting them to send representatives to their next convention to discuss the possibility of developing "closer connections." The ministerium's next convention was held in June 1819, in Baltimore. The New York Ministerium wrote to express interest in the venture as did North Carolina, and North Carolina's Gottlieb Schober was present in person to present his plan for such a cooperative venture. The plan, for which Schober reportedly used the constitution of the General Assembly of the Presbyterian Church as a model, called for the creation of The General Synod which would meet every three years. It would regulate the Lutheran publication effort, establish approved forms of worship, fix grades in the ministry, control the formation of new district synods, and serve as an arbiter in appeals from synods. Schober's plan was assigned to a committee for review and revision, and the result was the *Plan Entwurf* (Proposed Plan) which the ministerium adopted, reproduced in German and English, and distributed widely to synods and congregations.

In North Carolina Schober's dream received a radical challenge from a person who was emerging as his nemesis. In 1813 eighteen-year-old David Henkel attended the convention of the North Carolina Synod. Between conventions two pastors had granted him a license to serve as a catechist.[44] He came to the convention armed with requests from Lutheran congregations in Lincoln County that he be continued as a catechist. The convention agreed to the request, but ruled that in the future pastors would no longer have the authority to license candidates for the ministry between conventions. The following year he again requested the renewal of his license, and again the convention complied but adopted a resolution to the effect "that hereafter no uneducated person shall receive license to preach until he has studied with one of our pastors and is twenty-one years of age."[45]

At the 1815 convention David Henkel was advanced from the rank of catechist to that of candidate. The next year the desirability of having four ranks for those seeking ordination was challenged, no doubt by David Henkel or someone speaking on his behalf. But the synod re-affirmed its practice.[46] A recommendation that David Henkel be ordained as a pastor, a recommendation that he expected to pass, was instead defeated. The following year, 1817, the synod took three actions that subsequently contributed to the schism between the North Carolina and Tennessee synods. First, the synod decided to move from a fall convention date to Trinity Sunday. To allow an appropriate interval between conventions, it was agreed no convention would by held in 1818, but that the synod would next assemble on Trinity Sunday, 1819. Secondly, the convention approved for ordination at its 1819 convention several candidates. And, thirdly, it approved the publication of the book *Luther* prepared by Schober in connection with the anniversary of the Reformation. The volume included the rules and regulations of synod, listed the clergy members of the synod, and the candidates who were to be ordained at the next convention of synod. The name of David Henkel led the list of those approved for ordination at the 1819 convention.

The date for the 1819 convention, however, was the same date - Trinity Sunday, June 6 - set by the Pennsylvania Ministerium for its special convention on increased cooperation among synods. Schober and Storch felt that the North Carolina Synod should be represented at the Baltimore meeting, and therefore moved the meeting of the North Carolina Synod from June 6 to April 26. It was reported that all members of the synod had been notified of the change in meeting date, and those in attendance "unanimously, without an opposing word," approved the change.[47]

The year 1819 proved to be a notable one in the history of North Carolina Lutheranism. Reflecting on the April convention, the secretary commented:

> Is it not true that we never yet had such disagreeable labors before us as during the present Synod? Were there not such among them [i.e., the labors] that had more the appearance of law court business, than business belonging to the ministry of the Gospel? But were we not constrained to act as we did . . .?[48]

Not least among the secretary's concerns was the fact that developments had taken place which resulted in other Christians no longer looking upon Lutherans as charitably as they once had; he longed for the day when those for whom "Christ is all in all" would again be united in "love and cordial attachment."

David Henkel was present at the April convention. In view of the appearance of his name in the *Luther* listing of those to be ordained at the 1819 convention, he no doubt assumed he would realize his dream of ordination. However, the convention received several complaints about his conduct as a minister. There was Adam Costner who complained that Henkel had excommunicated him in "an improper manner." Henkel had offended Presbyterian clergy with criticisms of Calvinistic doctrines, and there were charges that he claimed the personal right to forgive sins and that he taught the Roman Catholic doctrine of the presence of Christ in the Lord's Supper. The charges with regard to heterodoxy in his understanding of the office of the keys and the Lord's Supper were not substantiated, but he apparently had antagonized representatives of other Protestant denominations. Under the leadership of Schober and Storch, the convention decided to punish the offending Henkel not only by refusing to ordain him as previously authorized, but also by reducing him in rank from candidate to his earlier rank of catechist. If, after six months, he could produce convincing evidence that there was peace in his congregations and that he had established good relations with folk in other denominations, then the president of the synod was authorized, not to arrange for his ordination, but to restore him to the rank of candidate.

On Trinity Sunday, 1819, Philip Henkel, several licentiates and lay delegates arrived at the Buffalo Creek church for the convention of the synod as originally scheduled.[49] President Storch was not present, so a letter was dispatched to him, indicating that if he were not present by 9:00 o'clock on Monday, the convention would be held without him. Storch dispatched a reply indicating that his health was not good, but that even if he were well, he would not attend. The convention had been held in April. The group that had assembled might use the church building for worship, but not to conduct an unauthorized convention.

Following worship in the church the next morning, those who had gathered at the Buffalo Creek church retired from the building and opened their convention in the shade of the trees in the church yard. Philip Henkel was elected president, Joseph E. Bell secretary, and the convention got down to business. Petitions were presented protesting the synod's April action with regard to David Henkel and urging that he be ordained as previously authorized and that Bell be ordained as well. The convention determined that the action of the previous convention with regard to David Henkel was invalid because the convention was not held on the constitutionally-designated date of Trinity Sunday.[50] The convention then authorized the ordination of Bell and David Henkel, and they were, "by the laying on of hands, and prayer, ordained Bishops (commonly called pastors) of the Christian Church."[51] Thus it came about that David Henkel, the central figure in the approaching split within the North Carolina Synod, was ordained "under an oak tree!"[52]

These developments were, of course, a lively part of the background for the confrontation that took place in Lincolnton at the end of May 1820. The synod stood on the verge of schism. Attempts were made to heal the breach while ostracizing David Henkel. Bell, who was ordained with David Henkel, at first sided with the Henkel party, but then went over to the hotel and made his peace with the North Carolina Synod. That body proceeded to declare his ordination at Buffalo Creek legal and valid. Laymen from White Haven, a congregation served by David Henkel, also joined the convention at the hotel and were accepted as delegates. In view of the convention's endorsement of Bell's ordination, the folk from White Haven asked that the convention also declare the ordination of David Henkel to be valid. This proposal was rejected because Henkel's situation was "infinitely different" from that of Bell. Henkel, it was claimed, had "shown no symptom of desiring to live in peace with us, and only last Monday had acted as dictator what doctrine we should preach, and otherwise had behaved with conspicuous incivility."[53]

While the leaders of the North Carolina Synod did not envision a unity that embraced the annoying David Henkel, they hoped to recover the allegiance of his brother, Philip. To that end, the synod decided to dispatch Bell to Philip with a message that the North Carolina Synod was willing to forget everything "that has occurred" and that the synod wished "to entreat him to re-unite with us again . . .", assuring him that he could expect to "be received with joy as a brother" if he would agree to live under the synod's constitution and submit to the will of the majority. Apparently Philip, in response to Bell's message, decided "to forgive" and "be reunited" with the body for whom he had labored for two decades. His decision was short lived, however. His brother, David, seems to have persuaded him against such a course of action.[54]

Leaders of scattered Lutheran congregations in North Carolina had come together in 1803 to form a bond of union, a synod. In a decade the mother synod of southern Lutheranism had congregations in four states, North Carolina, South Carolina, Tennessee and Virginia. But that unity was shattered in 1820 as resistance broke out against the attempt of the leaders of the synod to make Lutheranism over into an Americanized Protestant denomination. Soon conservative confessional forces were creating a unity of their own in the Tennessee Synod, a body that claimed congregations in the same four states as had the North Carolina Synod in 1820, congregations that sometimes represented divisions within congregations of the synods earlier on the territory.[55] In addition, the Tennessee Synod was receiving calls for ministerial service from as far south as Alabama and Louisiana and as far west as Missouri.

While fateful actions were taking place in North Carolina on Trinity Sunday, "that bluff, honest, homespun, good old man," Gottlieb Schober, was in Baltimore laying before the Pennsylvania Ministerium his vision of a united Lutheranism.[56] The *Plan Entworf* did not propose as powerful a new general body as Schober suggested. Nevertheless, there was opposition to it from the first. The ministerium itself adopted the measure by a vote of better than five to one. The Ohio Synod also voted approval, but again there was opposition.[57] The New York Ministerium concluded the plan took from them powers expressly granted to them by their own governing documents, so they rejected the proposal. It had been decided in Baltimore that the proposal would go into effect only if three of the four synods existing in 1819 should endorse it. Thus, the vote of the North Carolina Synod was crucial. With the Henkels having withdrawn from the Lincolnton convention, Schober was able to get the vote he wanted. North Carolina became the third synod to ratify the plan, so the president of the Ministerium of Pennsylvania announced that the General Synod would be officially organized at Hagerstown, Maryland, in October 1820.

The Henkels fought vigorously against the creation of the General Synod. David insisted that ". . . as many of us as know our Lord are already closely united - no human bulwark can make us more so." He argued that merely human organizations could hardly be expected to enrich what Christians have already received as a gift in redemption.

> Whosoever is justified by Christ, is also united to him; his soul being impressed with his lovely image, he is in fellowship with all saints and angels in the universe, whether they dwell in any of the regions here below, or in the high climes of bliss. The union of believers, like their King, is invisible - "their life being hid with Christ in God;" it therefore does not matter whether their human ceremonies and modes of government harmonize. All their union which is discoverable, is their uniform obedience to the Lord's commandments.[58]

At some points, however, David Henkel's attack on the General Synod was more than a theoretical discussion of the relationship of the spiritual reality of Christian unity to the tangible manifestations of that unity. Schober might take satisfaction that a German language hymnal designed to serve both Lutheran and Reformed was available, but David Henkel reportedly claimed that allowing Lutheran girls to marry Reformed boys and vice versa was like mating cows and horses. The Henkels had developed a printing press at New Market that produced worship materials.[59] Would the establishing of a general body with authority to prescribe acceptable worship materials mean the undermining of the *Henkel Press*? Was it necessary that there be uniformity in liturgy and hymnody? The Augsburg Confession declared it to be "sufficient for the true unity of the Christian Church, that the preaching be pure, according to the true understanding of the Gospel, and the sacraments administered according to divine Scripture; and it is not necessary for the true unity of the Christian Church, that the same ceremonies as established by men should be observed."[60] Was not the attempt to create a national body with exclusive authority to introduce new books of worship an attempt to undermine the diversity in worship which the Augsburg Confession clearly anticipated?

Following the Trinity Sunday convention of the North Carolina Synod, Paul Henkel visited Tennessee where a "conference" was held, presumably to plan a course of action in the event the 1820 convention of the North Carolina Synod should be unwilling to endorse the actions taken at the Trinity Sunday meeting. Among the possibilities undoubtedly discussed was that of creating a separate synod. But the *Plan Entwurf* declares that no new synod can come into being without the express authorization of the General Synod. Does not the suggestion that a synod has no legitimacy unless it is authorized by a superior body imply that all existing synods are illegitimate?

> Jejune must be the idea, and grotesque the pretension, for unchartered Synods in a conclave to pronounce other Synods illegal, merely because they are not chartered! Unchartered Synods give charters! Lo! what an exotic plant is this! at first germinated in hell, fostered by the old harlot in the garden of Rome; poisoning all that is pure, destroying all that is lovely; metamorphosed into a maniac demon, in the disguise of religion, is now proposed to be transplanted into the clarified soil of Lutheranism, which fills the agile mind with anticipated horrors of popery revived, even upon the unsullied shores of America.[61]

Another concern for David Henkel was the proposal that the new organization recognize various grades of ministry. He had been frustrated by the ladder of ascent from catechist to candidate to deacon to pastor. Such an arrangement seemed to him a mark of popery. From Henkel's perspective, attempts to modify "our present mode of church government" were unnecessary and should be resisted. Only let other Lutherans be unswerving in their loyalty to "the Augsburg Confession of Faith, and our love and union shall never be clouded."[62]

Despite the specific reasons David Henkel advanced for opposing the General Synod, one is left with the suspicion that the most compelling reason was the fact that, for persons connected with the North Carolina Synod, the words "General Synod" immediately called to mind one person alone: Gottlieb Schober. Henkel, "the small, lame stripling," had been so bold as to challenge the leadership of a man thirty years his senior, a man repeatedly elected to serve as an officer of the mother synod of Lutheranism in the South. To Schober it was the height of insolence for a young person to openly criticize his elders and those placed (by synodical election) in a superior position. To David Henkel, the person he was attacking appeared not as a rustic but good, old man, but as one intent on undermining the faith once delivered to the saints, a leader who was not entitled to the designation "Lutheran". The General Synod might not have come in for such scathing denunciations from David Henkel had the movement for its creation not been identified with Gottlieb Schober. And Schober might have been reconciled to the more conservative emphasis of the confessional party had it not been identified with Henkel.

But given the doctrinal stance which the new general body assumed in its effort to be inclusive and "American", and given Henkel's determination to be true to the understanding of Lutheranism set forth in the Augsburg Confession, an antipathy would probably have developed between the two parties regardless of the men who represented them. However, the clash of personalities was inevitable and underlies most of the reasons for the rupture. Bernheim's early description of the two men is given in equitable terms.[63] Henkel was presumptuous and earned some of the epithets he received. Schober's personality was overbearing, and his imperious manner is attested in Surratt's study.[64]

Thus, in helping create the General Synod, the leadership of the North Carolina Synod, especially Gottlieb Schober, inadvertently contributed to schism and the polarizing of Lutheranism in the Southeast. While proposals for uniting congregations of the Tennessee Synod with the congregations of affiliates of the General Synod in the South would emerge, the dominant theme of their interaction would for decades be colored by antagonism and acrimony.

The schism in North Carolina threatened the continued existence of the mother synod for Lutherans in the South. In 1821 there were only three ordained pastors, Schober and two others, who attended the annual convention of the synod; the following year Schober and three others. In 1823 Schober and five other Lutheran clergy attended the convention, but in 1824 again there were only three ordained pastors present since once again unity had given way to division within the North Carolina Synod. This time the pastors and congregations in South Carolina, led by one of the senior clergy of the North Carolina Synod, Godfrey Dreher, had withdrawn from the North Carolina Synod to create a synod of their own. This development not only produced a new synod composed almost entirely of former North Carolina Synod congregations; it would in time make an important contribution to the enlarging of that association of Lutheran congregations known as the Tennessee Synod.

The key figure in bringing the Tennessee Synod's brand of Lutheran confessionalism to South Carolina was Dreher, who in 1824 had been one of the organizers, and first treasurer, of the South Carolina Synod. Dreher was a conscientious churchman but also a prickly figure who became in the 1830s involved in a feud with Rev. Jacob Moser over the propriety of Lutheran revivalism. When the synod president, Stephen Mealy, attempted in 1834 to moderate their dispute, Dreher took umbrage. He concluded that he and his parishioners would be happier in independent Lutheran congregations than in the South Carolina Synod. In 1852, those congregations surrendered their independent status in favor of membership in the Tennessee Synod.[65] To persons like Dreher and the Henkels, it seemed that the creation of a national Lutheran church body would be the first step in transforming Lutherans in the United States into a Protestant denomination, perhaps receptive to the needs of the people but ready to jettison inconvenient elements of Old World Lutheran orthodoxy.

The movement toward national Lutheran unity among North Carolina Lutherans unwittingly jeopardized Robert Johnston Miller's lifelong dream of Lutheran-Episcopal merger in North Carolina. Miller had been ordained an Episcopal priest in 1794 by North Carolina Lutheran pastors. In 1821, he presented the North Carolina Episcopal diocese with a proposal from the North Carolina Synod for an exploration of merger between the two bodies. The effort foundered in 1822 when Episcopal leaders told Schober and other Lutheran leaders "TO OUR FACE THAT IT [MERGER] COULD NOT BE ADMITTED AS OUR ORDINATION WAS NOT VALID."[66]

Thus passed the possibility of a Lutheran-Episcopal church body in North Carolina based on similar liturgical and eucharistic practices and a generation of close interaction between Miller and the Lutheran Ministerium. In 1823, the Episcopal Diocese elected a new bishop, John Stark Ravenscroft, a staunch believer in the historic episcopate who feared that any "amalgamation" with Lutherans would have a "paralyzing" effect on his efforts to strengthen the Episcopal communion in the state, especially in its new mission field in western North Carolina.[67]

Like Ravenscroft in his concern for Episcopal identity, David Henkel and the leadership in the Tennessee Synod were not unconcerned about Christian unity, but they were convinced that unity achieved by agreeing to ignore points of disagreement was meaningless. They believed it to be more important for Lutherans to understand their confessional heritage than to embrace the latest fads among the Protestant denominations.

On the other hand, Gottlieb Schober and the leadership of the North Carolina Synod, in helping found the General Synod, created a body committed to "unity of sentiment among Christians in general, of whatever kind or denomination," and to the promotion of "general concord and unity."[68]

The two synods - divided on the issue of confessionalism vs. Christian unity - moved into the fourth decade of synodical life strengthened by the very differences which would later enrich their union and its contributions to the national Lutheran community. ✟

NOMINE JESU.

Dieses soll zur Nachricht und Zeugniß dienen daß H. *Daniel Scherer*
nach Ordnung der Evangelisch - Lutherischen Ministerial - Versammlung des Staats Nord-Carolina
und den benachbarten Staaten, ist geprüfet worden in seiner Erkenntniß der Evangelischen Lehre, und
den erforderlichen Fähigkeiten das Amt eines Evangelischen Lehrers zu verwalten; dem zufolge wird
Er hiemit dazu bevollmächtiget: öffentlich zu predigen, Catechismus - Unterricht zu halten, und zu
taufen, in den Gemeinden von *dem Staat Virginien Bottetourt*
County, Pentres & andern Gemeinen
und in allen andern
predigerlosen Gemeinden der Evangelischn Kirchen, wo es mit Recht mag gefordert werden, bis zur
nächsten Conferenz. Solches bezeugen wir die Beamten der besagten Conferenz mit unsern Namen
eigenhändig unterschrieben, und angedruckten Ministerial-Siegel, den 17ten *Oct.* 1815.

Jacob Scherer Secretair   *Philip Henkel Præs P. T.*

IN THE NAME OF JESUS

This shall serve as report and Certification that Mr. "Daniel Scherer" according
to the rule of the Evangelical-Lutheran Ministerial Association of the State of North
Carolina and the adjacent-states, has been examined in his knowledge of the Evangelical doctrine and in the necessary ability to administrate the office of an Evangelical teacher; accordingly he is herewith authorized: to preach in public, to hold
catechetical instruction, and to baptize, in the congregation "of the State Virginia,
Bottetourt County, Pentres and other congregations" and in all other preacherless
congregations of the Evangelical churches, where it may be requested by good reasons, until the next conference. That witness we the officials of aforesaid conference
with our names signing with our own hands, and the printed Ministerial-Seal, the
17th Oct. 1815.

/s/   Jacob Scherer, Secretary   /s/   Philip Henkel, Pres. P. T.

SEAL (Latin)

Ministerial Seal of (the) Evangelical Lutheran(s) in the
Carolinas and the neighbor states.

Peace be with you (Pax vobis)

Facsimile of Early Ordination Certificate,
With Translation

Gottlieb Schober
President, North Carolina Synod
1820-22, 1824-31

David Henkel
Secretary, Tennessee Synod
1824-25, 1826-28

Philadelphia, Dallas (1800)
Organized 1767

CHAPTER IV

SLAVERY, SECTIONALISM (1838-1860)

As the United States endured the prolonged trauma of civil war, a seminary professor observed, "Politicians, secular and religious journals, pamphleteers, men in all classes of society, freely lay the blame of this Rebellion, in great measure, or wholly, at the door of the Church; charging the ministry, more especially, with having caused it."[1]

Was there any real basis for blaming the church or, more particularly, its ordained leadership, for the division of the nation into two warring camps? In what sense could Christian leaders be accused of having contributed to the bloodshed that marked the years 1861 to 1865 in the United States?

Clarence C. Goen, a distinguished church historian who has researched the question over many years, concludes that indeed the church and its leadership were culpable. For at least the first thirty years of the nineteenth century, evangelical Protestantism clearly contributed to the unity of the United States. That same evangelical Protestantism found its most conspicuous manifestation in three national denominational organizations, the Methodist, the Baptist, and the Presbyterian. Those denominations could not sustain within their own organizations the unity God gave them in Jesus Christ, and, long before the firing on Fort Sumter in 1861, they had divided as churches into northern and southern denominations.

Thus, Goen concludes, "the denominational schisms presaged and to some extent provoked the crisis of the Union in 1861: they broke a primary bond of national unity, set before the nation a persuasive example of sectional independence, encouraged the myth of 'peaceable secession,' reinforced alienation between North and South, and heightened the moral outrage that each section felt against the other."[2]

By their participation in the trans-regional first and second Great Awakenings, the Baptists, Methodists, and Presbyterians had contributed to a sense of nationhood that transcended regional boundaries. The failure of these Protestant churches to maintain their own internal unity across regional lines had tragic consequences for the nation whose life they were called upon to enhance and ennoble.

Lutherans were less numerous than their Methodist, Baptist, and Presbyterian neighbors. The visible bonds of Lutheran unity which transcended state and region were strained but not ruptured prior to the outbreak of the Civil War. But if Lutherans did not provide an example of national scope on how to fracture unity, they nevertheless succumbed to the assumption that church life must follow the dictates of the local body politic in establishing organizational boundaries and in recognizing true brothers and sisters. By the end of July 1861, a leader in the Lutheran church in the Confederate States of America was urging the creation of "a General Synod South."[3] In fact, long before the creation of the Confederacy and the call for establishing a general church body for Lutherans in the South, the institution of chattel slavery and a growing sense of distinctiveness between North and South had prepared the ground for these developments.

Synodical Alignments

The North Carolina Synod in this environment was a growing church, but it suffered one division in 1842. Since 1813 a number of pastors and congregations in Virginia had found their ties to the larger world of Lutheranism through the North Carolina Synod. But in 1840 the synod received a petition from the pastors and lay delegates "who reside in southwestern Virginia" asking for permission "to form a new synod."[4]

NORTH CAROLINA SYNOD PRESIDENTS	
1838-40 William Artz	1851-52 Joseph A. Linn, Sr.
1840-41 Samuel Rothrock	1852-53 William Artz
1841-42 Henry Graeber	1853-54 Joseph A. Linn, Sr.
1842-43 J. D. Scheck	1854-56 Samuel Rothrock
1843-45 William Artz	1856-57 William Gerhardt
1845-46 J. D. Scheck	1857-58 Levi C. Groseclose
1846-48 Samuel Rothrock	1858-59 Joseph A. Linn, Sr.
1848-49 Jacob Brown Anthony	1859-60 William Artz
1849-50 Benjamin Arey	1860-61 Simeon Scherer
1850-51 W. G. Harter	

The Committee on Petitions rejoiced "that the number of our ministers in Virginia has increased to such an extent as to render the formation of a new synod practicable." At the same time, there was regret at the dissolution of ties enjoyed over many years.

Receiving the permission they sought, the Virginians met under the leadership of Pastors Elijah Hawkins and Jacob Scherer in September 1841. A constitution was drafted, and the following May "the Evangelical Lutheran Synod of Western Virginia and adjacent parts," later known as the Synod of Southwest Virginia, came into being.

Despite the departure of the Virginians, the synod grew within North Carolina. Congregations organized during this ante bellum period were: St. Matthew's, Salisbury (1838); St. Paul's, Statesville (1840); St. James, Concord (1843); Salem, Salisbury (1850); Bethel, Salisbury (1851); Trinity, Concord (1857); St. Paul's, Wilmington (1858); and St. Mark's, Charlotte (1859).

Meanwhile, other new congregations in the state were linking with the Tennessee Synod: Miller's, Hickory (1840); Christ, Stanley (1841); Sharon, Statesville (1842); Holy Communion, Banner Elk (1842); Mt. Pleasant, Boone (1845); Beth Eden, Newton (1850); Antioch, Dallas (1850); New Jerusalem, Lexington (1856); Bethphage, Lincolnton (1858); and Mt. Pisgah, Hickory (1859).

The Tennessee Synod, however, did not escape divisions. Its first came in 1848, growing out of a debate about the extent of the authority of the synod in dealing with its pastors. A committee of the 1845 convention of the synod summarized the first phase of the difficulties in this fashion:

> Whereas a charge of a serious nature is alledged [sic] against the Rev. Adam Miller, and as this Synod is not a judiciary, but an advisory body, and simply claims

the right of imparting her useful advice, ...and inasmuch as a majority of his elders have held a meeting, and have investigated the charge alledged [sic] against him; and...unanimously declared him innocent; and they see no cause why he should not resume his official labors; and as a respectable number of the members of his congregations concur with the decision of the elders; however, as there still seems to be a dissatisfaction existing in the matter, it is

Resolved, That the Rev. H. Goodman and J. Killian be appointed to take the voice of his congregations in a clear and distinct manner, as soon as possible; and if the voice of the congregations wish him to continue his official duties, that we, in that case, concur with them, provided they honorably acquit him."[5]

NORTH CAROLINA SYNOD CONVENTION SITES

1838 Zion, Wythe County, VA	1850 St. Matthew's, Rowan County, NC
1839 St. Paul's, Orange County, NC	1851 St. Stephen's, Cabarrus County, NC
1840 St. Michael's, Iredell County, NC	1852 Friedens, Guilford County, NC
1841 St. Peter's, Wythe County, VA	1853 Newton, Catawba County, NC
1842 Luther's Chapel, Rowan County, NC	1854 Bethel, Stanly County, NC
1843 Sandy Creek, Davidson County, NC	1855 Fredericktown, Dav. County, NC
1844 St. James, Concord, NC	1856 St. Enoch, Rowan County, NC
1845 St. Paul's, Orange County, NC	1857 St. Paul's, Iredell County, NC
1846 Union, Rowan County, NC	1858 St. Paul's, Alamance County, NC;
1847 Organ, Rowan County, NC	Lutheran Chapel, Rowan County, NC
1848 St. Paul's, Catawba County, NC	1859 St. James, Concord, NC
1849 St. John's, Cabarrus County, NC	1860 Sandy Creek, Dav. County, NC[6]

The convention unanimously adopted its committee's recommendation.

Adam Miller, Jr., a pastor who had been laboring in Lincoln County for more than a decade, had been charged in a paternity case earlier in the year. The mother of the child presumably named Miller as the father of her child. Friends advised Miller to institute legal action against the woman to clear his good name. He did so, a fact he later had cause to regret. Eventually, the mother of the child indicated in direct testimony to some of the elders in a congregation served by Miller, as well as in a sworn statement before a magistrate, that Miller was not the father of her child.

Nevertheless, when the elders tried to conduct a quiet hearing into the matter at Daniel's, Lincolnton, near the end of June 1844, "hundreds of persons assembled to hear the proceedings."[7] The elders concluded it was inappropriate, under the circumstances, to attempt an investigation of the charges.

Miller was urged by some to keep silent and await the outcome of the legal proceedings. He concluded, however, that he should seek a prompt decision from the elders of his churches, and they cooperated by agreeing to go ahead with their investigation, this time at Trinity, Vale. This time, the elders unanimously concluded that Miller was not guilty.

However, as noted in the committee's report, there still seemed to be "a dissatisfaction existing in the matter."

To Miller, the decision of the synod to send two persons into his parish and involve themselves in a matter already appropriately concluded by the elders of the parish must be protested. As Article IV of the synod's constitution made clear, the synod's role in relation to congregations "shall be to impart their useful advice."[8] To send in persons to conduct an election in his parish and sit in judgment on the character of his acquittal seemed to Miller to be more than the constitution authorized or allowed.

The matter being contested was not simply a question of whether the advice-giving function of synod could be stretched to cover the synod's action. The preamble to the synodical constitution made it clear that matters of church polity were to be determined by scripture alone.[9] The explanatory notes printed with the text of the constitution also made it clear that the synod was not to get into the business of adjudicating appeals from its congregations. "That there ought to be no appeals from the decisions of congregations, is evident from Matth. 18.15-20."

TENNESSEE SYNOD PRESIDENTS

1838-51 (not available)	1857-58 Alfred J. Fox
1851-53 Jacob Killian	1858-59 Jacob Killian
1853-54 Ambrose Henkel	1859-60 Adam Efird
1854-56 Abel J. Brown	1860-61 Alfred J. Fox
1856-57 James Kniceley Hancher	

Despite Miller's protest, the synod invited the pastor's seven congregations to vote once more on his guilt or innocence. Miller urged his parishioners to cooperate with the synodical representatives: Jacob Killian of Salem, Lincolnton, and Rev. Henry Goodman of Beck's-Pilgrim, Lexington. Of the 151 votes cast in the polling, 127 supported the elders' acquittal of Miller, so he continued to serve his congregations.

In October 1846 the synod held its convention at Daniel's, Lincolnton, one of Miller's congregations. As usual, Monday was devoted to getting the synod organized for its annual meeting, and on Tuesday the convention actually got down to work.

Wednesday morning, after quickly disposing of several items pertaining to publications, the delegates addressed the "unfinished business" pertaining to the convention's host pastor. It occupied the remainder of the morning. At noon the synod took a recess for half an hour, then "resumed the discussion, which continued till evening" when the convention adjourned for the day.

After opening devotions on Thursday, the delegates resumed discussion of Pastor Miller's case. The discussion consumed the morning and finally prompted a request for a single, coherent recitation of all the known facts in the case. W. W. McGinnis, lay delegate from Hebron in Cleveland County, was asked to perform the task when the convention re-convened following its thirty-minute pause for lunch.[10]

Most of the afternoon was given to McGinnis' recitation, after which the convention adopted a brief resolution declaring that the previous year's resolution that the judgment of Miller's congregations be obtained "in a clear and distinct manner" and that they "honorably acquit him" had not been complied with. Thus, it was clear the synod was not going to accept the decision of the parish.

At that point, Miller "withdrew himself from this body, and consequently placed himself beyond its reach; therefore the necessity of further action is suspended."[11] Miller's action prompted similar action by Michael Rudisill, an elder from St. Paul's, Newton; Daniel Rader, the delegate from St. Paul's, Newton; Ephriam Shell, delegate from St. John's, Conover; and John Hass, delegate from Haas', Newton.[12]

When the Tennessee Synod assembled for its convention in 1847, it was confronted by an unusually large number of petitions. Many of them related to Miller and the synod's action of the previous year. The convention decided that all the petitions should be read to the assembly, so a large portion of Tuesday morning was devoted to reading the petitions supporting Miller. In the afternoon those communications "sustaining the course of the Synod" at its previous convention were read. A committee was then authorized to review the petitions and recommend to the synod an appropriate response.[13]

The following morning the committee made its report, dividing the numerous petitions into three classifications. First, there were those from congregations supporting Miller who had followed his example and withdrawn from the synod. The committee concluded their petitions "require no action from Synod."

TENNESSEE SYNOD CONVENTION SITES

1838 Salem, Lincoln County, NC	1949 Beck's, Davidson County, NC
1839 Emmanuel, Sullivan County, TN	1850 Solomon's, Greene County, TN
1840 Pilgrim, Lexington, NC	1851 Koiner's, Augusta County, VA
1841 Rader's, Rockingham County, VA	1852 Salem, Catawba County, NC
1842 Trinity, Lincoln County, NC	1853 Emmanuel, Sullivan County, VA
1843 St. James, Greene County, TN	1854 St. Peter's, Lexington District, SC
1844 Zion, Catawba County, NC	1855 Emmanuel, New Market, VA
1845 Zion, Shenandoah County, VA	1856 Melanchthon, Randolph County, NC
1846 Daniel's, Lincolnton, NC	1857 Solomon's, Greene County, TN
1847 Buehler's, Sullivan County, TN	1858 Zion, Lexington District, SC
1848 Solomon's, Shenandoah	1859 Bethlehem, Augusta County, VA
County, VA	1860 St. John's, Catawba County, NC[14]

The second group of communications included one from George Easterly, a senior member of the ministerium who had been licensed by the first convention of the synod in 1820. He charged the synod with "having dealt with Mr. Miller contrary to our constitution and the scriptures." The petitioners in this second group called upon the synod to reverse its action of the previous year or face the withdrawal of additional congregations and individual members from the synod.

There were, in the third category, letters from congregations formerly served by Miller and from Pastors Ambrose and Polycarp Henkel, indicating that if the synod should reverse its previous action and invite Miller to return to pastoral duties, they, as pastors and congregations, would leave the synod.

The recommendation of the committee was that the synod deny the charge that it had violated "either its Constitution or the Holy Scriptures, and cannot therefore disannul its proceedings." The remainder of the morning was given to a discussion of the committee's report and recommendation. In the afternoon the discussion resumed, and after the matter had been "freely discussed," it was finally put to a vote. The committee's report was adopted with only two dissenting votes.

In August of 1848, Pastor George Easterly, who had withdrawn from the Tennessee Synod earlier in the year, convened a meeting of those who were unhappy with the action of the synod in the Miller case. Those attending decided to re-establish the Tennessee Synod on what they believed to be its founding principles, even using the constitution of the Tennessee Synod as their own.

Thus, the Evangelical Lutheran Tennessee Synod, Reorganized, came into being at a convention held in Greene County, Tennessee, on October 21, 1848. Miller, whose difficulties had prompted the debate about the authority of the Tennessee Synod in relation to its pastors, joined the new body in 1849 and was a mainstay of the synod until death claimed him in 1868.[15]

The Tennessee Synod, Reorganized, remained a small body, never having more than four pastors on its clerical roster at one time. But it did play a role in bringing to North Carolina a theological seminary. In 1884 the synod, consisting of three pastors, eight congregations and "about five hundred members" asked to be received into membership in the Joint Synod of Ohio. It was made clear that one of the strong reasons for joining was to provide for themselves educational institutions that would produce pastors.

Subsequently, for a time, the Joint Synod of Ohio did provide an educational institution in Hickory. St. Paul's Seminary was created as a "Practical English Seminary" for young men in the area who were already married and found it impossible to move to Columbus, Ohio, to pursue their preparation for ordained ministry. Academic and parochial departments were launched along with the seminary, but the educational efforts, begun in 1887, were discontinued in 1898.[16]

The second break in the Tennessee Synod came in 1860 when the synod received a petition from seven of its pastors serving in the mountains of eastern Tennessee respectfully requesting permission to create a synod of their own. A distinguished leader of the new body, Abel Jacob Brown, later recalled that the separation was not prompted by doctrinal differences or personal difficulties with other members of the Tennessee Synod.

But neither was the new synod created as a whim: "Synodical conventions every fourth year on their territory were too infrequent to sustain inspiration. The Synod was so cumbersome in size it could not function as a body effectively. Distance, poor mountain roads, time, inconveniences and expense were all too great for delegates to journey to the far reaches of Virginia and the two Carolinas."[17]

Meeting at Zion, near Blountville, Tennessee, at the end of December, eleven pastors and fifteen lay delegates created the Evangelical Lutheran Holston Synod. Taking its name from a river in the area, the Holston Synod took its understanding of Lutheranism from the Tennessee Synod with which its founding pastors had been identified.

They were a hardy crew: "Hampered by insufficient resources..., not one of them being fully supported by the church, but compelled to engage in some secular work to obtain the common necessaries of life, they occupied a unique position, and were scarcely known beyond the limits of their own pastorates or, at most, their own synod. Only two of them were classical scholars, and not one of them ... ever attended a Theological Seminary. But that does not mean that they had not studied and did not understand Lutheran Theology."[18]

Educational Institutions

In the North Carolina Synod, the period saw the opening of an educational institution of the synod.

Establishment of the institution stemmed from a persistant concern in the synod over the perennial shortage of clergy and the impact of secularism on traditional religious understandings and values. As early as 1812 the synod considered, and discarded, a proposal to create a school for poor boys and orphans. In 1818, Rev. Philip Henkel and Licentiate Joseph Bell asked the synod to support their starting a school for the preparation of pastors in east Tennessee, but the proposed school died in the controversy that led to the creation of the Tennessee Synod.

The pressure for a school was partly relieved when the North Carolina Synod joined forces with the other two synods (Maryland & Virginia, and West Pennsylvania) of the new General Synod to establish Gettysburg Seminary in 1826. Still, the synod in 1835 initiated study for a seminary within its own borders. But it decided the following year to settle for joint support of the South Carolina Synod's five-year-old seminary at Lexington, South Carolina.

Increasingly, North Carolina Lutherans also found themselves being challenged to review the question of making provision for the education of their young. The synod was called upon with growing frequency to endorse and encourage support for schools created and operated by other folk. In addition to the seminaries in South Carolina and Pennsylvania, the principal of the Virginia Collegiate Institute at Salem in 1850 wrote to the North Carolina Synod asking for their cooperation in promoting his school.[19] The following year the synod received another communication from the principal of the Virginia institution and a similar one from Pennsylvania College at Gettysburg. The committee reporting on these communications noted "the prosperity and efficiency" of these two institutions and recommended them "to the attention and liberality of the Members and Ministers of our Church...."

In a special convention in July 1852 at Concord, the synod elected a temporary board of directors for an institution and directed it to decide the question of the school's location. The site of Mt. Pleasant in Cabarrus County was selected. The synod, at its subsequent convention in 1853, decreed that the school, named Western Carolina Male Academy, be operated by a board of trustees elected by, and accountable to, the synod itself. Invitations were extended to Southern Seminary and the South Carolina Synod for support or at least endorsement; the acknowledgements, however, conveyed only expressions of best wishes for success.

The trustees purchased from Mathias Barrier sixteen acres of land overlooking Mt. Pleasant and then erected on the crest a three-story seven thousand dollar brick building. For a principal, the synod in 1854 elected Rev. William Gerhardt, a graduate of Pennsylvania College at Gettysburg who taught school for several years before attending Gettysburg Seminary and becoming ordained. The academy opened March 1, 1855.

The early developments at Western Carolina Male Academy encouraged supporters of the institution to urge its transformation into a degree-granting college. The initial success of Roanoke College in Virginia, as reported in the *Lutheran Observer*, probably also contributed to the proposal. In any event, the synod at its regular 1858 convention at St. Paul's, Alamance, asked the trustees of the institution to endow it with "the power of conferring degrees."[20]

At the time there were only four Lutheran colleges in the nation. Hartwick College opened in 1815 a few miles from Cooperstown, New York. Pennsylvnia College of Gettysburg, soon known popularly, and much later officially, as "Gettysburg College," was founded in 1832. In Ohio, Wittenberg College was chartered in 1845 in Springfield, and Capital University opened in Columbus five years later.

At Mt. Pleasant, the change from academy to college was made: two additional brick buildings were erected, science laboratories were installed, the library was enlarged, and the teaching staff expanded. The new name, North Carolina College, was adopted in January 1859.

While North Carolina Synod Lutherans could point with pride to "their" college, the Mt. Pleasant institution was not without its competitors. In fact, in 1860 North Carolina College was one of sixteen institutions of higher learning in the state. The state's resident population of college students totaled 1,540, with nearly one-third enrolled at the University of North Carolina at Chapel Hill.[21] In its first year North Carolina College and its preparatory department enrolled sixty-two persons, forty-six from North Carolina, fifteen from South Carolina, and one from New England.[22]

But, with the coming of the war in May 1861, North Carolina College, like most institutions of higher learning in the South, closed its doors. The president, Rev. D. H. Bittle, moved to Austin, Texas, where he operated a school for young women during the war.

Slavery

In the environment of both the North Carolina and Tennessee synods, slavery was a fact of life. When Henry Melchior Muhlenberg first set foot on the soil of the New World, he was promptly made aware of two forces that would shape the lives of folk "at the South" for generations to come. Landing in Charleston he observed that "the heathen slaves are so numerous here that it is estimated that there are fifteen for every white man." The presence of a substantial black population, for the most part held as chattel, was a force molding in distinctive ways the shape of the history of the South. A second force that would make a significant contribution to the development of the entire region was the fear of what the blacks would do if they escaped from slavery. As Muhlenberg observed, "They occasionally rebel against their masters in the country, a thing which occurred just two years previous, when they gathered together as a mob and mercilessly killed a number of English people and their children."[23]

It was not that slavery was something unheard of for European immigrants, but on coming to the American colonies they were confronted with human slavery in a form quite different from anything they had known previously or experienced personally.

> In British North America slavery was no exterior and distant phenomena, sealed off in remote regions as it was for Britain itself, but, in its most brutal form, an everyday fact of life in communities that were otherwise genteel, otherwise decent, and growing more tolerant, reasonable, and benign all the time. In plantation culture, and elsewhere where slavery was an important part of society, an accommodation was somehow made between brutality and progressive refinement. The savagery of chattel slavery was no new thing for people of the seventeenth and eighteenth centuries; brutality in human relations was commonplace, and took many forms. What was new was that chattel slavery, a condition considered appropriate for isolated work gangs at the remote margins of civilization, was here incorporated into a world of growing civilization.[24]

A Dutch ship stopping in Virginia in 1619 introduced the first slaves to the

American colonies. Eighty years later the black population in the colonies, ninety-five per cent of whom were slaves, probably represented no more than ten per cent of the total population.[25] As a result of a complex interweaving of relationships between slave traders from a variety of European countries, rulers of African tribes, Yankee merchants, and planters in the colonies of Latin and Anglo America and the Caribbean islands, the proportion of black to white population doubled in seventy years.

The black population was approaching half a million by 1770. Of the estimated nine to ten million Africans who were uprooted from their homeland and deposited in the Western Hemisphere through the slave trade, probably not more than five per cent were deposited in what is today the United States of America. But the influx of slaves into the colonies was so marked in the first six decades of the eighteenth century that blacks constituted nearly twenty-two per cent of the population by 1770, the highest percentage of the population ever achieved by black Americans.

The slave trade was not something invented by northern Europeans or Yankee traders. After the Islamic conquest of North Africa and Spain in the eighth century, the Arabs and Moors quickly discovered there was a ready market for slaves whom native traders would bring to commercial centers like Timbuktu. Some Arab slavers were still plying their trade fifty years after Robert E. Lee presented his sword to Ulysses S. Grant at Appomattox Court House in 1865. But the slave traders who transported black Africans to North American shores in the seventeenth and eighteen centuries were Europeans, not Arabs. The trade was early controlled by the Portuguese, their dominant place in the traffic soon being challenged, however, by traders from Holland, France, and England as well as Sweden and Germany's Brandenburg.

As England became a conspicuous player in the action, English colonies in the New World became increasingly prominent markets for slaves. The expanding wealth and power of commercial centers like London, Liverpool, and Bristol rested in part on the expanding market for slaves in English colonies. But it was not simply a case of mother country exploiting its colonies. Many slave ships found their home berth in Newport and Bristol, Rhode Island; others in ports such as Providence, Boston and Salem; and a few even in cities such as Portsmouth, New London, and New York.

When the slavery question became a politically divisive one in the United States, some southerners hastened to point out that skippers and businessmen from the North played a role in providing the slave population for the South. In fact, most of the slaves imported into the South came on foreign vessels, with probably not more than ten per cent being brought to southern markets by Yankee traders.[26]

By 1760 South Carolina was sixty per cent black, Virginia forty-one per cent and North Carolina, where the first Negro slaves were probably introduced by planters moving south from Virginia, approximately thirty-five per cent. The earliest North Carolina market for slaves was among the tobacco planters in the northeastern corner of the colony. The development of rice-planting in the lower Cape Fear River area and the production of naval stores in Craven, Edgecombe, and adjacent counties expanded the market for slaves after 1740.

"In 1756", records show, "Governor Dobbs reported to the Board of Trade that there were 77,561 'blacks' in the province, of which [sic] 1,420 were in New Hanover, 1,091 in Edgecombe, and 934 in Craven. On the other hand, Orange County had only 50 Negroes of a total population of 1,000, and Rowan had 54 of a total of 1,170."[27]

The census of 1790 reported a white population in North Carolina of 288,204 and a slave population of 100,572, reflecting the rapid rise of a largely white population in the Piedmont following the French and Indian War.

The wills of Phillip Rudisill in 1764 and Lawrence Schnapp in 1768 indicate that Germans settling in Piedmont North Carolina soon became involved in the ownership of slaves, although apparently none owned large numbers of slaves during the colonial period.[28]   Michael Braun, who along with Frederick Fisher gave more than one hundred acres of land for the Dutch Pine Meeting House (Union, Salisbury) was listed in the 1790 census as the owner of fifteen slaves, but he was an unusually wealthy German.

Across the state, the census of 1790 revealed that 30.7 per cent of North Carolinians were slaveholders, but only 12.4 per cent of the Germans held slaves. The Salisbury District consisted of the counties of Stokes, Surry, Rowan, Iredell, Guilford, Rockingham, Montgomery, and Mecklenburg. Two-thirds of all the German families in the Piedmont lived in this district where just over twenty per cent of the families owned slaves; but here "only 12.4 per cent of the German families belonged to the slaveholding class. The total number of slaves owned by the Germans in the piedmont was 760 and of these 602 were in the Salisbury District. Sixty per cent of the German slaveholders had but one slave and only ten families held eleven or more Negroes. The largest number belonging to an individual was nineteen."[29]

In Rowan County where Germans owned only 14.9 per cent of the slaves, nearly twenty-five per cent of all the county's free blacks found employment working for German farmers, an indication of the preference of the Germans for free labor rather than slave.

The noted traveller, F. A. Michaux, may have been too generous when he estimated that "almost all" the German families in Lincoln County in 1802 were slave owners, since in 1790 only 13.4 per cent had slaves. But it is clear that slave ownership increased markedly after 1790.

Nor was the sharp increase in the rate of slaveholding confined to Lincoln County. In 1790 there were but 516 slaves in Guilford County. In the following decade they increased 75.39 per cent, and in the next decade they increased another 62.1 per cent. The decade of the twenties produced more than a sixty-one per cent increase and the decade of the forties a push forward of another twenty per cent. Thus, there were more than thirty-six hundred slaves in Guilford County before the outbreak of the Civil War.[30]   As for the number of slaves owned by individuals who were of German extraction, Esther Phifer's ninety slaves in Cabarrus County in 1845 was probably the largest group of slaves owned by a single individual with a German surname who lived in the Piedmont.

Slavery in North Carolina generally had a more patriarchal character than was manifested in states in the Deep South where men with a reputation for brutality were sometimes imported to serve as overseers for hundreds of toiling blacks. The more humane character of North Carolina slavery was especially evident among Germans in the Piedmont. The owners and slaves lived on the same tract of land, ate food cooked in the same pots, wore clothes made from the same looms, and attended the same churches.[31]

Near the end of the nineteenth century, Niles J. Bakke interviewed a number of black North Carolinians who had been slaves of Lutheran masters, and they indicated they had been treated well. Some insisted that their masters never sold a slave, but the records indicate there were Germans who did. At the same time, there are also numerous indications of a fatherly concern demonstrated by German slave owners, as in the case of George Michael Heilig who in 1828 directed that when the mistress died, a particular slave "enjoy more liberty than before" and be cared for on the family farm for the rest of the slave's life. Another master who lived near a gold mine urged that his slaves be hired out only to "lenient and humane" persons who could be counted on to make "comfortable provisions" for their needs; in no case were they to be "hired out to a miner or a mining company."[32]

When Muhlenberg first reached Charleston in 1742, he was distressed to discover resistance to the idea of evangelizing the black population. Roman Catholics establishing themselves in the New World often demonstrated a marked concern for the baptism and conversion of their slaves, but South Carolina's population contained few Catholics. Muhlenberg learned that "the so-called Christians" in coastal Carolina were fearful lest a black person's conversion to Christianity imply liberation from slavery, an eventuality which introduced a larger fear among the whites that "the blacks would kill them all, and make themselves masters of Carolina."

Such fears were not confined to Charleston. An early Anglican missionary in eastern North Carolina reported that he had been teaching slaves the principles of the Christian religion, but that their masters would not permit him to baptize the slaves. Such an attitude reflected not only fear of slave revolt but familiarity with traditional Christian teaching regarding slavery. The church of the English colonists had long maintained that it was quite acceptable to hold "the heathen" in bondage, but that it was immoral to enslave a fellow Christian. Therefore, by 1700 all the southern colonies had promulgated laws which explicitly denied freedom to the slave by virtue of conversion to Christianity. But even colonial law did not allay the misgivings created by the earlier teaching that all Christians are brothers and sisters, and that enslaving a brother or sister in the faith was wrong.

Despite resistance in many quarters, concern for the spiritual welfare of the slaves grew. The first organized plan for bringing the Gospel to the slaves grew out of missionary concern articulated by the English clergyman, Thomas Bray. His work inspired a wealthy Huguenot refugee to create an endowment for an organization called the Associates of Dr. Bray. The organization's purpose was to provide Christian instruction for the children of slaves and to offer similar instruction to adult slaves who desired it.

From the 1730s to the outbreak of the American Revolution, funds from the Associates of Dr. Bray were dispatched to the American colonies to support the work of Anglican missionaries among the slaves, providing them with instructional materials and specific support for schools for the slaves. While the total impact of such work was modest, the associates were responsible for many blacks being exposed to basic Christian teachings; some learned to read, some converted to Christianity, and a few even became teachers of their fellow slaves.[33]

Anglican missionaries also received support from the Bishop of London who in 1727 dispatched a letter to the colonies urging the evangelization of the slaves and assuring slave owners that conversion to Christianity in no way altered a slave's "civil relations." This contention was later bolstered by scriptural arguments based on what present day biblical scholarship labels "incomprehensible distortions of biblical passages."[34]

With the rapid settlement of the South's back country in the second half of the nineteenth century, the erection of buildings to be used as places of worship and as schools became a common occurrence. In instances where congregations were formally organized, black members sometimes participated "in the very acts of incorporation. The absolute number of black church members was small at first (and before the nineteenth century total church membership was only a tiny fraction of the population). But slaves were attending churches, taking communion, being baptized and confirmed, listening to sermons, singing hymns, and gradually accepting the Christian world view."[35]

The Great Revival at the beginning of the nineteenth century established the dominant mode of Christian piety for the antebellum South, for both black and white church members. The continuing "seasons of refreshing" in the decades before the outbreak of the Civil War produced continuing, even if unspectacular, growth in the number of black persons worshipping in congregations that were predominantly white.[36]

The regions of the Carolinas and Virginia where the slave population was most heavily concentrated were the areas in which the Anglican church had its greatest strength. In the Piedmont and mountains where most of the Germans had settled, slaves were rarely to be seen, especially in the early years.

But as the Germans became more accustomed to their American environment, the purchase of a black to help with the work in the fields or in the kitchen became more common. Missionary Pastor Paul Henkel "owned a number of black slaves at various times in his life," and his son, Ambrose, who reprinted editorials against slavery in the *Volksberichter* on occasion, was also the owner of slaves at one time.[37] In Lincoln County, Pastor Arends reportedly owned "numerous Negroes," R. J. Miller of Caldwell County owned slaves, and Rowan County's Pastor Storch purchased a boy named Gem in 1789 and a girl named Sarah in 1791. Thus, the leading clergy in the formative years of the North Carolina Synod were familiar with what became known as the South's "peculiar institution."[38]

For the most part, Lutheran clergy accepted pastoral responsibility for black persons who were owned by members of their parishes. At Friedens, Gibsonville, during the pastorate of Philip Henkel, two children of Henry Kopp's slave were baptized on July 7, 1803. Kopp and his wife were the witnesses for the baptism. Presumably, however, some of the earlier concern about permitting slaves to become Christians lingered among members of the laity. After discussions at several conventions, the North Carolina Synod declared in 1809 that its pastors must be "permitted to baptize the children of slaves belonging to Christian masters and mistresses," provided these owners would assume responsibility for the Christian nurture of those baptized.

In 1814 it became apparent that the action of the Synod had not put the issue to rest. John Dreher, a dedicated layman from one of the synod's congregations in South Carolina, wrote to the synod urging "the necessity of instructing Negroes in the Gospel and of giving them an opportunity to hear the Gospel from our preachers." Returning to a consideration of what provision it should make for black persons, the synod passed a resolution calling on congregations to prepare places in their houses of worship for black persons and slaves so that they might "hear the word of God" and receive the instruction deemed necessary "to qualify them for admission into the Christian Church."

The synod's congregations in South Carolina had particular concerns about this action of their synod, so the synod authorized a Special Conference to be held in the Lexington District for the benefit of the South Carolina congregations. The conference was convened at the end of April 1816, the opening worship being conducted at Bethel and the business sessions at St. Michael's. Starting the conference with worship, C. A. G. Storch and R. J. Miller preached in the church building, while Gottfried Dreher and Gottlieb Schober preached "out of doors." "...The Reverend Mr. Shober addressed an assembly of Negroes in the woods, near the Church, on the subject of Christianity, and in the application particularly enforced obedience to their masters and mistresses, as a proof of their having adopted the doctrine of Salvation....."[39]

When the business sessions got underway, the officers of the North Carolina Synod read to the assembly the action of the synod at its 1814 convention regarding making provision for black worshippers in Lutheran church buildings. There was no question as to what the action of the synod had been, but there were those who questioned the feasibility of implementing the decision in its South Carolina congregations; there the synod's 1814 ruling "appeared to be much opposed."

Miller took the lead in arguing for the synod's resolution. Pointing out that the familiar command to preach the Gospel to every creature certainly included blacks and slaves, Miller went on to note that Abraham "was positively commanded to admit to circumcision" those persons whom he purchased, a rule that continued to be carried out in the Jewish "church." To allay the fears of slave owners that conversion to Christianity might mean emancipation, Miller recalled the content of the letter to Philemon; Paul sent the converted slave back "to his master in Asia."

"Serious deliberations" ensued at St. Michael's with the synodical rule eventually being affirmed, but with this addition:

"That it be left to every congregation either to prepare a place for the negroes, in the church or meeting-house, or make an addition to the same, or build a separate house for their use, if it is agreeable to the civil law of the state. And it was further resolved, to declare it to be the duty of the ministers & congregations by some means or other to have a care for the[ir] christian [sic] instruction, and by some means to give them an opportunity to hear the word of God."[40]

Other questions addressed by the 1816 Special Conference related to baptism.

(1) When should blacks and slaves be admitted to baptism? "....Before they are baptised [sic] they shall be sufficiently instructed in the rudiments of the Christian religion, and for some time...held on trial to prove their sincerity by their conduct."

(2) Are Christian slaves permitted to have their own children baptized? Yes, even "when only the father or mother" is a baptized Christian.

(3) Is it permissible to allow black Christians to serve as sponsors at a baptismal service? Yes, black persons who are communicant members in good standing may so serve. However, in cases where only the father or mother of a black child is a Christian, "sponsors are not absolutely necessary."

(4) When shall slaves and other blacks be admitted to the Lord's Supper? Not "immediately after baptism," but only after they have received "further instruction" and "a further trial" designed to prove "by obedience and humility their Christianity." Confirmation must precede admission to the Lord's Supper, but the timing of such matters is left to the minister and elders of the congregation to which the black or slave makes application for membership.

(5) Where may slaves commune? "....Such confirmed negroes [*sic*] can only receive the sacrament in the congregation to which his or her master or mistress belongs, and if they should belong to none of our congregations, in such [place] as is most convenient to the minister."

(6) May black Christians who are confirmed be denied access to the Lord's Supper? "Each minister can [*sic*] at any time refuse to admit any of them to the table, if he is convinced that the Christianity of the applicant admits of doubt, by general report of improper conduct."[41]

(7) Is it permissible for Christian black persons who are slaves to be married? Yes, they "shall promise to one another in a congregation of their kind, to remain faithful to one another, as long as they are not separated by their masters in being removed to a distance; but in this case, such [a] Christian who hath lost husband or wife in the manner aforesaid, cannot enter into a new connection without the consent of his or her minister and master or mistress, and it shall be the duty of the minister at the time of their entering into such connexion [*sic*] to explain and enforce the duties of the matrimonial state."[42]

Two months after the Special Conference, a leading Lutheran pastor in South Carolina wrote to the secretary of the synod that "the people generally appear to be satisfied with the resolutions formed at our meeting; they are willing and ready to put them in operation, but owing to an individual, the progress appears to be somewhat retarded." The "individual" was not identified, but his influence reportedly extended only to "such as have ever had an aversion to good order."[43] A few months later, the South Carolina pastor was much less sanguine about the outcome of the Special Conference. It seemed to him that "the evils that attended our special conference last spring" were at least in part the outgrowth of mistaken parliamentary procedure. By permitting "every person to speak their mind," and even engage in the debate, "many serious souls" left the meeting with hurt feelings.

On the other hand, there were those who were emboldened in their prejudices, "which has caused them to say more than they ought as people who profess to know the Lord." The writer urged the delegates to the fall convention of the synod at Brick Church, Guilford County, to take steps to preclude such unhappy developments by ruling that in any such gatherings in the future, unrestricted discussion and debate by any and all who happened to be present should be prohibited in favor of having "but one to speak at a time, and all points of disputes & controverseys [*sic*] to be laid over for a private hearing in the presence of the Preachers and Elders of the convention." Only by so doing, he believed, could one contribute to "the peace and unity of the Church."[44]

The North Carolina Synod's pastors in South Carolina who endeavored to comply with the synod's standards regarding black members continued to encounter problems. In 1820 J. Yost Meetze, who served St. Paul's, Pomaria; Bethel, White Rock; and Zion,

Lexington, reported to the synod that "he is prevented from administering the lord's supper [*sic*] because he admits negroes [*sic*] thereto, and baptizes them; he prays for a resolution to be made which is to be read in all our churches." The synod concluded that its rules as printed in *Luther* regarding the admission of black persons to membership in its congregations were clear. They suggested that Meetze and any others encountering such difficulties read to their congregation the appropriate passages from *Luther.*[45]

Unfortunately, in the early years pastors did not always present parochial reports to the synod, and when they did, official acts involving black persons were only occasionally identified in convention minutes. In 1819, for example, baptized slaves were reported by only three North Carolina Synod pastors: R. J. Miller (twelve), David Henkel (thirty-eight) and Daniel Sherer (four).[46] Two years later David Henkel reported confirming sixty-nine slaves and 156 white persons, he being the only pastor in the newly created Tennessee Synod to report the confirmation of slaves.[47] The following year he reported confirming thirty-two slaves and forty-seven white persons. His brother, Philip, reported the only other recorded ministerial act involving a black person, the baptizing of a slave.

In 1822 the Tennessee Synod found itself called upon to face directly the most basic question of all relative to slavery, namely, the legitimacy of chattel slavery itself. Conrad Keicher asked the question: Is slavery to be considered as an evil? In reply, the synod unanimously resolved that "it is to be regarded as a great evil in our land, and it [i.e., the synod] desires the government, if it be possible, to devise some way by which this evil can be removed". The synod also advised every minister to admonish every master to treat his slaves properly, and to exercise his Christian duties towards them.[48]

In the first decade of their synod's life, Tennessee Synod pastors frequently reported the baptism of slaves. Approximately 575 of the more than 800 baptisms of black persons reported by Tennessee Synod pastors between 1821 and 1865 were reported from congregations in North Carolina.[49]

In its 1814 discussion of ministry to black persons, the North Carolina Synod called upon its pastors "seriously to advise the deacons of their congregations to provide space in church buildings where black persons might "hear the Word, since it is not expedient that they sit among the white people...." For the most part, provision of separate seating in the same facility was preferred to erecting separate facilities or creating separate congregations for black Lutherans. The North Carolina and Tennessee synods had no clergy who devoted themselves exclusively to ministry among the blacks, and since there were more congregations composed of white persons than there were pastors available to serve them, the creation of black congregations did not provide an attractive option.

There was also the fact that creating separate black congregations raised the specter of slave revolt. From a more positive perspective, while Lutherans may not have endorsed the squire tradition in all its dimensions, they liked to stress the responsibility and obligations of individual slave owners. This involved assuming responsibility for all dimensions of the slave's life, including the religious.[50]

In the days before the cotton culture riveted slavery upon the South, persons who supported the abolition of chattel slavery, either gradually or immediately, were found on both sides of the Mason-Dixon Line. At least in the upper South, there continued to be significant anti-slavery sentiment until the 1820s. One of the expressions of this sentiment was the colonization society. At both the national and local level, persons worked to promote schemes which assisted in transferring American blacks to Africa. John Reck of St. John's, Salisbury, reflected the views of many when he characterized colonization societies as a reflection of "the benevolent spirit of our age."[51] The editor of Rowan County's *Carolina Watchman* later recalled that in this period of the 1820s "colonization was ardently cherished" in the area.

In the following decade, however, attitudes in the South underwent a significant change.[52] North Carolinians like David Walker helped contribute to the change. Walker, a free black in North Carolina, moved to Boston where he published in 1829 his *Appeal.* Embittered by the injustices he and other blacks had experienced, Walker pled in print for what hosts of white southerners feared most, namely, revolt on the part of blacks.[53]

January 1831 saw the launching of William Lloyd Garrison's militantly abolitionist periodical, the *Liberator*, which was also published in Boston. Garrison was uncompromising in his moral condemnation of the institution and in his demand for immediate emancipation of the slaves. Despite determined efforts to prevent the circulation of Garrison's paper in the slaveholding states, copies of the publication were discovered again and again in communities in the South, creating consternation and fear in the hearts of many slave owners.

In August 1831 came news of Nat Turner: "No ante-bellum Southerner could ever forget Nat Turner. The career of this man made an impact upon the people of his section as great as that of John C. Calhoun or Jefferson Davis. Yet Turner was only a slave in Southampton County, Virginia -and during most of his life a rather unimpressive one at that. He was a pious man, a Baptist exhorter by avocation, apparently as humble and docile as a slave was expected to be."[54]

Reading the Bible is said to have created in Turner a longing for freedom that eventually led him to run away from his master. While in flight in 1825, he believed the Spirit of God directed him to return to his master's plantation and perform a work on behalf of his fellow slaves. Obediently, Turner returned and devoted the next six years to plotting the insurrection that took place in August 1831.

The tragedy began at the home of Joseph Travis who owned Turner. Turner and his co-conspirators murdered Travis and his household. Then Turner led his associates to other houses in the area where all white persons were killed and slaves were forced to join in the revolt. Lasting only forty-eight hours, the insurrection claimed the lives of more than fifty white persons and produced "in the South something resembling a mass trauma, from which the whites had not recovered three decades later." The uprising was the chief propellant in launching Garrison and his *Liberator* to regional notoriety since in the popular mind the work of Walker, Garrison, and Turner were all part of the same nightmarish phantasmagoria. This blending of incentives to fear also produced a variety of denunciations, offers of rewards and pieces of legislation designed to curtail the influence of abolitionists.[55]

Garrison's strident calls for the immediate freeing of the slaves led in July 1835 to a citizens' raid on the Charleston, South Carolina, post office where abolitionist publications were removed from the United States mail and burned to prevent their distribution.[56]   Garrison's ability to arouse the ire of fellow Americans was not restricted to the South. In October he was dragged through the streets of Boston by an irate mob and was placed in jail for his own protection.

Lutherans in the Carolinas were not unaware of the furor created by the abolitionists, but they preferred not to discuss such issues at synodical conventions. However, the president of the South Carolina Synod decided in 1835 that the time had come for the Lutheran church to make itself heard on the question of abolitionism. Addressing the annual convention of that synod, he summarized the fears and concerns of many Carolina Lutherans.

> In common with thousands of sincere christians [sic] and patriots, the members of our communion have not failed to observe, and deeply to deplore the painful excitement, which has spread from one extremity of our country to the other, occasioned by the phrenzied [sic] schemes of the Abolitionists, who in arrogating to themselves the right to graduate [i.e., measure] the rectitude of conscience of their fellow citizens at the South, and to dispose of a large portion of our property, have proved themselves alike enemies to the Federal Compact by which we exist as a nation, forgetful of the Golden Rule, that we should do unto others, as we would have them do unto us - and reckless of the fundamental maxim of christianity [sic], that every man must stand or fall to his own master. The evils inflicted by the advocates of immediate abolition, have not been confined to the disturbance of our social and political relations, but have extended their disastrous results to the interests of religion itself. It is not my province to anticipate any action, which the Synod may think proper to adopt in reference to this all important subject. I would merely observe, that nearly every community of christians [sic] in our land, have declared their sentiments on this subject, and spoken in a language not to be misunderstood. The time has arrived when the voice of our own Church should be heard - temperately, but firmly - and when it should be made to appear in our printed Minutes, that whilst we yield to none in our devotion to our common country, we at the same time are not insensible that the Abolitionists are recreant to every principle of honesty, conscience, patriotism and humanity, in attempting to interfere with our internal and domestic affairs, in direct violation of the Constitution of our State and National Governments, and thereby to jeopard our lives and all that can make life desirable to us. Let them hear it to be our solemn and deliberate conviction, that were it not for the overruling Providence of God, their tender mercies for their brethren at the South, would ere this have caused the perpetration of atrocities in our neighborhoods and in our dwellings, at the bare mention of which the human heart sickens.[57]

The convention responded to the president's expression of concern, adopting a recommendation of its Committee on the Report of the President that called for the convention to embrace certain resolutions. A preamble to the resolutions deplored the abolitionist agitation which threatened "to sever the bonds of attachment which exist between master and slave." More importantly, the resultant interference with the South's "peculiar institution" was declared to be in opposition to the federal constitution, the natural rights of man to hold property, and the principles of the Christian faith as set forth in the Bible.

In the resolutions which followed, the synod did not hesitate to condemn "the conduct of the Northern Abolitionists." It promised to "hold no correspondence" with them, to return any "incendiary publications" received from them, and concluded with an expression of gratitude for the fact that "none of the ministers in our connexion [*sic*] in the United States have adopted the sentiments of the Abolitionists of slavery."[58]

The South Carolina Synod's expression of gratitude for the presumed fact that Lutheran clergy were not to be found among the abolitionists proved premature. The following year the synod took note that "some person or persons, in all probability of our own creed, living, perhaps, in the distant North," had attacked "in some of the Northern prints" pastors of the synod who owned slaves. The synod took time out to discuss what its response should be to "all such attacks." Noting that the discussion of issues raised by the abolitionists had already produced "painful results in the deliberative councils and churches" in some denominations, the South Carolina Synod resolved that it would "not at any time, enter into a discussion of Slavery, as agitated by the Abolitionists of the day."[59]

Although it was disturbing enough for southern Lutherans to learn that some Lutheran pastors "at the North" were espousing abolitionist sentiments, the year 1837 brought even more distressing news. A group of Lutheran pastors in New York, restive because their Hartwick Synod would not embrace a role of social activism, decided to create an organization that would more adequately reflect their point of view.

The result was the creation of the Franckean Synod, an organization that at its first convention declared its conviction that it was appropriate for ecclesiastical bodies to agitate for the abolition of the "crime", the "iniquity", the "*Sin of Slavery*."[60] Two years later the synod declared slavery a threat to "the rights and liberties of the free wherever it is tolerated" and "a disgrace to the government where it exists." The Franckeans were convinced that slavery encouraged and sustained "the most corrupt and depraved state of morals" and, thus, must be "an offence to God" and a provocation of his "just indignation": "It is the duty of Christians throughout the land to come out from the Babel of ruins, according to the divine command, lest its rotten and crumbling mass should fall on them and grind them to powder, the cries of 'the Union' and 'the peace of the Church' to the contrary notwithstanding."[61]

To win converts to its way of thinking, the Franckean Synod forwarded copies of its actions to the church press. Benjamin Kurtz, editor of the Lutheran church paper most widely circulated in the Carolinas, noted that this new synod required all its pastors to sign a double pledge, a pledge of total abstinence with regard to alcoholic beverages and a pledge of total abstinence from participation in, or the provision of support for, American slavery. Was the requirement of such a pledge commanded by Holy Scripture? Surely not! The fledgling synod was indulging in the "Ultraism" which Kurtz saw as "the mania of the age in which we live."[62] Kurtz declined to reproduce in the pages of his paper the new synod's resolutions against slavery.

When the Franckean Synod shared its initial abolitionist resolutions with the South Carolina Synod, that body felt called upon not only to return the mailing to the sender but to give public notice of its action. Ernest Lewis Hazelius, a pastor of the synod who served as the professor at Southern Seminary, reported the action through the *Lutheran Observer*, expressing the hope "the General Synod will not meddle with these matters, as political institutions have nothing to do with the Church of Christ."[63]

There had been a time when it was not uncommon to find white persons in the South who described slavery as an evil. As various schemes for ending slavery were considered by thoughtful southerners, it was increasingly popular to speak of slavery as a "necessary evil." But confronted by the challenge of a militant abolitionism which branded slavery as sin, pure and simple, it no longer seemed appropriate to admit slavery was an evil, even a "necessary" one.

In 1832, Thomas Roderick Dew of the College of William and Mary published *A Review of the Debates in the Virginia Legislature in 1831 and 1832*, in which he argued on economic grounds that slavery was, in fact, a positive good for both slaves and their masters. Five years later Chancellor William Harper of the South Carolina legislature published his *Memoir on Slavery* giving classic expression to Dew's "positive good" theory of slavery.

In the two decades prior to the publication of the *Impending Crisis*, the leadership in the South made it impossible for persons critical of slavery to gain a hearing. As it became clear that the anti-slavery forces in the South were losing the struggle to those who believed it imperative to stifle freedom of thought and discussion on the slavery question, many North Carolinians chose emigration. Looking back on the twenty years prior to 1856, Benjamin Sherwood Hedrick, the product of a German community in Davidson County, observed that nearly half of all his friends, relatives and neighbors had migrated to settlements in Ohio, Indiana, and Illinois. "They were going to seek homes in the free West, knowing, as they did, that free and slave labor could not both exist and prosper in the same community."[64]

The loss of this struggle for a society in which freedom of speech was cherished and differing points of view at least tolerated was to have profound ramifications for the South. For one thing, the church ceased to be the primary place where persons would wrestle with the moral issues growing out of chattel slavery. Instead, autonomous societies and reform agencies, spawned in the North by the Second Great Awakening, became the key agencies in the emerging struggle to rid the land of slavery. The church's gradualist approach to social change was replaced with a call for "immediate emancipation without expatriation."

> These modern abolitionists were distinguished from their predecessors by a number of factors: their youth in 1830; their agitation of national institutions as opposed to state and local authorities alone; their ability to reach a national audience through improved means of communication; their Northern audience's growing sense that slavery was alien to the progress presumably promised by industrialization; their ability to manipulate this belief in conjunction with sectional rivalries; their demand of moral perfection; and their wholesale attack on Southern society. The resulting alienation of Southerners from national institutions forced them to secede. Abolitionists' focus on slaveholding as a sin led to the division of Evangelical churches into slaveholding and free before the Civil War and also to the belated commitment of the Federal government to abolition as a war aim.[65]

Southern Lutherans responded to the new abolitionism by insisting that slavery was a purely political question; to continue to permit discussion of slavery in ecclesiastical conventions would be an unwarranted dabbling in politics by the church. Of course the church was expected to address moral issues, but Lutherans on both sides of the Mason-Dixon Line in the first half of the nineteenth century were inclined to see such issues as dancing, a proper keeping of the "Sabbath", and the consumption of alcoholic beverages as the really formidable ethical challenges of the day.[66]

Unqualified support for slavery became the South's litmus test for loyalty to one's state and region. As that came to be the case, abolitionists, including those who had hoped for a gradual elimination of slavery, became rare in the Carolinas. In the Tar Heel state, the mountain counties harbored few slaves and little enthusiasm for the system. In other sections of the state, only occasional pockets of resistance to the anti-abolitionist hysteria survived.

One such pocket persisted below Gibsonville in the southeastern section of Guilford County, in the area around the German Reformed's Brick Church and Mt. Hope. Dr. Eli W. Caruthers, a Presbyterian clergyman whose parish covered much of the section, is often credited with creating the abolitionist sentiment in the area since he was dismissed from the parish because of his anti-slavery activities. His dismissal, however, seems to have accelerated, rather than retarded, the growth of abolitionist sentiment.

In the late antebellum period, these congregations were served by Dr. George William Welker, a Pennsylvanian and an 1841 product of the German Reformed seminary at Mercersburg. For two decades, Welker's parishioners defended him from those who did not share his abolitionist and pro-Union views. When, however, secession became a part of the picture in 1861, the forces of division proved stronger than the forces for unity. Division at Brick Church led to the creation of a committee whose secretary, J. R. Huffman, notified the governor of North Carolina that, of the persons comprising Brick Church and Mt. Hope, many were "rank abolitionists," a fact not surprising since their pastor was "from Pennsylvania" and "a strong abolitionist."[67]

The rise of militant abolitionism made all denominations more concerned about the adequacy of their provision for black worshippers. Apparently a number of congregations of both the North Carolina and Tennessee synods provided space in their church buildings for black Lutherans during this period. When members of Friendship, Taylorsville, erected a building in 1832, its design included "a gallery." Occupants of the gallery included Jacob Bostian's slaves who at a service in 1839 constituted approximately fifteen per cent of the persons communing at Friendship.

When the congregation began construction of a new building in 1859, the question arose whether seats would be made available to blacks in the new building. The decision was recorded as being unanimously in the affirmative. In 1835 the members of Salem, Lincolnton, erected an addition to their building expressly to accommodate "people of color." Although there is no direct evidence, there were probably a number of additional congregations that made specific provision for black worshippers. But not all congregations in the North Carolina Synod did so, for in 1837 the synod again called upon its congregations who had not already taken the step to make available space for black worshippers.[68]

The rise of abolitionism provided an incentive to evangelize the slaves; those who charged white southerners with abusing their authority over blacks and with neglecting the spiritual welfare of their charges must be proven wrong.[69] This incentive was a late addition to others of long standing. From their earliest encounters with slaves, North Carolina's Lutherans had the gospel imperative to witness to all concerning God's love revealed in Christ. They also had the declarations of Holy Scripture calling on all persons, blacks included, to lead morally acceptable lives pleasing to their creator.

Through the exchange of minutes with other synods, the Lutheran Synod of North

Carolina received still another incentive to evangelize black persons. The minutes of the South Carolina Synod indicated that North Carolina's daughter synod was more zealous in evangelizing black persons than was the mother synod. In reporting on the minutes of other synods, a committee in 1845 pointed out that South Carolina Lutherans "have turned special attention to the colored population within the bounds of their respective charges, and have succeeded in gathering a goodly number into the Church."[70] Three years later, the synod's corresponding secretary noted that, of 459 baptisms in the South Carolina synod the previous year, 123 were black persons, of 181 confirmations forty-four were black persons, and that of 3,078 communicants, 439 were black persons. "It is a praiseworthy spirit in these brethren, seeing and ministering to the spiritual wants of these Heathen at Home, as well as those in distant lands."[71]

Motivation for mission is rarely an uncontaminated response to God's redemptive love. A concern not to be outdone by neighboring Lutherans to the south no doubt provided incentive for North Carolina Synod initiatives among blacks. And there were those who felt compelled to do something "to rebut abolitionist charges that slaveholders left their bondspeople in heathenish conditions."[72] Of course, many North Carolina Lutherans were concerned for the evangelization of the slaves because of the Pietistic tradition in which they stood. They shared the same piety and the same zeal to share the Gospel with others that prompted Bartholomaeus Ziegenbalg and Heinrich Pluetschau to sail from Europe as missionaries to India at the start of the eighteenth century.

In 1847 the roster of North Carolina Lutheran congregations included for the first time a "Colored Congregation." Presumably organized during the previous year, the congregation reported four infant baptisms, twenty adult baptisms and confirmations, and twenty-one communicants.[73] The following year, both J. A. Linn and J. B. Anthony were reported to be serving black congregations as well as their white congregations.[74] But while occasional congregations were established by North Carolina Lutherans exclusively for black persons, the typical pattern remained one in which overwhelmingly white congregations accepted into membership one or two black families owned by a member or members of the congregation.[75]

In 1849, Rev. Philip A. Strobel noted that in neighboring South Carolina, congregations were slow to reflect their concern for mission work among the blacks, with the notable exception of St. John's, Charleston. However, the example of the Charleston church had had its effect; now all but six of the synod's forty-three congregations contained black members. The previous year one-third of the synod's new members were black, so that nearly one-sixth of all members of the synod were now black.[76]

One of the most significant leaders of the Lutheran church in the United States in the nineteenth century was William A. Passavant, pastor of First Lutheran Church in Pittsburgh, Pennsylvania. Like many of the graduates of Gettysburg Theological Seminary during the tenure of President Samuel Simon Schmucker, Passavant was deeply concerned about the slavery issue.

More than a decade before President Lincoln issued the Emancipation Proclamation, Passavant was convinced that the days of slavery were numbered. Foreign competition in the raising of cotton and the exhaustion of soil in the South would, he felt, eventually produce an end to the South's "peculiar institution." But slavery was also being undermined, he believed, by educating and evangelizing the slaves. Such moral elevation of the slave community would operate with an even greater force than soil exhaustion and foreign competition. The demise of slavery could not come too soon, in Passavant's view. He took pleasure in reporting on a debate in Kentucky between a clergyman, John L. Waller, and a layman, Thomas F. Marshall. Waller contended that slavery was a divine institution, sanctioned and approved by God. To that assertion, Marshall gave a reply

> as pungent, as it was brief. "This gentleman," says Mr. Marshall, "has attempted to prove that the blessing of Heaven rests upon the institution of slavery. *I have too much respect for my God to attempt to defend him from such slander.*"[77]

As editor of a church paper, Passavant was also concerned to get the facts about the mission to black persons being carried out by Lutherans in the South. He decided to contact an experienced pastor ordained by the North Carolina synod in 1838, Philip A. Strobel. Strobel, then serving in South Carolina, was asked to report on work among blacks in that synod. After describing the recent rapid growth in black membership in the synod's predominantly white congregations, Strobel observed,

> But it may be asked what facilities are furnished to the slaves, for acquiring religious knowledge? Have they any means of becoming acquainted with the scriptures? As you have requested me to furnish nothing but facts, I must say, that in our church, few advantages are afforded them beyond the ordinary means of grace. They are, however, admitted in all our churches, where they can in company with their master enjoy the preaching of the gospel every Sabbath without let or hinderance [*sic*]. The Sacrament of Baptism is administered to them or their children, when desired, and they are invited in their turn, to surround our communion tables and unite with us in commemorating the dying love of our Common Master. In some few instances, special efforts are made to instruct our colored people, especially the young, in the doctrines and duties of christianity [*sic*].[78]

Recognizing that serious work among the slaves by Lutherans was still in its infancy, Strobel was confident it would continue its recent rapid growth.

Passavant also found himself drawn into the great national debate on slavery because of his key involvement in the development of the Pittsburgh Synod.[79] The synod, a small body at the time of its organization in 1845, made up in missionary zeal anything it may have lacked in size. In 1849 Benjamin Arey, the corresponding secretary of the North Carolina Synod, praised the Pittsburgh Synod with these words: "We hesitate not to say, that this synod is without parallel for its zeal and efficiency in building up the church and promoting all the benevolent enterprizes [*sic*] of the day. Would to God that we in particular, and all other synods of our church, could imbibe more of their spirit; and like them could become more efficient in accomplishing that part of the work which God has assigned to us."[80]

But the spirit and zeal of the Pittsburgh synod was, after 1857, viewed in a different light by many Lutherans "at the South." At the beginning of September of that year, the Middle Conference of the Pittsburgh Synod met in Lawrence County, Pennsylvania. Recalling that Americans liked to boast that their land was "the freest on which the sun shines," the conference observed the irony of the fact that it contained "between three and four millions of slaves."

These Americans were

> deprived of their natural rights, said in our Declaration of Independence to be inalienable; of liberty and the pursuit of happiness; they are deprived of the opportunity of mental improvement; they are shut out from the reading of God's Holy Word, and many of them from the most necessary religious advantages and privileges; they are worked, whipped, fed, bought and sold, and in every respect in which it is possible to treat human beings as brutes, they are so treated. Slavery makes tyrants and oppressors of masters, and menials and chattels of servants; it demoralizes the community, undermines our free institutions, makes us a by-word among the nations, and brings down the curse of heaven upon us as a people.[81]

The pastors and laymen assembled in Lawrence County recognized that a number of forces combined to support the enslavement of human beings in the United States. In the slave states, both the laws and public sentiment supported the institution, and the federal government upheld its constitutionality. In the free states, public sentiment was hardly overwhelming in its opposition to slavery. And there was the problem of the church. In the South it openly supported slavery, and this support for the institution was also supported "by the connivance of the Church in the North." These circumstances seemed to the Middle Conference of the Pittsburgh Synod to demand from them a clear articulation to "the Church and the world" of their own convictions on the subject.

> 1st. We hold that slavery, as it exists in this country, wars not only against the principles of the word of God, but against some of its express and plain declarations, and is therefore sinful.
> 2d. We hold that Christians, in their individual and associated capacities, are bound to testify against it, kindly but emphatically, in a language which cannot be misunderstood.
> 3d. We hold that Christians are solemnly bound to make their influence tell against this evil, as well at the ballot box as in their intercourse with their fellow-men.
> 4th. We hold, that whilst all political questions, as such, should be carefully excluded from the pulpit, as unbecoming its sacred character, as a moral question, the nature of slavery and the duty of Christians in relation to it, is a proper subject for pulpit discussion.[82]

The resolutions of the Middle Conference were printed prominently in *The Missionary*, a mission-oriented church paper with a number of readers in the South. Since the resolutions, however, were not enacted by a synod or expressly directed to synods, both the North Carolina and Tennessee synods took no official notice of the resolutions. The South Carolina Synod discussed the action of the Middle Conference and decided it, too, would make no official response. However, it called upon its most distinguished clerical member, John Bachman of Charleston, to compose a response to the resolutions. Bachman accepted the responsibility with reluctance; he was a man of peace and discussions of slavery in 1857 were more likely "to irritate than to convince." Was it not more appropriate that an issue like slavery should be debated in the secular, rather than religious, press? Of religious controversy he had seen enough, but Bachman accepted the responsibility, insisting only that he would not become involved in responding to any rebuttals that might be advanced to his presentation. In accepting the request of the synod, Bachman provided the most detailed defense of slavery to come from the pen of a Lutheran clergyman in the antebellum South.

Before addressing the specific resolutions of the Middle Conference, Bachman made some comments on the preamble. In so doing he touched on a number of the standard southern arguments in defense of slavery. A familiar one stressed the civilizing impact of slavery. The "lowest barbarians" had been brought to southern shores where hosts of them had been transformed into civilized Christians. Devout masters and clergy in the South had accomplished "a hundred times more than has been accomplished by all the missionaries of the Cross in Asia, Africa, and our Western wilds, from the time of the Reformation until this day," he contended.

As for the familiar abolitionist appeal to the Declaration of Independence, Bachman noted that this oft-quoted phrase could not have been understood by the signers of the Declaration to apply to slaves since the constitution, "framed eleven years afterwards, . . . plainly and indisputably guaranteed the rights of the master, and in a legal form sanctioned the institution of slavery." That constitution, he reminded the Middle Conference, had been signed by eight citizens of their own state, including the illustrious Benjamin Franklin.[83]

Bachman denied that slaves in the South were excluded from opportunities for religious development. All human beings should have access to religious nurture, and the Charleston clergyman was convinced that black persons and white persons belonged to the same species, the same human family. But while Bachman argued, contrary to some prominent scientists of the day, that the black person belonged to the human species, he insisted that an examination of free blacks, both in Africa and in more fully developed societies, indicated that they were an inferior variety of the human species.

This view was not peculiar to the South, he argued. "In our Northern States and Canada, they are everywhere regarded as an inferior race, and however the Declaration of Independence may by some be interpreted, they are not admitted as equals by the laws of many of the free States, nor by the laws of custom in any State. They are not invited to their tables, and a union with their daughters would be regarded as a degradation."[84]

What of brutality and the physical abuse of slaves? Yes, masters sometimes found it necessary to punish their slaves, and there were instances of actual abuse, but Bachman believed such abuse by owners was rare.

"When we assert that they, as a body, are kind and humane, we speak with confidence. The bond of attachment between the master and the servant is very strong. When sick, the latter are attended by the family physician; when aged and infirm, they are not sent to an alms house, or to beg on the highway, but are provided for at home; when in affliction, they are visited and comforted by the master and mistress and other members of the family, and when they die, they are buried and mourned over as parts of the household."[85]

But what of the laws passed by southern legislatures that made it a crime to teach a black person to read or write? How could one claim that black persons had access to opportunities for religious growth and development if they were not permitted to read and study the Holy Scriptures? Such laws had been passed, Bachman recalled, only because of the incendiary character of abolitionist literature which had been scattered abroad in the South.

Even so, the laws quickly became "a dead letter": "The churches of every denomination are all open to them, and in some the colored attendants are more numerous than the whites. When the heads of families retire from the holy communion table, the servants come forward and surround the same altar. Many servants are taught to read by the younger portion of the white members of the family, and the Bible is found in thousands of families among the colored population."[86]

Finally, in dealing with the preamble, Bachman raised the familiar concern about "outside" interference in a situation which he believed he and his fellow southerners best understood and were best equipped to address. What if a conference of a Lutheran synod in the South were to find itself confronted with proposed resolutions condemning Lutherans in Pittsburgh as "heathens and publicans" because of some mob violence that had taken place in their city? He felt confident the resolutions would not be adopted; surely "some pious brother of experience, mindful of the courtesies which should exist among men, and especially the kindness and charity which should characterize the Christian," would warn the assembly against meddling in the affairs of other persons, particularly when "our minds may have been misled by interested partisans."

In turning to the actual resolutions adopted by the Middle Conference, the Charleston pastor first addressed the assertion that slavery was contrary to the Word of God, hence, sinful. He reminded his readers that the Old Testament not only accepted the institution but in some instances mandated it. Slavery existed in the time of Jesus and the apostles and there is no evidence that they repudiated it. And there was the example of the Apostle Paul sending a runaway slave back to his master, even though the slave had become a Christian. It was not slavery which was sinful, Bachman argued, but its abuses, and these were just as abhorrent to Christians in the South as in the North. In his own state, the killing of a slave was classified as murder, and in rare instances when such a crime had been perpetrated, the offender had himself been executed.[87]

Bachman chose to address the three remaining resolutions of the Middle Conference at the same time. They related to the obligation of the Christian to bear witness against slavery, use the ballot box to defeat it, and acknowledge the propriety of dealing with slavery from the pulpit. A fundamental issue was the nature of the entire question of slavery; was it primarily a moral or a political issue? Bachman argued it was political. The most recent presidential election had seen one of the parties use as its slogan, "Free Speech, Free Press, Free Soil, Free Men, Fremont and Victory." The very plea of the Middle Conference, calling upon the Christian to use the ballot box to influence the course of events supported his contention that the issue was basically political, claimed Bachman.

But the Lutheran pastor was not primarily concerned about the ideological classification of a current topic of debate. Inviting clergy to use the pulpit as the place to voice their disparate opinions on the question of slavery, would, he was convinced, have a negative impact on the life of the church. Some northern church groups had already tried it. The result had been "nothing but bitterness and strife."

Every year one ligament after another, that bound us together as a nation, has been broken asunder. No sooner did any religious denomination assail the institutions of the South, and adopt resolutions reflecting on the moral and religious character of their ministers and people...than the Southern churches withdrew for the sake of peace, and organized Synods of their own. The Northern churches that have been engaged in these discussions, admit that they have declined in spirituality and in the number of communicants.[88]

Bachman believed it important that Lutherans had not permitted debate over questions like slavery to fracture the fragile unity of their denomination: "In the constitution of the General Synod . . . a clause is inserted which received the unanimous assent of all the Synods, which excludes these exciting and strife-engendering subjects from the control of the Synod, and confines its labors to its legitimate duties of promoting the great interests of the Redeemer's Kingdom. The effect has been most salutary."[89]

It seemed to Bachman that northern agitators hoped to unite the church in the northern states against slavery. Would that be a great advance? Understandings agreed upon in the United States constitution violated, strife between those who have lived in agreement, "bloody wars among brethren;" these surely would be the fruit of a really united northern front against slavery.

Was it not more appropriate for Lutherans to avoid debates calculated to fracture and alienate, and concentrate instead on the mission of the church? Surely if the great missionary heroes who had come to the American colonies to proclaim the Gospel could return and address their Lutheran successors in the 1850s, they would urge them to concentrate on their "high calling" of witnessing to God's love revealed in Jesus Christ, confident that in so doing their differences about political and social questions would "sink into insignificance."

On this altar of piety, hallowed by zeal and love, bury your disputes about symbolisms and platforms; leave to your statesmen the work of carrying on the intricate affairs of government, whilst you who are engaged in a higher calling, must "render unto Caesar the things that are Caesar's, and unto God the things that are God's." Thus, with a single eye to the glory of God and the salvation of souls, labor, by your faithful preaching of the gospel and your fervent prayers to God, to render every seat in your churches an anxious bench. "Let there be no strife between you, for you are brethren."[90]

For Bachman, the choice was clear. Concentrate on preaching the Gospel, whether to slave or free. The status of persons in a body politic is a political question. Let it be debated in the halls of politics; not in the church. While officially speaking only for himself, Bachman undoubtedly spoke for most Carolina Lutherans, lay and ordained, in 1857.

Sectionalism

A second factor, albeit inextricably intertwined with the first, contributed to the fracturing of the body politic, and, with it, the General Synod which North Carolina Lutherans had helped to create as a national bond of Lutheran unity. That factor was sectionalism, a consciousness of regional identity that became so strong and virulent as to rupture the republic and cause American to take up arms against American. In less than a dozen years after the constitution was drafted in Philadelphia in 1787, an issue arose that fostered significant theorizing about the nature of the union created by the federal constitution. That theorizing about an issue called "nullification", in turn, laid the groundwork for secession and civil war.

In 1798 a Federalist-dominated Congress passed the Alien and Sedition Acts, designed to curb the actions of Jeffersonian Republicans. A number of Jeffersonian newspaper editors and publishers who had publicly criticized the Federalists and their exercise of power were arrested and convicted as violators of the acts. This action prompted reflection on possible courses of action by those who felt the Alien and Sedition Acts were an unwarranted infringement on dearly won freedoms.

Two of the chief architects of the American experiment in democracy each drafted important documents suggesting what recourse might be had in such circumstances. The Vice President of the United States, Thomas Jefferson, drafted the Kentucky Resolutions which were introduced in the Kentucky legislature by John Breckenridge and adopted by that body in November 1798. One of Jefferson's fellow Virginians, James Madison, prepared the Virginia Resolutions which were adopted by the legislature of that state on Christmas Eve in the same year. Both Jefferson's resolutions and those penned by Madison recalled that the constitution was a compact agreed to by sovereign states, states that retained the right to interpret the constitution and pass judgment on laws passed under it.

The following year the Kentucky and Virginia legislatures went a step further, declaring that when they adjudged acts of Congress to be in conflict with their understanding of the constitution, the state could have recourse to nullification, that is, could declare the congressional act null and void within the bounds of their state. When the Jeffersonian Republicans gained control of Congress, the Alien and Sedition Acts were repealed. Jefferson and Madison would later insist that the resolutions they had prepared as a defense of the rights of the states were not intended to sanction disunion, but to reaffirm the role of the states as guardians of individual civil liberties. The theories they had advanced would not die easily, however.

In 1816 the Congress enacted the first protective tariff in the history of the young nation. When the tariff law was revised in 1824, the result was viewed by planters in the South as detrimental to their economic well-being while bringing advantages to Ohio, Kentucky and Pennsylvania. With the adoption of the "Tariff of Abominations" in 1828, the political savants attempted to use the tariff issue to unite regional interests for political gain.

Tempers waxed so hot over the tariff question that in 1832, the legislature of South Carolina convened a special state convention which adopted an Ordinance of Nullification in response to the latest act of Congress designed to address the tariff question. South Carolina declared the tariff legislation unconstitutional and without force within its borders, forbidding federal officials to collect such tariffs in the state after February 1, 1833, and threatening secession from the Union if the federal government used force to collect the revenues. President Andrew Jackson acted with firmness and issued a stern warning in the form of a Proclamation to the People of South Carolina which declared "disunion by armed force is treason." Congress responded to the President's request and provided him with the Force Bill to insure that the laws of Congress would be enforced in South Carolina. And they were.

In 1842 South Carolinians decided to send to the United States Senate their former governor, George McDuffie. He had served as a congressman during the Nullification crisis in 1832 and was an ardent exponent of states' rights. There were those who saw the presence of persons like McDuffie among representatives of the South as a liability rather than an asset. The editor of the *Lutheran Observer* remarked:

> We honestly believe that our Southern brethren have unintentionally contributed more to produce this anti-slavery sentiment than the Abolitionists. The latter by their intemperate and radical proceedings, have clearly abridged the rights of the poor slave, riveted the chains of his bondage, and awakened a deep sympathy in thousands of Northern bosoms in behalf of the honest slave-holder. But the uncompromising spirit of the South, and especially the harsh and lynching treatment received by some deluded abolitionists, and the high and untenable ground assumed by leading Southern statesmen, such for instance as Mr. McDuffie, have tended to neutralize that sympathy and greatly increase the number of anti-slavery men. Had the South permitted the North to carry on the war against and annihilate ultra abolitionism; or had they been less violent, things had not reached their present crisis.[91]

There may well have been Lutheran laymen in the South whose business interests made the tariff question one of vital interest for them. To the degree that that was the case, they were probably swept along in the increasing tendency to view political questions regionally. For Lutheran clergy, one of the first concerns to prompt thinking along regional lines was theological education. When the South Carolina Synod decided to launch a theological seminary in 1830, it was only the geographic remoteness of Hartwick and Gettysburg seminaries that prompted leading pastors to urge the creation and support of a Lutheran school of theology in the South. Even after the founding of the South Carolina Synod's school, occasional students and gifts of financial support from the Carolinas found their way to the seminary at Gettysburg.

But by 1843 there were other issues crowding to the fore. As the South Carolina Synod put it, "Resolved, That the moral, political, and local peculiarities of the South, require the churches here, to husband their own funds, and sustain their religious institutions under all circumstances."[92] Clearly, the emerging regional consciousness now involved more than geographic distance from the North.

The growing regional divisiveness within church bodies concerned the editor of the *Lutheran Observer.* Observing the growing tensions in the Methodist church during the first half of 1844, Benjamin Kurtz remarked that that body would soon succumb to a "speedily ripening division." To Kurtz' eye, it appeared that the American environment tended toward Congregationalism in church polity. Thus, attempts to address divisive issues would naturally lead to schism and the creation of multiple ecclesiastical entities, each with its own head. Ultimately, the time would arrive when every congregation large enough to support a clergyperson would have "her own bishop, and every bishop will have his own church."[93]

The next political crisis questioning the nature of the federal compact and the rights of the states came into focus during the war with Mexico (1846-48). David Wilmot, a congressman from Pennsylvania, succeeded in attaching to an appropriations bill an amendment which provided that slavery would not be permitted in any territory that might be gained by the United States as a result of the war with Mexico. The Wilmot Proviso was bitterly resented in the South.[94]

As political figures in South Carolina decried the Wilmot Proviso, the state's

Lutherans gathered for their annual convention.   The synod, in response to a recommendation of President John C. Hope, proposed that Lutherans in the South convene a Southern Church Convention "to unite the minds, feelings and energies of this division of our Church."   There was concern over the languishing state of the South's only Lutheran school of theology. Hope suggested that all the Lutheran synods in the South unite in establishing and operating a joint school of theology and a "collegiate institute" at a site other than Lexington, South Carolina, where the seminary had been located since Dr. Ernest Lewis Hazelius had succeeded John G. Schwartz as the professor of theology in 1833.

In addition to concern over the seminary, there were also those who believed that "the peculiar wants of our Church here...require a Southern Church paper."[95]   P. A. Strobel, who apparently was quite happy with the location of the seminary, reported in the *Lutheran Observer* that there were really only two reasons for the South Carolina Synod's proposal that a Southern Church Convention be held. First, there was the need to form "a closer bond of union," but, secondly, there was a need to improve the efficiency of mission efforts in the area.   Strobel, who had sought and received appointment as southern correspondent for the *Lutheran Observer*, opposed the suggestion that such a convention might lay the groundwork for a southern church paper for Lutherans.[96]

When the delegates to the convention of the North Carolina Synod assembled in May 1848, at St. Paul's, Newton, it was noted that a letter had been received from the corresponding secretary of the South Carolina Synod.   A committee consisting of Pastors Rothrock, Arey and Crim considered the letter and reported to the convention that, indeed, their sister synod to the south had proposed the calling of a Southern Church Convention.

The convention was to have as its leading objective the creating of "a union of the synods of South and North Carolina, West Tennessee and Western Virginia, in building the Church in the South West. To accomplish this it may be necessary to make our Theological Seminary more efficient by endowing other Professorships---and it may be made a question for this Convention, whether the publication of a religious periodical may serve as an auxiliary."[97]

The question of the seminary's location was raised with increasing frequency, and the decision to establish an academy in conjunction with the seminary posed the site question with greater urgency. Many believed it fortuitous that a church assembly was in the offing which would provide an opportunity for southern synods to confer about an appropriate site for these educational endeavors.

The North Carolina Synod's committee said the proposal from South Carolina met with their approval. They suggested that the convention meet early in the summer of 1849, agreed with the South Carolina Synod that "the delegation to said Convention might be particularly select," and suggested that North Carolina be considered an appropriate site for the meeting.[98]   It seemed fitting that the South Carolina Synod should determine the precise time and place for the convention as well as "the ratio of representation," which the North Carolina Synod's committee hoped "might be somewhat greater than the ratio of [its] delegation to the General Synod." The synod adopted the committee's report.

When the South Carolina Synod met in 1848, Bachman was clearly concerned about directions that might be taken by the projected Southern Church Convention. Reporting on the recent convention of the General Synod, the Charleston pastor stressed the importance of national unity for Lutherans, and did so with such effectiveness that the purposes of the projected Southern Church Convention were quietly re-phrased so as to prevent the convention from becoming a platform for divisive sectional interests.[99]

The following year, President Hope of the South Carolina Synod dispatched to the *Lutheran Observer* an announcement giving official notice of the South Carolina Synod's invitation to other synods to join them in the Southern Church Convention. Addressed "To Whom It May Concern," the announcement indicated Hope would be awaiting a reply from those interested in such a convention.[100]

Six weeks later the North Carolina Synod Lutherans gathered at St. John's, Concord, for their annual convention. In the course of the meeting, the synod's committee that reported on the minutes of other Lutheran bodies observed that "the most important matter claiming the attention" of the South Carolina Synod in 1848 was "the Southern Church Convention. This Convention was proposed to us by the brethren of the South, the objects of which were favorably received by this synod. But we are sorry to say that in our opinion one of the most important objects of the Convention, and one in which the most general interest was felt on the part of all the synods concerned, has been frustrated by the recent action of the synod of S. Carolina. The seminary, we presume, is now permanently located. A Southern Church paper does not meet our approbation."[101]

Despite the committee's clear disappointment that the relocation of the seminary would not be on the agenda for the Southern Church Convention, the committee proposed that the synod appoint delegates to represent North Carolina at the convention.

The synod responded positively to its committee's recommendations, voting to elect "two Ministerial and two Lay-delegates" to the convention to be held in Concord starting on "Friday before the first Sabbath in June." The pastors selected to represent the synod were J. A. Linn and J. D. Scheck. P. A. Seaford, Esq., of Rowan County and Christopher Melchor, Esq., of Cabarrus County were named the synod's lay representatives. The synod also voted to instruct its delegates "to oppose the establishment of a distinctive religious journal in our church, South," but in all other matters, the delegates were not bound.[102]

A month later, the Virginia Synod described the proposed Southern Church Convention as "deeply interesting to the Southern portion of the Lutheran church" and prayed that the convention's deliberations "may result in great and lasting benefit to the Church." But they did not elect or appoint delegates to the convention to be held in their neighboring state to the south.[103]

At last the day for the start of the Southern Church Convention arrived and "a number of brethren" met at Concord at the appointed time. Not only were there no delegates from Virginia; South Carolina, too, had failed to send a delegation.

The North Carolina Synod delegation recognized there was no point in formally organizing as a convention of the southern synods. Instead, reflecting their disappointment in the decision of the Board of Trustees of the Southern Seminary to leave the institution and its academy in Lexington District, South Carolina, the North

Carolina representatives at Concord turned their attention to the educational needs of the North Carolina Synod. What was needed, they believed, was a "Collegiate Institute within the bounds of the North Carolina synod." They recommended a called meeting of the synod four weeks later to consider further the education question.[104]

In July 1849 President Hope of the South Carolina Synod, provided "An Explanation" in the *Lutheran Observer* regarding the failure of the Southern Church Convention to materialize. The South Carolina Synod, which initiated the idea, was to appoint a committee to carry out correspondence with other synods and to serve as a committee on arrangements for the meeting. However, the synod "forgot" to appoint the committee! On his own initiative, President Hope went ahead and inserted a letter in the *Lutheran Observer* announcing the invitation to the convention.

Hope expressed disappointment that Editor Kurtz had run his letter announcing the Southern Church Convention in only one issue. Even that might have been expected to produce some sort of communication with the president of the South Carolina Synod, but Hope indicated he had heard nothing of the interest of other southern synods in being represented at the proposed convention. "No answers came, individually or officially -- neither by letter or otherwise."

In view of this lack of response, Hope decided not to dispatch the South Carolina Synod representatives: "Well, brethren, our Convention has failed -- I am sorry for it. But let us not despair. All that conventions can do for us, may be done yet. Some of you take the lead in the next movement of this kind --and by better management we will reach happier results."[105]

On the national political scene, the congressional adoption of the Compromise of 1850 was followed by a brief lull in the acrimonious debate over slavery. But with the enactment of the Kansas-Nebraska Bill calling for popular sovereignty as the means of deciding whether Kansas and Nebraska would be slave or free, the slavery issue resumed its prominent position in antebellum politics. Many folk from the South had moved into the Kansas territory, and the decision by Congress to let the settlers there decide whether their state would be slave or free produced a civil war in Kansas. Kansas became for the "free soilers" a challenge to demonstrate that the expansion of slavery into new territories could, in fact, be stopped. The rush to get new anti-slavery settlers into Kansas and the mobilizing of pro-slavery support in neighboring Missouri were the prelude to a "bleeding Kansas."[106]

In May 1856 Senator Charles Sumner delivered his "The Crime Against Kansas" speech in which the anti-slavery senator from Massachusetts attacked the Kansas-Nebraska Act, and its author, Senator Stephen A. Douglas of Illinois. By his own choice, a "moralist in politics," "Charles Sumner brought to the Senate an eloquence at once polished, classical, and offensively vituperative, an ego that managed to stand out even among the most egotistical assemblage in the United States, an unswerving set of high moral principles, and a sincere, abiding hatred of the institution of slavery."[107]

In condemning the attempted settlement of the slavery issue in the Kansas-Nebraska Act, Sumner indulged his penchant for dealing in personalities, attacking not only Senator Douglas who led the struggle to get the act passed but also Senator Andrew P. Butler of South Carolina who defended the rights of slaveowners in Kansas. Senator Butler consistently refrained from emotional rhetoric calculated to excite sectional feelings, but Sumner scorned him as "one of the 'maddest zealots' of 'tyrannical sectionalism'."[108]   When Sumner dealt in personalities, "he did so insultingly, and with apparent relish.   This habit, accompanied by a lofty, sanctimonious manner that was almost as infuriating as the actual content of his speeches, could not fail to inflame the rather easily ignited Southern temper."[109]

Senator Butler was not present to hear Sumner's attack but his nephew, Congressman Preston Brooks of South Carolina, was in the Senate gallery, heard it, and felt called upon to punish Senator Sumner for his attack on Senator Butler. Thus it was that shortly after the adjournment of the Senate at 12:45 p.m on May 22, Brooks entered the Senate chamber looking for the Senator from Massachusetts. Spotting Sumner at his desk in the rear row preparing copies of his "Crime against Kansas" speech for mailing, the congressman from South Carolina called out to him, and, as he advanced on the senator, calmly informed him of the reason for his visit.

Having reached Sumner, Brooks lifted the gold handled walking stick in his hand and brought it down with force on the head of Sumner. A flurry of blows from the cane followed, the Massachusetts senator ripping his desk loose from its moorings in a frantic effort to escape the seat that restricted his flight.[110] Despite his efforts to escape the fury of Brooks, the injuries Sumner received were so severe that he did not return to the Senate until December 1859.

Responses to this brief but dramatic episode were predictably sectional and "tragically ominous. Charles Sumner and Preston Brooks had blundered into the vintage where the grapes of wrath were stored, and the more vocal elements in the South frankly exulted at the news that a United States Senator had been clubbed into insensibility. Even the less extreme Southerners could not restrain a twinge of inner satisfaction; if there was regret here, it stemmed primarily from an awareness of the political profit the South's enemies could derive from the affair."[111]

Southerners applauded Brooks for defending the honor of his uncle. Northerners, increasingly indignant about developments in bleeding Kansas, were outraged by Brooks' attack on Sumner. Rev. William A. Passavant termed Brooks an assassin "whose cowardice is equalled only by his utter unfitness for the position he now holds in the Congress of the United States."[112] Benjamin Kurtz, whose readers were far more numerous in the South than were Passavant's, nevertheless joined Passavant in denouncing Brooks' action. Kurtz characterized Brooks' attack as "wanton and unjustifiable," indeed, an "outrageous act of violence," "one of the most disgraceful and alarming events of the time."[113]

Not all Lutherans in the South appreciated the attempt of Congressman Brooks to avenge his uncle and uphold the honor of the South. "Charitas", writing to the editor of the *Lutheran Observer*, noted that following the incident he had had occasion to travel "a good deal in the North." He found it difficult to imagine any course of action Congressman Brooks might have pursued that "could have prejudiced the cause of the South half as much as he has done, by this imprudent act."[114]

But there were those who not only appreciated Brooks' approach to maintaining southern honor; they were infuriated by the audacity of anyone who publicly criticized the congressman's action. Demonstrating this response was one of Brooks' constituents in Leesville, South Carolina. He rebuked Kurtz for his criticism of Brooks' conduct. To the writer's mind, the editor's criticism of Brooks established the fact that Kurtz was not what he pretended to be.

You pretend that you are a christian [*sic*]; but you are one of the devil's followers, or you would not be an exparte man, taking up as you have the Brooks and Sumner affair, assigning all the misconduct to our worthy representative, Col. Brooks, while you deem the speech of that Black Republican devil [Sumner] as just and right. I say you have no right to take up political matters, for you well know that the South is what keeps your paper alive. I say you are a Black Republican devil, and this is to inform you that you are to hold your tongue concerning Brooks, or you may have the pleasure of feeling the weight of a few pistol balls, and that before you are aware of it. Think not that Brooks constituents will suffer you to go on unchastised for your base and nefarious attempts to slur that honorable man. Now Kurtz, I say, hold your peace, you Black Republican devil, or your life may become extinct ere you are aware.[115]

After retiring from his editorship, Kurtz still remembered quite vividly the uproar created by his criticism of Congressman Brooks: "Of all the hornet-nests that it has been our misfortune to disturb, this was the most furious. In less than a fortnight we had a pile of letters on our table from the south, reaching well nigh the altitude of a lilliputian hay stack, menacing all the dire calamities that ever befell a luckless wight."[116]

As the mail received by Kurtz from the South made evident, many of his readers in South Carolina lived in the district served by Congressman Brooks. To one of those readers, the *Lutheran Observer* and its editor had "manifested a spirit toward the South and its peculiar institution, calculated to alienate every true Carolinian, both as to it and its editor, though it may be in every other respect faultless. I am sure every reader of that paper could not but see in what way the sympathies of the old gentleman run."[117]

The subscriber urged fellow Lutherans to join him in becoming an ex-subscriber to the *Lutheran Observer*, at least until it should lose its "fanatical aspect." Apparently, many heeded the subscriber's plea, since Kurtz later reported that his criticism of Brooks' conduct cost him two hundred or more of his southern subscribers.[118]

By the end of the decade of the fifties, thoughtful Christians in the South were beginning to ask if indeed the attempt to justify the South's "peculiar institution" had not gotten out of hand. The editor of a church paper published in Charleston reflected:

> The men of the Revolution and of the generation immediately succeeding, regarded it [i.e., slavery] in the light of an evil, to be gradually remedied if possible by removal or emancipation. Experience and maturer reflection proved the impracticability of either course, and the assaults of abolitionism induced a more thorough examination into the grounds, moral and religious, on which it rested. The Southern mind became satisfied that the relation was not without divine sanction, and that under existing circumstances it was the only one which could obtain between the two races brought together upon our own soil.[119]

Having arrived at this conviction, southern minds that had been uneasy about the question of slavery found temporary relief. "Here was a sufficient vindication of the Southern system - a true and incontrovertible position upon which its defenders might take their stand against every assailant." And for a time such a seemingly unassailable position seemed to satisfy. But, the editor observed, things seemed to be changing. No longer content simply to have a defense when charges were raised about the morality and appropriateness of chattel slavery, there has been manifested a disposition to break from our entrenchments and assume the offensive. Slavery has even been set forth as a necessary element towards the composition of a high and stable civilization - as a thing good in itself, without regard to the circumstances peculiar to Southern society - as in short the best mode in which labor and capital can stand associated. The sentiment of the South, and especially of South Carolina, seems verging toward the opposite extreme of a natural oscillation, passing from morbid sensitiveness into aggressive assertion.[120]

The editor was convinced that the one position was just as extreme and unwise as the other, and he was confident many thoughtful southerners would agree with him.

For three decades the recognition of differences in regional interests had mounted. As the conviction grew in the South that it was different, not only in its economic interests, but in its culture and values as well, the region betrayed an increasingly widespread willingness to make political realities correspond with these feelings of distinctiveness and independence.

To many southerners, it had long seemed imperative that the South maintain enough strength in the United States Senate to protect the region and its "peculiar institution" from the expanding influence of a sometimes hostile House of Representatives. Thus, the status of territories and prospective new states had long been a bone of contention, and had produced a number of compromises culminating in the Kansas-Nebraska Act of 1854. But several political factions unhappy with the Kansas-Nebraska Act came together to create a new political organization, the Republican Party. It was stridently opposed to the compromise tactics that for decades had enabled the United States to exist as a nation half slave and half free.

Convinced that slavery was morally wrong, the leaders of the new party criticized the Supreme Court's Dred Scott decision which denied that a slave or a descendant of a slave could ever be a citizen of a state or of the nation, and called for the return to captivity of captured slaves who escaped to freedom. Determined that in the future all new states admitted into the Union would be free states, the Republican Party represented in the eyes of many southerners an implacable foe. If the "Black Republicans" were successful in excluding slavery from the territories owned by all the states, slave and free, would they not promptly attack slavery in those states where it had existed continuously from the founding of the nation? Was it not clear that their fanaticism on this issue was such that they would trample under foot even that sacred compact, the Constitution of the United States, in order to achieve their aim? The rapid growth of the Republican Party, as reflected in the strong showing of Presidential Candidate John C. Fremont in 1856, made it clear the South could not simply ignore the new party as a lunatic fringe or passing aberration. The Republican Party's criticism of the Dred Scott decision of the Supreme Court, and the assumption on the part of many southerners that John Brown's raid on the arsenal at Harper's Ferry was evidence of the fanaticism and hostility of "Black Republicans", produced an environment in which the Democrats found themselves unable in their 1860 convention to agree on a party platform.

A Democratic Party split over slavery and related issues permitted Lincoln and the Republican Party to garner a majority of the electoral votes, even while failing to attract a majority of the popular votes. In the months before the presidential election in November 1860, a number of leaders in the South warned that entrusting the nation's highest office to the Republican Party's candidate would be viewed in the South as such a calamity that secession would be the only course of action left open for southern states.

South Carolina led the way. The election of Abraham Lincoln to the office of president in 1860 sparked the rending of the ties of political unity that had grown increasingly strained. "So, the legislature of South Carolina, which alone of all such bodies in the American states continued to choose Presidential electors, immediately called for the election of a sovereign convention when it learned of Lincoln's victory. This convention met in Columbia on December 17, adjourned to Charleston, and unanimously adopted an ordinance of secession on the twentieth."[121]

The next day a Cleveland, Ohio, newspaper recalled the process that had brought the nation to this point of crisis.

> For years the Union has, in fact, been dissolving. . . . The churches north and south divided. Then our Bible, Tract, and Missionary Societies, and finally the social relations [deteriorated] to an alarming extent. . . . The Secession of South Carolina, yesterday, was but the culmination of events which has been progressing for years.[122]

Early in the new year, six other states in the lower South followed the lead of South Carolina, and before Lincoln had taken the oath of office on March 4, 1861, delegates from those states had convened in Montgomery, Alabama, to create a provisional government and draft a constitution for the Confederate States of America. Lincoln believed that the Confederate states were mistaken in asserting a right to secede from the United States, and undertook to preserve the Union and protect United States property in the Confederate states. To that end, Lincoln decided to dispatch supplies to sustain the garrison at Fort Sumter in the harbor of Charleston, South Carolina. The Confederates moved quickly to lay siege to the fort when the commander refused to turn it over to the Confederacy.

On April 12, as he addressed a large crowd in Montgomery, Alabama, the Confederate Secretary of War, Leroy P. Walker, reported on the struggle for Fort Sumter and declared that "before many hours the flag of the Confederacy would float over that fortress," and that the same banner "would float over the dome of the old Capitol at Washington before the first of May."[123] On the first point, the secretary was correct; by the 14th Fort Sumter was a Confederate bastion. The secretary's second prophecy, reflecting a widely held Southern belief that an armed conflict between the North and the South must inevitably be one of short duration and of devastating consequences for the North, did not enhance Walker's reputation as a prognosticator.

Prior to 1860, few North Carolinians gave serious consideration to the possibility that their state might secede from the Union. After all, North Carolina was one of the original thirteen that created the United States. Nevertheless, Tar Heels did not hesitate to align themselves with other southern states when developments in the nation's capitol were deemed hostile to southern interests. North Carolina's congressional delegations had a consistent record of opposing all protective tariff legislation. The General Assembly labeled such tariff laws as "impolitic, unjust and oppressive." And North Carolina's congressional delegation regularly joined congressmen from other southern states in combating attacks on the institution of slavery.

With the rise of the abolitionism, North Carolinians became increasingly vocal in their defense of slavery and more aggressive in enacting harsh legislation designed to control both slaves and free blacks. When opposing tariffs and arguing for slavery, North Carolina stood solidly with other southern states. But when South Carolina in 1832 adopted its Ordinance of Nullification, denying any validity in South Carolina to the federal tariff laws of 1828 and 1832, North Carolina's General Assembly did not imitate their approach. Devotion to the Union they had helped to forge required that they brand the nullification doctrine propounded by John C. Calhoun as "revolutionary in character, subversive of the Constitution of the United States," and designed to produce "a dissolution of the Union."[124]

The relative balance between North Carolina's two political parties during the generation preceding the Civil War meant that in national elections neither party could assume that it had North Carolina in its pocket. The strength of the Democratic Party was in the eastern part of the state with its plantation economy and large slave population. In counties where slaves were least numerous, Whigs were strongest.

Since able North Carolinians were to be found in the ranks of both parties, the state often had persons serving in prominent posts in the parties and in appointive governmental posts. The Democrats were increasingly perceived as the more uncompromising on issues relating to slavery while North Carolina Whigs could not disguise their internal differences on the question of loyalty to the Union, splitting into groups called Federal Whigs and State Rights Whigs. Some of the latter eventually found their way into the Democratic Party.

The events that destroyed the political balance in North Carolina came in rapid succession in a five-year period. The annexation of the Republic of Texas by the United States in 1845 was opposed by North Carolina Whigs, and so was the Mexican War which broke out the following year, an "unjust war against a weak neighbor," they claimed. In the bitterly contested question of how to handle the slavery question in territory being added to the United States, Whigs worked to help shape the Compromise of 1850.

There were some who thought the compromise settled a thorny issue in an honorable manner, but there were southern Democrats who insisted it was a defeat for the South. North Carolina was invited to send a delegation to the Nashville convention of 1850, a meeting intended to provide Southerners with an opportunity to plan a common strategy. Newspapers that supported the Democrats generally urged participation in the convention; Whig papers like the *Carolina Watchman* published in Salisbury almost unanimously opposed involvement. The Whig governor refused to call a special session of the General Assembly to elect delegates, so North Carolina was not a participant in the Nashville convention. Continuing support for the Constitution and the preservation of the Union placed the Whigs again and again in positions that were unpopular with many Tar Heel voters.

Even though taking unpopular stands became commonplace for North Carolina Whigs, they could not go so far as to oppose the Kansas-Nebraska Act of 1854, which was immensely popular with the general population in the South. The Kansas-Nebraska Act and the creation of the Republican Party as a haven for anti-slavery forces virtually insured the disintegration of the Whig Party. The Republican Party with its anti-slavery stance could attract little following in North Carolina, so the state's

Whigs were left without a home. Some moved to the Know-nothing Party, but others disdained such a move. For the Democrats, who had taken control of North Carolina politics in 1850, political opposition was more and more ethereal as the crisis of secession approached.

The rise of the Republican Party with its unabashed anti-slavery stance galvanized simmering regional hostility. Fremont was selected to run as the Republican candidate for the presidency in 1856. The governors of Virginia, North and South Carolina met in Raleigh with prominent Democrats to discuss possible courses of action should Fremont prove the victor. Democrats like William W. Holden and Thomas L. Clingman urged secession by southern states as an appropriate course of action. Since the Democratic standard bearer, James Buchanan, won the election over Fremont and Millard Fillmore, the question of how the South might most appropriately respond to the election of an anti-slavery president did not have to be answered immediately.

North Carolina's long and strong attachment to the Union notwithstanding, a new mood was in evidence in the Old North State by 1856. The experience of a Rowan County native provides a case in point. Benjamin S. Hedrick, a scholarly and mild-mannered professor of chemistry at the University of North Carolina, let it be known that he opposed the extension of slavery into new states entering the Union, and would be happy to vote for Fremont if only he had the opportunity. The public outcry was immediate; his dismissal from the faculty, prompt. The threat of mob violence in Salisbury made it apparent that removal from his native state was his only assurance of safety.

The experience of another Rowan County native who once worked for a newspaper in Salisbury confirms the point. In 1857 Hinton Rowan Helper published *The Impending Crisis of the South* in which he sought to demonstrate that slavery was really harmful to the best interests of the South. Considered "incendiary literature" in Helper's native state, dispensing the publication in North Carolina was a crime punishable by imprisonment. A Guilford County clergyman, Daniel Worth of the Wesleyan Methodist church, distributed copies of the book anyway, and escaped a public whipping and a year of imprisonment only by following the example of Hedrick in fleeing the state.

The mood of many North Carolinians was changing: "Dominated by emotion, fear, and hatred, they would no longer tolerate calm reason, freedom of speech, or division of opinion on sectional and southern interests. Those who did not yield to the mounting hysteria of sectional hatred were suspected as loyal and patriotic southerners and were to be treated as enemies and traitors."[125]

North Carolinians demonstrated by their voting in 1860 that they overwhelmingly supported continuation as a part of the United States rather than secession. The caution of most political leaders in the state might suggest to some that North Carolina was affected by a "Rip Van Winkle sleep," but Governor John W. Ellis, a native of Rowan County who led the radical wing of the Democratic Party in the state, could not persuade the legislature to adopt his proposal for the calling of a state convention, even though his own party controlled the legislature.[126] While a prominent Democrat like William Holden would not hesitate to argue for the right of states to secede, he considered it unwise to rush into secession simply because Lincoln had been elected the nation's president. As late as the end of February 1861, there was not enough North

Carolina enthusiasm for "Southern independence" to authorize the calling of a convention to consider secession.[127]

Even the discussion of the mere possibility of secession disturbed some Tar Heels. At Friendship, Taylorsville, a congregational meeting was held before the worship service on February 24, and the following resolution was adopted unanimously:

> In consequence of the present distracted condition of our country and government we are in a crisis, momentous...and terrible in its appearance which demands of us prompt action . . . in order to secure our wellbeing . . . and notwithstanding it originated out of political and sectional operations, it nevertheless involves matter of faith and conscience, and thereby implicates the church, and, whereas, in a short time we must (we fear) take the first step towards sealing our destiny in future, and, whereas, we are biased in our minds and, to be feared, prejudiced to party we have reason to fear lest we take an unfortunate step for the first, therefore feeling our need of spiritual light and strength:
>
> Resolved: That we the members of Friendship Church, Alexander County, unanimously request our pastor [P. C. Henkel] to deliver a scriptural discourse today upon the distressed condition of our country, showing the scriptural and unscriptural movements of our country and rulers . . . showing how far the Church is to regard allegiance to ungodly laws and sovereignties, or rulers, and also showing the duty of subjects under Christian and Godly rulers, &c.[128]

But for many persons, President Lincoln's decision to send supplies to Fort Sumter provided an instantaneous clarification of a confused situation.[129] That decision also set in motion a quick succession of events leading to armed conflict. In a mere debate between those who wanted to break the ties created by the Constitution and those who wished to remain loyal to the Union, North Carolinians were overwhelmingly Americans. But when faced with Lincoln's request that the state furnish troops to the Union to help put down the "insurrection" in the South, regionalism asserted itself. Any hope of assuming the role of a "border state" evaporated with the decisions of Virginia and Tennessee to withdraw from the Union. From Mt. Pleasant in Cabarrus county, Rev. William A. Artz took pen in hand on May 14, 1861, to assure his brother in Hagerstown, Maryland, that members of the North Carolina branch of the family were "all well and doing tolerably well in our church and mill business. The great political excitement predominates over all other affairs and the duties of religion are much neglected."[130]

On the previous day Cabarrus County had elected "a man of Confederate sentiments" to represent them at the state convention to be held in Raleigh on May 20. He wrote: "This State will go out of the general Gov[e]rnm[en]t and go into the Southern Confederacy. We understand that the decree for our subjugation is gone forth; the time is come, and the blow will soon fall. The Old N. State is up and a doing; is preparing to meet it; and to show to the world that she will defend her rights at all hazards."[131]

But even as he recorded his reflections on the readiness of North Carolina to stand up for her rights, Artz could not escape a haunting premonition of disaster and a wistful expression of hope that at the last minute the tragedy might be averted:

> Our country rings with the sound of war; civil war; the most dreadful calamity that

can come upon a nation. We trust that all parties will pause on the brink and hearken to the voice of conscience and to the gospel of the Son of God which speaks peace and good will to men.[132]

On May 20, 1861, the Old North State dissolved its ties with the United States and adopted the Provisional Constitution of the Confederate States of America.[133]

Among Americans in the first half of the nineteenth century, no documents were so widely respected as authoritative and binding as the Holy Bible and the United States Constitution. Both documents were composed when slavery was an accepted part of the social order, and neither document decried slavery or called for its abolition. But new understandings spawned by the Enlightenment and by the continuing prodding of God's Spirit expanded the ranks of those who saw in slavery something incongruous with the lofty view of man and woman assumed by Enlightenment documents like the Declaration of Independence and by much of Holy Writ. The tide of Christian conscience, though hardly perceptible to contemporaries, was moving.

But Christian leaders in the South, Lutherans included, preferred to argue for the status quo. Change is usually threatening, and it seemed so much safer to take one's stand on traditional ways of interpreting the Bible and Constitution. Attempts to defend the institution of slavery grew so determined that they were permitted to spawn a virulent sectionalism, a sectionalism that would eventually rupture both the Union created by the Constitution and the unity God bestowed on the Church in Jesus Christ.[134]

Lutherans in North Carolina generally were not so prominently identified with slavery and sectionalism as to provide the leadership for the secession movement. In fact, some found a slave society so distasteful that they loaded their belongings into wagons and moved over the Appalachian Mountains to free states long before the series of crises that characterized the 1850s. But if those who elected to remain in North Carolina did not provide the South's leadership for sectionalism and secession, the fact remains that when a decision had to be made between standing against slavery and for the Union, or for slavery and against the Union, Lutherans like other North Carolinians had so long nurtured sectionalism over against unity that there was little doubt as to where they would take their stand.

Lutherans in the South in the closing decade of the twentieth century may find it difficult to understand how it was possible for their ancestors to identify themselves with slavery, sectionalism, and secession. But since understanding the mind-set of persons who lived in a different cultural setting may be impossible, one does well to avoid sitting in judgment on their conduct. As a noted Christian scholar has observed, "Each epoch is in the direct Presence of God, both in its greatness and its truth, and in its unfaithfulness to its better self."[135] In that Presence, Lutherans of an earlier day found both judgment and redemption; may their successors be equally blessed. ☦

North Carolina College (1892)
Founded 1855

Samuel Rothrock
President, North Carolina Synod
1839-40, 1845-47, 1853-55

Levi C. Groseclose
President, North Carolina Synod
1856-57

Ambrose Henkel
President, Tennessee Synod
1852-53

St. James, Concord
(c. 1890)
Organized 1843

CHAPTER V

eflecting on his personal experiences in the Civil War, the noted American, Oliver Wendell Holmes, Jr., observed, "The faith is true and adorable which leads a soldier to throw away his life in obedience to a blindly accepted duty, in a cause which he little understands, in a plan of campaign of which he has no notion, under tactics of which he does not see the use."[1] Such dedication and duty may be difficult for twentieth century Americans to comprehend, but the fact that such qualities were widespread when the North and South took up arms must be recognized if one is to account for the ardor with which soldiers, both North and South, embraced the conflict.

A Carolinian writing from a camp near Fairfax, Virginia, described for his young sister at home the parades held by Brigadier-General Bonham's brigade each afternoon. It was a "beautiful sight to see all those brave men formed in battle array, with glistening bayonets, flying banners, and beating drums, ready and anxious to meet the enemy...."

Despite the hardship caused by war, he was confident it was best not to dwell on the possiblities for tragedy: "Do not look too much upon the dark side of the picture! God may in his infinite mercy permit us ... to return to our home, and soon bless our distracted country with peace and tranquility. If he should see fit, however, to consign us to a bloody grave, and to continue this dreadful war, it is best to be happy whilst the future is veiled from us, and we can live in the hope of a better time coming."[2]

To play the role of hero in a contest whose justification seemed indisputable provided an adventure for young men, many of whom grew up on farms or in small towns and who never traveled far from home. Surely, their courage and the justice of their cause would produce a speedy victory!

With the outbreak of hostilities, North Carolinians were caught up in a wave of patriotic devotion to the cause of the Confederacy. The presumed "superiority of southern soldiers appeared to be confirmed by the initial Confederate battle at Big Bethel in Virginia. Even the death of Henry Lawson Wyatt of Edgecombe County, the first Confederate to be killed in battle, seemed to contribute to the confidence of North Carolinians, whose men constituted about half of the southern troops at Big Bethel."[3]

The June 10 skirmish at Big Bethel sustained for a time the widespread assumption that the war would be brief. But the young Carolinians who rushed to enlist soon discovered they had not chosen an immediate path to glory. Instead, these eager young men were confronted with months of repetitive drilling and the boredom associated with life in an army camp, a discouraging beginning for farm boys whose dreams of soldiering centered on early acts of heroism and bravery. Thus, even the prospect of moving from encampment to the field of battle often was welcomed by the untested soldier, although the welcome was tinged with fear.

In August 1861, the war took on a new reality for the Tar Heel State as the worst fears of some observers were realized. Mary Chesnut confided to her diary: "These inroads upon the Coasts have been my terror & despair from the first - but our government has such a knack of hoping - it looked for peace by every mail from Europe. So Micawber like - something will turn up - & no getting ready. Now the wolf is not at the door but in N. C."[4]

Federal troops invaded coastal Carolina and soon gained control over the access routes to the Albemarle and Pamlico sounds. No longer were North Carolinians required to go to Virginia to get their taste of combat. Soldiers, North and South, began to gain in eastern North Carolina their introduction to armed combat. Shortly before Christmas 1862, Horatio Newhall reflected on his first experience in combat a few days earlier near Kinston. The Confederate troops defending the town had "formed behind a large swamp, and the only road through it was guarded by the cannons...."

As his unit advanced toward the Confederate position, "cannonball, shell and bullets" ripped through the trees over their heads: "The black swamp mud was up to our waist and briars and grapevines grew wild, making it almost impossible to go ahead at all. We managed to push through it however and reach the other side about one-eighth of a mile. All through the swamp men were lying dead and wounded in the mud by dozens.... I had never seen a real battlefield before and it sickened me to see such a sight. Some dying, some dead and others going to the rear without help but bleeding badly. Rebels and union men lying together, large trees cut in two, broken muskets and horses lying in all directions...."[5]

An introduction to battle could produce varied reactions, including a concern about one's eternal destiny. A number of stretcher bearers followed in the wake of a regiment near New Bern. As one of them later recalled, he was suddenly "startled by the sound of a cannon;" then "whiz and spat came the ball. It struck the road about ten feet from me, spattering the mud into some of the boys' faces." Spotting several buildings in an open field, the stretcher bearers headed for the structures that soon became a hospital, but initially seemed little more than a convenient target both for enemy artillery and their own. Concluding they were in greater danger in the buildings than outside, they finally decided to make a run for it.

In retrospect, it seemed miraculous to Amos Steere, one of the bearers, that their flight from the structures and across the open field was successful: "I felt the need of religion then if I ever did, and wished that I might be a Christian so that I shall in time of battle and at all other times be prepared to meet my God in peace. I have met with no change of heart as yet, but only [long] for the time to come when it will be as easy for me to do right as it is for me to do wrong."[6]

An officer who had been a lawyer in civilian life sensed that his military experiences might have a deadening effect on his moral sensitivity. He wrote to his wife: "War is fast becoming the thing natural, tho' abhorrent to my feelings. I go at it just as I used to go at law-suits. Still I am not by any manner or means fond of the profession. The idea of being continually employed in the destruction of human life is revolting in the extreme. Necessity, imperious and exacting, forces us along and we hurry through the dreadful task apparently unconscious of its demoralizing influences and destructive effects both upon the nation and individuals."[7]

Throughout the war there continued to be remarkable feats of heroism and valor. After the Battle of Gettysburg, families at Daniel's, Lincolnton, for example, recounted with pride the information they received about the exploits of David A. Coon, a son of their congregation. On the third day of the July 1863 battle the young lieutenant was "wounded nine times, left for dead, captured, and then imprisoned" for the remainder of the war.[8]

But early enthusiasm for the conflict, whether on the part of civilian or soldier, was later tempered with reality. The president of the Lutheran synod of North Carolina reflected:

> Our lately happy country has been converted into a nation of soldiers-brethren armed against each other. Peaceful pursuits are laid aside, and war has become the all-absorbing topic; belligerent armies have mustered to the conflict, which has been prosecuted with a determination and fierceness, which have no parallel in our previous history. As the God of Providence has permitted the counsels of our best statesmen to fail, and all suggestions of an amicable adjustment to be set aside, we may well conclude that He has permitted the crisis to occur for inscrutable purposes.[9]

By the end of 1862 letters written by soldiers to their families at home were less likely to extoll the glory of battle and soldiering. Moral standards soon reflected deterioration, and morale a perceptible decline. Stories of valor and heroism were replaced by accounts of desertion and the desire to return home. Long after the war ran its course, veterans rarely embraced the pain of reflecting on the carnage at Antietam or Gettysburg.

Instead, they would revel in some fleeting moment, real or imagined, of individual accomplishment or heroism in which they were involved. Stories based on such moments might make it appear that the war was an heroic adventure, but grandchildren would discover packets of faded letters in attic trunks, letters that revealed how an early unquestioning devotion to a cause could be undermined by continuing physical hardship, by the repeated experience of seeing human flesh gored by mini ball and grape shot, and by prolonged separation from loved ones.

Chaplains

With long experience in such matters, the United States government recognized the value of offering spiritual care to its soldiers through provision for an army chaplaincy. As early as 1863 the United States War Department declared chaplains noncombatants and indicated it would not hold Confederate chaplains as prisoners of war. It was assumed that clergy could make a positive contribution to the military without bearing arms. ". . . In an era when morale and firepower were equally important during battle, a clergyman's bravery may well have been a valuable resource to his regiment."[10]

Those entrusted with the responsibility for shaping a military force for the Confederacy virtually created a replica of the Army of the United States except that initially it "made no provision for chaplains. It was a deliberate exclusion on the part of President Jefferson Davis and the legislators. It offered an insight into the importance the Provisional Congress attached to the office of chaplain, and reflected an attitude which changed only slightly with the passage of time."[11]

The decision to exclude chaplains from the Confederacy's military table of organization produced "a howl of protest." The Confederacy's Secretary of War, LeRoy Pope Walker, concluded a report to President Jefferson Davis by urging "the passage of a law empowering this Department to appoint chaplains for the service. Military experience demonstrates the importance of religious habitudes to the morality, good order, and general discipline of an army in the camp or in the field. If we expect God to bless us in our struggle in defense of our rights-to terminate, in all probability, only after a protracted and bloody war-we must recognize Him in our actions."[12]

In view of the furor it created, the Confederate government reviewed its decision regarding chaplains, and in early May the Confederate Congress authorized President Davis to appoint military chaplains. However, the legislation lacked details. For example, there was no indication of what rank the chaplains would hold. "Although available pictures show chaplains wearing the uniform of a captain, and they were commonly thought to have the rank of captain, all legislative efforts to confer the rank were defeated."[13]

Nothing was prescribed in the legislation concerning age limitations, if any; what the chaplains' duties might be was not specified; nor were the conditions under which they were to serve. The initial legislation did provide for a salary half way between that of a first and a second lieutenant; however, that eighty-five dollar figure was reduced to fifty dollars lest the chaplaincy attract "clergymen who were interested only in material gain...."[14] A Mississippi judge who supported the decision to reduce the chaplain's pay to fifty dollars per month "claimed the chaplains were not entitled to as much pay as company officers, as the latter worked every day, while the chaplains preached once a week and were free the remainder of the time."

While the Confederacy gave its chaplains no rank, it made clear its intent by providing that they should receive the ration of a private rather than that of an officer. North Carolina clergy were especially discouraged from enlisting as chaplains since, while serving under the State of North Carolina, they enjoyed the rank of major and received pay of $150 per month. Nevertheless, many clergy offered their services; for example, the Protestant Episcopal church with fewer than two hundred thousand members furnished sixty-five chaplains, at least fifteen of them coming from the ranks of the fifty-three Episcopal priests in North Carolina.[15] In April 1862, the Confederate government finally agreed to raise the chaplain's pay to eighty dollars per month, and with the provision of forage authorized in 1864, the chaplain's annual compensation increased to $1,325 plus forage for his horse.[16]

In the spring of 1862 fewer than half the Confederate regiments had chaplains, and that ratio of chaplains to regiments tended to persist. At one point sixteen North Carolina units in the same command were "without any religious guidance."[17]

Many unit commanders were devout Christians and would have welcomed chaplains had the churches been prepared to provide them. Thomas Jonathan "Stonewall" Jackson, a Presbyterian whose Christian faith was renowned, secured chaplains in only forty-four of his ninety-one regiments despite his personal plea to the General Assembly of the Presbyterian Church.[18]

By 1863 the South was suffering from a serious shortage of military manpower. The earlier Confederate practice of permitting ordained enlisted men to transfer to an available chaplaincy slot was discontinued. Also, the Confederacy did not see fit to exempt theological students from the draft. Thus, despite the protest of church leaders, student bodies in schools of theology in the South were decimated as the Secretary of War for the Confederacy sought to provide as many soldiers for the army as possible.

The first Christian group in the South to move in a specific and tangible way to minister to men in the armed forces was the Southern Baptist Convention. The convention's Board of Domestic Missions was the catalyst for the work, its corresponding secretary contacting early in 1862 the missionary secretaries in each of the state conventions. The secretaries at the state convention level were urged to ask congregations to (1) help fund the church's ministry to men in the armed forces and (2) to release their pastors for occasional visits with the men in uniform.[19]

Before the Lutheran synods in the South organized themselves to minister to men in the armed forces, some pastors responded to the need as they perceived it. When a unit of soldiers passed through a town, local clergy would often attempt to minister as best they could. Where clergy found themselves relatively close to an army encampment, they went to the camp to conduct worship services. And it was not unusual for a pastor to leave his parish to visit a wounded relative or parishoner with the army and, while there, conduct services for the military unit. In 1862, for example, Rev. Samuel Rothrock of Salisbury made "three trips to the war front to visit his son, who was wounded at Sharpsburg, and to preach to the troops and visit wounded ones in hospitals. He had bodies of some, presumably parishoners, exhumed and brought to Rowan Co., for burial."[20]

Another pattern emerged as some pastors, especially younger ones, elected to don an army uniform themselves. Alexander Phillippi, the organizing pastor for St. Mark's, Charlotte, moved to Lynchburg, Virginia, to organize a mission. But his move coincided with the outbreak of hostilities, and he soon gave notice to the president of the Western Virginia Synod of his decision to enlist in the army so he could defend his country and, at the same time, preach the Gospel to fellow soldiers.

He became a field officer and had the full duties of chaplain in the twenty-ninth Virginia Regiment, remaining in the army until the end of the war. Chaplains like Phillippi who devoted themselves full-time to the military were apparently "able to serve the troops much more effectively than other ministers who tried to reach the soldiers camping near their communities or passing through on their way to battle."[21]

Except when troops engaged the enemy, Sunday was the chaplain's day in the Confederate Army. If a Protestant, he was expected to preach and lead in worship. As religious interest grew among the officers and men, chaplains often found it necessary to conduct two Sunday services. By 1865, many commands provided worship services each day.[22]

In conducting service, chaplains had to assume there would be distractions. The Sabbath calm was often punctuated with the pounding of horses hooves. In warm weather, the hum of insects was to be expected. The smell of bacon frying over a near-by fire, or the yells of soldiers in an adjacent unit as they encouraged men engaging in fisticuffs challenged the preacher's efforts to retain the attention of his audience.

And there could be the sound of gunfire: "The effect of the big guns was largely psychological. A soldier could listen intently to his chaplain near heavy action at the front lines, but an occasional shell in camp made him fidget. He was ready, if not willing, to die in battle, but the prospect of losing his life to a Sunday fluke made him uneasy."[23]

Sermons delivered by chaplains were apt to be shorter than those of their civilian counterparts, sometimes requiring only fifteen minutes, rarely ever more than a half hour. Since so many services were held outdoors, particularly in the early years of the war, weather was often a strong inducement to sermonic brevity. "Chaplain Wilton Kennedy once shortened his message to the twenty-eighth North Carolina Regiment because he could not bear to detain his congregation on the wet, cold ground."[24] Given the shortage of chaplains, services scheduled by the chaplain were rarely cancelled because of something as transitory as inclement weather. Soldiers neither expected nor received a medal for standing in the rain for thirty minutes to hear a sermon.

For Protestant chaplains, Sunday worship and its sermon were the high point of the week's work, but contrary to the opinion of the Mississippi judge cited earlier, the chaplain's duties were not restricted to one day a week: "Chaplains counseled the disturbed, visited the wounded, baptized the converted, solemnized marriages, distributed tracts and bibles, conducted prayer meetings and Bible classes, administered the sacraments, and undertook other general pastoral functions...."[25]

By the fall of 1863, it became more difficult to stem the tide of discouragement in the ranks of the Confederates. It was apparent that early expectations of a short conflict had been unrealistic. Chaplains were not immune to the change in mood. A chaplain serving with the cavalry under Gen. Jubal Anderson Early in Virginia submitted his resignation "on account of domestic affliction." The general declined to recognize the stated reason for the resignation, but accepted the resignation anyway since it was clear the chaplain's "heart was so little in the Cause he would no longer be useful."[26]

And when chaplains were captured in combat, they experienced the same interrogations to which other prisoners of war were subjected. Chaplain John Magill of the Fifty-second Regiment, Virginia Volunteers, was captured, and at Fort Delaware, Maryland, where he was confined, was interrogated by the commander of the prison, Brig. Gen. Albin F. Schoepf. In an attempt to discourage the prisoner, the general reported to the chaplain that Confederate Gen. Ambrose Powell Hill had been killed, the army of Gen. Robert E. Lee routed and forty thousand prisoners captured. He then asked the chaplain for information he might have on the state of Confederate forces. "My information, Sir, is pretty much the same as yours and in addition I hear Genl. Ewell is bleeding to death from a wound in his wooden leg." The chaplain's witticism was not appreciated by General Schoepf.[27]

In many respects it is impossible to estimate the impact made by chaplains on the soldiers. But three million Americans were exposed to an environment where chaplains, some three thousand committed to the Union and possibly one thousand in Confederate ranks, who represented a variety of Christian traditions, sought to bring the challenge and solace of God's Word to human beings living under physical hardship and intense psychological stress. Many commanders believed that the ministry significantly strengthened the troops. Gen. John B. Gordon observed that the efforts of chaplains "banished from the heart all unworthy passions, prepared the soldier for a more heroic endurance; lifted them above their sufferings, nerved them for the coming battles; gave them a higher conception of duty; imbued them with a spirit of cheerful submission to the decrees of Providence; sustained them with a calmer and nobler courage; and rendered them superior to danger."[28]

And the influence of clergy in uniform did not disappear the moment the war ended.

For the span of a generation, social and political reforms and forward movements in religion and education were rooted in the hopes and fears and resolutions of the tense years of war.[29]

With the prolongation of the conflict, synods began to face up to the challenge of providing for a systematic approach to ministry to persons in the military. Meeting at St. Mark's, Charlotte, on April 30, 1863, the North Carolina Synod adopted the following proposal submitted by Rev. Daniel I. Dreher of St. James, Concord:

> Whereas, It is the duty of this Synod to signify its concerns for the spiritual welfare of our soldiers in the Confederate Army, by some substantial token of its regard, therefore
>
> 2. Resolved, That this Synod do send ministers to serve the army as volunteer Chaplains, for the term of twelve months -- one minister serving one month at a time.
>
> 3. Resolved, That the various congregations be called upon to contribute for this purpose, means to defray the expenses of such ministers as may serve in the army as above designated.
>
> 4. Resolved, That a committee of three be appointed by the President to ascertain the names of the ministers who are willing to go as volunteer Chaplains, to the army.[30]

When the Tennessee Synod met at St. John's, Conover, in October 1863, Pastor Henry Goodman of Zion, Hickory, served notice that, at the proper time, he would "call the attention of Synod to the importance of performing missionary labors in the army."[31] He did so and a committee was created to address the concern. Later in the convention the committee, chaired by Rev. Alfred J. Fox, presented the following proposal which was adopted:

> Whereas, this Synod is fully aware of the great necessity of doing something to supply our own soldiers in the Confederate Army with the preaching of the Gospel by our ministers,
>
> 1st. Resolved, That we establish an Army Mission in the following manner: Let as many ministers in connection with this synod as will subscribe this resolution, be obligated to perform missionary labors in the Confederate army, for the period of one month in each year, if our funds and the situation of the army will permit.
>
> 2d. Resolved, That two ministers go at the same time, and that in rotation, being chosen by lot at each annual meeting of synod.
>
> 3d. Resolved, That their expenses, at least, be defrayed by donations obtained from the congregations by solicitation.[32]

The committee's report also provided for the election of a treasurer for the Army Chaplain's Fund who would receive funds from congregations and disburse them as travel reimbursement to the pastors serving as short-term chaplains. Thus, the Tennessee Synod joined the North Carolina, South Carolina and Virginia synods in designating a committee to foster and support its efforts to serve men in the military. For the Lutherans in the South the typical pattern was to entrust responsibility for mission work among men in uniform to either special committees or existing committees having responsibility for other mission work.

The committees often found their new assignment difficult to implement. In

Virginia the officers of the synod's Education and Missionary Society found their attempts to coordinate a volunteer chaplaincy service thoroughly frustrating. They wrote to each pastor who had indicated a willingness to share in the program, but not one could make himself available while the Army was in winter quarters "and in a posture to be benefitted by such labor."

When the fighting moved into the Richmond area, several clergy indicated they were ready to join the troops, but the committee "deemed that an unsuitable time to send transient Chaplains into the army, because it would be impossible to labor efficiently amongst troops constantly in motion. Even regular Chaplains find less opportunity to fulfill their calling during such pressing times; and it was judged by us that those who would go with a view of devoting but a month would find still less opportunity of doing good. Under these circumstances we declined to make appropriations."[33]

In view of the continuing shortage of chaplains and the limited effectiveness of the short-term visits to the army by civilian clergy, some used the printed word. In the summer of 1861 a Salisbury newspaper noted that "various religious organizations" in that community had established the Rowan Bible Society to purchase religious literature for distribution to the soldiers. Early in 1862 the newspaper described the operation of the General Tract Agency of Raleigh which selected and published tracts such as "*A Mother's Parting Words to her Soldier Boy*" and "*The Precious Blood of Christ, or How a Soldier Was Saved.*" The agent for the agency explained, "We are striving to supply our whole army with these gospel truths. There is increasing evidence that this means of grace is being blessed of God to the great spiritual good of many of our soldiers."[34]

Many Lutherans in the South believed it desirable to place a church periodical or newspaper in the hands of the church member away in the army. There was talk of creating a "southern" church paper during the 1850s, but it took the actual outbreak of hostilities to produce such a publication. *The Southern Lutheran* was initially published in Charleston by a committee of the South Carolina Synod. In May 1864, the General Synod of the Evangelical Lutheran Church in the Confederate States of America met at Organ Church, Salisbury. In a report from Attorney Robert G. Chisholm of Columbia, South Carolina, who was handling the financial accounts for the *Southern Lutheran*, the convention learned that in addition to receiving $3,251 for "Soldiers' Papers", the periodical had collected $2,173.60 in support of "Army Missions".

The action of the several synods to provide a ministry to men in the armed forces, however, fell short of meeting the need. The convention called for the appointment of a committee "to present an appeal" to Lutheran pastors in the southern synods, "urging them to visit our armies and at least for a short time preach the Gospel to our brave soldiers." Pastors J. P. Smeltzer and T. S. Boinest, along with Mr. A. F. Graeber of the North Carolina Synod, were assigned the task. The convention also named Pastors A. R. Rude and G. D. Bernheim and Mr. R. G. Chisholm to its "Executive Committee on Army Missions."[35]

Despite the pre-war antipathy between the Tennessee Synod and southern synods related to the General Synod, Rev. J. R. Peterson introduced at a convention of the Tennessee Synod the following preamble and resolutions which, "after a free interchange of opinions," were adopted unanimously:

> Feeling as we do, the great want of a Religious Periodical in the families of our connexion, and as the Southern Lutheran is the only paper of Lutheran character now published in the Confederate States, be it therefore,
> Resolved, That this Synod most cheerfully recommend the Southern Lutheran to the families composing our congregations, and that the Ministers connected with this Synod be encouraged to introduce it into our families.
> Resolved, That a collection be taken immediately after the sermon today for the purpose of sending the *Lutheran* to the soldiers.[36]

With a circulation generally in the range of one thousand to fourteen hundred copies, it could hardly be said that the *Southern Lutheran* covered Dixie like the dew. Nevertheless, with half its circulation going to men in the army where reading material was in short supply and, hence, read by more persons than the original recipient, it was a significant instrument of nurture and outreach.

Revivals

The Second Great Awakening which emerged at the end of the eighteenth century provided the Christian community in a rapidly expanding nation with a remarkable tool for church growth. That tool, the revival, continued into the Civil War era and beyond as a social force of considerable significance. During the first half of the nineteenth century, successive waves of revivalism arose, crested and subsided. Revivals found their place in the Civil War armies as well. The army revivals were not an isolated phenomenon, but were a part of the increasingly dominant expression of Protestant Christianity in America. "The revivals in the Civil War armies were linked most closely to the so-called 'businessman's' revival of 1857, which had begun in several major cities and then spread throughout the country just prior to the war."[37]

Like other revivals associated with the Second Great Awakening, the army revivals operated on the principle of stressing only those matters on which Christians were generally in agreement and avoiding those subjects on which Christians were known to disagree: "Those who took part in the revivals were not concerned with theoretical issues of theology or church polity, but simply with the experience of conversion and dedication to Christian living. In this regard, the army revivals were quintessentially American, that is, laying stress more on participation and practicality than on contemplation and speculation. The leaders of the revivals were concerned more with *results* than with process."[38]

As early as the second year of the war, revivals became "a distinct feature of life in the Southern camps," some of the earliest apparently taking place in Jackson's corps. "The first group within Jackson's corps to be seriously affected was Trimble's brigade, including regiments from North Carolina, Georgia, and Alabama."[39]

The soldiers not only contributed to the success of the army revivals by providing the congregations and the converts; they even built log chapels so that services might be conducted more effectively during winter encampment: "When troops moved to a new location their axes rang continuously for a week or more, building for the glory of God. As religious interest mounted, chapels required enlargement. Construction reached amazing proportions in the final winter of the war, and according to one estimate every brigade between the Appomattox and James Rivers had a house of worship. Most accommodated from 300 to 500 persons and were usually crowded."[40]

Revivals were the key ingredient in transforming the Confederate armies into some of the most religious fighting units ever to undertake combat, comparable in religious fervor even to Cromwell's famed Roundheads. At least one hundred thousand Confederate soldiers experienced conversion during the conflict, many conversions being the product of the "massive revivals that occurred on several occasions throughout the conflict...."[41]

The Army of Virginia's invasion of the North in the summer of 1863 temporarily curtailed the revivals but, "by the fall of 1863, what Southern churchmen later called the 'Great Revival' was in full progress along the defensive line by the Rapidan and Rappahannock rivers. This revival lasted throughout the winter and into the spring of the next year before it was finally terminated by Grant's attacks in May 1864. According to reports from the army, approximately 7,000 men (or about ten percent of Lee's soldiers), were converted in that period, and at least 32 out of the 38 infantry brigades were touched by the revivals. Even in brigades that had shown little interest in religion during the first two years of the war, a religious interest gripped the soldiers."[42]

Virginia was the site of many revivals among Confederate troops, particularly from October of 1863 to the spring of 1864. However, the summer of 1864 saw revivalism among Confederate forces in Virginia reach its peak, and by this time some observers were convinced that revivals were having an "unsual and critical effect on the performance of the troops in battle." The usual willingness of the convert to attribute the conversion experience to the work of the Holy Spirit and the consequent reliance on the Spirit to guide and sustain in the faith encouraged soldiers converted in the Virginia revivals "to surrender the hope that they could ever win the war by their own efforts."

In retrospect, it seems "a sort of religious ecstasy took possession of the army" during the last twelve months of the conflict. The bravery of the troops at times exceeded all reasonable levels of commitment to a cause, the men's dedication suggesting the soldier was "assisting at his own funeral." Instead of relying on their military leaders, the mood shifted to an expectation of "a miraculous interpostion of supernatural power." "A cognizance of the ultimate futility of human aspirations pervaded the camp...."[43]

Lee's Army of Virginia was not the only Confederate fighting force to experience revivals. Revivals broke out in the Army of Tennessee in the winter of 1862-1863 and gained momentum as the year progressed to the excitement attendant on the Confederate victory at Chickamauga in September 1863. But with the defeat inflicted on the southern forces at Missionary Ridge in late November, large-scale prayer meetings came to an end for the Army of Tennessee.[44] In fact, as their subsequent encampment revealed, the disaster at Missionary Ridge apparently had a deep impact on Confederate revivalism and morale generally.

Following the Missionary Ridge debacle, Confederate troops withdrew to Georgia where they established an encampment at Dalton. There, during the winter of 1863-64, numerous conversions were reported, but an "unusually pressimistic air" pervaded the troops.[45] Indeed, after Missionary Ridge, soldiers in the Army of Tennessee seemed increasingly to understand that, while God may be the guarantor of spiritual victory, spiritual victory does not necessarily translate into worldly success. After the Atlanta campaign, revivalism in the Confederate armies in the West declined.

Religion may have bolstered military morale in the early days of the war, especially as news of victories was reported by the Confederate armies. "Revivals and conversions in the camps, the piety of high officers (and low soldiers), the service of an Episcopal bishop as a military commander, sermons assuring congregations that God favored the Confederacy, and prayers pleading for that same favor by means of military victories-- all cast the mantle of a holy crusade over the cause."[46]

As the tide began to turn, however, circumstances called for new understandings. At first, the defeats could be interpreted in a positive light; later, Christian interpretations of the conflict actually undercut an already declining morale.[47]

The Home Front

The fact of the war came home early to folk in North Carolina. Synodical President John D. Scheck noted that the war had begun amid "clouds of doubts and apprehensions," but "then followed a brilliant succession of victories which swept every cloud from the horizon." But then came lengthening casualty lists, military reverses, and "a sky darker and stormier than ever before."[48] Benjamin Arey, who served as president of the synod before the war, learned that his sons Theophilus and Charles were both killed on September 17, 1862, at the battle of Antietam. A third son, Luther, was so severely wounded during the war that he died shortly after the close of the conflict. The tragedy of lives snuffed out and bodies crippled called for some kind of explanation of what was happening.

Early in its life as a publication, *The Southern Lutheran* carried "A Soldier's Prayer" on its front page. "Arise, O Lord, lift up Thy hand; forget not the humble. Give us help from our trouble, for vain is the help of man." The petitioner sees his enemies as "lively and strong;" and believes that those who "hate us wrongfully are multiplied." To contend with an enemy is a serious matter in itself, but how galling to discover that someone formerly close and trusted is that enemy! "Our own familiar friend, in whom we trusted, hath lifted up his heel against us." "Deliver us, O God, out of the hand of the wicked." "O Lord, though our iniquities testify against us, do Thou it for Thy name's sake."[49]

Women found themselves called upon to assume responsibilities exceeding those they had known before the conflict began. There were not only expanded responsibilities in the home and on the farm; soldiers needed shirts for their backs and bandages for their wounds. And if they left the home or farm, women often encountered a strange new world.

> Our women are now in a nice condition - traveling, your false hair is developed & taken off to see if papers are rolled in it - & you are turned up instantly to see if you have pistols concealed - not to speak of their having women to examine if you are a man - in disguise. I think these times make all women feel their humiliation in the affairs of the world. With men it is on to the field - "glory, honour, praise, &c, power." Women can only stay at home - & every paper reminds us that women are to be violated - ravished & all manner of humiliation. How are the daughters of Eve punished.[50]

What did it all mean? President Adam Efird of the Tennessee Synod saw the

South as being involved "in a war of self defense, for the preservation of our religious, social and political liberties." There was no doubt in his mind that "the cause in which our country is engaged" was "a just one."

At the same time he could speak of the conflict as a "cruel and ungodly war": "Yet while we look upon the Lord as being on our side politically, and notwithstanding the success of our arms against a reckless foe; the losses, trials and bereavements experienced by our people more or less in all portions of our country, bring the conclusion that the Lord is holding a controversy with his people, and with all nations of the earth."[51]

The president of the Southwestern Virginia Synod, Elijah Hawkins, was convinced that the South was being invaded by the arms of an "implacable foe" who sought nothing less than the "entire subjugation" of the southern populace "to the control of a tyrannical military despotism." Prayer was important to insure that God would accompany "the army of Israel" as it went off to give battle to the invading forces from the North. Military developments had interrupted normal communications between Lutherans in the South and those in the North. But Hawkins expressed the hope, if not conviction, that the Lutheran church was really one family even though presently divided: "I hope that thus separated, she still can sing, 'by faith we meet around one common mercy seat.'"[52]

Economic Conditions

To a young boy growing up in Concord during the war, one concern seemed to dominate all others. Paul B. Barringer later recalled, "Anxiety for the men at the front was ever present; many of them came home wounded, and there were many funerals."[53] But other concerns soon began to manifest themselves as people on the home front made the adjustments demanded by war and a wartime economy.

North Carolina had been slow to cast its lot with the secession movement, but once the decision was made, it gave strong support to the military effort of the Confederacy. With its sparce population, North Carolina saw a higher proportion of its male population go to war than any other state. Forty thousand North Carolina lives, a larger number than from any other Southern state, were sacrificed in the South's attempt to establish itself as a separate nation.

At home, there were boys considered "too young" to go off to the army, and there were the aged and the infirm. There were farm wives and sweethearts, plantation mistresses and black mammies. In some respects it mattered little whether one were male or female, black or white, of a prominent family or a poor one. All faced an increasing array of scarcities growing out of the blockade of southern ports, the South's inadequate transportation system, speculation and, in the early years, hoarding.[54] And there were the mounting requirements of the military for supplies. The need for fiber for clothing and tents for the troops resulted in handsome houses being stripped of their draperies and carpets. Lovely wall paper was peeled from walls to provide the local print shop with paper.

> Writing paper, envelopes, account books, and wrapping paper were all scarce during the war. Letters were written on the poorest quality paper that blotted and splotched until the writing was hardly legible. Much of the paper produced in the South was soft and hard to manage. When it became impossible to obtain regular writing paper,

even of the poorest quality, Southerners turned to substitutes. Wrapping paper, blank pages of books, scraps of old letters, and even prescription blanks were used to write the tenderest billet-doux or the most business-like letter. Envelopes were as hard to obtain as writing paper, but the people managed to make their own. They were made of brown wrapping paper, while old letters, wallpaper, once used envelopes, and even pictures were turned so that the blank side remained on the outside.[55]

Bronze church bells were lowered from their steeples and towers, melted down, and made into howitzers or gun caps, and "the sabbaths were silent."[56]   Since all match factories were "at the North," pieces of flint and steel were recovered from closets and other places of storage. At night, hearth fires were carefully heaped with coals and ashes to preserve the embers until morning.

The diet changed, not as radically as for those who joined the army, but substantially none the less. Tea and coffee quickly disappeared. Folk learned to brew a type of tea from roots of the sassafras tree. Parched corn, or a mixture of parched rye, wheat and browned sweet potatoes provided coffee substitutes. The rye, wheat and sweet potatoes were blended into a paste that was then cut into cubes and dried. Submerging the dried cubes in hot water produced an ersatz coffee.[57]   The Union blockade of the Carolina coast also brought a halt to the importation of sugar. As "white Sugar" disappeared, substitutes were found. The Palatines who settled near Fredericksburg, Virginia, in the early eighteenth century had introduced the honey bee to America. Honey now became one of the most popular substitute sweeteners in the South, and "bee gums" (i.e., homemade bee hives consisting of a short section of a hollow black gum tree) multiplied rapidly.   The brown sugar crust which formed on barrels of sorghum was scraped off to make "short sweet'nin," the liquid sorghum being used by the less affluent as "long sweet'nin."

Dried beef and pork were reserved for the soldiers, so efforts were made at home to increase production of domestic fowls: chickens, ducks, turkeys, guineas and peacocks.

The wives and children of many Confederate soldiers, particularly those residing on small farms in the Piedmont and mountain regions of the South, suffered increasing privation.

One citizen satirically recommended that the army "knock the women and children of the mountains in the head, to put them out of their misery." Somewhere between 20 and 40 percent of North Carolina's population required poor relief from the state. In Georgia, fully half the state expenditures were devoted to poor relief by 1864.[58]

Disease and Illness

Hunger and malnutrition were distressingly familiar as the conflict persisted. Disease and illness refused to take a holiday. There were cases of the dreaded small pox in Concord during the war. Chills and fevers were commonplace since quinine was two hundred dollars an ounce in gold when it could be had at all. In the fall of 1862 Wilmington suffered an outbreak of yellow fever that claimed more than one thousand lives in sixty days.[59] Morphine was urgently needed for medicinal purposes, so many gardens contained beds of poppies.

As the months of conflict lengthened, it seemed clear to President John Bachman of the General Synod in the Confederate States that something more was involved than occasional shortages of items once in plentiful supply. Was it not the case "that the sins of our nation have brought down upon us the visitations and punishments of God?" As proof of that visitation and punishment, Bachman pointed to the fact that there was "scarcely a residence in our Southern land which has not become a house of mourning." There was reason to rejoice in some apparent victories on the field of battle, "yet we have met with many reverses, and our whole Southern land has become one vast graveyard, where the bodies of our sons and brothers lie mingled with the mouldering remains of their murderous foes."[60]

What national sins provoked such an outpouring of God's punishment? To Bachman there was no doubt as to the sin that should lead the list: the fact that "the burdens and distresses of this war have been very unequally distributed." It was bad enough, in his eyes, that coastal sections of the Confederacy bore so much of the weight of the conflict. But when the fortunes of war drove numerous folk from the seaboard into the interior, "what sympathy or substantial comfort did the poor exiles receive? Whole communities seemed ready to prey upon their necessities. They were compelled to pay any price for homes to shelter them, for food and clothing which the unprincipled extortioners saw fit to demand. Hunger presses on the poor sufferers, their children are clamorous for bread, and some unprincipled planters demand twenty dollars per bushel for corn...."[61]

North Carolinians knew what Bachman was talking about when he discussed inflation and price gouging. In Mocksville where the city fathers authorized payment of seventy-five cents per day for "good able bodied hands" in the summer of 1857, the rate had reached $1.50 per day by the end of the summer of 1862. As the early months of the war became years, "opportunistic farmers and unscrupulous blockade runners continued to sell their goods at the highest prices the market would bear. Bacon jumped from 33 cents to $7.50 per pound, wheat went from $3 to $50 dollars a bushel, and coffee was selling at $100 per pound."[62]

The scourge of inflation had its impact on individual citizens, whether church members or not. After the loss of Vicksburg and the withdrawal of Confederate forces across the Potomac River, inflation in the South worsened.

"The only remedy", one historian observed, "seemed to be to run the printing presses faster. By the spring of 1864 it took $46 to buy what $1 had bought three years earlier."[63]

The impact of inflation was also felt by organizations, including Lutheran congregations. In 1863 Friendship, Taylorsville, pledged to pay its pastor seventy-four dollars "and some corn." The following year the commitment jumped to $350 plus eight and one-half bushels of corn and two bushels of wheat.[64]

Blockade-running, with its promise of transforming cotton into urgently-needed military and civilian supplies, made a few Carolina entrepreneurs wealthy. As the war progressed and the South lost more and more of its ports, Wilmington, where Lutherans established their first congregation in the eastern half of the state in 1858, became a city of strategic importance to the Confederacy. Wilmington's port was difficult for off-shore vessels to patrol, and it had many features that made it an ideal site for blockade-running. With cotton selling for three cents a pound in the South and twice that amount in England, there was adequate incentive to risk the occasional loss of a vessel to the United States Navy.

It was not unusual for fortunes to "be made almost overnight. A number of successful steamers piled up millions of dollars in profits for their owners. It was possible for a large vessel loaded with 1,000 bales of cotton to realize a profit of a quarter of a million dollars in two weeks on the inward and outward run."[65]

Thousands Scarred

Except for some profiteers and blockade runners, North Carolina's families were ravaged by the war. In addition to the forty thousand men who died in uniform, thousands more

> were scarred and damaged, left with only their courage and their pride. Millions of dollars in local, state, and Confederate revenue were spent for naught as well. Investments, savings, loans, and currency, all were rendered worthless with no hope of reparation. Countless banks, mills, stores, and schools were closed forever. Blighted crops, empty barnyards, fallen fences, and broken dreams, all had to be dealt with in the midst of defeat.[66]

North Carolina at the time of the conflict was an overwhelmingly rural state. As late as 1850 it remained the most sparsely populated of all the states in the eastern United States. In 1860 North Carolina could boast only six towns with populations of two thousand or more.[67] Thus, it was not difficult to create a manpower shortage in the state.

The early shortage of males became more acute as the war progressed, its impact being felt in the church as well as on the farm and in the factory. When the pastor celebrated the Lord's Supper at St. Luke's, Lexington, in 1864, there were only eighty-one male participants but 139 women.[68] In studying the history of their congregations, many Lutheran pastors serving older churches in North Carolina, would agree with the finding of Rev. Sidney D. Steffy of St. John's, Concord, who concluded: "These were the darkest days in the history of the congregation, not even excepting the perilous times of the Revolutionary War."[69]

As the war drew to a close, the depredations of hostile troops ceased to be a matter experienced only by North Carolina families living in coastal sections. From east Tennessee, Union Gen. George F. Stoneman led a six-thousand-man cavalry force on a raid into western North Carolina, and Gen. William T. Sherman invaded the state from neighboring South Carolina. Tar Heels in increasing numbers became acquainted with "Bummers" and their expertise in foraging.

A Union officer, with first-hand knowledge of its work in the South, described a military unit assigned to foraging as "an institution by itself": "I doubt whether the history of war shows an organization equal to it in scientific and authorized stealing. These squads are composed of about twenty men each, selected for their great personal bravery and reliable character as soldiers. They are always commanded by picked officers, whose duty it is to scout the country and gather everything that can be used by the Army. Nothing escapes them; they go miles in every direction from the main column...."[70]

The devastating results of the war and its impact on the male population in the

South impressed even the conquerors. Thomas Ward Osborn of Sherman's staff, writing from Johnson County in late March 1865, commented: "The people of the North can form no conception of the barrenness of the South in able bodied men; they have all been absorbed. An able bodied white man of military age is a curiosity in the South. Governor Brown of Georgia says there are only 1,400 men in the state fit for military duty, not now in the Army. The mayor of Columbia told General Howard there were 1,450 in South Carolina. Thus, the largest state and the most treasonable state in the South together cannot furnish 3,000 men, not enough to stand a morning skirmish without being annihilated. Lee's Army, said to be 65,000 men, and Johnston's of less than 40,000 will be pretty much exhausted before the summer is out. There are no large armies from which to draw reinforcements, as was the case last summer...."[71]

Desertion

By 1864 it was clear the early enthusiasm for the war, which seemed to overwhelm all opposition, began to fade. Four Union officers who, as escaped prisoners of war, made their way from near Charleston to Winnsboro and Rock Hill and then across western North Carolina, found families who were ready to support them in their flight. Near Dallas a "Mr. W---" and his wife provided the fleeing Yankees with a hearty meal.

> That night, sitting before the cheerful blaze on his great hearth, he told us the story of North Carolina mountain loyalty, proving to us that freedom still had brave defenders among the hearty forest-men of the old North State. He told us of the cruel persecutions to which Union men, in his section of the country, had been subjected by the Confederate authorities, but that, notwithstanding their tribulations, they had remained faithful to their principles. He belonged, he said, to a society called "The True Heroes of America," a sort of Union League, whose chief object was to keep Unionists out of the Confederate army. Thousands of good and true men were members of this order.[72]

Moving on westward through Burke and Caldwell Counties, the Union officers entered territory where the spouses of deserters were encountered more frequently. The same qualities of industry, courage and self-sacrifice that won plaudits for so many feminine supporters of the Confederate cause were also displayed by their counterparts whose chief concern was an end to the war and the restoration of the "old flag." Observing that the women who prepared their meal were also capable of discussing the war and reflecting their faith "that the old Union would be preserved," a New Jersey officer commented, "The women whom I met along upon the mountains of Western North Carolina and Eastern Tennessee, while surrounded by terrible dangers, were as heroic as any whose noble deeds are recorded in our country's annals."[73]

The loss by the Confederacy of major battles and the increase in suffering on the part of the soldiers had its impact on desertion statistics. But their flight was not just a flight from hardship and danger; it was a flight to home and loved ones in need. At the end of 1863 Lt. Col. Aden Cavins reported on conversations with captured Confederates.

> But when they were shut out from their homes, their friends, and the dear ones that aforetimes smiled happily around their firesides, they were subdued---not by federal bayonets or the fierce rattle of our dreadful musketry, but by sentiments deeply established in the constitution of man: love of home, wife, father, mother or children.

There is a point beyond which few can go. One may endure any physical hardship, to gratify a feeling, a prejudice or a whim, or suffer death rather than a real or supposed dishonor. But most men are subdued when the ties of early life are sundered and all the joyous memories of 'home, sweet home' are trampled under foot. When, therefore, the rebels are driven from their homes and their places become occupied by our soldiers; when they are separated from their families by long and tedious days, they will give up the contest.[74]

By early 1864, the desertion problem reached serious proportions for the Army of Northern Virginia. On the 22nd of February, General Lee issued his General Order No. 4 which, among other things, provided that when military units were on the march, one man in ten was to have bayonet fixed and a loaded pistol at the ready, in case any of the nine tried to flee military responsibility.

North Carolinians were reminded in dramatic fashion of the desertion problem. An attempt by Gen. George C. Pickett to wrest New Bern from the control of United States troops was unsuccessful, but netted the Confederates approximately three hundred prisoners of war, twenty-two of whom were discovered to be former Confederates who had joined the First and Second North Carolina Union Volunteers. The twenty-two were declared deserters, and were hanged at Kinston on February 28. The troops of Gen. R. F. Hoke's brigade assembled for this mass execution, and then heard a lengthy sermon delivered by Chaplain John Paris. The chaplain saw the executions as possible instruments of good since through them "the eyes of the living might be opened to view the horrid and ruinous crime and sin of desertion," which had become so prevalent. Paris blamed the desertions on forces at work on the home front.

NORTH CAROLINA SYNOD PRESIDENTS

1861-62 J. D. Scheck	1864-65 Jacob Crim
1862-63 Daniel Isaac Dreher	1865-66 Jacob Brown Anthony
1863-64 Gotthard Dellman Bernheim	

I am fully satisfied, that the great amount of desertions from our army are produced by, and are the fruits of a bad, mischievous, influence that is at work in the country at home. If in this bloody war our country should be overrun, this same mischievous home influence will no doubt be the prime agent in producing such a calamity. . . . These malcontents profess to be greatly afflicted in mind about the state of public affairs. In their doleful croakings they are apt to give vent to their melancholy lamentations in such words as these: "The country is ruined!" "We are whipt!" "We might as well give up!" "It is useless to fight any longer!" "This is the rich man's war and the poor man's fight!"[75]

As the war progressed, it became apparent to some that victories like Sabine Cross Roads, Kennesaw Mountain and Cold Harbor could not compensate for the frightful toll exacted by Chancellorsville, Gettysburg and Chattanooga. As suffering became more pervasive and persistent for the troops in the field and supplies including food more difficult to come by, brave men increasingly dreamed of reuniting with loved ones just one more time before they were called upon to make the supreme sacrifice.

As the numbers of deserters mounted, those who reached home found the authorities resorting to desperate measures to stem the tide. Instead of producing meek compliance, such measures often strengthened determination to resist. When a man like Bill Estes, hiding out in the shadow of Grandfather Mountain, learned that the authorities had strung up his son to a tree by his thumbs in an effort to force him to tell his father's whereabouts, the fugitive was not immediately converted into a disciple of law and order.

And since deserters could not return to their farms and homes, they turned to robbery as a means of survival. The winter of 1864-65 in much of the Piedmont and mountain country was marked by a rash of robberies.[76] The robbers often enjoyed considerable popular support, especially in Randolph and Caldwell Counties.[77]

Not all of those who attempted to hide out in the hills or to flee from their military unit were successful. A Stanly County soldier serving in Virginia decided early in 1865 that, "although he was in rags and half starved," he must go home to see his wife and children one more time. The fugitive soldier was captured, however, and returned to camp where he was promptly court-martialed and sentenced to be shot the following day. The evening of March 3 he penned a letter to his wife, Nancy.

> My dear wife:
> I have to state to you the sad news that tomorrow at 12 o'clock that I have to die. I have to be shot to death for starting home to see my wife and dear children. . . .
> Dear wife, don't grieve for me. Try and not. I drempt last night of seeing you, but I shall never. You shall see your husband no more. I want you to raise my children in the way they should go. . . .
> With all my love,
> Joe[78]

NORTH CAROLINA SYNOD CONVENTION SITES

1861 St. Paul's, Wilmington	1864 Mt. Carmel, Cabarrus County
1862 Organ, Rowan County	1865 St. Michael's, Iredell County[79]
1863 St. Mark's, Charlotte	

Impact on Churches

The density of Lutherans in North Carolina at the outbreak of hostilities was quite similar to that of Lutherans in other southern states. In fact, the general pattern of southern church life was clearly established for southern states by 1850. At that juncture, the Methodists were the most numerous, followed by the Baptists, Presbyterians, Episcopalians and Lutherans, in that order. That pattern prevailed in North Carolina ten years later, except that the Lutherans had slipped by the Episcopalians and were the state's fourth largest denomination.[80]

The impact of the war on the churches in the South was substantial. When the North Carolina Synod's Central Conference met at New Bethel, Richfield, on September 28, 1861, Rev. Joseph A. Linn, who was serving St. Matthew's, Salisbury, and Luther's, Richfield, reported that forty-one men from his parish had volunteered for the Confederate army, "leaving their seats vacant in the house of God." Rev. Jacob B. Anthony, serving New Bethel and St. John's, Concord, noted that a great many young men had volunteered from his parish also, and "that eleven young men had made a public profession of religion and had been confirmed into the Church before leaving home. Thrice he had been called upon to hold religious services with departing soldiers and their friends."[81]

Conventions could not be held at the times and places they were planned. Communications were few and far between; on one occasion a synod president reported that he had received only one official communication since the previous convention. In 1864 the Tennessee Synod found it necessary to resolve, "That, in view of their proximity to the enemy, all of the Virginia brethren be excused" from attending the annual convention, even though attendance was normally considered mandatory.

A pastor of the Holston Synod where only grape wine was considered acceptable for use in Holy Communion recalled that

> during and just after the war..., when almost every article of necessity was scarce and hard to procure, real grape wine was so scarce as to be almost impossible to find. In consequence, many churches, other than Lutheran, made use of blackberry wine in the administration of the Lord's Supper.[82]

TENNESSEE SYNOD PRESIDENTS

1861-62 Adam Efird	1864-65 John M. Smith
1862-63 Timothy Moser	1865-66 Jesse Reuben Peterson
1863-64 Jesse Reuben Peterson	

Churches found their plans for building or improving facilities put on hold. The building that served Sinking Springs congregation was older than the Tennessee Synod itself. In the late 1850s the congregation started to erect a brick structure sixty feet long and forty feet wide to replace their old building. With the opening of hostilities, construction ceased, not to be resumed until after the war was over. During the period of construction, people came to church and sat on the floor sills. Many brought their muskets to the worship service.[83]

But the major impact of the war on the churches stemmed from the economic deprivation of the region and, consequently, of the Lutheran families. Pleas by a Lutheran pastor for help in rebuilding a church structure "destroyed at the time the army of Gen. Sherman passed through that village" failed to produce any significant response among impoverished southerners, despite their antipathy toward Sherman. The petitioner broadened his plea:

> Brethren of the clergy, North and South, in our destitute condition aid us in the re-erection of our church edifice. Many of you in the North, who are in better circumstances than we in the South, and who are men of influence, I still remember - such as Drs. Morris, Schmucker, Baugher, Brown, Stork, Anspach, Krauth, Martin, Reynolds, Seip, Conrad, Diehl, Pohlman, Passavant, Schmucker, jr., W. D. Strobel, P. A. Strobel, and others; and some recently from the South, such as Bros. Anthony, Scheck, Smithdeal, Blackwelder, etc. Come, brethren, all of you, and all others whom I have not mentioned, English or German, make collections for us, and send your contributions . . .[84]

Many years had to pass before Lutherans in the South could recover either the numerical, or the financial, strength they enjoyed before the creation of the Confederacy.[85]

Lutherans in the South during the period of the Civil War were not isolated from the general currents of religious thought and practice. The revivalism found in military camps was very much a part of life on the home front as well.

Rev. Elijah Hawkins, who headed the Southwestern Virginia Synod, noted that "many of our young men, who were efficient members of the church, have had to unite with the army, in defense of their common country, and are thus exposed to all the temptations peculiar to that school of vice. Notwithstanding these commotions I have heard of several revivals of religion in the churches."[86]

At St. Matthew's, Cleveland, Rev. M. M. Miller was pleased "to let the Church see that amidst the calamities and distractions of our country," God was still "willing to hear and answer prayers." He reported in the early fall of 1861 on a "protracted meeting" at St. Matthew's that began on the Thursday night before the second "Sabbath of September": "The Lord poured out his spirit upon his people and sealed his truth upon the hearts of sinners. Christians were revived, as showers of Divine Grace were poured out upon them. Truly the hearts of Christians were greatly refreshed, and their souls were filled with inexpressible gladness, while sinners came falling at the foot of the Cross, and jailer-like, cried out, 'Sirs, what must I do to be saved,' or 'Lord, save us, we perish.' During the meeting, which lasted eight days and nights, between forty and forty-five persons were happily converted to God, and publicly professed Christ before the world, and went on their way rejoicing."[87]

TENNESSEE SYNOD CONVENTION SITES

1861 St. John's, Lexington District, SC	1864 St. Mark's, Gaston County
1862 Grace, Catawba County	1865 St. Peter's, Catawba County
1863 St. John's, Catawba County	

Licentiate Whitson Kimball of Lutheran Chapel, China Grove, reported a "protracted meeting" that took place the same month which resulted in sixty persons professing "faith in Christ, and thirty-one joined the Church."[88]

Since the dominant religious ethos in the South in the nineteenth century was revivalistic, it also was individualistic. Starting with a personal conversion experience, it issued into individual attempts to lead a personal life that avoided those things in life labeled "sin" and embraced deeds of kindness, generosity and hospitality. Lutherans in the Carolinas were also influenced by this kind of thinking. Reports on "membership" produced only information on communicants, not on the number of persons accepted into the covenant community through God's gift of Holy Baptism.

What is less clear is why this understanding of Christianity, which was by no means confined to the South, failed to produce in the South a broad concern for the moral condition of society in general. In the early decades of the century, some Christians in the South, including Lutherans, could be recruited to support the American Colonization Society as well as societies promoting temperance, respect for the Sabbath, and a ban on duelling.

But in general, Christians in the South were not likely to think of themselves as erecting the Kingdom of God on southern soil. They were much more likely to think of themselves as persons addressed by the parable of the wise or foolish virgins, persons who must strive to avoid personal sloth and drowsiness lest they be overtaken by an apocalyptic consummation of history. Why were Christians in the South less concerned about transforming society into a healthier, holier place than they were to triumph over personal sins and vices? It has been argued that "the shock caused by the rise of abolitionism dispelled completely thoughts in any Southerner's mind that a formal synthesis might be formed between public duty and private devotion."[89]

Did the fact that Christians in the South failed to wed themselves to the idea of creating the Kingdom of God in Dixie impact the contribution of religion to the Confederate war effort? That has been suggested: "The highly individualistic religion of the South, with its overriding emphasis on personal salvation, generally failed to serve a proper social function. Rather than strenghtening the resolve of the Southern people to support the struggle for political independence, religion in the South actually undermined the Confederate war effort."[90]

When living the Christian life is reduced to personal efforts to improve one's performance in practicing certain virtues and avoiding certain vices, it is much easier to leave to God the destinies of peoples and of nations.

Synodical Alignments

In 1859 the General Synod included among its twenty-six member synods the synods of Kentucky, Maryland, North Carolina, South Carolina, Texas, Virginia, and Western Virginia. When the body met in Pittsburgh that year, each synod from the South was represented by synodical officials, suggesting the importance the synods attached to this relationship.[91]

The North Carolina Synod met at St. Paul's, Wilmington, in early May 1861. The previous year the synod had elected its delegation to the biennial convention of the General Synod to be held in Lancaster, Pennsylvania, in 1861. But South Carolina seceded from the Union in December, four other states followed in January, and the Confederate States of America was organized in February. Ten states had already cast their lot with the Confederacy by May, and even as Lutheran delegates assembled in Wilmington, legislators in Raleigh were debating the withdrawal of North Carolina from the federal union. Given the "distracted condition" of the country, did it make sense to send delegates from the North Carolina, or any other southern synod, to the convention of the General Synod in Pennsylvania?

President Daniel H. Bittle of North Carolina College, elected in 1860 to serve as a delegate to the 1861 convention of the General Synod, helped the North Carolina Synod address the new situation. Why not accept the fact that it was not practical to send delegates to Pennsylvania just now?

Instead, let the synod invite General Synod delegates from all member synods in the South to assemble in Salisbury, North Carolina, in May 1862, "for the purpose of endorsing the proceedings of the next meeting of the General Synod if practicable; otherwise to take such steps as may best promote the future harmony and prosperity of that portion of the church represented by the absent delegates."[92]

By the end of May, however, there were new factors to consider. North Carolina seceded from the Union and joined the Confederacy. There were Lutherans who believed that such a move need not involve armed conflict. Was it not true, asked the pastor of St. James, Concord, that when Abraham and Lot found they could not live together without their herdsmen engaging in controversy, Abraham "sought peace in separation?" Should not the Abraham from Illinois have followed a similar course?[93] And by the end of May also, the *Lutheran Observer*, which had long struggled to serve as a national church paper, came out clearly and unequivocally for the Union, leaving Lutherans in the South feeling betrayed by their own church paper.   As a Virginia Lutheran exclaimed to the editor,

> It is a matter of life and death with us - our homes, the virtue of our wives and daughters, and our all is at stake in this terrible struggle, and yet you send the Observer with its influence . . . against us. Great God Almighty, do you wish to make our church paper an instrument to assist in our extermination? . . . I think it very hard in you, when we are your brethren, and yet a united church, that you should array the Observer against us right at a time when we expect the bloodiest struggle that was ever witnessed on this continent.[94]

As it turned out, one of President Daniel Bittle's reasons for holding a Southern Church Convention quickly disappeared. He had suggested such a gathering might ratify actions taken by the General Synod at its Lancaster convention. However, before the end of July the battle of Bull Run had taken place in Virginia, and it was decided to postpone the Lancaster convention for a year. But as Bittle's suggestion for a ratifying convention lost its meaning, his proposal for a convention "to take such steps as may best promote the future harmony and prosperity" of the Lutheran church in the South seemed increasingly desirable and necessary. When the newly organized Georgia Synod met in convention in July, the president expressed his conviction that "it will become necessary to hold a Church Convention at an early day, at some central point, to organize a General Synod South."[95]

North Carolina's invitation to other southern synods to join in sending delegates to a convention in Salisbury a year later elicited a positive response in some quarters. In early September the Synod of Western Virginia, meeting at St. John's, Wytheville, took stock of the situation. By that time it was clear that the meeting proposed by the North Carolina Synod for Salisbury was needed, not, indeed, to endorse the actions of the General Synod of the United States, but to create a comparable organization for the Confederate States in America. The Wytheville convention unanimously adopted the following resolutions received from its committee on the president's report:

> 1. Resolved, That we, the members of the Evangelical Lutheran Synod of Western Virginia, in full view of our accountability to God, believe that the time has arrived, in the providence of God, when our ecclesiastical connection with the late General Synod in the United States ought to be, and that the same is hereby dissolved.
> 2. Resolved, That we will heartily cooperate with the Lutheran Church South in the formation of a General Synod in the Confederate States of America, in building up literary and theological institutions, in establishing a Lutheran Church literature, and in all the benevolent enterprises of the day.
> 3. Resolved, That we cordially approve of the action of the North Carolina Synod, at its last session, in recommending the call of a Convention of the Lutheran Church South, to meet in Salisbury, N. C., on the Thursday preceding the third Sabbath in May next, and that delegates be appointed by this body to said Convention in the same ratio of representation to which we were entitled under the

Constitution of the late General Synod of the United States.[96]

As the fall progressed, other Lutheran synods in the South that had been affiliated with the General Synod in the United States followed the example of the Synod of Western Virginia in cutting their ties with the General Synod and electing delegates to the proposed convention in Salisbury. The Tennessee Synod which had been unwilling to approve membership in a general body prior to 1861 also elected commissioners to attend the organizational meeting for a general body for the South.

The 1862 assembly in Salisbury, however, turned out to be a disappointment. Western Virginia's delegates wrote they could not come because of traveling conditions. Only two of Tennessee's delegates reached Salisbury and only one from South Carolina. No one appeared from either Georgia or Virginia and even North Carolina was missing two of its lay delegates, despite the fact that those in attendance delayed the start of the meeting an entire day. The exigencies of wartime frustrated attempts to hold a meeting even though all prospective participants agreed it was a meeting of great importance. Those present decided they should not, without a more general representation, proceed to create a general body for Lutherans in the Confederate states. Instead, after electing Nicodemus Aldrich as president and appointing four committees, the convention voted to re-schedule its assembly to September 25.

Unfortunately, conditions were not more settled in September, so Aldrich did not convene the assembly at that time. When the Tennessee Synod met at Grace, Newton, the following month, a number of North Carolina delegates to that body were convinced an unwise decision had been made the previous year in authorizing commissioners to organize a general body in the Confederate states. Despite the recommendation of President Timothy Moser that the commissioners be continued, the synod declined to do so.[97]

It was not until May 20, 1863, that the organizational convention was convened. The North Carolina Synod's delegates were Pastors D. I. Dreher of St. James, Concord; J. A. Linn of St. Matthew's, Salisbury; and G. D. Bernheim of St. Mark's, Charlotte; along with three laymen, Ransom Winecoff, Esq.; Christopher Melchor, Esq., of St. John's, Concord; and Col. John Shimpoch of St. James, Concord.

President Aldrich noted that those assembling in Concord did so, "not to rejoice, but to lament - not to speak of the prosperity of Zion, but to consider her distracted condition, and to behold her once fair proportions marred by the evil passions of misguided men."[98]

Early in the War, Elijah Hawkins, president of the Synod of Southwest Virginia, stated his convictions with regard to the church's new situation. It was not the role of the church to "meddle with political contests nor engage in sectional strife," he observed, but the Lutheran church was now confronted with a new situation. Those bodies formerly united under the name of Luther now found their association "interrupted by warlike hostilities between her localities." "Our own sunny South, dear to us by all the ties of nature and religion, is invaded by an implacable foe . . ."

What did this portend for Lutherans? Hawkins was convinced that Lutheran synods in the South must create for themselves an umbrella organization for their new nation. ". . . Our fate, our history and success are identified with that of our anticipated happy growing Confederacy . . ."[99]

President Aldrich agreed, but he believed it important that the reasons for their actions be clearly understood: ". . . It has been for no light or trivial cause our ecclesiastical connection with that portion of the Church embraced in the 'General Synod of the United States of America' has been annulled. So far as sympathy and harmony of action is concerned, the Northern and Southern portions of our Church have for years been divided."[100]

It seemed to Aldrich that the "household of faith" had been torn apart because "the Northern portion" of that household had surrendered to "a spirit of fanaticism," a spirit that contrasted with the South's spirit "of conservatism." The presiding officer was indignant that, with the outbreak of hostilities, "the Northern Church" not only failed to protest Lincoln's decision to resort to arms; it, "by a formal resolution, declared it to be the duty of the government to prosecute this war even to our subjugation." In separating from their former "brethren" Aldrich insisted neither "malice nor revenge" was involved. They were simply following the biblical injunction to withdraw from association with "every brother that walketh disorderly."

Those representatives of five district synods who assembled in Concord agreed. Following the presentation of the president, Pastor Bachman of St. John's, Charleston, South Carolina, asked for the floor. He had played a key role in persuading his own synod to unite with the old General Synod and twice had been elected to the general body's highest office. He now submitted a motion to the convention which invited the body to declare itself to be the "General Synod of the Evangelical Lutheran Church in the Confederate States of America." The motion was adopted unanimously. The convention then elected Bachman to succeed Aldrich as their president.

The committees appointed at the Salisbury session of the convention were invited to present their reports. In addition to the decision to create a separate general body in the South, the two most significant actions of this convention in the realm of Christian unity were responses to committee reports: the adopting of the *Book of Worship*, and the adopting of the constitution.

In creating their own general body, the southerners hoped to establish one that would be more inclusive of district synods than had been the case with the General Synod created in 1820. The approach to inclusiveness used by that body was to minimize matters of doctrine. Its constitution contained no doctrinal article, and it only required that its member synods hold "the fundamental doctrines of the Bible as taught by our Church."[101]

Lutherans who were concerned about the confessional identity of their tradition, such as the Tennessee Synod, with whom Lutheran pastors in the Carolinas and Virginia were in close proximity and frequent contact, found the General Synod's approach to inclusiveness unacceptable. Both the North and South Carolina synods, in urging the creation of the General Synod South, called for the creation of a body "on the basis of the Augsburg Confession." President Aldrich, who soon became pastor of St. Mark's, Charlotte, reminded the delegates that the Lutheran church had always grounded its creedal affirmations in that confession, "but at the same time she has never aimed to bind the consciences of her children beyond the limits of God's Word."[102]

Rev. John B. Davis of Virginia presented the report of the Committee on the Constitution. The second article, which defined the doctrinal basis of the new general synod, "elicited an animated, free, yet fraternal discussion - each member conscious of a great responsibility, solicitous of establishing such a platform as would secure the future unity of the Lutheran Church in the Confederate States, and without burdening any one's conscience in reference to the doctrinal symbols of the Church."   The first two sections of Article II provided an explicit doctrinal basis for the new body. First, there was an acknowledgement of the Old and New Testaments as "the only infallible rule of faith and practice." Then came recognition of the Creeds and the Augsburg Confession as setting forth the "fundamental doctrines" of Holy Scriptures. There were, however, those present who were concerned about such an unequivocal endorsement of the Augsburg Confession. After all, Lutherans in the United States had often dissented from the confession's interpretation of baptism and the Lord's Supper. Were consciences now to be coerced into agreement?

The convention decided to retain its previously-adopted statements regarding scripture, the creeds and the Augsburg Confession, but added the following caveat as a third section of the doctrinal article: "Inasmuch as there has always been, and still is, a difference of construction among us with regard to several articles of the Augsburg Confession; therefore we, acting in conformity with the spirit and time-honored usage of our Church, hereby affirm that we allow the full and free exercise of private judgment in regard to those articles."[103]

A second concern felt by some had to do with church polity: in particular, the authority and power to be vested in the regional body. There were those who believed the original General Synod was less attractive to district synods because it was strictly an advisory body. It could not even hear appeals from its member synods, and, while it could develop or endorse books of worship and other publications, it had no power to make the use of such publications obligatory.

President Aldrich had made it clear that he believed that, in creating a general body for Lutheran synods in the South, this organizational impotence should be corrected. Thus, in the proposed constitution the General Synod South was made the highest denominational court of appeal for cases dealing with doctrinal or disciplinary issues that might be referred to it. The constitution also authorized the General Synod South to provide an order of worship or liturgy "which shall be observed in every part of the Church." The constitution was adopted unanimously. ♱

St. Luke's Lutheran Church
1861 - 1926

St. Luke's, Lexington (1861)
Organized 1788

Daniel Dreher
President, North Carolina Synod
1861-62

G. D. Bernheim
President, North Carolina Synod
1862-63

Timothy Moser
President, Tennessee Synod
1861-62

St. Paul's, Wilmington (1860)
Organized 1858

CHAPTER VI

SURRENDER AND ITS AFTERMATH (1866-1869)

he light spring breeze moves across southside Virginia and into North Carolina's Halifax County as dusk settles. At Hascoosea, the summer home of the Edmonstons, Kate, the mistress of the household, seems strangely preoccupied as she seats herself at the writing desk in her room. Oblivious to the breeze rustling the curtain and making the lamp flicker, she takes in hand her journal and her eyes fall on an entry written only two days ago: "If we but stand by our President & our Army and present a stubborn, dogged resistence, we will yet conquer."

Now she takes pen in hand and slowly begins to write:

> April 16, 1865. How can I write it? How find words to tell what has befallen us? *Gen. Lee has surrendered!* Surrendered the remnant of his noble Army to an overwhelming horde.[1]

On April 9, 1865, the surrender of Gen. Robert E. Lee to Gen. Ulysses S. Grant took place twenty-five miles east of Lynchburg, Virginia, at the site of the court house for Appomattox County. A native son of North Carolina who devoted a lifetime to the study of his region reflected some eighty years later on the ravages and waste of the war.

> The Civil War was not worth its cost. It freed the slaves, upset a social and economic order, strengthened the powers of the national government, and riveted tighter upon the South a colonial status under which it had long suffered.
>
> What good the war produced would have come with time in an orderly way; the bad would not have come at all. Its immediate effects on the South were glaring and poignant; those more fundamental were less evident and long-drawn-out. The war generation bore the brunt, and it was they who had to grapple hardest with the new problems.[2]

NORTH CAROLINA SYNOD PRESIDENTS

1866-67 Samuel Rothrock	1868-69 L. A. Bikle
1867-68 Nicodemus Aldrich	1869-70 W. A. Julian

For those still in uniforms of Confederate gray, the cessation of hostilities had a distinctive perspective. There would be time enough for them eventually to join the folk on the home front in trying to comprehend the deeper meaning of struggle and defeat. But for now, it was enough that the incessant marching on ill-shod feet was over, the din of battle silenced, the frightful carnage stopped.

First, a day or two of rest; then start the long dreamed-of journey home. For many the trip itself made them aware that they were not returning to the South they had known.   And arriving at home in western North Carolina only confirmed the transformation that had been wrought. Although it was the end of April, many fields were unplanted - since seed was in such short supply, the ground had not even been broken. Also, tools were a scarce commodity and, when available, usually worn out. Fields that once boasted large herds of cattle and hogs now could muster only a few scattered creatures, and persons who still possessed a mule or horse were fortunate. Burned-out buildings served as grim reminders that Yankee raiders had passed through Carolina.[3]

It was disorienting to discover the once-familiar surroundings of home so different. But it was not just the external world that was different: "Everything had changed; they themselves had changed. Lads of twenty returned witnesses to death and carnage unimaginable in a normal lifetime. Missing limbs and bandaged wounds bore silent testament to their combat, yet veterans betrayed the deepest scars, the ones etched on their souls, by vacant expressions in haunted eyes. They stared at houses and barns gutted, gardens and fields grown wild, fences and sheds flattened or spent for firewood. Even people whose houses had not been physically destroyed sensed the loss of something equally precious: the happiness and security that define a home, the emotional and spiritual roots that anchor it, the sense of community that nourishes it."[4]

To invest so heavily in a cause believed to be just and yet suffer defeat produced not only dismay but disorientation. As one historian has recently observed, "Before all else, one must appreciate the confusion that followed Confederate defeat. An angry pause descended upon the land. The stillness of history struck different people at different times, in different places, depending on when the news of surrender overcame them and when they decided that this gloomy report, unlike so many previous ones, was not rumor but the harshest of truths.   The effect, momentarily gut-wrenching, paralyzed, immobilized them. For some people, the moment lasted only a few hours. For others, it dragged on over the course of days, weeks, years, lifetimes."[5]

NORTH CAROLINA SYNOD CONVENTION SITES

1866 Trinity, Cabarrus County	1868 Lau's, Guilford County
1867 St. John's, Salisbury	1869 Friedens, Guilford County;
	Salem, Rowan County

Inevitably, as persons began to recover from the initial disorientation, attempts were made to find scapegoats. At times it seemed a "universal hue & cry. This one caused our failure - the other one - here - there - every where. I say every man who failed to do his utter most aided - every man who could & did not fight caused it. I do not see that any did their duty but the dead heroes - the wounded maimed - & those sturdy souls who first went into it - & were found at their post under arms when the *generals* gave them up to the Yankees."[6]

The Lutherans, as well as other church members in the South, did not escape the bewilderment of the antebellum period. They believed their cause was righteous and deserving of God's blessing.   After all, that sacred compact, the United States Constitution, had, in their eyes, been flagrantly violated. At the same time, southerners were convinced that God ruled over all things, even mundane day-to-day happenings. Since God permitted the Confederate forces to suffer defeat, it could only mean that, as a result of their sinfulness, southerners had failed to properly interpret God's will and purpose. No doubt sinfulness had brought down the wrath of God upon them, but they were inclined "to be rather vague about the nature of that sinfulness, usually dredging up the old failings of dance or drink. . . . When the former Confederates considered the central issues of the war, secession and slavery, few talked of sinfulness. In the years immediately after the war, in fact, southerners reasserted the righteousness of the South's position on both these issues."[7]

Southerners continued to believe that the Bible, the bedrock of their religious faith, made it clear slavery was not, in itself, sinful. As a Presbyterian body pointed out, it was true that southerners "may have to lament before God, either for neglect of duty toward our servants, or for actual wrong while the relation lasted," but they have no need "to bow the head in humiliation before men, or to admit that the memory of many of our dear kindred is to be covered with shame, because, like Abraham, Isaac, and Jacob, they had bond-servants born in their own houses, or bought with their money...."[8]

In the final analysis, it was not deemed necessary to understand precisely what sin had offended the Almighty, or determine at precisely what point there was a failure to discern and follow God's will; after all, God's wisdom so far surpasses human comprehension as to make ludicrous man's attempts to comprehend the Divine. It was enough to recognize that sin was present and that humble contrition was appropriate for those who acknowledged their guilt.

Rather than persistently probing the question of guilt, it seemed more appropriate to resume in so far as possible the kinds of community and church activities experienced before the war and to recover a sense of gratitude to God for blessings that remained. Devastating as was the war and its aftermath, Lutherans in the South could still discern causes for thanksgiving.

As President Peter Schickel noted in his report to the Southwestern Virginia Synod, there was peace: "though we failed to secure our Independence, our prayers have been answered, if not in form, in spirit. The great Prince of Peace has once more restored to us a cessation of hostilities as a nation, if not in the way we looked, hoped, and prayed for; yet in God's own way and time. It becomes us to bow with humble submission before the heart of Jehovah, saying, 'Father, not our, but thy will be done.'"[9]

Although the distractions of the post-war period were not conducive to home mission activity, the North Carolina Synod did receive during the five-year period four new congregations: Ebenezer, China Grove (1867); Macedonia, Burlington (1869); Holy Trinity, Mt. Pleasant (1869); and St. Luke's, Mt. Ulla (1869).

TENNESSEE SYNOD PRESIDENTS

1866-67 Adam Efird	1868-69 J. M. Smith
1867-68 A. J. Fox	1869-70 Thomas W. Miller

Despite losing three pastors during the same period, the Tennessee Synod also grew, adding to its rolls Philadelphia, Granite Falls (1865); and in 1867 both Sardis, Hickory; and St. James, Newton (1867).

Impact of War

Many fortunate enough to make it back home would join "Adelphos" in confessing that, as far as material possessions were concerned, "I lost all I was worth during the war, and had to start afresh at its close."[10]   Early after the end of the conflict, Barnas Sears, former president of Brown University, toured the South in connection with his new responsibilities as general agent of the Peabody Education Fund which would make a monumental contribution to education in the post-bellum South. Sears concluded that there were two million children in the South and that "about two-thirds of them" were living in poverty.[11]

North Carolina, which began a school program with legislation in 1840 and gradually accumulated $2,850,000 in a "permanent school fund," found the fund had evaporated by 1865. Paper currency and stocks and bonds churned out by Confederate printing presses during the war years were now worthless. Food was in short supply. The South's modest antebellum industry and manufacturing struggled to survive as a pall of poverty blanketed the land. For those Carolinians whose labors or good fortune had brought relative comfort before the war, there were times when remembering the past in the midst of current privation would be enough to make them join Mary Chestnut's lament: "There are nights here ... when I could tear my hair & cry aloud for all that is past & gone."[12]

TENNESSEE SYNOD CONVENTION SITES

1866 Beck's, Davidson County	1868 Salem, Lincoln County
1867 Cedar Grove, Lexington District, SC	1869 Emmanuel, New Market, VA

The textile industry was barely able to function. As early as 1813 several mills were operating in the state.[13] By 1860 North Carolina could boast thirty-nine mills, more than any other state in the South. But the experience of Mountain Island Cotton Factory in Gaston County was typical. Prior to the war it was one of the largest textile mills in western North Carolina. The incessant running of the mill during the war years left the mill's machinery worn out. But the owners were now too impoverished to replace the machinery, so they could only try to keep the equipment patched together and let the mill limp along producing what little it could. Fortunately, as in the typical mill village in the post-war period, employees at Mountain Island each had a small tract of several acres within half a mile of the mill where each could grow vegetables for his family, tether a cow, and raise a few pigs.[14] Without these modest amenities, life for those who found employment in a mill would have been bleak.

And the general economic destitution of the region was just as real to farmers and planters as to mill owners and their employees. In launching a magazine for Lutherans in the South in 1866, the editor recognized that even the modest subscription price of $1.50 per year was beyond the reach of hosts of potential readers. Thus, he devised a pay-as-you-go plan: "As money is yet very scarce in many parts of the South, some might prefer to pay 15 cents on the receipt of each number. To any, therefore, who cannot raise the money to pay for the *Lutheran Visitor* at once, we give them the privilege of paying monthly."[15]

In fact, the economic plight created by the fall of the Confederacy threatened to rob hundreds of southern landowners of their property. An article appearing in a

Boston newspaper early in 1866 described the condition and alerted northern capitalists that this was an excellent time to buy land in the South since half of the real estate in the region was in the hands of persons who, in fact, were bankrupt. The land would have to change hands in the next twenty-four months, so here was an excellent opportunity for the Yankee entrepreneur. The article aroused the ire of a southerner who edited a church paper.

> What a malevolent triumph would this be to those pretended partakers of the religion of Jesus! Rubbing their fists with inexpressive glee, they say one to another, "our glorious Union and pious armies have robbed the South of their slaves, of their mules and horses, of their jewelry and silver; we have stolen or burnt their cotton, corn, rice, and sugar; we have cut their levees and overflowed their plantations; we have burned up their fences, gin and sugar houses; we have made their land utterly desolate, and brought poverty and ruin to every household; come, now, let us whose homes have not been desolated by fire and sword, - we who have fattened and grown rich on their misfortunes, let us go down before they recover, buy their land for a song and drive them from the country."[16]

The plight of the South presented the entrepreneur with varied opportunities to improve his fortunes. For example, southerners in many areas were without mail service for a time. One who had recently returned north after spending time in the South noted that he was "well aware of the great inconveniences to which the Southern people are subjected on account of lack of mail facilities." He assured folk at the South that there was no longer any reason for them to be deprived of mail service.

The difficulty was not that there were no persons in the South who were willing to serve as mail carriers. Many would have been happy to accept the employment, but were prevented from receiving government employment because they could not swear that they had never taken up arms against the United States Government. Southern Lutherans were alerted to the fact that Bryan Tyson, "a national Union man, (late of North Carolina)," could and would take the necessary oath, contract for mail routes identified for him by southerners, and sub-contract the routes "upon satisfactory terms" to southerners desiring to be mail carriers. Thus, for a fee the enterprising Tyson proposed personally to "form the connecting link between the Southern people and the United States Government."[17]

The economic advances in the North during the war seemed to cry out for exportation to the South in the aftermath of the conflict. Representatives of the business community in the North were interested not only in providing mail service and in purchasing former plantations in the South. Railroads seemed a promising investment, there were coal fields to be exploited, and investing in North Carolina's turpentine and lumber business promised a good return on one's invested capital. Some even imagined that through such investing in the South they could help to transform the region into a likeness of the North, thus enhancing the unity and homogeneity of the Nation.[18]

The church could not escape the turbulent times that transformed the society of which she was a part. The war robbed the church of "some of her brightest ornaments", young men "of talent and hopeful promise" devoured by an "unfeeling and insatiable war." The problem of the loss of promising candidates for the ordained ministry was coupled with the problem of inadequate support for the clergy who were available to serve the congregations. The loss of manpower on the battlefield and the abolition of slavery contributed to a diminution of

> our agricultural resources. This, connected with the loss of money once current, has greatly impoverished the country, leaving very little in the hands of the masses of the people after disbursing their taxes.[19]

Despite the evidence of loss and poverty on every hand, the president of the North Carolina Synod believed "most of our pastorates are able to afford a comfortable living to their pastor," but he conceded that "none amongst us receives such support." This circumstance, he believed, had already resulted in the fact that "some of our most efficient ministers have been forced to resign their churches and engage in secular pursuits."[20]

A committee of the Tennessee Synod observed that all that body's

> congregations in North Carolina have suffered much by the terrible conflict through which the country has passed - some by the loss of members, others by alienation among the members caused by the course each felt it to be his duty to pursue during the war.
>
> The impoverished condition of the country also tends to prevent a speedy return of the former prosperity of the church. Most, if not all, of the ministers find themselves under the necessity of engaging in secular pursuits in order to obtain for themselves and families the necessaries and some of the conveniences of life. All these things have a very depressing influence upon the prosperity of the church.[21]

The external circumstances of the people were clear enough. In some locales the destitution was "truly distressing, and devastation general." A delegate to the General Synod South convention in 1866 who edited a Lutheran magazine observed that even the South's oldest residents acknowledged that "the most stringent state of monetary affairs" existed which they had ever known. A pastor who was less than enthusiastic about his church's growing concern for "uniformity" and "liturgy" lamented other changes between the *then* and the *now.* It appeared to him the traditional hospitality extended to visiting clergy was evaporating.

Formerly, when a local pastor had announced a "protracted meeting" for his congregation and alerted the people to the identity of any guest preachers who would be assisting with the services,

> there was a commendable rivalry among his people as to who was to have the pleasure of extending their hospitalities to these servants of God sent temporarily into their midst. But now, judging from observation, the only sensation produced by such an announcement is the mustering of reasons why each family of the congregation cannot entertain these expected visitors; and "they all, with one consent, began to make excuse." *Then* the pastor, unless by special request, had not the opportunity to have the helping brother as his guest. *Now,* has he a home, necessity is laid upon him to entertain one or all who may be present, simply because his people do not offer to bear the *burden,* as they evidently regard it. . . .
>
> *Then* when the brother descended from the pulpit he was met by a crowd, and saluted with many a pressing invitation; "won't you go home with me?" *Now* the

altar, aisle and door are kept clear. The brethren hurry out as soon as the benediction is pronounced, or *modestly* stand aside, and in action at least, say -- "Go on, thou chosen of the Lord, we are not worthy that thou should'st so much as come under our roof; go thou with our pastor, his house is holy, and there abide."[22]

The pastor's sarcasm was probably misplaced. The familiar hospitality would return and persist for many decades. But in the years immediately after the war, families that formerly delighted to welcome guest pastors to tables laden with the produce of farm and forest often found themselves unable to provide the bare necessities for their own household. They would have been embarrassed to have guests discover the true extent of their poverty.

Devastation and impoverishment were not confined to urban targets of the recent invading armies - cities like Atlanta, Savannah, Columbia and Charleston.

Whole regions of country have been overrun, - private residences entered, clothing and valuables carried off or destroyed, forage and provisions hauled away in the carriages and wagons found on the farms, - and frequently the residence, outbuildings and farming implements all consigned to the flames. How can those thus reduced to a bare subsistence, afford to give according to the demands and necessities of the Church? Even Church buildings have been robbed of their communion service and other valuables, and in some instances have been reduced to ashes. Our institutions of learning have been greatly injured by the loss of funds invested in bonds and stocks which became depreciated and worthless.[23]

Conditions were so extreme that some Lutherans in the South swallowed their pride and asked assistance from Lutherans "at the North." In the summer of 1870, the acting president of the North Carolina Synod contacted the Executive Committee on Missions of the Ministerium of Pennsylvania, requesting two hundred dollars to supplement the salary of the new pastor, Jacob Grabenstein Neiffer, who had just taken up his responsibilities at St. John's, Salisbury. President Bikle submitted his request, and within sixty days learned from Rev. Beale M. Schmucker, the committee's secretary, that one hundred dollars was assured and a duplicate amount would be forthcoming if "the funds on hand would allow." Bikle proposed that the annual convention of the synod create a committee to respond to "the generous and liberal donation of the Pennsylvania Synod's Executive Committee on Missions."[24]

Both for the church and for southern society in general, the aftermath of the war called for profound economic adjustments, but more was involved than economics. From the perspective of southerners, a once-familiar way of life was undergoing radical change. Amid the poverty and desolation of defeat, "there was a feeling of unrest and dissatisfaction everywhere."[25]

How would the United States deal with those who had elected to support the cause of southern independence? What did the assassination of Abraham Lincoln portend for the fate of the conquered people?

Since the United States Congress was not in session at the end of the war, President Andrew Johnson alone was obligated to determine how the southern states would be restored to the Union. As the Constitution did not provide for such action, the president did what he thought proper. His plan, the one that Lincoln had tentatively designed, was to accept the states back into full fellowship as quickly and as easily as possible with only the most essential restrictions.[26]

The South waited and speculated as to what would be forthcoming from Washington. "My idea is the drunken tailor [Johnson] will soon issue a proclamation & define our position. *Then,*" observed Mary Chestnut in May of 1865, "we will settle some where here or *move on.*"[27] Five days later the diarist would lament, "The same bitter endurance of life here [in South Carolina] - & certainty that worse is coming."

Near the end of May 1865, Johnson named William Woods Holden, the publisher and editor of the *North Carolina Standard,* to serve as provisional governor of North Carolina, and the process of returning North Carolina to the Union began. Holden called a constitutional convention which met in October and again in May and June 1866. The state's secession ordinance was nullified, slavery abolished, and the Confederate debt repudiated, but the attempt in August to secure passage for the state's new constitution was not successful.

Early the following year, a plan endorsed by Johnson for the readmission of southern states was formulated. Congress rejected the plan and, with it, the presidential approach to Reconstruction.

> It was in large measure to test the attitude of the Southern states - or more likely simply to confirm what the Radical Republicans already knew - that the Fourteenth Amendment was passed by Congress in June 1866 when none of the eleven Southern states were represented. It was promptly submitted to the states for ratification. Its acceptance would determine whether a Southern state could again be represented in Congress and thus returned to membership in the Union. When the amendment was rejected, Congress began to implement its own terms under which the states might be restored.[28]

In March 1867, Congress passed, over the presidential veto, an act "to provide for the More Efficient Government of the Rebel States" which, along with three additional acts adopted shortly thereafter, placed North Carolina and other Confederate states under military rule, made clear the provisional character of all state governments in former Confederate states, and set forth procedures to be followed by states seeking re-admission to the Union. These procedures included the adoption of a state constitution consistent with the Constitution of the United States. In North Carolina a new constitution was drafted in the early months of 1868 and adopted in April. With the legislature's ratification of the Fourteenth Amendment on July 4, the way was cleared for the state to return to the Union with its legislators returning to the halls of Congress later the same month.[29]

Thus, as a Congress dominated by radical Republicans began to shape its scheme for reconstructing the South, it appeared to many white persons in the region that two disasters were in the offing, military rule under the Yankees and elections in which black persons cast ballots that carried just as much weight as those cast by white persons. Given the economic desolation, the unavoidable uncertainty, and the persistent fearfulness of those whose fate was in the hands of their conquerors, some in the South considered the possibility of emigration, and some did, in fact, leave.

The idea of leaving the South to establish hearth and home elsewhere occurred to some before war's end. For example, as early as the capture of Vicksburg by Union forces in July 1863, Capt. William Nugent wrote to his wife, "We are now driven to fight to the bitter end, [even] if ... [our defeat] itself be the result. The ruling majority are contending to emancipate our slaves, and if the negroes are freed the country, as a general thing, is not worth fighting for at all. We will be compelled to abandon it and seek some more congenial climate."[30]

Emerging from the initial shock of defeat, some Southerners decided to move to Brazil or Mexico. Brazil seemed especially attractive to those who had difficulty reconciling themselves to the new status of black persons in the South. Slavery was still permitted in the Amazon republic, there was "a thriving cotton industry," land was inexpensive, and extended payment plans were readily available.[31]

An estimated eight to ten thousand southerners actually moved to Brazil, while much smaller numbers decided to try Mexico, Venezuela or Honduras. Why such drastic action? Dr. D. M'Neill Turner, of Abbeville, South Carolina, wrote a series of letters to a doctor in Hampton, South Carolina, explaining why he believed emigration was an appropriate option. The letters were published in the Abbeville *Banner,* and the editor of the *Evangelical Lutheran,* Rev. Nicodemus Aldrich, considered them of sufficient interest that he reprinted them on the front page of his publication.

Turner was devoid of optimism about the political future of the South, but it seemed to him a worse calamity than the loss of political rights and influence was in the offing: "My views may appear harsh; but I am forced to entertain them. I am thoroughly convinced that our fiendish enemies will be satisfied with nothing short of the total destruction of society as it formerly existed in the Confederate States."[32]

If the southern way of life which northerners found so objectionable was to be expurgated, it would require more than merely depriving southerners of "former political privileges." The ownership of land carries with it certain power to influence social patterns and developments. It would only be a matter of time, Turner contended, before those who labored to acquire land, build it up, and defend it, will see themselves dispossessed.

"Good men may hoot at the idea of confiscation; and Thaddeus Stevens may be regarded as 'a brainless wit,' 'a baptized infidel,' 'a raving maniac,' or anything else equally lovely; but the masses are far better prepared to receive the idea of confiscation than they were that of abolitionism. It will not require thirty years to render the former palatable. Nay, the utterances of Stevens and Wade are so harmonious to the ears of many, that even such men as Gerritt Smith are taking alarm. In honied [sic] speech, as if they really felt the impulses of humanity, they utter their remonstrances against the ills with which the poor South is threatened."[33]

Of course, the pretext would be things like "making the South pay for the expenses of the war" and "punishing rebels," but Turner was convinced that discerning men recognized that "Southern sentiment" would not be destroyed as long as white southerners still held significant tracts of land.

And Lutherans learned from their church paper that Turner also was convinced that those who had conquered the South would not hesitate to create in the South "a conflict of races" in an effort to achieve their ends. Members of Congress were hardly unaware, Turner noted, of how the culture established by the French families in Haiti was destroyed. Was it not the North's desire to use race in the same way in the prostrate South?

"The people of the South", he wrote, "submitted too readily to the Civil Rights bill and the Military bill. The anticipated conflict did not occur. Something more must be done. Emissaries must be dispatched all over the land to stir up strife. The people of all classes at the South are too quiet. There can be no Hayti [sic] while such stillness predominates. But Haytian [sic] scenes must be re-enacted, [before] the Southern sentiment may be effectually buried."[34]

Turner admitted he did not really think the South could be turned into another Haiti, at least not in all respects, but he believed the attempt would be made since such an approach (i.e., racial strife) would provide "an occasion to the malicious and vindictive foes of the South for the enactment of such laws as will utterly subvert Southern society. I think that as to social character, we are a doomed people. Our late military leaders, our prominent civilians and others, may manifest as much servility to the powers that be as they can; all will prove of no avail. Mordecai has given mortal offence to Haman, and he must hang for it! The decree has gone forth. It is like a law of the Medes and Persians. Do you see in all this no reason for emigration? Shall we be satisfied to remain here not merely politically but socially degraded?"[35]

Instead of emigration to a foreign country, some southerners chose emigration from the South to what only recently had been "enemy country," namely, the North, and, in particular, New York City. They sold whatever belongings they had in the South and moved to the North in the hope of there finding better opportunities for building a new life. An estimated sixteen thousand southerners moved to Yankeedom in the decade of the 1860s, and the decade of the 1870s saw several thousand more join them.

But "emigration fever" soon ran its course. "As months and years passed, more and more people who had spoken enthusiastically of emigration accommodated themselves to Yankee rule."[36] Discouraging as were the prospects, social, political, and economic, most former Confederates could not desert the soil for which they had risked their lives, the familiar hills of home, the family and friends who shared their confusion and impoverishment, the cemeteries where parents and grandparents lay waiting for the day of resurrection. So in the aftermath of the war there were also those "determined, relentless folk" who resolved to stand by the South and attempt to rebuild lives and fortunes.

Of those remaining at home in the South, however, some were ambivalent about their course of action. In August of 1865, North Carolinian Armand L. DeRosset reflected on the strange situation in which his self-expatriated brother in England found himself. Southerners caught in Europe at the end of the war found themselves without country or home, ". . . exiles and wanderers upon the face of the earth;" surely "their fate is indeed to be commiserated. . . . But still how much better off they are than we, here, in our once happy, sunny South, once happy, but now the present and future to us any thing but pleasant, crushed and ground down by an over-whelming military despotism."[37]

But even those who bewailed their fate and that of their beloved South harbored the hope and expectation that one day things would get better. Thus, as one analyst has suggested, in creating the character of Wilkens Micawber, the "grand procrastinator" and persistent survivor, Charles Dickens inadvertently provided many southerners with a role model. They did not elect some direct course of action and plunge into it; rather, they moved cautiously if at all, waiting to see what would "turn up." The past represented smashed dreams and destroyed hopes. Surely the future would hold something better.[38]

While a precise measurement of the importance of black-white relations in the shaping of life in the southern United States is impossible, it is equally impossible to exaggerate the importance of those relations in that process. "The 'peculiar institution' that as late as 1840 had seemed to astute observers to be on a course of ultimate extinction, rent the nation. It galvanized the South - a region of long-standing diversity as to religion, politics, class, economics, history and custom - into unified military action, ideological conformity, and a high degree of religious (if not denominational) homogeneity."[39]

That the enslavement of fellow human beings left emotional scars on masters as well as slaves is suggested by the remark of a Carolinian in April of 1861: "The only thing we fear in this war is that the Yankees will arm our slaves and turn them against us."[40] The specter of a Denmark Vesey or Nat Turner was not easily dispelled.

Before the end of 1861, slave owners in the South were breathing a sigh of relief. The fear that, while those of military age were off fighting the war, the blacks would rise up to destroy the women, old men and children left at home, proved unfounded. In fact, the editor of a church paper announced that the war was enabling slavery to be seen "in its true light" by the entire world, to be seen as an asset rather than a liability:

> While the ruling race go forth to war, the servile till the land and raise the staples of subsistence and commerce in the usual quantity. The North verily thought that slave insurrections would break out simultaneously with the war. This was their rod of terror over us, their boast and final resort - they would raise insurrections, or rather, they would give an opportunity, and servile insurrections would be general and spontaneous. Well, the war has been going on long enough to convince them that all their calculations were cast in error. Since the abolitionists that were among us have been scared out and driven off, the negroes have been quieter than ever.[41]

The Emancipation Proclamation and the surrender of the Confederacy produced a radically different situation. What was now to be the fate of black persons in the South?

"The Emancipation Proclamation", one observer noted, "had relieved them from all duty of service to their masters; but it had also relieved the masters from all duty of providing for and protecting their slaves. By a stroke of the pen four million slaves had been transformed into vagrants and paupers."[42]

Whose responsibility was it to respond to the needs of the freedmen? The communities and states in the former Confederacy were in no position to assume such a responsibility, even if the North had been willing to entrust such a responsibility to them. Should Congress assume the responsibility, a Congress composed "almost exclusively of Northern men, who did not understand the negro, never had lived among the negroes, had no real affection for the negro, and could not understand his temperament . . ." Would it not be preferable to invite the former slaves to assume as much responsibility for their own adjustment and development as possible?

"Enfranchise him; give him the ballot, and with it all the rights and privileges and prerogatives of citizenship. Apply the principle of the Homestead Act. Use the abandoned lands in the South, and, if necessary, confiscate the lands of the rebels, and give each negro a lot for cultivation - forty acres was proposed."[43]

But would there not be a cry of outrage from landowners if their last remaining vestige of material possessions were taken? In five Southern states black persons were more numerous than whites, and in a sixth the two races were almost equal in number. What if the white South took exception to granting control of government to the black population, still largely uneducated and without experience in exercising political responsibility? "It would be a just punishment. But the South would not long object. In a few years - five at the most, said Charles Sumner - the South would conquer its prejudice sufficiently to allow the late slaves to be their equals at the polls. Sumner was better acquainted with political theories than with human nature."[44]

With all of its potential pitfalls, this was the course of action decided upon: black persons should immediately be entrusted with full political responsibility. A clergyman who devoted himself to the herculean task of educating the new electorate in the South observed in retrospect that the results of the policy adopted in Reconstruction demonstrated that "the ballot in the hands of ignorance is as effective an instrument for self-destruction as for self-protection."[45]

To many Lutherans in the South as well as their neighbors, it seemed that post-war developments revealed the hypocrisy of the victors. Why had the North taken military action against the South? Was it not claimed that the conflict was being waged "for the integrity of the Union of States?" But now "that victory has perched upon the banner of the North," the victors were imposing on Southerners patterns of social relationships perceived by them to be intentionally degrading and humiliating, relationships designed to sow "among us the seeds of bitter dissention." As Congress substituted its several acts for the presidential plan for Reconstruction, the Charlotte editor went on to lament that disputes among Southerners were springing up as to how best to respond to this radically new social situation:

> brother is arrayed against brother upon political points; the spirit and principles of the Gospel are ignored; churches have been split in twain, and our ministers standing between the porch and the altar, are weeping over the sins of the people.[46]

Black persons in North Carolina demanded that "the oppressive laws which make unjust discriminations on account of race or color be wiped from the statutes of the State."[47] In 1866 the General Assembly validated the marriages of the former slaves, gave them the same rights enjoyed by white persons in courts of law and equity, gave blacks protection from fraud and ignorance in entering into contracts with white persons, and, except in the case of rape, made the criminal law equally applicable to white and black person alike.[48]

For a time it appeared the Congress of the United States would see to it that blacks in the South actually experienced a new birth of freedom. But there were hosts of political issues to be resolved before such an eventuality could come to pass. For example, the former slaves had each been counted as three-fifths of a person in deciding how many representatives a state might elect to Congress. But now black persons must each be recognized as a full person. How could that be done without suddenly bestowing on the defeated South twelve new seats in Congress? The vying of Democrats with Republicans and the contest between the White House and Congress for control of the reconstruction effort resulted in the black person in the South ultimately receiving far less than had been anticipated in May of 1865.

And in the South there were significant forces opposed to the social change which Congress demanded. One of those forces was the Ku Klux Klan, whose first secret lodge was established in Tennessee late in 1865. The Klan quickly spread into other southern states, and made rapid strides in North Carolina. In its campaign to create fear as a deterent to the integration of the races, the Klan in North Carolina was credited with "260 outrages, including 7 murders and the whipping of 72 whites and 141 Negroes."[49]

But the Klan was not the only force at work shaping the future relationship between black and white persons in the South. Planters needed laborers. Some believed the South should seek to import laborers from Europe. Noting that the region had suffered "the entire destruction" of its labor system and that it had become "absolutely necessary that laborers of an entirely different class" be introduced to the Southern scene, the North Carolina Synod went on record as being willing to cooperate in any scheme which showed promise of transferring laborers from "the now crowded Districts of Protestant Germany" to the sunny South.

The synod's Committee on Foreign Emigration asked and the convention agreed that "a Committee of Correspondence be appointed, whose chairman shall take immediate steps to lay this matter before Pastors of Lutheran churches in Protestant Germany, stating the deep interest exhibited by this body, and the great anxiety our people have expressed to secure immigrants, as co-laborers with them in cultivating the soil, and various other pursuits."[50]

But on every hand there were the former slaves, now without jobs. Planters and freedmen "came together to form a new system that was, in many respects, very like the old. The freed slave, now a 'sharecropper,' continued to live in a rent-free house on the planter's land and was paid for his labor not in regular wages, but by a share of the crop produced on the acreage designated as 'his.' The cropper was in theory free to leave at any time if he did not care to continue working for a particular planter, and the high rate of interplantation mobility indicates that many did move. But the fact remained that the share-cropper's freedom consisted almost entirely of freedom to move from place to place within the plantation network. Few were equipped by training or habit - or lured by the prospect of better opportunities elsewhere - to abandon the cotton fields altogether."[51]

Soon, relations between white and black Carolinians, like relations between blacks and whites in the South generally, settled into a recognizable pattern. Without digging in their heels in opposition to change, southerners, white and black, experienced elements of continuity in the patterns of organization in their society.

A prominent North Carolina clergyman observed: "Indeed on many plantations freedom for the Negroes did not bring about much change. The little homes occupied by them continued to be the places of their habitation. Thousands of slaves refused to leave kind masters and mistresses, and the work and social life went on about as in former days."[52]

The sharecropper pattern of organizing southern farm labor persisted well into the twentieth century.

But the sharecropper pattern of organization was not the only social configuration to emerge in the aftermath of the war. Many blacks, perhaps recognizing that former patterns of social organization would tend to persist if they remained in the same place associated with the same persons, elected to migrate into towns. They often arrived with no means of support. Having heard rumors that the government that had freed them would provide them with "forty acres and a mule," they confidently expected the government to take care of their needs.

And through a newly-created federal agency, the Freedmen's Bureau, an attempt was made to assist the former slaves, whether they elected to migrate into town or preferred to become share croppers: "The bureau supervised the drafting of contracts and work arrangements for the freedmen, and before it was abolished in 1872 its agents registered black voters. Emergency food and shelter were provided, schools were established, and military courts heard their complaints."[53]

The patterns of race relations that emerged in rural and urban areas reflected a resistance to change which appears in most cultures but which assumed a peculiar prominence in the South. Despite the disruption created by the Civil War and the political fact of emancipation, "traditional familial and religious bonds" persisted, "enabling southern communities to revive a racist system, regain political ascendancy, and rebuild their economy. Ironically, then, the war for union did not destroy the culture of the South. Indeed, southern culture survived precisely *because* of its local attachments and its peculiar community structure."[54]

But whereas relations between black and white persons in the antebellum and war periods, while undeniably racist and, on the part of the whites, at best paternalistic, were often characterized by good will that made it possible for black and white Christians to worship together, the period of Reconstruction began to change all that: "Ill will generated between the races during Reconstruction virtually ended mixed religious congregations, and the separation was not always voluntary. In Wilmington, for instance, Union general Schofield *ordered* the Methodists to select a minister satisfactory to the blacks."[55]

The closing decade of the century saw forces at work in race relations in the South that would further widen the social chasm between black and white persons in the region and its churches.

Synodical Alignments

The end of the fighting and the collapse of the Confederacy posed some immediate and local problems for Christians. In denominations using liturgical prayers, the petitions often included intercessions for the nation's governing authority. Since Lincoln was so widely despised in the states that comprised the Confederacy, it was not difficult to fall in step with the times and pray instead for President Jefferson Davis. But with the end of the war, was it possible simply to substitute President Andrew Johnson, whose plebeian origins and fondness for drink were widely touted in the South, for the respected Mississippian, President Davis?

Mary Chestnut noted that Episcopal leaders in her community were not of one mind. For example, when "praying for the President" of the United States was discussed, "John Elliot said his conscience would let him - & Gnl. R. Anderson joined him, as right to pray for the powers that be. Another clergyman said he would find it hard to pray for the health & prosperity of a man -when he wished him dead! Mr. Trapier was for praying for Jeff Davis to the last gasp - & when that was denied us, to shut up the churches awhile - not to be in such a hurry to be Yankeecised."[56]

For Christians in the South whose denominations divided into northern and southern branches prior to or during the Civil War, an inescapable question arose at the end of the conflict. Could northern and southern branches of the denomination reunite, and if they could, should they?

Leaders in North Carolina's German Reformed community, a community with whom the Lutherans were often closely associated, expressed the conviction that their household of faith was fortunate. Despite the heated rhetoric in the political arena, the political schism, and the armed conflict, "we have calmly kept ourselves from strife and divisive words or counsel, and there is not a word in all our records to divide us or offend a Christian brother. We may then dwell in peace and unity. Neither, so far as we can see, is there one act or word in the records of our Church North that is marked by bitterness; but our [southern] churches have been hailed with delight on the return of peace, and all brethren speak to us words of love and kindness. Let us then as a Church maintain the unity of our whole body, and let it be our task to cement the bonds that shall make our country one. . . ."[57]

In 1866 the Classis of North Carolina heard read a letter from the Synod of the German Reformed Church expressing "most hearty feelings of regard, Christian sympathy, brotherly kindness and charity, together with sincere regret that adverse circumstances" had resulted in the North Carolina Classis not being represented at recent conventions of the synod. The "earnest hope" was expressed by the synod that the classis would promptly resume sending its customary delegation to synodical conventions, and, in fact, the classis voted to send delegates to the very next meeting of the synod.[58]

Lutherans were among those Christians whose denominational structure had been fractured as a result of the war. Thus, they, too, faced the question of reuniting with Lutherans in other regions of the United States in a national organization. Of the seven southern and border states whose Lutheran synods were part of the General Synod of the United States at the start of the war, only two (Kentucky and Maryland) remained members of the General Synod five years later. The other five synods had adjusted to a new political reality, removed themselves from the general synod, and created a separate umbrella organization for the Confederate states.

In 1866 those five synods once more faced a new political situation; would they quietly return to their former places as members of the General Synod of the United States? Rev. J. C. Roehm, president of the synod of Texas, dispatched a letter to the General Synod on behalf of the district synod he represented. The letter reflected a strong attachment to the General Synod and deplored "the unjustifiable event" which ruptured relations between the Texas and General synods. Roehm expressed the hope that "active relations" might soon be reinstated between the two bodies, despite the fact that Texas was financially unable to send delegates to the 1866 convention of the General Synod at Fort Wayne, Indiana.[59]

The North Carolina Synod also explored the question of re-uniting "with Synods of like faith with ourselves in the North." The issue was "discussed at great length," but the proposal of Rev. John Samuel Heilig of Trinity, Concord, that the synod rescind its action of 1862 terminating its relationship with the General Synod in the United States was finally defeated.[60]

Southern synods that withdrew from the General Synod in the course of the war often found it difficult to lay aside memories of the recent conflict in favor of Lutheran unity. The General Synod in the United States had publicly denounced the actions of the southern states in withdrawing from the Union and characterized the creation of the Confederate States of America as "rebellion" against duly constituted authority, a rebellion

> most wicked in its inception, unjustifiable in its character, inhuman in its prosecution, oppressive in its aims, and destructive in its results to the highest interests of morality and religion.[61]

President Lincoln was assured by the Lutheran leaders in the northern General Synod that they were asking their people to pray to God for the success of the Union armies that there might be a speedy deliverance from the "treason and anarchy" being fostered by the seceding states. The General Synod also made it clear that its criticisms were not just of political leaders or militarists in the South. No, "those Synods and ministers" in the South who formerly were members of the General Synod were singled out for the General Synod's "most decided disapprobation" because of their "open sympathy and active co-operation" with the Confederate cause.

The end of hostilities did not produce an instant change in attitude. Meeting a year after the war, the General Synod in the United States expressed the hope that since the great "rebellion" had been put down, the passage of time would eventually make it possible for the church, "North and South," once more to encounter each other "on common ground." Nevertheless, it seemed appropriate to the convention publicly to affirm that they did not wish to soften "a jot or a tittle" their wartime denunciation of the South's action.

Fourteen months after the close of the armed conflict, Lutherans in the South came together once more in Cabarrus County, North Carolina, this time for the third convention of their General Synod of the Evangelical Lutheran Church "in the Confederate States of America." This proved to be a meeting that profoundly influenced the continuing development of Lutheranism in the South. In the absence of President Anders Rudolph Rude of South Carolina, Rev. Edwin Abiel Bolles, who had served as agent for the Confederate States Bible Society, was asked to preside through the election, at which time the convention selected Rev. Thomas William Luther Dosh of Virginia, a future pastor of St. John's, Salisbury, to chair the convention.

For those southern Lutherans gathered at St. John's, Concord, in 1866, the mere recalling of the official title of their organization was a reminder that the political changes forced upon the South necessitated a revision in their constitution. A committee consisting of Pastors Josiah Pierce Smeltzer, Gotthard Dellman Bernheim, David McConaughy Gilbert and Joseph Iranaeus Miller along with lay delegates Col. J. S. Pifer of Virginia and Jacob Duls of St. Mark's, Charlotte, was appointed to review the constitution "and suggest such amendments as our present circumstances as a Church render proper and necessary."[62]

Naturally, the long and bitter conflict was still prominent in the minds of all, but there was a concern to turn from what might have been and get on with the tasks at hand: "It is to be expected that the interests of religion should receive a shock proportionate to the magnitude of the excitement incident upon such a conflict of arms as that through which we have so recently passed. During the prevalence of such commotions the Church will, naturally, rock and reel amidst the restless billows of human passion, ever and anon in danger of being driven from her moorings.

> Now, that the storm is over, and quiet is being restored, the opportunity is offered those having management of the Church to exert themselves in repairing the injuries done during the raging tempest.[63]

A contributor to the church paper observed: "As a church we cannot but admit that we have said and done many things whereof we should be ashamed, and it is time that all bitterness, and wrath, and anger, and clamor, and evil speaking, be put away with all malice; and that we be kind one to another, tender-hearted, forgiving one another, 'even as God for Christ sake has forgiven us.'"[64]

Should the synods represented at Concord simply reject the sectional sentiments that had been built up in recent years and return to the fold of the General Synod of the United States? Should they actively encourage synods in other regions to unite with them in an organization that had its origins in the former Confederate States of America?

G. D. Bernheim noted that such questions were discussed "at great length," but the discussion culminated in the following resolution: "Resolved, That we deem it impracticable to make any overtures to our sister Synods [note the use of the term sister] at the North, to become united with us in the General Synod, nevertheless, whenever any applications for union with us shall be submitted by any Lutheran Synod in North America, it shall become the duty of the General Synod properly to consider the same; but undue anxiety for the uniting of other Synods with us might be misunderstood or misinterpreted."[65]

The church in the South suffered severe monetary losses as a result of the war; and in material things like buildings and property the war had also taken its toll. But it seemed clear to some, at least, that the losses created by the war were not to be computed solely in material terms.

Was it not also to be lamented that many who bore the name of Christ had suffered a decline in piety? "Civil or social discords and conflicts afford no school for good morals, - they are ever at variance with religion and sound morality. Dissensions of any kind are well calculated to lead us astray from duty, but how much greater the danger of being swerved from the path of moral virtue when the feelings and passions become so excited as to rend asunder a great people and array the disagreeing parties against each other in deadly conflict."[66]

The Committee on the State of the Church at the 1866 convention of the General Synod South took comfort, however, in the fact that not every Christian suffered a decline in morals in turbulent times. Some encountering "such scenes of excitement" cling with greater tenacity to their religion and experience a growth in piety, even while their fellow Christians "who are not truly sincere" have their moral standards undermined.

How was one to understand the new relationship between Americans "at the North" and those persons whose region had so recently sought to assert its independence? There were those whose perspective on the now concluded military struggle suggested not so much two hostile nations vying with each other as "a great people" torn asunder.

But not everyone was eager to be recognized as "one people" with those who resided "at the North." Nor was everyone ready to "forgive and forget" the national trauma that had invaded even the life of the church. When the editor of *The Lutheran Visitor* reported on the refurbishing and re-opening of Wentworth Street Church in Charleston, South Carolina, in the fall of 1866, he could not refrain from pointing out that the renovation had been made a necessity "by the shelling of our northern brethren(?)."

The General Synod South's Committee on the State of the Church was no doubt realistic when it observed, "In some instances there exist feelings of alienation, with heart burnings and a spirit of contention, that has assumed sufficient magnitude to threaten the unity of the Church. All who feel willing to listen to the voice of the Church, and seek her and their good, deplore these dissensions. It should be our aim to cultivate unity of spirit and purpose, and feelings of friendship and brotherly love throughout our whole communion. A captious, domineering spirit is the bane of all vital piety, and should be shunned with as much dread as a deadly, pestilential contagion."[67]

"Harmony and unity" in the church were clearly the goals to be pursued, the committee believed, but the promotion of these desirable qualities within the Lutheran household of faith would require "delicate legislation": "Carefully should we cultivate that 'charity which suffereth long, and is easy to be entreated.' Antagonistic opinions and alienated feelings should give way to a spirit of conciliation, if we hope for the unity and perpetuity of our Church."[68]

The North Carolina Synod which met a month before the general convention of southern synods in Concord in 1866 had debated at considerable length the question of returning to membership in the original General Synod. While those desiring an immediate return to membership failed to persuade a majority of delegates to vote with them, they did succeed in providing that North Carolina's delegates to the convention of the General Synod South the following month be instructed "to inquire as to what steps can be taken to form a union with sister Synods North." They did so, and found that there was some concern to lay aside the bitterness engendered by the years of conflict, but the General Synod South was not yet ready to sacrifice its own existence in the interest of a larger Lutheran unity.

The wounds were deep and would take time to heal. Lutherans in the South included the words "in North America" in the new title of their supra-synodical organization in an effort to emphasize the fact that they did not wish their general body to be perceived as a remnant of entrenched sectionalism. But in fact, Lutherans in the former Confederacy for many years found the focus of their quest for Lutheran unity in the region, rather than across the continent.

The General Synod South decided to dispatch a letter to the congregations in its member synods indicating why it was necessary to "maintain our separate organization as a General Synod." The three pastors assigned the responsibility for preparing the letter were Joseph I. Miller, Gotthard D. Bernheim, and Thadeus Street Boinest. To these pastors there were four good reasons to continue a general body.

First, the Lutheran church in the South would be hampered in carrying out its mission unless it had educational institutions, particularly a theological seminary, on its own territory. Given the impoverished condition of the South, the synods in the region would have to combine their efforts to support such educational institutions. A regional organization provided the natural structure for such cooperative efforts.

Second, while congregations in the South could utilize religious literature and publications developed by Lutherans in other regions, failure to develop literature and publications in the South would leave the southern church with less than full development as an ecclesiastical body. A regional organization could foster the development of literature and support a publishing effort.

Third, Lutherans in the South wanted to affirm their confessional identity. The affirmation was not expected to win applause in the northern General Synod, but it could possibly prevail in a regional body.

And, finally, the old general body seemed "convulsed and torn by internal dissensions;" hardly inviting to those who "desire peace." The authors of the "Pastoral Letter" avoided recriminations about the verbal condemnations adopted by the northern body.[69]

Despite the concern of some Lutherans in the South to avoid recriminations and even to recover active fellowship with Lutherans north of the Mason-Dixon Line, the experience of Reconstruction persistently undercut the transformation of such concerns into a broad consensus.

In fact, as a historian of the Virginia Synod has observed, at times it appeared "feelings of fraternity to the church in the north approximated total eclipse." Illustrative of that fact is the decision of the editor of the *Lutheran Visitor* to draw on biblical phraseology if not ideology in opposing any attempt at reunion with northern Lutherans: "What God hath put asunder let not man join together."[70]

At the 1866 convention of the General Synod South, it was necessary to revise the constitution to eliminate at least the designation "Confederate States of America." However, the committee appointed to propose revisions to the constitution did not content itself with proposing for the organization a new name, "Evangelical Lutheran General Synod in North America." It also recommended the deletion of the third section of Article II of the constitution, that section permitting "the full and free exercise of private judgment" with regard to those articles of the Augsburg Confession whose continuing validity was debated by some Lutherans. In adopting the committee's recommendation to eliminate Section 3, Article II, of its constitution, the general body endorsed a stricter confessionalism.

To reinforce its centralizing of power and emerging confessionalism, the General Synod South called upon the committee preparing the "Pastoral Letter" explaining the necessity of continuing the general body also to explain to the constituency why the organization must have some delegated power and a clear confessional identity.

After pointing out that the justification for continuing the General Synod South as a separate organization was not based on a desire either to create or sustain "sectional animosity" but only out of a concern for "the glory of God and the prosperity of our beloved Zion in the South," the authors of the "Pastoral Letter" addressed the controversial issues of confessionalism and delegated power.

As for the move to make the body more explicitly confessional, it was argued that the lack of progress made by the Lutheran church in the United States, "North and South, is to be accounted for, in a great measure, by the extreme latitudinarianism which she has taught and practiced. It has been too much the practice of her ministers to seek to make the impression on the public mind that, in no important particular, do we differ from other denominations."[71]

Such doctrinal indifference contributed, they believed, to the "easy transition" of Lutheran pastors and lay persons from the Lutheran to other denominations. Since Lutherans have "an historical prestige and a Confession of Faith" that would enable them to stand tall among the many denominations on the American scene, why "not avail ourselves of the armor furnished to our hands, and get to ourselves a name and position which shall be the glory of Protestantism?

"Let us, then, at this particular juncture of our Church, plant ourselves firmly upon the 'Augsburg Confession,' the proud bulwark of Protestantism, despite all opposition, from whatever source, arrayed against us.

"God honored our Church as the instrument to break the fetters of Popery in the time of the Reformation, and, if we are true to ourselves, she is destined yet to take no secondary place among evangelical denominations."[72]

In addition to confessional integrity, the "Pastoral Letter" argued that one thing more was essential if the Lutheran Church in the South was to assume its proper place among the evangelical denominations: "As ministers, we should accept, in good faith, the legislation of those to whom we delegate authority to enact laws for the Church at large. We should study those things that make for peace, and things whereby one may edify another. Having now, as a body, legislative and judicial authority, (which might have been assigned as another reason for continuing our present organization,) we can expect a higher degree of efficiency and prosperity, if we will only accept, in the spirit of fraternal love, the result of the combined wisdom of our legislative body."[73]

Not all Lutherans in the South appreciated the new tack taken by the General Synod South with regard to confessionalism and centralizing power. The editor of the *Lutheran Visitor*, Rev. Joseph I. Miller, assured his readers that "one of the chief excellencies" of the Lutheran Church was the fact that it "allows the fullest exercise possible, of individual opinion." No one need cry "Wolf!" until he published something in conflict with this hallowed Lutheran principle.

The cry of "Wolf!" was raised by Rev. Christian Beard who was concerned about the contrast between the traditional attitude "of our Church" toward doctrinal matters and the doctrinal stance called for by the recently-amended constitution of the General Synod South.[74] Beard recalled that the new version of the constitution had been "warmly opposed" when it was presented to the Virginia Synod for adoption. In fact, the convention of that body was equally divided between those who agreed to the new form of the constitution and those who opposed it. The editor of the *Lutheran Visitor* was also president of the Virginia Synod when it voted on the revised constitution for the General Synod South, and he cast the deciding vote in favor of the new constitution.

Beard called attention to three provisions of the constitution of the old General Synod with which he and his fellow pastors had been acquainted in antebellum days. First, that constitution had recognized that "No General Synod can be allowed to possess or arrogate unto itself the power of prescribing among us uniform ceremonies of religion." Second, that earlier governing document had accepted the fact "that liberty of conscience, and the free exercise of private judgment in matters of religion, are natural and unalienable rights of men" which all governments, civil and ecclesiastical, were bound to respect.

Finally, proposed regulations for governing the life and practice of the church must be considered in the light of the New Testament by "every individual church" which will then adopt or reject the proposal. In the recent action of the General Synod South, it appeared to Beard a very different spirit was manifested.

First, there was this new *Book of Worship* "with its forms, ceremonies, prayers, responses, &c., and now they ask that all ministers in every Synod in connection with the Gen. Synod, shall use this book of worship. And why? We *must have uniformity*."[75]

Beard was quite willing to admit that the liturgical developments reflected in the *Book of Worship* were admirably suited to the worship life of some Lutheran congregations. But to others, including, presumably, the congregations he served, these developments were "very objectionable." But the crucial issue was not the suitability of the forms of worship, but the cherished liberty to take or leave particular worship forms as might seem appropriate to any particular congregation and/or pastor. This newly revised constitution for the General Synod South was staking out a claim to power "never claimed by the old General Synod, and never imposed by Jesus Christ or his Apostles."

And then there was this burgeoning confessionalism. The General Synod North did not set forth a confessional basis in its constitution of 1820, and gave the Augsburg Confession only limited recognition by requiring professors at her theological seminary to acknowledge it as a Lutheran document. The body's model constitution for district synods also encouraged a similar recognition, one that permitted the individual pastor to consider himself a Lutheran even while repudiating the sacramental character of Baptism and the Lord's Supper. The Virginia Synod had been content to require its pastors to subscribe to the fact that "the fundamental doctrines of the word of God are taught in a manner substantially correct in the Augsburg Confession." The Virginia pastor appreciated this kind of "liberty" in relation to confessional statements.

> But the General Synod in N. A. requires of us to adopt the Augsburg Confession, in an unqualified manner. Heretofore we adopted it as containing the fundamental doctrines of the Christian religion. Now we are asked to adopt it without any qualification - adopt it as a whole; and thus profess to believe it, whether we do or not. Yea, there are doctrines in that venerable Confession that many of us do not believe; and yet those young apostles of liberty, notwithstanding our conscientious scruples, insist that we must adopt it without any qualifications; and in the face of all this, tell us that they are the friends of liberty. If so, leave us the liberty we have so long enjoyed as a church. We ask no more. But do not try to fetter the consciences of your brethren, and then, with the same pen, proclaim that you are the friend of liberty. May God save us from such freedom.[76]

There were, no doubt, other pastors who shared Beard's views, but the main stream of Lutheranism in the South had chosen a new direction from which it would not be turned aside in a quest for a superficial unity. Unity would be a prominent concern, but it would be a unity growing out of common confessional commitments and shared worship forms. Thus, while the North Carolina Synod also had some pastors who were much concerned about their loss of "liberty" under the new constitution of the General Synod South and while revivalism and occasional resistance to the use of the *Book of Worship* would continue to surface among Lutherans in the Old North State, the majority of North Carolina Synod pastors and congregations were clearly to be identified with the "main stream."

Publications

But the North Carolina Synod had its differences with the General Synod South. One issue on which the district synod differed with the general body was the church paper. The *Lutheran Observer* published in Baltimore enjoyed a wide circulation among Lutherans in the South in the period before the war, partly because its editor, Benjamin Kurtz, deplored the extremism of the abolitionists and was concerned to see the unity of Lutherans in the United States fostered rather than fragmented.

In the North Carolina Synod, President William A. Artz in 1844 urged the synod to recognize the value of having this publication become a weekly visitor in the homes of its parishes. He was confident that those wishing to "stir up our people to greater activity and more enlarged and liberal views on matters pertaining to the prosperity of our Zion and the kingdom of God" ought to strive to "circulate the *Lutheran Observer....*"[77]

The attitude of the *Lutheran Observer* toward the Augsburg Confession and toward revivalism made it unacceptable to those Lutherans in North Carolina who had cast their lot with the Tennessee Synod. Yet that body too recognized the need for a church paper as an instrument of communication and a bond of unification. Since it did not have a paper of its own and did not appear to be in a position to launch its own publication, Dr. Samuel Godfrey Henkel in 1845 proposed that the synod recommend to its members "the *Lutheran Standard,* of Ohio, and the *Lutherische Kirchenzeitung,* of Pittsburgh, Pa.," since those papers had "taken a stand against 'new measures'."[78]

The convention decided to postpone a decision on the question for one year since many delegates were not familiar with the publications in question. The following year the synod noted that the Western District Synod in Ohio "warmly recommend to us the *Lutheran Standard.*"[79] However, the Tennessee Synod was so deeply embroiled in the controversy that gave rise to the Tennessee Synod Reorganized that it could not deal seriously with the endorsement of publications. It contented itself with alerting its constituency that the *Lutheran Standard* and the *Lutherische Kirchenzeitung* "may be very profitably read...."[80]

As the issues polarizing the nation were debated in the late 1840s, the need was voiced in the South for a new Lutheran church paper. In the North Carolina Synod, there were those who believed it important to maintain support for the *Lutheran Observer* rather than take chances on a new Lutheran publication. Thus, in 1851 the synod once more endorsed the Baltimore publication as "a paper well calculated to promote the interests of our church" and resolved that it would "endeavor to promote its circulation among our churches."[81]

Prior to the war, the *Lutheran Observer* managed to retain most of its Southern subscribers, at least until the Brooks-Sumner affair. With the outbreak of hostilities and the unmistakable alignment of the *Lutheran Observer* with the Union cause, the need for a church paper for Lutherans in southern synods was no longer debatable.

The South Carolina Synod took unilateral action which it hoped would find favor with other synods in the Confederacy. Assuming that it was just a question of time until all Lutheran synods in the Confederate States severed any relations they may have had with the General Synod, the synod announced through its officers their conviction that

> Our earliest efforts should...be directed to the establishment of a paper, which might strictly be regarded as the organ of the whole Southern Church, to be ultimately under the management and control of a General Synod.[82]

Since it would be some time before a southern General Synod could be established and assume the responsibility for publishing a paper, the South Carolina Synod assumed responsibility for getting the paper started. In August 1861, the weekly first made its appearance. The North Carolina Synod announced that "we heartily rejoice in the successful labors of our South Carolina brethren in establishing a Lutheran Church paper," and encouraged its support by "our church members."[83] In the absence of a synodical paper of its own, the president of the Tennessee Synod, Alfred J. Fox, promptly encouraged that body to support the *Southern Lutheran,* and the following year his successor called the synod's attention to the fact that they were still without a church paper and that that fact was felt keenly in many homes of members. President Adam Efird went on to "recommend that if practicable our Synod do something in this direction," but the synod took no action on the president's proposal.[84]

Two years later, however, Jesse Reuben Peterson was more successful. He presented the following preamble and resolutions which, "after a free interchange of opinions," were adopted unanimously:

> Feeling as we do, the great want of a Religious Periodical in the families of our connexion [sic], and as the *Southern Lutheran* is the only paper of Lutheran character now published in the Confederate States, be it therefore, Resolved, that this Synod most cheerfully recommend the *Southern Lutheran* to the families composing our congregations, and that the Ministers connected with this Synod be encouraged to introduce it into our families. Resolved, That a collection be taken immediately after the sermon today for the purpose of sending the *Lutheran* to the soldiers.[85]

The offering produced $163 in the inflated currency of 1864.

When delegates met in Salisbury in May 1862, as a convention of the "Evangelical Lutheran Church in the Confederate States of America," President Nicodemus Aldrich apprised the convention "of the financial condition of our church paper, the *Southern Lutheran,* and its present prospects." It was North Carolina Synod Pastor Joseph Alexander Linn, the secretary of the convention, who shaped the convention's support for its fledgling publication.

> Resolved, That this Convention regard as of primary importance the existence of a church paper, and that we are highly pleased with the literary and religious character of the *Southern Lutheran,* and that we hereby most earnestly request all the pastors in the Confederate States to make an earnest appeal to the benevolent in their respective charges, as also to endeavor to increase the number of subscribers to said paper.

> Resolved, That this Convention truly appreciate the self-denying and arduous efforts of the Editing Committee, in maintaining the existence of the paper to the present time, and hereby receive our most hearty thanks for the labor performed.[86]

On motion of Rev. Daniel Isaiah Dreher of St. James, Concord, the convention asked President Aldrich to dispatch a "circular letter" to the Lutheran pastors in the Confederate States "informing them of the pecuniary wants of the *Southern Lutheran,* with the request that they take immediate action for its maintenance."

When the General Synod South met at Organ, Salisbury, in May 1864, it was clear the body's publishing effort was in financial trouble. President John Bachman alerted the convention that *The Southern Lutheran* "has been saved from being discontinued by the liberality and strenuous efforts of a few of our members," aided most efficiently by South Carolinian Robert G. Chisholm, Esq. Bachman rehearsed the benefits derived from a church paper, and expressed confidence that the convention would "enter into such arrangements" as to insure "that the benefits of *The Southern Lutheran* will be perpetuated." Following the president's report, the convention heard reports from the financial agent for the paper as well as its editorial committee. A convention committee responsible for responding to these reports addressed directly the question of the publication's financial plight.

> Our funds are now exhausted, and our weekly expenses are increased in large ratio, so that unless help comes, and that speedily, its weekly visits to our soldiers and our families must inevitably soon cease. Brethren, this ought not to be - indeed, it must not be - and immediate steps must be taken to provide means for its continuance. The balance sheet shows only $48.40 in hand on May 1st, and two numbers have been issued since, which will bring us, to-day, in debt to the printer to the amount of three or four hundred dollars.[87]

The committee proposed among other things that the convention resolve "That measures be immediately taken to procure funds for the continuation of the *Southern Lutheran.*" The discussion of this proposed resolution culminated in a series of resolutions which first of all called upon clergy and congregations to renew their efforts to secure support for the publication. A resolution singled out for appreciation "the ladies" from Organ and other congregations who, as visitors at the convention, raised six hundred dollars for the support of the paper.

Before the convention adjourned, a lay delegate advanced a proposal to raise five thousand dollars for the paper by securing fifty one-hundred dollar subscriptions. "Twenty names were pledged for $100 each on the spot." It was hoped that by placing before the entire constituency this approach to funding the remaining subscribers could be secured. With the rapidly declining fortunes of the Confederacy, however, the days of the *Southern Lutheran* were numbered. The paper apparently ceased publication in January 1865.

A year later a monthly magazine entitled *The Lutheran Visitor* was launched by a Staunton, Virginia, pastor, Joseph I. Miller. This publication soon attracted more than five hundred subscribers, many of them residing in North Carolina, but the magazine failed to quench the desire on the part of many for a weekly church paper. When the General Synod South met in June 1866, that body declared that such a publication "should be immediately established." An arrangement was worked out whereby the Charlotte pastor, Nicodemus Aldrich, served as publisher of the weekly paper for the General Synod South and Rev. Gotthard D. Bernheim served as editor.

The agreement arrived at by the General Synod, Aldrich, and Bernheim determined the paper's name, size, doctrinal position, and the financial basis for its operation. It also included a proviso to the effect that at the end "of any Synodical year," the General Synod could, if it so desired, "sever all connection" with the publication. In August *The Evangelical Lutheran* began publication, but the publication did not flourish. In May 1867 President T. W. Dosh of the General Synod South suggested to the convention of that body that in the future one editor have entire responsibility for the publication.

The convention's Committee on the President's Report agreed, but urged that "to secure its more extensive circulation, they recommend that the Editor act under the supervision of a committee of publication, whose duty it shall be to consult the desires of the Church of the South in general, in reference to the character of the articles issued in the paper, so as to avoid, as far as practicable, the controverted points of the Church and prevent sectional disputations."

In May 1866 Editor Bernheim had moved from Charlotte, and the following year he asked the Staunton convention of the General Synod South to relieve him of his responsibilities as editor of *The Evangelical Lutheran.* The Committee on Church Literature proposed Rev. A. R. Rude as "our official representative in the editorial management of the paper." It also proposed that the convention enter into an agreement with Pastor Aldrich, an agreement which he drafted and presented to the committee.

Under Aldrich's proposal, he would continue to issue the paper under the same name, provided the General Synod South continue to recognize the paper as its official organ and promote its circulation. He agreed to work with "an associate Editor" who could contribute articles as the representative of the sponsoring body and review all articles by Aldrich which could be construed as "of a doubtfull [sic] character." Aldrich also agreed to make available to his associate the financial records of the paper so as to enable the associate editor to report to the General Synod South "concerning the financial managment, and surplus funds of the paper."[88]

The publication enjoyed but a brief life. Editor Miller of *The Lutheran Visitor* heartily endorsed the new journalistic venture. When Lutherans in the South did not promptly adopt it as their church paper, Miller indicated he was "truly sorry to see so little interest manifested towards sustaining" *The Evangelical Lutheran.* He suspected the problem might be "a lack of confidence in its doctrinal status," indicating that "the ministers in the Va. Synod, and of the Synod of Western Va., are all unswerving advocates of genuine revivals of religion."

When word circulated that *The Evangelical Lutheran* "is opposed to the extension of the Redeemer's kingdom by this means," the Virginia pastors refused to recommend it to the members of their congregations. Miller himself was an advocate of revivals, but he supported *The Evangelical Lutheran* and urged others to do so because he did not believe the paper was really anti-revival.[89] What if *The Evangelical Lutheran* failed? Would southern Lutherans go back to their paper of yesteryear, the *Lutheran Observer*? Miller believed that was impossible:

Are we willing that a paper shall come into our families, weekly, flinging it into our teeth, that some loved one, or brother, or husband, or father, whose blood was freely poured out as a libation to the goddess of Liberty, was *a traitor against God and man*? From the last *Lutheran Observer* we quote one sentence from its Washington correspondent "B," to show you the animus of much of its matter. "As a great Christian government we can afford to be magnanimous, but with the untold sorrows of a *rebellion* which cost billions of money and half a million lives, this *indiscriminate pardon* does not make *treason odious*." We are traitors. And treason must be made *odious,* is the doctrine of our Northern Church papers. Can we as an honest people, who acted during that great crisis, as much, to say the least, with the fear of God before our eyes, as did they, submit to have this charge continually rung in our ears?[90]

The editor's attempt to gain support for southern publications by playing on the sectionalism theme was not a success, at least not in North Carolina. The following year, he noted with consternation an article appearing in the *Lutheran Observer* in which the editors reported that the first two weeks in April had brought an unusual amount of mail from the South, all of it containing subscriptions and the payment in advance for those subscriptions.

"From North Carolina, especially", they wrote, "we have most encouraging proofs of the popularity of the *Observer,* and at various points clubs have been formed, ordering the paper. This affords gratifying proof, that the ancient revival spirit has not died out in the Southern churches, but still glows warmly in the hearts of our Lutheran people."[91]

The editor of *The Lutheran Visitor* quotes this item from the *Observer* in order to take exception to it since it seems to suggest that the Lutheran church papers in the South are not supportive of revivals in religion. Miller insists that both the *Evangelical Lutheran* and *The Lutheran Visitor* are supporters of "genuine revivals."

In retrospect, it seems clear that the *Evangelical Lutheran* "fell victim to the unsettled state of doctrine and practice among its constituents."[92] When it came to the catechism and revivals as approaches to adult church membership, the North Carolina Synod was a house divided.

Some were sure revivals were signs of God at work in the midst of the people, while others were just as convinced that revivalism "had a tendency to divert the mind from the regular Means of Grace as set forth in the Word of God, as well as from a reliance on the promises contained in Divine Revelation, to a dependence on the feelings or emotions, for salvation."[93]

Bernheim's conservative confessionalism which made him an admirer of the newly-created General Council did not sit well with those who were unhappy with the stance embraced by the General Synod South. Aldrich, on the other hand, probably lost the paper some support in both the confessional and the revivalistic camps when he tried to convince readers that one could appropriately support both protracted meetings and strict adherence to the Augsburg Confession.

The delegation from the North Carolina Synod that attended the convention of the General Synod South at Newberry, South Carolina, in 1868 noted that

With one exception the regular business was transacted with great unanimity, and the best feeling prevailed. We regret to state that, in the discussion of the church paper, there was wanting, to some extent, that spirit of christian [sic] love and due regard to the interests of the church which should ever characterize the deliberations of an ecclesiastical organization. A strenuous effort was made to commit the General Synod to the support of a new paper, but it was steadily resisted by the undersigned, as they believed that such action of Synod would involve the Editor of *The Evangelical Lutheran,* a member of this body, in great pecuniary loss, and seriously reflect upon his christian [*sic*] integrity.[94]

As a result of the debate, the General Synod South concluded it could no longer endorse any particular paper as its official organ or any editor as its official spokesperson. The publication of church papers was thus left to "individual enterprise," a decision that spelled the doom of *The Evangelical Lutheran* which needed the endorsement of the General Synod South, and failing to receive it, had to suspend publication in August 1869.

Seminary

A second area of concern that revealed a marked difference of opinion between the North Carolina Synod and the General Synod South was a Lutheran school of theology for the South. Given its size relative to other synods holding membership in the General Synod South and its location between Virginia and South Carolina, two of the other large member synods, the North Carolina Synod Lutherans could not understand why a theological seminary for the general body should not be located on their territory.

Despite three decades of struggle, theological education for Lutherans in the South as represented by the institution at Lexington, South Carolina, had never been a thriving operation.

And like the colleges in the South, it had not fared well during the Civil War. The seminary sponsored by the South Carolina Synod was the only Lutheran school of theology in the South when the conflict broke out, and there were only three students enrolled. They promptly enlisted in the army and before the war ended two of them had been killed.[95] The seminary closed during the second year of the war, and in June, 1866, it was still without a student body.

It appeared that, for the foreseeable future, one seminary would be more than adequate to serve the entire Lutheran church in the South. As Pastor Smeltzer stated in 1866: "One Theological Seminary, located in some central position, having an efficient faculty, is all that the Lutheran Church needs, or will need for years to come. Such a Seminary the Synods of the General Synod [South] could have, and successfully maintain. Colleges may spring up wherever they can be supported, but we need but one Seminary, and that should be of the highest order."[96]

The constitution adopted in revised form in 1866 called for the General Synod South to "devise plans for seminaries of education and missionary operations." (Article V, Section 4). The North Carolina Synod voted "to heartily cooperate with the General Synod in the establishment of a first class Theological Seminary, to be under the immediate control of the General Synod."[97]

The following spring there were significant new developments with regard to funding the seminary. The president of the General Synod South wrote to the clergy and congregations related to the general body:

Dear Brethren:- It is hereby recommended, that the Sabbath nearest to the 31st of October ensuing, be observed, by appropriate religious exercises, as the Seventh Jubilee of the glorious Reformation inaugurated by Doctor Martin Luther. It is suggested that collections be taken in aid of the Educational Institutions of the Church. These collections can be reported to the several District Synods, and appropriated as said Synods may direct. In the application of the funds thus collected, the claims of the General Synod's Theological Seminary should be kept prominently in view.[98]

The Editor of *The Evangelical Lutheran* was strongly supportive of the idea of a special appeal in connection with the anniversary of the Reformation, and indicated he was sure President Rothrock's recommendations would be followed "as far as the impoverished condition of our Church will admit." Editor Aldrich went on, however, to express concern about two aspects of the special observance.

First of all, it seemed to him unfortunate that the call was for an observance on a single Sunday: "An occasion of such importance as the release of the human mind from the fetters of servile priest-craft and gloomy superstition, and its induction into the glorious light and liberty of a pure Gospel and a more spiritual faith, should call forth a more extensive demonstration than that embraced in a single Sabbath."[99]

It seemed to him that something as significant as the 350th anniversary of the Reformation should provide the church with a year-long celebration.

Aldrich was also concerned about reports he had received concerning developments in Virginia. The Virginia Synod had voted to participate in the special observance called for by the General Synod South and elected to devote the offerings they received as a part of the observance to the support of the theological seminary. That, of course, was quite acceptable to the editor of *The Evangelical Lutheran,* but the Synod had gone on to stipulate that the offerings were to go to the seminary "only on condition that it is located within her bounds." For a single synod to presume to dictate the location of the general body's school of theology seemed to Aldrich a betrayal of the spirit of cooperation developing among the synods in the South. Surely, he argued, the General Synod South

> should be allowed to consider the interests of the whole Church and locate the Seminary where ever, in her judgment, those interests would be most widely promoted, without the least regard to synodical preferences. If the preferences of the brethren composing the Synod of South Carolina were consulted, they doubtless would retain the Seminary within their bounds, but considering only the welfare of the whole church they have said nothing about location, but left that matter to the determination of the General Synod, and this should be the action of all our Synods.[100]

Some North Carolina congregations required little prodding to insure their participation in the Jubilee celebration. On the second Sunday in December, St. John's, Concord, responded to the special occasion by gathering an offering of $170 to be devoted to the "erection and endowment of a Theological Seminary in the South."[101] The following spring, in his role as president of the North Carolina Synod, Nicodemus Aldrich noted in his report to the convention that Lutherans in the United States and abroad were celebrating the 350th anniversary of the Reformation. He acknowledged that some North Carolina congregations had already recognized this significant anniversary, but commented that "it would be well if some systematic plan could now be proposed which would result in practical benefit to our Synod and the Church at large."[102]

The Committee on the President's Report recommended, and the convention agreed, that clergy who had not "lifted a collection" in connection with the celebration of the "Jubilee of the Reformation" be "required so to do as early as practicable and forward the amount to the Treasurer of Synod. We further recommend that a joint effort be made by the brethren at such time within the year as they may think most suitable to collect funds for such [a] specific Church enterprise as may be thought most important in the judgment of this Synod."[103]

In the spring of 1868, the General Synod South met in Newberry, South Carolina, where the seminary was located. There the North Carolina Synod delegation learned that its sister synod to the South had transfered "its Seminary to the care and supervision of the General Synod, giving it the power to change its locality, &c., to suit the present emergency of the Church, provided the individuality of the Theo. Seminary of South Carolina be perpetuated, and the alumni not deprived of their Alma Mater."[104]

On learning that the issue of site was yet to be determined, the North Carolina Synod named the Rev. G. D. Bernheim agent in the state of North Carolina to obtain offers for the location of the new theological seminary. Other synods also designated agents to prepare proposals from their several states as all strove to demonstrate their ability to provide for the seminary in a way that was "tangible and efficient."[105]

In a unilateral move, perhaps designed to influence the general synod's selection, President L. A. Bikle challenged his North Carolina Synod to start its own seminary. In the spring of 1869, he announced that

> The establishment of a Theological Seminary within the bounds of this body, temporarily at least, has become an absolute necessity. The duty will devolve upon us to make some provision for the education of our theological students at home, as the pressing wants and limited resources of Synod will prevent us from sending them either North or South to be educated. I recommend that, for the present, a Theological Department be created in N. C. College, and that the Ministers of this Synod, residing in Mt. Pleasant, be constituted a Faculty to superintend and perform, free of charge, the duties of said Department.[106]

The Committee on the President's Report called on the convention to adopt the president's recommendation and asked the board of trustees of North Carolina College for permission "to use temporarily, two lecture rooms in the North building of said College" for the synod's seminary.[107] Its recommendations were adopted.

Concordia Synod

During the Civil War the Virginia pastors and congregations associated with the Tennessee Synod had been unable to attend the synodical conventions. The Virginia Conference of the Tennessee Synod, which in 1856 began holding periodic meetings, held its first post-war convention at Rader's Church at Timberville, Virginia, in October 1865.

The convention proceeded in routine fashion, information being gathered about the state of the churches, persons being licensed to serve congregations, sad note being taken of the fact that two sons of the conference who had been studying theology, Henry Miller and Martin Luther Wetzel, had been killed in the recent conflict.

Then, perhaps inspired by the example of the Holston Synod, a committee without fanfare or warning cast "a firebrand" into the deliberations.[108]   The committee proposed that the conference schedule a meeting for the following May at which time the conference would be made into a synod. There was no organized opposition to the surprise move, so the resolution was adopted, although one pastor asked that his negative vote be recorded.

When the scheduled meeting was held the following May, it was well attended, and enthusiasm for transforming the conference into a synod seemed to be running high. It was decided to petition the Tennessee Synod for permission to continue and then hold a follow-up convention in November.

In October, the Tennessee Synod, meeting at Beck's, Lexington, considered the request of its Virginia Conference and "gave its unanimous, though reluctant, consent to the venture."[109]   The synod indicated that when the new body organized itself, pastors holding membership in the Tennessee Synod would be granted "an honorable dismission" so they could unite with it.

The following month the Virginia Conference met. On receiving a report of the synod's action, the conference adopted a proposed constitution, declared itself to be the Evangelical Lutheran Concordia Synod of Virginia, and set the date for its first convention in October 1867.

It seems probable that Pastor Socrates Henkel was not present at Beck's when the Tennessee Synod approved the transforming of the Virginia Conference into a synod. He was the person who, when the issue was first raised at the 1865 convention, asked that his negative vote be recorded. During the eleven months from the constituting convention to the convening of the first regular convention in October 1867, he seems to have persuaded most of the new synod's pastors and congregations that it would be better to revert to their earlier status as a conference.

At any rate, when the appointed time came for the first regular convention of the Concordia Synod, only three pastors and their lay delegates appeared. Rev. Henry Wetzel was all for classifying the new synod as aborted and going home. However, Pastors George Schmucker and James E. Senecker persuaded him to remain and participate in the convention.

The Tennessee Synod later declared the effort a failure, and despite the request of the pastors involved, refused for several years to dismiss them to create the Concordia Synod. In 1871 President Alfred J. Fox of the Tennessee Synod reminded the delegates that three of "their" pastors had "for some time, neglected to attend the Annual Conventions of this Synod, and in a very obstinate and irregular manner insist upon being recognized as a separate Synod, and annually assemble and transact business."[110]   A committee was created "to consider this vexed affair." While still insisting that the action of the Virginia Synod pastors who organized the Concordia Synod was "irregular and schismatic," the Tennessee Synod decided it was the better part of wisdom to remove their names from its rolls.

For a decade the little synod struggled to survive, but in 1877 it capitulated to reality and asked to be received as a conference of the Joint Synod of Ohio.[111]

Meanwhile, the majority of the potential members of the Concordia Synod returned to their earlier status as members of the resuscitated Virginia Conference of the Tennessee Synod.

Tennessee and North Carolina Synods

The Tennessee Synod was not without interest in sharing with other Lutherans in the South the benefits of membership in a larger Lutheran fellowship. In 1867 it dispatched Dr. Alfred J. Fox to the convention of the General Synod South in Staunton, Virginia. A committee consisting of A. R. Rude, David Frederick Bittle and T. W. Dosh was named to confer with this "commissioner" from the Tennessee Synod. The committee noted that their interview with Fox "afforded satisfactory evidence of the truly Christian and Lutheran character of the Synod" which he represented. In an effort to allay any fears the Tennessee Synod might have regarding the doctrinal orthodoxy of the General Synod South, the committee proposed and the convention adopted the following:

> I. Resolved, That we will cordially receive said Synod as an integral part of this body, on the truly Lutheran basis which we have adopted, and in accordance with which we feel bound as an ecclesiastical body to withhold our sanction or imprimatur from any religious publication, of whatever form, which shall inculcate principles opposed to the doctrine of the Augsburg Confession as construed and defended by our Church, in her symbolical writings.
>
> II. Resolved, That we feel in like manner bound to appoint or employ no professor in our theological schools who shall teach doctrines at variance with our time-honored Confession.[112]

Fox was favorably impressed with his visit and communicated to the convention of the Tennessee Synod his positive impressions along with the action of the General Synod South. As was often the case at conventions of the Tennessee Synod held in South Carolina, the attendance was poor at the September 1867 convention, and it was decided to defer action on the significant issue of uniting with the General Synod South until the following year.[113] A special committee consisting of Pastors Jesse R. Peterson, Polycarp Cyprian Henkel and Dr. Fox and Laymen Ambrose Costner, Esq., and M. L. Cline was asked to study the matter and present their report at the convention at Salem, Lincolnton.

The committee indicated at the 1868 convention that it had not had sufficient time to study the issue and, meanwhile, Fox, who had become president, had presented the synod with a proposal that to some seemed even more promising than uniting with the General Synod South. Recognizing that the Tennessee Synod had spawned several synods including the Tennessee Synod, Reorganized, the Holston Synod, and, more recently, the Concordia Synod, President Fox proposed that all these former members of the Tennessee Synod be invited to unite with the Tennessee Synod in a joint synod arrangement. Through such an approach, each body would become a district synod within the joint synod which would serve as the umbrella organization.

A committee consisting of Pastors Henkel, Fox and Timothy Moser and Laymen Ambrose Costner, Esq., and F. L. Herman of Catawba County was asked to explore this proposal. Since the convention itself did not provide adequate time for a full exploration of the proposal, it was decided that in the interim between conventions Fox should pursue the matter with the Holston Synod to determine its interest.

The following year, the Tennessee Synod continued its committee on the possibility of uniting with the General Synod South. But it asked that the group exploring the possibility of transforming the Tennessee Synod into a joint synod move at once to arrange for "a free conference" between the Tennessee and Holston synods on the subject, said conference to be held at Grace, Newton, as early as possible after the adjournment of the convention of the Tennessee Synod.

Meanwhile, the Tennessee Synod also moved to heal an old breach that occurred in 1820. In 1868 President Aldrich of the North Carolina Synod included these comments in his annual report to the synod.

> My residence in Charlotte has furnished frequent opportunities for interviews with our brethren of the Tennessee Synod, in which the disposition to lose sight of old issues was quite manifest. We recommend that a corresponding delegate be elected to represent this Synod at the next annual convention of that body, to convey our friendly and christian [sic] greetings to them as brethren of the same household of faith, and to request that a delegate be appointed in turn to meet with this Synod at its next convention.[114]

The North Carolina Synod clearly considered this a matter of great importance. It not only approved the proposal but named its president, Prof. Louis Albert Bikle, to be its delegate, and asked its recording secretary, Pastor Aldrich, to serve as Bikle's alternate. As it turned out, Aldrich actually represented the North Carolina Synod at the next convention of the Tennessee Synod. Noting the action of the North Carolina Synod and the presence of Aldrich, a committee at the convention of the Tennessee Synod commented, "We heartily reciprocate the fraternal feelings of these brethren, and welcome the presence of Rev. Mr. Aldrich among us."[115]

In response to a presentation by Aldrich, the convention named Rev. John M. Smith to represent them at the 1869 convention of the North Carolina Synod. This formal exchange of representatives was frequently supplemented by pastors of one body attending sessions of the other body when the convention was held in their proximity.

Education

In the North Carolina Synod during this period, attention turned to synodical ownership of a second school in Mt. Pleasant, a school for girls. The school, Mt. Pleasant Female Seminary, became affiliated with the synod as a result of events set in motion a decade earlier, in 1858.

L. C. Groseclose, the synod president at that time, challenged the synod to convert its Western Carolina Male Academy to a college and at the same time laid before the convention another challenge: "Not only do we need a college for the thorough education of the sons, but we need, and ere long must have, a college to educate the daughters of the church. No nation or people can be what they should be without female education. If education is, for a time, to be exclusively confined to either sex, let the females have the preference."[116]

The president went on to explain that while "an ignorant, coarse-bred, uneducated mother" could not be expected to rear "refined and intelligent children," well-educated mothers could be counted on to "educate their children."

The proposal to educate young women was not a novel idea in North Carolina.

As early as 1802, Salem Boarding School was created by the Moravians and provided an excellent educational program for young women. The Methodists established Greensboro Female College in 1838, and just four years later the Episcopalians founded St. Mary's in Raleigh. New Garden Boarding School (Guilford College), established by the Society of Friends in the 1830s, also admitted women.[117]

While the challenge issued to the North Carolina Synod by Groseclose did not immediately produce a college for women, Susan Biglow Bittle, the wife of President D. H. Bittle of North Carolina College, opened in Mt. Pleasant a private school for young women in 1859. The catalog for North Carolina College reported that Mt. Pleasant Female Seminary was "now in successful operation under Prof. G. F. Schaefer": "Its seclusion is altogether favorable to study, and the student is here preserved from those allurements of vice and extravagance that too generally beset Schools in more public places. By act of the Legislature, all gambling, exhibitions of an immoral tendency, juggling, and the sale of spirituous liquors, are prohibited under a heavy penalty within three miles of the College."[118]

Mrs. Bittle gave oversight to the school until she and her husband removed to Texas in the first year of the war.

In 1866 Pastor G. D. Bernheim purchased the assets of the female seminary. In September of that year the school re-opened with Bernheim as principal and his wife, Elizabeth Clayton Bernheim, serving as assistant principal. An advertisement for the school announced its "advantages" as

> Economy - The Seminary is located in an agricultural and rural community, where the price of boarding is moderate, and expensive dress is not required. Health - Pure air, good water, and where the pupils will not be so closely confined as in city life. A Thorough Education - The pupils of this Seminary will not be advanced to the higher branches of learning, before they are thoroughly acquainted with those studies which are of greater service to them in their every day duties and requirements of life.- Besides, as Rev. mr. [sic] Bernheim and lady have been long engaged as instructors of young ladies in the city of Charleston, S.C., they bring into this Seminary all the benefits of their experience.
> Mount Pleasant is situated nine miles east of Concord, the nearest Railroad station on the North Carolina Railroad, midway between Charlotte and Salisbury, where pupils can obtain public conveyances to take them to the Seminary.
> *******
> The patrons of the Seminary may be assured that the moral and religious training of its pupils will be considered a matter of primary importance.[119]

Having purchased the school and operating it for several years, Bernheim in 1868 offered it to the North Carolina Synod for the same price he had paid: two thousand dollars. Further, he offered to raise for the synod the funds necessary to make the purchase.

The synod reflected on the offer, concluded that it was "highly important to the prosperity of our Church, that this Synod have under its supervision and control a first class Female Seminary," and accepted the offer.[120]

Bernheim promptly fulfilled his part of the bargain, and the North Carolina Synod found itself sponsoring institutions of higher learning for both young men and young women.

Impact on Church

The Lutheran church in the South shared the region's difficulties in the Reconstruction Era. Immediately after the war, the North Carolina Synod was distressed to discover that several of its congregations were so filled with internal strife and alienation "that they no longer agree upon any thing connected with the peace and prosperity of Zion."[121] The president of the synod noted that these difficulties focused "upon questions growing chiefly out of the war," and usually ended up with one party or the other "against their pastor."

The places used for worship by a number of congregations were damaged or fell into serious disrepair during the war years. Other facilities were actually abused in the course of the conflict. President Aldrich noted in his 1868 report to the synod that St. Paul's, Wilmington, had been used as a hospital both during and after the war, "and on account of its shameful abuse by the parties who last occupied it, was rendered unfit for religious services."[122]

Both the North Carolina and Tennessee synods were plagued throughout their early years by a perennial shortage of clergy. The war period with its interruption of the educational programs of a number of candidates and its demands for chaplains aggravated the shortage. And in the decade following the war several respected pastors of the North Carolina Synod elected to join the migration north; Levi C. Groseclose and Nicodemus Aldrich to Illinois; William Alexander Julian to the Franckean Synod in New York; John L. Smithdeal and John Daniel Scheck to the Eastern Pennsylvania Synod; John S. Heilig, John H. Mengert and Philip Melanchthon Bikle to the Maryland Synod; and Jacob Brown Anthony to the Central Pennsylvania Synod.

Leaders of the Tennesseee Synod expressed their regret that a number of their clergy "have not felt it their duty to remain and labor" for the welfare of their synod, but "have gone where the wants of the church were not so pressing as among ourselves or might have been more easily supplied."[123]

While a number of Lutheran clergy left North Carolina after the war, there were also clergy moving into the synod. From Georgia came John D. Bowles; from South Carolina came Adam David Luther Moser; from the Hartwick Synod in New York came Philip A. Strobel; from the Eastern Pennsylvania Synod Louis W. Heydenreich; from Virginia came John B. Davis, David Melanchthon Henkel and Jacob Grabenstein Neiffer; from the Southwestern Virginia Synod came William E. Hubbert; and from the Florida Conference of the Methodist Episcopal Church came Charles Herman Bernheim.[124]

Sobering as was the shortage of clergy, the economic situation confronting the Lutheran church in the South, and the unsettled social situation following the Civil War, not all was gloomy. For those who measured the vitality of the church in terms of conversion experiences, there was hope in the fact that "revivals of religion now and then occur," suggesting that God had not deserted His people entirely. At St. John's, Concord, Pastor Groseclose launched a protracted meeting in December, 1867, that ran for twenty-two days, involved nine clergy, and the preaching of forty-four sermons. The church records note that "There were in all about 70 conversions, nearly all of whom were members of the church."[125] In commenting on a revival in Athens, Georgia, in which the Methodists, Baptists and Presbyterians cooperated and which numbered "by the several hundred" its converts, a Lutheran editor was moved to pray,

We trust our "Chastening is yielding the peaceable fruits of righteousness." God grant, that our whole section, so heavily scourged, may receive a new baptism from the Holy Ghost.[126]

Church offerings were modest, but many persons seemed willing to give what they could. As early as 1867 the treasurer of the North Carolina Synod could report receipts of nearly $130 from more than thirty synodical congregations. In 1875, the synod's pastors reported their congregations had local expenses in excess of twenty-one hundred dollars; "general" expenses of more than nine hundred dollars; and the synod itself received in excess of two hundred dollars.[127] Most of the institutions created by the Lutheran church in the South prior to the war were again in operation and others were "being opened under hopeful prospects." Surely, "a brighter day" was dawning. ✝

Mt. Pleasant Female Seminary
Founded 1859

L. A. Bikle
President, North Carolina Synod
1867-68

W. A. Julian
President, North Carolina Synod
1868-69

Alfred J. Fox
President, Tennessee Synod
1866-67

Macedonia, Burlington
Organized 1869

CHAPTER VII

FROM SERVANT TO LEADER (1870-1902)

As the horror of the Civil War and the pathos of Reconstruction passed, the North Carolina Synod turned with renewed seriousness to the needs of the synod and its congregations. New efforts were directed to clarifying distinctive Lutheran practices, educating ministers, providing pastoral leadership for congregations, developing missions, and aiding disabled pastors. Internal enrichment was the theme, while external concerns such as synodical alignments were placed, for the most part, on hold. The period, however, began and ended on intersynodical relationship notes: ushering in the period was the dissolution of one relationship in 1871; closing the period was the 1903 renewal of interest in a restored relationship.

The environment of the period was one of a region and state which approached the close of the century as it began the century; economically, socially, and politically, North Carolina was a rural state. At mid-century less than three percent of the population could be considered urban and only the port city of Wilmington claimed as many as five thousand inhabitants. While the state could not boast a business center to compete with Richmond or Charleston, growth was taking place. Between 1860 and 1900, the population doubled to almost two million. And in the two decades following 1886, nearly two hundred cotton mills were built, drawing more than 150,000 residents off the farms and into towns and villages to work in mills.

NORTH CAROLINA SYNOD PRESIDENTS

1870-71	Whitson Kimball	1882-84	S. T. Hallman
1871-72	Samuel Rothrock	1884-85	J. A. Linn
1872-73	W. H. Cone	1885-86	William A. Lutz
1873-74	J. D. Bowles	1886-90	F. W. E. Peschau
1874-76	Samuel Rothrock	1890-94	George H. Cox
1876-78	L. A. Bikle	1894-96	B. S. Brown
1878-79	G. D. Bernheim	1896-98	V. R. Stickley
1879-80	L. A. Bikle	1898-00	C. A. Rose
1880-81	Samuel Rothrock	1900-02	Charles B. Miller
1881-82	V. R. Stickley	1902-04	R. C. Holland

Focusing on the past and the Civil War did not prove detrimental to religion. Renewed reflection on the war provided an occasion for recognizing that honor could be triumphant even, perhaps especially, when military victory proved impossible. The reflection strengthened the conviction that spiritual goals, rather than material ones, were the only ones really worth pursuing. At the same time, the South, as well as other parts of the nation, became increasingly concerned with the theme of national reconciliation. The theme became prominent in politics, in literature, and in religion.

North Carolina Synod Lutherans in 1870 were impatient to see the General Synod South move decisively on the question of a theological seminary, and they were not the only ones who were discouraged with the slow progress. When delegates to the convention of the General Synod South gathered in Winchester, Virginia, in June 1870, they heard the president of that organization, Rev. David McConaughy Gilbert, declare that many had been looking forward to this convention "as promising to be of greater importance than any we have yet held." The president indicated to the delegates that,

NORTH CAROLINA SYNOD CONVENTION SITES

1870	Lutheran Chapel, Rowan County	1887	St. Michael's, Iredell County
1871	Pilgrim, Davidson County	1888	St. James, Concord
1872	Organ, Rowan County	1889	St. John's, Cabarrus County
1873	St. Paul's, Rowan County	1890	St. John's, Salisbury
1874	St. Paul's, Wilmington	1891	St. Enoch, Enochville
1875	St. John's, Cabarrus County	1892	St. Paul's, Rowan County
1876	St. Enoch, Rowan County	1893	Lutheran Chapel, China Grove
1877	St. Peter's, Rowan County	1894	Organ, Rowan County
1878	Friedens, Guilford County	1895	St. Michael's, Iredell County
1879	Bethel, Stanly County	1896	St. James, Concord
1880	Holy Trinity, Mt. Pleasant	1897	St. John's, Cabarrus County
1881	Sandy Creek, Davidson County	1898	Macedonia, Burlington
1882	St. James, Concord	1899	St. John's, Salisbury
1883	St. Stephens, Cabarrus County	1900	First, Albemarle
1884	Ebenezer, Rowan County	1901	Friedens, Gibsonville
1885	Bethel, Rowan County	1902	St. James, Concord
1886	Union, Rowan County		

One of the first things to claim your consideration will be the question, either of the entire abandonment of, or the adoption and vigorous prosecution of proper measures to establish among us, a Seminary for the preparation of Candidates for the Gospel Ministry. It seems as if we had hitherto been only dallying with that subject; just doing enough to make a show of having such an enterprise in hand, but we owe it to ourselves, and to the Church at large, now, to have done forever with the procrastinating spirit which has characterized much of our legislation in this matter, and to say openly whether we really want and intend to have such an institution or not.[1]

A special committee charged with presenting to the convention a plan for the seminary began its report on Saturday morning, but the issue proved divisive and had to be "laid over until the afternoon session." The "considerable discussion" on Saturday afternoon again failed to settle the matter.

On Monday the matter was finally resolved, but not to the satisfaction of the North Carolina delegation. Charlotte, Concord and Lincolnton had been proposed to the general body as possible sites for its theological seminary. The General Synod South decided against these sites, but selected instead, for a time, Mt. Pleasant.

The convention, however, no sooner arrived at this decision than a motion to reconsider the issue was introduced and prevailed. The reconsideration resulted in the school of theology being awarded to Columbia, South Carolina. The two South Carolina pastors, A. R. Rude and J. P. Smeltzer, who were selected as the faculty for the school in 1867, were re-elected to that role.[2]

But two years later, Synod President Abel J. Brown saw little progress:

> The subject of a Theological Seminary has . . . more or less engaged the attention of our General Synod at all our meetings. At its last session, after long discussion, and a full and free interchange of opinions, it was determined to locate the Seminary at Columbia, S. C. The Board of Directors elected a Professor of Theology, made provisions for Assistant Professors, should the interests of the Seminary require them, and proposed a plan for raising funds to carry on successfully its operations. But, for reasons which I shall not attempt to enumerate, comparatively nothing important has resulted from that action.[3]

TENNESSEE SYNOD PRESIDENTS

1870-71	A. J. Fox	1887-88	J. S. Koiner
1871-72	S. Henkel	1888-89	J. C. Moser
1872-73	A. J. Fox	1889-90	A. L. Crouse
1873-74	J. M. Smith	1890-91	W. P. Cline
1874-75	L. A. Fox	1891-92	J. Paul Stirewalt
1875-76	J. R. Peterson	1892-93	A. L. Crouse
1876-78	S. Henkel	1893-94	I. Conder
1878-79	P. C. Henkel	1894-95	J. F. Moser
1879-80	J. R. Peterson	1895-96	P. C. Wike
1880-81	S. Henkel	1896-97	John N. Stirewalt
1881-82	A. J. Fox	1897-98	J. C. Moser
1882-83	S. Henkel	1898-99	J. P. Stirewalt
1883-84	J. R. Peterson	1899-00	E. H. Kohn
1884-85	C. H. Bernheim	1900-01	J. C. Moser
1885-86	J. M. Smith	1901-02	W. A. Deaton
1886-87	R. A. Yoder	1902-03	A. R. Beck

Faculty could not be employed and facilities for the school could not be purchased until funds were made available, and they had not been secured in sufficient quantities to make either feasible. Only one student had enrolled for theological studies, and, fearful lest he himself prove an obstacle to the success of the school, Pastor Anders R. Rude resigned his professorship. Brown confessed that, "under existing circumstances," it seemed to him "exceedingly difficult, if not impossible, to attain sufficient unanimity of views and concert of action to establish such a Seminary as would fully meet our wants and be a blessing and an honor to the Church."[4]

In the same year of 1872, the General Synod South decided to move the seminary to Salem, Virginia, but North Carolina by then had disassociated itself from the general synod and declined to recommend the Virginia institution.

Instead, North Carolina renewed efforts in 1873 to establish its own seminary, this time by resolving to create a twelve-thousand-dollar endowment fund for the proposed institution. All ministers were authorized to act as agents and collect funds for the project.[5] But a convention inquiry about progress the following year revealed that no funds had been raised.

TENNESSEE SYNOD CONVENTION SITES

1870 St. Peter's, Lexington County, South Carolina
1871 Philadelphia, Gaston County
1872 Rader's, Rockingham County, Virginia
1873 Zion's, Lexington County, South Carolina
1874 Pilgrim, Lexington
1875 Mt. Calvary, Page County, Virginia
1876 St. John's, Lexington County, South Carolina
1877 Coble's, Guilford County
1878 St. Matthew's, Shenandoah County, Virginia
1879 St. James, Lexington County, South Carolina
1880 St. Peter's, Catawba County
1881 Emmanuel, New Market, Virginia
1882 St. Jacob's, Lexington County, South Carolina
1883 Concordia College, Conover
1884 St. Mary's, Shenandoah, Virginia
1885 St. Peter's-Meetze's, Lexington County, South Carolina
1886 College Chapel, Dallas
1887 Bethlehem, Augusta County, Virginia
1888 St. Peter's, Lexington County, South Carolina
1889 Holly Grove, Ilex
1890 Mt. Calvary, Stony Man, Virginia; St. James, Catawba County
1891 St. Paul's, Lexington County, South Carolina
1892 Holy Trinity, Hickory
1893 Emmanuel, New Market, Virginia
1894 St. John's, Lexington County, South Carolina
1895 St. Andrew's, Hickory
1896 St. Matthew's, Tom's Brook, Virginia
1897 Mt. Tabor, New Brookland, South Carolina
1898 Daniel's, Lincolnton
1899 Solomon's, Forestville, Virginia
1900 Cedar Grove, Lexington County, South Carolina
1901 Lutheran Chapel, Gaston County
1902 Rader's, Rockingham County, Virginia

The synod was called on to reconsider its seminary arrangement ten years later, in 1883. When the general synod that year voted to close the Salem seminary, the South Carolina Synod announced its intention to take over the seminary and operate it at Newberry. It asked the North Carolina Synod to assist in the undertaking by providing some of the support for a professor. But North Carolina declined the request, preferring instead to recommend that its students obtain their theological education at either Philadelphia or Gettysburg.[6]

Later, when the general synod's seminary was reopened, this time near Charleston, South Carolina, the North Carolina Synod assumed proportionate financial support and steered its students toward it. In the late 1890s, when the seminary enrollment ranged from six to ten, there was usually one student each from the North Carolina and Tennessee synods. In the 1901-02 session, the seminary enrolled fifteen students, four of them from the North Carolina Synod.

The General Synod South's seminary decision, coupled with its earlier publication decisions, helped to cool the North Carolina Synod's ardor for the intersynodical organization it helped to form. When the delegates of the North Carolina Synod made their report to their colleagues in North Carolina, they observed that at the Winchester sessions "nothing of special interest was transacted" and they were not impressed with

> the efficiency of the General Synod. There seems to be a disposition on the part of several District Synods to propose and adopt important measures for selfish purposes, and not for the general welfare of our church, South. They apparently forget that said body is a *general* body, organized to legislate for the benefit of the whole church, and not for the promotion of private or local interests. Such "clannishness" if continued, it must be evident to every reflecting mind, will not only impair the future usefulness of the General Synod, but eventually prove its destruction.
>
> Will it not be well to inquire at this time, what advantage to the church will it be to continue in connection with a body, which has, in all probability, served its day?[7]

The convention found the views of their delegation persuasive and, as the secretary of synod noted, the delegation's "report was *unanimously* adopted."

Even as it questioned the long-term usefulness of the General Synod South, the North Carolina Synod harbored a concern for Lutheran unity. It was no longer a question of holding membership in the General Synod South or the General Synod North. Another option emerged.

In 1864 growing frustration with the General Synod North and its leadership as personified in Prof. Samuel Simon Schmucker of Gettysburg Seminary led to the creation by the Pennsylvania ministerium of a rival seminary in Philadelphia. When the General Synod North met at Fort Wayne, Indiana, in 1866, it refused to seat the delegation from the Pennsylvania ministerium. The action led to a call "to all synods which confess the Unaltered Augsburg Confession" to send representatives to Reading, Pennsylvania, in December "for the purpose of organizing a new general body upon distinctively Lutheran principles." Thirteen synods responded to the call, and The General Council of the Lutheran Church in North America was established the following year with twelve member synods.

So, as the North Carolina Synod's convention at Lutheran Chapel, China Grove, in August 1870 wrestled with the issue of broader affiliation, the options were General Synod South, General Synod North and General Council.[8] Without committing itself to a particular organization the North Carolina Synod

> Resolved, That . . . the time has come when those sections of our Church, one in faith and practice, should be connected in one General body.

Resolved, That our delegates to the next meeting of our Southern General Synod be instructed to present the above resolution for the action of that body.[9]

When the Tennessee Synod met in early November, the Committee on Letters noted that several pastors unable to attend the convention had written in to ask that they be excused and to express themselves on the question of a possible merger. Jacob Killian favored "a union with the North Carolina Synod, provided it can be done upon a safe foundation." Irenaeus Conder found himself "somewhat favorable to a union with the General Synod South." Christian Moretz "expresses himself favorable to a union with some central Southern body," while Henry Goodman was "unfavorable to a union with any other body."[10] A committee reviewing the minutes of other Lutheran bodies had nothing positive to say on perusing the minutes of the General Synod and of the General Synod South.

But the minutes of the first convention of the General Council evoked an enthusiastic response. This body "has planted itself firmly upon the unaltered Augsburg Confession, and interprets it in the light of the other Symbolical Books and confessional writings. We regard its organization, under such favorable auspices, as prophetic of a brighter day for the Church in this country. True to the Confessions, its energy and talents and resources must, we firmly believe, uproot the old leaven of unsoundness and fanaticism, and gather into itself the whole of the Lutheran church in America united in one common faith and uniform practice. May the time soon come!"[11]

The committee earlier created by the Tennessee Synod to study the feasibility of uniting with the General Synod South at last presented its report. They indicated that while their extended study of the question had revealed "many things..., which would make such union desirable, we have also found many other things, which seem, to your committee, to indicate that union with that ecclesiastical body is, at present, of such doubtful propriety, that we are wholly unprepared to recommend such a connection and, therefore, most respectfully ask, that your committee be excused from further consideration of this matter."[12]

The convention adopted the report and discharged the committee.

The North Carolina Synod's 1870 convention at China Grove revealed a fading interest in general synod affiliation but demonstrated a renewed interest in relations with the Tennessee Synod. In his report, President Whitson Kimball observed:

> Our Synod is slowly, but gradually, and steadily improving; becoming more doctrinal and uniform in her system of worship. We anticipate with gratitude the day when the distinctive characteristics of the Lutheran Church will be unfurled in every congregation within the bounds of this Synod.
>
> The efforts to unite the Synods of North Carolina and Tennessee have been blessed, and we believe that the long wished for, and much desired period is now at hand, when these two bodies will unite upon the great doctrines of the Lutheran Church; when we will regard each other in good faith, and work together harmoniously, for the glory of God, the advancement of Christ's Kingdom, and the salvation of souls.[13]

A reunion of the North Carolina and Tennessee synods seemed a more appropriate objective than trying to work within the framework of the General Synod South.

To foster the goal of unity, the North Carolina Synod named a committee of five to meet and work with a like committee from the Tennessee Synod in formulating a plan for reuniting the two bodies. The North Carolina Synod delegation included Pastors Levi C. Groseclose, Nicodemus Aldrich, and Simeon Scherer, along with Capt. J. A. Fisher and Dr. Paul A. Sifford. The pastoral representatives of the Tennessee Synod were Dr. Alfred J. Fox, John M. Smith and Timothy Moser, serving with lay representatives Col. Alexander Conrad of Pilgrim, Lexington, and Ambrose Costner, Esq., of Salem, Lincolnton. Meeting in Mt. Pleasant on April 25, 1871, the committees formed a joint committee or conference, designated Fox as their presiding officer, and selected Aldrich as secretary.

When the discussion of proposed theses began the following day, the discussion was "animated" but "there was not the slightest feeling of asperity manifested, between the members of the two Synods." As it turned out, the differences in theological perspective were not between the North Carolina Synod delegation and the Tennessee Synod delegation but within the ranks of the North Carolina Synod delegation. One of the North Carolina Synod pastors and the two laymen found themselves entirely in agreement with the Tennessee Synod proposals, but the other two North Carolina Synod pastors were not happy with the wording of two of the propositions advanced by Tennessee. Fox reported to the Tennessee Synod convention at Philadelphia, Dallas, in October that the division within the North Carolina Synod delegation made it unnecessary for the Tennessee Synod representatives to argue for their point of view: "As there were two parties among them - one fully representing the views of our Synod, and the other the opposite views; our committee was greatly relieved in the discussions, having little more to do than to listen to their discussions."[14]

Finally, "a few very slight verbal alterations in the two propositions to which exception was taken" permitted the conference to adopt the proposed Basis of Union unanimously.

The document was printed as a circular, and 250 copies were made available to each synod for study and action. In two parts, the Basis included a section devoted largely to the confessional stand on which there was agreement but which also included statements on worship, catechization and discipline. The second section provided succinct statements on a variety of points of doctrine.[15]

The North Carolina Synod meeting at Pilgrim, Lexington, in August 1871 voted to "heartily endorse and adopt" the Basis, while also agreeing to withdraw from the General Synod South. Fox, who attended the convention as the representative of the Tennessee Synod, noted that consideration of the Basis of Union "elicited some animated discussion," but he did not hesitate to commend the majority of members of the North Carolina Synod as thoroughly Lutheran.

> From all that I could learn, from private interviews, with various of its ministers, and from their public discussions, I am fully convinced that a majority of its members are decidedly Lutheran in theory and practice - and a few of them may be regarded somewhat ultra. A few, however, seem still to be anxious to retain some of the un-Lutheran customs, which unhappily found their way into the Synod, in days when she, like too many other Lutheran Synods in this country, was not as well informed and watchful in these things as she should have been. I am encouraged to believe, that, in no very great while, that Synod will have expurgated herself from every trace

of un-Lutheranism in practice, as she has nobly done in theory.[16]

The Tennessee Synod met six weeks later, and after adopting "some explanations" of certain statements in the Basis, unanimously voted to approve the work of its committee.

Secretary John M. Smith of the Tennessee Synod communicated his body's action to President Samuel Rothrock of the North Carolina Synod, stressing the fact that, while Tennessee stood ready "to consider further steps towards the consummation of a union of the two Synods," it was the "sense of the Tennessee Synod, that at the present time, a union in the form of a 'Joint Synod,' would be preferable to . . . one of consolidation." President Rothrock, in reporting to his synod, explained that

> it is believed that difficulties, of a very grave nature, interpose themselves to a union of the two Synods by consolidation. Neither Synod would feel disposed to relinquish its historical identity by merging its name into that of the other. Hence it would be necessary to assume a new name, which would maintain and perpetuate the historical identity of each Synod. But, the consolidated Synod, under its assumed name, would not be known in the Deeds conveying property to the church and educational purposes, nor in our College charters, and hence legal difficulties, of a very grave nature, might readily spring up and give rise to troublesome litigation, and cause divisions and alienations of kindly feeling. But a Union, by an occasional meeting in Joint-Synod, each Synod maintaining its separate and independent organization, might be productive of good, and promotive of greater unanimity of sentiment and harmony of feeling.[17]

Reminding the North Carolina Synod that it had at its previous convention dissolved its relationship with the General Synod South and presently stood "in an isolated condition without connection with any General Body," the president urged the convention "to form a union with the General Council."

The committee chaired by Pastor Bernheim which responded to the report of the president addressed both the issue of membership in the General Council and the question of merger with the Tennessee Synod. The committee reminded the convention that it had previously committed itself to joining a general body that was "sound in the faith, that is likely to bind the church in the unity of the spirit and the bond of peace." While the committee applauded the General Council for "its soundness in the faith and for the high character it sustains," it did not see in the council a "general organization likely to bind the church in the unity of spirit and the bond of peace. . . ." Therefore, the committee declined to recommend membership in the General Council. The convention agreed.

As for the synod's relationship to the Tennessee Synod, the committee did not hesitate to ask the convention to declare "that a union between the North Carolina and Tennessee Synods is not only practicable but desirable." The committee agreed that "union" did not need to imply "consolidation;" the "joint-synod" approach with each body "maintaining its separate and independent character" seemed acceptable to the committee.

The committee apparently anticipated that even the conditional merger would be opposed. There were many congregations like Organ, Salisbury, the convention host, where stories of bitter struggles between North Carolina Synod folk and "the

Henkelites" were part of living traditions.[18] The committee called for the creation of a special committee "to prepare an address setting forth all the advantages of this union," the address to be made available to all the pastors of the synod along "with instructions that it be read from their respective pulpits."

To muster its arguments for merger, the synod called on Bernheim, Rothrock and Aldrich, along with Laymen J. M. Eddleman of Lutheran Chapel, China Grove, and George E. Ritchie, Esq., of St. John's, Concord. The committee asked that its address be considered "calmly, and in a Christian spirit."

While it prefaced its report with two biblical quotations, "That they all may be one" (John 17:21) and "Stand fast in one spirit, with one mind, striving together for the faith of the Gospel" (Philippians 1:27), the committee did not see fit to elaborate a biblical or theological rationale for the proposed union. Instead, it set forth eight advantages to the merger such as better understanding of each other, greater cooperation between members of the two bodies, a stronger missionary outreach, a larger public influence, a reduction in unchristian strife and contention, a more effective use of limited pastoral resources, and a renewal of the lives of congregations.

"It is also felt," the committee stated, "that if we wish to extend the boundaries of our church in our State, we must establish our own Theological Seminary. Either Synod by itself is not sufficiently strong to establish this great and much needed institution. Unitedly we can endow such a 'school of the prophets,' and only then will we become a church strong in our own State. Where our sons are educated for the ministry, there in most cases, will they remain."[19]

The committee contended that the "separate and independent actions" of the two synods no longer reflected differences in doctrine but were now largely "hereditary prejudices." But there were those who would surrender their freedom to interpret the Bible and conduct worship as they saw fit only with great reluctance, if at all. The committee tried to provide reassurance.

> We know there is apprehension on the minds of some, that by this union, they will be restricted in their practices, or in their own language, "their christian [sic] liberty will be assailed." As regards this view of the matter, there is not the least ground for fear. We are to enter upon this union in a spirit of toleration, and as each Synod retains its identity, there is to be no interference on the part of either with the other[']s peculiar rights and privileges. Whatever distinction there may be in each other[']s practice, must be borne with in true christian [sic] charity, until God, by His grace, operating upon our hearts and minds, will enable us to see "eye to eye."[20]

Only "the general affairs" of the church, not, presumably, the inner workings of congregational life, would be shaped by the new joint body.

In September the Tennessee Synod reviewed the actions of the North Carolina Synod the previous month and decided to "heartily endorse" the resolution of the North Carolina Synod to the effect "that a union of the two Synods in a Joint Synod is both practicable and desirable." It insisted it was "ready to meet the North Carolina Synod in a joint convention at any time and place, and on any basis of lay representation that may be agreed upon by the Presidents of the Synods...."[21]

On Wednesday, April 30, 1873, the delegates to the seventieth convention of the North Carolina Synod gathered at St. Paul's, Salisbury. President William Henry Cone reported to the convention that the Tennessee Synod had endorsed North Carolina's actions of the previous year, noting that, lest they prove an impediment to union, the Tennessee Synod had even rescinded its several proposed amendments to the joint document developed at Mt. Pleasant.

"The fraternal regard shown, in so doing," he added, "is very commendable, and augers well for such a harmonious Union as we desire. In view of the fact, that all difficulties have been removed, it remains for this Synod to take further steps, with regard to the Union."[22]

On Thursday morning, as the convention resumed its deliberations, Dr. Fox of the Tennessee Synod arrived as that body's corresponding delegate. He was "cordially received and invited to a seat, and requested to participate in our deliberations." But if the Lincoln County pastor expected to see the North Carolina Synod ratify and build upon the Basis of Union he and the other representatives of the two synods had hammered out at Mt. Pleasant two years earlier, he was disappointed. The secretary of the North Carolina Synod did not see fit to enlighten future generations about the issues actually discussed by the convention when it turned its attention to the question of merging with the Tennessee Synod. He contented himself with this summary: "After resuming the consideration of the miscellaneous business of the [Friday] morning session, and discussing it awhile, the following resolution was passed:

"Resolved, That in view of the difference of opinion among the members of this Synod, in regard to forming a union with some other ecclesiastical body, the subject lie over without further agitation, to be decided at the meeting of this Synod in 1878."[23]

The seemingly endless discussion and frustration attendant upon serious, ecumenical dialogue had taken their toll. To a majority, it seemed best to declare a five year moratorium on the issue of merger.

But there were those within the North Carolina Synod who were not satisfied with the action taken. When the synod's Western Conference met in the fall of 1873, it unanimously adopted a resolution calling upon the president of the North Carolina Synod to arrange for "a colloquium between the Tennessee and North Carolina Synods." President John D. Bowles promptly dispatched to President John M. Smith of the Tennessee Synod a letter regarding the matter. Smith responded that, in light of the five-year moratorium declared by the North Carolina Synod, he could not support the calling of an interim colloquium.   Bowles' efforts to explain North Carolina's 1873 action as "having nothing to do with" the proposed colloquium failed to convince Smith. The North Carolina Synod was reminded of the official offer of the Tennessee Synod to meet with the North Carolina Synod in a joint convention "at any time and place" agreed upon by their presidents, but, in light of the failure of Smith to respond to Bowles' explanation of North Carolina's moratorium on merger talks, the North Carolina Synod concluded "it inexpedient to consider the proposal to hold a Conference of the two Synods." The resumption of serious conversations about unity between the North Carolina and Tennessee Synods would have to await a later day.

The South suffered much during Reconstruction, the actions of a Republican-dominated Congress convincing southerners that any white native of their region possessed of a sense of honor must oppose the Republican Party. The vigorously-contested elections in the fall of 1876 ended the domination of Republicans in Raleigh, and, while Rutherford B. Hayes extended Republican power in the nation's capitol, he had no sooner assumed presidential responsibilities than he began removing federal troops from the South, a move that more than compensated southern Democrats who had struggled to defeat him in the November election.

And what was the legacy of the first ten years after the Civil War for those who resided "at the South?"

> Reconstruction, though marking a distinct advance in humanitarianism and public education and in some aspects of social, economic, and political democracy, was humiliating to North Carolina and the South generally and was in many ways a worse experience than the war. It produced lasting racial and sectional hatreds; complicated the Negro problem; compelled an abnormal, illogical, and harmful political unity of the whites; made racial and sectional prejudice the basis of political alignment; encouraged lawlessness, political manipulation, and corruption; and diverted political attention from realistic social and economic issues. But after nearly a decade of troublous Reconstruction home rule was established, Negro-Republican dominance was over, "white supremacy" was triumphant; and the state government and most of the local governments were again in charge of the tradition ruling class.[24]

The departure of federal troops from southern communities produced rejoicing among white southerners. At the 1877 convention of the North Carolina Synod, President Bikle could not refrain from extending to the visiting representative of the South Carolina Synod "congratulations" on South Carolina's "deliverance from oppression and misrule. Galling indeed must have been the yoke you were compelled to wear, and trying, most trying to Christian patience. But the night has passed and the light of day appears. The clouds have been dispelled from your political firmament and the sunshine of a bright and happy future is yours."[25]

In 1874 the synod noted that the General Council headed by Dr. Charles Porterfield Krauth had issued an invitation to all Lutheran synods "unreservedly" accepting the unaltered Augsburg Confession as their own confession to join with the council in planning a colloquium on the Augsburg Confession. An attempt in 1871 by the General Council to promote such a conference on a national scale secured a hearing in the South only among some representatives of the synod of Virginia. But this time, the North Carolina Synod promptly designated its representatives to work with the representatives of the General Council and other synods in planning such a colloquium. The Tennessee Synod also went on record approving the initiative.[26]

The General Council's project was also brought to the attention of the General Synod South. At that body's Savannah, Georgia, convention, the Committee on Letters and Petitions reported that notice of the proposed gathering had been received not only through the minutes of the General Council's 1873 convention, but also through a letter from the convention's English secretary, Dr. Beale M. Schmucker.

> The overture thus officially laid before us is so clear and unequivocal in its design, as to allay all that suspicion with which some of us have regarded previous efforts professing a similar object. The reading of it, and the statements made by the Rev. Dr. Frey before this Synod, assure us that it solely contemplates a greater unity in the one true faith of our church without any reference to the present general organizations as such.
>
> A closer union between all the parts of the Lutheran Church in this land is

sought, not by legislation or through formal organic connection, but by a voluntary conference of those bearing the same name, and holding the same confession, "that by a candid and fraternal expression of views" on points concerning which there is a difference of interpretation, we may all "by the grace of God be brought to a greater unity of spirit."[27]

The General Synod South moved ahead under the impression that it could be a full-fledged participant in planning for the colloquium. It named J. I. Miller to head a committee to help plan the event, but Miller reported that, when his committee attempted to fulfill its responsibility, it "received no response."

Instead of producing a conference to which Lutheran bodies elected delegates or representatives, the General Council initiative created a "Free Lutheran Diet." The agenda was fixed in advance and confined to the presentation and discussion of thirteen essays prepared and read by prominent Lutheran pastors and seminary professors.

The invitation to participation was a broad one: "All Lutherans, clerical and lay, without respect to synodical connections, are invited to seats and membership in this Diet, with the privileges of participation in the discussions."[28]

Since the participants were not representing anyone but themselves and had to assume responsibility for their own expenses, the proceedings did not encourage the participation of Lutherans far removed from the site of the diet. However, since the diet was held in Philadelphia, more than one hundred pastors, largely from the northern General Synod and the General Council, were able to attend as were more than fifty laymen and fifteen students of theology. The diet and a second one held the following year aired "sharp differences of opinion" as well as "much friendly discussion." At the very least the diets helped re-establish lines of communication between Lutheran leaders in the General Synod and the General Council, communication that had been limited and sometimes hostile since the creation of the General Council.

The General Synod South was aware of the potential significance of the 1876 gathering initiated by the General Council. It seemed to the delegates that a closer relationship among Lutherans adhering to the unaltered Augsburg Confession "would greatly advance the Lutheran faith in our beloved land, and thereby contribute to the glory of God, and the salvation of souls," so they voted to send delegates to the next conventions of both the northern General Synod and the General Council, provided the former body rescind any standing resolutions "compromising the Christian character of the ministers and church" represented in the General Synod South.[29]

Even as it sought closer bonds with the two general Lutheran bodies, the General Synod South extended an overture to the two district synods of North Carolina and Tennessee.

> Whereas, The Evang. Lutheran Synod of North Carolina was once an integral part of this body; and
> Whereas, Commissioners from the Evangelical Lutheran Tennessee Synod once held a conference with this body, with a view to a similar organic connection; but from considerations, neither directly nor indirectly communicated to us, the one withdrew and the other withheld said connection; therefore,
> Resolved, That we most respectfully, fraternally, and sincerely invite said Synods to a re-consideration of their action in taking their present position, and with a view to the greater unity and concentration of our Church in the South, we most

earnestly urge them to canvass impartially the propriety of uniting with us upon our basis of an unreserved acceptance of the Augsburg Confession.

Resolved, That we are the more constrained to make this overture for the closer fellowship of our Southern Church by the assured permanence and prospective growth of the work already accomplished by us as a General Synod in the promotion of sound doctrine and a more earnest church life among our ministry and laity.[30]

The minutes of the 1877 convention of the North Carolina Synod reflect no awareness of this action of the General Synod South, nor is there any noting of it the following year.

However, a return to the General Synod South was initiated in 1880. The synod voted that L. A. Bikle "be sent by this Synod, as a commissioner, to the Evangelical Lutheran General Synod in North America, at its approaching meeting to be held in Richmond, Virginia, to enquire into the doctrinal position of that body, with a view to an organic union with it."[31] Bikle's report was encouraging, and the synod voted at its next convention to reunite with the body it left a decade earlier.

Five years later, in 1886, the general synod expanded into the new United Synod of the Evangelical Lutheran Church South, uniting all the Lutheran synods of the South Atlantic states. The new synod, boasting 33,544 communicants at its 1887 convention in Savannah, included North Carolina among its members for the remainder of the period.

At the same time, the North Carolina and Tennessee synods maintained fraternal relations. In 1883, ten years after North Carolina declared its five-year moratorium on merger discussions, the synod was engaged with Tennessee in the formulation of a cooperative agreement on mission development. A committee of Dr. Bikle, Pastor Rothrock, and D. R. Hoover met with the Tennessee representatives, Rev. A. J. Fox, Rev. P. C. Henkel and Ambrose Costner, to formulate the agreement:

> The object of our appointment being to mature and submit for the consideration and adoption by said Synods in Convention assembled, some expedient, judicious, equitable plan or policy to prevent conflicts between these Synods in their efforts to extend the Redeemer's Kingdom on earth, in the occupancy of places, the establishment of mission points, the erection of church edifices, the organization of congregations, &c. - conflicts calculated to disparage the efforts at and the prosperity of such places, establishments, erections, organizations, &c., as are already occupied and inaugurated by the one or the other of these Synods, and in process of existence, we submit the subjoined plan or policy as practicable and effective:
>
> I. That inasmuch as the aforesaid Synods confess and teach in accordance with the Confessional basis of the Evan. Luth. Church as set forth in her Symbols, and while the said Synods so confess and teach, neither Synod, in its efforts to promote the Gospel and cause of Christ, shall occupy places, erect churches, establish missionary points, organize congregations, &c., where such things have already been instituted by the other, in villages or towns whose inhabitants do not exceed 2,000 souls; and so too in regard to churches and church work in the country or communities....
>
> II. That in towns or cities having more than 2,000 inhabitants, and large enough to support two or more Lutheran Churches, it may be advantageous for both Synods to operate, without any view of conflict or infringement.

III. That when or where either of said Synods has a member or members residing in [a] community, village, or town, already occupied by the other..., it shall be the duty of that Synod to advise such member or members to unite with those already occupied with the Redeemer's Kingdom at such place or places.

IV. That in all proper efforts to promote the interests of the church, friendly, Christian relations shall be maintained and cherished between the two Synods, each respecting the rights of the other, as it becomes Christians to do in the dissemination of the Gospel and in the promotion of the church.[32]

The need for the agreement was raised by a confrontation when the North Carolina Synod began work in Hickory, where Tennessee already had a congregation. After the agreement was worked out, the North Carolina members of the intersynodical committee admitted to their convention that "the Mission in that place ought not to have been undertaken."[33] In response, the convention delegates proposed to Tennessee a solution: a congregation at nearby Newton, with a church building "in good condition", would be given to Tennessee with the understanding that North Carolina would be permitted to retain the Hickory church. But Tennessee refused the offer and declined to appoint a committee for negotiating. In 1886, the Committee on Missions of the North Carolina Synod recommended that the mission "be left under the care of Rev. J. C. Moser, of the Tennessee Synod."

The Hickory matter had barely been put to rest when, in 1888, one of the leading pastors of the North Carolina Synod, B. S. Brown, was denied transfer into the Tennessee Synod. The denial, according to North Carolina sources, was because "his views on the formula of the administration of the Holy Lord's Supper; on self-administration of the Lord's Supper; and on pulpit and altar fellowship, do not accord with the principles of this [Tennessee] Synod as laid down in the Summit Rule, and since defined by the resolution adopted at Conover in 1883, and at Dallas in 1886."[34]

The North Carolina reaction was supportive but not aggressive: "We rejoice to find that he [Brown] stood so firmly on the confessions of the church and refused to go beyond them in accepting opinions or practices, that are no where required or distinctly stated in the symbols of our church."

The exchange soon faded. Tennessee sent a fraternal delegate, Rev. W. P. Cline, to the next North Carolina convention as a messenger "of its desire for peace."[35] Cline addressed the North Carolinians "in a short, kind address", and President F. W. E. Peschau assured him "of the kindest feelings of fraternal love on his part and of our Synod, for him and his Synod."

Twelve years later, the relations were so cordial that President Charles B. Miller noted that an "annual Lutheran Reunion was again held in August, 1901, and was a large, enjoyable, and profitable gathering of North Carolina and Tennessee Synod Lutherans. This reunion," he added, "should be continued and encouraged."[36]

Alpha Synod

At the end of the Civil War, the church in the South, as well as the general society, had to adjust to the new status of the "colored people." Although the North Carolina Synod entered this ministry, it was the Tennessee Synod which first articulated the need:

The colored people among us no longer sustain the same relation to the white man they did formerly, and that change has transferred the individual obligations and responsibility of owners to the whole Church. . . . These colored people are considered firm adherents to our Church, and we feel it is our imperative duty to assist them in adopting such measures as will meet best the necessities of their present condition. . . .

Some of them were formerly members of our congregations, and still claim membership in them, but owing to the plainly marked distinctions which God has made between us and them, giving different colors, etc., it is felt by us and them, also, that there ought to be separate places of worship, and also separate ecclesiastical organizations, so that everyone could worship God with the least possible embarrassment.[37]

Following the lead of the Tennessee Synod, the North Carolina Synod accepted the strategy of providing separate congregations and preachers for black Lutherans. The black Lutheran preacher was not restricted to preaching, but could administer the sacraments, catechize, and perform weddings and funerals "among those of his own race." Recognizing that blacks seeking ordination would not immediately possess the credentials of white candidates, the examination of candidates focused on matters like "motives and mental and moral qualifications."[38]

Two years after the Tennessee resolution, in 1868, North Carolina licensed a native of Guilford County, Michael M. Coble, for work "among those of his race". Three other candidates joined him. All four were licensed to preach, but were not ordained. They did not attend synod conventions, but reported to the convention through the local white pastors to whose general supervision they were assigned.

In 1880 the synod received a request from its Eastern Conference that David James Koontz be examined and, if found appropriately prepared, ordained as a missionary to work among blacks in North Carolina. The synod meeting at Mt. Pleasant accepted the recommendation. The examination was satisfactory, and Koontz preached before the convention as it assembled in the chapel at North Carolina College, using as his text John 3:14-15. On May 1 he was ordained at Holy Trinity, Mt. Pleasant, with G. D. Bernheim serving as preacher for the occasion. Later, in 1884, two other blacks, Samuel Holt and Nathan Clapp, were ordained.

Koontz, who earlier was called "the only ordained colored Lutheran minister in the world" by the *Lutheran Visitor*[39] saw his congregation of fourteen grow into four congregations with forty communicants in 1885. His Concord congregation built a church in 1883 with funds from the General Synod North. His congregations gave an annual contribution to the North Carolina Synod, "which, although modest, was larger than the contributions of some white congregations."[40]

North Carolina soon realized it could not sustain the ministry alone. It made overtures to the general synods, asking for full relief, or at least some help, first to the General Synod South and later to the General Synod North. But no help came.

President William A. Lutz in 1886 recommended that the synod advise the three colored ministers "to engage in secular occupations for their support."[41] Two years later, the synod also sought help from the Maryland Synod.

In 1889, the synod's Committee on Work Among the Freedmen reported that the Maryland approach was without success, but Maryland had suggested that the Freedmen be allowed to form their own synod. The committee also reported receipt of a petition from the three black ministers for permission to form a separate synod. In the same report, the committee recommended authorization for W. Philo Phifer, a licentiate from the Maryland Synod, to raise funds for erecting a black Lutheran church in Charlotte.

On May 8, 1889, at St. John's, Concord, the synod's four black pastors and their lay delegates met with the four white officers of the synod to organize a separate body, the Alpha Synod of the Evangelical Lutheran Synod of Freedmen in America. Pastor Koontz was elected president. Minutes of the meeting were published with the minutes of the next convention of the North Carolina Synod, which also contributed twenty-five dollars to the new synod "to enable them to hold their property in Concord."[42]

Two years later, the synod still provided moral support to the ministry. The synod convention responded to a request for recognition from the Charlotte black congregation, St. Mark's, by acknowledging the congregation and its pastor, who was Phifer, as "truly Lutheran and in the common faith with us."[43] It also authorized one of the Charlotte white pastors to exercise oversight of the ministry.

It was at the beginning of 1891, following Koontz' death the previous year, that Phifer, acting in his capacity as secretary of the Alpha Synod, wrote to the president of the Lutheran Church - Missouri Synod, asking for help. The matter was referred by the Missouri Synod to its Mission Board which dispatched three of its home missionaries to North Carolina to investigate the situation. The Missouri Synod pastors met with "the preachers Phifer, Holt, and Clap[p]" of the Alpha Synod in the cabin of a black family at Burlington, the Missourians having been ousted from the local hotel when it was learned that they, though white, were missionaries to black persons.

The meeting of the Missouri Synod representatives with the pastors of the Alpha Synod proved revealing: "Easy catechetical questions were put to these preachers, but only a few were correctly answered. The theological examination was not satisfactory to the committee, but it saw in the field a door which the Lord had opened, hoped that the preachers in course of time might be utilized, and advised the Board to take charge of the field, provided a man could be found who would instruct the preachers and superintend the mission."

The Mission Board accepted its committee's recommendation, and promptly turned to a member of the committee, Missionary Nils Jules Bakke, with an invitation to launch the work in North Carolina. Thus, in September, 1891, Pastor Bakke became the first Missouri Synod pastor to labor for that synod on North Carolina soil. He made Grace, Concord, his base of operations.

By 1903 the Missouri Synod opened Immanuel College in Concord for the education of black students and the preparation of black pastors. The school soon moved to Greensboro, where it continued for about fifty years.[44]

In 1911 Bakke reported active work on behalf of the Missouri Synod at twenty-two sites in North Carolina stretching from Wilmington on the coast to Winston-Salem and Charlotte in the Piedmont.[45] Parochial schools were associated with a number of the churches. Typically, in addition to providing instruction in reading, writing and arithmetic, the schools placed "emphasis ... on Bible history and Luther's *Small Catechism*. All pupils had to memorize the Ten Commandments and their meaning as well as the Apostles' and Nicene creeds."[46]

Polity and Practice

The role of the North Carolina synodical organization was spelled out in its constitution (Chapter I, Section 3):

> It shall be the duty of this Synod to see that the rules of government and discipline prescribed in the formula, are observed by all the congregations and ministers within its bounds, to receive appeals from decisions of Church Councils and of Conferences, when regularly brought before them, and review and reverse or confirm the decisions to which they refer; to examine and decide on all charges against ministers, that of heterodoxy alone excepted; to form and change Pastoral Districts; to provide supplies for destitute congregations; and to devise and execute suitable measures for the promotion of piety, and the general prosperity of the Church.[47]

The responsibility for deciding on charges of ministerial heterodoxy was excluded from the duties of the synod because such charges were heard by the ministerium, the organization of pastors which customarily met in connection with the annual convention to approve candidates for ordination and act on other matters related to the clergy.

The synod's role in the life of the church was revealed further in the set of standing resolutions customarily printed with the annual convention minutes. The set of resolutions, which were subject to amendment from year to year, appeared in 1871 in this form:

> I. Resolved, That we recommend to the Church Councils the propriety of adopting the plan of collecting the Pastor's salary by assessment.
>
> II. Resolved, That in accordance with our Church discipline, chap. 6, section 3, the Church Councils be instructed to require every member of the Church, to contribute to the support of the Gospel, except such as in their judgment are too poor to do so.
>
> III. Resolved, That no minister in our connection shall be allowed to take charge of vacant congregations until they shall have satisfactorily met their obligations with their former pastor.
>
> IV. Resolved, That each charge shall have an annual settlement with its pastor, and that each pastor be required to present to Synod annually, a written statement of the amount promised for his support, and the amount received by subscriptions and donations from each Church.
>
> V. Resolved, That the Church Councils be required to send to Synod by their Delegates, a written report, stating the manner in which their Pastor discharges his obligations to his charge.
>
> VI. Resolved, That these reports from Pastors and Councils be read in Synod by the Secretary.

In addition to its own constitution, the synod in 1880 printed with its convention minutes a "Proposed Constitution for the use of Congregations in the N. C. Synod." In later years, it began urging congregations to adopt a constitution and submit it to the synod for approval.

In a further governance act, the synod in 1886 sought incorporation and was issued a charter which was ratified on February 2, 1887.

A special convention was held in 1902 to attend to a series of constitutional revisions carried over from previous meetings. The convention was held at St. Mark's, China Grove, on June 24-25. Amendments were approved allowing for a lay delegate from each congregation (rather than each parish), instituting the position of statistical secretary, and creating an Executive Committee composed of the officers of the synod, the conference presidents, and an additional layman. Other amendments authorized the president to receive clergy by transfer from other synods, and restricted beneficiary aid to students who had completed the sophomore year in college and to seminarians attending Lutheran Theological Southern Seminary.[48]

Both the changing constitution and the act of incorporation reflected the evolvement of the synod from a clearing house for pastoral assignments to a promoter of accepted Lutheran beliefs and practices among its congregations.

Church Publications

Although North Carolina's withdrawal from the General Synod in 1871 stemmed partly from publication disagreements, the withdrawal did not solve the publication problem. North Carolina had a new problem of providing, if necessary on its own, a church paper that would enhance Lutheran consciousness among parishoners and provide a medium for communication.

In the March 1872, Samuel Rothrock of Rowan County went to Mt. Pleasant "to attend a conference to start a church paper." His diary gives no particulars, but he was presumably one of the North Carolina Synod pastors who met with counterparts from the Tennessee Synod to discuss their common concern for a church periodical. One of the most involved pastors of the Tennessee Synod was Alfred J. Fox of Lincoln County who made several trips to Mt. Pleasant to participate in the negotiations in 1872 and 1873 that culminated in the establishment of *Our Church Paper*.[49]

It was not the North Carolina Synod alone which could take comfort in the creation of *Our Church Paper*. The Tennessee Synod welcomed "with much pleasure" the advent of the publication, "a religious journal, published at New Market, Virginia." The synod appreciated the general appearance of the new publication, but was even more impressed with "the soundness of the doctrines and practices which it inculcates."[50]

The New Market publication became the newest but not the only Lutheran periodical available to members of the North Carolina and Tennessee synods. The publication endorsed by the General Synod South, *The Lutheran Visitor*, continued to be published in Salisbury (but edited by South Carolina and Virginia pastors) until 1878 when it was moved to South Carolina. There was also the Baltimore journal, *The Lutheran Observer*, which continued in sufficient popularity to merit selection by the congregation of Cold Water, Concord, for placement in the cornerstone of its new 1881 building.

Other publications also competed for Lutheran subscribers. Around the turn of the century, there were efforts to establish Lutheran periodicals with a stronger local flavor. In addition to increasing the coverage of matters close to home, such papers provided their editors with an avenue for advancing personal views of church doctrine and practice.

For example, in January 1898, Pastor Crouse of Friendship, Taylorsville, began publishing *Our Church Record*, a monthly parochial paper. For two years, he printed it on his home printing press and distributed the paper without charge.

Some of the members were so pleased with it that they, at different times, gave the pastor money to help pay for the paper. During the second year, they with the other congregations in the pastorate decided that the paper should be enlarged and be issued as a subscription paper, which was done. Instead of four pages the paper at the beginning of the third year became an eight page paper. The people also instructed the pastor to send it to every family. This has been done except in a very few cases. . . . The congregations annually pay what is needed, over the amount received on subscription, to pay the expense of printing and mailing the paper. The names of all persons baptized, confirmed, married and buried by the pastor are printed in this paper. A good record is thus kept. Elections of officers and other principal items of business are noted. Many of the people have preserved all these papers, and they have a good history of the last seven years of the life of the congregation.[51]

Crouse, a key figure in the theological controversies that marked the life of Lutheranism in Catawba and Alexander counties around the turn of the century, often used the parish paper to articulate his position in those discussions.

Missions

Although not specifically cited in the purpose of the synod, the promotion of new congregations was a constant interest of the North Carolina Synod. In 1871, President Whitson Kimball, a leading spirit in the home mission field, recommended the employment of a missionary "whose duty it shall be to supply all the vacancies, within the bounds of the Synod, and gather up our scattered Lutherans, organize them into congregations, and build churches." The challenge, however, went unanswered.

Despite the absence of a missionary, there was home mission activity. With the help of interested pastors, the tempo for organizing congregations picked up after 1870.

During the first twelve years of the period, ten congregations were formed: Christ, Spencer (1870); Christiana, Salisbury (1871); Center Grove, Kannapolis (1876); Mt. Olive, Mt. Pleasant (1878); Cross of Christ, Concord, and St. Mark's, Salisbury (1879); First, Albemarle, and Grace, Salisbury (1880); Mt. Hermon, Concord (1881); and Concordia, China Grove (1882)

In 1883, the synod inaugurated its first Executive Committee on Home Missions; the committee consisted of three pastors, Samuel Rothrock, S. T. Hallman, and W. A. Lutz, along with laymen I. F. Patterson and the Hon. H. C. McAllister. The committee held its organizational meeting June 15, 1883, and elected L. A. Bikle "Missionary for the State at large, with a salary of $800 per annum."[52]

On September 25, Bikle presented to the committee a report on his activities - along with his resignation. He concluded that (1) immediate results were anticipated which could not be realized and (2) "the Synod was not in a condition to sustain a prospecting Missionary."[53]

In 1886, President W. A. Lutz reported that, "Never before, perhaps, in any one year has the Synod exhibited so much activity in mission work, both Home and Foreign."[54]

While the president could report much activity, not all the news was good. The Forsyth Mission was "in a very unhealthy condition" since the strongest congregation (Nazareth, Rural Hall) would not accept the ministry of the missionary, E. P. Parker. From the Lexington mission, begun in 1881, the congregational secretary reported they "considered the mission hopeless" and wanted to dispose of their property. The two congregations comprising the Davie Mission were "in a helpless condition," while the Mooresville Mission had never been given "a place in any charge" nor had it ever been placed under the care of a pastor.[55]

During the period between 1883 and 1890, only one congregation was organized. Amity, Cleveland, was formed in 1885.

In 1890, the Advisory Board of Missions and the Executive Committee once again proposed that the synod employ a home missionary, named a "missionary pastorate." It cited mission development at Lexington, Durham, Mocksville, Mooresville, Greensboro, Kannapolis and Elkin, and noted calls for "our immediate assistance" from Goldsboro, Raleigh, New Berne (sic), Winston "and others." It recommended the employment of Rev. J. W. Kimmel, of Nebraska, as State Missionary at a salary of nine hundred dollars per year. But the convention turned down the proposal for lack of funds.

Even so, the earlier pace of five new congregations per decade quickened. The period of 1891-1901 alone saw eleven congregations organized: Augsburg, Winston-Salem (1891); St. Matthew's, Wilmington (1892); Lebanon, Cleveland (1893); St. Mark's, China Grove (1894); Sharon, Gibsonville (1894); Mt. Zion, Richfield, and Emmanuel, Rockwell (1895); Peace, Gibsonville (1898); Faith, Faith, and Haven, Salisbury (1899); and Wittenberg, Granite Quarry (1901).

In 1902, President Charles B. Miller observed that the work in missions was "healthy and promising" and cited mission points that included Burlington, Davie County, Forsyth County, Albemarle, Chestnut Hill (Salisbury), Spencer, St. Andrew's (Concord), and the Davidson pastorate.

The synod noted with appreciation the work of W. A. Lutz as president of the Board of Church Extension and the importance of the Church Extension Fund. The fund, started with seventy-five dollars given by St. Enoch, Enochville, had grown to $2,014.69. The growth could be attributed partly to the 1889 action of the synod calling on pastors to receive an offering for the fund either on Reformation Day or at Christmas.

The period also saw the emergence of the Lutheran Seaman's Mission in Wilmington, primarily through the efforts of the port city pastor, F. W. E. Peschau. The synod approved the establishment of the ministry in 1889 as a response to the large number of Scandinavian and German seamen, all Lutheran, arriving in Wilmington. The mission was placed under the fostering care of Peschau. Two years later Synod President George H. Cox reported on his visit to the mission in March. Regular services were conducted on Sunday afternoons and Wednesday evenings. The services, led by Peschau, were conducted in the Scandinavian language in the Luther Memorial Building of St. Paul's church.

During the 1870-1902 period, a total of twenty-two congregations were formed in the North Carolina Synod, bringing the baptized membership to 11,615.

Meanwhile, twenty-four other congregations in the state of North Carolina were added to the roster of the rival Tennessee Synod. The first twelve-year period, when North Carolina added ten congregations, saw Tennessee welcome only four: Holy Trinity, Hickory (1876); St. Matthew's, Kings Mountain (1876); St. John's, Cherryville, and Good Shepherd, Mt. Holly (1881).

In the next seven years, however, while North Carolina was picking up only one new congregation, Tennessee added ten: Holy Communion, Dallas, and Mt. Olive, Hickory, and Holly Grove, Lexington (1885); St. Timothy, Hickory (1887); Shiloh, Hickory, and St. John's, Statesville (1888); Ebenezer, Catawba, and St. Luke's, Monroe (1889); and Lebanon, Lexington, and Mt. Gilead, Mt. Pleasant (1890).

During the final eleven years, while North Carolina added eleven, Tennessee accepted ten congregations: St. Luke, Taylorsville, and Cedar Grove, Vale (1892); St. Andrew's, Hickory, and St. Martin's, Maiden (1893); Mt. Hermon, Statesville (1896); St. Paul's, Dallas (1897); St. Luke's, Conover, and Holy Trinity, Gastonia (1899); and Mt. Calvary, Claremont, and St. Paul's, Crouse (1902).

Other Tar Heel congregations organized during the period chose to associate with the Joint Synod of Ohio. Among them were St. Mark's, Claremont (1887); St. John's, Lenoir (1889); St. Luke's, Taylorsville; Mt. Zion, Conover (1893); and St. Paul's, Hickory (1901).

Pastors

Even though Lutheran pastors sometimes found it necessary to supplement their income by what might be regarded as "secular" employment, they did not take lightly their ordination vows. Nor was the carrying out of those vows something that could be handled by assigning to them the hours one had left over when other "necessary" tasks had been completed. Regularly providing worship leadership and preaching for three, four or five congregations was the pastor's most frequent and conspicuous role. Weddings, funerals and baptisms also loomed large on his schedule. And of course there was the matter of the visiting of parishioners. R. A. Yoder of the Tennessee Synod was one who involved himself in pastoral visitation, despite the fact that most of his ministry was centered in educational work. After a day of teaching at Concordia College, or later at Lenoir College, he would set off in his buggy to the home of a parishioner for supper. He would spend the night with the family, have an early breakfast with them, and then depart to visit another family or return to the parsonage.

"Baptism of a child in the home", according to his biographer, "was not infrequently a part of these visits, though infants were often brought to the church service for this rite. Plans for weddings were made at friendly meals. Matters of doctrine or church policy were discussed with the heads of families. When a member of the parish was critically ill, Yoder and his wife would go to the home of the patient and often remained until the patient died or got better."[56]

During a "communion season" the pastor's weekend schedule likely began with arrival at a church on an early Saturday afternoon. Young persons being prepared for confirmation joined him for a session devoted to the explanation and recitation of sections of Luther's *Small Catechism*. In the late afternoon, the pastor conducted a service of self-examination and confession for members of the congregation who expected to commune the following day. Then he went home with a family in the congregation, enjoyed a modest supper, engaged the adults in conversation after supper, and retired early.

On Sunday morning after breakfast, the pastor and the host family returned to the church for the worship service culminating in Holy Communion. After the service, and often some consultation with leaders of the church council, the pastor visited with the family that had asked for the privilege of hosting him for Sunday dinner. This was no modest affair, but the finest fare to be found in the smoke house and pantry. Since it was such a special occasion for the host family, other guests often were invited to join in what might be the host family's outstanding social event of the year. The afternoon was a time for the women to socialize and the men to converse, the pastor taking leave sufficiently early to arrive home before dark.

Of Holston Synod pastors in the 19th century, George H. Cox wrote:

> Their visits to their parishioners were, in deed and in truth, "pastoral visits." They recognized this part of their work as one of the greatest and most important means for accomplishing good. It brought them into close contact with the thought and feeling and life of the people, and gave them a great grip upon their hearts. It was the usual custom that, when the pastor came, the whole family would lay aside whatever else they had to do, gather around the fireside and engage in conversation upon purely religious subjects; scarcely anything else being mentioned. It was a rare thing for the pastor to come and not find some Biblical question awaiting his explanation. In this way he was both encouraged and enabled to follow up the work done in the pulpit, and could, and did take the opportunity to reprove wrong doing and correct erroneous opinions.[57]

Housing for the pastor and his family was provided by only a few congregations or parishes, but it was increasingly a matter claiming their attention. Yoder served twelve Tennessee synod congregations during his ministry which began in 1879, but only two of them owned parsonages. One of them was Emmanuel, Lincolnton, which was given a parsonage for Yoder after he took up his work there. "The house is new," he wrote, "contains nine rooms, is centrally located, has water and sewage and electric lights. The friends who bought it for the church paid $3,500 for it."[58]

In 1902, A. L. Crouse and his family moved into the newly-completed parsonage adjoining St. Paul's, Taylorsville. It was owned by three congregations: St. Paul's, Salem and Friendship. Construction started about 1895 during G. E. Long's pastorate, and several rooms were completed at that time so Long could occupy them. Crouse lived in Hickory, but when he learned that members of the parish were planning to dispose of the partially-completed parsonage, he urged its completion. They completed it and then persuaded him to move from Hickory to occupy it. This he did for two years, but then returned to his "own home" in Hickory.[59]

For transportation, the pastor of course was usually dependent on the horse, although, toward the close of the period some made use of the bicycle. Crouse sometimes cycled on a vehicle given by his children, who with the aid of parishioners, collected three thousand metal tags off chewing tobacco to acquire the two-wheeler. But he used it only for short trips. For longer trips, he rode a young mare; it may have been slower, but it was easier, and it allowed him to read and write in transit.

For all their travels and labors, the pastors were not paid handsomely. At St. Luke's, Tyro, in 1872, the total paid on the pastor's salary by ninety members amounted to $197.25.

Some pastors received more. The 1883 financial report for the year included the salaries of pastors, as provided by eighteen parishes. D. J. Koontz, the black missionary, received the lowest salary, $120; F. W. E. Peschau at St. Paul's, Wilmington, received the highest, $1,200. The average for the eighteen was $425.83, the median $400.

Yoder, ordained in 1879, never received more than five hundred dollars in the first twenty-five years of his ministry. But, his biographer reports,

> The small amount of money was somewhat compensated for by the agricultural products and other items which were given to Yoder by parishioners. If a farmer had a good crop of apples, a peck or a bushel found its way to the parsonage. One pig out of a large litter might be given to the preacher when he came on his next visit. If the farmer's wife put up peaches or pickles, or if the family made cider, some of the product was sure to be given to the pastor. When the new minister took up his residence in the midst of the members of the congregation, and from time to time thereafter, it was the custom for most of them to call at the pastor's house, each bringing a pound of foodstuff.[60]

Congregations

In terms of number of congregations, the North Carolina Synod was not a significant force in the religious life of the state. In 1870 the synod boasted thirty-nine congregations. By comparison the Methodists claimed 1,193; the Baptists, 986; Presbyterians, 204; and Episcopalians, seventy-seven. The Lutherans, including the congregations of the Tennessee Synod, followed in fifth place with seventy-three congregations.[61]

Growth during the period was moderate. By 1880, the synod had increased its congregations to forty-eight. An additional seven were added during the next decade, and the synod closed out the century with sixty congregations. During the same thirty-year period, the communing membership grew from 4,201 to 7,230.

Worship

The sharing of common worship materials is a significant force in promoting Christian unity. Among early German immigrants to the New World, often among the family belongings transported from Europe to America, were two books: a Bible and a hymn book.

For German-speaking Lutheran and Reformed immigrants to Pennsylvania, the hymn book of choice was usually a work widely referred to as the *Marburg Hymnal*. The popularity of this work, and the fact that so many families arrived in America without any books of any kind, prompted Christopher Saur of Germantown, Pennsylvania, to produce an American printing of the *Marburg Hymnal* in 1752.

As German folk moved from their initial places of settlement in Pennsylvania to Virginia and the Carolinas, the *Marburg Hymnal* often made the journey with the family. Families who were among the early settlers at St. John's, Concord, for example, had copies of this work, and it was probably the most widely used book of worship among the Lutheran and Reformed settlers in the Carolinas in the eighteenth century.[62]

South Carolinians continued to use the *Marburg Hymnal* into the nineteenth century, but a competitor appeared on the scene in North Carolina in 1797. From Michael Braun's print shop in Salisbury Francis Coupee and John Martin Schlump published "a thirty-page collection of Lutheran hymns (without music) entitled *Sammlung von erbaulichen Gesaengen, zum Gebrauch bey dem oeffentlichen Gottesdienst fuer die Deutschen Gemeinen in Nord-Carolina.*"[63]

With the creation of the Henkel Press in New Market, Virginia, the Lutheran church in the South developed another source of worship materials. In 1810 the Henkel

Press produced *Das Neu-eingerichtete Gesang-Buch* by Paul Henkel, a work that was especially popular in the Carolinas. Among the works drawn upon by Henkel in compiling his hymnal were the *Marburger Gesang-Buch, Das kleine Davidische Psalterspiel*(a work first published in America by Saur and used mostly by Mennonites and Dunkers in America), *Neandris Harfenspiel* (a Mennonite hymnal), *Geistliche Lieder* by Bernhard H. Sasse, and an interdenominational work entitled *Das Neu-Eingerichtete Gesang-Buch* published by Saur in 1752.[64] Henkel himself contributed several hymns to the collection: "It would not be an exaggeration to state that his *Das Neu-eingerichtete Gesang-Buch* was, in all probability, the most successful religious work in German produced on the New Market Press. It achieved an estimated printing well in excess of twenty-five hundred copies and was printed twice within three years."[65]

Among English-speaking Christians in the South, hymns began very early in the nineteenth century to be accompanied by musical settings in the form of shape-notes, and it was not long before hymns, irrespective of their source were "invariably circulated in shape-note form." The shape-note system of notation was introduced in New England about 1800 in *The Easy Instructor* to facilitate sight reading among semiliterate folk.

> The shape of the note, independent of its position on the staff, indicated its musical pitch (fa was represented by a triangle, sol by a circle, la by a square, and mi by a diamond). The method was transported into the South by singing school teachers who came down out of Pennsylvania into the Shenandoah Valley. These itinerant singing masters were hardy souls who became as well known, and as warmly welcomed, as peddlers or Methodist circuit riders. They came into a community, held their schools for 10 days, and then left for another community where they once again taught their method.[66]

One of the earliest Southern shape-note tune books was published in 1816 by Joseph Funk, a Mennonite who titled his work *Choral Music*. His descendants established a singing "normal" school at Singers Glen, Virginia. This school became the training site for numerous singing teachers who wandered throughout the rural South.[67] The popularity of singing schools and collections like *The Sacred Harp* helped to preserve congregational singing in the South at a time when Calvinistic congregations in other regions were moving toward a low point in that art.[68]

To the degree that music was cultivated outside the church in the South, it was largely a matter of concern for women or those often transient music teachers whose speech reflected the fact that France, Italy or Germany was their land of origin. As female seminaries emerged for the education of young women, music promptly assumed a conspicuous place in their curricula. Susan Biglow Bittle, when she opened Mt. Pleasant Female Seminary in 1859, assured the public it provided "the usual English branches" of instruction as well as "Latin, French and Music." Later known as Mont Amoena Seminary, it became "an island of culture in the difficult years following the War Between the States." Even schools located in remote communities strove to provide musical instruction.[69]

One of the first responsibilities assumed by the General Synod South was to provide a book of worship for Lutheran congregations in the Confederate states. At the first session of the first convention, a committee was appointed to prepare a hymnal and catechism and another was named to prepare a liturgy.

The chairman of the hymnal committee, President William D. Roedel of Wytheville Female College in Virginia, was an experienced hymnologist, having just published his *Carmina Ecclesiae*. In preparing the hymnal for the General Synod South, he drew more than three hundred hymns from the hymnal published by General Synod North in 1850. Nearly 150 additional hymns were selected from a variety of current hymnals. Roedel also provided the committee's translation of Luther's *Small Catechism*. He presented his committee's report to the Concord session of the first convention on May 22. Action on the report was deferred four days in order to give the delegates time to examine the work. When the vote was taken, the committee's work was accepted as presented except that the numbering of the Ten Commandments in the catechism was revised to make Luther's numbering conform to that of the book of Exodus.

The committee charged with the responsibility of preparing a liturgy had a much more difficult assignment, primarily because the worship practices of Lutherans in the South were extremely varied.

In the Holston Synod, according to George H. Cox:

> They did not use the liturgical forms of worship as we now do, but each pastor conducted as it seemed best to him and his people. Upon a certain occasion, before I was ordained, and when I had not preached but once or twice, Rev. J. K. Hancher came to my home, late on a Saturday afternoon, and asked me to fill his appointment at old Zion Church, on the next day, as he had been called away to officiate at a funeral service. I consented; and that there might be no confusion, I asked how he conducted the service. Said he, "O well, we sing a little, and pray a little, and then preach like thunder for about two hours."[70]

A contributor to the *Lutheran Visitor* in the spring of 1870 gave a similar description:

> Many . . . will breathe a silent prayer, then look about to see who is there. Every time the door opens all look around, perhaps awaiting the minister. Presently the minister enters and immediately ascends the pulpit. Whilst he is finding his text and the hymns, the choir sings an introductory. He arises, gives out his hymn, reads a portion of Scripture, observing no Pericope, and perhaps reading Luke ii at Easter, or Mark xvi, at Christmas. He then prays and all are silent, from the fact that no one knows what he intends to pray for. He then gives out another hymn, after the singing of which he announces his text and preaches the sermon, prays again, sings another hymn, and dismisses.

As early as 1812 the North Carolina Synod decided it must develop a liturgy for use in the congregations, but "for weighty reasons" the liturgy was not prepared immediately. The following year, it was decided to postpone the development of a synodical liturgy until contact could be established with the Pennsylvania ministerium to see if "in their opinion it would not be practicable and necessary to compile a complete Liturgie for the use of our church in every state. Until this could be effected, an extract might be made from Leiler's Liturgie...."[71]

Thus, a short time later the Pennsylvania president received a letter from the secretary of the North Carolina Synod, Gottlieb Schober, inquiring about their reaction to a proposal for the development of a "complete Agenda or liturgy . . . which could be used throughout America." Schober expressed his own opinion that such a move could preserve for future generations of Lutherans "unity in the Symbols of our Church" and guard against "innovations."[72]

In 1846 Rev. Benjamin Arey alerted the North Carolina Synod to the fact that the General Synod had raised a question of producing "a new liturgy." Arey kept this concern before the synod and, in 1851, was one of three pastors named to a committee to study matters pertaining to a liturgy and present the synod with its recommendations.

A short time later, the Tennessee Synod, which as early as its second year of existence called on Rev. Paul Henkel to prepare a liturgy that would be both scriptural and consistent with commitment to the Augsburg Confession, began to confront the question of liturgy again. A committee of nine selected in 1857 was replaced by a committee of three the following year. At convention after convention, however, the committee could apparently report little progress, and in 1864 the committee was discharged.

When the Lutherans from across the South who gathered at Concord in 1863 turned their attention to worship materials, the question of liturgy was still unresolved by current usage. Many congregations would have stoutly denied that they used a liturgy. In most congregations, however, there was a set form to the worship service, even if the form was adopted unconsciously.

The vocal participation of the congregation in most worship services was limited to the singing of the hymns, and since hymn books were usually in short supply, the pastor was often expected to "line out" the hymn, the congregation joining him in singing the line of the hymn he had just spoken. In a very few congregations there was use of a liturgy that involved participation by both the pastor and the congregation.

Objections to liturgical worship centered around the familiar concern about formalism in worship and the fact that rural congregations, an appropriate designation for the majority of congregations in each of the member synods, were assumed to be incapable of using such a worship tool. Many folk in rural congregations were poor readers, and almost all lacked training in music.

After two days of debate on a liturgy proposed by its committee chaired by Rev. Anders R. Rude of Ebenezer, Columbia, South Carolina, those opposing its adoption finally agreed that the proposed liturgy might be printed in the new *Book of Worship* provided it was understood that the use of any part of it would be optional.

Promptly following the convention, the North Carolina Synod instructed its delegates to the next convention of the General Synod South to seek the publication of an edition of the *Book of Worship* without the liturgy. After the book was published in 1868, however, the synod embraced the new liturgy fully, using it pointedly throughout its 1870 convention.

The Tennessee Synod, which was not a member of the general synod, gave the hymnbook only mild approval, recommending instead that its congregations use the *Church Book,* which was published shortly after the *Book of Worship* by the General Council.

While earlier worship centered on the minister, the *Book of Worship* involved the congregation.   It promoted congregational singing of liturgical responses and congregational standing for parts of the service.

One pastor reported, on first try, "only one person stood up, beside my family." But he continued: "the next Sunday we had a full house at St. Enoch, and fifteen stood up. A member of the choir came after service, and asked me to meet the choir that afternoon and train them. . . . They all learned to sing the glorias and responses. Soon the congregation, with a few exceptions, joined in the service."[73]

But the 1872 convention heard that, in one parish, "the opposition was violent and determined."

Rev. Charles H. Bernheim found such resistance to the liturgy at St. James, Concord, that he consulted with the synod president about suspending its use. President Rothrock indicated to the synod in his annual report that he did not consider it appropriate to advise Bernheim to suspend the use of "our prescribed forms of religious worship."

Because North Carolina later severed its connection with the synod which produced the *Book of Worship*, President Rothrock in 1872 raised the question whether the Formula of Government and discipline in the book was still binding or whether it was not necessary for the synod to vote formally on adopting the book. The convention declined to vote, but the use of the book continued.

One congregation, St. Michael's, Iredell County, petitioned the synod in 1873 to use in their services the "old edition of Lutheran Hymns", instead of the *Book of Worship.* The convention responded that the congregational vote to exclude the *Book of Worship* was "injudicious, and will be productive of the destruction of the peace and harmony of the church." It recommended use of the *Book of Worship* and also the old General Synod's *Hymn Book* "but that they use exclusively, in their worship, such hymns, only, as are found in both Hymn Books."[74]

In the first decade after the Civil War, the initial stock of 10,807 copies of the *Book of Worship* was exhausted. The General Synod South in 1874 created a committee consisting of T. W. Dosh, S. A. Repass, and J. P. Smeltzer to revise the book of worship as well as enter into a new contract for its publication.[75]

Despite lingering resistance in some North Carolina Synod congregations to the *Book of Worship* and in Tennessee Synod congregations to the *Church Book,*

the introduction of these books worked a revolution. For the first time many congregations knew what it meant to use a distinctively Lutheran order of service. The special identity which this discovery gave to a congregation extended quite naturally to the synods as a whole. This new feeling of unity, coupled with the consciousness of a peculiarly "Lutheran" heritage, became the foundation upon which all later work of the General Synod South was built. Its effect can not easily be measured, but the more one comprehends the influence which the *Book of Worship* exercised, the more one realizes how basic it was to all the other areas of cooperation among southern Lutherans.

Liturgical unity was promoted further by the appearance in 1888 of the *Common Service,* developed in a cooperative effort by the General Synod, the General Council and the United Synod of the South. The service was established on the principle of the common consent of the pure Lutheran liturgies of the sixteenth century and was eventually incorporated in many Lutheran service books and hymnals.[76]

The introduction of the *Book of Worship* produced a new appreciation for the potential role of the choir and musical instruments in worship.

Music claimed more attention. St. John's, Salisbury, created its "first formal choir on record" in 1881.[77] Lutheran Chapel, China Grove, one of the first congregations in the area to develop a trained choir after the Civil War, sponsored "singing schools" to which other churches in the area sent persons for training in choir work.

In 1892, the synod president noted that St. Paul's, Salisbury, had installed a new organ at a cost of $184, and that St. John's, Salisbury, had installed a new pipe organ at a cost of twelve hundred dollars.[78] Five years later, St. John's budgeted sixty dollars for its organist (but seventy-five dollars for the janitor).[79]

In addition, as early as the fall of 1867 synodical conventions began to take official notice of special choir work in connection with its annual gatherings.[80]

Musical instruments to support the worship of Lutheran congregations were not unknown prior to the Civil War, but they were a rarity in rural churches. Because its pipe organ was so unusual among the Rowan County churches in the late eighteenth century, Zion Evangelical Lutheran Church became known as "Organ Lutheran Church," and it continues to use the name today. Its instrument was built by Capt. John Stirewalt, a member of the congregation.

As the *Book of Worship* began to shape the worship life of congregations in the South, the availability of musical instruments became a more widely-publicized fact. An early issue of *The Lutheran Visitor* carried advertisements for musical instruments and publications including advertisements for Baltimore firms that sold Knabe Pianos, Colton's Piano Fortes and Melodeons and Estey's Cottage Organs. The publisher of the *Visitor* also advertised his musical periodical, *The Musical Advocate and Singer's Friend* (published monthly) and his firm's book of musical settings for popular hymns, *The Harmonia Sacra, Being A Collection of Church Music.* The magazine's editor, Rev. J. I. Miller of Staunton, Virginia, who also served as president of the General Synod South, advertised the fact that he was the "authorized agent for Estey for the State of Virginia": "No Church need be without that invaluable accompaniment to their singing, A GOOD INSTRUMENT, since they can be supplied with one of Estey's Cottage Organs, for from $100 to $350, which in tone and power is scarcely inferior to the Pipe Organ."[81]

J. F. Rueckert, a professor of music in Wilmington, also marketed "first class pianos & organs," and assured the state's Lutherans that "orders from the country" would receive his prompt attention. Charles M. Stieff of Baltimore reported he had "Parlor and Church Organs, some 20 different styles on hand from $50 and upwards," and invited North Carolina Lutherans to contact him for a catalog that would include a listing of "over 1000 southerners" including two hundred North Carolinians who had purchased pianos or organs through his firm.[82]

Still, the worship setting was sometimes distracting. A. L. Crouse describes worship in the old eight-sided frame church at Friendship, Taylorsville: "The windows are of good size, and had board shutters. These were usually left loose during the service, and, when the wind blew, slammed furiously. Added to this racket was frequently the howl of several vigorous babies and larger children. Sometimes a few dogs came in and scurried about with tails and bristles up, and when some of the elders fell upon them with clubs, the confusion was sufficient to make any preacher 'lose his place.' But for the most part the service of the sanctuary was of the most quiet and devout character."[83]

Church services were generally held on alternate Sundays, sometime less frequently. It was in 1877 that Salem, Lincolnton, moved from having only one worship service per month to two.[84]

When R. A. Yoder served a three-church pastorate "in 1885, the normal scheme was to hold services at St. James [Newton] two Sundays each month; at Grace [Newton] on one other Sunday, supplying a mission point at Starrtown in the afternoon; and at Salem [Lincolnton] on the other Sunday, preaching at a mission point in Maiden that afternoon."[85]

Not until 1888 did St. John's, Concord, begin worship services every Sunday, despite the fact that it was one of the oldest and largest congregations in the synod.

Although revivals were not generally held, many pastors, according to Hugh George Anderson, held "protracted meetings" each year. Rev. Simeon Scherer reported on his meetings in 1870:

> The meetings from first to last were characterized by unusual attention to the preaching of the Word, a slow but gradual increase of prevailing seriousness and deep solemnity, with comparatively little outburst and noisy excitement, just as we prefer.

But, Anderson observes, another pastor described the meetings with a bit more color: "When Rev's. Linn, Scherer, Scheck, Groseclose, Kimball and Shell got on fire with their themes . . . the people cried out, 'Men and brethren, what shall we do?'"

Anderson continues: "Some pastors used these revival-like services to replace catechization. In 1866, one parish reported 123 conversions. Within the Tennessee Synod, however, and among some pastors of the North Carolina Synod, these methods came under sharp attack."[86]

Pastor A. L. Crouse of the Tennessee Synod wrote that, although the Lutheran rule had always been to catechize new members, the exception to the rule was becoming more common: "This exception was the high pressure, quick process system; and its method was to steam through as quick as possible, sing up to the altar and give the right hand, then reviving the church. And in this way the exception has revived many congregations to death."

The North Carolina Synod attempted to resolve the matter of protracted meetings by asking a special committee of Nicodemus Aldrich and L. C. Groseclose to prepare a statement on the matter.

It confessed failure: "Whilst uniformity in practice is desirable, and whilst our ministers should feel themselves obligated to adhere as much as possible, to Lutheran practices, yet in the judgment of your committee, it is not advisable to adopt any resolution that may distract and divide the church within our bounds. We therefore, must patiently abide the time when God will enable us to see eye to eye."[87]

Role of Laity

Auxiliary organizations made their first appearances as an outgrowth of an earlier mission organization.

Early in their history the North Carolina and adjacent synods sought to develop support for mission work through the creation of a mission organization. Because the most conspicuous obstacle to mission expansion was the shortage of clergy, a two-pronged effort was attempted through organizations intended to sustain both ministerial education and home mission activity. It was typical, for a period of time, for the annual synodical convention to be turned over to an Education and Missionary Society so that there might be a presentation on one of the themes. Such presentations were accompanied by the "lifting" of an offering in support of the society. From time to time, pastors were also encouraged to create in their parishes local auxiliaries of the parent society.

The funding provided by the annual society meetings was useful, but inadequate to meet the ministerial education and mission expansion opportunities. In the Southwest Virginia Synod, a committee was created in 1879 to study the problem. Citing "the characteristic devotion of women in every good work," the committee proposed that women be asked to create "co-operative associations" in each congregation or parish "to aid in raising the funds so much needed."[88] Two years later, in 1881, the Women's Missionary Society of the Evangelical Lutheran Synod of Southwestern Virginia came into being.

In 1884 the emerging women's auxiliaries and missionary support organizations received a boost when William P. Swartz, a son of a Tennessee Synod pastor serving as missionary to India, toured the congregations of the Southwestern Virginia Synod and spoke at a Sunday School mass meeting in Botetourt County, generating interest and enthusiasm for the world mission of the church. Soon Swartz was visiting congregations in South Carolina where, in February 1885, women from twelve congregations assembled at Redeemer, Newberry, to create the Women's Missionary Society of the South Carolina Synod.

PRESIDENTS, NORTH CAROLINA SYNOD WOMAN'S HOME AND FOREIGN MISSIONARY SOCIETY

1886-88 Mrs. J. S. Fisher, Concord	1894-97 Mrs. J. Q. Wertz, China Grove
1888-89 Mrs. W. G. Campbell, Concord	1897-99 Mrs. J. H. C. Fisher, Mt. Pleasant
1889-91 Mrs. W. R. Brown, Heilig's Mills	1899-00 Mrs. J. Q. Wertz, China Grove
1891-93 Miss Ella Belle Shirey, Mt. Pleasant	1900-02 Miss Ella Belle Shirey, Bear Poplar
1893-94 Mrs. W. R. Brown, Organ Church	1902-04 Mrs. J. A. Linn, Mt. Pleasant

In less than ninety days Swartz was at St. James, Concord, meeting with the representatives of six local missionary societies that had been established in North Carolina, helping them organize a executive committee that would, in turn, create a synodical society.[89] The organization took place in the home of Mrs. Josiah S. (Laura Plunkett) Fisher in Concord on April 24, 1885.

Acceptance spread quickly, especially among the synod's clerical leadership. At its convention the same year, the synod endorsed the plans and constitutions for the "Woman's Home and Foreign Missionary Society of the North Carolina Lutheran Synod." It also recommended that all congregations consider establishing societies.

Within a year, the societies numbered fourteen with an aggregate membership of 320. Congregations reporting societies were St. Luke's, Bear Poplar; St. Mark's,

Charlotte; St. Paul's, Wilmington; St. Enoch, Enochville; Lutheran Chapel, China Grove; Holy Trinity, Mt. Pleasant; Union, Salisbury; Grace, Salisbury; Bethel, Franklin; St. James, Concord; Trinity, Concord; Prosperity, Concord; St. John's, Cabarrus County; and Center Grove, Kannapolis.

Under the guidance of its Executive Committee, the synodical organization held its first convention April 29, 1886, in Concord. Twenty-four delegates attended, reporting total contributions for the year of $275. In addition to adopting a constitution and by-laws, the delegates elected Mrs. Fisher as the charter president. Also elected were five vice-presidents: Mrs. J. S. Heilig, Mrs. J. B. Davis, Mrs. J. D. Shirey, Mrs. R. A. Brown and Mrs. A. M. Brown. Other officers named were Miss Julia Shirey, corresponding secretary; Miss Lillian Slough, recording secretary; and Mrs. John A. Cline, treasurer.

Minutes of the inaugural convention were printed and bound with the 1886 minutes of the synod. But, when the 1887 synod minutes included only an abstract of the women's proceedings, the auxiliary decided to print their minutes at their own expense. They did so in 1888 and have done so ever since.

In 1888, the organization promoted the observance of a Week of Prayer in late October.

At the inaugural convention, the delegates voted to divide undesignated funds equally between home and foreign missions. Within three years, it encouraged a variety of practices for the promotion of gifts. It suggested use of the Mite Box (a box kept in the home for deposit of frequent, small gifts), as well as a special birthday offering. It also asked minister's wives to give the marriage fees received on the date nearest Christmas. The expenses of the annual convention were funded by the payment of five cents per member per year. Honorary memberships for a year were available for one dollar and could be awarded to member and non-member alike, including men. The honorary membership practice, begun in 1889, continued for sixty years.

CONVENTON SITES
NORTH CAROLINA SYNOD
WOMAN'S HOME AND FOREIGN MISSIONARY SOCIETY

1886 St. James, Concord	1895 Organ, Rowan
1887 St. Enoch, Enochville	1896 St. Enoch, Enochville
1888 St. John's, Salisbury	1897 St. John's, Salisbury
1889 Holy Trinity, Mt. Pleasant	1898 Bethel, Rowan
1890 Lutheran Chapel, China Grove	1899 St. Mark's, Charlotte
1891 St. Mark's, Charlotte	1900 Lutheran Chapel, China Grove
1892 St. Peter's, Rowan	1901 St. Paul's, Rowan
1893 Union, Rowan	1902 Augsburg, Winston-Salem
1894 Holy Trinity, Mt. Pleasant	

Initially, the women sent undesignated funds to the Board of Missions of the United Synod South, with the request that they be divided between home and foreign objectives.

The primary foreign mission objective was Japan. Rev. R. B. Peery of the North Carolina Synod and Pastors C. K. Lippard and A. J. Stirewalt of the Tennessee Synod served in Japan as missionaries of the general synod.

In 1892, the organization began appropriating only one-half of the contributions annually to the missions board, sending the balance to the North Carolina Synod for mission points within the synod.

Later, in 1900, the president, Mrs. J. Q. Wertz, lamented the women "were still without a project of their own, and the only thing they had to show for their prayers and gifts was the memorial window in Augsburg, Winston-Salem."[90] Soon thereafter the convention adopted the Macedonia, Burlington, building project as the "Women's Special."

The early women's conventions were held in association with the synod convention in the spring. The date, however, was moved in 1890 to August to avoid the conflict.

The society grew rapidly. By 1895, nine years after organization, it had expanded from fourteen societies to twenty-eight, reporting a membership of 511. Gifts had grown by 1896 to $1,063.

From the concept of a woman's auxiliary grew other similar organizations.

The first was an organization for children. The synod's original authorization for a woman's organization included an implied provision for a children's society, visualized as a department of the woman's organization but often also associated with the congregational Sunday School.

The first Children's Missionary Society was organized in 1886 at St. Luke's, Bear Poplar, by Mrs. J. D. Shirey. One of the early certificates of membership read: "This is to certify that Bachman Miller of St. Luke's Sunday School has contributed 25c to the Children's Foreign Missionary Society of the Lutheran Church and is hereby constituted a member for one year." The second society was formed in 1889 at Holy Trinity, Mt. Pleasant.[91]

The contributions received by the children's societies were sent, in accordance with an 1886 action of the synod, to the treasurer of the synod and "accredited upon the assessments of the various congregations for Foreign Missions."[92] In 1893, however, the women's convention directed that contributions be transmitted to the Board of Missions of the United Synod South.

The first tabulated report of the societies, in 1895, showed nine local children's organizations, 265 members and offerings of $93.17. Congregations reporting organizations were Grace, St. Luke's, St. Mark's (China Grove), Trinity, Salem, Holy Trinity, St. John's (Cabarrus), St. John's (Salisbury), and Center Grove.[93]

The following year, the women's organization named Miss Ella Belle Shirey as the first children's secretary. It announced that the societies should seek one hundred dollars annually to be used for the support of a native Japanese worker, to be known as the "Children's Helper."

In addition to the children's societies, an organization for young people emerged during the same period. The earliest report of a young people's organization appeared in 1888 from Mont Amoena Seminary where a Young Women's group had formed.

But another youth organization of national scope, the Luther League, had gained the attention of the synod, which appointed a special committee of Pastors M. G. G. Scherer and J. D. Shirey to look into the matter. They recommended, in 1894, that the Luther League and its publication, *Luther League Review,* be commended to the congregations.

Six leagues were organized the following year, and eight were represented when the state Luther League organization was formed at St. James, Concord, on October 31, 1896. The local leagues, with memberships totaling 231, were located at St. John's, Salisbury; Holy Trinity, Mt. Pleasant; Macedonia, Burlington; St. James, Concord; St. Mark's, Charlotte; St. Andrew's, Concord; Augsburg, Winston-Salem; and St. Paul's, Asheville (a mission congregation served by Clarence Brown Cox). The Mt. Pleasant league reported the largest membership: fifty-four members.

The synod, at its next convention, approved the state league constitution but asked that the organization refrain from uniting with the national league "until further developments."[94]

In addition to membership in the auxiliaries, lay members of the church served the synod in other ways. As in earlier years, the treasurer of the synod continued to be a layman, even after the death of I. Frank Patterson of Albemarle in 1896. In an election on March 10, the Executive Committee of the synod chose another layman, J. D. Heilig of Salisbury, to fill the post.

One of the most significant developments in the Lutheran church in the South in the second half of the nineteenth century was the expanded role of the laity. And one of the areas of church life in which that expansion was conspicuous was the Sunday School. In its earliest forms the Sunday School was viewed primarily as a tool of social control, something that would enable the established social order to assimilate the children of the poor who might otherwise become destructive of that order. Gottlieb Schober seems to have been the staunchest advocate of Sunday Schools among the early North Carolina Synod pastors.

In 1812 at its convention at St. John's, Conover, the synod endorsed Sunday Schools: "As many of our children have no opportunity to receive instructions by a regular school, it was resolved, that Sunday Schools should in all our congregations be publicly recommended from the pulpit."[95]

Four years later the synod again urged that "whenever possible" pastors seek to establish Sunday Schools "in all our Churches." The schools were no longer to be viewed simply as instruments for improving society that might be placed in the hands of an educated secularist. Schools sponsored by Lutheran congregations were to be supervised by the pastor "and shall be opened and closed with singing and prayer."[96]

Desirable as might be the pastoral supervision of Sunday Schools called for by the North Carolina Synod in 1816, the fact was there were not enough pastors to go around. In a situation where congregations could receive the service of a pastor only once a month or less, the Sunday School was soon recognized as having potential for sustaining congregational life in the absence of a pastor. For five years following 1820, Union, Salisbury was without the services of a pastor except for a period of a few months when they apparently were served by a young licentiate. By 1825 the congregation was "mournfully destitute," but in the spring of 1827 a Sunday School was organized at Union and in just a few months the school boasted 120 pupils and twenty teachers.[97] By 1830 there were pastors who could report they related to more Sunday Schools than congregations.[98]

While the North Carolina Synod had its ardent promoters of Sunday Schools in persons like Schober and Reck, it is clear many pastors did not consider it a part of their calling to foster such enterprises. In 1840, only four of the twelve pastors attending the annual convention of the synod reported having Sunday Schools in their parishes.[99]

In the wake of the Second Great Awakening more and more persons came to believe that conversion, rather than the mere teaching of morals, was the best way to establish social controls and insure a stable society. Thus, by the 1830s Sunday Schools were increasingly evaluated on the basis of the number of conversions they could report.[100]

The fact that in the antebellum period most North Carolina Synod pastors supported revivals or "protracted meetings" meant that the North Carolina Synod generally looked with favor on Sunday Schools.

At the same time, the resistance of the Tennessee Synod to revivalism and their caution regarding interdenominational ventures resulted in their being less eager to promote Sunday Schools. However, since Christian education had always been such an integral part of the Lutheran tradition, a potentially useful educational tool could hardly be ignored.

In the era after the Civil War as North Carolina Synod Lutherans began to join their Tennessee Synod counterparts in reaffirming a distinctive heritage including the baptism of children in their infancy, the question of Christian nurture through such agencies as the Sunday School took on a new urgency. Increasingly Lutheran pastors viewed the Sunday School as a resource that could be adapted to the uses of a church that stressed the catechism rather than revivals, and this new appreciation for the Sunday church school created significantly expanded opportunities for lay persons to serve their Lord through the program of the church. As a contributor to *The Lutheran Visitor* observed, the expansion of the Sunday School movement brought "the laity to the front in church work."[101]

Never before had a congregation been able to offer to so many of its members, men and women, an opportunity to participate in a meaningful congregational activity on a continuing basis. But the opportunities for lay participation in the Sunday School movement were not confined to the local congregation. Sunday Schools were increasingly bound together into conferences or even state-wide associations. In the conventions held by these associations, lay persons were far more numerous than clergy so they were able to exert a degree of leadership and authority they had not known in other church meetings such as synodical conventions. In the summer of 1883 a Virginia Synod Sunday School and congregational convention at Fisher's Hill brought together an estimated four to five thousand Lutherans, establishing the fact that "the Lutherans of the Valley are not the least of the tribes of Israel."[102]

Happily, Lutheran clergy seemed not to have felt threatened by this emergence of lay leadership. By 1870 the North Carolina Synod had Sunday Schools organized in approximately three-fourths of its congregations. The Tennessee Synod saw their ratio of Sunday Schools to congregations grow "from one to three to better than one to two."

Given the environment in which the Lutheran congregations in the South functioned, many Lutheran pastors continued to regard the primary aim of both Sunday School and confirmation class as conversion. However, when the editor of *The Lutheran Observer* voiced such views on behalf of the Sunday School, he was challenged by Pastor Crouse of the Tennessee Synod who insisted Sunday Schools should not be designed to try to convert young people who had already been baptized. Rather, they should be viewed as instruments of missionary outreach to those outside the Christian fellowship.

Institutions

When the period opened in 1870, the North Carolina synod owned two educational institutions, both situated at Mt. Pleasant.

North Carolina College, closed during the Civil War, had been reopened for three years. Rev. L. A. Bikle served as president and presided over an enrollment of eighty-one boys, many of them "preparatorians" who paid less tuition than the college-level students and failed to generate the revenue needed by the institution.

Although the enrollment climbed by 1873 to 130, the year brought with it a three hundred dollar deficit which quickly ballooned to a four thousand dollar debt over the next four years.

In 1875, the Committee on Church Institutions and Education noted the college was not flourishing as it should with regard to enrollment and influence. There were 105 enrollees.

"The causes of the want of this prosperity," the committee said, "we conceive to be several.

> First: the College is not sufficiently advertised in the secular press. Judicious expenditure of printer's ink always brings in a rich return. The Merchant, who does not advertise his goods and place of business, cannot expect a large and profitable trade.
>
> Again another cause for the want of prosperity, is the absence of an endowment fund, that the teaching force might be increased. The Board of Trustees put into the field an agent for this very purpose, and he collected several thousand dollars. We recommend that this agency be continued until the amount of $20,000 be raised, as was presented by your committee last year.

NORTH CAROLINA COLLEGE PRESIDENTS

1868-1874	Dr. L. A. Bikle	1887-1889	Dr. J. G. Schaidt
1875-1877	Dr. J. B. Davis	1889-1896	Dr. J. D. Shirey
1878-1881	Dr. L. A. Bikle	1896-1899	Dr. M. G. G. Scherer
1882-1883	Dr. G. H. Bernheim	1899-1900	Prof. Edgar Bowers (Acting)
1883-1887	Dr. G. F. Schaeffer	1900-1902	Rev. W. A. Lutz

> Another cause for this want of prosperity, is the manner of employing the faculty of the College. They have heretofore been elected by the Board of Trustees with a fixed salary for each one of the Professors, grading these salaries according to the position occupied in the Faculty of the College. We would recommend that this plan be changed. Let the Professors that are and may hereafter be elected take the College and by their own energy and worth increase the number of their students and pay themselves out of the tuition proceeding therefrom. The plan heretofore pursued has left undeveloped the latent energy of the corps of Professors, whilst it has gradually but surely involved the College in debt, until it now amounts to $1,500.

The committee went on to report the resignation of both President Bikle and one professor. Rev. C. F. Bansemer was selected by the board to succeed Bikle and Rev. J. H. Turner was named to fill the faculty position.

"The buildings of the College are in bad repair," the report continued. "The late storm has considerably damaged the College buildings, which has been repaired in part, by the help of the friends in the neighborhood. The interior of the buildings are in a bad condition and it will require an outlay of $400 to $600 to fix it up properly, which must be done this ensuing vacation. Synod recommends that every Minister lift a collection in each Church for this special purpose at their next communion season."[103]

The convention adopted the report.

To buy some time for liquidating the debt and repairing the property, the synod convention in 1877 agreed to offer the school "to a faculty that would take charge of it and conduct it in accordance with its chartered design upon their own responsibility." Three professors (Bikle, Ludwig and Rev. S. S. Rahn) accepted the proposition and entered into a three-year agreement with the college board of trustees. The faculty received the operating income and free use of the property and was responsible for the operating expenses. The board was responsible for repairs and insurance on the property.

The faculty did its part. In the first year, it erected a new fence around the campus and replaced several roofs despite a disappointing enrollment of only seventy students. But the board did not gain much headway. It did not reduce the debt; in fact, accrued interest increased the debt.

The lease arrangement was terminated by the synod convention at the end of the three-year term, and the board was ordered to resume operation of the school. As a result of a partly-successful congregational assessment program, the debt was reduced from thirteen hundred to eight hundred dollars but there was no provision for its further reduction.

FEMALE SEMINARY PRESIDENTS, PRINCIPALS

1855-1858 Rev. William Gerhardt	1874-1876 Rev. P. A. Strobel, Mrs. E. M. Strobel
1859-1861 Rev. D. H. Bittle	1876-1882 Prof. L. H. Rothrock
1866-1867 Rev. L. A. Bikle	1882-1883 Rev. G. F. Schaeffer
1867-1868 Rev. C. F. Bansemer	1885-1891 Rev. J. Adolphus Linn
1870-1871 Rev. D. I. Dreher	1892-1897 Rev. C. L. T. Fisher
1871-1872 Prof. W. A. Barrier	1897-1902 Rev. H. N. Miller
1872-1874 Mrs. W. E. (Virginia Ribble) Hubbert	

Meanwhile, across town, Mt. Pleasant Female Academy in 1870 was headed by Rev. D. I. Dreher and enrolled fifty-seven pupils. Although its enrollment remained stable, it also soon experienced financial difficulties.

Conditions continued to deteriorate at both institutions until, despite efforts by the synod to reduce the debts and increase enrollments, they were both forced to close for a period in the 1883-84 year. Prior to the start of the year, the synod convention had taken two steps to remedy the problem, voting to merge the schools into a single co-educational institution, and directing a special committee to "investigate the chances for a consolidation of the N.C. College with either Newberry or Concordia College or both. . ."[104] Newberry was owned by the South Carolina Synod; Concordia, by the Tennessee Synod. Neither, however, was interested in consolidation, nor were the Mt. Pleasant schools merged, because North Carolina College was soon reopened "on a plan that promises success."[105]

The plan that promised success was developed by the college treasurer, Jonas Cook, who proposed that "a College Benefit Association" be created, its membership to consist of two hundred persons who promised to pay to the association ten dollars a year for five years. Members enjoyed a ten-dollar per year reduction in any tuition bills they might be called upon to pay. Congregations holding memberships could send to the college tuition-free any students "having the ministry in view."

The board of trustees, in adopting the plan, decided to re-open the college when one hundred memberships were secured. Rev. J. A. Linn was named agent to solicit memberships. The college resumed operation in January 1884, but to make this possible, some "friends of the College" had to subscribe two memberships. Despite the "extreme severity of the weather," approximately sixty students enrolled.

The girl's school also re-opened after a short period and in 1885 was reported "in a flourishing condition" with a three hundred dollar debt described as "not very great."[106] Despite the optimism, the synod observed in the following year that the needed endowment for North Carolina College was not practical, and it expressed continuing interest in conferring with the Tennessee Synod about merging educational work. Talks with the sister synod, however, were not seriously pursued until fifteen years later.

During the final decade of the century, conditions at the two schools stabilized. North Carolina College dropped its financial loser, the Preparatory Department, and, through the special solicitation successes among congregations, boosted its endowment by five thousand dollars. The girl's school, which changed its name in 1892 to Mont Amoena Female Seminary, increased its enrollment by 1897 to a record 112 students.

But all was not well. Both institutions continued to fight chronic indebtedness, with North Carolina College's remaining at four thousand dollars. North Carolina College's enrollment dropped to fifty-six in 1900. Mont Amoena suffered the indignity of losing its most popular and successful principal, Prof. C. L. T. Fisher, to a potentially-serious competitor, a new college for girls at Charlotte sponsored by the United Synod South.

The proposed discussions with the Tennessee Synod, suggested in 1886, resurfaced in 1899 when the college trustees challenged the North Carolina Synod convention once again to help improve attendance and liquidate the debt. The convention responded with the oft-repeated argument that the location of the college was a strategic problem. The delegates directed that a committee be appointed to solicit bids for other locations for the college and report its findings to the next convention, or to a called convention if necessary.

The committee, after advertising in church journals and in daily newspapers of Charlotte, Salisbury, Greensboro and Winston, received two bids. The city of Salisbury offered sixteen acres of land and cash of eighty-five hundred dollars if the college were placed there. The Tennessee Synod, which abandoned Concordia College in 1891 for the more spacious campus of Lenoir College in Hickory, also entered a bid. It offered half interest in the building and grounds of Lenoir College (valued at ten thousand dollars), twelve building lots in Hickory and equal representation on the board of trustees if the college were merged with Lenoir.

Two conventions were required for consideration of the proposals. At a called meeting at St. John's, Salisbury, on February 20, 1900, the delegates, citing the small attendance, concluded that the matter should be deferred to a regular convention. At the regular convention, held at First, Albemarle, on May 3, the delegates rejected the Tennessee Synod offer, primarily because of practical difficulties in joint management. But they hesitated to accept the Salisbury offer because of Mt. Pleasant opposition to relocation itself. Salisbury was asked to keep its offer open for one year, but the offer was not re-submitted at the following convention.

Conditions improved at North Carolina College in 1901. The Mt. Pleasant community renovated the college buildings, enrollment jumped to a record 102, and the faculty and alumni devised plans to build a memorial hall.

The success, however, was temporary. At its 1902 convention, the church delegates learned that North Carolina College had "few students" and "fewer faculty." Conditions had deteriorated to the point that the convention voted to suspend operations for one year. It also authorized a special committee to inquire whether the Tennessee Synod was still interested in merging educational interests.[107]

Conditions at Mont Amoena were more stabilized. Although the girl's school lost some students because of a North Carolina College decision to admit women to its junior and senior classes, its 1901 enrollment of ninety-two was followed by a 1902 registration of ninety.

The new Lutheran women's college in Charlotte, opened in 1897, was named Elizabeth College. Despite its potential competition to Mont Amoena, its founding was not opposed by the synod. At a special convention eight years earlier, the synod delegates reported by vote "that we have heard with pleasure the remarks of Capt. W. A. Barrier [a charter trustee of Mont Amoena] respecting the founding of a Lutheran Female College at Charlotte, and that we reaffirm our endorsement of this enterprise by Synod, and invite Capt. W. A. Barrier to canvass the congregations of Synod to secure aid in behalf of the proposed Seminary."[108]

The institution also had community support. The city of Charlotte gave the site and ten thousand dollars toward the building construction cost.

It was readily embraced by the synod because it was situated on the synod's territory, it was designed to serve Lutheran women at the bachelor's degree level, and its governing board was comprised only of Lutherans. It was not, of course, owned by the synod: the property was deeded and held in trust for the United Synod South.

It was an institution in which the synod could take pride. Its twenty-acre campus was graced with an attractive seventy-thousand-dollar building. It opened with an enrollment of ninety-four students and a staff of eighteen teachers and officers. Its aim was "to afford a first-class college for the daughters of the Lutheran church."[109]

The synod's Committee on the State of the Church reported to the annual conventions the status of Elizabeth, alongside those of North Carolina College and Mont Amoena. It gave unabashed praise to the new college, describing it as the "finest institution for the education of women in the Lutheran church in America."[110] By 1902, the enrollment had advanced to 119, and the property was valued at $250,000.

In addition to North Carolina College, Mont Amoena and Elizabeth, there were several parochial schools operated by North Carolina Synod congregations. At the close of the period, in 1902, however, the only parochial school was at St. Paul's, Wilmington.

The Tennessee Synod was associated with three Lutheran schools in the state.

Dallas Academy, near Gastonia, was reactivated by a Lutheran minister, Marcus Lafayette Little, in 1882. In addition to teaching, he raised ten thousand dollars in gifts, counting among the school's donors Jonas Hoffman, Henry Setzer, David Mauney, L. L. Sugg, Ambrose Costner and John M. Rhodes. Among Little's associate teachers were Rev. L. A. Bikle, Rev. L. L. Lohr and John M. Roberts, the editor of the *Lincoln Courier.* Graduates included physicians, ministers and teachers, particularly Lutheran women teachers of North and South Carolina.

After Little's death in 1891, the school was developed into Gaston College for Girls and Young Women. For many years, Prof. S. A. Wolf served as principal. Although it was not funded by the church, the school offered free tuition to one pupil from each Lutheran congregation in the area.

Another school in the Tennessee Synod territory was Holly Grove Academy near Lexington. It was founded in 1885 by Rev. W. P. Cline with the collaboration of Peter Kepley, Peter Yount, Henry H. Conrad, William Fritz, Haley Myers, William Beck and others.

Concordia High School at Conover enjoyed a more formal synodical relationship. It opened in 1877 under the direction of Dr. P. C. Henkel, Rev. John M. Smith and other local pastors. After it was chartered in 1880 as Concordia College, the Tennessee Synod moved to closer affiliation, finally accepting the institution under its "fostering care" in 1883. The arrangement gave the synod the privilege of nominating the college's trustees and requiring the trustees to report annually to the synod. Two years later, the synod designated Concordia for the education of its ministerial candidates and assessed its congregations eight hundred dollars annually to fund the salary of the theological professor.

Limited space, however, prompted some of the Concordia leaders in 1890 to urge removal of the college to the fifty-six-acre campus of Highland Academy at nearby Hickory. When the synod turned down the proposal, the Concordia president, Rev. R. A. Yoder, and three other clergy members of the faculty and board, decided to leave Concordia anyway and start a separate school at the Hickory site without synodical support. The school opened in 1891 under the name of Highland College but changed the name in the middle of its first year to Lenoir College, honoring the donor of the campus property, Walter W. Lenoir. One hundred and forty-nine students attended during the first year.

Although the Tennessee Synod did not immediately impart its "fostering care" on the new college, it did direct ministerial students to study under one of its professors, Rev. Andrew L. Crouse.

It was in 1895, after the remaining trustees of Concordia College offered that institution to the Evangelical Lutheran Synod of Missouri, Ohio, and Other States, that the Tennessee Synod adopted a resolution pledging "hearty moral and financial support" of Lenoir. The college, in return, agreed to increase its board membership from six to thirteen, and to permit the synod to nominate the seven new members and all future vacancies occurring on the board.

Yoder served as president of Lenoir until 1901, when he relinquished the reins to a Lenoir graduate and former professor who was teaching at Elizabeth College, Rev. Robert Lindsay Fritz.

While both the Tennessee and North Carolina synods demonstrated an interest in educational institutions, the North Carolina Synod during this period also inaugurated support of a social ministry institution - an orphanage.

In 1887, without synod impetus, an orphanage was opened on the estate of Rev. William S. McClanahan, near Salem, Virginia, because a brother of McClanahan's had died in Texas, leaving several small children in McClanahan's care. Two of the children were Dr. G. W. McClanahan, and Mrs. R. C. (Mary McClanahan) Holland. With the aid of an executive committee comprised primarily of Lutherans, William S. McClanahan directed the operation of the home as superintendent, and his niece, Mrs. Holland, assisted as matron, housekeeper, teacher, and office helper.

Although the orphanage was not located within its boundaries, the North Carolina Synod expressed interest in the home and commended support of the institution to its congregations. The action reflected the absence of an orphan home within the synod and anticipated what actually happened before the end of the period - some North Carolina children were cared for in the Virginia home. Regular reports of the home were submitted annually to the synod.

In 1897, the orphanage was taken over by the United Synod, of which the North Carolina Synod was a member. The home was relocated on Boulevard and Florida Streets in Salem, and the name was changed to Lutheran Orphan Home of the South.

Enrollment in the home in 1899 totaled twenty-seven children, including six from North Carolina.

Despite its interest in the orphan home, the synod did not engage in other social ministry activities, such as issuing statements on social issues. One statement, however, was issued. In 1896, the convention adopted a resolution condemning Cuban oppression. It was introduced by Lay Delegate Jonas Cook and Rev. W. A. Lutz. The resolution stated: "Inasmuch as the enjoyment, anywhere, of civil and religious liberty is a priceless boon of the great reformation by Luther; and recognizing the inalienable right of all peoples to self-government: We hereby express our unfeigned sympathy for the Cubans in their struggle for liberty and independence, deploring the atrocities committed by combatants on either side."[111]

Finances

The synod's treasury during the period served as a funnel for a variety of contributions flowing from the congregations to specific objectives, such as missions, ministerial education and educational institutions. Congregations were also asked to assess amounts for the operation of the synod itself, to cover such expenses as the printing of convention proceedings and paying travel expenses for fraternal delegates to other synodical conventions. The expenses of the synodical treasury totaled only a few hundred dollars but began increasing toward the end of the period, advancing from $309 in 1900 to $418 in 1901, $543 in 1902 and $693 in 1903.

Synodical Alignments

The Tennessee Synod, which had already experienced three splits, suffered a fourth in the last decade of the century. The division centered on the synod's institution at Conover, Concordia College.

When the synod in 1891 declined to designate a theology professor at the college and instead recommended the new Highland College at Hickory for its beneficiary aid students, the trustees of Concordia felt betrayed.

Hoping to have their school remain identified with confessional Lutheranism, the

Concordia trustees turned to the Mission Board of the German Missouri Synod and invited that body to provide faculty for Concordia College.

In December 1891, Pastors William Dallmann of Baltimore and Frederick Kuegele of Augusta County, Virginia, paid Conover a visit at the request of the Board of English Missions of The English Missouri Synod. This synod grew out of the English Lutheran Conference of Missouri which had been organized in Gravelton, Missouri, in 1872 by two Tennessee Synod pastors along with a pastor of the Holston Synod.[112]

After conferring with Dallmann and Kuegele, the Board of Trustees at Concordia resolved to call a professor "from the Missourians, to be President of Concordia College, Literary Professor, and pastor of Concordia Congregation, to have full liberty in the pulpit and at the altar according to his conscience bound in God's Word."

By the end of July, Rev. W. H. T. Dau had been installed as the new president of Concordia College and a young graduate of the seminary in St. Louis, G. A. Romoser, had joined him on the faculty.

Meeting in Chicago in 1893, the English Missouri Synod received a formal offer from the Board of Trustees of Concordia to take over the school. The synod, consisting of twenty-eight congregations served by sixteen pastors, accepted the school, retaining Dau in the president's office.

For a number of years the faculty at Concordia supplemented their modest salaries by supplying vacant congregations in the Conover area, a fact that enabled them to bring a number of Tennessee Synod congregations into the Missouri Synod. At the same time, Concordia College began to emerge as the chief center for the mission activities of the Missouri Synod in the Southeast.

The arrival of Missouri Synod pastors to labor among North Carolina's black population was not resented by either the North Carolina or the Tennessee synods. But the presence of Missouri Synod pastors in what had been Tennessee Synod congregations did produce ill will because the newcomers failed to unite with the Tennessee Synod. This practice, coupled with the developments in Conover, caused some to suspect a plot to undermine the Tennessee Synod by infiltrating its congregations.

A Free Conference in October 1893 brought together Tennessee and Missouri synod pastors at Hickory in an effort to arrive at a common understanding of one of the differences separating the two synods: predestination. A second conference was held three months later in Conover, but a resolution of the differing points of view was not forthcoming.

The situation was also aggravated by the fact that the public airing of views on election revealed that the Tennessee Synod's professor of theology, Rev. A. L. Crouse, really held the Missouri position on election rather than that espoused by his colleagues in the Tennessee Synod. When it became clear that he could not in good conscience accept the Tennessee Synod position, Crouse, even though one of the founders of the institution, resigned his position at the Tennessee Synod college, which opened under the name of Highland but was renamed Lenoir College during its first year. Eventually four Tennessee Synod pastors and four congregations moved from the Tennessee Synod to the Missouri Synod as a result of the predestinarian controversy.

Lutherans in North Carolina still bore a common name and professed allegiance to the Reformation heritage. But as they moved into the twentieth century, their congregations related to three different supra-synodical organizations, the United Synod South, the Joint Synod of Ohio, and the Lutheran Church - Missouri Synod. To a leader of the Tennessee Synod, the North Carolina situation seemed confused because there actually were present three different kinds of Lutheranism.

The first refused to be bound by anything more than the Augsburg Confession, believing that that was all that should be required to insure Lutheran identity. From the perspective of the Tennessee Synod, this was the "weakest type" since it laid its adherents open to the suspicion that, by refusing to subscribe to the entire *Book of Concord,* they did not really believe the teachings of the Augsburg Confession.

A second type of Lutheranism in the Tar Heel State was described as requiring acceptance of the Lutheran Confessions in their entirety, but failing to bring its own "teaching and practice" into conformity with the doctrines set forth in the documents contained in the *Book of Concord.*

The third type, involving not only the acceptance of the documents contained in the *Book of Concord* but conformity of teachings and practices to the doctrines set forth in the confessional writings of the Lutheran tradition, was, predictably, assumed by the speaker to describe the kind of Lutheranism represented by his own Tennessee Synod.

A recovery of Lutheran unity in North Carolina would clearly require getting to know and trust one another as well as professing loyalty to the Lutheran confessions.

✝

Elizabeth College
Founded 1897

R. A. Yoder
President, Tennessee Synod
1885-86

St. Paul's, Burlington (1893)
Organized 1770

Alpha Synod Church Building (1993)
Charlotte, N. C.
Congregation Organized c. 1891

George H. Cox
President, North Carolina Synod
1889-93

Tennessee Synod Ministers, Lay Delegates
Holly Grove, Lexington
November 8, 1889

CHAPTER VIII

TOWARD UNION (1903-1920)

he first two decades of the twentieth century - known in American history as the Progressive era - were a time of hope, anxiety and energetic action for many white, middle-class North Carolinians. The two decades were also the time when the Tennessee Synod and the North Carolina Synod moved more closely together and, in 1920, finally healed their century-long schism. Progressivism and Lutheran unity in North Carolina were, in reality, closely related historical changes.

Progressivism was a white, middle-class movement led by professional men and women - physicians, teachers, engineers, journalists, lawyers, social workers, and ministers- who sought to advance education, protect public health, preserve the natural environment, outlaw alcoholic beverages and democratize politics. Although black leaders in the South shared these concerns and white Progressives worried about racial injustice, the Progressive movement in the South sought social reforms which would not challenge segregation or immediately alter the place of blacks in a hierarchical social order.

In hoping that social progress would eventually ameliorate the plight of blacks, white Progressives exhibited their American optimism about human nature; if the scourges of ignorance, disease, alcohol and privilege could be eliminated through education and cooperation, they reasoned, then the native intelligence and natural virtue of the people would come to the fore.[1]

Robert A. Yoder of Catawba County, one of the most prominent figures in North Carolina Lutheranism during the first decade of the twentieth century, exemplified progressive values and worked diligently to promote public and church supported education within the confines of a conservative social order.

Yoder was a teacher and Lutheran college president, a Tennessee Synod pastor, and an elected public official. He was continuously engaged in various education, political and religious controversies which, in addition to his crushing workload, contributed to his early death at the age of 57. As president of Concordia College in Conover, he first resisted and then oversaw the move of the college to Hickory to become Lenoir College. As the underpaid, overworked Superintendent for Public Instruction for Catawba County from 1884 to 1894, he struggled to improve the training of teachers and sought without success to extend professional training to black teachers.

The controversy over moving Concordia College to Hickory spawned a theological dispute when disgruntled trustees turned to the Lutheran Church - Missouri Synod for support. Suspecting a Missouri design to lure churches away from the Tennessee Synod, Yoder emphasized the theological difference between the two Lutheran church bodies over the issue of salvation by grace (Missouri upheld predestination). Yoder's skill as a theological debater not only stemmed defections to Missouri, his leadership also reminded the Tennessee Synod of its confessional Lutheran heritage. Thus made conscious of its own theology and confident of its orthodoxy, the Tennessee Synod under Yoder's influence entered actively into the work of the United Synod South, which elected Yoder its president in 1902 and in 1904. Yoder used that office to promote education and domestic and foreign missions.[2]

NORTH CAROLINA SYNOD PRESIDENTS

1902-04	Robert C. Holland	1911-15	M. M. Kinard
1904-08	George H. Cox	1915-19	C. A. Brown
1908-11	V. Y. Boozer	1919-21	Jacob L. Morgan

In the election of 1919, Morgan was named the synod's first full-time, salaried president. In an associated action, the synod rescinded an earlier action creating the salaried position of synodical missionary, which Morgan filled prior to his election.

Like other progressive clergymen and educators, Yoder believed that institutions devoted to human betterment, and comprised of men and women of good will, ought to grow in size, increase in activity, and reach out to the larger society. The cooperation between the Tennessee Synod and the United Synod South between 1900 and 1920 was an example of this progressive faith in the efficacy of human service institutions. Like other churches, Lutherans in North Carolina became imbued after 1900 with a sense of duty to make the state and nation a more humane place by embracing the educational, humanitarian and scientific spirit of the modern world.

Missions

The concept of a synodical missionary would not die in the North Carolina Synod. The opportunities for new congregations were plentiful, and synodical leaders felt the Lutheran church was losing ground to other denominations because insufficient time was given to the development of new churches. The task required the full-time attention of a pastor.

NORTH CAROLINA SYNOD CONVENTION SITES

1903	St. John's, Salisbury	1912	St. Mark's, Charlotte
1904	Christiana, Rowan County	1913	St. John's, Cabarrus County
1905	Pilgrim, Davidson County	1914	Macedonia, Burlington
1906	St. John's, Cabarrus County	1915	St. Paul's, Salisbury
1907	Salem, Rowan County	1916	St. James, Concord
1908	Lutheran Chapel, China Grove	1917	First, Albemarle
1909	Faith, Rowan County	1918	Augsburg, Winston-Salem
1910	First, Albemarle	1919	Union, Salisbury
1911	St. Paul's, Wilmington	1920	St. Mark's, China Grove

At its centennial convention at St. John's, Salisbury, in 1903, a call was voiced for the employment of a synodical field secretary. The matter was referred to the Executive

Committee.

At the next convention, the Executive Committee recommended and the convention approved, without funding, the employment. Later the convention reconsidered its action, and J. H. Rehder of St. Paul's, Wilmington, offered to raise one thousand dollars for the missionary's salary if the pastors and delegates would poll their congregations for additional support. The challenge was accepted, and the congregations pledged $720. A committee was formed to seek an additional $280 so that the two thousand dollars in support would be available.

While the financial support was sought, some intersynodical efforts were undertaken. The Northern and Southern conferences worked together with Rev. D. I. Offman of the Tennessee Synod for a time in providing a ministry to "Lutherans at Landis, a new mill-town in Rowan county. But, at length, believing that more could be accomplished by one man serving them, and inasmuch as Rev. Offman was most conveniently located for the work, and that most of the Lutherans living there were members of his pastorate, our men withdrew from the work, giving it all over to Rev. Offman."[3]

The position of synodical missionary was finally created in 1905. Rev. Edward Fulenwider began the work on January 1, using Lexington as his primary site, but also giving general oversight to the areas of Thomasville, High Point and Greensboro. During the next two years, three congregations were formed: First, Lexington, and Calvary, Spencer (1905); and St. James, Rockwell (1907). Fulenwider, however, then accepted the call of the Lexington congregation to become its regular pastor, in the process vacating the new synodical position.

Succeeding Fulenwider as synodical missionary was Rev. Jacob L. Morgan, a 1902 ordinand who had been serving two congregations at Enochville. He assumed duties July 1, 1907, in High Point, but worked also at Greensboro, Mooresville, Landis and exercised oversight of work at Kannapolis. His schedule required that he preach at High Point in the morning and at Greensboro in the afternoon on three Sundays each month. On the other Sunday in each month, he led services at Mooresville in the morning and at Landis in the afternoon. On the fifth Sunday, he preached again at Mooresville.

TENNESSEE SYNOD PRESIDENTS

1903-04	R. H. Cline	1911-12 J. P. Stirewalt
1904-05	E. L. Wessinger	1912-14 L. L. Lohr
1905-06	J. P. Stirewalt	1914-16 C. K. Bell
1906-08	E. J. Sox	1916-18 A. R. Beck
1908-09	J. C. Moser	1918-21 B. D. Wessinger
1909-11	W. J. Boger	1921 W. A. Deaton

The mission at Greensboro, First Church, was opened in 1907. Woman's Memorial (Emmanuel), High Point, followed in 1908. During the next two years, Morgan developed two more congregations: St. Mark's, Mooresville (1908); and Trinity, Landis (1911). Grace, Thomasville, was also formed in 1911, although its organization was not directly related to Morgan's work.

Despite the addition of congregations, Synod President V. Y. Boozer chided the

1911 convention for the small net increase in communicant membership. The annual net gain for ten years had not been more than 150, he said. He felt the problem lay in the pastor's ministering only to Germans and Scandinavians: "We seem to think we have no right to try to lead to Christ other unchurched and unsaved people. Why should we depend solely on immigration and Lutheran settlements for fields in which to garner for the Lord?"

Moving to Raleigh, Missionary Morgan helped to organize Grace, Liberty, in 1911 and Holy Trinity, Raleigh, in 1912. When he accepted a call in 1916 to become regular pastor of the Raleigh church, the synodical missionary position was again left vacant. The synod convention was urged by the Rowan County Minister's Association to continue funding the position, but the synodical Committee on the President's Report argued that it was "not feasible at this time."[4] In the following year, however, Rev. John Baxter Moose of Bluefield, West Virginia, a native of Cabarrus County ordained by the North Carolina Synod, was called to fill the position.

Meanwhile, new congregations continued to appear. Calvary, Concord, was founded in 1913; Kimball Memorial, Kannapolis, in 1914; and Holy Trinity, Charlotte, in 1916.

TENNESSEE SYNOD CONVENTION SITES

1903	St. Peter's, Lexington County, South Carolina
1904	Mt. Moriah, Rowan County
1905	St. Paul's, Page County, Virginia
1906	St. Thomas, Lexington County, South Carolina
1907	St. Matthew's, Kings Mountain
1908	Emmanuel, New Market, Virginia
1909	St. Paul's, Lexington County, South Carolina
1910	Emmanuel, Lincolnton
1911	St. Peter's, Shenandoah County, Virginia
1912	St. Jacob's, Chapin, South Carolina
1913	Holy Trinity, Hickory
1914	St. Mary's, Mt. Jackson, Virginia
1915	Mt. Tabor, New Brookland, South Carolina
1916	Good Shepherd, Mt. Holly
1917	Rader's, Timberville, Virginia
1918	Mt. Horeb, Chapin, South Carolina
1919	Solomon's, Forestville, Virginia
1920	Emmanuel, Lincolnton

While the North Carolina Synod was welcoming thirteen congregations during the 1903-1920 period, the sister Tennessee Synod added twelve churches to its North Carolina Conference.

Six of the new Tennessee congregations were formed during the first five years. Both Grace, Bessemer City, and Mt. Hebron, Hildebran, organized in 1903. They were followed by St. Paul's, Startown (1905); New Jerusalem, Hickory (1906); Bethlehem, Hickory (1907); and St. Stephen's, Lenoir (1908).

The importance of the mission program was underscored in 1909 by R. A. Yoder.

As president of the recently created Board for Home Missions and Church Extension of the United Synod South, Yoder prepared two articles on home missions for the *Lutheran Church Visitor*, (March 4 and April 15, 1909).[5] He wrote: "If the Lutheran Church is to grow with the growth of this marvelously developing Southern country..., if she is to fulfill her mission among men, and be faithful to the Master's great commission, then she must project her Home Mission work on a broader basis...."

Since October was designated as the time for gathering funds for the cause, Yoder wrote a letter to each Sunday School and each congregation in September through the church paper, reminding them of the opportunity to support an important work of the United Synod. In October he offered special envelopes for receiving the offering for those congregations and Sunday Schools that requested them.[6]

During the next eleven years, the Tennessee Synod added six congregations. Bethany, Hickory, and St. John's, Hudson, organized in 1910, and St. Matthew's, Granite Falls, followed in 1911. St. John's, Taylorsville, opened in 1915; Grace, Hendersonville, in 1916; and Holy Comforter, Belmont, in 1917.

A report to the Tennessee Synod on missions in 1917 sounded a positive note. It indicated that the mission points in the North Carolina Conference were

> all enjoying the services of regular pastors, except the Hendersonville Mission. The Rev. Dr. M. M. Kinard of St. John's congregation, Salisbury, while on his vacation, is supplying the work here during August. A letter from the place expresses the great pleasure of the congregation at his services, also the very encouraging outlook of the work here. Negotiations are pending with the United Synod Board of Home Missions looking toward the placing of a permanent pastor here under the charge of said Board. All our other missions are in a healthy and prosperous condition.

Publications

The focus on mission development following the turn of the century was not matched by a focus on a single Lutheran periodical until late in the period. In 1906 some of the constituent synods in the United Synod South were served by *Our Church Paper*, others by the *Lutheran Visitor*. The United Synod South had created a third publication, *The Southern Lutheran*, to serve as its own official organ. In this year Tennessee Synod Pastor R. A. Yoder of Emmanuel, Lincolnton, recommended to the United Synod South that it purchase the two privately owned papers and then consolidate them with *The Southern Lutheran*, a move he believed would give the official organ of the United Synod South wider circulation, would effect a useful economy in operation, and would contribute to a greater "unity of faith and practice in our Synod."[7]

Despite Yoder's call for a single publication, an additional Lutheran publication appeared the same year in an adjacent county. The *Catawba Lutheran* began publication and continued publishing through 1922, possibly 1923, as an organ of the Lutheran Pastoral Association of Catawba County. Editors included C. Luther Miller (1906, 1909), W. A. Deaton (co-editor, 1909), J. H. Wannemacher (1912, 1914), E. J. Sox (1915), C. I. Morgan (1917), V. L. Fulmer (1918), John C. Peery (1919), F. L. Conrad (1920, 1921), A. R. Beck (1922). Places of publication included Newton, Lenoir and Granite Falls.

With the merger creating the United Lutheran Church in America in 1918 appeared *The Lutheran*, a biweekly which was promoted increasingly among congregations during the latter part of the period.

Pastors

Meanwhile, the first two decades of the new century saw the Lutheran synods experiment with two new projects for pastors: assistance for disabled ministers, and ordination of foreign ministers.

During the early years of the period, the establishment of a fund "for the relief or support of indigent, disabled, or superannuated ministers" was undertaken by the North Carolina Synod.[8] Responding to a persistent challenge over several years, the synod convention in 1903 formulated plans for the Disabled Ministers Fund.

Each minister and each congregational member was assessed for the fund. Ministers receiving annual salaries of less than six hundred dollars were assessed 0.5% of their salaries; those with higher salaries were assessed one percent. In addition, an annual three-cent assessment was placed on each member of a congregation in the synod. The funds would be disbursed by the Executive Committee of the synod.

Response to the assessments was weak, and in 1904 the convention delegates authorized the creation of a board of directors for the fund, with responsibility for devising ways and means for raising the funds. Three years later it approved a constitution for the fund.

Disbursements from the fund were made for about a decade, but the small fund failed to attract additional gifts and ultimately disappeared.

During the same period, three Japanese pastors were ordained or enrolled by the North Carolina Synod, and a fourth was ordained by order of the Tennessee Synod, although they did not serve in the territories of the synods. The unusual arrangement was necessitated by the absence of a regularly-constituted Lutheran body in Japan. Their listing on the North Carolina synodical roster was made at the request of a mission board of one of the general synods within the United States.

Hikoshiro Aoyama, a native of Okazaki, Japan, graduated from McCormick Seminary in Chicago and was received into the Lutheran church about 1913 and enrolled as an ordained minister by the North Carolina Synod. He later served Japanese pastorates in Hakata and Kobe and as a professor at the Lutheran Seminary in Kumamoto.

Toranosuke Chiga, native of Nagasaki, Japan, studied theology at Aoyama Gakuin, Tokyo, and entered the Methodist ministry. In 1919 he resigned from the Methodist church and was ordained by the North Carolina Synod. He served Japanese pastorates at Hakata and Karatsu.

Kochichiro Takimoto, born at Wakayama, Japan, graduated from Pacific (Presbyterian) Seminary in California and served as an evangelist and pastor of the Church of Christ in Japan before transferring to the Lutheran church in 1911. He was ordained by order of the North Carolina Synod in 1917 and served pastorates at Kumamoto and Momodani, Osaka. He also taught at the Lutheran seminary in Kumamoto and, in 1920, became president of the Japan Lutheran Church.

Another Japanese minister was ordained by order of the Tennessee Synod. He was Tsunenari Wasa, a Buddhist priest before his conversion to Christianity. Ordained in 1918 at Kurume, Japan, he served pastorates at Saga City and in Saga Prefecture.

Worship

The dawn of the twentieth century introduced to many Lutheran worship settings at least three new elements: electric lights, music editions of worship books and individual communion cups.

During the first decade of the century, many of the congregations began searching for ways to install electric lights, an improvement which could cost as much as sixty-five dollars in larger churches. In 1908, for example, St. Mark's, China Grove, announced that an offering for the "Electric Light Fund" would be taken at the Sunday morning communion service on December 27.[9]

Music editions of worship books became popular. Earlier, the *Common Service Book*, a twelve-cent small, thick black book containing only the words without musical setting was used; the organist had a book of tunes from which a tune of appropriate meter was selected. Later, however, music editions of the worship materials appeared and gained acceptance. In 1909 the United Synod convention authorized a music edition of the *Book of Worship*.

The use of individual communion cups became an issue. The church council of St. John's, Salisbury, considered the change from a common cup in 1913, but it wasn't until three years later the change was actually made. At Lutheran Chapel, China Grove, the women asked in 1919 that the individual cups be introduced, but it was nearly a decade before the practice was implemented. Even then, it provoked the resignation of two members of the church council.

Special services commemorating the Reformation were popular, often featuring a guest preacher and sponsored by groups of congregations. The 1908 service at St. John's, Salisbury, was sponsored by the Rowan County Lutheran Pastors' Association. The speaker was J. E. Whitteker of Lancaster, Pennsylvania. Fourteen clerical members of the association were present. Although the event did not attract many representatives from the rural pastorates, it was attended by a large number of non-Lutherans in the city so that the host church "had the auditorium of the church and Sunday School rooms all thrown together and completely filled."[10]

The four hundredth anniversary of the Reformation, in 1917, was an occasion for unusual special services. St. John's, Salisbury, was the site for a special "Quadri-Centennial" Reformation Service sponsored by the United Synod of the South on November 1.

In the North Carolina Conference of the Tennessee Synod, a year-long 1917 observance was held with each of twelve pastors delivering Reformation sermons at twelve different parishes. The preachers and their topics were: W. A. Deaton, Lutheranism vs. Rationalism; W. E. Murray, The Faith of Our Fathers; E. J. Sox, The Mission of the Lutheran Church; J. D. Mauney, What the World Owes to the Lutheran Church; D. L. Miller, The Lutheran Church, Conversion & Santification; J. A. Yount, The Lutheran Church & The Sacrament of the Altar; W. D. Wise, The Lutheran Idea of Worship; W. J. Roof, The Lutheran Church and the Word; F. M. Speagle, The Lutheran Church and Christian Education; V. L. Fulmer, The Lutheran Church and Regeneration; C. I. Morgan, The Priesthood of All Believers; and W. D. Haltiwanger, The Lutheran Idea of Christian Life.

Women's Auxiliary

The women's auxiliary in the North Carolina Synod, formed in 1885, advanced to the point by 1903 that it was considering joining in the formation of an intersynodical women's association under the aegis of the United Synod South. But it received no encouragement at that time from the North Carolina Synod. Later, sometime after 1905, the North Carolina synod relented, and the women sent six delegates to Dallas, North Carolina, for the organizing convention of the Woman's Missionary Conference for the Southern Lutheran Church.

NORTH CAROLINA SYNOD
WOMEN'S MISSIONARY SOCIETY
PRESIDENTS

1902-04 Mrs. J. A. Linn, Mt. Pleasant	1915-17 Miss Constance Cline, Concord
1904-06 Mrs. V. Y. Boozer, Salem	1917-19 Mrs. John M. Cook, Concord
1906-12 Mrs. J. A. Linn, Rockwell	1919-21 Mrs. F. A. Bissinger, Wilmington
1912-15 Mrs. R. L. Patterson, Charlotte	1921-22 Mrs. John M. Cook, Concord

In 1909 the North Carolina women were cited for their help in funding the construction of the High Point church building. Gifts of $4,130 for the project were given by members of the Woman's Home and Foreign Missionary Society and earned for the church the distinction of being the first to be built by the society. The initial church name, Woman's Memorial, was later changed to Emmanuel.

The society's interest in home missions was, of course, matched by its interest in the mission work in Japan. In 1909 there were six missionaries in the field from the United Synod South, and four years later the women's and youth societies of the general synod had undertaken support of two women missionaries, Misses Mary Lou Bowers and Martha Akard. In 1917, the general synod board dispatched from North Carolina two sister missionaries, Misses Annie and Maud Powlas, who received substantial support from the women's groups.

NORTH CAROLINA SYNOD
WOMEN'S MISSIONARY SOCIETY
CONVENTION SITES

1903 Holy Trinity, Mt. Pleasant	1913 Lutheran Chapel, China Grove
1904 Macedonia, Burlington	1914 First, Albemarle
1905 St. Enoch's, Enochville	1915 St. Paul's, Wilmington
1906 St. James, Concord	1916 Macedonia, Burlington
1907 St. Mark's, Charlotte	1917 Holy Trinity, Mt. Pleasant
1908 St. Mark's, China Grove	1918 Faith, Faith
1909 Augsburg, Winston-Salem	1919 Organ, Rowan
1910 St. John's, Salisbury	1920 St. James, Concord
1911 St. John's, Cabarrus	1921 St. Mark's, Mooresville
1912 Holy Trinity, Mt. Pleasant	

In addition to missionary support, the women assumed for a number of years the entire support of a kindergarten project in Japan at six hundred dollars per year, and they established the Holland Memorial Scholarship Fund which produced seventy-fve dollars annually for a Japanese theological student.

In the Tennessee Synod, the churches began the century without a synodical women's organization although local societies were growing in number. In 1913, when the number of societies stood at thirty-five, a synodical organization was formed. The unit took the name of Women's Missionary Society of the Evangelical Lutheran Tennessee Synod. Its formation was initiated at the synod convention at Holy Trinity, Hickory, in October. The organizational meeting was held the following month at St. Andrew's, Hickory. Twenty delegates were present, including two from the South Carolina Conference of the Tennessee Synod.

TENNESSEE SYNOD
WOMEN'S MISSIONARY SOCIETY PRESIDENTS

1913-15 Mrs. W. J. Boger, Mt. Holly   1917-20 Mrs. W. J. Boger, Newton
1915-16 Mrs. J. K. Efird, New Brookland, SC 1920-21 Mrs. A. P. Rudisill, Dallas
1916-17 Mrs. E. H. Kohn, Mt. Holly

As in the North Carolina society, the Tennessee society gave emphasis to home and foreign missions. Its members contributed to congregations in Monroe and Statesville and directed overseas support to the Japan Home for Women Missionaries. In 1916, support was also sent to the general synod missionaries, Misses Bowers and Akard. Offerings in 1920 totaled $1,510.

TENNESSEE SYNOD
WOMEN'S MISSIONARY SOCIETY CONVENTION SITES

1913 St. Andrew's, Hickory   1918 Good Shepherd, Mt. Holly
1914 St. John's, Statesville   1919 Zion, Hickory
1915 Baptist Church, New Brookland, SC 1920 Holy Communion, Dallas
1916 St. James, Newton   1921 ARP Church, Mooresville
1917 Lutheran Chapel, Gastonia

The name of the North Carolina society was changed in 1916. From the original "Woman's" Home and Foreign Missionary Society, it was changed and shortened to "Women's" Missionary Society.

The new name conformed to that used among the general synods which merged in 1918. At the time of the merger, the societies of the merging churches came together to form the Women's Missionary Society of the United Lutheran Church in America. Among the delegates from the United Synod South to the merger convention were four representatives of the North Carolina society: Miss Constance Cline, Mrs. John M. Cook, Mrs. G. W. McClanahan and Mrs. Y. Von A. Riser. Miss Cline was elected to the governing board of the new WMS. When her term expired the following year, Mrs. Cook was elected to the board for a three-year term.

The North Carolina society was the first among the synodical societies in the new church to have a field secretary. Miss Constance Cline assumed the duties in the latter years of the period. Succeeding her in the position were Mrs. Riser and Mrs. Cook.

Youth and Child Work

Throughout the period, the North Carolina society continued to foster youth and child work. Among its regular officers at the synodical level were a president and treasurer of young people's work and a secretary-treasurer of children's work.

The women's program for young people supplemented the synodical Luther League organization, formed in 1896, by providing a forum for the promotion and support of missions. Aimed initially at girls, the local women's-program groups assumed the name of Girl's Guild. The first appeared at St. Mark's, Charlotte, in 1902. Its chief project was support of a teacher in Japan. Other Girl's Guilds were organized at St. James, Concord, and St. Mark's, China Grove, in 1906, and St. Peter's, Rowan County, in 1907.

In 1907, membership in the guilds was opened to boys, and the name was changed to Young People's Missionary Society. By 1912, twenty-five societies had organized in the North Carolina Synod.

Initially, the Young People's Societies were not organized into a synodical organization, but they did send delegates to the women's conventions. Their coordination at the synodical level was provided through the women's society and particularly through the position of General Secretary of Young People's Work. Miss Marie Yeager of Charlotte, elected in 1910, was the first to serve in the post. She was succeeded by Miss Constance Cline in 1912, who served until 1916.

Separate identity for the Young People's Societies was initiated in 1916. Delegates to the Women's Missionary Society convention, meeting at Macedonia, Burlington, authorized the representatives of the youth groups to hold a separate business session during the convention and elect officers. The youth named Miss Ida Brown Efird of Winston-Salem president, and elected Miss Mary Cline of Concord treasurer. The youth work secretary, Miss Constance Cline, also served on the new executive committee. At its subsequent convention, in 1917, the women's society gave permission for the youth to hold a separate convention and to appropriate and disburse funds.

The first convention of the Young People's Federation was held August 13-15, 1918, at Sharon and Friedens, Gibsonville, with thirty-eight societies represented. Prof. L. L. Smith of China Grove was elected president, but he resigned before the end of his term and was succeeded by Miss Ruth Brown. S. White Rhyne of Charlotte succeeded her as president in 1920.

In the Tennessee Synod, Young People's Missionary Societies predated those in the North Carolina Synod. In 1901, societies were reported in three congregations of the North Carolina Conference. Both St. Matthew's, Kings Mountain, and Holy Trinity, Hickory, reported twenty members; Emmanuel (no location given) gave no member count but reported eighteen dollars in benevolence contributions.[11] The society at Good Shepherd, Mt. Holly, was organized in 1909.

In 1914, the Tennessee women reported seven youth societies. In addition to the Mt. Holly organization, there were Young People's Missionary Societies at Bessemer City; Holy Communion, Dallas; Oakview Hall at Lenoir College, Hickory; St. Andrew's, Hickory; Zion, Hickory; and St. John's, Statesville. Three years later, the women's society rolls contained the names of eleven youth societies with a total membership of 120.

In addition to the Young People's Societies, the Tennessee Synod had a number of Luther Leagues. The first step toward an association of leagues was initiated in 1913 by the league at St. John's, Statesville, when it invited youth groups from nearby counties to send representatives to a constituting meeting. The youth met on November

20, approved the formation of the District Luther League of Western North Carolina and elected as the first president M. F. P. Troutman, the president of the host league. The representatives continued to meet semi-annually until they held their first annual synod-wide convention on September 2, 1920, at St. Michael's, Troutman. The district organization was apparently intersynodical in membership: St. John's, Statesville, was in the Tennessee Synod; St. Michael's, Troutman, in the North Carolina Synod.

In addition to the leagues for teen-agers, some congregations organized Junior Luther Leagues for younger boys and girls. By 1921, however, the state league carried on its roster only two such groups: Holy Trinity, Hickory, and St. Stephen's, Hickory.

As time approached for the merger of the North Carolina and Tennessee synods, nothing in the church was more fragmented than the youth program. Within each synod, there were both Young People's Societies and Luther Leagues. Sometimes both organizations were represented in the same congregation.

Action by the new national merged church helped to resolve the issue. At its Washington, D. C., convention in 1920, the ULCA endorsed the Luther League as the official organization to coordinate youth activities in the church. The convention also urged organization of leagues along synodical lines.

The ULCA action was endorsed by the new North Carolina Synod at its Burlington convention in June 1921. In effect, the synodical action gave approval to a youth merger which had already be initiated.

Early in 1921, the president of the Tennessee Luther League, George Nelson, invited the officers of the Young People's Federation in the North Carolina Synod to join in creating a committee to plan a youth merger coincident with the synodical merger.

The committee met twice, on February 28 in Salisbury, and on July 27 in Hickory. It recommended a merger convention in Dallas on August 25 at 2 p.m.

First to act on the recommendation was the federation in the North Carolina Synod. At its fourth annual convention, at Salem, Salisbury, on August 16, the federation adopted the recommendation, and President S. White Rhyne announced that it stood ready to merge with the young people of the Tennessee Synod to form the State Luther League of North Carolina.[12]

The Tennessee Synod Luther League, newly organized and meeting for only its second convention, assembled at Holy Communion, Dallas, on August 24, the day before the merger. It also approved the recommendation.

The merger at Dallas was effected on schedule, and the new organization was given the name of Luther League of the United Evangelical Lutheran Synod of North Carolina. Fifty-four Young People's societies of the two synods joined with twenty-four Luther Leagues to form the new youth association.

Men's Auxiliary

In addition to the refinement of the women's and youth auxiliaries, this period also brought initiatives leading to the formation of a men's auxiliary.

In North Carolina, the origin of the church men's group was tied indirectly to the Laymen's Missionary Movement, a national interdenominational effort launched in 1906 to promote mission education in the major denominations. In the Lutheran General Synod, the movement took form in 1911 under the name of Lutheran Laymen's Missionary Movement. Funded by the gifts of laymen, the Lutheran movement hired field secretaries to promote every-member visits, the use of dual-pocket offering envelopes, congregation budgets, and quarterly statements to contributors.

The movement came to the graphic attention of the North Carolina Synod when delegates to the synod convention convened in 1911 at St. Paul's, Wilmington, to find a local unit of the movement within the host congregation.

A meeting sponsored by the movement was scheduled during the convention on Thursday afternoon, during the period when the ministerium met. Speakers at the meeting included Rev. E. C. Cronk, general secretary of the movement for the United Synod South, and five laymen: C. W. Polvagt, James P. Cook, J. Roun Smith, W. W. Koch and Dr. T. F. Costner.

Later in the convention, the delegates recommended consideration of the movement by all congregations. Its educational plans, the resolution stated, increased interest in missionary, charitable and educational programs of the church, and its financial system boosted offerings for both benevolence and local work.

Further exposure in the North Carolina Synod was created when the United Synod South phase of the movement held its 1912 convention, directed by Cronk, in Salisbury. In the *Lutheran Church Visitor* of January 25 George B. Cromer, a prominent South Carolina Lutheran layman and chairman of the executive committee for the event, observed that preparations for the event made it clear it would be "the greatest convention of representative Lutherans ever held in the South."

Speakers for the event included J. Campbell White, the general secretary of the Laymen's Missionary Movement, and Robert E. Speer, a leader in the Student Volunteer Movement and the secretary for foreign missions of the Presbyterian Church, U.S.A. Rev. M. L. Stirewalt of Lenoir College spoke on the place of mission studies in a church college curriculum, and R. L. Fritz, president of the college, also addressed the assembly.

Other program participants included Rev. R. L. Patterson, pastor of St. Mark's, Charlotte, and president of the Board of Home Missions and Church Extension, and Rev. W. H. Greever, editor of the *Lutheran Church Visitor*. Program notables included the popular pulpit orator, Simon Peter Long, and Edwin Trail Horn of Lutheran Theological Seminary at Philadelphia, president of the Board of Foreign Missions for the General Council. Missionary A. J. Stirewalt, Philadelphia Seminary Dean Henry Eyster Jacobs, and Newberry College President J. Henry Harms were also among the participants.

Following the event, the president of the North Carolina Synod, M. M. Kinard, praised the movement with the observation that "we need this to bestir our latent forces."[13]

During the next year, the congregation of St. John's, Salisbury, organized a men's group meeting under the name of the "brotherhood."[14] Prof. G. F. McAllister of Mt. Pleasant Collegiate Institute was the speaker at the initial meeting, scheduled as a Reformation event. In his presentation, McAllister used the brotherhood meeting to reflect on the contribution of Cronk and the Lutheran Laymen's Movement to the life of the Lutheran church.[15]

In 1914, the movement again appeared on the agenda of the synodical convention, this time introducing the concept of the Lutheran Brotherhood. At the Friday afternoon session, during the regular business meeting, a report was presented by

Arnold H. Snider of St. John's, Salisbury, from the Committee on the Laymen's Movement. On Friday evening, which was termed on the convention agenda as "Laymen's Evening", Mr. Snider, one of several speakers, presented an address on "The Lutheran Brotherhood: Its History and Purpose." Other topics addressed during the evening were: "The Call of the Church to her Men" by Prof. G. F. McAllister; "Our Men and the Use of their Money in the Church," by W. F. Aberly; "The Laymen's Place and Opportunity in the Church Today," by Dr. C. E. Reitzel; and "Our Men and the Sunday-school," by Prof. W. L. Cooper.

At the following synod convention, in 1915, the delegates endorsed the Lutheran Brotherhood Movement, resolving "that a committee be appointed from a congregation having a Brotherhood; This committee to be at the disposal of any congregation desiring to organize a Lutheran Brotherhood."[16] The men chosen to serve on the committee were Snider, J. D. Barrier of Charlotte and C. A. Cook of St. James, Concord.

Later in the same convention, the delegates took action relating to the Laymen's Missionary Movement. Dr. Cook first stated that "if the North Carolina Synod desires the Laymen's Missionary Movement to continue its distribution of literature in the Synod a co-operating committee should be appointed as formerly." In response, the delegates authorized the appointment of the committee. Snider was also appointed to this committee, to serve with Professor McAllister and J. M. Moser.

Three years later, the "Laymen's Evening" appeared again on the synodical convention agenda, this time presided over by Snider. There were three speakers on the general theme: "Some of the Vital Needs of the Christian Church Today and at the Close of this World-War to Maintain Her Hold Upon Men and to Fulfill Her Divine Mission in the World."

At this 1919 convention, the North Carolina Lutheran Brotherhood was organized, and Snider was named president.

A national brotherhood organization was strongly commended to the congregations by the new synod president, Jacob L. Morgan. "The Lutheran Brotherhood of America," he said, "has come into existence for this purpose. It is here to serve our church and our nation. It is a National Lutheran Brotherhood. I most heartily commend this organization to the manhood of our Synod, and urge them to a hearty cooperation with the same."[17]

Morgan's enthusiasm for the Lutheran Brotherhood of America, however, was not shared by the ULCA. At its second convention, in 1920, the national church received from its Executive Board a series of recommendations for the formation of a men's auxiliary. The board reported it had given

> Much consideration...to the matter of the organization of the Lutheran Brotherhood, the determination of its sphere of operation and its relations. The judgment of the Board with reference to these matters was that the Brotherhood should be organized in the same way as the Woman's Missionary Society and the Young People's Societies, and the functions of the Committee on Brotherhoods should be similar to those of the corresponding Committees for the Societies just mentioned. The support of the educational interests of the Church by the Brotherhood has been encouraged as eminently worthy and as constituting at least one definite line of work for that organization. In regard to relations with the Lutheran Brotherhood of America the

position taken by the Executive Board was that, inasmuch as that Brotherhood was a war emergency organization, each general body of Lutherans should have its own Brotherhood and that, if desirable, these Synodical Brotherhoods may federate through appointed representatives.[18]

Meanwhile, in the Tennessee Synod, the organization of a synodical brotherhood was authorized by the synod at its 1919 convention. The organization was defined as an "auxiliary to the Lutheran Brotherhood of The United Lutheran Church in America." It had as its object to distribute literature published by the "United Lutheran Brotherhood, so that every man shall feel the impulse of being connected with a Continent-wide movement, as an organic part of it."[19]

The constitution of the synodical brotherhood required no dues or assessments of local organizations, but voluntary contributions were "much needed and most welcome."

The brotherhood's annual convention was held in association with the meeting of the synod; the assembly was composed of all members of local brotherhoods "or other organizations of men in the Synod's congregations." Each local organization was entitled to one vote.

The constitution provided for the five-member executive committee, including the president and secretary-treasurer, to be elected by the synod at its annual meeting. Brotherhood elections, however, were not recorded in the minutes of subsequent meetings of the synod.

At the congregational level, brotherhoods first appeared in the Tennessee Synod in 1920. That year, William K. Mauney initiated the organization of a group at his church, St. Matthew's, Kings Mountain, at about the same time that Hon. Bismarck Capps helped to form a group at Holy Trinity, Gastonia.

The Kings Mountain and Gastonia units gave aid and encouragement to others in the area which followed: Holy Communion, Dallas; St. John's, Cherryville; Lutheran Chapel, Gastonia; Emmanuel, Lincolnton; St. Mark's, Charlotte; and Christ, Stanley.

"These Brotherhoods," President Morgan of the North Carolina Synod later wrote, "formed a group which came to be known as the Gaston District Brotherhood. Many of the early meetings were held in mild weather as picnics, and a favorite spot for these was at Dallas, N.C. Later the district meetings were set for the fifth Sundays . . ."[20]

Sunday School

In addition to working through auxiliary organizations, the laity took leadership roles in the Sunday School.

Response to the Sunday School at Friendship, Taylorsville, in 1905, according to Pastor Crouse in the Tennessee Synod, was lukewarm: "In theory (the church members) are not opposed to them, and do not raise a voice against them, but simply let them alone. If any of the members want to attend Sunday-school and profit by the work, it is all well enough with the others, but they prefer to be excused. Sunday-school work has been carried on at times during the summer, but the school always hibernates."[21]

Other schools were more popular. At St. Mark's, China Grove, the 1908 school enrolled 230 and had an average attendance of 155. St. John's, Salisbury, in 1909 had twenty-five teachers and three hundred students. A larger school was conducted at St. Paul's, Salisbury, which had one of the synod's largest Sunday Schools at the time.

The school at St. John's assembled at 9:45 a.m. on Sundays. But in 1909 the school was moved to Sunday afternoons for the winter and spring.

The Sunday School curriculum during the first decade of the century varied among the congregations. At Friendship, Taylorsville, studies focused on *The Catechism for Little Children, Luther's Small Catechism,* and the *Bible.*[22] At St. John's, Salisbury, the Men's Bible Class, with an enrollment of fifty, was led in an hour of systematic study by the pastor using Joseph Stump's *Bible Teachings* and J. A. W. Haas' *Biblical Literature.* The class also studied the Augsburg Confession.

The role of the laity in the church also included the simple moral support demonstrated by many laypersons in different ways. The account of one 1907 loyal Lutheran was included in a periodical report on the meeting of the North Carolina Conference of the Tennessee Synod at an undisclosed site:

> Revs. A. L. Crouse and J. S. Koiner were visitors in Conference. But perhaps the most interested visitor was Mother Townsand, of Watauga County, who left her Mountain home and made a trip of 60 miles in a wagon over mountain roads in order that she might see this conference, which she loves, in session. It makes one recall the missionary journeys of Paul Henkel as she related the incidents of the trip - how that her neighbors called her foolish, that she slept one night in a barn with her sturdy sons who accompanied her - all that she might attend Conference. Possible she is four score years, yet such a faith! Such church love! Regularly she attended all the sessions, save Sunday, when she was too ill to do so. Sixty miles to see Conference! And some do not go 60 rods![23]

Institutions

The plight of North Carolina College in 1902 which prompted the North Carolina Synod to cease its operations led eventually to creative arrangements for operation and management.

In 1903, the synod entered into an agreement with Prof. G. F. McAllister and Rev. H. A. McCullough to operate the institution under a name and with a curriculum of their choosing, as long as it was approved by the board of trustees.

The school assumed the title of "Collegiate Institute," later acquiring the name of Mt. Pleasant Collegiate Institute (MPCI), and began operations as a secondary school and junior college. It opened with an enrollment of over fifty students, most of them local, instructed by a staff of three teachers. In 1907 a modified military system was introduced, and the following year McAllister assumed, alone, full responsibility for the conduct of the institute.

The synod's other Mt. Pleasant institution, Mont Amoena Seminary, suffered a serious loss when its multi-purpose building was destroyed by fire on November 30, 1911. Recovery came, however, with the acquisition of more land and replacement of the building near the old site. The new three-story building, situated on a seven-acre campus, contained fifty-eight rooms, was steam heated, electrically lighted and featured a modern water system providing pure water from a deep-drilled well. The cost of construction was thirty thousand dollars.

The principals of Mont Amoena Seminary during the period were two pastors: J. H. C. Fisher, from 1902 to 1914, and R. A. Goodman, from 1914 to 1921.

In the Tennessee Synod, Lenoir College at Hickory maintained a steady enrollment through most of the period, starting the period with 243 students in 1903 and closing the period in 1921 with an enrollment of 310. The year of 1918-19, bringing with it an influenza epidemic weakening a small enrollment already depleted by the wartime draft, almost closed the school, but the Armistice brought with it enrollment stability.

The college fortunes were boosted in 1916 when the institution received an "A" rating from the State Board of Education, placing it academically in a select group of ten institutions, including the University of North Carolina, Davidson, Elon, Guilford, Meredith, Salem, State Normal, Trinity and Wake Forest colleges.

Lenoir College, as well as MPCI and Mont Amoena, were affected by the emergence of the public school system in North Carolina during the period. The development moved the church schools to discontinue their primary departments. A later state action, introducing the six-month school system in 1918, pushed some of the private schools, including Lenoir, to drop their pre-college or preparatory departments as well.

Although the Tennessee Synod entertained no aspirations for a seminary in its territory, the North Carolina Synod kept alive its dream to host a theological institution. The hopes brightened in 1909 when the United Synod South concluded it should move its seminary from Mt. Pleasant near Charleston. Late in the year, the Northern Conference of the North Carolina Synod promoted the consideration of Salisbury as a site, and a substantial offer was made on behalf of the city. In addition, the general synod received an offer from another North Carolina Synod city, Charlotte. But neither bid was accepted, and the seminary was relocated two years later at Columbia, South Carolina.

The North Carolina Synod, during the period, continued to promote support of the general synod's Lutheran Orphan Home of the South at Salem, Virginia. Special gifts were encouraged from the congregations and were transmitted regularly by the synod. A popular means of support among the congregations was to encourage Christmas offerings of children. One congregation, St. John's, Salisbury, in 1905 sent thirty dozen eggs to the home.

The synod's involvement in the temperance movement sweeping the country at the time was limited to a single resolution. In one of its earliest statements on a social issue, the synod convention in 1908 admitted that "drink evil is one of the greatest curses of our time, a blight upon temporal welfare, and a burden to the churches and the Kingdom of God."[24]

The convention voted to "encourage its constituency and all others to the utmost devotion in the cause of temperance, both in preaching the Gospel to the repentence of drinkers and the building up of the sentiment that will prevent the traffic in intoxicating liquors."

It also stated that "we approve the present civil movement in this State, . . . and it is our judgment that we should adopt and faithfully use the present opportunity to banish this iniquity from our State." The resolution was introduced by Layman B. B. Miller and two pastors, B. S. Brown and J. A. Linn.

In a manner similar to the synod's reaching into Virginia to support a children's home, it reached during this period into South Carolina to support a home for the aged and helpless.

The home, given to the South Carolina Synod, was received through the alert action of Dr. Walton H. Greever. Mrs. Malissa Lowman had mentioned to Greever that her offer of the property to the State of South Carolina had been declined and she did not know what would become of her invalid children after her death. Her estate included one thousand acres of land, buildings and village property near White Rock, South Carolina, valued at forty thousand dollars.

Greever suggested that she donate the property to the South Carolina Synod. The residence was given the name of Lowman Home for the Aged and Helpless. Greever also developed plans to raise ten thousand dollars for repairs to the buildings, and to provide equipment for operating the home.

Dr. W. P. Cline became the first superintendent and served for twelve years. Greever served as president of the board for twenty-one years.

At the outbreak of World War I the property had a superintendent's home, a six-room home for residents, a new barn, and several farm buildings. Finances, however, were a problem throughout the early years, and by 1916 the indebtedness was over seven thousand dollars. Annual expenses ran about two thousand dollars a year; contributions in 1917 were only $72.73 and in 1918 sank to forty-five dollars.

In 1914, the home was accepted by the United Synod South, of which the North Carolina and Tennessee synods were members. Later, following the merger of the general synods in 1918, the home was turned over to the Lutheran synods of the South, again including North Carolina and Tennessee, to support and maintain. The affiliation, of course, enabled North Carolina and Tennessee to offer the services of the home to their members, some of whom retired there.

Late in the period, in 1921, the North Carolina Synod was presented with an opportunity to establish its own orphan home. Daniel Efird Rhyne, a wealthy Lutheran industrialist of Lincolnton, offered to the synod the Lithia Springs property and one hundred acres of land valued at seventy-five thousand dollars, for an orphanage, provided the synod would raise one hundred thousand dollars to improve and maintain the property. Although some sources indicate the synod accepted the offer, the funds needed to seal the contract were never raised.

Finances

The impact of the Laymen's Missionary Movement and its promotion of techniques to improve individual giving was felt among many congregations even before the first local movement group took form in Wilmington in 1911.

When Rev. C. A. Brown became pastor of Lutheran Chapel, China Grove, in 1908, he introduced the envelope system and, according to one member, "revolutionized" the financial operation of the congregation.

"Until this time", the member continued, "we still practiced the old custom of taking subscriptions for the pastor's salary, mostly from the heads of families, collecting what we could during the year, borrowing when necessary and making a final settlement with the pastor at the end of the year. If the pastor managed to get enough of the salary for a mere existence during the year and a final settlement at the end of the year in time to get a good Christmas dinner, he was lucky.

"Since the adoption of the envelope system, we have been able to pay the pastor promptly at the end of each month."

After the general synod sponsored the movement's convention in Salisbury in

1912, many of the techniques espoused by the movement appeared in the congregations. Most congregations promoted weekly offerings for missions. Within three months after the Salisbury convention, Union, Salisbury, under the leadership of Rev. L. B. Spracher, adopted the use of the duplex envelope system. In November 1920, the men of St. John's, Salisbury, gathered on a Sunday afternoon to conduct an every-member visitation, with the effort generating pledges in excess of eight thousand dollars.[25]

Archives

The archives of the North Carolina Synod were maintained during the period at North Carolina College. In 1902, however, the "archivarius" raised a question about the safety of the records, and the synod convention called for the creation of a committee of three to investigate the possibility of securing a fire-proof vault, the committee to report at the called convention of synod.[26] It is not clear that this committee was appointed or that it reported at the special convention in June.

Eighteen years later, the synodical minutes report that the archives were housed for a time in the vault of Elizabeth College in Charlotte.[27]

Synodical Alignments

Both the North Carolina and Tennessee synods entered the twentieth century as members of the United Synod South, this mutual affiliation nurturing an environment for closer cooperation.

Interaction between the two synods was ample. Representatives worked side-by-side in the general synod. Also, a series of annual reunions of all Lutherans in the state, begun in 1900, continued throughout the period.

Another cooperative effort was the 1904 Free Conference of Pastors. The colloquim, sponsored by the North Carolina Synod and the North Carolina Conference of the Tennessee Synod, was held at St. John's, Salisbury, and attended by twenty-five pastors of the North Carolina Synod and fourteen ministers of the Tennessee Synod.

The Free Conference discussions were based on the premise that the two groups should cooperate in educational and mission projects. In education, it was suggested there be one or two Lutheran colleges in the state performing "genuine college work" and a sufficient number of preparatory or fitting schools "to do their own work and also serve as feeders."[28] In missions, it was agreed neither body should start a mission in a town or community which was "preoccupied" by the other.

A more enduring interaction was initiated in 1908 with the appointment of a joint committee to plan a school for Sunday School teachers. The project was initiated at the invitation of the North Carolina Conference of the Tennessee Synod and accepted promptly by the North Carolina Synod. The Tennessee representatives to the committee were Rev. John Hall, Rev. James F. Deal, and Mr. John J. George. The North Carolina members were Dr. M. M. Kinard, Rev. H. A. McCullough and Prof. G. F. McAllister.

"This was," according to Jacob L. Morgan, "the first united work on a state-wide basis undertaken by the two Synods since 1820."[29]

The first school was held in July 1908 at St. James, Concord, with North Carolina as host. The registration totaled 150. Guest faculty members included Rev. W. L. Hunton of Philadelphia, and Rev. and Mrs. E. C. Cronk of Atlanta. North Carolinians comprised the balance of the faculty.

The second followed on July 21-23, 1909, at Lenoir College with Tennessee as host.

The series of annual joint normal schools continued for seven years, at sites usually alternating between Lenoir College and Mont Amoena Seminary. The pattern was interrupted in 1916 when the project chairman moved from the state.

The single catalyst leading to union was initiated in 1913 by the Tennessee Synod. Its special committee, appointed to plan the celebration of the four hundredth anniversary of the Reformation in 1917, invited North Carolina to join Tennessee in merger discussions so the observance could be celebrated "at some central place by a united Lutheranism in the State of North Carolina."[30] The North Carolina Synod promptly accepted.

The Joint Commission on Union met three times, twice in Charlotte and once in Salisbury, during the winter of 1914-15. Under the leadership of Dr. E. H. Kohn of Tennessee as chairman and Prof. George F. McAllister of North Carolina as secretary, it formulated a tentative basis for merger.

North Carolina, at its 1915 convention, adopted the basis, but Tennessee strengthened the language opposing secret societies. Historically, Tennessee stood strongly against membership in "oath-bound secret societies", while North Carolina had been more tolerant. The issue was a stumbling block, partly because of doctrinal differences, partly because some pastors held insurance through the lodges. Although efforts to resolve the issue continued, the four hundredth anniversary of the Reformation was celebrated by a divided synod.

The year of 1917, however, did not pass without a step toward Lutheran unity taking place within the state. On November 7, the United Synod South, meeting at St. John's, Salisbury, received a proposition that it join two other general synods in forming one body to be known as the United Lutheran Church in America (ULCA). The other two synods had already given their approval: the General Synod at its meeting in Chicago, the General Council, in Philadelphia.

Representatives of the General Synod and General Council urged the Salisbury assembly to adopt the proposal, citing "the urgency of the present crisis in political, economical and religious life of America and the world demand for the concentrated and united effort of the Lutheran church."[31]

The drama of the moment was not lost on the local newspaper:

> . . . more than thirteen million Lutherans in America are today awaiting the action of the United Synod South now in session in this city.

The convention delegates voted the following day, on November 8. The proposal was adopted on a unanimous vote, and ratification by the district synods, such as North Carolina and Tennessee, was predicted. And both synods came through. At its 1918 convention at Augsburg, Winston-Salem, the North Carolina Synod gave unanimous approval with a rising vote and the singing of "Now Thank We All Our God."

On November 15, 1918, in New York City, the "Great Merger" was consummated.

The national merger nudged the North Carolina and Tennessee synods to work harder at a union. One of the principles of the new ULCA required that territories of member synods be geographical and not overlap. That principle told the two synods in North Carolina that if they did not merge, they should realign their boundaries.

A new joint committee, the Commission on Basis and Constitution, was headed by Professor McAllister as chairman and Rev. M. L. Stirewalt of the Tennessee Synod as secretary. It met twice in August 1919, drafting a report and constitution. The Tennessee Synod, meeting the following month in Forestville, Virginia, approved the documents with one amendment. When, however, North Carolina met the following May at St. Mark's, China Grove, it adopted the commission version of the documents and simply received the Tennessee amendment as information. In response, Tennessee, meeting on October 20, 1920, at Emmanuel, Lincolnton, reconsidered its earlier action and approved the commission report and constitution without amendment. The meeting was the one hundredth, and final, convention of the Tennessee Synod.

The merger convention met in Salisbury on March 2, 1921. Present were ninety-six ministers and eighty-eight lay delegates. Each synod had convened in special session the day before, the Tennessee Synod at Haven church and the North Carolina Synod at St. John's. A joint worship service in the morning was led by the presidents of the merging synods: Rev. Jacob L. Morgan of North Carolina and Dr. W. A. Deaton of Tennessee. Preacher for the service was Dr. M. G. G. Scherer, secretary of the ULCA and a former member of the North Carolina Synod. In the afternoon session, the delegates approved a constitution and by-laws, proposed resolutions, and elected officers.

President Morgan of Salisbury and the North Carolina Synod was elected president. Rev. H. Brent Schaeffer of Kings Mountain and the Tennessee Synod was elected secretary, and Dr. Ernest Houseal Kohn of Mt. Holly, also of the Tennessee Synod, was named statistical secretary. The choice of treasurer was obvious: James D. Heilig, who had served the North Carolina Synod in that capacity since 1896, was chosen.[32]

At the time of the merger, the North Carolina Synod had seventy-seven congregations, and the Tennessee Synod had 119, including seventy-nine in North Carolina, twenty-three in Virginia and seventeen in South Carolina.

Since the Tennessee Synod was not incorporated, it was necessary, in order to make the merger legal, that it be ratified by at least a majority of the congregations of that synod. By the deadline of May 1, ninety-four congregations reported ratification to the secretary; three voted not to ratify.[33]

The merger convention was followed by separate meetings of the two synods on June 7-8 in Burlington to transact the business incident to the closing of separate records. The delegates came together June 8-10 at Macedonia, Burlington, in an adjourned session of the March convention to take over the work of the two synods. Later in the session, the new synod ordained its first three ministers: Earl K. Bodie, Paul L. Miller and George W. Nelson.

The seal adopted by the new synod encircled the portrait of Martin Luther above clasped hands symbolizing the reunion that had been quickened by the Reformation anniversary observance. ✝

M. M. Kinard
President, North Carolina Synod
1910-14

Pilgrim, Lexington (1904)
Organized 1754

Portion of North Carolina Synod and Ministerium
Macedonia, Burlington
May 6-10, 1914

"Old Main"
Lenoir College
Founded 1891

W. A. Deaton
President, Tennessee Synod
1921

CHAPTER IX

The reunion of the North Carolina Synod and the Tennessee Synod in 1921 began a forty-two-year period of assimilation and gradual growth. Under the leadership of its most aggressive mission developer, Rev. Jacob L. Morgan, the new synod gave renewed attention to new congregations. It also consolidated its educational interests in one college and joined forces with other synods to strengthen the seminary and develop a summer camp. In the latter stages of the period, it wrestled with the painful choice of giving up its newly-restored traditions for the sake of broader Lutheran unity in the 1963 national merger.

The period of the ULCA in the reunited North Carolina Synod began during a period of national concern with implementing, and later disposing of, Prohibition and continued through a succession of upheavals. The depression of the 1930s not only affected the mood and gifts of the church members, but ultimately displaced many blacks in the South. As farmers were forced to reduce cotton acreage, blacks migrated from southern farming communities by the thousands to seek employment in the North. At first, they found World War II-created jobs in the armed forces or in defense factories. But after the war, their frustrations erupted in the 1950s in demonstrations and riots that touched all facets of life, reaching even into the church pews of the North Carolina Synod.

ULCA SYNOD PRESIDENTS
1921-47 Jacob L. Morgan
1947-49 Voigt R. Cromer
1949-62 F. L. Conrad

When the North Carolina Synod merged with the Tennessee Synod in 1921, the choice of a president was not difficult. Rev. Jacob L. Morgan, the president of the North Carolina Synod since 1919, was one of only two synodical presidents in the United Lutheran Church in America with full-time experience.

A native of Rowan County, Morgan graduated from the synod's school, North Carolina College, and from Lutheran Theological Southern Seminary before being ordained by the synod in 1902. He first served a parish of two mission congregations: Haven, Salisbury; and Christ, East Spencer. He was serving his second parish of St. Enoch, Enochville, and Trinity, Landis, when in 1907 he accepted a call to become field missionary of the synod. He served in that position at High Point and Raleigh until 1917 when he became pastor of Holy Trinity, Raleigh, after having organized it in 1912. He resigned the pastorate in 1919 when he was elected the first full-time president of the synod.

Although his initial election by the merger convention was for a five-year term, Morgan was elected to successive terms sufficient to establish the longest presidential tenure of the synod: twenty-six years, not to mention the preceding two years as head of the prior North Carolina Synod.

When he retired from the office in 1947 and was named president emeritus, associates credited him with preaching three thousand sermons, holding 1450 conferences with congregational officials, attending five hundred meetings of church councils, presiding over 151 meetings of the executive, mission, and ministerial education committees, and attending 135 meetings of college and seminary boards.

Morgan also served as delegate to all conventions of the ULCA while in office and served on its Board of Foreign Missions, Board of American Missions, and Executive Board.

In North Carolina, he ordained 123 candidates for the ministry, installed 368 pastors, participated in 117 dedications, thirty-four rededications, thirty blessings and sixty-eight cornerstone layings. Under his administration, thirty-seven congregations organized, seventy-eight new houses of worship were built, and 116 church plants were equipped with additional educational facilities.

ULCA SYNOD CONVENTION SITES

1921 St. John's, Salisbury;	1943 St. John's, Salisbury
Macedonia, Burlington	1944 St. James, Concord
1922 St. Matthew's, Kings Mountain	1945 St. John's, Cabarrus County;
1923 St. Mark's, Charlotte	Organ, Rowan County
1924 Lutheran Chapel, Gastonia	1946 Augsburg, Winston-Salem
1925 Holy Trinity, Hickory	1947 St. John's, Salisbury
1926 (no meeting)	1948 St. John's, Salisbury
1927 St. John's, Salisbury	1949 Augsburg, Winston-Salem
1928 Augsburg, Winston-Salem	1950 Beth Eden, Newton
1929 St. James, Concord	1951 St. Paul's, Wilmington
1930 St. James, Rockwell	1952 St. Andrew's, Hickory
1931 Beth Eden, Newton	1953 St. John's, Salisbury
1932 First, Albemarle	1954 First, Greensboro
1933 Mt. Moriah, China Grove	1955 St. Paul's, Wilmington
1934 St. Paul's, Wilmington	1956 Haven, Salisbury
1935 Emmanuel, High Point	1957 First, Greensboro
1936 Holy Trinity, Hickory	1958 St. Paul's, Wilmington
1937 Ascension, Shelby	1959 Augsburg, Christ, Winston-Salem
1938 St. Matthew's, Rowan County	1960 Holy Trinity, Hickory
1939 St. John's, Cherryville	1961 St. Mark's, Charlotte
1940 St. Andrew's, Hickory	1962 St. Paul's, Salisbury
1941 St. Andrew's, Hickory	1962 St. John's, Salisbury
1942 St. Andrew's, Hickory	(constituting convention)

Three years before Morgan's retirement, in 1944, the synod made provision for a headquarters facility. A large brick residence at 115 South Ellis Street, Salisbury, was purchased and served both as a home and an office for the president.

Elected by the 1947 convention to replace Morgan was Rev. Voigt R. Cromer, pastor of Holy Trinity, Hickory. The son of a one-time Tennessee Synod pastor,

Cromer was born at Rhodhiss and graduated from Lenoir Rhyne College in 1925 and Southern Seminary in 1928. While attending the seminary he also earned an M.A. degree at the University of South Carolina in 1927. Following ordination by the South Carolina Synod in 1928, he earned the S.T.M. degree at Hartford (Connecticut) Seminary and pursued later graduate work at Union Theological Seminary in New York City.

After a two-year pastorate at St. Luke's, Summerville, South Carolina, Cromer returned to North Carolina, serving at Emmanuel and St. Luke's, Lincolnton (1930-36) and St. James, Concord (1936-41). He assumed duties at Holy Trinity, Hickory, in October 1941.

During his second year as synod president, Cromer was elected to the presidency of Lenoir Rhyne.

His successor, Dr. F. L. Conrad, was elected by the 1949 synod convention at its regular meeting at Augsburg, Winston-Salem. Conrad, the synod secretary for fourteen years, was a native of Davidson County and a descendant, on both his father's and mother's sides, of early German Lutheran settlers in that area. He graduated from Lenoir Rhyne in 1916 and Southern Seminary in 1919.

Ordained in 1919 by the Tennessee Synod, Conrad began his ministry serving two years as pastor of the three-church pastorate composed of Philadelphia, Granite Falls; St. John's, Hudson; and St. Matthew's, Caldwell County. In 1921, he accepted a call to Emmanuel, High Point, where he served until his 1949 election to the presidency.

Conrad served as president for thirteen years. He was also a member of the ULCA Board of American Missions, as well as other boards and committees of the national church. His retirement in 1962 coincided with the ULCA merger with other Lutheran bodies and marked the close of an era in North Carolina Lutheranism.

The presidency was the only full-time position of the synod until 1955. In the preceding year, delegates to the synod convention instructed the Executive Committee to call a full-time director of evangelism. But the committee, confronted with pressing needs in other fields, asked the subsequent 1955 convention in Wilmington to approve instead the office of assistant to the president.

The change was endorsed, and the call to the position was accepted by Rev. Ernest L. Misenheimer, Jr., pastor of Center Grove, Kannapolis, and chairman of the synod's Committee on Stewardship. To the new position were assigned the duties of promotion and supervision of stewardship, evangelism, missions and public relations.

Misenheimer, who assumed the position July 1, 1955, set up office in the shrinking space of the synodical headquarters on South Ellis Street.

Two additional full-time positions were filled briefly before the close of the period.

In 1958, the position of secretary of Christian education was approved by the convention. Purpose of the position was to direct religious education and youth activities in the synod under the supervision of the president and Executive Committee.

Jane Sigmon, one of the first two women to graduate with the M.A. Degree in Christian Education from Southern Seminary, accepted appointment to the post. A native of Newton and graduate of Lenoir Rhyne, she served as parish worker at First, Albemarle, prior to beginnning seminary studies.

Sigmon assumed duties on September 1, 1958, but resigned in the fall of 1959. The vacancy was not filled because of anticipated organizational changes which were not resolved until the 1963 merger.

The position of full-time superintendent of home missions was created in 1961 and filled by Rev. David F. Johnson on October 1. The following year, however, the ULCA Board of American Missions called Johnson to perform similar duties in the new position of regional director for the board. Johnson, therefore, vacated the synodical position after twelve months, and it remained unfilled.

With the growth of the synodical staff came the realization that the converted South Ellis Street residence did not provide adequate space. The residence was therefore sold, and a nine-acre tract of land on Klumac Road near Highway I-85 was purchased. Ground was broken for a synodical headquarters building on March 12, 1961, and President Conrad and Pastor Misenheimer moved into the new building January 19, 1962. In addition to office space, the structure included a vault, archives room and chapel. Total cost for the land, building and furnishings was $211,000.

Synodical Alignments

Although the reunion of the North Carolina and Tennessee synods in 1921 brought many Tar Heel congregations under one roof, it also introduced into the synod fifty-four congregations outside the state: specifically, those in South Carolina and Virginia which were members of the former Tennessee Synod.

The congregations forming the South Carolina Conference numbered nineteen, in eight parishes: Mt. Horeb, St. Jacob's, St. Peter's and St. Thomas, Chapin; St. Andrew's, Columbia; St. Paul's and Grace, Gilbert; Bethlehem, Irmo; Cedar Grove and St. James, Leesville; Pilgrim, St. Peter's and Zion, Lexington; Holy Trinity and St. John's, Pelion; St. John's, Pomaria; Emmanuel, Mt. Hermon and Mt. Tabor, West Columbia. Serving the conference were nine pastors, including two in retirement.

In the year following the merger, in 1922, the conference was transferred into the South Carolina Synod.

The congregations making up the Virginia Conference numbered thirty-five, in eleven parishes: Edinburg (Salem, St. Jacob's, Zion); Forestville (St. Mary's, Solomon's); Manasses (Bethel, Trinity, Zion, St. Luke's); Mt. Nebo; New Market (Emmanuel's, Mt. Zion); Orkney Springs (Bethel, Morning Star, Powder Springs, St. Paul's); Rockingham (McGaheysville, St. Jacob's, St. Paul's, Trinity); Shenandoah (St. James, St. Luke's, St. Paul's, St. Peter's); Stoney Man (Beth Eden, Grace, Morning Star, Mt. Calvary); Timberville (Raders, St. John's, St. Paul's); and Tom's Brook (Mt. Calvary, St. David's, St. Matthew's, St. Stephen's). The congregations reported thirty-five hundred baptized members and thirteen pastors, including three in retirement.

The Virginia Conference initiated transfer proceedings at its 1923 meeting at Zion, Edinburg, and was received by the Virginia Synod in 1924.

For the first time since 1803, the territory of the North Carolina Synod was restricted within the boundaries of the state of North Carolina.

Throughout the balance of the period, North Carolina remained one of the thirty-three synods of the ULCA. Its seniority in the national church was arguable. In terms of composition and boundary lines, the synod dated from 1924 (or possibly back to 1921) and was the youngest in the ULCA. But from the perspective of the long-time constituent congregations, the synod dated from 1803. This view was reflected in the title of the minutes of the 1921 merger convention, which was described as the "One Hundred and Eighteenth Annual Convention of the United Evangelical Lutheran

Synod of North Carolina." This age count made North Carolina the third oldest among the constituent ULCA synods. In terms of confirmed and communing membership, it ranked tenth among the thirty-three in 1950.

The synod was one of the early participants in the North Carolina Council of Churches, organized in 1935. Purpose of the council was "to promote Christian fellowship among Protestant communions in North Carolina, serve as a medium of inter-church counsel and advise in matters affecting the progress of Christianity in the State."[1] The Lutherans participated initially in a consultative relationship, pending approval by the ULCA. Lutheran representatives also attended the council meetings.

Polity and Practice

In the early years of the period, some organizational principles in the new synod were designed to help in assimilation. President Morgan pressed for three practices: conference alignments including congregations from both of the prior synods, pastoral calls to ministers of the opposite prior synod, and a synodical publication.

The new conference boundaries required re-orientation. The old synodical line ran roughly north to south through Statesville and Charlotte. In the new synod, three conferences were formed. The Eastern Conference stretched from the coast west through Winston-Salem and Lexington. The triangular Southern Conference included Albemarle, Gastonia and Salisbury. The Western Conference covered the territory not included in the other two conferences. The alignment was continued until 1936 when the synod was redistricted into four more compact conferences.[2]

A study of the organizational structure of the synod was authorized by the 1958 convention, inspired by the work of the ULCA Commission on Organizational Structure which reported in 1954. The North Carolina study was undertaken in response to an expanding program which had "created new situations and called for additional personnel"[3] The committee, comprised of seven ministers, seven laymen and eight consultants, was chaired by Harry E. Isenhour of Salisbury, a member of the ULCA commission.

The report of the committee, submitted to the 1960 convention, contained, in addition to recommendations, a revised constitution and by-laws. The convention gave one day to consideration of the report, acting on some of the recommendations. The constitution and by-laws, together with proposed amendments, were postponed to the next convention.

At the next convention, in 1961, the pending merger of the national church appeared imminent, and the convention voted again to postpone action on the constitution. The postponement this time was for a period "until the meeting after the anticipated formation of the Lutheran Church in America, or until the regular meeting in 1963, whichever comes first."[4]

The 1963 regular meeting came first, but by then the formulation of a constitution which conformed with LCA polity took priority. The essential elements of the committee's document were therefore incorporated into the merger constitution.

During the ULCA period of the synod's history, women first began to take elective roles in the work of the organization. The first woman delegate to a convention of the synod was Mrs. Ernest Houseal (Catherine Ehrhardt) Kohn of Good Shepherd, Mt. Holly, a native of Philadelphia, Pennsylvania, who attended the 1927 convention at St. John's, Salisbury. Among the earliest trustees of synodical institutions was Mrs. J. S.

Efird of Albemarle, who served in 1931 on the governing board of Mt. Pleasant Collegiate Institute. The first woman to serve as North Carolina delegate to a ULCA convention was Mrs. E. R. Lineberger of Lumberton, president of the synodical Women's Missionary Society, who was elected in 1952.

Publications

The 1921 merger was cemented in part by the publication of a synodical paper. The 1922 convention of the synod received memorials from four conferences asking for a monthly publication.

The *North Carolina Lutheran* was first published in January 1923, edited by Rev. A. R. Beck, pastor of Beth Eden, Newton, and former editor of *The Catawba Lutheran*. The eight-page periodical included monthly announcements and agendas of coming events, summaries of conventions, letters and topical articles, occasional sermons, and an editor's column of personal notes on pastors and congregations.

In 1932, for the first time in its ten-year history, the *North Carolina Lutheran* operated at a deficit. Rates were revised, making individual subscriptions fifty cents per year.

Also, in 1935, the Committee on the *North Carolina Lutheran* cut the costs of publication with the hope of increasing circulation and reducing the operating deficit. Subscriptions increased from 1,400 to 4,250 and the annual operating deficit was reduced but not eliminated.[5]

Beck retired as editor in 1937 after fourteen years because of the press of pastoral work, and the synodical Executive Committee named as his successor Rev. B. E. Petrea, pastor of Union, Rowan County. In connection with the change, a sub-committee of the Executive Committee asked for a number of changes in the publication itself. The page size was reduced from 10x13 1/2 to letter size, the format was spruced up, lengthy articles were eliminated, more congregational news was sought, and a limited number of advertisements were permitted.

When Petrea resigned in 1950, subscriptions for the paper had advanced from four to seven thousand.

With the 1950 change in editors, the responsibilities were divided between two positions: an editor, and a business/circulation manager. The Executive Committee also determined that the two positions be filled by synodical convention election for one-year terms.

The first editor to be named by synodical election was Rev. Roscoe B. Fisher, pastor of St. Stephen's and St. John's, Lenoir. Hugh C. Petrea of St. John's, Salisbury, was elected business/circulation manager, to be replaced the following year by the election of Dr. George H. Rhodes, retired pastor of First, Albemarle.

After two years in office, Editor Fisher resigned to pursue graduate study. He was succeeded by Rev. David F. Cooper, pastor of Good Shepherd, Brevard, who also served two years before accepting a call to serve as mission developer in Texas. Rev. Stafford L. Swing, pastor of Mt. Olive, Hickory, served as editor for three years before declining re-nomination in 1957.

Swing was succeeded by Jeff Norris of Hickory, a member of the Lenoir Rhyne staff and first lay editor of the publication, who served for ten years.

Missions

The home mission emphasis of the new synod was established during the first convention after the merger, but the emphasis germinated two years earlier. The need for money to finance the construction of mission churches and parsonages was made specific by President Morgan when he issued a challenge to the old North Carolina Synod in its 1920 convention: "This Synod should have an endowment fund of not less than $50,000.00, the principal of which to be used as a loan fund to assist needy missions in this Synod in their building operations, and the interest accruing therefrom to be a donation fund out of which to make initial investments for new missions in this territory."[6]

Morgan's plea went unanswered in 1920, but it was heard when he renewed it to the first convention of the new synod.

The convention, held November 14, 1922, at St. Matthew's, Kings Mountain, was greeted with the announcement by one of the host congregation's members, W. A. Mauney, that a fund would be created specifically for home mission and church extension work in the synod. Ten laymen of St. Matthew's, Mauney reported, had pledged one thousand dollars each for a permanent loan fund and had challenged other laymen in the synod to help build the fund to a minimum of one hundred thousand dollars. The project, later promoted through the state men's auxiliary, eventually assumed the name of Brotherhood Loan & Gift Fund and provided loans to mission congregations for church construction.

At the same convention, the synod took steps to re-establish the synodical missionary posts which had been abandoned by the predecessor synods. With the 1921 merger and a doubling of congregations and resources, renewal of the work became possible.

Called to the eastern field missionary position in 1922 was the newly-ordained S. White Rhyne. Rhyne served for four years, organizing Trinity, Rocky Mount, in 1923 and serving as its first pastor before resigning to become executive secretary of the ULCA Board of Parish Education.

In the western part of the state, the synod in 1923 created a parallel position which was filled by N. D. Yount, a 1918 ordinand of the Tennessee Synod and former pastor in the Watauga parish. As field missionary, Yount worked for two years in the Asheville area, surveying, developing and organizing missions. He organized three congregations: Ascension, Shelby, and St. Mark's, Asheville, in 1923; and St. Andrew's, Andrews, in 1924. He vacated the post in 1925 to become pastor of the two-church parish composed of Grace, Bessemer City, and Ascension, Shelby.

In addition to the four organized by the field missionaries, other congregations were formed. During the first decade of the new synod, eight other churches were added to the roll: St. Mark's, Lenoir (1922); Grace, Boone, and St. Paul's, Durham, and Good Hope, Hickory (1923); Holy Trinity, Troutman (1924); St. Luke's, Charlotte, and Bethany, Kannapolis (1928); and Alamance, Alamance (1929).

In 1933, President Morgan, in his report to the synod, observed:

> One of the greatest tasks of the Christian Church is to minister to human souls. And it seems to us that the need for such service has never been greater than at this present time. People are discouraged over world conditions, and are longing for something different. It is quite possible that many do not realize the source from which to hope for relief. Some are still relying on material support, others are looking to politics, while a vast multitude are confused and blindly groping their way. In the

midst of such conditions, the Christian Church should find her opportunity for timely service.

There are people in every community who are not identified with the Christian Church, who afford a challenge to us to try to win them to Christ, and thus add spiritual joy to their souls. We should not wait for the depression to get over in order to try to do this, but right now, while people are realizing their helpless state of life, is when they may be reached. Furthermore, the Church needs to find recruits these days, for her own benefits. She needs it in order the better to combat the evil with which she is surrounded. And then she needs it to help make up for financial losses. The business man realizes these principles. Then why should the children of this world be wiser than the children of light?[7]

The Committee on the President's Report called on the synod to make "the matter of 'soul saving' a special objective during the coming year. We feel that under the present depression there are better days ahead for the church, for depression, too, causes men to think of God, of His Word, of His Church and of His Service. It is a great day when God can get men to think."

The recommendations of the committee, chaired by George H. Rhodes, included: "That there be an exchange of pulpits and pastors during the year and an intensive campaign for the ingathering of souls inaugurated, and that the local congregation should visit all lapsed members, and try to win and reclaim and hold all those who rightly belong to her." The recommendations were adopted.[8]

The report of the Committee on Evangelism included a schedule for a year-round program of evangelism in the congregation. The schedule for October-November included a "Week of Evangelistic Services" and the "Advent-Christmas" schedule included a "Sunday Night Evangelistic Sermon Series." The schedule for "Lent-Easter" included an "Intensive Spiritual Appeal to Catechumens."[9]

A review of the synod's mission development strategy was precipitated by a 1935 proposed restructuring of home mission work in the ULCA. The ULCA policy to make loans available only to new churches would not keep open for the synodical Mission Committee the option to establish missions in communities where Lutherans were scarce. Despite the concerns expressed by the Mission Committee, the convention adopted a resolution offered by Rev. E. K. Cooper approving the action of the ULCA at Savannah "unifying Home Mission Developments under the Board of American Missions...."[10]

At the same time, the Evangelism Committee called for a revival of the idea of "A Lutheran Church in Every County of the State" with a goal of entering five new counties each year so that by 1950 there would be a Lutheran church in every county. The convention also approved this goal.[11]

The depression and war, however, slowed mission development in the second decade, when only seven congregations were organized: Calvary, Morganton (1933); St. James, Fayetteville (1936); St. David's, Kannapolis (1938); St. John's, Asheboro, and Good Shepherd, Goldsboro, and Redeemer, Kannapolis (1939); and St. Paul's, Hamlet (1941).

The third decade saw the formation of ten churches: Messiah, Salisbury (1942); Trinity, Sanford (1944); Holy Trinity, Chapel Hill, and Reformation, Taylorsville (1946); St. Andrew's, New Bern, and Advent, Spindale (1949); and Good Shepherd,

Brevard, and Resurrection, Kings Mountain, and St. Mark's, Lumberton, and Atonement, Wilkesboro (1951).

Mission development was supported in the 1950s by three different synod-wide outreach efforts.

Three Mass Lutheran Evangelism Rallies were conducted in the fall of 1951 to kick off sixty-five simultaneous Preaching-Teaching Missions among congregations. The first of the rallies, held in Raleigh on September 16, featured as speaker Dr. Wynne C. Boliek of the South Carolina Synod. The other two were held simultaneously on September 23. The speaker at Salisbury was Dr. L. Boyd Hamm, also of the South Carolina Synod; the speaker at Hickory was Dr. F. Eppling Reinartz, secretary of the ULCA. More than fifteen hundred workers and leaders attended the rallies, which included workshop sessions for evangelism workers.[12]

Five years later, in 1956, the Area Mission Week was held in the synod for the first time as part of a regular ULCA program. The program was launched on Sunday afternoon, January 22, with an area rally at First, Greensboro, attended by eight hundred church council members, lay visitors and congregational leaders. Speaker for the rally was Dr. J. A. Keisler, Jr., ULCA regional director of evangelism. Twenty-eight participating churches in the area conducted special services and training sessions each night of the week under the leadership of visiting ministers from a four-state area.

During the week, 416 visitors called on 1,460 prospects. Fifty-two prospects expressed a desire to transfer, fourteen declared a reaffirmation of faith, and 189 enrolled in pastor's classes. Many of the calls were made in a snowstorm, prompting one prospect to ask what church sent out visitors in such weather and then explaining, "I just wanted to know, for that's one church I don't want to join."

The third special project, held in 1957, was the Charlotte Area Evangelism Mission, at St. Mark's, Charlotte. The February event included a closing rally at Ovens Auditorium, attended by three thousand Lutherans from North and South Carolina. Speaker for the event was Dr. Oscar W. Carlson of Baltimore. The music was led by a 340-voice choir directed by Rev. Douglas Fritz of Kings Mountain.

The area evangelism missions continued in the North Carolina Synod for fifteen years through 1971. Congregations in each district were involved in a mission each third year. Each series of area missions carried out a different theme and followed a different format.

Another educational event for congregational leaders begun in the fifties was a triennial school held at Lenoir Rhyne. In 1957 this venture began as the Stewardship Sector Project School. It's purpose was to train leadership for the ULCA-wide stewardship growth program. In 1960 the school was enlarged to include both stewardship and evangelism leaders and in 1969 social ministry was added.

The school was held each third year from 1957 through 1975, and again in 1979. Registration was usually between four hundred and five hundred.

The special evangelism efforts of the 1950s may have contributed to the explosion of new congregations. The final decade of the period produced a record twenty-eight new congregations, ten during the first five years: Kure Memorial, Kure Beach (1952); Messiah, Hickory (1953); Christ, Charlotte, and Our Saviour, Jacksonville (1954); Redeemer, Charlotte, and Holy Trinity, Reidsville (1955); and Faith, Conover, and Good Shepherd, Hickory, and Prince of Peace, Kinston, and Prince of Peace, Salisbury

(1956).

The eighteen congregations formed during the final six years of the period included: Our Saviour, Dallas, and Christ, Winston-Salem (1957); Christ, Durham (1958); Christ, Greensboro, and St. Timothy, Havelock (1959); Good Shepherd and St. Thomas, Charlotte, and Our Redeemer, Greenville, and Holy Cross, Lincolnton, and Holy Cross, Mocksville, and Gloria Dei, Salisbury (1960); Messiah, Burlington, and Our Father, Greensboro, and Ascension, Wilson (1961); New Covenant, Archdale, and Incarnation, Charlotte, and Our Saviour, Southern Pines, and Epiphany, Winston-Salem (1962).

The synod's attention was directed to world missions on March 31, 1935, when the daughter of the synod president, Gladys Morgan, became the first North Carolinian to be commissioned a medical missionary to a foreign field.

The commissioning service was held at St. John's, Salisbury, where she was a member. The service was led by Dr. S. W. Herman of Harrisburg, Pennsylvania, president of the ULCA Foreign Mission Board. He was assisted by Dr. P. E. Monroe of Lenoir Rhyne, a member of the board; Dr. M. L. Stirewalt, pastor of St. John's; and Synod President Morgan. The candidate was presented by her mother, who was a member of the executive board of the Women's Missionary Society of the ULCA.

Missionary Morgan held degrees from Lenoir Rhyne, University of North Carolina and the Woman's Medical College of Philadelphia. She also pursued medical research for a year at the University of Geneva in Switzerland. In addition to her medical studies, she was trained in music, Bible and catechetical work. She sailed from New York on April 10 for missionary duties in India.[13]

Pastors

Immediately following the 1921 merger, the process for a congregation's calling a pastor played a role in the amalgamation of the synod. Where conditions justified, vacant parishes were encouraged to call a pastor formerly associated with the opposite synod.

"These new associations," President Morgan observed, "contributed materially to a closer fellowship and a more complete understanding between pastors and people who had once been separated by Synodical lines and affiliations."[14]

Shortly after the merger, the synod was presented with a new opportunity to help its retired ministers. Prospects for success were improved over those of the 1903 effort because the larger resources of the ULCA, not only the synod, would be involved.

The church-wide Ministerial Pension and Relief Campaign, launched in 1928, sought four million dollars to provide better church pensions. Annual payments to pensioners at that time were three hundred dollars. The campaign, promoted broadly in North Carolina, promised to generate annual income of two hundred thousand dollars which could be used by the church to boost significantly the annual pension payments.

The salaries of pastors during the Depression era ranged widely. In 1933 the synod's Committee on the State of the Church indicated that, of ninety-eight congregations reporting, the highest pastor's salary was $3,600, the average $1,599. Nine congregations paid $2,000 or more. "The others report salaries running from $850 to $1,800, many of which are not paid regularly."[15]

Two years later, the committee noted that only one congregation in the synod provided its pastor with an automobile and reported the following salary ranges for pastors: two pastors received annual salaries ranging from $200 to $600; twelve, from $700 to $1,000; thirty-eight, from $1,100 to $1,500; fifteen, from $1,600 to $2,000; three, from $2,100 to $2,500; three from $2,600 to $3,000; two, from $3,100 to $3,600.[16]

Some congregations provided a parsonage in addition to the salary. In 1933, Bethany, Kannapolis, acquired a new brick-veneered parsonage for M. L. Kester and his family. The cost was approximately three thousand dollars for "a splendid ten-room" facility.[17]

The synod typically ordained a handful of new pastors each year, but in 1955 it ordained the largest single class in its history. A total of thirteen were ordained in the service on June 12 at Kimball Memorial, Kannapolis. Included in the group were three ordinands from the host congregation: R. Earl McCombs, Charles McCombs and Frank Perry.

The growth in chaplaincy services, both in the military and in institutions, required the services of more ordained clergymen, and many North Carolina Lutheran pastors responded to the call.

During the period, a total of seventeen served as chaplains in the Army.

Serving during World War II were John D. Barringer, 1942-46; George H. Cooper (who served as National Chaplains' Association president), 1941-46; Wayne M. Daubenspeck, 1936-38, 1940-54; Claude V. Deal, 1942-47; Roy L. Fisher (awarded five theatre ribbons), 1943-54; John R. Himes, 1943-63; Jason W. Oxner, 1943-45; C. Ross Ritchie, 1942-46; Walter A. Sigman, 1943-46; Charles F. Steck, Jr., 1936-50; and J. Edgar Stockman, 1941-46.

Serving in the Army during the Korean Conflict, the Vietnam War or during peacetime were Keith J. Beam, who entered the Army in 1960; James R. Boggs, who entered in 1957; Clarence K. Derrick; William E. Hall (twice awarded the Bronze Star for combat service), 1952-54; George C. Kahl, who entered the Army in 1965; and Carl S. King, who entered in 1963.

Serving as Navy chaplains were eleven North Carolina Lutherans: Glenn L. Barger, 1943-47, 1950-54; Carl A. Brink, who entered in 1962; James Butt; Richard Duncan; Glenn S. Eckard, 1942-53; Ted E. Edwards, who entered in 1962; Donald W. Herb, 1945-47; Ernest R. Lineberger, Jr., who entered in 1951; Don M. Michael, who also entered in 1951; Herbert W. Stroup, Jr., 1945-46; and Jack E. Tretheway, 1960-64.

The Air Force chaplaincy during the period included the following clergymen from the synod: C. Cecil Adderholdt, 1951-53; John D. Barringer, who entered in 1948; W. Gilmer Boggs, who entered in 1956; James W. Kinney; Martin L. Shaner, 1941-63; Voigt M. Sink, who entered in 1943; Jasper J. Smith, who entered in 1956; and Thomas O. Stelling, 1951-53.

Other members of the synod serving as institutional or industrial chaplains included: Edgar C. Cooper, North Carolina State Prison System, 1937-39, Federal Penitentiary, Atlanta, Georgia, 1945-46; J. Arthur Linn, North Carolina Lutheran Homes, Hickory; A. Wike Lippard (first full-time chaplain in a North Carolina state mental institution), Broughton State Hospital, Morganton, 1949-64; Harold E. Rhoads, Veterans Administration, Washington, D. C.; George G. Robertson, Veterans Administration, Wisconsin, who assumed duties in 1965; Charles F. Steck, Jr., Industrial Chaplain, Carolina Freight Carriers Corp., Cherryville, 1957-59; Robert G.

Walker, Lenoir Rhyne College, who assumed duties in 1961; and Harold M. Yoder, South Carolina State Hospital.

Worship Practices

By the 1930s, the *Common Service Book* had been widely distributed in the synod. In 1933, the synod's Committee on the State of the Church reported that "nearly all congregations use the Common Service, with a few showing objection to its use."[18] Two years later, the committee confirmed that the book was used extensively.

Most parishes consisting of a single congregation held two worship services each Sunday: The Service in the morning, and Vespers in the evening. Matins was used only with the Easter sunrise service. Few congregations conducted a midweek service, but most observed the major festivals of the church year: Christmas, Easter, Pentecost, Reformation and Thanksgiving.[19]

Communion was administered four times a year in the typical congregation, but very few congregations held a separate confessional service.

Congregational worship, however, was altered a quarter-century later with the 1958 introduction of the *Service Book and Hymnal.* The book, reflecting twelve years of planning and work by eight Lutheran bodies, differed from the *Common Service Book* liturgy by offering two musical settings instead of one. The service also introduced intonations for use by the worship leader. The liturgical word content remained largely unchanged, but the music differed.

North Carolina Lutherans were introduced to the new worship materials in March 1958 through ten area workshops, planned by the synodical Committee on Church Music. The first setting for the service, with intonation, was demonstrated, and other features of the book were previewed.

The *Service Book and Hymnal* was also used exclusively at the 1958 synod convention, held at St. Paul's, Wilmington. Delegates and visitors not only worshipped through use of the new liturgical setting, but they sang the Matins and Vespers services as well.

By fall, many congregations were introducing the book to their members. St. John's, Salisbury, began using eight hundred copies of the volume, priced at four dollars each, on the first Sunday of October, World-Wide Communion Sunday. Two years later, it introduced the hymn-of-the-month as a pedagogical approach to the use of the new book. A new hymn was sung by the choir the first two Sundays in the month; the congregation joined in singing the same hymn on the third and fourth Sundays. A monthly article in the parish news letter reported the names of the composer and the author of the hymn, along with a history of the words and the melody.[20]

Frequency of communion during the period slowly increased. In 1933, only one congregation of the synod offered communion as many as five times per year. In 1955, St. John's, Salisbury, increased the number of its administrations to twelve per year and four years later advanced it to sixteen.

In the same year of 1962, St. John's voted to begin using lay assistants in the administration of the Lord's Supper.

Women's Auxiliary

As a part of the 1921 synodical merging process, the women's societies of the North Carolina and Tennessee synods met jointly in August to form the Women's

Missionary Society of the United Evangelical Lutheran Synod of North Carolina.

The meeting was held in Mooresville, with the Tennessee women meeting separately for a closing session in the Associate Reformed Presbyterian Church. The North Carolina group met at St. Mark's Lutheran Church, where the constituting convention also assembled. Principals in the merging action were the president of the North Carolina society, Mrs. F. A. Bissinger, and the president of the Tennessee group, Mrs. A. P. Rudisill.

The structure of the new society was modified during the first fifteen years to transfer responsibility for organizing new groups from the synodical to the conference level. The option became practical with the development, over the years, of strengthened organizations among the four conferences.

Annual conventions of the society were attended by delegates and visitors representing congregational units. Two consecutive conventions, however, were hampered by external conditions. The normal three-day meeting was shortened to one day in 1944 because of an outbreak of infantile paralysis. The following convention was cancelled because of war-time gas rationing: the business actions were approved by the delegates through mail ballots. Local units hosted the conventions until 1946, when the society began meeting on the campus of Lenoir Rhyne.

WOMEN'S ORGANIZATION PRESIDENTS

1921-22	Mrs. John M. Cook,	St. James, Concord
1922-25	Mrs. G. W. McClanahan,	Friedens, Gibsonville
1925-28	Mrs. J. L. Morgan,	St. John's, Salisbury
1928-31	Mrs. J. F. Crigler,	St. Mark's, Charlotte
1931-34	Mrs. J. A. Moretz,	Holy Trinity, Hickory
1934-37	Mrs. G. W. McClanahan,	Christiana, Granite Quarry
1937-40	Mrs. L. E. Blackwelder,	St. Mark's, Mooresville
1940-43	Mrs. E. R. Trexler,	Mt. Moriah, China Grove
1943-46	Mrs. Aubrey Mauney,	St. Matthew's, Kings Mountain
1946-49	Mrs. M. C. Yoder,	St. Andrew's, Hickory
1949-52	Mrs. E. R. Lineberger,	Christ, East Spencer
1952-55	Mrs. Ray R. Fisher,	Augsburg, Winston-Salem
1955-58	Mrs. Paul B. Beatty,	St. Mark's, Charlotte
1958-61	Mrs. George R. Patterson,	Holy Trinity, Hickory
1961-64	Mrs. Paul Stout,	Grace, Thomasville

Active roles were played by North Carolinians in the national women's organization. Throughout the ULCA period, at least one Tar Heel served in an elective position in the governing board, except for a six-year period starting in 1952. At the time of the North Carolina-Tennessee merger in 1921, Mrs. John M. Cook of St. James, Concord, was serving a three-year term on the board. On her retirement in 1922, Mrs. G. W. McClanahan of Friedens, Gibsonville, was elected to two successive three-year terms.

In 1928, Mrs. Cook was elected treasurer and began a twelve-year period as national officer, serving from 1937 to 1940 as statistical secretary. During her tenure as officer, she was joined by another Tar Heel, Mrs. J. L. Morgan of St. John's,

Salisbury, who served on the board from 1932 to 1940. When both Mrs. Cook and Mrs. Morgan retired in 1940, Mrs. L. E. Blackwelder of St. Mark's, Mooresville, succeeded them, serving six years. She was succeeded in turn by Mrs. E. R. Trexler of Mt. Moriah, China Grove, from 1946 to 1952. After a six-year interval, Mrs. L. C. Powles of St. James, Rockwell, was elected to the board to serve until the merger.

The North Carolinians also hosted the fourth biennial convention of the national society in 1924 at St. John's, Salisbury. And, during the period, Week of Prayer programs for the general society were written by four North Carolinians: Mrs. Cook, Mrs. J. F. Crigler of St. Mark's, Charlotte; Sister Catharine Stirewalt of St. John's, Salisbury; and Miss Inez Seagle of Emmanuel, Lincolnton.

In the early years of the new organization, its home mission emphasis was guided for a period by the national society which took for its biennial objective one term of work in Konnarock, Virginia, and Watauga County, North Carolina. In addition to supporting the two projects through gifts to the national society, the synodical group provided leadership for the work in Watauga County. Miss Cora Pearl Jeffcoat of Boone was commissioned as a parish worker in the county in 1923, and later, Miss Amy Louise Fisher of Holy Trinity, Mt. Pleasant, daughter of former WMS President Mrs. J. H. C. Fisher, went to Boone as a parish nurse.

WOMEN'S ORGANIZATION CONVENTION SITES

1921	St. Mark's, Mooresville	1935	St. Mark's, Charlotte
1922	Emmanuel, Lincolnton	1936	St. Paul's, Wilmington
1923	St. John's, Statesville	1937	Holy Trinity, Hickory
1924	St. Andrew's, Hickory	1938	Holy Trinity, Gastonia
1925	St. Mark's, Charlotte	1939	Macedonia, Burlington
1926	Macedonia, Burlington	1940	Haven, Salisbury
1927	St. Paul's, Wilmington	1941	Emmanuel, High Point
1928	Emmanuel, High Point	1942	Augsburg, Winston-Salem
1929	St. Mark's, China Grove	1943	St. John's, Salisbury
1930	St. John's, Salisbury	1944	St. James, Concord
1931	Emmanuel, Lincolnton	1945	(cancelled)
1932	St. James, Concord	1946-47	Lenoir Rhyne/
1933	St. John's, Statesville		St. Andrew's, Hickory
1934	First, Albemarle	1948-62	Lenoir Rhyne

The home mission emphasis was not limited to support through the national organization. During the ULCA period, the society gave three hundred thousand dollars to the national organization, but it also contributed more than two hundred thousand dollars

to mission development in North Carolina. Most of the home mission funds were distributed through synodical channels, but some gifts were directed to specific projects. The society contributed funds toward the erection of the St. Mark's, Blowing Rock, church in memory of Miss Constance Cline. Pews in the Asheville church were given as a memorial to Miss Ella Belle Shirey, and contributions to the Hudson church were made in memory of Rev. and Mrs. C. O. Lippard. A total of thirty-eight North Carolina churches were helped by the missions offerings of the society during the period.

Foreign mission support was channeled largely through the national organization. But the synodical society gave an additional seventy-five thousand dollars during the period for the support of particular missionaries, especially women missionaries from North Carolina. In 1929, it assumed the support of its first missionary, Miss Clara Sullivan of Hickory, for a term of five years in the China field. Cost of the project amounted to one thousand dollars per year. In addition it contributed fifteen hundred dollars in 1946 for the purchase of a station wagon for her use in China. The society also gave significantly to the support of two other North Carolina missionaries, Misses Maud and Annie Powlas of Barber Junction, who served in the Japanese mission field.

Other special projects were undertaken. A contribution of four hundred dollars was made to Lutheran World Action in 1940. A gift of two hundred dollars was made for several years in support of a weekday religious education consultant of the North Carolina Council of Churches. During the three-year period starting in 1949, the society joined with the societies in the South Carolina and Georgia-Alabama synods to raise twenty thousand dollars toward the erection of Mission Hall at Lutheridge; the North Carolina share of the project was twelve thousand dollars. A 1949 gift to Lenoir Rhyne established an annual two-hundred-dollar Maud & Annie Powlas Scholarship to assist women students entering full-time Christian service.

The society also contributed an electronic organ in 1960 to Lenoir Rhyne for use in Monroe Auditorium, and furnished an auxiliary room in 1961 for the new synodical headquarters in Salisbury.

In 1950, the society altered some of its funding policies in response to general society actions. The national organization discarded the concept of dues, for members and synodical groups, and urged the practice of free-will offerings. In North Carolina, the new practice was adopted; twenty percent of the gifts received at the synodical level were retained, and the balance was forwarded for the work of the national organization.

In the same year, the synodical auxiliary assumed the administration of the Patterson Memorial Fund, an endowment fund established by the sons and daughters of the former synod treasurer, I. Frank Patterson and his wife, Maria. The fund's annual income, which totaled twenty-five hundred dollars in 1962, was restricted by the donors to be used "in a manner which is in accord with the practice and objects of said Society in the use of its general funds."[21] Although some gifts were made to other projects, such as the furnishing of lounges at the Hickory and Albemarle units of Lutheran homes, distributions were normally designated for scholarship support of North Carolina Lutheran and foreign students.

Five years later, the name of the auxiliary was changed by action of the national organization at its triennial convention in Cleveland. The change, designed partly to merge the Women's Missionary Societies and Ladies Aid Societies which co-existed in some congregations, resulted in the new name of United Lutheran Church Women (ULCW).

As the ULCA neared its 1963 merger, the ULCW organization on the national level held its own constituting convention in July 1962 in Minneapolis to form the new Lutheran Church Women (LCW) of the LCA. The North Carolina unit followed with a constituting convention October 6 at Augsburg, Winston-Salem, in preparation for the new organization to become effective on January 1, 1963.

The synodical organization, which began the period in 1921 with ninety-eight local societies representing 2,451 members, approached the merger with 179 units and an active membership of 10,842. During the period, it contributed more than one million dollars to the work of the church.

Children's Work

Although the women's synodical auxiliary relinquished its interest in young people's societies with the 1921 formation of the synodical Luther League, it continued support of children's societies, which were given the new name of Light Brigade with the merger.

At the merger convention, North Carolina reported fifty Light Brigade organizations with 1,428 members and contributions of $2,517.96. The Tennessee society reported thirteen groups with 464 members and annual gifts of $158.84.

Programs of the local Light Brigades were based on mission study books prepared by an interdenominational committee later known as the Friendship Press. Lutheran leaders prepared guides for three divisions: Little Lights, Lamplighters, and Torchbearers.

The Light Brigade promoted a twelve-point efficiency standard among local units. In 1923, four of the ninety-two brigades in North Carolina reached the twelve-point level, and fifteen others made the ten-point honor roll.

Support of missions was promoted through monthly dues and use of Thank Offering boxes. Missionaries supported by the Light Brigade included Miss Annie Powlas, missionary to Japan; Miss Christina Erickson, India; Miss Mary Bauer, Africa; and Miss Cora Pearl Jeffcoat, Watauga County. The gifts also supported other projects such as a milk fund, the Puerto Rico oppressed and the Queen Louise Home in the Virgin Islands.

In 1926, North Carolina reported the organization of 111 brigades and became the first synodical society to reach the goal of one brigade in each local WMS.

In 1928, Light Brigade rallies were introduced. Five rallies were held in the state, attended by fifty-seven brigades and 1,122 children. In 1935, eleven rallies were attended by ninety-one brigades and two thousand children. The last rally was held the following year.

Mrs. Julia Hall of St. John's, Cherryville, was elected at the 1921 merger convention to the position of superintendent of the Light Brigade and served for eight years. Succeeding her in the position were Mrs. J. Lewis Thornburg of St. Paul's, Durham, 1928-31; Mrs. J. F. Crigler of St. Mark's, Charlotte, 1931-33; Mrs. E. R. Trexler of Mt. Moriah, China Grove, 1933-36; and Mrs. R. L. Conrad of Emmanuel, High Point, 1936-39.

In 1939 the national Light Brigade moved from WMS affiliation and was placed under the jurisdiction of the Parish and Church School Board of the ULCA. It was renamed the Children of the Church. At the time of the change, North Carolina reported 112 brigades with 4,124 children and annual gifts of $2,617.59.

Emphasis of the new Children of the Church was placed on program as contrasted to organization. Weekly weekday sessions were urged, with focus directed not primarily on missionary work but on the total work of the church. Study was designed for beginner, primary and junior departments. Free-will offerings were encouraged.

The North Carolina work in Children of the Church excelled among synodical programs. In 1941 and 1942, it was recognized by the Parish and Church School Board for the largest festival attendance and offering in the ULCA. In 1941, the North Carolina program ranked first in total offerings and maintained that rank for ten years, except in 1945.

In 1946, North Carolina and St. John's, Salisbury, hosted the ULCA service of dedication of Children of the Church gifts. Representatives of the ULCA boards were present to receive the gifts from the hands of North Carolina children, who represented the Children of the Church of the ULCA. Present for the January 27 event were 1,360 persons, including more than eight hundred children.

Participation in the Children of the Church was highest in the years following World War II. In 1946, participating congregations numbered 137; the following year, the number of participating children totaled 6,573. The record high offering of $4,383.16 was reported in 1950.

The first synodical secretary of the Children of the Church program was Mrs. J. Lewis Thornburg of St. John's, Statesville, who assumed the duties in 1939. Succeeding her in the position were Mrs. J. D. Sheppard of St. Mark's, China Grove, 1941-42; Mrs. Earl K. Bodie of Bethany, Kannapolis, 1942-47; Mrs. Olin W. Sink of Holy Trinity, Charlotte, 1947-49; Mrs. Barbara Yount Rudisill of St. John's, Cherryville, 1949-52; Mrs. Jacob L. Lackey of St. Timothy, Hickory, 1952-55; Mrs. Samuel Sox of First, Greensboro, 1955-58; and Mrs. C. P. Fisher, Jr., of St. James, Rockwell, 1958-62.

In 1953, during Mrs. Lackey's tenure, the Children of the Church activity was merged into a new Parish Education Committee program of Children's Work, which included Sunday School, Weekday Church School, Vacation Church School, and the Christian Home. Festivals continued to be held each fall in the local congregations, but a new logo of the program was "Stewart the Steward", a cartoon character promoting stewardship, who danced through the pages of "Let's Go!", a monthly newsheet designed for boys and girls. A separate illustrated issue of the newsheet designed for use by congregations in the synod and featuring North Carolina projects, was written by Mrs. Lackey.

Local offerings in the Children's Work program were distributed equally between the local congregation and benevolence causes, with one-fourth retained at the synodical level and the remainder forwarded to the ULCA. Synodical projects during the next decade included a children's worship center at St. Mark's, Lumberton; baptismal fonts at Messiah, Hickory, and Kure Memorial, Kure Beach, and Atonement, Wilkesboro; the Lenoir Rhyne Development Fund; and books for the Powlas sisters in Japan.[22]

As the year for the 1963 merger approached, the Children's Work secretary position was terminated and the duties subsumed in the synodical parish education staff position.

Luther League

By virtue of the 1921 merger convention of youth organizations, youth work in the synod was organized within the structure of the Luther League of America, the official youth auxiliary of the ULCA, with the Luther League of North Carolina as the synodical auxiliary.

The synodical league functioned through delegates sent by congregational leagues to annual conventions. The delegates, with guidance from the Luther League of America, determined policies and programs for the synodical program and offered direction to the congregational groups. In addition, the delegates elected officers and an executive committee for the Luther League of North Carolina.

Initial purpose of the league focused on education, missions, and life service. But, in the 1950s, the purpose was revised into a five-fold program of Christian vocation, evangelism, missions, social action, and recreation. Congregational leagues used programs centering on one or more of the topics as developed by the national league.

LUTHER LEAGUE PRESIDENTS

1921-23 E. R. Lineberger, Gaston County
1923-25 Curtis Wise, Rowan County
1925-27 Frank Cauble, Lincoln County
1927-28 Herman Fisher, Salisbury
1928-31 Luther Mauney, St. Andrew's, Hickory
1931-33 Joe Moretz, Holy Trinity, Hickory
1933-35 Catharine Stirewalt, St. John's, Salisbury
1935-37 Irene Sox, St. Andrew's, Hickory
1937-39 David Cooper, Emmanuel, High Point
1939-41 Elmer Troutman, Holy Trinity, Hickory
1941-43 Carl Litaker, St. John's, Statesville
1943-45 Mabel Seagle, Emmanuel, Lincolnton
1945-47 Evelyn Troutman, Holy Trinity, Hickory
1947-49 Betty Scott Lentz, St. John's, Salisbury
1949-51 Ray Cline, St. John's, Concord
1951-53 Jeff Norris, Macedonia, Burlington
1953-54 Sue Culp, First, Albemarle
1954-56 George Keck, St. Andrew's, Hickory
1956-57 Judy Ford, St. John's, Cherryville
1957-59 Edwin Ricks, Trinity, Rocky Mount
1959-60 Wendy Brokhoff, St. Mark's, Charlotte
1960-61 Elizabeth Herion, Holy Trinity, Mt. Pleasant
1961-62 Linda Lockard, Augsburg, Winston-Salem

In addition to congregational league meetings, members were given opportunity to partipate in district meetings and state conventions. The state conventions, and to some extent the district meetings, included: inspirational and educational addresses by leaders of the synod and the ULCA; workshops on Bible study, program and organization; and business sessions for the election of officers, adoption of budgets, and reports from officers and committees.

Stewardship emphasis in the Luther League resulted in support for a variety of church programs. The synodical league receipts ranged from three thousand dollars in the earlier years to eighteen thousand dollars in 1960. Mission congregations in the synod were always a target for the league's benevolence. Among other projects were the seminary, Lowman Home, Lutheridge, Lenoir Rhyne, war-time service centers in North Carolina, Lutheran Children's Home of the South, and North Carolina Lutheran

Homes, in addition to the Luther League of America.

The education programs directed toward congregational leagues took several forms, according to Rev. Brady Y. Faggart, Jr., writing in 1963:

> The LINC program, "Leagueing in N. C.," was used between 1953 and 1957, with trained teams visiting local Leagues. This was replaced by an annual President's Conference and the caravaning program of the LLA. In this latter program, North Carolina youth supplied large numbers of caravaners, almost one-third of the total in 1960. District meetings, held twice a year, attracted large numbers of Leaguers for inspirational, education and fellowship programs; in 1959 total attendance for district meetings reached 2,000. Publications of the synodical League included "Edmilise," which was merged with the Luther League section of the *North Carolina Lutheran* in 1956, newsletters from various presidents, and *League Lens*, a printed newsletter begun in 1962. An annual *League Calendar* was produced to aid in program planning. Throughout the period, an "efficiency standard" was developed with specific suggestions to guide congregational Leagues. "Standard Leagues," completing certain points on the standard, were recognized, and annual awards were given to two Leagues for outstanding work.[23]

As the synod neared the 1963 merger, the synodical league reported local leagues in 180 congregations with an aggregate membership of thirty-seven hundred members. The number of members was divided equally between intermediate and senior groups.

The synodical league played an active role in the activities of the national Luther League. Rosa Sox of St. Andrew's, Hickory, was elected second vice president of the national organization when it was hosted by North Carolina leaguers at St. John's, Salisbury, June 2-5, 1927. Eva Peeler of St. John's, Salisbury, served as recording secretary from 1929-33, and J. W. Cobb of St. John's, Cherryville, was elected second vice president in 1937 and also named to the national executive committee, serving in that capacity until 1946.

Other Tar Heel leaguers serving on the national scene included Ray A. Cline of St. John's, Concord, the first Southerner and the youngest person to serve as president (1951); Sue Culp of First, Albemarle, secretary (1955) and executive committee member; George Keck of St. Andrew's, Hickory, executive committee member (1955); Judy Ford of St. John's, Cherryville, the first female to serve as president (1957); Edwin Ricks of Trinity, Rocky Mount, executive committee member (1959); and Ruth Whittecar of St. John's, Salisbury, secretary (1961).

Men's Work

At the time of the 1921 merger, there was no active synod-wide men's organization. In the Tennessee Synod existed eight congregational groups informally associated for social events, but not united in a formal organization. In the old North Carolina Synod, the North Carolina Lutheran Brotherhood had been formed in 1919 but remained to be activated. An effort to initiate activity was renewed by the synod on the day prior to the merger, March 1, 1921, by authorizing the appointment of a synodical Committee on Brotherhoods.

Appointed to the committee were two ministers (E. A. Shenk of First, Greensboro, and H. Brent Schaeffer of St. Matthew's, Kings Mountain) and three laymen (P. M. Edge, J. H. Dinglehoff and Leon E. Sloop).

The following year, in 1922, the committee reported to the new synod its difficulty in forming new organizations. It commended the work that had resulted in the groups organized in Gaston, Cleveland, Lincoln and Mecklenburg counties.

One of the barriers to the formation of local brotherhoods, according to Harry E. Isenhour of Salisbury, was the lack of guidance at the national level. The ULCA Brotherhood had been organized with an office in Cincinnati, Ohio, but "most of its activities consisted of an occasional visit to a synod and 'mail' contacts throughout the ULCA. It had no well developed program for the new congregational Brotherhoods that existed, other than largely a social nature. No well defined objectives had been adopted and what little dues collected were supplemented out of the ULCA treasury to keep the organization intact.[24]

LUTHER LEAGUE CONVENTION SITES

1921	Holy Communion, Dallas	1940	Beth Eden, Newton
1922	St. Paul's, Wilmington	1941	Kimball Memorial, Kannapolis
1923	Emmanuel, Lincolnton	1942	St. Mark's, Charlotte
1924	St. James, Concord	1943	St. John's, Salisbury
1925	St. Matthew's, Kings Mountain	1944	Kimball Memorial, Kannapolis
1926	St. Mark's, China Grove	1945	Emmanuel, Lincolnton
1927	First, Albemarle	1946	Macedonia, Burlington
1928	Holy Trinity, Gastonia	1947	Holy Trinity, Hickory
1929	Macedonia, Burlington	1948	St. John's, Concord
1930	Augsburg, Winston-Salem	1949	St. Paul's, Wilmington
1931	St. John's, Statesville	1950	St. James, Concord
1932	Holy Trinity, Hickory	1951	First, Albemarle
1933	St. John's, Salisbury	1952	Center Grove, Kannapolis
1934	St. Mark's, China Grove	1953	St. John's, Salisbury
1935	Emmanuel, Lincolnton	1954	Lenoir Rhyne
1936	Macedonia, Burlington	1955	Lenoir Rhyne
1937	Holy Trinity, Mt. Pleasant	1956	Lutheridge
1938	Lenoir Rhyne	1957-62	Lenoir Rhyne
1939	St. Paul's, Wilmington		

The national organization, he added, had no model constitutions for synodical, district or even congregational brotherhoods. Its own activity focused on a meeting which was held in connection with each convention of the ULCA.

Despite the challenge, a temporary synodical brotherhood was organized at the regular district meeting held at Holy Trinity, Gastonia, on the fifth Sunday of April in 1923. Hon. Bismarck Capps of the host congregation was named president, and O. B. Robinson was elected secretary.

The two officers and other interested laymen then met with Avery R. Rhyne, president of the Gaston District Brotherhood, at St. Mark's, Charlotte, on November 6 to complete the permanent organization. The constitution and by-laws, drafted by Harry E. Isenhour, were adopted. Elected officers were Capps, president; Rhyne, vice-president; Isenhour, secretary; and R. W. Graeber, treasurer.

Later in the month, the state brotherhood met in connection with the convention of the synod and reported twenty congregational units had been organized.

The following spring, on May 4, 1924, the Central District Brotherhood was organized at Salisbury with six congregational units. The number had increased to twelve when the state organization reported to the synod six months later.

Other district organizations followed quickly. The Western District Brotherhood was formed January 30, 1927, in Hickory, by five brotherhoods representing ninety members. The Northern and Eastern districts were added before the close of 1928.

MEN'S ORGANIZATION PRESIDENTS

1923-27	Bismarck Capps, Holy Trinity, Gastonia
1928-29	W. K. Mauney, St. Matthew's, Kings Mountain
1930	W. L. Kinney, Augsburg, Winston-Salem
1931	E. B. Graeber, Holy Trinity, Raleigh
1932	W. P. Hooker, Emmanuel, High Point
1933	Roy S. Safrit, Salisbury
1934-35	S. J. Marion, St. Andrew's, Hickory
1936	T. L. Stryker, Augsburg, Winston-Salem
1937	Paul E. Monroe, Holy Trinity, Gastonia
1938	James L. Fisher, St. John's, Salisbury
1939-40	Aubrey Mauney, St. Matthew's, Kings Mountain
1941-45	Zeb B. Trexler, St. James, Concord
1946-47	Luther Boliek, St. Andrew's, Hickory
1948-49	H. D. Frye, St. Stephen's, Hickory
1950-51	Harold Krause, Augsburg, Winston-Salem
1952-53	Fred R. Smyre, Holy Trinity, Hickory
1954-55	M. Allen Fritz, Good Shepherd, Goldsboro
1956-57	G. Dewey Arndt, Holy Trinity, Raleigh
1958-59	John J. Lentz, Trinity, Sanford
1960-61	Harry M. Arndt, Mt. Calvary, Claremont
1962-63	Paul Ritchie, Salisbury

The first synodical brotherhood banquet was held November 19, 1924, at Lutheran Chapel, Gastonia, and attended by three hundred.

Following the banquet, the annual synodical brotherhood met at Holy Trinity, Gastonia, and offered to manage the synod's Loan & Gift Fund. The offer was accepted by the synod at a later convention. Although the Loan & Gift Fund pledges topped one hundred thousand dollars, payments were slow. Receipts at the end of 1930 totaled $7,307.94; at the end of 1931, $13,165.08. Still, the first loans to mission churches were made in 1931.

After the Depression, the Loan & Gift Fund assets grew more rapidly. They reached the thirty thousand dollar level in 1939 and advanced to $52,977 in 1943. By 1947, the pledged amount of one hundred thousand dollars was reached, and the brotherhood had also begun raising an annual gift for additional support where it was most needed by mission churches. In 1952, the contributions totaled $45,821.54, increasing the assets of the fund to $250,116.36. Included in the total was $168,884.05 in the revolving loan fund and $81,272.31 set aside for gifts.

The fund's growing demand for investment and management supervision resulted in the synod's 1953 creation of the "Home Mission Foundation of the United Evangelical Lutheran Synod of North Carolina." The funds were transferred from the Brotherhood Executive Committee into the foundation, where they could be administered by a twelve-member Board of Trustees which was elected by the brotherhood Executive Committee and approved by the synodical Executive Committee. The brotherhood continued to raise funds through the Loan & Gift Fund organization, a network of committees throughout the state.

MEN'S ORGANIZATION CONVENTION SITES

1924-33	(not available)	1952	First, Albemarle
1934	St. Matthew's, Kings Mountain	1953	St. John's, Salisbury
1935-37	(not available)	1954	Emmanuel, High Point
1938	Holy Trinity, Mt. Pleasant	1955	St. John's, Salisbury
1939	Holy Trinity, Gastonia	1956	St. Mark's, Charlotte
1940	St. John's, Salisbury	1957	First, Greensboro
1941	St. James, Concord	1958	St. Andrew's, Hickory
1942	St. John's, Salisbury	1959	St. Paul's, Salisbury
1943	St. James, Concord	1960	St. James, Concord
1944-45	St. John's, Salisbury	1961	Holy Trinity, Hickory
1946	Holy Trinity, Gastonia	1962	Beth Eden, Newton
1947-51	St. John's, Salisbury		

In 1959, the gift fund was broadened to permit financial aid for ministerial students, in addition to grants for mission churches. The policy was also adopted to allocate ninety percent of all unrestricted gifts to the loan fund, with the remaining ten percent going to the gift fund.

When the synod entered into the 1963 merger, the revolving fund of the Home Mission Foundation totaled $434,330.20, including funds on loan to twenty-one mission congregations.

In addition to the Loan & Gift Fund, the state brotherhood promoted a program designed to stimulate lay service in support of the church. At its 1928 convention, held November 8 at St. James, Concord, the delegates adopted the four-point efficiency standard of the national brotherhood. But eight years later, the national brotherhood, meeting in Springfield, Ohio, replaced the four points with six objectives to which the state organization also subscribed: "(1) win the unsaved for Christ, (2) bring back the lapsed member, (3) develop the church life of our boys, (4) increase the attendance of men at the services, (5) practice and promote Christian Citizenship, and (6) meet the obligation of the whole church."[25]

In 1948, the national and synodical brotherhoods adopted a new set of ten objectives:

> Evangelize. (1) Win the unsaved for Christ and bring back the lapsed member. (2) Deepen and enrich the Spiritual and Intellectual life of the men. (3) Increase attendance at church services.
> Educate. (4) Foster an intelligent and appreciative understanding of the whole work of the whole church.
> Energize. (5) Promote Christian Fellowship - locally, nationally,

internationally. (6) Encourage men of the various Lutheran bodies to draw close together in understanding and cooperation. (7) Stimulate the practice of Stewardship of time, talents and money. (8) Strengthen the home so that it may be a real school for Christian living. (9) Promote aggressively a Christ-centered, experience centered and guided Boy's Work program, such as Scouting. (10) Encourage our men as Christian citizens to exert an individual and collective Christian influence in the community and to participate actively in the affairs of government.

The number of brotherhoods continued to rise. From fifty-seven organizations in 1930, the number advanced to eighty in 1941, 105 (largest in the ULCA) in 1944, and 124 in 1951.

In 1946, the state organization adopted the dues plan of financing, as recommended by the national group.

The annual Brotherhood Lay Retreat was inaugurated in 1950 with an event at Lenoir Rhyne held prior to the annual brotherhood rally. In 1953 the retreat attracted fifty-seven laymen and fifty-five visitors from forty-two brotherhoods; the rally at St. Andrew's, Hickory, was attended by 250. Interest in the retreat, however, waned later, and the final event was held in 1961.

The program of sponsoring Boy Scout troops gained official recognition in 1953 with the designation of Aubrey W. Mauney of St. Matthew's, Kings Mountain, as the synodical Director of Scouting. At the time, the brotherhoods in the state reported sixty-two troops in the synod with 1,171 members.

The year before, in 1952, the brotherhood inaugurated the annual Lutheran Scout Camporee at Lutheridge. Seventy-five scouts and twenty-one leaders attended. Five years later, attendance increased to 297 scouts and seventy-six leaders, and in 1962, the event attracted 417 scouts and leaders.

The fame of the North Carolina scouting program spread in 1956 when the National Lutheran Committee on Scouting inaugurated the Lamb Award to recognize outstanding service by Scout leaders and directors. Among the first recipients of the award were two Lutheran Tar Heels: W. Harold Little of Hickory and Aubrey Mauney. Other North Carolinians receiving the award later were Dr. J. Lewis Thornburg of Lutheridge, Roscoe R. Coggins of Kannapolis, Rev. Claude V. Deal of Landis, Charles A. Dyer of Camp Lejeune, Henry Herman of Hickory, Fred H. Rudisill of Lincolnton and Paul Holscher of Rocky Mount.

In 1958, the brotherhood, meeting in its thirty-sixth convention at St. Andrew's, Hickory, on November 18, changed its name to "United Lutheran Church Men of the Lutheran Synod of North Carolina" (ULCM). The change was made to conform with the name adopted by the national organization two years earlier. The change was also recommended, but not required, for the six districts and 132 congregational units in the organization.

During the ULCA period, the North Carolina men's organization contributed top leadership to the national organization. Harry E. Isenhour of Salisbury served as president of the ULCA Brotherhood from 1932 to 1936, and Zeb B. Trexler of Concord was elected to the same position for two two-year terms beginning in 1944. Later, in 1959, Aubrey Mauney of Kings Mountain was named president of the ULCM at its biennial convention in South Bend, Indiana.

The state men's organization also hosted the national Lutheran Church Men organization at its constituting convention in 1962. The meeting, attended by three hundred delegates from the United States and Canada, was held from August 30 through September 1 at Lenoir Rhyne and St. Andrew's, Hickory. The new organization became operational on January 1, 1963.

After entertaining the national convention, the state ULCM group held its final convention on November 14 at Beth Eden, Newton, and then reconvened to constitute the new Lutheran Church Men state organization. Official convener of the meeting was Rev. J. Wilford Lyerly, secretary of the newly-constituted North Carolina Synod of the Lutheran Church in America.

Summer School for Church Workers

The Summer School for Church Workers, an intersynodical project that declined in use shortly before the 1921 merger, was revived after the merger.

The typical daily schedule for the one-week school included morning sessions on church music, Bible study, leadership training for all Sunday School departments, and organization conferences for the Women's Missionary Society, Light Brigade, Luther League, and pastors and church council members.

The afternoon period was given to recreation, and the evening hours were devoted to twilight services, Vesper services, and lectures. Guest lecturers often included representatives of the ULCA Division of Parish Education, and missionaries to foreign countries from the synod.

The school sites alternated each summer between MPCI and Lenoir Rhyne. In 1934, however, the synod joined with the South Carolina Synod to sponsor the Carolina Summer School for Church Workers, which was held July 23-29 at Blue Ridge Assembly Grounds near Black Mountain. Within two years, the Georgia-Alabama Synod joined in the sponsorship, and in 1940 the Florida Synod participated. Blue Ridge was the perennial site, although one school, in 1936, was held at Kanuga Lake near Hendersonville.

War-time travel restrictions, however, stopped the intersynodical gatherings at Blue Ridge after 1941, and the North Carolina Synod reverted to its own school the following summer. For a site, the school leaders could hardly turn down the offer of President P. E. Monroe at Lenoir Rhyne: eight dollars per registrant for the six-day period, the fee to cover registration, room and board.

The travel restrictions did not handicap the school at Lenoir Rhyne, even in 1945, when the U. S. Office of Defense Transportation notified school leaders that "not over 50 (attendees) using public transportation facilities may attend. All others must use private means of conveyance."[26]

The Summer School for Church Workers continued at Lenoir Rhyne through 1952. In 1953, it moved to the new Lutheridge Assembly Grounds.

In the early years of the summer school, in 1925, a supplementary organization, the Lutheran State Sunday School Association, was formed. The association, which developed a network of fourteen regional districts for Sunday School promotion and teacher training, began holding separate conventions in 1928 and continued the practice until 1935 when it dissolved and its objectives were re-incorporated into the summer school program.

Educational Interests

At the time of the 1921 merger, the educational interests of the two synods centered on three institutions. MPCI was a junior college of recognized standing with property valued at $65,000, and an endowment of $5,000 plus $15,000 in subscriptions secured by notes. Mont Amoena reported property of $66,000 with a fund of $4,000 on hand and a debt of $7,000. Lenoir College, a four-year college ranked Class A by the State Board of Education, held property valued at $230,000 and a debt of $30,000.

The merged synod agreed at the outset that it should support only one standard A-grade college and that college would be Lenoir, but it also agreed that the other two institutions would be continued as then conducted. A Board of Educational Institutions was created to govern the work in all three institutions.

The board functioned for eighteen years, although when Mont Amoena closed in May 1927, the responsibility of the board was reduced to two institutions. In 1931 the MPCI facilities were leased to the school's president, Professor McAllister, to continue its operation, but he surrendered the lease two years later and the school closed. The board also ceased to function shortly thereafter, after designating the Lenoir Rhyne board as its successor.

Lenoir College, which entered the merger under the leadership of Rev. John C. Peery, altered its name in 1923 to "Lenoir Rhyne" to honor Daniel E. Rhyne, a Lutheran textile manufacturer of Lincolnton who initiated the college's endowment fund, covered many of its operational deficits, and funded its major building.

Rev. H. Brent Schaeffer served as president from 1927 to 1934, when the college constructed three major buildings and received regional accreditation.

During the administration of Dr. P. E. Monroe (1934-49), a dormitory and library were constructed and the post-war student enrollment jumped from three hundred to eight hundred, beginning a growth trend that continued for two decades.

Shortly after President Voigt R. Cromer assumed office in 1949, the North Carolina Synod approved participation in a six million dollar Christian Higher Education Appeal of the ULCA which was launched in 1950. The national appeal included $144,000 for Lenoir Rhyne, and to this amount the synod added a $500,000 goal in addition to a supplemental goal for Southern Seminary. North Carolina set the pace in the ULCA for gift response, exceeding all its goals and providing funds for a dormitory at Lenoir Rhyne, as well as library property for the seminary.

In 1955, the synod convention approved another capital campaign in support of the college. The goal for the Development Fund campaign, $1.5 million, was also met, helping to fund construction of an auditorium, gymnasium, dormitory, and two classroom buildings.

Four years after the second campaign for Lenoir Rhyne, the synod launched another campaign, this time in concert with four other synods for the Expansion Fund of Southern Seminary. Other synods participating in the effort were South Carolina, Virginia, Georgia-Alabama, and Mississippi.

The campaign was prompted by a backlog of facility and endowment needs accumulating, without benefit of a campaign, over several decades. Under the leadership of President John L. Yost, the seminary had grown, by 1955, to enroll seventy students, employ a faculty of eight and expand its offerings for women. Its annual budget approximated one hundred thousand dollars.

A forecast of the needs was indicated earlier by the seminary Board of Trustees in its 1953 report to the constituent synods. It reported the duties of the president and faculty had been reorganized to allow the president more time for field work and promotion. There was a need, it explained, to "beat the bushes for additional funds to meet financial obligations - perhaps, the President's own salary."[27]

The goal of $750,000 was set to fund construction of a chapel, married student apartments, student union, administration building, president's home and faculty houses.

The campaign, conducted during the first quarter of 1959, exceeded not only the goal, but most expectations. Final receipts from the six synods totaled $1,111,800, and more than half the amount came from North Carolina.

President Yost, a native of Rowan County and former pastor of Redeemer, Atlanta, Georgia, who assumed the presidency in 1945, resigned at the close of 1960. He was succeeded in office by the former ULCA secretary, Dr. E. Eppling Reinartz.

Before Yost's retirement, however, the seminary in 1961 inaugurated in cooperation with the ULCA Board of Higher Education a Pastor's Institute. It also initiated other new ventures in theological circles such as the Southern Seminary Seminars on Theology of Life, conducted annually at Lutheridge, and the Columbia School of Theology for Christian Laity.

Lutheridge

In addition to supporting educational institutions, the synod during the ULCA period entered into the joint development of a Lutheran assembly ground.

The concept was introduced early in the period, partly because of the need for a site for the annual Summer School for Church Workers. In 1924, a committee of the synod proposed the site of Vade Mecum near Rural Hall for an assembly ground.

"But other members of Synod", according to the *North Carolina Lutheran*, "thought that site not sufficiently within the summer resort territory, and strongly advocated other sites throughout the summer resort sections of western North Carolina."[28]

Twenty-two years later, in 1946, the synod's Executive Committee, on the recommendation of its Assembly Grounds Committee, purchased a tract of 172 acres of wooded land at Arden, between Asheville and Hendersonville, for use by the North Carolina, South Carolina and Georgia-Alabama synods. The Mississippi Synod joined in the sponsorship in 1952. The cost was $34,500.

Planning for the facility was directed by an intersynodical Board of Trustees headed by Clarence L. Whisnant of Bethany, Hickory, chairman; Dr. C. A. Linn of Atlanta, Georgia, vice-chairman; B. T. Bodie of Columbia, South Carolina, secretary; and Oscar Pitts of St. Mark's, Asheville, treasurer. The name - Lutheridge - was suggested by Secretary Bodie.

In 1949, Dr. J. Lewis Thornburg resigned as pastor of St. Mark's, China Grove, and assumed duties as first executive director of the assembly grounds.

Ground was broken in the summer of 1950 for development of the grounds and construction of six initial buildings at a cost of one hundred thousand dollars. Included in the group were the Efird Hall Administration Building, Lineberger Dining Hall, and four family-type cottages.

The first organized summer program was held in 1951. It provided seven weeks of camping sessions for junior, intermediate and senior youth.

By 1953, a total of 1,434 guests, including the Summer School for Church

Workers, made annual use of the facility. Nine years later, prior to the synodical merger, the one-year registration of students, leaders and weekend guests totaled 6,942.

Social Ministry

During the ULCA period of its history, the synod continued to support the Lutheran Orphan Home of the South at Salem, Virginia.

In 1948, the home changed its name to Lutheran "Children's" Home of the South to reflect the changing character of its residents. Few residents were orphans. Most were disturbed children, products of families broken by strife, alcoholism, mental illness or desertion.

In the decade to follow, the nature of the home's services changed as well. Child care grew more individualized. The maximum size of the cottage groups dropped from thirty to sixteen "to create a more homelike atmosphere, reduce tensions and enable the staff to work more constructively with the children."[29]

The care also grew more specialized. The children experiencing the most difficulty in school received the assistance of tutoring by college students or a staff teacher. Those with personality problems were referred to the guidance center or to a psychiatrist for examination and consultation. The home also arranged its schedule to enable a specialist in child mental health to meet with groups and individuals, when necessary, on Saturday mornings as a further step in helping the children toward mental maturity.

In the 1950s, the home also began extending its services beyond the campus. Recognizing the value of care in an actual family environment, the home began providing casework services to the families of the resident children. It also facilitated more foster care and adoption. In 1963, twenty percent of the children received care through these extended services.

The synod's affiliation with the home continued to grow. From the date of its founding until 1963, approximately 355 North Carolina children received care in the home or through its placement services, and the churches and individuals of the synod contributed $367,000 through the synodical apportionment and direct giving.

The synod contributed about one-third of the funding for the home's plant renewal in 1961-62. Two of the four cottages were renovated extensively, the dining room and kitchen were refurnished and re-equipped, outdoor recreational facilities were enlarged and additional office space was provided. Over $115,000 was spent on the improvement. Renovation of the other two cottages was undertaken in 1963 at a cost of one hundred thousand dollars.

Superintendents of the home during the period included Rev. E. W. Leslie, George Santmiers and Rev. and Mrs. Paul Sieg. Upon the resignation of the Siegs in 1928, Rev. T. A. Graves assumed the post and served for ten years. He was succeeded in 1938 by T. C. Rohrbaugh who served twenty-two years. Following Rohrbaugh's retirement in 1961, Assistant Superintendent Bruce E. Wilds was elected superintendent.

Meanwhile, at White Rock, South Carolina, the synod maintained its relationship with the Lowman Home for the Aged and Helpless. It contributed in 1962 the sum of $26,341 toward the home's general budget of $163,500.

The home expanded its facilities, constructing three buildings in 1927 and two dormitories in 1932. In 1956 it initiated a cottage program for residents who wished to live on the grounds but were willing and able to look after their own daily needs. Two cottages and a nurses' home were added during the 1950s and an infirmary in 1963. Capacity of the home increased to 104, with thirty-four of the beds occupied by North Carolinians. At the close of the period, the assets of the home totaled $1.2 million.

Serving for twelve years as the home's first general superintendent was Dr. Leroy E. Blackwelder, a North Carolinian who was pastor at St. Mark's, Mooresville, before assuming the home duties. When he retired in 1961, he was replaced by Rev. J. Kenneth Webb of the South Carolina Synod.

In addition to its affiliations with the children's home and Lowman Home, the synod entered into a relationship with a boys' home. Sipes Orchard Home, near Conover, opened in 1945 to provide a refuge for underprivileged boys. It was established through a donation of land and other property by Mr. and Mrs. Vernon O. Sipe of Conover. The home was not owned by the North Carolina Synod, but by the Eastern District of the American Lutheran Church, and it was promoted by the brotherhood of that district as a service project.

The charter of the home, however, permitted the North Carolina Synod to elect one minister and one layman to serve on the Board of Directors, and the synod happily exercised that privilege. Under the leadership of Superintendent John G. Odom, the home in 1962 reported a capacity admittance of forty-two boys, and assets valued at $291,000.

The synod entered into another type of social ministry in the late forties when it responded to a challenge of the National Lutheran Council to help with the relocation of Europeans displaced by World War II. Under the direction of the Lutheran Resettlement Committee of North Carolina, headed by Rev. J. L. Norris of Macedonia, Burlington, 259 refugees (149 adults and 110 children) were relocated in the state in April 1949. Most of the refugees were Latvians, although two physicians in the group were Hungarians.

During the period, the synod also developed its own institutional ministry to the elderly. The movement was prompted in part by a 1956 survey by the Committee on Social Missions which showed that 247 persons needed institutional care or probably would need it in the near future. The needs obviously would exceed the capacity of the Lowman Home, which served not only North Carolina but three other synods.

In 1959, the synod created the "Board of Trustees for an Institutional Ministry to the Aging and Helpless," which changed its name the following year to "Board of Trustees of North Carolina Lutheran Homes." Officers of the board were Dr. A. Wike Lippard of Calvary, Morganton, president; Rev. John A. Pless of St. Luke's, Lexington, vice president; B. S. Brown, Jr., of Kimball Memorial, Kannapolis, secretary; and Dr. John C. Herion of Holy Trinity, Mt. Pleasant, treasurer. Selected as the board's executive director was Dr. J. L. Norris, pastor of Grace, Hendersonville, who assumed the duties in 1960.

Several communities in the state made offers of building sites and cash donations in their bids for the first unit of North Carolina Lutheran Homes. There were two Hickory bids, one by Prof. W. H. Little, the other by Mr. and Mrs. Albert D. Eckard. The Eckard bid, including cash of $30,000 and property northeast of Hickory near St. Stephen's church, was accepted. The bid also included an undesignated gift of $25,500 by Mr. and Mrs. Clarence Bost.[30]

A synod-wide appeal for $225,000 was launched in January 1961 to help fund construction of the first unit. Among the contributions were the gifts of the state Luther League Penny Parade: 212,963 pennies. The gift was delivered to Executive Director Norris by the league president, Libby Herion of Mt. Pleasant.

The first unit, constructed and furnished at a cost of $335,000, opened on October 7, 1962. With a capacity for fifty-six residents and a staff of twenty-eight, the facility operated under a license of the State Board of Health which designated it as a combination nursing and boarding home for the aged and infirm.

Cost of care during the first year was $160 per month for ambulant residents, $175 for invalid residents. The operational revenues of $66,600 included a supplement from the North Carolina Synod of $29,256. The unit began operation with an indebtedness of $130,000.

The synod's social work included a 1954 historic step in ministry to the blacks of the state. Since the formation of the Alpha Synod, the ministry had been neglected by the synod, although ministry to blacks had been conducted as missionary enterprises by the Missouri Synod and the American Lutheran Church.

President Conrad believed that it was time for the synod to take responsibility for ministry within its own boundaries. He had indicated his position in previous reports to the synod, and with the synod's approval in 1953 he appointed a Commission on Negro Work, Dr. M. L. Stirewalt, Jr., chairman, and Rev. R. F. Shelby, Jr., secretary.

The commission reported to the convention in April 1954. Its recommendations were adopted calling for the appointment of a committee to supervise a "grass root program of Christian education in race relations."[31] The program was to be conducted in each congregation of the synod, and financial support was approved for the committee, the program, and for beneficiary aid to black ministerial students. The Mission Committee was authorized "to call White or Negro pastors as may be needed in order to begin a ministry among the Negroes."

A few weeks later the United States Supreme Court ruled on the case of Brown vs. Board of Education. This ruling and the resistance from some elements in the synod impeded the development of the ministry until the work of the Social Ministry Committee and the Task Force on Justice and Social Change in the 1960s.

Financial Support

Congregations within the synod were not always pleased with the financial support of their members. Even St. John's, Salisbury, with nearly one thousand adult members, was not exempt. In 1923, it became concerned about unpaid pledges and employed an "official collector" who received ten percent of all unpaid pledges he collected. The system was discontinued as being unsatisfactory, but it was revived ten years later only to be dropped permanently when the collector resigned after two months. In 1937, the congregation experimented with the publication of a listing of member pledges and amounts paid but also discontinued that practice after the second year.

For the synod itself, the apportionment method of funding synodical projects (asking congregations to give in proportion to their membership size) was used most often during the ULCA period of the synod's history, but the method was not completely successful.

As early as 1930, the topic attracted discussion on the convention floor to the extent that J. A. B. Goodman was prompted to observe later in "A Layman's Impressions at Synod":

But one subject that interested me most was the "Apportionment Subject," one of the "Biggest in the Synod," and so many of our churches not near coming up, many not more than half, and on some parts, notably the "Ministerial Pension Fund." Brethren, this will never do, and it is a burning shame, and let's every one get out of it. Please excuse me, but if a little poor church of about 150 members, like Mooresville, when not over a half dozen members own their own homes, and the town hard hit by the cotton mills being on half time, yes, when these poor people can always pay their apportionments in full, have subscribed $1,300 to Ministerial Pensions, and already paid $900. What ought not the congregations every one do? I know it is hard times, but that is not the cause; we are just asleep, and some Wide Awake Laymen in each church, ought to wake us up, good and strong.[32]

A special stewardship committee noted that seventeen congregations paid in full their apportionments in 1932, ninety-nine made partial payments and forty-three "paid nothing at all." The synod's receipts from congregations were down nearly six thousand dollars from the support received in 1931.[33]

The Depression was felt most strongly in 1933. President Morgan commented in his report to the Synod:

This has been a year of trying circumstances for the most of our pastors and congregations. Quite a number of our people are out of employment, while others are working on short time and for reduced incomes. This has made it particularly difficult to handle the financial part of the church program. However, when we compare our situation with that of other church bodies, we are made to feel that our people have done quite as well as others have. In fact, when we think of the many reverses which have come over the business world, we should feel deeply grateful to almighty God that our Church has fared as well as it has.[34]

He went on to note that those having investments "are receiving but small income from it." Yet, congregations have gone ahead with building programs in

the years when business conditions were favorable, all of which were counted commendable, but which now call for special efforts in order to finish paying for such improvements. This makes it more difficult for such churches to contribute as largely as otherwise they could to the benevolent causes of the Church. Another occasion of the shortage in benevolent funds for the general work, is the fact that all too many congregations fail to give anything to that cause, while many others give only nominal amounts.[35]

The extent of the Depression's impact was reflected in various reports of the 1933 convention minutes. Southern Seminary reported its support from the synod dropped from $1,314.58 in 1931 to $209.05 in 1932. In his own report to the synod, the statistical secretary declined to compare financial data with the prior year, stating that the reason was obvious. The salaries of the recording and statistical secretaries were reduced from $125 to $50; the salary of the treasurer from $500 to $200. At the request of the president, his salary was reduced (again) by ten percent, down to $2,700 and later to $2,400.

The synod failed to meet apportionment obligations to the Lowman Home for the year 1932 and to Lenoir Rhyne for a period of 18 months. The custom of sending fraternal delegates to sister synods was discontinued, and greetings were conveyed by letter instead. Subscriptions to *The Lutheran* in North Carolina declined from 1,375 in January 1929 to 667 in January 1933; subscriptions to the *North Carolina Lutheran* declined from 2,025 in January 1929 to nine hundred in January 1933.

In 1935, the response to the synod's apportionment was worse: of the 160 congregations in the synod, only twelve paid their apportionments in full. The Committee on the State of the Church could not fault the techniques: 126 congregations conducted an Every Member Canvas during the year, 106 churches prepared an annual budget, 115 used offering envelopes. Some of the churches used the pledge system, some subscriptions, and some free-will offerings.

Only once during the period was the apportionment method successful. In 1942, every one of the 165 congregations paid its apportionment in full.[36]

Because the method did not set well with the concept of free-will offerings, the 1953 sesquicentennial convention at St. John's, Salisbury, voted to discontinue the apportionment method after 1953 and rely on the "covenant" method. Congregations were asked, "out of gratitude to God, to give to the benevolence work of the Church according as He has prospered them."[37] If the covenants from the congregations fell short of the synod's budget, it was agreed, the Stewardship Committee would ask congregations to increase their covenants.

The covenant arrangement did not apply to the institutional benevolences, such as Children's Home, Lowman Home, Southern Seminary, Lutheridge and Lenoir Rhyne. Synodical support for those objectives continued to be apportioned to congregations on the basis of their communing memberships.

The results of the first year of covenant giving, in 1954, were not encouraging. Two-thirds of the congregations failed to increase their giving in proportion to the budget increase of the synod, and revenues trailed the budget.

At the 1955 convention, when a second shortfall loomed, the delegates authorized the Stewardship Committee to ask the congregations to reconsider their covenants. The congregations were asked to give the "figure that would have been their 1955 apportionment figure based on 20% increase in the Synodical budget since 1953."

The situation had not improved when the delegates gathered for the 1956 convention. The covenants for the current year, Presidential Assistant Misenheimer reported, fell below the synodical budget by $38,500. The delegates voted that, if the covenant receipts prevented the synod from remitting its full ULCA apportionment of $237,000, the Stewardship Committee would be authorized to conduct an emergency appeal later in the year. The emergency appeal was held in December, but it raised only twenty-two thousand dollars. The synod elected to make its full remittance to the ULCA, but its own budget experienced a nineteen thousand dollar deficit.

The three-year venture with covenants did not promise improvement. The differences between total congregation covenants and the synodical budgets had grown larger, not smaller, from $10,000 in 1954, to $12,000 in 1955 and $39,000 in 1956.

Delegates to the 1957 convention at First, Greensboro, however, hesitated to abandon the Covenant Plan altogether. They voted to continue the plan but to provide a floor for the covenants based on communing members. They also voted to move to a unified budget which included quotas for the synodical institutions, Lutheran World Action, and other items.

In 1958, the synod reverted to the concept of apportionments, although the term given to them was "minimum assignments." It also expanded the assignable budget by adding a "Part D" in which was listed the "opportunities ready for realization as soon as funds are available."[38]

On the national level, the ULCA did not cringe from the apportionment word. At its Harrisburg convention, the church adopted a fortieth anniversary year special budget of twice the benevolence it anticipated in 1957 (i.e., seven million dollars) or approximately fifteen million dollars. "American missions was to make a big breakthrough. Foreign missions was to catch up on capital projects in affiliated churches." "Double apportionment" was the cry. The result of $11.5 million fell short of double apportionment but did spark a fifty-six percent increase in benevolences.[39]

Shortly after the Covenant Plan experience, the synod received a bequest of an endowment which promised to extend the work of the synod beyond the bounds of its own budget. The Michael Peeler Fund was created in 1959 by the will of John Michael Peeler, a Salisbury wholesale distributor, to provide income "to be used by the synod each year wherever it is needed most for the advancement of the Kingdom of God."[40] The will also proposed that the synod appoint two laymen and one pastor to manage the endowment and report to the synod each year. Elected first trustees of the fund were Rev. Frank K. Efird, Harry E. Isenhour and J. E. Fisher, all of Salisbury. The fund, initially valued at $612,885, produced income of $27,500 in 1961 and $30,000 in 1962.

The initial 1961 distribution of the Michael Peeler Fund income helped finance the construction of the synod's synodical headquarters building. In recognition of the distribution, the Executive Committee of the synod designated the facility's chapel-conference room as the Michael Peeler Memorial Room.

World War II

The impact of World War II on the synod was not as heavy as it was on the congregations, but it was felt and reflected in some of the wartime conventions.

One session of the 1943 convention, at St. John's, Salisbury, was plunged in darkness, according to the *North Carolina Lutheran* reporter, Rev. L. Boyd Hamm of Macedonia, Burlington:

> The Rev. Walton A. Greever, D.D., LL.D., secretary of the United Lutheran Church, was the official representative of the Church. His presence and his message were profitable, pleasing and challenging. While he was speaking on Wednesday evening we experienced a statewide blackout, but he went on with his message in the dark. . . . It was during his appeal for the million-dollar fund for Lutheran World Action that the black-out came.

At the following convention, in 1944, the synod held a special memorial service, recognizing the nineteen members of synodical congregations who died in the war. Leader of the service was Dr. John Hall, retired Army chaplain of Hickory, and the preacher was Rev. Voigt R. Cromer. At the 1946 convention at Augsburg, Winston-Salem, a similar service was held in memory of the 186 congregational members who died in the armed services. The address was delivered by Army Chaplain Claude V. Deal, and a service flag was displayed indicating that 5,564 members of synod congregations had served during the war.

The convention during the year before, in 1945, was held with special governmental permission. An application to hold the convention was submitted to the Office of Defense Transportation and transmitted by Representative A. L. Bulwinkle of the Eleventh Congressional District, a Gastonia Lutheran. The permit was granted by R. H. Clare, secretary of the War Committee on Conventions.

"However," his permit letter continued, "the committee earnestly requests your cooperation in doing everything possible to minimize attendance at this meeting, if it cannot reasonably be deferred."

The synod secretary, Pastor Conrad, responded to Clare's request by notifying the congregations that the only ones permitted to attend the convention were pastors, lay delegates, officials, or those having a part in the proceedings. He also asked that rides to the convention be shared to conserve gasoline and tires.

Merger

Late in the period, the synod became aware of a new relationship on the horizon. The ULCA entered into merger discussions with three smaller church bodies: American Evangelical Lutheran Church, Augustana Lutheran Church, and Finnish Evangelical Lutheran Church (Suomi Synod).

In North Carolina, the discussions attracted only casual interest, partly because none of the three churches merging with the ULCA had congregations in North Carolina: the synod congregational roster would not be altered by the merger. The discussions did arouse the interest of the synod when the negotiators suggested a merging of the North Carolina and South Carolina synods as a means of reducing the number of synods in the proposed church. The proposal, however, was soon dropped, even before the two affected synods could muster opposition.

The merger negotiators, working under the banner of Joint Commission on Lutheran Unity (JCLU), formulated in 1961 an Agreement of Consolidation for the ULCA and submitted it to the synods for consideration. Ratification by two-thirds of the ULCA synods was needed for merger plans to proceed further.

North Carolina considered the agreement document at its 1961 convention at St. Mark's, Charlotte. The motion for approval was introduced by Dr. Voigt R. Cromer, president of Lenoir Rhyne and a member of the ULCA delegation to the JCLU. The convention approved the motion unanimously, and a special committee was appointed to draft a constitution and by-laws. The sixteen-member committee, known both as the Little JCLU and the Committee on Operational Activities, was chaired by Dr. John L. Yost, Jr., pastor of Holy Trinity, Hickory.

The potential for merger problems surfaced during the synod's regular 1962 convention at St. Paul's, Salisbury, in May. Formal action on the merger documents was not scheduled until the synod met in September in a constituting convention, but some of the major issues were introduced at the May meetings for preliminary reaction.

The actions of the May convention raised doubts that the synod could enter the merger in agreement with the principles of the new church, which was to be named the Lutheran Church in America (LCA). The convention voted, for example, not to accept the synodical name recommended by the LCA; instead of the proposed "North Carolina Synod of the Lutheran Church in America", the delegates voted to retain the current name of "United Evangelical Lutheran Synod of North Carolina."

The delegates also questioned the type of synod-LCA relationship proposed by the LCA. They voted not to accept the JCLU proposal that the synod amend its charter to restrict the powers of the synod to "those permitted by the laws of the Lutheran Church in America."[41]   Instead, they approved the operational committee proposal which only gave the synod the privilege to "affiliate" with the LCA.

On the last day of the convention, however, the delegates softened their stand. They approved proposed LCA constitutional wording that linked the powers of the synod to the laws of the LCA, rather than embrace the operational committee wording which linked the powers of the synod to the constituent congregations and the synodical charter.

"The question at issue," Cromer told the assembly, "is whether the church is a federation of synods or whether it shall be a coming together of congregations in a meaningful central church. . . . If we enter into any kind of common effort, we delegate some of our privileges and rights to the common agencies . . ."

Support for the JCLU position was argued by Dr. Albert H. Keck, Jr., pastor of St. Andrew's, Hickory: "A minister in the new church is a minister of the church (not the synod), and he can move from one synod to another without appearing before an examining committee. This is my idea of the church: the church is one. The LCA structure gives us an opportunity to demonstrate to the outside world the oneness of the church."

The hesitancy of the convention to embrace the LCA polity prompted the ULCA representative, Dr. Harold Haas, to quip that North Carolina may prefer to create a triad of The American Lutheran Church, Lutheran Church in America, and "Lutheran Church - North Carolina Synod."

On the national level, the needed synodical approval was received, and the new church, named the Lutheran Church in America, was constituted on June 28, 1962, in Detroit. Participating in the formation were one thousand delegates representing the four merging churches, including delegates from the North Carolina Synod.

The following month, the North Carolina synod's Executive Committee announced that, despite the synodical convention action in May, the name of the new synod would be "North Carolina Synod of the Lutheran Church in America." The committee had determined that the name for the synod was actually adopted when the synod approved the merger documents at its Charlotte convention in 1961. The old name, adopted in 1921, would give way to the new name on January 1, 1963.

The other merger issues, however, could not be resolved in time for the synodical constituting convention, held September 21 at St. John's, Salisbury. The president-elect of the LCA, Dr. Franklin Clark Fry of New York City, convened the meeting, and the retiring synod president, Dr. Conrad, presided. But the constitution prepared by the operational committee was not in harmony with LCA polity, so the committee chairman, Dr. Yost, moved that the constitution be accepted only as rules of procedure until it could be adjusted to conform with LCA requirements. In the meantime, the rules would enable the new synod to begin operation.

The convention, scheduled for four sessions, ended after the third session because of the constitution deferment. Before adjourning, however, the delegates did adopt a budget for 1963 and elect officers and members of boards and committees.

Balloting for the president of the synod first resulted in the election of Dr. Yost, the chairman of the operational committee, but he declined the office, citing his preference for the pastoral ministry. Subsequent balloting named as the president Rev.

George R. Whittecar, pastor of St. James, Concord.

In other elections, the convention named the officers of the expiring synod: Rev. J. Wilford Lyerly, secretary; and Charles S. Heilig, treasurer.

The North Carolina Synod was the only one of the thirty LCA synods to fail to adopt a constitution at its constituting convention. Although not in full compliance with the new LCA, however, it was permitted to install its new officers and staff. The ceremony took place on January 13, 1963, at St. James, Concord.

In spite of, or perhaps because of, the difficulties, the preacher of the installation sermon was the architect of the new church and its first president, Franklin Clark Fry. After the service, Fry met with the synod's new Executive Board at the nearby Hotel Concord to explain why the North Carolina's rules of procedure were inconsistent with the LCA Approved Constitution for Synods.

A key issue, Fry reported, was the control of the financial structure of the synod. The synod's rules gave exclusive control to the synod; the LCA proposed that in each synod the control be shared with the LCA to insure that all synods contribute equitably to churchwide funding.

Another difference hinged on whether a synodical auxiliary should be primarily accountable to the synod or to the churchwide auxiliary. Also, there was the question whether a district within a synod should be comprised solely of congregations and their pastors or whether the membership should include retired ministers. Other differences related to the role of the vice pastor, the tenure of synodical officers, the power of the LCA to amend certain portions of the synodical constitution, and the division of responsibility between the synod and the LCA Board of American Missions.[42]

To resolve the differences between the synod's rules of procedure and the LCA's polity, the Executive Board appointed a special committee to prepare, in consultation with a representative of the LCA Executive Council, an acceptable constitution and by-laws. Named to the committee were Whittecar, Rev. Paul L. Morgan of First, Greensboro, and Attorney B. S. Brown, Jr., of Kannapolis.

The revised constitution, recommended by the special committee and approved by the Executive Board on March 28, was submitted to the 360 clerical and lay delegates assembled at First, Greensboro, for the 1963 convention on April 29.

"Delegates," reported the *North Carolina Lutheran*, "who had debated the constitution in 1960 and again in 1961, and again in 1962 and 1963, tensed into silence as the negative vote was called, chuckled a sigh of relief as the single 'no' was voted, and applauded heartily as President George R. Whittecar declared, 'The motion to adopt is carried.'

"Dr. Malvin H. Lundeen, secretary and official representative of the Lutheran Church in America, hurried to the rostrum.

"'It gives me pleasure to announce,' he stated, 'that this document which you have adopted is approved by the Executive Council of the Lutheran Church in America.'

"'You mean you're letting us in?' inquired President Whittecar.

"'Yes,' said Dr. Lundeen. Both men joined in the roar of laughter." ☩

F. L. Conrad
President
North Carolina Synod
1949-63

Jacob L. Morgan
President
North Carolina Synod
1919-47

Voigt R. Cromer
President
North Carolina Synod
1947-49

Synod Church House
South Ellis Street, Salisbury, N. C.
1944-62

Lutheran Homes Hickory Unit
Opened 1961

Ray A. Cline
President
Luther League of America
1951-53

Mrs. John M. Cook
Treasurer
Statistical Secretary
ULCA Women's Auxiliary
1928-40

Harry E. Isenhour
President
ULCA Brotherhood
1932-36

Efrid Hall
Lutheridge
Grounds Acquired in 1946

CHAPTER X

LCA IN NORTH CAROLINA (1963-1987)

Leading the North Carolina Synod into the new Lutheran Church in America was the first president in its history who was not ordained by the synod, or educated in one of its colleges or its seminary. George R. Whittecar, a native of Kansas, graduated from Midland College and Western Seminary at Fremont, Nebraska. He also pursued graduate study at Tulsa University.

Licensed in 1934 and ordained the following year by the Kansas and Adjacent States Synod, Whittecar served pastorates in Beloit, Kansas, and Tulsa, Oklahoma. He also served as synodical secretary in 1941-42 and president in 1942-45 before moving to North Carolina to become pastor of St. James, Concord, in 1951. During his twelve years in the synod prior to becoming president, he served as a delegate to ULCA conventions, an elected member of the ULCA Board of Social Missions (1950-62), and vice-president of the North Carolina Council of Churches (1961-63).

The new synod of 192 congregations and 230 pastors began with a headquarters staff of three full-time executives. In addition to Whittecar, the staff included Rev. Ernest L. Misenheimer, Jr., the assistant to the president since 1955, and Rev. J. Wilford Lyerly, who filled the new post of full-time secretary.

When Lyerly was first elected secretary of the synod in 1953, the office was a part-time position and he also served as pastor of Messiah, Salisbury, and later as mission developer of Christ, Winston-Salem. When he was re-elected at the 1963 constituting convention, the duties of the full-time position were expanded to include those of statistician, archivist, necrologist, news bureau director, assistant in home missions, and synod headquarters manager.

The trio was joined on February 1 by a fourth full-time synodical executive, Rev. Brady Y. Faggart, Jr., who filled the post of secretary of Christian education, which had been vacant since 1959. Faggart, a native of Concord, served as pastor of St. Mark's, China Grove (1960-63) before assuming the post.

When Faggart resigned three years later, in 1966, to become executive director of Lutheridge, he was replaced by Rev. Robert L. Troutman. A native of Iredell County, Troutman served as pastor of Bethel, Salisbury, before joining the synodical staff.

At the installation of Troutman, the synod introduced the pectoral cross for use with the office of the president. The three hundred dollar solid gold cross with an amethyst (symbolic of vitality and humility) was presented to Whittecar by the chairman of the Committee on Music and Worship, Rev. Thurmond C. Plexico, pastor of St. James, Concord. The ceremony took place at St. John's, Salisbury, on January 28, 1968.

Troutman served as secretary of Christian education for two years, when he resigned to succeed Faggart at Lutheridge. In Salisbury, he was succeeded by Rev. Terry W. Agner, pastor of St. Mark's, China Grove.

By 1970, the synodical headquarters on Klumac Road not only housed the four executives, but a growing audio-visual library as well. The collection of over 750 items, managed by the president's secretary, Virginia Casey, reported the highest circulation of any of the LCA synods.

The synod staff suffered its first major emergency July 20, 1970, when President Whittecar entered Rowan Memorial Hospital in Salisbury with chest discomforts, later diagnosed as a light heart attack. Following four months of recuperation, including one month at the Salisbury hospital and another month at Duke University Medical Center, he returned to the office on a limited schedule on November 15. During his absence, he delegated, with the approval of the Executive Board, his synodical responsibilities to Misenheimer, the assistant to the president.

Secretary Lyerly resigned in 1972 to accept the call to serve as pastor of St. Andrew's, Mt. Airy, a mission congregation he organized three years earlier. Succeeding him was Rev. David Martin, pastor of Good Shepherd, Goldsboro, for the previous three years.

The fourth administrative assistant position was added in 1973 when Rev. Richard W. Rhyne, a native of Charlotte and pastor in Greensboro, joined the staff with duties in the area of social ministry.

Two years later, in 1975, Treasurer Heilig resigned after forty-six years in office. Because his father, James D. Heilig, served as his predecessor in office from 1896 to 1929, the event marked the close of a seventy-nine-year era of treasurer service by the same family. In honor of the retiring treasurer, the Executive Board named the synod's audio-visual library the Charles S. Heilig Multi-Media Library.

The treasurer selection process also changed as a result of the 1962 restructuring. The post was not filled by convention balloting, but by Executive Board election from among members of the Executive Board or the staff administrative assistants. For Heilig's successor, the board selected a fellow-member, Marcus C. Smith, a Salisbury City School administrator and member of St. John's, Salisbury.

SYNOD PRESIDENTS (Bishops after 1979)
1962-78   George R. Whittecar
1978-82   Ernest L. Misenheimer
1982-91   Michael C. D. McDaniel

As President Whittecar neared the 1978 close of his term in office, when he would be constitutionally ineligible for re-election, the convention debated changes affecting the office. In 1975, it reduced the president's term of office from five years to the LCA-recommended four years. The following year it gave tentative approval to supplementing the ecclesiastical balloting process with a search committee which would select at least three names for inclusion on the nominating ballot. When it came time in 1977 to amend the constitution, however, the amendment failed to receive the needed two-thirds majority vote.

The 1978 convention went about the election of a new president with the traditional ecclesiastical ballot. Elected on the fifth and final ballot was the senior administrative assistant, Dr. Misenheimer, who joined the president's staff 23 years earlier.

A native of Albemarle, Misenheimer received his education at Lenoir Rhyne and Southern Seminary prior to his 1940 ordination by the North Carolina Synod. He began his ministry as assistant pastor of St. John's, Salisbury (1940-43). Before joining the synodical staff, he served as pastor of St. James and Immanuel, Rockwell (1943-49); St. Mark's, Mooresville (1949-51); and Center Grove, Kannapolis (1951-55).

Continuing on the synodical staff into the Misenheimer administation was one executive, Martin, the secretary and administrative assistant for leadership ministries.

Filling the slot vacated by Misenheimer was the synod's second full-time lay staff officer, James A. Chesky, a retired Navy officer from Norfolk, Virginia. He assumed the position of administrative assistant for resource ministries.

Replacing Agner on the staff was Rev. Robert A. Shoffner, from the staff of Holy Trinity, Hickory. He assumed the position of administrative assistant for parish life ministries. Replacing Rhyne on the staff was Rev. Richard C. Little, a native of Lincolnton and pastor of Prince of Peace, Greensboro. He became the administrative assistant for outreach ministries.

The title of "Bishop" was conferred on the North Carolina Synod president in 1980 by action of the national LCA convention. The delegates, meeting in Seattle, adopted the title for application to the presiding officers of the national church and all of its constituent synods. Recipients of the title included not only the LCA's "Bishop" James R. Crumley, Jr., but North Carolina's "Bishop" Misenheimer as well.

Misenheimer used the title for only two years, not being eligible for re-election because of age. His successor was Dr. Michael C. D. McDaniel, elected at the 1982 convention on the fifth and final ballot.

A native of Mt. Pleasant, McDaniel graduated from University of North Carolina at Chapel Hill, Hamma Divinity School, and University of Chicago. He also did post-doctoral work at the University of Hamburg in Germany. Ordained by the North Carolina Synod in 1954, he served pastorates at Faith, Faith (1954-58), and in Savannah, Georgia (1958-60), before accepting work as associate director of evangelism in the ULCA Board of Social Missions (1960-62). After serving a pastorate in Chicago, he joined the religion faculty of Lenoir Rhyne in 1971 where he served at the time of his election to the office of bishop.

Following McDaniel's election, the headquarters was staffed by two continuing assistants (Chesky and Little) and two new ones. In place of Martin and Shoffner, the new staff included Rev. Richard R. Campbell and Rev. Mark W. Menees.

Campbell, former pastor of Holy Trinity, Charlotte, became minister for parish life; Menees, a former pastor of Mt. Olive, Hickory, became minister for leadership.

The McDaniel team stayed intact throughout his first term until 1986 (when he was re-elected on the first ballot). In that year, Campbell accepted a call to St. Matthew's, Charleston, South Carolina, and was succeeded by Dr. Leonard H. Bolick, pastor of St. James, Fayetteville. In the same year, Little accepted a call to Advent, Charlotte, and was replaced on the staff by Rev. Richard J. Goeres, pastor of Holy Cross, Lincolnton.

Synodical Alignments

Despite its recalcitrance, the North Carolina Synod enjoyed a trustworthy relationship once within the LCA. Two North Carolinians, Dr. Frank K. Efird of St. John's, Salisbury, and Dr. Voigt R. Cromer of Lenoir Rhyne, were charter members of the LCA's Executive Council.

Their roles in LCA leadership typified the Tar Heel influence that continued throughout the life of the LCA. Among those serving in elective or appointive positions were Luther G. Boliek of Hickory (Deaconess Board), Dr. Raymond M. Bost of Hickory (Board of Publication), Bachman S. Brown, Jr., of Kannapolis (Commission on Study of Nature and Function of the Congregation), Dr. Glenn R. Frye of Hickory (Board of World Missions), Judy Ford Houser of Cherryville (Division of Parish Services, Executive Board), Wallace Jorgenson of Charlotte, Tom Kadell, Dr. Albert Keck, Jr. (Board of Publication), Dr. Gerhard Lenski of Chapel Hill (Board of Social Ministry), Dr. Paul Lutz of Greensboro (Division for Mission in North America, Division for Parish Services), Bishop McDaniel (Board of Publication, Lutheran/Orthodox Dialogue Commission), President Misenheimer, Stephen Misenheimer of Salisbury (Youth Commission), Dr. Carveth P. Mitchell of Charlotte (Board of Pensions), O. Leonard Moretz of Hickory, Jeff Norris of Hickory (Commission on Church Papers), Rev. Richard J. Perry, Jr., of Charlotte (Division for Parish Services), Joe C. Ridenhour of Kannapolis, Dr. Austin Shell of Southern Seminary, President Whittecar, and Dr. John L. Yost, Jr., of Hickory.

SYNOD CONVENTION SITES

1963 First, Greensboro	1969 Macedonia, Burlington
1964 Kimball Memorial, Kannapolis	1970 Lenoir Rhyne/St. Andrew's, Hickory
1965 Macedonia, Burlington	1971 St. John's, Salisbury
1966 Bethany, Hickory	1972 Convention Center, Durham
1967 St. James, Concord	1973 Lenoir Rhyne/Holy Trinity, Hickory
1968 Holy Trinity, Raleigh	1974-93 Lenoir Rhyne, Hickory

Other North Carolinians served in key LCA staff positions. Rev. Ralph E. Eckard, a native of Alexander County and graduate of Lenoir Rhyne, was named an assistant to the LCA president in 1963. He was still serving in the position in 1968 when another Tar Heel, Rev. Brady Y. Faggart, Jr., became an assistant to the president. In 1973, when the number of presidential assistants was reduced, the two North Carolinians, Eckard and Faggart, were the only assistants serving President Robert J. Marshall.

In 1978, Rev. Edgar R. Trexler, Jr., a native of China Grove and graduate of Lenoir Rhyne, was elected editor of the LCA periodical, *The Lutheran*, and served throughout the remaining life of the LCA.

Even with a voice in the LCA corridors, the North Carolina Synod experienced a difficult adjustment during the early years of the LCA. After the first five years, President Whittecar assessed the price and benefits of the adjustment in his annual report:

> Certainly we have found some valuable assets in the merged church. Our fellowship has been broadened by the addition to our immediate circle of more than 2,000 congregations with their ministers and institutions. They have brought insights,

ways of working, and traditions that have been new to us, and in various ways these have enriched our lives. New vitality has come with the new educational curriculum (under preparation before the merger but introduced about the time the merger became effective). Our program of theological education has been revised and renewed with the Master Plan for Theological Education, the interm program for theological students and programs of continuing education for ministers. We have sharpened our process of guiding and supporting candidates for the ministry and various other church occupations. We have a unified program for American Missions which involves synodical and board cooperation. Our social ministry institutions and programs have been more closely identified with the church. Our districts have served to bring the church's programs closer to the congregations.

The problems that we have had have grown largely out of slowness on the part of some to understand the nature of the merger, which required three basic changes in our organization structure. One, the congregations became identified primarily with the Lutheran Church in America, only secondarily with the synod. Two, the synods were reorganized as agencies of the Lutheran Church in America in given areas rather than as independent bodies that together comprise the church. Three, the ministry became identified with the Lutheran Church in America rather than with particular synods. As our people have come to recognize and accept these principles in our life, the problems connected with merger have diminished.

Ecumenical Relations

After the initial settling-in with the LCA, the North Carolina Synod gave more attention to its relationships with other Lutherans and other Christians. This was particularly true in the McDaniel administration, when the synod was led by a bishop with special enthusiasm for the ecumenical potential.

Overtures with the Lutheran Church - Missouri Synod were actually initiated by the Missouri Synod. In 1971, its Southeastern District adopted the following resolution:

> Whereas, the Lutheran Church in America congregations within our District boundaries have been generous in sharing their resources; and
>
> Whereas, they have been careful to make it known that we are welcome at all their functions and workshops; and
>
> Whereas, they have, almost without exception, been open and caring in their relationship with us; and
>
> Whereas, part of the task of the Church is to build one another up in the faith; therefore
>
> Be it Resolved, that we let them know of our thanks, and
>
> Be it Further Resolved, that they receive invitations and encouragement to attend all of our District functions and workshops.[1]

The North Carolina Synod's Executive Board responded by resolving "that we acknowledge with gratitude the content and spirit of this resolution, that we seek every opportunity for mutual cooperation, and that a response of appreciation be conveyed to the proper office."

Several evidences of cooperation later came to the synod convention attention. In 1974, a representative of the Missouri Synod district, Rev. Lester Wolfe of Winston-Salem, participated in a panel discussion on ecumenism during the synodical proceedings. In 1983, McDaniel was invited by the district president, Richard T. Hinz, to speak at the district's annual pastor's conference. In the same year, the synod received by transfer two ministers of the Missouri Synod, Rev. Harold I. Haas and Dr. Harold G. Kupke, who were professors at Lenoir-Rhyne.

In 1984 McDaniel, addressing the Missouri Synod district convention in Charlotte, held out the hope for building better relations and invited the district to authorize the creation of a regular dialogue. The district accepted the invitation, and, a month later, District President Hinz was greeted with a similar response when he addressed the synod convention at Lenoir-Rhyne.

In 1985, Hinz acknowledged before the next synod convention in Hickory that he found "hope in this moment that pastors and congregations, yours and ours, are sensing a greater role than ever before in demonstrating their common thanks to God with neighboring Lutheran congregations, in searching for the ways in which our partnership in the Gospel can be expressed and in pushing for greater . . . understanding among us."[2]

Talks by representatives of the synod and the district began in October 1985 at Augsburg, Winston-Salem, and continued in alternate months for a year.

Relations with the American Lutheran Church Southeastern District were even more frequent and cordial. The mutual recognition, which was present even in earlier years, became more evident in 1982 when national conventions of the LCA, the ALC and the American Evangelical Lutheran Church voted to begin work on the formation of a new church.

Talks with Episcopalians and Roman Catholics grew out of discussions on the congregational level, such as those initiated among Hendersonville clergy as early as 1975. The participants in Hendersonville (Rev. Karl Park of Grace Lutheran, Rector Alex Viola of St. James Episcopal and Father William Pharr of Immaculate Conception Roman Catholic) undertook the discussions to develop clearer understandings of their common beliefs and to explore ways of cooperative ministry to the community. By 1981, the activity involved other nearby churches and led to a series of meetings to plan a conference on ecumenical cooperation. Participating in the planning meetings, in addition to the three initial churches, were Nativity Lutheran at Arden, Good Shepherd Lutheran at Brevard, St. John-in-the-Wilderness Episcopal at Flat Rock and Sacred Heart Roman Catholic at Brevard.

The first Hendersonville conference of Lutheran, Anglican and Roman Catholic (LARC) representatives was held at St. James Episcopal Church in October 1981 and attended by seventy clergy and laypersons. Its recommendations called for a series of seminars designed to explore further the differences and similarities among the churches, a sharing of music resources, cooperative projects in social outreach, establishment of an ecumenical library, and an exchange of worship leadership.[3]

Earlier in the same month, McDaniel's installation as bishop was the occasion for the first instance in history when an Episcopal bishop participated in the installation of a Lutheran bishop. The Episcopal participant was Bishop William G. Weinhauer of the North Carolina Episcopal Diocese.

At the synod's 1983 convention Weinhauer served as preacher for the opening day evening service and later discussed with delegates the progress of the Lutheran-Episcopal dialogue then underway.

"Both Episcopalians and Lutherans," he said, "have moved to the point where they are calling each other fellow Christians and sister churches, something which neither Church had ever done before."

At the close of his visit, Weinhauer presented Bishop McDaniel with a copy of *The Book of Common Prayer.*

McDaniel in the same year participated in the installation of Bishop Robert W. Estill of the North Carolina Diocese and preached at the annual conventions of the Eastern and Western North Carolina Episcopal dioceses. He was also host for the national Lutheran/Catholic Dialogue Commission that year and participated in a public dialogue on Martin Luther with Bishop Michael J. Begley of the Charlotte Roman Catholic Diocese.

On November 10, the LARC Conference in Hendersonville sponsored a joint celebration of the five hundredth anniversary of Luther's birth. The service, held in the newly-constructed Grace Lutheran Church, was led by three bishops: Catholic Begley, Episcopalian Weinhauer and Lutheran McDaniel.

In 1984, McDaniel was awarded the honorary LL.D. degree by Belmont Abbey, the Roman Catholic liberal arts college at Belmont in recognition of his, and the synod's, contributions to Catholic-Lutheran relations.

History was made at the 1985 synodical convention when delegates voted unanimously to give seat and voice to the rector of Grace Episcopal Church of Whiteville. The action stemmed from the convention's related vote to receive into the synod the Lutheran congregation of Christ the King, Whiteville. By a special arrangement between the bishop of the diocese of East Carolina, the Most Rev. B. Sidney Sanders, and McDaniel, and approved by the LCA, members of the LCA mission in Whiteville became a congregation united with Grace Episcopal, with the rector, Father Robert T. Schriber, authorized to serve also as the pastor of the Lutheran congregation.

The Whiteville Lutherans worshipped with the Episcopalians, and the two congregations used both the Episcopal *Book of Common Prayer and Hymnal* and the *Lutheran Book of Worship.* The Episcopal vestry and the Lutheran council both were represented in an overarching governing body, and benevolence offerings were sent to both the synod and the diocese.

Similar creative Lutheran/Episcopal arrangements were adopted at Newland and at Robbinsville in succeeding years, actually fulfilling agreements reached between North Carolina Lutherans and Episcopalians 164 years earlier in 1821, but never implemented in the intervening years.

Relations between Lutherans and Roman Catholics grew closer in 1985 with an exchange of letters between LCA Bishop James Crumley and Pope John Paul II. A diplomatic mission of nine synod bishops, including North Carolina's McDaniel, was appointed by Crumley to visit the world's leading religious leaders, including those of the Roman Catholic Church.

The group went to Istanbul for a visit with the patriarch of Eastern Orthodoxy, Demetrios I, and to England for talks with Anglican Archbishop Robert Runcie. But the highlight of the three-week trip was a week in Rome, where the Lutherans met with the leading cardinals of the Roman Catholic Church and had a private audience with the pope.

On his return, McDaniel invited the two Roman Catholic bishops in North

Carolina to begin regular conversations concerning ways to build understanding and cooperate in proclaiming the Gospel. The frequency of the conversations grew over the next years from two to four or five times annually.

In May 1986, McDaniel delivered the annual address for the Ecumenical Institute sponsored by the Baptists of Wake Forest and the Roman Catholics of Belmont Abbey.

The LARC concept, born in Hendersonville in the west, also took root in the eastern part of the state, where an initial meeting was held in the fall of 1986. Meanwhile, in the west, the development of relations with the bishop of the United Methodist Church in Western North Carolina, as well as the bishop of the African Methodist Episcopal Zion Church, led to their inclusion in annual "LARCUM" conferences.

The expanded movement entertained 125 clergy and lay members at an ecumenical conference for theological discussion at Lenoir-Rhyne on August 28, 1987. Theme for the event was "Ministry in Ecumenical Perspective." In addition to Bishop McDaniel, leaders in the conference were Dr. Bevel Jones, III, of the Western North Carolina Conference of the United Methodist Church; the Most Rev. John F. Donoghue, of the Roman Catholic Diocese of Charlotte; and Dr. William G. Weinhauer, of the Western Diocese of North Carolina, Episcopal Church. Dr. Geoffrey Wainwright, professor of theology at Duke Divinity School, was the guest speaker.[4]

Throughout the LCA period, the synod continued participation in the North Carolina Council of Churches. In the early years, President Whittecar served two years as president of the council. In 1980, the synod amended its constitution to create a seven-member Committee on Ecumenical Affairs with responsibilities to coordinate ecumenical activities and serve as synodical representatives to the House of Delegates of the council.

The synod also contributed leadership at the national interdenominational level. Dr. Arthur Larson, a member of St. Paul's, Durham, and a Duke University law professor, was elected vice-president-at-large of the National Council of Churches of Christ in the United States of America at its 1966 convention in Miami Beach. Rachel Cobb of Holy Trinity, Raleigh, later served on the council's General Board.

Polity and Practice

The new North Carolina Synod began in 1963 with six operational committees: stewardship, evangelism, parish education, American missions, social ministry, and education for the ministry and other vocations. The number of committees, however, grew during the period; by 1982, the synod had added other committees in the areas of educational ministry, youth ministry, music and worship, world missions, campus ministry, justice and social change, Lutheran World Relief/World Hunger, and environmental concerns.

Its district organization also expanded. It began the period with six districts: eastern, central, northern, southern, northwestern and southwestern. Fourteen years later, in 1977, a portion of the Eastern District was used to form a seventh district, named Coastal.

One area undergoing constant change during the first half of the period was the annual convention of the synod. In the second year, 1964, approval was given to three new features: a recognition of the ministers living within the bounds of the synod who have been ordained fifty years or more, a social event for the pastor's wives or widows, and a convention banquet when possible.

A change in 1967 was more traumatic. The long-standing practice of convening on Monday evening was altered to allow the convention to start on Monday morning. Changing the opening time enabled the delegates, later at adjournment, to depart for their homes on Wednesday, rather than Thursday, reducing the need for overnight housing by one night.

Three years later, however, the delegates urged a reconsideration of the convention dates, and also the convention sites. They asked the Executive Board to schedule the 1971 convention on a weekend, to permit more participation by lay delegates. Also, while meeting at Lenoir Rhyne for the first time in several years, they expressed a willingness to return to the college campus as an economy measure: they asked the Executive Board to reconsider an earlier decision to meet at St. John's, Salisbury, in 1971 and at the Durham Convention Center in 1972. Instead, they said, hold both conventions - and other future conventions - at Lenoir Rhyne.

Study of the proposals led the Executive Board to mixed conclusions. It agreed to reschedule the Salisbury convention for a weekend, but it found that weekend dates were not available for the Durham convention. At the same time, it moved more cautiously with respect to sites. The board cited the advantages of moving the convention: more delegate variety, synodical exposure in more communities. It concluded that plans should continue for conventions in Salisbury and Durham, but conceded to returning to Lenoir Rhyne in 1973 and in alternate years, not every year, thereafter.

The schedule was followed, with St. John's, Salisbury, hosting the convention for the sixteenth time and the Durham site introducing the delegates to a convention center, and its higher costs, for the first time.

When it came time to consider an alternate site following the 1973 convention at Lenoir Rhyne, the question appeared to be already settled. There were no invitations, and no funds for the bigger convention budget.

The weekend convention became a pattern, but not without a price. Clergy delegates, especially those living in the area of the convention, sometimes ducked the closing session in order to preach in their own churches.

The 1976 convention, for example, adjourned its Saturday evening session for lack of a quorum, but discovered it was still without a quorum when it attempted to resume business Sunday morning. The meeting continued, reports were heard and sense votes were taken on recommendations, but the formal work of the convention was left for the Executive Board to finish.

The Executive Board took steps to prevent a reoccurence of the quorum problem in 1977. It declared the Sunday of the convention as "Synod Sunday," encouraging lay leadership in congregational worship and asking the Worship and Music Committee to prepare optional services for congregational use on that day. Congregations, reminded that their pastors were constitutionally required to attend the convention, were urged to help the pastor fulfill that obligation.

While convention practices required extended consideration by the Executive Board and the convention delegates, a question of a congregation's privilege to condition its apportionment payments was resolved by the board alone. St. John's, Concord, reported dissatisfaction within the congregation with some policies of the church, and it asked for instructions on how to prevent its contribution from being used to support such policies.

The board responded in effect that such a procedure should not be possible: "In view of further complications relative to stipulations regarding distribution of benevolent contributions, the Executive Board established a policy not to accept benevolence moneys from congregations whose purpose it is to bypass one of the established programs of the church and the regular channels of the church and inasmuch as it is inconsistent with Article XIII, Item 5, of the Constitution of the N. C. Synod."[5]

The change of another practice required convention approval, which was readily given. The Lenoir Rhyne Board of Trustees proposed that a limit be placed on the number of consecutive terms that can be served by its trustees. The Executive Board of the synod liked the idea and suggested that it apply to all other boards as well. The convention agreed, amending the constitution in 1971 to limit elective members of boards to serving no more than three consecutive three-year terms on the same board.

Changes in the administrative structure of the synod were undertaken by the 1972 convention following a two-year special study. Conducting the study was a committee chaired by Joe Bookout, a Charlotte banker. The other members were Bachman S. Brown, a Kannapolis attorney; John T. Beam, Jr., Gastonia industrial personnel officer; and two pastors: C. Marion Starr of Kimball Memorial, Kannapolis, and R. Douglas Fritz of St. John's, Salisbury.

The committee concluded that the synod staff should emphasize grass-roots service to congregations and pastors. The staff should function as a flexible team ministry of officers and staff for more effective use of resources, and there should be a redistribution of functions of staff and officers, especially with respect to the presidency.

It recommended, and the convention approved, an elected synod president with four administrative assistants. The positions of assistant to the president, secretary, and secretary of Christian education became administrative assistants, elected by the Executive Board, not the convention. The positions of secretary and treasurer became part-time positions, to be filled annually by the Executive Board from either the administrative assistants or members of the board. The membership of the Executive Board was increased from twelve to eighteen.

Further amendments to the constitution and bylaws were made in 1977, but they were made by the LCA Executive Council, not the synod. The extensive renovation was undertaken to achieve four purposes: (1) to reflect changes in church structure following the 1972 LCA study of function and structure, (2) to eliminate masculine nouns or pronouns when referring to either male or female, (3) to transfer to the bylaws material that reflected rules or procedures that were not essential to the corporate structure, and (4) to eliminate duplications or reflect changes in practice or procedures.[6]

During the same period the synod undertook a long-range planning study, using the resources of the LCA planning services. The two-year study included a survey of 259 leaders in the synod and produced a set of thirty goals in 1979. The five top goals on the list related to evangelism, stewardship, youth ministry, pastors and parish education. Lowest priority was given to the goals relating to outdoor ministries (rank: 26), conventions, deans and districts, fund-raising, and the headquarters building (rank: 30).

Made a part of the synodical and congregational policy in 1983 was an alcohol and drug statement adopted by the convention. The statement discouraged the use of alcoholic beverages at church functions and outlined procedures for use whenever alcohol is served. It promoted congregational use of educational programs on alcohol and alcoholism and making facilities available to Alcoholics Anonymous. It also outlined synodical procedures if alcoholism affects the performance of church professionals.

Synodical Publication

The *North Carolina Lutheran*, edited by Jeff Norris, continued monthly publication into the merged church without obvious change until 1965. Then, as a complement to the biweekly publication of *The Lutheran*, the synodical paper moved to biweekly publication, alternating with the publication dates of the national journal. In the conversion, the synodical paper also changed its format, maintaining the same page size but expanding from three columns to four columns. The pages in each issue were reduced, from eight to four.

The practice of publishing biweekly, however, continued for only one year. To reduce confusion, and once again to synchronize with *The Lutheran* frequency, the paper became a semi-monthly, appearing on the first and third Wednesdays and reducing its yearly number of issues from twenty-six to twenty-four.

Following Norris' resignation in 1967, he was succeeded by the associate editor who had served since 1959, Rev. Paul L. Conrad, pastor of St. Paul's, Statesville. Conrad resigned after two years and was replaced by Rev. George W. Shuford in 1969.

During Shuford's editorship, the publication frequency was reduced from twenty-four to sixteen issues per year because of increased printing costs.

When Shuford, the pastor of St. Luke's, Conover, died suddenly in 1978 following nine years as editor, the interim post was filled for five months by Rev. Karl Park of Grace, Hendersonville.

Shuford's successor, Rev. John E. Wertz, pastor of Christ, Stanley, supervised further alterations in the *North Carolina Lutheran* two years later, in 1980. The page size was increased from letter-size to 11 x 17, and the number of columns was advanced to five. The paper, formerly published sixteen times per year, was restored to a monthly publication.

In the same year, the tenure of the editor - and the business manager - was changed by constitutional amendment from one year to three years to permit the publication officers to engage in more long-range planning.

In the first year of his three-year term, however, Wertz resigned the office for health reasons. He was succeeded in 1981 by Elsie Hamilton, a member of Holy Comforter, Belmont, a Gastonia newspaper reporter and the first woman editor of the *North Carolina Lutheran*.

Under Hamilton's guidance the publication earned a first-place award in the 1986 synod publications contest sponsored by the LCA Department of News and Information. More than two hundred entries from seventeen of the LCA's thirty synods were judged in the contest. The award to the *North Carolina Lutheran* credited the publication with the best coverage of a synod convention.

Missions

The division of responsibility for organizing and developing mission congregations in the new merged church underwent adjustment during the early years. The new division was spelled out by the synodical Committee on American Missions following a meeting in early 1962 with Dr. Donald Houser, executive secretary of the national Board of American Missions (BAM):

> . . . the Synod and BAM share in finding fields of mission churches, the board to survey fields on request of the Synod, and after approval of such fields for occupancy, the board to develop them in cooperation with the Synod. The providing of temporary places of worship becomes a responsibility of Synod, but the providing of parsonages and church sites rests with the board. The Synod, together with prospective members of the mission congregation, will supply initial equipment. The Synod will organize congregations following board approval. In calling pastors, the Synod will recommend, the board will approve, and the congregation will call. In supporting pastors, the Synod will recommend, the board will give salary aid, and the congregation will provide salary according to its ability. Congregations confronting special problems can come in for board assistance with Synodical recommendation. The financing of mission churches is a matter for the board in cooperation with the congregations.[7]

The last sentence in the statement, making the financing of mission churches a matter for the board and the congregations, omitting reference to the synod, presented an awkward situation for a synod which prided itself on investing generously in a Home Mission Foundation. But there were compensating benefits, noted in the same committee report:

> The predecessor Synod was deeply involved in the financing of parsonages and church sites for mission congregations, using its credit to borrow money on behalf of particular projects or congregations until permanent financing could be arranged through the board, the Home Mission Foundation, or other sources. The office of the treasurer of the new Synod inherited a number of such obligations on January 1, 1963, as indicated in the Treasurer's Report. However, it is the understanding of the committee that the Board of American Missions intends to take up these loans and repay the Synod so as to take the Synod out of the interim financing business.

Other benefits were noted by the synodical committee secretary, Rev. Hugh E. Baumgartner, Jr., in his report to the convention. He referred to a report outlining the "preemption system, which eliminates competition between the various Lutheran bodies in a specific area," and he urged cooperation between the various churches in each area. He also mentioned "the generous assistance provided by the Board of American Missions and indicated that at the present time, some $769,000 has been invested in loans and salary aid", in addition to interim financing, which the board was in the process of assuming.

The role of the Home Mission Foundation became clearer the following year:

> Clarification of the place of the Loan and Gift Fund of the Lutheran Church Men and the Home Mission Foundation in the mission program of the Synod was made during the year. It is understood with the Board of American Missions that the Home Mission Foundation will make funds available for first mortgage loans for mission churches or parsonages in the North Carolina Synod.
> In the case of a congregation needing a loan for such construction purposes, the

Board will arrange for it to be made by the Home Mission Foundation, including the same in the over-all financial program for the congregation. Interest will be charged at low rates. Thus, the Foundation will be a source of funds for the Board that will make it unnecessary for the board or congregation to borrow commercially, and doing so at a considerable saving of interest to the congregation. Congregations in the Synod will become eligible for such low-interest loans from the Foundation in the order in which they make application to the Foundation.[8]

In the first decade of the new church, the synod welcomed into membership sixteen congregations: Nativity, Arden; A Mighty Fortress, Charlotte; Christus Victor, Fayetteville; and St. Philip's, Raleigh (1963); Christ the King, Cary; and St. Michael's, High Point (1964); Resurrection, Greensboro (1965); Redeemer, Gastonia; Living Word, Laurinburg; and Our Saviour, Welcome (1966); Christus Victor, Durham; and Christ, Jonesville (1967); Advent, Charlotte; and St. Andrew's, Mt. Airy (1969); Shepherd of the Sea, Atlantic Beach (1971); and Prince of Peace, Greensboro (1972).

The second decade of the merged church brought into the synod only five new congregations: St. Peter's, Southport (1973); Shepherd of the Hills, Sylva (1974); Lord of Life, Garner; and Community in Christ, Huntersville (1977); and Living Saviour, Charlotte (1979).

During the last five years of the LCA period, however, the synod received six congregations: King of Glory, Clemmons; and Good Shepherd, Raleigh (1983); Messiah of the Mountains, Burnsville; and Christ the King, Whiteville (1985); Reconciliation, Wilmington (1986); and Cross and Crown, Matthews (1987).

One enduring evangelism project begun in the LCA period was the Carolinas' Evangelism Conference sponsored by the North and South Carolina synods and the LCA Commission on Evangelism. The event was born of ideas inspired by the Omaha Mid-America Pan Lutheran Conference on Evangelism in 1960. Evangelism leaders in the two synods were looking for an event "to awaken the interest of the congregations in evangelism opportunities to share the good news of the Gospel; to acquaint the evangelism leaders with the resources of the church to equip people for witnessing; to provide motivation for sharing the faith; and to send the participants home with joy and enthusiasm for the task."[9]

After years of planning, the first of the Carolinas' Evangelism Conferences was held February 8-10, 1965, at St. Mark's, Charlotte, with capacity crowds attending each session. The conference was one of three which the LCA Commission on Evangelism helped to fund with participating synods. The other two conferences were held in Atlanta and Washington.

The planning committee for the first six conferences, spanning a fifteen-year period, was chaired by Dr. Ernest L. Misenheimer, administrative assistant to the president of the North Carolina Synod.

The event, continued biennially throughout the period, typically attracted six hundred pastors and lay leaders from the two Carolinas. A rally in Ovens Auditorium, added to the program in 1978, was attended by more than two thousand Lutherans.

In 1977-78, the Charlotte event served as the centerpiece for the synod's version of the Evangelical Outreach Program developed and produced by the LCA and the American Lutheran Church. The two-year program, headed by Rev. David Misenheimer of A Mighty Fortress, Charlotte, chairperson of the synod's special task force, included five other activities. The Lenten/Easter Preaching Workshop, held at Lutheridge February 2-4, 1977, was the opening event. It included presentations by Dr. William Lazareth and Pastor/Evangelist James Stephenson and was attended by one hundred LCA and ALC pastors.

The closing activity, the Fall Training Events in 1978, was designed to help congregational leaders in the areas of parish visitation, media evangelism, catechization and integration of new and restored members, and Bible study and witness. Other activities in the program were special presentations by Misenheimer at the 1977 spring district meetings, church council visitations, and Bible Study and Witness programs in volunteer congregations.

During the period, the synod's ministry at colleges and universities of the state received increased attention.

In 1965 the synod authorized a special capital funds campaign among congregations for Lutheran campus ministry facilities at eleven non-Lutheran institutions in the state. The campaign, named CAMPUS, sought six hundred thousand dollars for facility needs at Chapel Hill, Boone, Charlotte, Cullowhee, Durham, Greensboro, Greenville, Raleigh, Salisbury, Wilmington and Winston-Salem.

The effort, directed by the Lutheran Laymen's Movement Fund Raising Service, was launched January 23 at Catawba College, Salisbury, with LCA President Franklin Clark Fry as speaker. After the second year of the three-year campaign, 149 congregations reported gifts of $530,000.

The North Carolina Synod also contributed one of its own pastors to the campus ministry program. Rev. Robert G. Walker, chaplain at Lenoir Rhyne, was called in 1966 to serve as southeastern regional director of the National Lutheran Campus Ministry. One of six national field staff members, Walker served a territory bounded by Charleston, West Virginia; Memphis, Tennessee; and Miami, Florida. He continued to serve throughout the remainder of the LCA period.

In addition to the minority and student ministries, the synod formalized a hospital chaplaincy program in the Durham area.

The ministry had its beginnings in the work of Rev. Henry A. Schroder, pastor of St. Paul's, Durham. Schroder was asked by the National Lutheran Council to serve as contact pastor for servicemen at Camp Butner during World War II.

After the war, as the Butner facilities were converted into health care institutions, Schroder began ministering to the patients. He was also called upon to visit families at the expanding Duke University Medical Center.

In 1964 the synod's Social Ministry Committee asked Schroder to survey the need for a designated Lutheran ministry in the area. His survey showed that the twenty-one institutions served a population of nine thousand persons.

The LCA Board of Social Ministry agreed to support, on a declining scale over five years, a Lutheran chaplain for the area, the initial support to fund one-half of the budget for the ministry. The synod provided the other half of the early funding, increasing it to full support at the end of the five-year period. The initial grant from the LCA was fifty-two hundred dollars: the synod invested $3,081 from the earnings of the Michael Peeler Fund.

Selected as first chaplain of the new program was Dr. J. White Iddings of First, Albemarle, who served as contact chaplain for the National Lutheran Council at Moore

General Hospital, Oteen, during his earlier ministry at St. Mark's, Asheville. He assumed the duties of the new Durham post in July 1965.

The primary focus of the ministry was visitation, counseling, and the provision of the Holy Communion for Lutherans who were institutionalized in the Durham area. The ministry was supervised by an advisory committee composed of Lutheran pastors in the area and a representative of the synodical staff.

In 1968 the Missouri Synod also began a chaplaincy in the area, assigning Rev. Frederick A. Stiemke to the work. A division of labor was worked out which permitted Stiemke to focus his ministry on persons receiving psychiatric care and Chaplain Iddings to continue his ministry to persons in general hospitals and other institutions.

In 1977 Rev. David M. Franzen was called to the chaplaincy after Iddings retired.[10]

The synod's support of world missions during the period was primarily through the LCA. Two events, however, brought the cause of world missions closer to home for Tar Heels.

In 1969 a North Carolina pastor who served as a missionary to Malaysia, Rev. Carl M. Fisher of Rockwell, was elected president of the Lutheran Church in Malaysia and Singapore. A missionary since 1962, he was elected to a four-year term. At the time of his election he also served as president of the Association of Missionaries in Malaysia and Singapore.

Eleven years later, in 1981, the synod's college, Lenoir-Rhyne, hosted one of the LCA's two Global Mission Events for that year. The four-day program, which focused on both domestic and international missions, was sponsored by twelve synods in partnership with the LCA Division for Mission in North America and the Division for World Mission and Ecumenism.

Pastors

Early in the LCA period, the synod convention was prompted to help resolve a conflict between church policy and statutory law regarding ministerial confidences. The LCA constitution required: "In keeping with the historic discipline and practice of the Lutheran church and to be true to a sacred trust inherent in the nature of the pastoral office, no minister of the Lutheran Church in America shall divulge any confidential disclosure given to him in the course of his care of souls or otherwise in his professional capacity, except with the express permission of the person who has confided in him or in order to prevent a crime."[11]

In North Carolina, however, there was no protection in the statutory law. If a Lutheran minister should be required by a trial judge to divulge such confidential communication, he or she would be required to either violate the laws of the LCA or be subject to punishment for contempt of court.

The 1966 synod convention responded to the need with adoption of the resolution:

> That the General Assembly of the State of North Carolina is respectfully requested at its next regular session to enact legislation so as to provide that no ordained minister, the laws of whose church prohibit the disclosure of confidential communications between a minister and a communicator, shall be required to testify in any action, suit or proceeding concerning any information which may have been confidentially communicated to him in his professional capacity under such circumstances that to disclose the information would violate a sacred and moral trust,

when the giving of such testimony is objected to by the minister.[12]

A more frequent problem relating to the pastoral ministry was balancing the supply of ministers and the congregational need for pastors.

President Whittecar addressed the problem in his 1969 report to the synod, citing an unusually large number of congregations without regularly-called pastors. At times, he wrote, the shortage was fifteen to eighteen percent.

A contributing factor was the problem of pastors for small congregations. During the previous year, he observed, three joint parishes became independent, doubling the collective need from three pastors to six. The synod had only two parishes left with more than one congregation.

"Now," he continued, "it would seem to be the time to re-assess the mission of some of our smaller congregations to see if some ought to merge and make new starts in their ministries."[13]

Seven years later, however, the reverse side of the problem emerged to reduce the movement of pastors and give rise to further analysis of the situation by Whittecar:

> The movement of ministers from parish to parish and in and out of special ministries is a normal part of our church life and often contributes to the good spirit and encouragement of ministers and congregations alike. However, the close balance . . . has slowed down the calling process. Frequently this has led to frustrations and tensions between pastors and people.
>
> Personal disruptions in minister's families have added to the problem. In addition, two factors have come into the life of the church in this generation that help complicate the movement of pastors: the minister's wife who works outside the home in her own career, and home ownership by pastors of congregations. . . .
>
> The best way for the church to use the commitment and abilities of those who offer themselves for service in the ministry is to be diligent in opening new opportunities for persons to serve. Growing congregations can call more than one pastor. New congregations can be planted. New ministries in extra-congregational settings can be established, such as institutional and military chaplaincies, campus ministries, and social ministries. Older small congregations can be renewed so that they can call pastors to serve them.[14]

The following year, he discussed the problem from the perspective of the skills required of the parish pastor:

> The ordained minister has changed radically in this generation. Increasing demands are made on our ministers by their congregations and the complexities of the social order. Members of the congregations seem to have more need for pastoral counseling and personal service. Our pastors need skills that were not required in earlier years, and the competition they have for the time and attention of people is intense. Our parish pastors are on the front line of the church as we contend against the secularism and the confusion in the world about us. They deserve our honor and appreciation.[15]

Although not necessarily related to the supply and demand of pastors, nor ministerial skills, the synod in 1973 altered a policy which tended to restrict the freedom of a congregation to call a pastor. The change allowed congregations to call a pastor at any time. Under the previous policy, if one congregation was in touch with a pastor about changing churches, another congregation could not contact him until after he decided whether to accept or reject the first call.[16]

Three years later the synod also altered its policy regarding district membership for pastors. During the 1963 merger discussions, the LCA position limiting district memberships to active parish pastors was accepted with reluctance by the synod. But in 1976, the topic had ceased to become an issue, and the synod used the opportunity to restore full district membership to the retired and other non-parish pastors residing in the district.

A 1979 attempt to help pastors on leave from a call, however, was not as successful. The convention consented to the appointment of the Task Force to Study the Feasibility of Providing a Temporary Assistance Fund to Help Pastors on Leave from Call. But the conclusions of the task force were not affirming.

"As Christians," the report observed, "members of the North Carolina Synod have an equal responsibility to care for all people, Christian and non-Christian, clergy and lay. Preparation for the ordained ministry in no way carries with it a guarantee of a call to ministry or financial support outside of a call to ministry. Many Christians are at present unemployed and suffering financial hardship. Whether they be clergy or lay, the church has a responsibility to them."[17]

In response, the Executive Board recommended that financial assistance not be provided, and the following convention agreed with the board.

In the same year of 1979, the synod ordained its first woman pastor. Christine L. Bohr, a member of Gloria Dei, Salisbury, was among the nine people ordained during the synod convention at Lenoir Rhyne on June 10 in an event that came nine years after the LCA approved women for ordination. Bohr assumed duties as pastor of St. David's, Kannapolis, on July 1.

During the latter years of the period, the role of the pastor assumed new priority in the synod. The bishop became more active in the management of the call, giving increased assistance to congregations in finding a new pastor.

The same emphasis was assumed by the synod's committee charged with preparing and examining candidates for the Gospel ministry. New energies were spent in tightening the committee procedures, enhancing the shepherding of candidates, and in continuing annual retreats for seminarians.

Additionally, an annual retreat was held for those new to the ministry and the synod in order to provide both a practical introduction to the life of the synod and inspiration for achieving the synod's ministerial ideals.

Congregations

The North Carolina Synod entered the LCA period in 1963 with 195 congregations. During the twenty-five year period it gained a net total of eighteen congregations, ending the period in 1987 with 213 congregations. The baptized membership reflected gains in all years except two (1981 and 1983), advancing from 71,346 to 83,945 for an averge annual increase of 504 members. The ministers on the synod's clerical roster increased more rapidly than either congregations or members, advancing from 230 to 335.

Worship

Worship among the synod's congregations was dramatically altered by the 1978 introduction of the *Lutheran Book of Worship* as a successor to the *Service Book & Hymnal.*

Six of the synod's congregations were among the 114 congregations in the nation which participated in the 1977 pre-publication testing of the materials. Three of the congregations were in Salisbury: Organ, St. John's and St. Paul's.   The other participants were St. Luke's, Charlotte; St. Mark's, China Grove; and St. James, Concord.

The synod assisted in introducing the hymnal by selecting teams of musicians and pastors to conduct sixteen workshops in the state.

Rev. Robert E. Allen, the North Carolina *Lutheran Book of Worship* coordinator, alerted congregations and members to the degree of worship change in a *North Carolina Lutheran* interview: "Every practicing Lutheran must be patient and reasonable in his expectations of the new worship manual. This book has dared to do the impossible in attempting to be the book of the whole Lutheran family. It is not just for LCA-ers. Both those who have never ventured beyond one dimension of the *Service Book & Hymnal,* as well as those who have been out to pasture liturgically, will need to study the book carefully to appreciate its flexibility, which is one of its central gifts."[18]

With the introduction of the *Lutheran Book of Worship,* lay persons became more prominently involved in the leadership of worship.   Choir members and other worshippers often served as cantors, lectors, and assisting ministers.[19]

A strong emphasis on worship continued throughout the period, with Bishop McDaniel making it the first of seven objectives with which he challenged the synod after his election. It remained at the heart of the "Parish Renewal" emphasis which led the synod toward higher levels of stewardship. Among the activities of the synod's Committee on Worship was the production of a quarterly journal, *Soli Deo Gloria,* edited by Dr. and Mrs. R. Harold Terry of Macedonia, Burlington, and distributed widely in the LCA.

The frequency of communion in the congregations increased during the period. McDaniel commented in his 1986 report to the convention that "while we do not have any recent statistics on the matter, hardly a week passes in which I do not hear of another congregation which has restored weekly communion."[20]

Lutheran Church Women

During the LCA period, the number of active Lutheran Church Women congregational units fluctuated, ranging from 185 in 1971 to 204 in 1985. Active members ranged from a high of eleven thousand members in 1964 to a low of nine thousand in 1980. The financial operation grew dramatically: nine years after the LCA merger, in 1974, the disbursements totaled eighty-nine thousand dollars and ten years later, in 1984, the organization reported income of $130,000.

Special projects of the synodical auxiliary varied.

In 1967-68, the North Carolina women's unit joined with the South Carolina unit to collect and ship linen supplies for Phebe Hospital in Monrovia, Liberia. Included in the shipments were seventeen hundred diapers, seven hundred receiving blankets, 350 adult gowns and 350 sheets.

In the decade of the seventies, the interest focused on adult literacy. With the help of the national auxiliary, the state conducted workshops for the training of tutors and helped to organize community literacy councils. It also appointed Catherine Safrit of St. Paul's, Salisbury, as unit literacy coordinator to enlist and train tutors as volunteer reading aides.

SYNODICAL LUTHERAN CHURCH WOMEN PRESIDENTS

1961-64 Kathleen Stout, Grace, Thomasville
1964-66 Ruth Fisher, Augsburg, Winston-Salem
1966-70 Rachel Cobb, Holy Trinity, Raleigh
1970-74 Mary Elizabeth King, St. James, Concord
1974-77 Kay Conrad, Epiphany, Winston-Salem
1977-80 Catherine Norris, St. Andrew's, Hickory
1980-82 Sarah Ingle, St. Mark's, Charlotte
1982-87 Betty Carr, Holy Trinity, Hickory

Other projects during the decade included the making of Chrismons for Christmas trees at the Albemarle Lutheran Home and the synodical headquarters, collecting supplies for Kiomboi Hospital in Tanzania, and funding the purchase of materials for a mission school in Tanzania. The organization also urged a change in state laws to protect adolescents who were truant or had run away, but had not committed crimes.

Projects in the 1980s included the collection of old cloth in support of work at Kilimanjaro Christian Medical Center.

In 1982, the synodical unit took the lead in renewing a discouragement of commercialism in the church. It not only promoted free-will giving rather than money-making projects in its own convention action, but it urged the synod convention also to reaffirm the LCA's 1964 statement on commercialism. The synod convention did so the following month. The actions rationalized that "the selling of goods or services in the name of the church vitiates the clear relationship between the giving of the Christian and the mission of the church and further weakens the life of the church and a true sense of stewardship."[21]

As it did during the ULCA period, the North Carolina women's auxiliary contributed leadership to the national LCW organization. Although no Tar Heels served on the national Board of Directors for the first five years, their presence was continuous during the remaining twenty years. Catherine Norris of St. Andrew's, Hickory, was elected to the board in 1968 and served for three years. Replacing her was Ruth Fisher of Augsburg, Winston-Salem, who served from 1971 to 1977. Fisher was succeeded on the board by Kay Conrad of Epiphany, Winston-Salem, who was elected in 1977. In 1980 Virginia Stackel of St. Mark's, Charlotte, was elected vice-president of the organization, and at the end of three years was named a member of the board for the 1983-87 period. In addition, Sarah Ingle, also of St. Mark's, Charlotte, joined the auxiliary professional staff in 1983 as secretary for spiritual growth and renewal.

The unit also contributed leadership to the interdenominational Church Women United in North Carolina with Rachel Cobb of Holy Trinity, Raleigh, assuming the presidency in 1975.

The state auxiliary continued to administer the Patterson Memorial Fund, awarding in 1985 scholarship grants totaling twenty thousand dollars.

Inter-Lutheran activities also received the support of the North Carolina Lutheran

Church Women. In 1972 the unit joined with the American Lutheran Church Women and the Lutheran Women's Missionary League to sponsor a study meeting on Japan. The event, attended by five hundred, was held at St. Andrew's, Hickory. It featured an address by Barbara Voelkert of High Point, representing the Lutheran Church - Missouri Synod, and recognized two former ULCA missionaries to Japan, Maud Powlas of Barber Junction and Mabel Linn of St. Andrew's, Hickory. In 1976, again at St. Andrew's, Hickory, the three organizations sponsored a Shalom Conference featuring peace activists John and Mary Schramm as speakers.

Ten years later, the LCW joined with the American Lutheran Church Women and the (Catholic) Women in Action for Mission to sponsor the Theological Conference for Women at Sacred Heart College at Belmont. Participants attended from six southern states.

Youth Ministry

Although the Luther League in North Carolina entered the LCA period with strong identification at the synodical level, local leagues were not always clearly linked on the congregation's organizational chart and appropriately associated with other youth programs. The problem was noted by the synodical Youth Committee in its 1964 report to the synod convention: "Youth work in many congregations at present, is under no central direction - such as the Church Council, or one of its committees. Boy Scouts may be sponsored by the LCM; Girl Scouts by LCW; Luther League by the Committee on Christian Education. The defined objectives for the various youth programs (Boy Scouts, Girl Scouts, Luther League, Vacation Church School, Weekday Church School, Sunday Church School) are seldom gathered and evaluated, with duplications of objectives and gaps in desired objectives being noted."[22]

LUTHER LEAGUE PRESIDENTS
1963-64 Robert N. Peery, Jr., Beth Eden, Newton
1964-65 Myra Seitz, St. James, Newton
1965-66 David Misenheimer, Haven, Salisbury
1966-67 Robert Shoffner, St. Paul's, Burlington
1967-68 Michael W. Frye, Mt. Moriah, China Grove

The committee and the synod's Executive Board, therefore, urged church councils to provide for a subcommittee of the Committee on Christian Education and give to the subcommittee responsibility for coordinating the youth activities of the congregation.

The seemingly innocent emphasis on youth, not Luther League, proved to be a harbinger. Three years later, in 1967, the synod's Executive Board approved the Youth Committee's pursuance of "further development of the emerging concept of youth ministry."

The action was stimulated by an announcement that the LCA Commission on Youth Activities planned to award financial grants to several synods, including North Carolina, to explore creative and experimental youth programs. The exploration involved employment in the 1967 summer of an associate in youth ministry "to continue synodical introduction of Youth Ministry as the emerging philosophy of youth work in the LCA, and to provide direct assistance to congregations in youth work. . ."[23]

Robert Shoffner of St. Paul's, Burlington, the president of the North Carolina

Luther League Unit, was named the associate. But shortly before he assumed his summer duties, he reported to the synod convention some of the background for the new concept:

> A realization that the present structure of the Luther League is not serving the needs of the youth in the church has come, and is coming to some slowly and to others more abruptly. Thus within the NCLLU the major thrust during the past year has been to help the youth become aware of themselves and to develop their potentialities in the ministry of the church. Many of the activities which the NCLLU has offered the youth have involved the youth individually but have failed to help them to diverge into the surrounding church and develop their ministry there. . . . Youth ministry institutes and a seminar replaced the traditional leadership schools and seminars. This step in change was taken so that the emphasis could be shifted from the "program centered" to "person centered" involvements for those participating. . . . Although the NCLLU is one of the few units in the LL-LLA that has fulfilled its pledges over the past few years, a decline in the financial response of the youth is being seen. This may, to some extent be due to the fact that many of the youth feel that their pledges are not being used by the unit and international structures in a way which is helping the youth to meet their needs.

In the summer months to follow, the traditional Luther League convention was held at Lenoir Rhyne but other youth events were also staged. Youth ministry institutes were held at Dallas, Winston-Salem and Wilmington, a two-week workcamp for youth served the residents at Murdock Center for Retarded Children at Butner, and a one-week workcamp served residents at the Hickory Lutheran Home.

Shoffner's reasoning for a change in youth ministry was shared by his successor in the state Luther League presidency, Michael W. Frye of Mt. Moriah, China Grove. In his Luther League report to the synod the following year, Frye echoed the call for a change: "It is the feeling of both the Executive Committee and the Youth Committee that both the youth and the adults of the synod should work hand in hand to extend the work of the church in North Carolina. In order to do this, the classification stigma of a youth auxiliary must be lifted and replaced by a more effective program in which the youth and adult members of the congregation work on equal terms to fulfill their mission to their community."

The North Carolina Luther League Unit, representing 160 local leagues, held its last convention in 1968. In accordance with the LCA action in Atlanta the same year, the state league merged with the synodical Youth Committee, a new committee of nine adults and nine youth. The state league closed its books on December 31, 1968, distributing its treasury balance to the LCA league ($2,538.40) and the synodical Youth Committee ($1,000).

"I do not consider this a final report of the Luther League," said Frye, who presided over the closing state league convention, "rather as the prologue to a very important history which will have great significance to all of us in the years ahead."

Robert Peery, the state president in 1963-64, also served as president of the Luther League in America in 1964 and 1965. He became the third North Carolinian to head the national organization in its forty-seven-year history.

The new Youth Ministry program sponsored a variety of synodwide events in 1968. An August one-week Seminar on Interpersonal and Self Growth at Lutheridge, coordinated by Mrs. Robert Thompson, was attended by twenty persons and four leaders. A one-week Junior High Leadership School the same month at Lenoir Rhyne attracted thirty-six youth; co-deans for the event were Rev. Gary Safrit and Mary Stamey. The Christian Youth Caravan, directed by Dr. Joe Glass of the Lenoir Rhyne faculty, conducted area leadership events at Lincolnton and Kannapolis.

Other 1968 activities included a two-week "Youth Ministry in Action" team coordinated by Rev. Harry Robinson of St. Paul's, Durham, and involving three youth with residents at Murdock Center, Butner. Also, Rev. and Mrs. Peter Setzer of Holy Trinity, Gastonia, pioneered with a one-on-one camp for retarded children for one week in August at Burnsville; the camp brought together fifteen Lutheran youth and fifteen retarded youth from Butner.

New activities introduced in the summer of 1969 were a three-day "convention style" Youth Rally at Lenoir Rhyne in June and a one-week Burnsville camp in August with youth from a Charlotte ghetto.

In 1971 the state Youth Ministry program participated initially in a project of the LCA Commission on Youth Ministry which provided a youth staffer to serve in the synod. The staffer served as a consultant to congregations, trained and supported Youth Ministry Consultation Teams, and trained and supported pastors and lay adults in Youth Ministry concepts and skills.

The staffer, who worked under the direction of the synodical secretary of Christian education, was Mary Ann Moller of Hoquiom, Washington. She served for one year starting July 1, 1971, working with seventy congregational groups.

The program of youth staffers continued for the remainder of the LCA period, with other young adults from other areas of the church serving in the synod for one-year terms.

The Youth Ministry program, in the opinion of Rev. T. C. Plexico, pastor of St. James, Concord, needed an organized and structured group at the district and synodical level to give more specific guidance and direction to congregations in the area of programs and projects. He proposed such a group on the floor of the 1977 synod convention, but the motion failed.

The following year, in 1978, Plexico renewed his motion, but it was referred, on motion by Rev. Richard B. Graf, Jr., of Macedonia, Burlington, to the Youth Convo, the group of youth who attended the synod conventions each year and, in separate sessions, studied its issues. The Convo proposed that a special task force be formed to study the matter, to which the synod convention agreed. The task force presented its report to the 1979 convention, recommending no additional youth structure.

Five years later, however, the 1984 convention endorsed a recommendation of Bishop McDaniel and the Youth Ministry Committee that a task force be appointed to create a new synod-wide youth organization.

Growing out of that action was the organization of Lutheran Youth in North Carolina (LYNC) in the summer of 1985 on the campus of Lenoir-Rhyne. The organization, which represented ninety-five congregational groups at its formation, added eighty-seven units during the second year. The initial LYNC president, elected in 1985, was Anna McMahan of Holy Trinity, Gastonia. She was succeeded by Tammy Jones of Ascension, Shelby, elected in 1986.

Men's Auxiliary

The LCA was less than three years old when, at its 1966 convention in Kansas City, the delegates voted to discontinue the Lutheran Church Men as a churchwide auxiliary. The action was taken despite a memorial of the North Carolina Synod opposing the move. In a bow to the interests of North Carolina and several other synods, the LCA convention did agree that "at the option of each synod, synodical organization for men may be constituted."

In North Carolina, there was little hesitation about the next step. Five months after the Kansas City action, on November 2, 1966, the constituting convention for a successor men's auxiliary in North Carolina was held at Holy Trinity, Hickory.

The name given to the new organization was "Lutheran Men of North Carolina," later changed to "North Carolina Lutheran Men" (NCLM). The constitution provided for a synodical organization with duties and powers for "(a) promoting the establishment of an auxiliary of men in congregations of the synod, (b) helping and guiding congregational auxiliaries, (c) promoting such projects on a synodical and congregational level as are not in conflict with the policy of the synod, (d) organizing and overseeing Lutheran Men districts, (e) providing leadership training, (f) arranging for retreats and convocations, (g) holding conventions, (h) adopting budgets, (i) reporting to the Synod."[24]

MEN'S AUXILIARY PRESIDENTS

1962-63	Paul Ritchie, Salisbury
1964-65	Harry E. Faggart, Jr., Incarnation, Charlotte
1966	W. A. Kluttz, Greensboro
1967	Harry B. Fesperman, Grace, Thomasville
1968	Ray A. Cline, St. John's, Concord
1969	G. C. Miller, Haven, Salisbury
1970-71	Martin C. Pannell, Faith, Conover
1972-73	Harold F. McKnight, Christ, Charlotte
1974-75	George Page, Salisbury
1976-77	David C. Fleming, St. Mark's, Charlotte
1978	Elbert Bowman, Friendship, Taylorsville
1979-80	Carl Webb, St. John's, Cherryville
1981-82	Ed Martin, St. Thomas, Charlotte
1983-84	Elmer Lutz, New Jerusalem, Hickory
1985-86	Max Faggart, St. Thomas, Charlotte
1987-88	Harry Arne, St. James, Fayetteville

The stated purpose of the organization was "to support the program of the North Carolina Synod of the Lutheran Church in America and to carry forward its life in the congregation and districts."

Three projects from the predecessor auxiliary were carried forward: the Loan & Gift Fund, Scouting, and help in recruiting full-time Christian workers. A Loan & Gift Fund goal for the first year was set at sixty thousand dollars in contributions.

Presenters at the constituting convention were Rev. Marshall F. Mauney of West Columbia, South Carolina, devotional leader, and Dr. H. George Anderson of the

Southern Seminary faculty, speaker. Four hundred people attended the closing banquet held at Lenoir Rhyne.

The new organization became effective immediately following the expiration of the national Lutheran Church Men on December 31, 1966.

In 1971, the new organization ventured forth by employing its first salaried person. Rev. Walter N. Yount of Calvary, Concord, was engaged as executive director with the duty "to promote the work of Lutheran Men throughout the synod with particular emphasis on the Loan & Gift Fund program of the organization."[25] Yount served until 1982 when he was succeeded by Dr. John W. Cobb of St. John's, Statesville.

In the closing years of the LCA period, when it became known that a churchwide men's auxiliary was not planned in the proposed new church, the NCLM spearheaded an effort calling for a men's organization. It also funded a steering committee which, for two years, conducted the preparatory work leading to the formation of the churchwide auxiliary.

During the period of the LCA, the number of congregational units chartered by NCLM varied, ranging from a low of 39 in 1974 to a high of 92 in 1977 and again in 1987.

MEN'S AUXILIARY CONVENTION SITES

1963	Haven, Salisbury	1976	Haven, Salisbury
1964	St. John's, Cherryville	1977	St. Mark's, Charlotte
1965	Trinity, Rocky Mount	1978	Lutheran Chapel, Gastonia
1966	Holy Trinity, Hickory	1979	St. Stephen's, Hickory
1967	St. Paul's, Salisbury	1980	St. John's, Concord
1968	St. James, Concord	1981	Grace, Thomasville
1969	Grace, Thomasville	1982	Bethlehem, Hickory
1970	St. Luke's, Charlotte	1983	Salem, Salisbury
1971	St. Stephen's, Hickory	1984	Augsburg, Winston-Salem
1972	Ebenezer, China Grove	1985	Calvary, Concord
1973	First, Greensboro	1986	St. Mark's, China Grove
1974	St. Stephen's, Hickory	1987	Christ, Charlotte
1975	St. James, Concord		

Contributions to the Loan & Gift Fund also varied. The amounts reported to the synod conventions for three years were: $24,859.43 in 1984, $18,736.26 in 1985, and $23,770.48 in 1986.

The Home Mission Foundation continued to grow during the LCA period. At the close of the period in 1987, the foundation reported assets of $1,474,530, with loans outstanding to twenty-nine mission congregations.

Synodical Lay Leadership

About a third of the LCA period had passed when women were elected for the first time to membership on the synod's governing board. The 1972 convention broke the gender barrier by electing two women to the Executive Board. Betty Jo Litaker, librarian and member of St. John's, Statesville, was elected on the second ballot, and Catherine B. Norris, kindergarten teacher and member of St. Andrew's, Hickory, was named on the fourth ballot. Both were elected to three-year terms.

Later in the decade, in 1978, the synod initiated recognition of lay professionals in the church by granting them seat and voice in the synodical conventions. At the same time, it bound the lay professionals to convention actions relating to them.

Over the next two years, the synod formulated further policies relating to lay professionals. It stressed that synod convention attendance be a part of the lay professional's job description with expenses paid by the local congregation. It required a church council employing either a certified or non-certified lay professional to consult with the synod president about potential candidates. The synod also required that, when a certified lay professional resigns, the church council notify the synod president, and the lay professional consult with the synod president.

Institutions

The North Carolina Synod began its life in the LCA with a capital campaign for Lenoir Rhyne. The 1963 Fund for Progress was first planned by the Hickory college to fund a set of projects during the 1961-65 period, but a prior commitment of the synod postponed the college plans. The synod convention approved the campaign in 1959 but stipulated that it not begin until 1963.

The college sought two million dollars for a women's dormitory, an administrative office building, expansion of the library facility, and enlargement and improvement of the stadium.

Under the leadership of Glenn E. Ketner, a member of St. John's, Salisbury, the solicitation was launched on January 27, 1963, the first month of the LCA period, and closed on March 23. The responses, however, fell short of the goal, totaling $1,448,932. Five years later, on February 9, 1968, the campaign receipts had risen to $1,813,795.[26]

Included in the campaign gifts was a $150,000 commitment of the synod for a Lenoir Rhyne professorship, approved in a rising vote at the 1965 convention at Macedonia, Burlington. The commitment was funded through annual gifts from the income of the Michael Peeler Trust Fund over a period of ten years. At the time of the approval, the annual gift of fifteen thousand dollars represented about half of the annual income from the trust fund.

The president of the college, Dr. Voigt R. Cromer, resigned for health reasons in 1967 following an eighteen-year administration. He was succeeded in office by the academic dean, Dr. Raymond M. Bost, a native of Maiden ordained by the synod in 1952. Bost became Lenoir Rhyne's seventh president in its seventy-seventieth year of operation.

In 1970, the synod approved a proposal of the college Board of Trustees which gave the board more voice in the selection of college trustees and permitted, for the first time, non-Lutherans to serve on the board. The change in practice was effected by increasing the board membership from twenty-four to twenty-seven and granting the board exclusive authority to nominate for (but not elect) six of the board seats, three of which could be filled by non-Lutherans. The synod retained the privilege of electing all twenty-seven trustees, and it required that the position of chairman of the board continue to be filled by a Lutheran.

Elected at the same 1970 convention was the first non-Lutheran to serve on the Lenoir Rhyne board: George M. Chapman, an Episcopalian who graduated from the college and practiced law in New York City.

Unrelated to the trustee-selection process was a suggestion of the national church that all LCA synods enter into covenant discussions with the colleges and universities they supported. In response, the North Carolina Synod and the Lenoir Rhyne Board of Trustees formed a joint committee to formulate a covenant statement summarizing how each organization expected to help and be helped by the relationship. The statement, approved by the 1972 synod convention, included a requirement that it be reviewed at five-year intervals.

After nine years in office, Bost resigned the presidency in 1976 to become president of the Lutheran Theological Seminary at Philadelphia. The college, which earlier in the year hyphenated its name to become "Lenoir-Rhyne", selected for his successor a Lutheran philosophy professor from Minnesota and the college's first non-ordained president, Dr. Albert B. Anderson.

Anderson arrived on campus in the fall of 1976, in time to help launch the synod's second campaign of the period for Lenoir-Rhyne. The institution, which earlier in the decade raised $1.9 million in the Hickory community toward its $3.5 million Strategy for the Seventies improvement, needed an additional $1.2 million for endowment, for the replacement of one classroom building (Yoder) and for the renovation of another (Rhyne). The synod's Forward Together Campaign, chaired by Rev. Brady Y. Faggart, Jr., pastor of First, Greensboro, was conducted among the congregations of the synod, resulting in gifts and pledges of $1,589,623.

At the close of 1982, Anderson resigned the presidency to become development officer at Luther College in Iowa. Serving the college as acting president during the following twenty-month interim was Albert M. Allran, a retired Hickory textile executive and member of the Board of Trustees.

Assuming the presidency in 1984 was Dr. John E. Trainer, Jr., a native of Pennsylvania and graduate of Muhlenberg College, Wake Forest University and University of Oklahoma. The biology professor moved to Lenoir-Rhyne from Jacksonville University in Florida, where he served as vice president for academic affairs.

During the twenty-five years of the LCA period, the college expanded its campus from sixty to one hundred acres, the enrollment grew from eleven hundred to fifteen hundred students, and the endowment advanced from one million to ten million dollars. The annual budget expanded from $1.4 to $12.3 million, and the total assets increased from nine million to twenty-nine million dollars.

Meanwhile, in Columbia, South Carolina, the synod-supported Southern Seminary increased its annual operational budget from $167,000 to $1.7 million. Its total enrollment, including the graduate school, ranged from a low of 154 in 1962 to a high of 190 two years later. Its 1974 enrollment of 130 students seeking ordination was an institutional record. Although attendance during the period remained stable, women seminarians grew more common, increasing to twenty percent of the total enrollment.

The president, Dr. F. Eppling Reinartz, retired in 1970 and was succeeded by Dr. Hugh George Anderson, who had taught church history since 1958 and headed the seminary's graduate studies program.

During Anderson's administration, the North Carolina Synod participated in the seminary's 1973 Outreach Appeal for two million dollars for facility development. Dr. Voigt R. Cromer of Hickory headed the appeal's North Carolina phase which resulted in pledges and gifts exceeding $550,000.

An earlier North Carolina gift funded the 1975 construction of the Abel C. and Martha J. Lineberger Memorial Library, made possible by a contribution from the Lineberger Foundation, through the interest and influence of Dr. J. Harold Lineberger of Belmont.

Anderson resigned at the close of 1981 to become president of Luther College. Succeeding him as the seminary president in 1982 was Dr. Mack C. Branham, Jr.

During the third month of Branham's administration, the North Carolina Synod's Executive Board approved a plan to boost the seminary endowment by establishing a $250,000 Michael Peeler Professorship. The project was funded through annual contributions from the income of the synod's Michael Peeler Trust Fund.

At Lutheridge, the synod's other institution which was jointly owned with other Southern synods, the 1963 merger made no change in the ownership and operation. But a change in synodical lines reduced the number of its constituent synods from four to three: North Carolina, South Carolina and Southeastern. During the LCA period, Lutheridge expanded its program from a summer camp to a year-round conference center. Facilitating the expansion was the 1977 installation of heat in the Lineberger Dining Hall.

Between 1963 and 1988, the mountain facility increased its annual disbursements from $185,000 to $690,000. Its assets grew from $863,000 to $2,500,000. At the end of the period, the number of people registering for its activities during the twelve-month period exceeded fourteen thousand.

Dr. J. Lewis Thornburg, the first executive director of Lutheridge, retired in 1966 following seventeen years in the position. He was succeeded by Rev. Brady Y. Faggart, Jr., of Salisbury, former synodical Christian education secretary, who served for two years before moving to New York City to serve as an assistant in the LCA president's office.

Rev. Robert L. Troutman, who like Faggart was synodical Christian education secretary, assumed the position of Lutheridge executive director in 1969 and served throughout the remainder of the LCA period.

Complementing the Lutheridge mountain facility in the western part of the state was the purchase by the synod of an oceanfront facility on the North Carolina coast, at Kure Beach, in 1966. The fifteen thousand dollar purchase by the synod, financed by funds from the Michael Peeler Trust Fund and Luther League Penny Parades, included two lots and a former motel on Highway 421 five blocks south of Kure Beach square.

Named Kure Beach Lutheran Retreat Center, the facility opened in 1967 and served twenty-four church groups in 1968. Forty-eight groups - about twelve hundred people - used the center in 1969, and seventy-nine groups, in 1970.

In 1983, the old motel structure was replaced by a new facility comprised of three buildings connected by decks. One building, single-storied, served as an assembly-dining facility and included a kitchen. The other two buildings, both two-storied, provided living and sleeping quarters. The spaces could be adapted to accommodate forty-six youth, or thirty adults, or twelve couples, or eight families.

In addition to the new facility, a nearby house was acquired to supplement the main center. The house, which included four bedrooms, two baths, a kitchen, living room and large enclosed porch, accommodated twenty-four youth. A second cottage was added to the complex the following year.

Three years after opening the Kure Beach Center, the synod's Camping Committee began acquisition of 554 acres on the Cape Fear River near Sanford for a center to serve the spiritual needs of those engaged in boating and other outdoor recreational activities.

The need for a staff person to help the committee raise funds, acquire and develop the property, and direct the operation of the oceanfront center at Kure Beach, prompted the creation of the position of director of outdoor ministries, which was approved by the 1972 synod convention. Rev. David L. Castor, chairman of the Camp Committee, accepted the call extended by the Executive Board to become the first director.

A contest to name the Cape Fear facility was won by Mrs. D. F. Currie, a member of St. James, Fayetteville. Her entry: Agape Camping, Conference and Retreat Center.

The camp opened on July 14, 1974. Activities of the initial summer included congregational youth retreats and workdays, scout campings, and adult day retreats. Participants during the first year numbered more than one thousand. Full-time services were provided by a manager living on the site. In addition to the manager's residence, the facilities included a bath house, picnic tables, nineteen trailer sites and tent pads in the tent-camping area.

In 1978 a lodge was constructed at Camp Agape. It provided twenty-four bedrooms, two large meeting rooms, a dining room, kitchen and larger deck. The $210,000 cost was funded through gifts raised by North Carolina Lutheran Men, and the lodge was dedicated in 1982 in honor of the organization's former executive director, Dr. Walter N. Yount of Concord.

The development of both Camp Agape and Kure Beach, as well as Lutheridge, were aided by the synod-wide Camping and Conference Ministry Appeal in 1980. Pledges and gifts to the campaign totaled ninety-eight percent of the $1.6 million challenge goal.

Three years later, in 1983, the synod convention authorized the formation of the Lutheran Outdoor Ministries, Inc., with responsibility for operation and maintenance of the two eastern retreat centers. The formation also provided for a Board of Trustees to be elected by the synod.

At the close of the LCA period, the two centers were operating jointly on an annual budget of two hundred thousand dollars, hosting each year thirty-five hundred campers at 250 camping events.

Social Ministry

One reluctant separation forced by the LCA merger was the divorce of the North Carolina Synod from the Sipes Orchard Home for Boys.

The relationship that existed prior to the merger was so informal that it did not meet the requirements inherent in the LCA. A key requirement, known as the "representative principle," stated that "in interchurch associations the official representatives of churches should never be expected to sit on a parity with individuals who represent only themselves or at most organizations which are less than churches."[27]

At the Sipes home, the composition of the Board of Directors failed to meet that requirement. The board consisted of seven members representing the Eastern District of the American Lutheran Church, two representing the North Carolina Synod, a pastor and a layman elected by Mt. Zion ALC Church, and nine additional members who needed not be members of good standing of either church body.

The variance from the representative principle compelled the synod, at its second convention in 1964, to notify the Sipes Home directors that it would not replace the representatives it elected in 1963. The representatives, Henry Herman of Conover and Rev. D. F. Swicegood of St. Stephen's, Hickory, had been elected to three-year terms. The expiration of their terms in 1966 would automatically discontinue the formal relationship.

The convention emphasized that the action did not "express any loss of interest or dissatisfaction with the program or management." It also noted that the action did not affect the personal relationships of members of the synod who served on the board and did not officially represent the synod.

In 1966, when the synod's formal relationship with the home came to an end, the home cared for forty-seven children, operating on an annual budget of sixty-four thousand dollars. John G. Odom, the home's first superintendent, continued to serve in that capacity.

Separation from the Sipes home was not the only disassociation initiatied by the 1964 convention. It also set in motion the withdrawal of ownership and support of the Lowman Home for the Aged and Helpless, but for a different reason.

The North Carolina Synod had thirty-one members residing in the Lowman Home. Seventeen were paying their own way, and fourteen resided there at the expense of the synod. The synod's support of the home, based on its confirmed members in good standing, was $26,400. But if the synod purchased the care for the fourteen residents who were not paying, its annual expense would be only $18,366. The synod was entitled to place fifty residents in the Lowman Home, but surveys indicated that most members of the synod preferred the synod's own Lutheran Home, even if they had to wait two years for admittance. The convention also noted that withdrawal negotiations with Lowman Home might take four to six years for completion.

The convention voted to initiate withdrawal proceedings, ending a relationship which dated from 1911. The synod's representatives on the home's Board of Trustees terminated their service in 1966, and synodical support of the home ended the following year. For the Lowman Home, North Carolina was not the only synod terminating its association; the Virginia Synod also withdrew its ownership and support at the same time.

At the time of North Carolina's withdrawal, the Lowman Home cared for 163 residents, including twenty-six from North Carolina. The home operated on an annual budget of $325,000, with assets of three million dollars. Serving as superintendent was J. Kenneth Webb.

The synod's disassociation with Lowman Home coincided with a 1966 revelation that the synod's own Hickory Lutheran Home, only five years old and newly out of debt, should expand from fifty-six beds to eighty.

The change, recommended by the LCA Board of Social Ministry to improve economy of operation, was made under the direction of the new executive director, Rev. John A. Pless, former pastor of St. Luke's, Lexington. Pless succeeded Dr. J. L. Norris following Norris' retirement in 1966.

Expansion of the Hickory unit did not jeopardize the synod's plans for a second unit at Albemarle, but it did require an upgrading of the Albemarle plans and, because of the higher cost, more time to secure funding.

A capital fund campaign titled CONCERN (Care of North Carolina Elderly Right Now) was launched in 1969 with Dr. Carveth P. Mitchell of St. Mark's, Charlotte, serving as general chairman. The basic goal of $575,000 was sought to help fund the Albemarle unit (which was under construction at the time) and pay off the expansion debt of the Hickory Unit. The campaign also had a challenge goal of $1,375,000, which included eight hundred thousand dollars for construction of the proposed third unit of Lutheran Homes at Salisbury. In 1973, the pledges and gifts to CONCERN totaled $1,067,000.

The Albemarle unit, designed as a fifty-bed infirmary, received its first residents in 1971.

The Salisbury unit opened in 1976. It accommodated sixty residents in skilled care, twenty-five in intermediate care, and twenty-five in the Home for the Aged.

At the time of the Salisbury opening, the Hickory unit served forty-eight residents in skilled care, sixteen in intermediate care, and sixteen in the Home for the Aged. The Albemarle unit had a capacity of fifty-four beds, all in skilled care.

Two years later, in 1978, Rev. Robert Q. Beard assumed the position of executive director following the death of Pless.

Growing needs in the three units and in other areas compelled the synod to mount another special appeal for Lutheran Homes in 1985. The basic goal of $1.5 million was sought to provide $470,000 for additional beds at Hickory, $375,000 for additional beds at Salisbury, and $355,000 for additional beds at Albemarle. The remaining three hundred thousand dollars was needed for planning and development of proposed sites in Wilmington, the Research Triangle Area, and Charlotte. Within six months after the appeal began, pledges and gifts from 180 congregations exceeded the basic goal and set a record in LCA fund-raising.

The funds helped to make possible the $2.4 million addition to the Hickory unit in 1986. The addition, named Luther Manor, included thirty rest home beds and thirty intermediate care beds.

The corporate structure of North Carolina Lutheran Homes was reorganized late in 1985 under the new name of "Lutheran Services for the Aging" (LSA). The change created a parent company with subsidiaries for specialized functions and placed the three home units in a subsidiary named "Lutheran Nursing Homes." The restructuring offered the advantages of greater flexibility in planning and decision-making, more effective management, sheltering of assets, and opportunity for more pan-Lutheran and non-Lutheran participation in the subsidiary boards.

In addition to the homes provided through synodical channels, other homes appeared in the eighties as a result of congregational efforts. Lutherhaus, a fifty-apartment complex for the elderly and handicapped, opened in Hickory in 1980 sponsored by the St. Andrew's and Bethany congregations.

In Burlington, the Macedonia congregation, through the use of a four-million-dollar bequest of Wade Coble, completed the Twin Lakes Center in 1983. The main building of the center contained thirty-six skilled nursing beds, thirty-seven intermediate care beds, and thirty efficiency apartments. The center also included a separate Independent Living section, composed of a cottage, four duplexes, sixteen one-bedroom apartments and sixteen two-bedroom apartments.

Early in the LCA period, when the synod operated only one Lutheran Home, consideration was given to the establishment of a hospital. In late 1963, President Whittecar reported receipt of an expression of interest in making a "sizeable" gift toward a first-grade Lutheran hospital. The matter was referred to a special committee of three physicians, a hospital administrator and a pastor which reported in late 1964 its findings:

> In light of available resources, the cost of building and operation, the number of hospital beds available in the state of North Carolina, and the known plans for enlargement of existing institutions; and, being aware that our Synod is supporting causes now in operation which require a resonable stewardship of our people to maintain and expand, the Special Committee recommends to the Executive Board of the North Carolina Synod that the Synod not enter into a program of receiving gifts and making plans for erecting and operating a Lutheran Hospital as proposed at this time.[28]

The recommendation was approved by the Executive Committee in early 1965.

Although reluctant to undertake a hospital, the synod was eager to expand its ministry to children and families. Eleven years later, in 1976, the Social Ministry Committee urged the Lutheran Children's Home of the South to extend its off-campus child-care and family services more aggressively into North Carolina. The home, under the leadership of Roy Hendrickson, executive director since 1967, adopted the "North Carolina Program" and employed a Tar Heel social worker, Bill D. Brittain, to give full-time direction to the services.

Working out of an office at Holy Trinity, Raleigh, Brittain directed the home's new North Carolina Office of Services to Families and Children into a quickly-spreading program. Improvements in the state juvenile justice system were promoted with the assistance of the state LCW unit. Coordination was given to a youth need-assessment survey conducted by the Wake County Citizens for Improved Youth Services. Assistance was given the Family Aid Program in Catawba County in providing financial aid and counseling services. An emergency shelter care program for youth was established in Mecklenburg County, and four shelters were placed in operation in 1978.

At the home base in Virginia, Hendrickson retired in 1977 and was succeeded by Ronald Herring, who helped to guide the home into a re-evaluation of its planning principles. The 1978 study suggested that the home focus in three directions:

> 1. Serving youth with more complex needs at the institution in Salem, Virginia, who cannot reside with their families, and for whom other community services, such as foster care, or group homes, are not viable.
>
> 2. Decentralization of services to other geographic locations in North Carolina and Virginia to serve both congregational and community needs as needs and resources would dictate.
>
> 3. Development of the Salem campus to serve multiple needs (in addition to residential care) and to participate and respond to the needs in the Roanoke Valley.[29]

The following year, however, the North Carolina Synod undertook its own study to determine whether it should continue to work through the Virginia home to serve North Carolina needs. A 1979 special task force, chaired by Frances Frock of St. Andrew's, Hickory, recommended that the synod terminate its relationship with the Salem home and create its own agency to continue and increase the child-care and family ministry.

"If North Carolina had its own program," the task force reasoned, "the synod could have more involvement in the program, and there could be more interaction in the Synod Mission Profile and Long Range Planning. If the agency were closer at hand, the synod could be more sensitive to its needs and respond more readily. In addition, the North Carolina agency would be more likely to feel a stronger accountability to the concerns and interests of the North Carolina people."

The 1980 synod convention, noting that there were no North Carolina children at the Salem home, agreed with the task force.

The new agency, named Lutheran Family Services of North Carolina (LFS), was new in name only and continued under Brittain's direction to expand its services. In addition to nine group homes (serving forty-five children daily), it maintained a network of twenty foster homes. It opened its first family counseling education and enrichment office. It began offering refugee sponsorships for Cuban and Haitian families and the establishment of thirty foster homes for Indochinese children. The following year, in 1981, it established its first day treatment center; the facility in Sanford, with a capacity for five youths, was funded through a contract with Lee-Harnett Mental Health Center.

By 1983, LFS managed twenty-two group homes for children, five day treatment centers, seventy-five youth in foster care and a family counseling center. The agency had a daily child-care capacity of 235 children and youth, which made it the second largest private agency in the state.

The services of the agency were grouped in 1987 into five divisions: children's division, adoption services, refugee resettlement, prison ministry and family ministry.

The children's division included twenty-five group homes (including new ones in Wilmington, Lenoir and Asheville), eighty foster homes licensed to serve one hundred children per year, independent living units (for older teenagers) and in-home family services ministering to a total family in a home setting.

The adoption services included an international adoption agency (World Child, Inc.) which was formed with three other Lutheran social ministry organizations. The refugee resettlement services included the resettlement of 202 Montagnards who arrived in November 1986 to resettle in Raleigh, Greensboro and Charlotte. The prison ministry began with employment of a full-time family worker at Wake Advancement Center in Raleigh.

The family ministry division serviced counseling, education and enrichment centers in Charlotte, Raleigh, Greensboro and Salisbury. Retreats on marriage and family enrichment and related topics were also offered at Lutheridge.

At the close of 1986, the LFS had assets of $1.3 million and operated on a budget of $5.1 million.

Another social issue attracting synodical staffing during the LCA period was race relations. The staffing, however, did not come until after several years of contentious discussion.

The synod's first substantive resolution on race relations since the 1954 convention was introduced at its 1964 convention at Kimball Memorial, Kannapolis. The resolution, proposed by the Social Ministry Committee, called on the delegates to:

> remind each congregation of the inclusiveness of the Gospel and of its duty to include in its ministry all persons who are within its area of concern and who do not have a living relationship to Christ, without distinction as to race, color, national origin, economic or cultural status. . . .
>
> We call on the members of the congregations of the Synod to welcome as fellow members and co-workers for Jesus Christ, all persons who qualify by reason of faith without regard to race, color, national origin, or other conditions of life.[30]

Strong opposition was voiced by several lay delegates, reported the *North Carolina Lutheran.*[31] One reported "almost unanimous opposition" in his congregation, and another warned that ratification "will be construed as an endorsement of the mob in the street and brotherhood by law."

In reply, Rev. Frank C. Perry of Chapel Hill pleaded for "a church that is unafraid to say unambiguously what it means in race relations. We cannot abrogate our responsibility in this field."

The discussion included a report by Dr. Voigt R. Cromer that the Lenoir Rhyne Board of Trustees in the spring of 1963 adopted a resolution eliminating race as a discriminatory factor in the admissions policy of the college. Five Negroes were enrolled in the 1963 summer session, and one had applied for the regular September term.

After one hour of debate, the resolution was adopted. As affirmation of its intent, the convention also voted down a subsequent motion to instruct delegates to the LCA to vote against the proposed Race Relations Statement of the LCA Board of Social Missions.

Five years later, however, President Whittecar saw no progress. "We have no congregations that are made up of Negro people," he reported to the 1969 convention, "and only a very minimal token integration of church membership in two or three congregations. We have adopted in our church life the same patterns that have generally prevailed in our racially segregated society."[32] He urged each congregation and pastor to consider specific ways to effect outreach.

To help the congregations, the Executive Board responded to a 1968 LCA convention resolution and created a President's Task Force on Justice and Social Change. Purpose of the task force was to assist congregations in meeting problems related to poverty and social injustice, as well as racial prejudice. The task force of thirteen members, organized in the summer of 1969, was chaired by President Whittecar.

Efforts of the task force to participate in the churchwide Priority Program on Justice and Social Change resulted in a series of six 1970 Encounter Retreats. The retreats included dialogues with black participants. In addition to retreats for pastors, there were retreats for members of the Executive Board, members of the Task Force on Justice and Social Change and resource persons. Similar programs for church councils were recommended. Directing the series of programs on a part-time basis was Rev.

Richard W. Rhyne, pastor of Prince of Peace, Greensboro.

In a parallel development, the synodical Stewardship Committee in 1972 asked that the Executive Board and congregations of the synod be urged to comply with Project Equality. The request meant that all agencies and committees would, in so far as possible, deal with businesses which abided by certain guidelines laid down with respect to equal employment regardless of race or sex. Adherence to the request during the next year required the Executive Board to consult the guidelines in matters such as the investment of funds and the selection of convention facilities and meeting services.

The following year, in 1973, the Executive Board approved the creation of a fourth position of administative assistant to the president with fifty percent of the time devoted to justice and social change. The remainder of the time was devoted to the Social Ministry Committee and associated institutions, the Environmental Task Force, Task Force on Family Living, Project Equality, and Lutheran World Relief. Accepting a call to the position was Pastor Rhyne.

Ensuing activity in justice and social change included a workcamp for Indian, black and white youth, a teacher education workshop on human relations, linkage of Lutheran congregations with county Hunger Coalition projects, consultations on labor-management concerns in the textile industry, and sponsorship of a internship involving Lutheran congregations and the Indian community.

In 1979, the first three blacks assumed leadership roles in the synod. In June, the first black Lutheran pastor since Alpha Synod days joined the synod: Rev. Eugene Powell, former campus pastor to Chicago city colleges, accepted a call as mission developer in Raleigh. In September, Rev. Earlean Miller, native of Illinois and the first black woman to be ordained in the LCA, became pastor of Prince of Peace, Greensboro. In December, the synod's new full-time position of director of minority ministries was created, funded jointly by the synod and the LCA Division for Mission in North America. Rev. Richard J. Perry, Jr., of Gary, Indiana, served as first director, locating his office in Charlotte with the offices of the North Carolina Family Services of Children's Home of the South.

Five years later, the Task Force on Justice and Social Change gave way to a standing Committee on Inclusive Ministry. The new committee was charged with the responsibility to "provide direction in inclusive ministry for congregations, . . . and to conduct an annual evaluation and submit a written report to the appropriate boards and cabinets of synod and to the Lutheran Church in America Division for Missions in North America."

In 1986 the synod convention, at the committee's recommendation, approved a set of goals designed to advance the inclusive ministry. It called for a ten percent increase in the minority membership in the synod, a regular review of policies and practices to eliminate racism, the establishment of ecumenical relationships with predominantly black denominations for the purpose of dialog and cooperation, and a two percent increase in minority appointments and elections.

At the same convention, the synod recorded a historical first by electing three persons of color or with primary language other than English. An Asian, Dr. David Chou of Hickory, was named a trustee of Southern Seminary, and two blacks, Cheryl L. Troutman of Greensboro and Renee Palmer of Raleigh, were elected to the board of Lutheran Family Services.

Progress in minority ministry as the LCA period ended was determinable. The 1986 parochial reports revealed an enrollment of 450 baptized and more than three hundred confirmed people of American Indian, Asian, black and Hispanic backgrounds. That was a ten percent increase over the reports of 1985. And, the Inclusive Ministry Committee reported to the 1987 convention that it was "pleased that twenty-two people of color and primary language other than English are able to be at this convention."

Still, Director Perry had misgivings: "We rejoice that people are sharing the good news with the rich diversity of people in their communities. However, I want to express a word of caution. I am very concerned that the synod has not grown in its Black membership. The synodical records show that in 1888 and 1889 there were about 200 Black Lutherans. In 1986, there were 185 baptized Black Lutherans. Living in a state that is more than 20 percent Black causes me to wonder what we really are doing in the area of witnessing within the Black community."

Nevertheless, at the LCA convention in Milwaukee that year, the North Carolina delegation included a higher percentage of women and people of color than the delegation of any other synod except Metropolitan New York.

In addition to its inclusive ministry efforts, the synod practiced its social ministry through regular clothing drives of Lutheran World Relief. Under the direction of Rev. Donald Deal of Dallas, the synod's congregations joined with the North Carolina congregations of the American Lutheran Church and the Lutheran Church - Missouri Synod to contribute twenty-two tons of clothing in 1962. They also contributed a record twenty-one tons during the 1963 Thanksgiving Clothing Drive alone.

The pan-Lutheran spirit also spread to refugee resettlement, even before the ministry was assumed by Lutheran Family Services. In 1975, the congregations of the synod joined with those of two other Lutheran bodies to help resettle refugees from Vietnam and Cambodia. The Lutherans, according to Richard Rhyne, administrative assistant to the president, were challenged with a goal of fifty families, but over seventy congregations responded, offering assistance to over 120 families and three hundred persons. Rhyne was later designated the North Carolina director of resettlement service for the Lutheran Immigration Refugee Service of the Lutheran Council in the USA.

Other social ministry actions of the synod during the LCA period took the form of resolutions urging action on the part of congregations and its members. The objectives included World Hunger (1975), handicap accessibility (1978), Polish refugee resettlement (1982), Bread for the World (1984) and ecology (1985).

The topics of other social ministry resolutions debated (but not necessarily adopted) by conventions in the seventies included Vietnam (1972), amnesty for Vietnam exiles (1973), capital punishment (1974), criminal justice (1977), Indian treaty rights (1978), insanity pleas (1978), liquor by the drink (1979), abortion (1979) and Medicaid (1979).

Resolutions debated in the 1980s included the Nestle infant formula (1981), Equal Rights Amendment (1981), fundamentalist methods of political action (1981), Voting Rights Act (1982), nuclear armaments (1982), Namibia struggle for independence (1982), war and peace in a nuclear age (1983), alternatives to incarceration (1983), corporal punishment (1983), state sales tax on food (1983), violence (1984), nuclear weapon investments (1984), alcoholic beverage advertising (1985), AIDS education

(1986) and South African investments (1986).

Finances

In the synod's financial operations, its budget and apportionment process was enhanced with two improvements: the 1970 apportionment formula and the 1974 Synod Mission Profile.

In 1968 a new by-law was added authorizing the Executive Board to recommend each year a formula for assigning congregational apportionments. The formula for the 1970 budget reduced by one-half the apportionments of congregations with less than one hundred members and added the difference to the congregations with more than two hundred members. Later other changes were made to create more categories of congregations according to membership.

In 1974 the synod introduced the development of a mission profile featuring a three-level ("essential," "urgent," "desirable") budget for 1975. The mission profile provided a statement of mission, goals and objectives for each committee, board and agency along with a three-year program projection. The development of the program budget was directed by the administrative assistant to the president, Dr. Ernest Misenheimer.

Attention was also given to synodwide appeals for gifts. The constant presence of the capital funds campaign stimulated action by the 1965 synod convention to limit the campaigns to not more than one within a three-year period.

The need for a limit was described by Rev. Paul Morgan: "Since 1950, the synod has been contributing to one or more appeals every year; from 1954 to 1960, the treasurer of synod was receiving receipts for at least two appeals, and since 1961, receipts for at least four appeals."[33]

The response of the convention was to adopt a by-law amendment setting the one-at-a-time limit. It defined the capital funds campaign as "one in which all congregations of Synod are asked to participate with the intention of presenting the cause to all members of the congregations." It also defined what is not a campaign: "An approach by representatives of the Synod or one of its institutions to individuals or groups of members within the congregations to request gifts for special purposes shall not be considered as a capital funds campaign."

At the time of the 1965 action, the synod was completing the Lenoir Rhyne two-million-dollar Fund for Progress appeal which began in 1963. The following two years, 1966 and 1967, were reserved for the six-hundred-thousand-dollar Campus Ministry campaign, to be followed in 1968 and 1969 by the LCA's $6.5 million national ACT (Act in Crisis Today) appeal for inner-city ghettos, migrants and minority groups.

The $575,000 CONCERN campaign for Lutheran Homes (1969-71) was followed by the Southern Seminary's $550,000 Outreach campaign (1973-75) and the Lenoir-Rhyne $1.2 million Forward Together campaign (1976-79). Overlapping the Lenoir-Rhyne campaign was the 1977 LCA's Strength for Mission appeal for twenty-five million dollars.

Prior to the close of the Lenoir-Rhyne campaign in 1979, the synod amended its campaign by-law further to lengthen the period between campaigns. The amendment provided that there would be a one-year interval between campaigns when there would be no campaign activity in the synod.

Accordingly, there was a one-year delay before the Conference and Camping

Ministry Appeal (1981-83) was launched and another delay before the Lutheran Homes Building for Living Appeal (1985-87) began.

During the LCA period from 1963 to 1988, the budgeted expenditures of the synod advanced from $1.1 million to $3.1 million. The assets of the Michael Peeler Trust Fund grew from $665,000 to $2.8 million and its annual distributions to the synod increased from $30,000 to $106,000.

During the period of McDaniel's service as bishop, the synod resumed, for the first time in two decades, its practice of remitting one hundred percent of its benevolence share to the national church. The achievement was repeated the following two years.

Merger

The shadow of the close of the LCA period was seen as early as 1982. Dr. John L. Yost, Jr., of Charleston, South Carolina, the churchwide representative to the synodical convention that year and a former North Carolinian who helped usher in the LCA period in 1963, reported that affirmative votes at three national conventions in September would result in a merger on January 1, 1988.

At the following convention Kay Conrad of Winston-Salem was introduced as a member of the Commission on the Formation of a New Lutheran Church, and she and LCA representative Bishop Kenneth Sauer reported on the work of the commission and answered questions.

The 1984 convention delegates were led by Dr. J. Larry Yoder of Lenoir-Rhyne, a member of the Executive Board, in a review of sense motions relating to the new church, and the 1986 delegates voted on ten merger issues which were reported to the commission. At its 1987 convention, the synod approved an "Agreement and Plan of Merger."

The tendency toward union so permeated the synod and the LCA that H. George Anderson observed that the successor church "owes its existence to the unremitting efforts of its parent. The LCA actively worked for its own demise. Its constitution required it to 'strive for the unification of all Lutherans within its boundaries in one church and to take constructive measures leading thereto.' Conventions of the LCA repeatedly made that mandate their own as they authorized committees to seek organic union with sister Lutheran bodies."[34]

At the national level, the Evangelical Lutheran Church in America was formally constituted by delegates representing the Lutheran Church in America, American Lutheran Church and the Association of Evangelical Lutheran Churches in Columbus, Ohio, April 30-May 3, 1987.

Among those elected to leadership in the new 5.3-million member church were seven North Carolinians. Bishop McDaniel was elected by the Conference of Bishops to represent Region IX on the ELCA Council, and the nine bishops on the council elected him as their chairman. Edgar Trexler of Philadelphia was named to edit the church periodical. Gail A. Starr of Durham and Dr. Kay O. Conrad were named to the Board for Congregational Life. Dr. Paul E. Lutz of First, Greensboro, was elected to the Board for Higher Education and Schools, and Eloise D. Thomas of St. Matthew's, Wilmington, was selected for the Social Ministry Organizations Board. Bachman S. Brown, Jr., of Kimball Memorial, Kannapolis, was named to the Nominating Committee.

The constituting convention of the North Carolina Synod of the ELCA was held

May 30-31, 1987, at Lenoir-Rhyne following the last convention of the North Carolina Synod of the LCA the day before. The presiding officer, appointed by the ELCA Transition Team, was Former Bishop Ernest L. Misenheimer.

Chief items of business included the adoption of a constitution and program budget, and the election of officers, Synod Council, boards and committees.

Dr. James R. Crumley, Jr., bishop of the LCA, was the speaker for the convention banquet, and Rev. David A. Wobler, bishop of the Southeastern District of the ALC, preached at the closing worship service.

A total of 746 delegates, pastors and visitors registered for the convention. It brought together 230 congregations and eighty-five thousand Lutherans into the new synod.

As the North Carolina Synod moved toward adjournment of its final convention as a part of the LCA on May 29, a tribute to the retiring synod was led by Rev. David K. Huddle of St. John's, Salisbury, chairman of the convention Committee on Reference and Council:

> We give thanks and praise to Almighty God for the long and dedicated history of the North Carolina Synod of the Lutheran Church in America. We have been blessed to be "the People of God" in this place for these past twenty-six [*sic*] years.
>
> We remember with thanksgiving all those who have faithfully served this Synod throughout its history . . . individuals, institutions, auxiliaries, and congregations. We pray God's continued Grace, Blessing, Guidance, and Direction as we bring to a close one era of ministry, and move forward into new and exciting challenges as together we "share the Spirit."   ♱

Ernest L. Misenheimer, Jr.
Synod President/Bishop
1978-82

George R. Whittecar
Synod President
1963-78

Michael C. D. McDaniel
Synod Bishop
1982-91

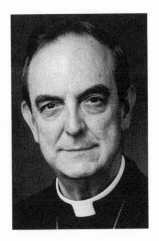

Synod Church House
Klumac Road, Salisbury, N. C.
1962-89

Synod's First Woman Ordinand

Chris Bohr (Fifth from left), with Gene Baker, Herman Yoos, III, James Cone, Ed Tilley, Jeff Cloninger, Bob Hilton, Jeff Lingle, Gene Peeler

June 10, 1979

Charles S. Heilig
Synod Treasurer
1929-75

Edgar R. Trexler, Jr.
Editor, *The Lutheran*
1978-

CHAPTER XI

Epilogue: ELCA in North Carolina (1988-1993)

The 1988 merger brought to North Carolina Lutherans a new synod of 229 congregations. Included in the group were the 213 congregations formerly associated with the LCA.

Although the new synod included no congregations from the merging body of the Association of Evangelical Lutheran Churches, it did contain sixteen congregations formerly associated with the American Lutheran Church.

One of the sixteen congregations was welcomed back into the synod after an absence of 168 years. Old St. Paul's, Newton, organized in 1755, was a charter congregation of the North Carolina Synod in 1803 but joined the Tennessee Synod in the 1820 division. Later, in 1848, it aligned itself with the Tennessee Synod, Reorganized, and thereby became associated, in 1884, with the Joint Synod of Ohio, a predecessor of the American Lutheran Church.

Six of the other new congregations also came to the North Carolina Synod by way of the Joint Synod of Ohio: Miller's, Hickory (1840); Mt. Pisgah, Hickory (1859); St. Mark's, Claremont (1887); St. Luke's, Taylorsville (1892); Mt. Zion, Conover (1893); and St. Paul's, Hickory (1901).

The other ALC congregations joining the North Carolina Synod in the merger included: Christ, Greensboro (1959); Good Shepherd, Charlotte (1960); Grace, Raleigh (1963); Abiding Saviour, Durham (1965); Resurrection, Rocky Mount (1976); Mountainside, Robbinsville (1982); Family of Faith, Harrisburg (1983); Church of the Saviour, Newland (1983); and Abiding Saviour, Asheville (1987).

Other Changes

In addition to the former ALC congregations, the merger brought other changes.

Some were simple changes in terminology. The Executive Board of the synod became the "Synod Council." The annual synod convention became the synod "assembly." Districts became "conferences" - again. The synodical headquarters address, on a street named for a motel, was changed to "1988 Lutheran Synod Drive." The national church office was no longer called New York, but Chicago.

Other changes were more substantive. A new elective office of vice-president was created, to be filled by a lay person who served as presiding officer of the Synod Council. Also, the synod became a constituent of a second seminary, Trinity Seminary in Columbus, Ohio, and an additional camping/conference facility, Lutherock, near Newland.

Some adjustments were learned by trial and error. Despite good intentions, the constituting convention failed to elect the prescribed mix of men and women to the Synod Council: in its effort to insure adequate female representation, the convention elected too many women. Consequently, the Synod Council, at its initial meeting, found it necessary to unseat two women and replace them with men.

The first annual assembly, held at Lenoir-Rhyne in May 1988, reported registration figures hinting at the size and vitality of the new synod. The attendance of 884 included 305 ordained pastors, 395 lay delegates, ten associates in ministry and 174 registered visitors. In contrast with prior years, ministers were outnumbered: they constituted only forty-three percent of the voters, as compared to fifty-six percent the year before.

Staff

The North Carolina Synod of the Evangelical Lutheran Church in America came into being on January 1, 1988, with three changes in leadership. Elected to the vice-president position was the Tar Heel who served on the national Commission for a New Lutheran Church, Dr. Katherine O. Conrad of Epiphany, Winston-Salem. The native of Columbia, South Carolina, was a teacher and former president of the synodical Lutheran Church Women.

Serving as secretary of the new synod was Margaret Winter of Grace, Raleigh, a realtor and former president of the American Lutheran Church Women. Assuming the treasurer position was Donald W. Moose of Faith, Faith, a graphics company owner.

The new synod elected as its first bishop the Rev. Michael C. D. McDaniel. His reappointments of his former staff - James A. Chesky, Rev. Mark W. Menees, Rev. Richard J. Goeres and Dr. Leonard H. Bolick - were confirmed by the new Synod Council.

The year of 1989 marked the first sabbatical leave granted to the synod's chief executive. McDaniel was granted leave for the first quarter of the year to accept an invitation to lecture at Oxford University on "Lutheran Theology in the Light of the Ecumenical Movement." While serving in that capacity, he represented the Lutheran World Federation on the Lutheran Council of Great Britain. He also tutored Oxford undergraduates in Reformation history.

In May of the same year, the synod assembly authorized the replacement of the headquarters building at a cost of $1,240,760. The replacement was needed to provide additional space and avoid the need to substitute new material for the potentially-dangerous asbestos in the old building.

The new structure provided twice as much space. In addition to offices for the staff, the building included conference rooms, a chapel, media center, combination mailroom and printroom, a lunchroom and refreshment center, and an archives room with adjacent research area.

Later the same year, Pastor Goeres resigned to accept a call to a South Carolina parish and was succeeded by the synod's first female assistant to the bishop. Sister Carol Burk, a graduate of Southern Seminary and a deaconess on the staff of St. Andrew's, Hickory, since 1984, assumed the position serving primarily as director of the synodical multimedia center. Also joining the staff was Rev. Maria-Alma R. Copeland, the first black female ordained by the ALC, who assumed duties as director of multicultural ministries. A native of Gastonia, Copeland graduated from Pacific Lutheran University and Luther Northwestern Seminary before her 1985 ordination by the ALC's Ohio District.

In 1991, McDaniel declined to run for re-election as bishop. The three-term bishop announced prior to the assembly that he had accepted an offer to return to the faculty of Lenoir-Rhyne and to create a Center for Theology.

For its new bishop, the 1991 assembly turned to the senior ordained member of the staff, Rev. Mark W. Menees. The second youngest ELCA bishop at age 41, Menees had served on the McDaniel team since 1982. A native of Tennessee, he was a theological graduate of Vanderbilt University who began his ministry as a Methodist pastor before his ordination by the Lutheran church in 1979. Before joining the synodical staff, he served as one of the pastors of Mt. Olive, Hickory.

At the same assembly, Dr. Jane P. Mitcham of Charlotte, a native of Statesville serving as a staff member of Lutheran Family Services, was elected to succeed Conrad as vice-president. Several months later, however, she accepted an appointment to the full-time staff of the synod, relinquishing her vice-president position to Faith Ashton of Chapel Hill. Ashton, a member of Christus Victor, Durham, was a university research analyst and also president of the synodical women's organization. Elected to succeed Secretary Winter was Rev. Daphne L. Burt, a 1987 ordinand of the Southeastern Synod serving as pastor of Bethany, Boone. Assuming the duties of treasurer was H. D. Fry, Jr., of St. Stephen's, Hickory, succeeding Mr. Moose who declined re-election.

In the ranks of the full-time staff, Bolick was the only carry-over from the McDaniel team. Chesky, Burk and Copeland were succeeded by Rev. George L. Rhyne of Salisbury, Rev. Elizabeth K. Kearney of Winston-Salem, and Dr. Jane P. Mitcham. Rhyne, a 1977 ordinand, was called from service as pastor of St. Mark's, Salisbury. Kearney, a 1981 ordinand, was assistant pastor of Epiphany, Winston-Salem.

Synodical Alignments

The ELCA structure introduced with the 1988 merger a new ingredient in the form of regional organizations of synods. The region served congregations, synods and the national church, and facilitated programs for missions.

The North Carolina Synod became a part of Region IX which included also the Virginia, South Carolina, Southeastern, Florida and Carribean synods. Among the nine regions of the ELCA, the southeastern ranked eighth in size and second in giving per capita. It was described as the fastest-growing region and characterized by more diversity in color and language. Dorothy Jeffcoat, stationed in Atlanta, served the region as coordinator.[1]

The synod's outreach beyond ELCA synods extended early to the Lutheran Church - Missouri Synod. The new North Carolina Synod, at its first assembly in 1988, endorsed the continuation of the Forum for Theological Discussions. The discussions were begun in 1985 at Ebenezer, Greensboro, under the leadership of Dr. David J. Ludwig, a Missouri Synod clergyman and psychology professor at Lenoir-Rhyne, and continued in the new church under the chairmanship of Dr. J. Larry Yoder, ELCA pastor and religion professor at Lenoir-Rhyne. Two parties to the discussions, the LCA synod and the ALC district, were themselves merged into the ELCA in 1988, but their new entity, by this action, indicated a desire to continue discussions with the Missouri Synod district. Purposes of the discussions were to enhance the relationship, increase the understanding, and intensify the witness of Lutherans in the region.[2]

Three years later, the relations were symbolized in a ceremony before the 1991 assembly in the signing of a covenant citing twelve points promoting understanding and cooperation. Joining Bishop McDaniel in the ceremony was Dr. Richard T. Hinz of Washington, D. C., district president of the Missouri Synod. The document was the only such covenant between Missouri Synod and ELCA members anywhere in the world.

The synod also affirmed its interest in Episcopalian relations during the initial assembly. On the recommendation of the Committee on Ecumenism, the assembly approved participation in a joint Lutheran-Episcopal study of the document, "Implications of the Gospel," the third document of the national Lutheran-Episcopal Dialog released in April of the same year. Plans were drawn for the study group, or groups, to meet monthly from September 1988 to January 1989, then lead parish or congregational groups in Lenten study during the following February and March.

In addition, the 1989 assembly adopted a Lutheran-Episcopal Covenant declaring cooperative interests of the synod with the Episcopal Diocese of Western North Carolina.

At the same 1989 assembly, the delegates heard a rare ecumenical presentation which included two Roman Catholic bishops. Participating in the panel with Bishop McDaniel were the Most Rev. John F. Donoghue of the Charlotte Diocese and the Most Rev. Joseph Gossman of the Raleigh Diocese.

Two years later, the three bishops signed a covenant describing sixteen activities promoting Lutheran-Catholic understanding and cooperation. The signing took place in a special service on Pentecost Sunday, May 19, 1991, at First, Greensboro. This was the second such covenant in the nation to be approved between Catholics and Lutherans, the first having been signed the previous year by the Lutheran and Catholic bishops of Chicago.

In the same year, the synod negotiated an agreement with the AME Zion denomination for annual continuing education events to be held for the pastors of both denominations at the AME Zion seminary in Salisbury.

The synod's ecumenical strides under the leadership of Bishop McDaniel were given special recognition in a hymn commissioned by the synod for its 1992 assembly. The hymn, titled after the assembly theme of "God's People, One in Witness," was written by Dr. and Mrs. R. Harold Terry of Macedonia, Burlington, and dedicated in honor of McDaniel "for his distinguished leadership toward church unity."

Synodical Publication

With the merger, the synodical publication, the *North Carolina Lutheran*, ceased to be printed and mailed independently and became an insert for the national publication, *The Lutheran*. The change, recommended as a part of the merger planning by the Task Force on Communications, reduced the costs to congregations which subscribed to both publications on an every-member basis.

Elsie Hamilton continued as editor of the periodical through 1990, when she resigned following nine years in office. Succeeding her as editor was Marsha McLamb, a member of Holy Trinity, Gastonia.

Missions

In its first year as an ELCA synod, North Carolina and Lenoir-Rhyne hosted the ELCA's Global Mission Event, held in July 1988. The event was produced as a "free university," permitting participants to select from dozens of mission presentations and to talk with missionaries and others involved in the mission emphasis of the church.

Keynote speaker was Bishop Dinesh Chandra Gorai of the ecumenical Church of North India. Preacher for the Sunday worship service was the ELCA bishop, Herbert W. Chilstrom of Chicago.

Two years later, the synod joined with the South Carolina Synod to resume sponsorship of the Carolinas Evangelism Conference at St. Mark's, Charlotte, in January 1990. Bishop Chilstrom returned to the synod to help with the event as a co-leader with his wife, Rev. E. Corinne Chilstrom. For the first time, a youth rally was added, and conference planners were overwhelmed when the expected fifty youth swelled to seven hundred.

At the synod assembly four months later, the delegates endorsed the synod's participating in the ELCA's new Companion Church Program, designed to give opportunity for synods to share and learn with a church abroad.   On the recommendation of the Global Mission Committee, the synod entered into an informal association with the Lae District Lutheran Synod of Papua, New Guinea. At the following assembly, in 1991, the bishop of the Papua synod, Rev. Robert Gesungtau, greeted the delegates and presented Bishop McDaniel with a large, hand-carved wooden cross.

Three additional congregations were organized and welcomed into the synod: St. Luke's, Shallotte (1989); Living Waters, Cherokee (1989); and Spirit of Joy, Weddington (1991).

The Home Mission Foundation continued into the new synod to assist new congregations, providing mortgage loans to twenty-nine missions. During the first four years of the new synod, the assets of the foundation increased from $1.7 million to $2.0 million.

Pastors

Coming to the early attention of the new synod were two aspects of pastoral preparation: the call of the ordained ministry, and the call of a congregation.

The need to help young people, and others, respond to the call of the ministry prompted the synod to produce in 1991 a videotape for use in its congregations. Titled "Like Falling in Love," the tape was produced with a thirty-thousand-dollar grant from the Michael Peeler Trust Fund and made available free with promotional posters and a discussion guide to all congregations of the synod, and to the bishops of all ELCA synods.

The merger itself, however, precipitated a change in the timing of the ordination of seminary graduates.   The reason was explained by Rev. David M. Franzen of Durham in commenting on the changes in the ordination approval process. After the merger, he said, the candidates were more likely to receive first calls in any of the church's sixty-five synods. This meant it took longer to complete the call process, and it became less likely that the seminary seniors would be ready for ordination at the time of the synod assembly.[3]

Role of the Laity

The constituting convention for the women's organization in the new synod was held October 2-3, 1987, at First, Greensboro, with more than four hundred in attendance. Formal name of the new organization was "North Carolina Synodical Women's Organization of Women of the Evangelical Lutheran Church in America," sometimes shortened to "North Carolina Women of the ELCA" (WELCA).

Activities of the new organization were divided into three program areas: growth, community and action. Seventy percent of the annual budget, totaling $155,550 in 1990, was transmitted to the churchwide organization.

The new organization assumed responsibility for administering the Patterson Memorial Fund, which in 1992 awarded more than twenty-seven thousand dollars in scholarship grants.

Assuming the WELCA presidency in 1988 and serving in the office for four years was Faith Ashton of Christus Victor, Durham. She was succeeded in 1992 by Kaye Beaty, a member of Holy Trinity, Gastonia.

The women continued the tradition of predecessor bodies in contributing leadership to the national organization. Esther Arne of St. James, Fayetteville, was elected treasurer at the first national triennial convention, held in 1990 in Anaheim, California.

Although the women entered the merger from a position of strength, the youth were caught in the early stages of re-organization. The two-year-old Lutheran Youth in North Carolina (LYNC), LCA, with its retiring president, Tammy Jones of Shelby, presiding, formed the nucleus for the constituting convention of the Lutheran Youth Organization, ELCA. It also elected to go with the same name: Lutheran Youth in North Carolina.

The convention, held July 23-24, 1987, at Lenoir-Rhyne, resulted in the election of Nancy Snyder of Holy Trinity, Raleigh, as first president. Succeeding her in office were Marc Hewitt of First, Greensboro (elected in 1988), Cathy Summer of St. John's, Cherryville (1989); Erin Cram of St. Mark's, Asheville (1990); Christopher Johnson of A Mighty Fortress, Charlotte (1991); Omar Bell of Abiding Savior, Durham (1992); and Bryan Phillips of Good Shepherd, Raleigh (1993).

Two representatives of the synodical youth, from the same family, were elected to national offices during the convention of the ELCA Lutheran Youth Organization in San Antonio in 1988. Boua Sy Ly was elected vice president, and her younger brother, Nhia, was elected to a three-year term on the Multicultural Advisory Committee. The native Laotians immigrated with their parents to the United States in 1976 and joined the congregation of First, Albemarle.

The men's synodical organization retained the name of "North Carolina Lutheran Men" at its 1987 constituting convention. But the name gave way the following year when the national organization held its constituting convention and adopted the name "Lutheran Men in Mission." Thereafter, the synodical group used the name of "North Carolina Lutheran Men in Mission."

Harry O. Arne of Fayetteville, elected first president of the synodical group, resigned in mid-1988 when he was elected first president of the national organization. At the synodical level, the unexpired term of Arne was completed by Harry W. Blume of Calvary, Concord, former vice-president of the organization. Blume continued in office for an additional year until he was replaced in 1990 by John L. Barger of Bethlehem, Hickory, who in turn was succeeded by Clarence L. Pugh of St. Andrew's, Hickory, elected in 1993.

The North Carolina LMIM was supported by chartered congregational units ranging in number from 106 in 1990 to 108 in 1991. Its annual budget ranged from $16,447 in 1990 to $19,042 in 1992.

At the national men's organization level, Arne gave presidential leadership for four years. In addition to his initial election in 1988 at Texas Lutheran College, he was elected to a second two-year term at the LMIM biennial assembly at Newberry College in 1990.

Institutions

Lenoir-Rhyne, the synod's college, entered the early years of the ELCA period with student enrollments ranging from 1584 in 1987 to 1659 two years later, then dropping to 1617 in 1991. The budget grew from $13.4 to $19.8 million; assets advanced from thirty million dollars to forty-four million; the endowment increased from ten million dollars to nineteen million.

The endowment growth was aided by a 1991 synodwide campaign for two million dollars. The gifts were used to fund the Martin Luther Scholarship Endowment to provide financial assistance to North Carolina Lutheran students attending the college.

At the Southern Seminary in Columbia, South Carolina, enrollments ranged from 160 to 170 with continued growth in the number of women students. Women, who constituted thirty-five percent of the enrollment in 1988, increased to forty-four and fifty percent the following two years before dropping back to forty-two percent in 1991. Expenditures increased from $2.0 to $2.5 million. Total assets in 1990 amounted to $12.6 million, including an endowment of six million dollars.

The seminary's Lutheran Theological Center in Atlanta became a joint venture in 1990 of Southern Seminary and Trinity Seminary. When the director, Dr. Carl Ficken of Southern, took a sabbatical leave in early 1990, his substitute was Rev. Rudolph R. Featherstone of Trinity.

Presidential leadership at the seminary changed with the retirement of Dr. Mack C. Branham, Jr., in August 1992. His successor in office was Rev. H. Frederick Reisz, Jr., senior pastor at University Lutheran Church in Cambridge, Massachusetts.

A part of the synod's merger process in 1988 was getting acquainted with its second seminary, Trinity. The Ohio institution, formed in a 1978 merger of Hamma Divinity School of Springfield and Evangelical Theological Seminary in Columbus, enrolled 265 students, including two from the North Carolina Synod. Thirty percent of the students were female, and fifty percent were "second career" students. The twenty-six-member faculty was headed by President Frederick W. Meuser, III, who was succeeded shortly thereafter by Rev. Dennis A. Anderson.

Joining the North Carolina Synod's clerical roll were two members of the Trinity staff: Dr. Paul Harms, professor of homilectics; and Dr. James M. Childs, Jr., academic dean. The elected synodical representative to the Trinity governing board was Dr. Marcus C. Smith of Salisbury, who served later as chairman of the board.

Another institution introduced to the synod by the merger was Lutherock, a 420-acre mountain camping and conference facility near Newland operated by some of the ALC congregations prior to the merger. For three years, Lutherock continued to operate as a separate facility under the direction of the ALC director, Rev. Mark P. Radloff.

In 1991, Lutherock merged with Lutheridge, to create Lutheridge/Lutherock Ministries, Inc., supported jointly by the North Carolina, South Carolina, Southeastern and Florida synods. Assuming duties as executive director of the parent company was

Rev. F. Wayne Williams, former camp director for the Virginia Synod. At Lutherock, Radloff continued as director. At Lutheridge, Dr. Robert L. Troutman, whose resignation after twenty-two years as executive director coincided with the merger, was succeeded by Fred L. Park of Nativity, Arden, in the retitled post of director.

The program of Lutheran Outdoor Ministries, with Rev. David L. Castor as executive director, continued into the ELCA period with the management of Kure Beach Retreat Center and Camp Agape. Approximately thirty-five hundred campers participated in the program each year. Annual expenditures during the period rose from $206,000 to $309,000.

Social Ministry

Lutheran Services for the Aging, aided by the two million dollar "Building for Living" synodical campaign prior to the merger, added two facilities during the ELCA period.

Crescent View Retirement Community, a joint project of LSA and Lutheridge/Lutherock Ministries, opened at Arden in 1991. The rental retirement project offered seventy-eight independent-living apartments and twenty assisted-living units.

Trinity Oaks opened in 1993 adjacent to the Lutheran Nursing Home in Salisbury. Designed as a continuing care retirement community, it contained 125 independent- and twenty assisted-living apartments.

Prior to the opening of Trinity Oaks, the LSA president and chief executive officer, Rev. Robert Q. Beard, retired. At the time, the ministry offered over four hundred beds and employed more than three hundred workers. Forty-five percent of its residents were Lutheran. Assets totaled $21.8 million, and annual operating expenses exceeded ten million dollars.

The LSA statistics did not include those of the Lutheran Retirement Ministries of Alamance County, Twin Lakes. Under the supervision of the executive director, Dr. Clyde J. Christmas, the center added thirty retirement units in 1988 and an additional fifteen in 1989, completing a $2.5 million Independent Living section named Luther Court. The expansion increased the number of retirement units to 110, in addition to the institution's 36 skilled-nursing beds and thirty-seven intermediate-care beds. Assets of the center totaled $14.2 million, and the annual operating expenses were $4.1 million.

Meanwhile, Lutheran Family Services continued to expand its services. In 1990 the name of Lutheran Family Services of North Carolina was changed to Lutheran Family Service of "the Carolinas" to reflect the response the agency had given to a South Carolina Synod request through the opening of counseling centers in that state.

In 1991, the newest program serving developmentally disabled adults was announced. The service was provided through two group homes (in Cherryville and Winston-Salem) for autistic adults, and two other homes (in Ahoskie and Woodland) for developmentally disabled adults.

"It was a great year," reported President Bill D. Brittain of Raleigh. "Our over 400 employees, backed by our church communities, provided services to over 5,000 individuals throughout the Carolinas."

The effectiveness of Lutheran Family Services was recognized outside the church. The service was named 1991 "Agency of the Year" by the National Association of Social Workers in North Carolina. The award was based on service to clients, adherence to the association's code of ethics and contributions to the knowledge base of social work.[4]

The agency, with assets of $2.9 million, experienced 1991 disbursements totaling $11.3 million.

Reflecting its roots in a children's home, the LFS continued to search out children in need. In 1988, four hundred children received care in twenty-three children's homes from Wilmington to Asheville. In addition, seventy trained foster families provided care to 109 children.

"The children in LFS care," Brittain pointed out, "are among the most troubled in the state. Most come from disturbed families where they have been abused or neglected. Many have behavioral problems, learning disabilities, physical handicaps, or are mentally retarded; most have a combination of two or more of these problems. Work with them, and with their families, is both challenging and rewarding."

In addition to the institutional expressions of social ministry, social statements debated and adopted by the annual assembly were used by the synod to address the needs of society.

The needs of minorities reflected a concern the synod attempted to demonstrate in its own practices. The new synod began with a commitment to a five-year goal of ten percent representation by minorities in synod assemblies, councils, committees, boards and other organizational units. The minority representation could be fulfilled either by persons of color or persons whose primary language was other than English.

Acquired Immune Deficiency Syndrome (AIDS) also received attention. At the request of the 1990 assembly, the Social Ministry Committee established an AIDS task force to educate both lay and clergy members of congregations concerning HIV infection and AIDS.

Other social statements debated, but not necessarily adopted, by the assemblies included child abuse (1990), recycling (1991) and violence (1992). In 1993 alone, the assembly debated the the the state sales tax on food, a state lottery and education on child abuse.

Finances

After six years of the ELCA period, the synod reported assets of $3.6 million and annual budget expenditures ranging from $3.4 to $3.7 million. The Michael Peeler Trust Fund, whose assets jumped from $2.8 to $5.2 million, made annual distributions to the synod ranging from $175,000 to $222,000.

In 1988, the synod registered the highest per capita giving to benevolence among the sixty-five synods of the new ELCA. The following year, it contributed to the ELCA one hundred percent of its benevolence share.

Concern within the synod, however, was voiced regarding the level of funding received by its institutions from the ELCA. Both the Southern and Trinity seminaries, as well as Lenoir-Rhyne, reported in 1990 that their church financial support had decreased from pre-merger levels, when the support was provided primarily by the synod. The response of the synod assembly was to memorialize the ELCA to "consider establishing a method of financial support wherein synods make direct contributions to the colleges and seminaries."[5]

With respect to the perennial capital fund campaigns, the new synod shared the disdain of its predecessor. The LCA synod, in its final convention in 1987, expressed a hope the campaigns could be avoided. As an alternative, it proposed the creation of an endowment which would generate income comparable to the amount of gifts typically raised in a capital funds campaign. Institutions or other programs seeking capital funds could apply for grants from the endowment yield rather than conduct synod-wide solicitations.

The concept was reaffirmed in the first year of the new synod when the Synod Endowment Fund, which at the time contained only seven hundred dollars, was boosted with a thirty thousand dollar addition voted by the Synod Council from a 1988 Michael Peeler Trust Fund distribution.

Specific plans for phasing out the campaigns were sketched by the 1990 synod assembly and detailed by the 1991 assembly. The plans called for a one-year interval following the 1991-93 Lenoir-Rhyne campaign and a similar interval following the scheduled Lutheran Family Services appeal in 1994-96. A period of seven years will then be reserved for the final campaign, to be conducted for the benefit of the Synod Endowment Fund. The final year of the campaign will be 2003, when the synod observes the two hundredth anniversary of its founding.

Although the year 2003 will mark the bicentennial of the first Lutheran synod to be founded in North Carolina, it is fitting that this account be closed with events that occurred a little more than a decade prior to that event.

The year 1991 was not only a time of transition in the leadership of the synod, and the centennial of the synod's college, but also the two hundredth anniversary of the first meeting of the Lutheran Ministerium of North Carolina. At that first meeting, the new ministerium ordained a candidate for the ministry on behalf of the Episcopal church; and, although both this pastor and a Moravian pastor were active in the subsequent organization of the North Carolina Synod, it was the first Lutheran synod to be organized on a clear and uncompromising dogmatic foundation.

This extraordinary tradition of confessional ecumenism has been maintained throughout two hundred years in various ways. In their *History of the Evangelical Lutheran Synod and Ministerium of North Carolina*, Bernheim and Cox write:

> That the Synod, as such, held the true Lutheran position, the Word of God, the only and infallible rule of faith and practice, and the confessions of the Church as correct interpretations of that rule, is evident from the fact that in her first Constitution she says (Article IV.): "No one shall be ordained to the ministry until the ministers who examine him are fully satisfied that he has a sufficient and satisfactory acqaintance with the New Testament in the Greek language, his faith (doctrines of the Church), and the Latin language." There can be no question but that the expression "Doctrines of the Church" then meant and had reference to the Lutheran confessions, and hence, in this article of the Constitution, there is the subscription to both Word and confessions... From this position she has never receded. So far as authentic records are concerned, there are no evidences that she ever modified, denied, or rejected any article of the Lutheran faith, but has ever pressed on to a deeper consciousness and a fuller and clearer statement of what she believes.[6]

In their account of "how the Synod gradually developed her Lutheran consciousness, more and more forcibly," the authors go on to report that, at the second annual convention in 1804, a motion was passed to print the Augsburg Confession "so that all members of the congregations may obtain them at small price;" and, when the constitution was revised in 1817, the Augsburg Confession

> was the first officially declared specific confessional basis of the Synod, and it was the first formal and public avowal of the recognition of the Augsburg Confession by any Lutheran Synod in America.[7]

It was thus here, in the foothills of the Blue Ridge Mountains in North Carolina, that the evangelical catholicity of the Augsburg Confession took firm root in American soil; and, the effort to remain faithful to the Word of God and the dogmatic confessions in the Lutheran *Book of Concord* has resulted in the continuing formation of enlightened leadership among both the lay and clergy of the synod. It is precisely the strength of such leadership, and their achievement of excellence in many aspects of Christian life and witness, that has given the synod the necessary confidence to strive for the realization of Christian unity.

As this first two-hundred-year period came to a close, it was not only the case that Lutherans in North Carolina were more nearly "all one body" than ever before, but that those Lutherans were leading the way toward that reunion of all Christians in one body for which Jesus prayed in his great high priestly prayer (John 17): "that they may all be one . . . so that the world may believe that you have sent me."

Although North Carolina Lutherans, like all Christians of every time and place, were sinners in need of forgiveness and, in the final analysis as compared with God's will, "unprofitable servants," it was nevertheless true that to a remarkable degree and in an astonishing variety of aspects, the North Carolina Synod was, by the last decade of the twentieth century, at the forefront of Christian leadership.

In its emphasis upon worship and the centrality of Word and Sacrament as the source of the Christian life, its level of stewardship, its bold leadership in ecumenism, its energetic attention to Christian education, its strong nurture of rising generations, its planting of new missions, and its care for people in every circumstance of life through vibrant social ministry organizations, the North Carolina Synod was faithfully upholding its heritage as the oldest Lutheran synod in continuous existence in the Western Hemisphere.[8]

It is for the remembrance of this great heritage, and with the prayer that those who read it will be inspired to carry it to greater heights still, that this history has been written. May God bless this synod, as He has so richly done in the past, that through all the winds of change that are now so strongly blowing, we and our descendants may stand firm, all one body, in Jesus Christ our Lord.   ☦

Mark W. Menees
Synod Bishop
1991-

Katherine O. Conrad
Synod's First Vice President
1988-91

Lutheran/Roman Catholic Covenant Signing

F. Joseph Gossman, Raleigh Diocese; Michael C. D. McDaniel, Lutheran Synod; John F.
Donoghue, Charlotte Diocese

First, Greensboro
May 19, 1991

NOTES

Chapter I. The Scattering (p. 1)

1. There were approximately 225,000 German-Americans in the Colonies at the outbreak of the American Revolution. It is usually assumed this group represents an immigration of sixty-five to seventy-five thousand, but it may be closer to one hundred thousand. Moltmann, *Germans to America*, p. 9.
2. Muhlenberg, *Journals*, Vol. I, p. 8.
3. *Gottlieb Mittelbergers Reise nach Pennsylvanien im Jahr 1750 und Ruekreise nach Deutschland im Jahr 1754*, quoted in Harmut Bickelmann, "The Venture of Travel," in Moltmann, *Germans to America*, p. 47.

     With the development of steerage and the increasing demand for passenger space, the transportation of colonists became more significant from an economic point of view. Captains were paid according to the number of emigrants they transported, so they crammed into the steerage as many persons as they could. The stench and vermin often began to take their toll of the passengers before the ship left harbor.

     > Under these circumstances many children died, especially with a stormy sea. Indeed, of many families no one survived, neither children nor the parents themselves. In letters from Portsmouth, where the embarkation took place, it was reported to London that upon a single ship even before the departure eighty of the emigrants died. Hundreds of the others lay sick therein and seemed to want to follow the dead. The cause of the mortality could be sought partly in the close crowding and partly in the fact that the shipmaster did not provide the people with good and wholesome food. But even the death of the emigrants meant gain for the shipmaster, for then upon the voyage he had to feed less people. *Pennsylvanien im 17. Jahrhundert*, p. 66 ff., as quoted in Todd, *Von Graffenreid's Account*, p. 51.

4. Holborn, *The Reformation*, p. 322.
5. *Ibid.*
6. Holborn, *1648-1840*, p. [22].
7. Cobb, *German Immigration*, p. 6.
8. The annexation of Alsace was completed in 1681 with Louis' capture of the Imperial city of Strassburg. Carl Hammer, Jr., "Emigration From the Palatinate," in Roscoe Fisher, *Michael Brown*, 2nd ed., 1977, p. 3.
9. Holborn, *1648-1840*, p. 76.
10. *Ibid.*, p. 94.
11. Cobb, *German Immigration*, p. 8.
12. Roeber, *Palatines, Liberty and Property*, pp. 46-47.
13. *Ibid.*, pp. 42-43.
14. Glatfelter, *Pastors and People*, Vol. I, pp. 59, 61; Vol. II, p. 19. DeMoulin-Eckart, *Geschichte Der Deutchen Universitaten*, p. 275.
15. Including the following Henkels: Paul, Benjamin, John, Joseph, Solomon, Philip Augustus, Ambrose, Andrew, David, Charles, Polycarp Cyprian, Socrates, and David Melanchthon;

and these Stirewalts: Paul Jacob Melanchthon, Julius Luther Quintilian, Quintius Spiner Vespasian, John Nathaniel, Jerome Paul, Arthur Julius, Martin Luther, Jr., and Martin Luther, Sr.; compiled from Junkin and Junkin, *Henckel Family Geneaology;* and [Norman,] *Life Sketches.*

16.   Knittle, *Palatine Emigration,* p. 4.

17.   Bailyn, *Peopling,* p. 69.

18.   Hammer, *Rhinelanders on the Yadkin,* p. 22.
       The "newlanders" often found their work facilitated by the circulation of pamphlets and books such as Pastor Joshua Kockerthal's description of South Carolina and how to get there published in German in 1706. Kockerthal (d. 1719) had not visited America when he wrote his widely circulated pamphlet, but the pamphlet was so influential that a predecessor of Ziegenhagen at the German Court Chapel (St. James) in London, Rev. Anton Wilhelm Boehme wrote a series of tracts to correct impressions created by Kockerthal's work. Boehme's pamphlets were published in book form under the title *Das verlangte nicht erlangte Canaan.* Todd, *Von Graffenried's Account,* pp. 13-14.

19.   Eisenberg, *Lutheran Church in Virginia,* p. 3.

20.   Sheftall, *Germans in the Southeast,* p. 9.

21.   An account of this attempt at colonization is found in Section 9, Chapter I, of Bernheim, *German Settlements.* See also Sheftall, *Germans in the Southeast,* pp. 10-11.

22.   Cobb, *German Immigration,* p. 8.

23.   Faust, *German Element,* Vol. I, p. 58. Faust argues that there were five major causes of German immigration in the eighteenth century: (1) religious persecutions, (2) the tyranny of autocratic rulers, (3) destructive wars, (4) crop failure and famine, and (5) economic bankruptcy. *Ibid.,* p. 60.

24.   Knittle, *Palatine Emigration,* pp. 6-11. Knittle notes that religious disputes played a part in the complex of factors prompting emigration, but argues convincingly against ranking religious persecution as the primary factor.

25.   Muhlenberg, *Journals,* I, p. 28. Muhlenberg notes that there were reportedly two hundred "Palatines" on an English ship anchored near his own, but that he is not really sure "what kind of Germans" are on the other ship since "the English call everybody who comes from Germany and Holland 'Palatines'."

26.   Holborn, *The Reformation,* p. 323.

27.   Linn, "The Salzburgers," p. 26.

28.   Holborn, *The Reformation,* p. 368.

29.   Wentz, "Salt," p. 23.

30.   Cobb, *German Immigration,* p. 9.

Chapter II. A Move Toward Unity (p. 13)

1.   Clay, Orr and Stuart, *North Carolina Atlas,* pp. 5-6.

2.   In explaining the failure of the Germans as a group to assume "cultural importance" for the South as a whole, Randall M. Miller observes, "German immigration to the South encompassed too broad a time span, was too irregular, and drew from too many diverse sources within 'Germany' to impose a single cultural order anywhere. Still, large numbers of Germans settled in the southern region from the colonial period through the nineteenth century, and within their areas of concentration they built and maintained German subcultures that thrived into the modern era in several instances, at least in attenuated forms." Randall Miller, "Germans," p. 429.

3.   Faust, *The German Element,* Vol. I, p. 7.

4. Williamson, *North Carolina*, Vol. I, p. 277.

5. Todd., *Von Graffenreid's Account*, p. 225.

6. *Ibid.*, p. 318.

7. The Pennsylvania statute is quoted in Lefler and Newsome, *North Carolina*, 3rd. ed., 1973, p. 63.

8. Bailyn, *Peopling*, p. 109.

9. Holloman, "Early Settlers," p. 61.

10. Eisenberg, *Lutheran Church in Virginia*, p. 17. Eisenberg helpfully reprints the entire document, "Mary Pool vs John Caspar Stoever."

    Biographical sketches of Stoever and his son appear in Glatfelter, *Pastors and People*, pp. 138-43.

11. Kornegay, *Kornegay History*, p. 6. The structure was designated "the Palatine Church or the High German Chapel." Kornegay quotes from the Craven County Deeds for 1740.

    The headwaters of the Trent are located east of U.S. Highway 258 just south of Jonestown in Jones County. Its meandering course roughly parallels N.C. Highway 41 in a northeasterly arc almost to Pollocks on the edge of Great Lover Swamp. Then it swings southeasterly through Trenton to Pollocksville, then turns northeasterly toward Rhems and New Bern.

12. More than forty Palatine protesters of this action dispatched a petition to King George II in July 1747. Holloman, "Early Settlers," p. 61, where the names of the petitioners are listed.

13. Sheftall, *Germans in the Southeast*, p. 8.

14. Eisenberg, *Lutheran Church in Virginia*, p. [5].

15. Linn, "Salzburgers," pp. 41-42.

16. Bailyn, *Peopling*, p. 113.

17. J[acobs], *Lutheran Cyclopedia*, p. 265. Joshua Kocherthal's German pamphlet was in its fourth edition by 1709. Cf., Todd, *Von Graffenreid's Account*, pp. 13-14.

18. Strobel, *The Salzburgers*, p. 64. The site was immediately adjacent to land claimed by an Indian tribe, so the governor envisioned his new colonists as providing a helpful buffer of protection for the more heavily populated coastal area. After two years, the chief Salzburger settlement was relocated several miles closer to the Savannah River since experience showed that the original site was unhealthy, quite apart from the danger of Indian attack. Sheftall, *Germans in the Southeast*, p. 18.

19. The third group of Salzburgers were accompanied by other immigrants including Protestants from England and Scotland as well as some Moravians. Two Anglican missionaries, John and Charles Wesley, were also on this ship. Governor Oglethorpe hoped to settle this group of immigrants at Frederica on St. Simons Island as a buffer against the Spaniards in Florida. Most of the Salzburgers ended up joining the Ebenezer settlement, but a few volunteered to join the group going to Frederica. *Ibid.*, p. 19. The Spanish threat was removed after 1742, and ten years later Frederica was a deserted village.

20. George Whitefield to Thomas Jones, Sept. 18, 1740, quoted in Strobel, *Salzburgers*, pp. 111-12.

21. Muhlenberg, *Journals*, Vol.I, p. 60. Muhlenberg had been asked by the "Reverend Fathers" at Halle to visit the Salzburgers and invite Pastor Bolzius to accompany him to Pennsylvania and help him get established there. As it turned out, Bolzius accompanied him only as far north as Charleston, South Carolina.

22. *Ibid.* The modest church building that Muhlenberg admired was replaced with a permanent structure erected during the period 1767-69.

    The leaders of the Salzburger settlement, Pastors Boltzius and Gronau, found a kindred spirit in Muhlenberg: "We are very fond of our dear Mr. Muhlenberg...," Boltzius noted in the journal kept by the Georgia pastors. Gronau said of Muhlenberg's visit, "We have never had such a blessed period in Ebenezer." George Jones, *Detailed Reports,* Vol. 9, pp. 209, 212.

23.   The article is cited by W. Richard Fritz, "Beginnings--Before 1803," in McCullough, *Lutheran Church in South Carolina,* p. 21.

24.   "Historic Philadelphia," in Tait, *1976 Bulletin Almanac,* p. 283.

25.   This means of describing the location of German settlements in Penn's colony is based on that developed by Philip S. Klein and Ari Hoogenboom, *A History of Pennsylvania.* New York: McGraw-Hill, 1973, p. 37, as cited in Baltzell, *Puritan Boston,* p. 116.

26.   Maldwyn Jones, *American Immigration,* p. 29.

27.   Guenter Moltmann, "German Migration to America in the Colonial Period and the Redemptioner System," in Moltman, *Germans to America,* p. 30.

28.   Eisenberg, *Lutheran Church in Virginia,* pp. 20-21.

29.   Meining, *Shaping of America,* p. 289.

30.   Bailyn, *Voyagers,* pp. 14-15. In addition to the "Great Philadelphia Road" just described, some elected to go southward from Lancaster, Pennsylvania, to Frederick, Maryland, and thence to Warrenton and Amelia Court House in Virginia. Those taking this route then proceeded on south and entered North Carolina, passing near present day Oxford and Hillsborough. Anderson, *Foundations,* pp. 3-5.

31.   Bailyn, *Voyagers,* pp. 15-16.

32.   Sherrill, *Annals of Lincoln County,* p. 8. Preslar, *Catawba County,* p. 19. Conrad Yoder "became the founder of the Yoder family in North Carolina." Yoder, *Yoder Family,* pp. 5-7.

Gary Freeze in his new history of Catawba County observes that "in 1747, only about forty households were to be found anywhere west of the Yadkin River, an area reaching back about thirty miles to the north and east. Within four years the number would more than double between the Yadkin and the Catawba, but only a few families joined the Sherrills at their four homesteads beyond the [Catawba] river. Most of these were Germans who followed Henry Weidner to Jacob's Fork.

In the first eight years of settlement ... about sixty families, according to various estimates, settled to the west of the river in what is today Catawba, Lincoln, Gaston, and Cleveland counties." Ms., chap. 1, pp. 16-17.

33.   Letter dated Aug. 24, 1755, *Colonial Records,* Vol. V, p. 356; quoted in Hammer, *Rhinelanders,* pp. 78-79.

34.   The first group of Moravians to settle in North Carolina consisted of twelve young men who came to the tract called Wachovia in November 1753 from Pennsylvania. The following year the original twelve at Bethabara were joined by additional settlers, and in 1759 a second community, Bethania, was begun three miles from Bethabara. When the first group of Moravians colonists arrived directly from Europe, they were given the challenge of creating Salem "which was intended for a manufacturing town." Williamson, *North Carolina,* Vol. 2, pp. 72-78.

35.   R. D. W. Conner was convinced there was at least one Lutheran congregation near the Haw River as early as 1745, but whether the congregation was Frieden's, Gibsonville; St. Paul's, Alamance; or Low's, Liberty, is not clear. Morgan, *Lutheran Church in NC,* p. 19.

36.   Dr. Thomas J. Haupert, Director of The Moravian Archives in Winston-Salem, notes that, with Salem as his base, Soelle's tours took him approximately eighty miles northeast of Salem, eighty miles west, forty miles southwest, and sixty miles southeast. His travels are recorded in "Diary of the Rev. George Soelle, March 23, 1771-April 12, 1773," a translation by Kenneth G. Hamilton which, along with the original diary, is in The Moravian Archives.

It may be that Soelle considered himself a member of both the Lutheran church and the Unity of Brethren. As early as 1744 Zinzendorf developed his concept of Tropen, a term derived from the Greek tropoi peideias, "methods of training." "He believed that the evangelical churches were one in essentials but that each possessed its own special talent for training souls in accordance with its traditions. Hence there should properly be a Lutheran, a Reformed, and a Moravian 'trope'-later even a Methodist-within the Unity of Brethren, so that souls would be educated for eternity in conformity with the peculiar emphasis of each." Hamilton and Hamilton, *Moravian Church,* p. 101.

37. It was also reported in Weis, *Colonial Clergy,* p. 94, that Wortmann served Lutherans in Savannah, Georgia, in 1760-61, before taking up his Charleston ministry. Documentation for this ministry was not discovered by C. A. Linn in preparing his history of the Lutheran Church of the Ascension. Linn, *Two Hundred Years.*

Wortmann's mobility and short pastorates presumably related to Muhlenberg's characterization of him as "a powerful speaker in the pulpit, but in his social relations he was a hot-tempered bully and battler." Muhlenberg, *Journals,* Vol. II, p. 319.

38. By September 1810 Laurentz was employed by Ambrose Henkel to assist with the Henkel Press, and young Wortmann should be credited with transforming the New Market business from a "rather amateurish printery into a going concern." Quoted in Dolmetsch, *German Press,* p. 22.

Whether Wortmann, Soelle, or Peter Brugell should be recognized as the first regularly ordained Lutheran pastor to reside in North Carolina is a question not easily resolved. W. T. Whitsett reported in his pamphlet, *Pioneer Lutherans in North Carolina,* p. 22, that a Pastor Samuel Burgell preached to Lutherans on the Haw River prior to his move to Virginia in 1755. Eisenberg was not able to identify Samuel Burgell, but appropriately noted the similarity to the name of a pastor, Peter M. Brugell, who was serving the New River settlement in southwest Virginia in 1788. Eisenberg, *Lutheran Church in Virginia,* p. 99.

39. McCullough, *Lutheran Church in SC,* p. 27.

40. Leonard, *Southern Synod,* p. 20.

41. Gary Freeze suggests the possibility of the celebratory service in 1764, the building project having apparently been launched in 1759 or 1760. Paul and Froney Anthony deeded ten acres to the "christian churches Lutarin and Presbetaren" in 1771. Ms., chap. 1, pp. 33-34.

42. Wall, *Davie County,* pp. 241-42. The Cattons, in describing the removal of Daniel Boone's family from Pennsylvania to the Shenandoah Valley to this area where Soelle ministered describe it as "the wild Yadkin River country of frontier North Carolina...," an apt characterization. Catton, *Two Roads,* p. 13.

43. On Aug. 21, 1768, Governor Tryon worshipped with Pastor Suther and the Cold Water congregation. The governor was sufficiently impressed with Suther's sermon to appoint Suther chaplain to the Rowan and Mecklenburg battalions of the militia. Bostian and Cruse, *Dutch Buffalo Creek,* pp. 44-45.

Suther, twelve siblings and their parents set out for America in 1739. The father and two daughters died and were buried in England. Samuel was the only member of the family to survive an unusually harrowing crossing of the Atlantic, one that consumed four months and involved weathering thirteen storms. When he grew to adulthood, Suther went to Pennsylvania where he became a parochial school teacher in Philadelphia and, later, in Germantown. It is also reported that he taught in Maryland, Virginia, and Georgia, as well as Carolina. Leonard, *Southern Synod,* p. 129. From 1751 to 1760, he was in the German settlement in Orangeburg District, South Carolina, presumably as a teacher. He may have been studying theology under the local Reformed pastor, John Giessendanner, at the same time. McCullough, *Lutheran Church in SC,* p. 13. Glatfelter, *Pastors and People,* Vol. II, p. 172.

44. Leonard, *Southern Synod*, p. 130. Leonard suggests that it was probably such attacks on Lutheran doctrine and Suther's strong words, growing out of his perception that the Lutherans did not share his ardent patriotism, that led to his being "excluded from Low's Church." A number of members of Brick Church were participants in the disastrous battle of Alamance. "The Reformed members almost to a man were at one with the preacher in his patriotic sentiments."

45. The Anglican priest, Theodorus Drage, identified the German petitioners as persons on Second Creek. He made no mention of petitioners in neighboring Mecklenburg County, and when Johann Bohl of The Hague presented Rintelmann and Layrle with a host box for use in communion services in North Carolina, the engraving on it indicates it was "presented to the Ev. Lutheran Church in Rowan Co. in North America." However, it has often been assumed that the petitioners represented not only Second Creek in Rowan, the Hickory Church that gave birth to Zion (Organ), but the Dutch Buffalo Creek (St. John's, Concord) settlement as well. The assumption that the Mecklenburg Germans participated in the embassy to secure a resident pastor for southern Rowan may be related to the fact that the Lutheran pastor secured through these efforts, Adolph Nussmann, served Organ for only one year before removing to St. John's, Concord, where he spent the remainder of his ministry and life. A German with whom Nussmann corresponded, J. C. Velthusen, seems to have understood that the Dutch Buffalo Creek congregation "consented to" the attempt to secure a pastor in Europe.

   Again, it has often been assumed that Rintelmann was a member of the Hickory Church, while Layrle came from Dutch Buffalo Creek. However, it has not been possible to confirm Layrle's identification with Dutch Buffalo Creek, and his ownership of land in Rowan County suggests he may have been a member of the Hickory Church, or the church in Salisbury. Layrle's suggested identification with St. John's, Concord, may grow out of the fact that his son, Christopher, was a member of that congregation. Bostian, *Dutch Buffalo Creek*, p. 34.

46. Ruth Blackwelder provided the sketch on Nussmann which appears in [Norman,] *Life Sketches*, pp. 1-4. The sketch appearing in the Powell, *Dictionary of NC Biography,* Vol. 4, pp. 381-82, was prepared by Gary C. Roth.

   After arriving in North Carolina, Nussmann married a daughter of Christopher Rintelmann. His first wife died after providing him with three children. As a second wife, Nussmann married a daughter of Christopher Layrle who bore him four children.

47. With the perennial shortage of properly educated and certified clergy, it is understandable that congregations would often be victimized by pretenders to the clerical office and former clergy who had been removed from office in Germany. Rev. Christian Eberhard Bernhardt who came to Rowan County in 1787 spoke of wandering preachers, "men who, like roaming knights, traverse the land, and after no longer being able to make their living because of the evil conduct of their profession -- become preachers." Quoted Cline, "Adolph Nussmann."

   An early constitution of St. John's, Concord, resolved that the congregation should "have nothing to do with the vagrant preachers in this land, who are either unlearned intruders or educated men deposed in Germany." Calhoon, *Religion and American Revolution,* p. 34.

48. In a biographical essay on Arends, George W. Shuford notes that, despite the survival of a copy of the information contained on Arend's ordination certificate, the precise date of his ordination is still open to question. [Norman,] *Life Sketches,* p. 8. W. Richard Fritz demonstrates that there is also reason to question the site of the ordination, even though the copy of the ordination certificate carries the address, "Second Creek, Rowan County, N. C." McCullough, *Lutheran Church in SC,* pp. 89-92. While many questions remain

concerning Buelow and the ordination, the validity of the ordination seems not to have been questioned, not even by Nussmann. Nothing has come to light to explain Buelow's use of the title "Missionary and Inspector over South and North Carolina."

49. Escott and Crow, "Social Order," p. 374.

   For a helpful description of the manner in which the conflict impacted Germans on the North Carolina frontier, see the section "Securing the Revolution: Conflict and Combat," in Chapter 1 of the new Gary Freeze *History of Catawba County.*

50. Bernheim, *German Settlements,* p. 270.

51. McCullough, *Lutheran Church in SC,* p. 94.

52. Dolmetsch, *German Press,* p. 6.

53. Austin Allran, "John Godfrey Arends," in Powell, *Dictionary of NC Biography,* Powell, Vol. I, p. 40.

54. Steffey, *St. John's, Cabarrus County,* p. 10.

55. Moose, *Adolph Nussmann,* p. 8.

56. A second edition of the catechism ran to 254 pages. Widely circulated among Lutherans in North Carolina, it was known as the North Carolina Catechism.

57. An early sketch of Storch by Sprague appears in Jensson, *American Lutheran Biographies,* pp. 768-69. Storch expanded his ministry to include what is now Lutheran Chapel, China Grove, in Jan., 1789. Phillips, *Lutheran Chapel,* p. 3.

58. Velthusen reported that Roschen, who had relatives in Charleston, was so eager to serve as a missionary in Carolina that he offered to pay his own way to America. Boyd and Krummel, "German Tracts," No. 1, p. 121. Roschen was convinced that "An American wife is in our circumstances infinitely better adapted" than a spouse brought over from Europe. *Ibid.,* p. 126. Roschen's letters to Germany provide many insights into life in the Carolinas in the last decade of the eighteenth century. His trip from Charleston to Davidson County is described in Boyd, "German Tracts," No. 2, p. 242.

59. Holborn, *1648-1840,* p. 139.

60. Pellens, "North Carolina and Niedersachsen," p. 35.

61. Strobel, *Salzburgers,* p. 222.

62. Anderson, "First Synodical Organization," p. 282. Strobel accounts for the respected career of Bernhardt after leaving Ebenezer by saying Bernhardt "was converted" after he moved to Carolina. Strobel, *Salzburgers,* p. 223.

63. Eisenberg, *Lutheran Church in Virginia,* p. 100.

64. Anderson, "First Synodical Organization," p. 283, footnote 12.

65. Finck, "Paul Henkel," p. 27.

66. *Ibid.,* p. 28.

67. The Presbyterian revival in the area reportedly began in mid-August at Cross Roads Presbyterian Church to the north of the present site of Mebane in Alamance County. Some weeks later it began to make its impact at Hawfields Presbyterian Church to the south of Mebane, then moved into Guilford, Rowan and Iredell counties. Keever, "Lutheran Preacher's Account," p. 41.

68. The crowd that gathered for the services was astonishingly large for that time and place, but reports of 20,000 to 25,000 are probably exaggerated. Weisberger, *They Gathered,* p. 31.

69. *Ibid.*

70. Finck, "Paul Henkel," p. 29.

71. *Ibid.*

72. Heidelberg was located east of the present site of Mocksville. A few years after Henkel left the parish in 1805, the congregation relocated in the Jerusalem community south of Mocksville on the road to Salisbury, at the same time taking a new name for the congregation, New Jerusalem. Still later the congregation moved about two miles east of

the Jerusalem community and established Reformation Lutheran Church, popularly known as Cherry Hill. Morgan, *Lutheran Church in NC,* pp. 190-91. Wall, *Davie County,* pp., 35-36, 238-39.

73.   Finck, "Paul Henkel," p. 32. Camp meetings were held by Presbyterians and Methodists in North Carolina before the turn of the century. Rehobeth Church in Catawba County dates its camp meeting tradition from 1794 when Daniel Asbury, William McKendree, William Walters and other preachers united in conducting a camp meeting under Methodist auspices. The blending of the camp meeting and the emotionalism of the Great Revival was to split many Presbyterian congregations, but enabled the Methodists and Baptists to become the dominant religious bodies in the State. Keever, "Lutheran Preacher's Account," pp. 40-41.

The crude setting in which Henkel observed this revival was soon to be replaced at Southern camp meetings by a brush arbor.

In the process of clearing a wooded grove of most of its trees and brush in order to accommodate an encampment, a brush arbor was created by leaving several selected trees standing that ran up to a substantial height. Branches on the selected trees - if any - were stripped to a height of at least 10 or 12 feet. This left the upper branches to come together over the clearing, producing a natural canopy above the meeting's activities. The foliage offered shade and some protection from the elements, and lamps could be attached to the trunks of the trees in order to provide light for night services. Such arbors had to be large, covering up to half an acre or more, since camp meeting crowds usually numbered several hundred or even a few thousand. Beneath an arbor enough plank seats were constructed to accommodate such a crowd, with separate sections for white men and women and another section for blacks, and a preacher's stand raised several feet above the ground. Participants camped in tents pitched on the arbor's periphery." Bruce, "Brush Arbor," p. 118.

74.   Finck, "Paul Henkel," p. 35.

75.   *Ibid.,* p. 36.

76.   *Ibid.,* p. 39.

77.   Brawley, "Wood Grove."

78.   Finck, "Paul Henkel," p. 40.

79.   *Ibid.,* p. 42. A recent analysis of Paul Henkel's opposition to revivialism is found in Baur, "Paul Henkel and the Revivals," pp. [113]-122.

80.   Finck., "Paul Henkel," p. 44.

81.   Gobel and Matthews, *Glorious Hill,* p. 1.

Chapter III. Division (p. 45)

1.   The upper, newer portion of the building probably contrasted rather sharply with the older, weathered portion of the building, a fact that may have led to the painting of the entire facility white not long after it was used by the Lutheran Synod of North Carolina. Later generations knew the structure as the old White Church.

The early Germans who settled in Lincolnton included both those of the Lutheran and those of the Reformed persuasion, "the Dutch Presbyterians and Dutch Lutherans" as they were designated in a deed drawn for the property on which their church building was erected. They had already erected a house of worship on the land when Christian Reinhardt and Andrew Heedick secured a deed for the land in January, 1788. Brown, *Our Enduring Past,* p. 32.

2. Socrates Henkel, *Tennessee Synod,* p. 20. Henkel's description of the interchange outside the church in Lincolnton does not identify the representative of the North Carolina Synod who presented the questions to the Henkel party, but the description would seem to suggest that it was a central figure in the dispute, Gottlieb Schober, the secretary of the synod. Bernheim noted from earlier descriptions that Schober was one characterized by "a lofty independence, an ardent temper, and a character decidedly affirmative," one who "frequently experienced difficulties, and encountered points other than pleasant, in his pilgrimage through life . . . which a disposition more pliant could have averted." Bernheim, *German Settlements,* p. 441.

3. *Luther* is actually titled *A Comprehensive Account of the Rise and Progress of the Blessed Reformation of the Christian Church.* Baltimore: Schaeffer & Maund, 1818. The constitution appears on pp. 152-56.

4. Robert J. Miller to Gottlieb Schober, July 17, 1816.

5. The officer who called for the moving of the convention to the hotel was presumably either Schober or Storch, most probably the former. Socrates Henkel, *Tennessee Synod,* p. 22.

    In describing the effect on the North Carolina frontier of too few pastors and teachers, Nussmann did not hesitate to speak of the "fanatic enthusiasm" that tended to prevail in areas he could not reach with his ministry, this even before the camp meeting had its North Carolina beginnings in 1789 or 1790. Storch, while not clear about what constituted an appropriate designation for developments associated with the Second Great Awakening, said he was reluctant to brand them "Fanaticism". Bernheim, *German Settlements,* p. 351.

6. Morgan, *Lutheran Church in NC,* pp. 383.

7. Quoted in Nichols, *Romanticism in American Theology,* p. 2. Adopted by English Calvinists at a London convocation (1643-49), the Westminster Confession articulated an understanding of Calvinism that would play a critical role in shaping Puritanism in New England.

8. *Ibid.,* p. 22.

9. Weisberger, *They Gathered,* p. 21.

10. The Second Great Awakening or Great Revival gained momentum in the East in the years immediately following the American Revolution. It spread to the South and over the mountains into trans-Appalachia, launching a succession of waves of revivalism that continued into the Civil War era.

11. Clark, *Methodism in Western NC,* p. 31. Rock Springs Camp Ground near Denver grew out of this first camp meeting. Rock Springs has hosted an annual gathering from 1797 to the present except for one year in which there was an epidemic.

    In addition to Rock Springs near the border of Lincoln and Catawba Counties, Lutherans found their Methodist neighbors attending camp meetings at Wesley Chapel Camp Ground near Plateau in Catawba County, at Shepherd's Cross Roads and Union Camp Meeting in Iredell, at Union on Deep Run in Randolph and at Mt. Gilead in Montgomery.

12. Matthews, "Second Great Awakening," p. 209.

13. Morgan, *Lutheran Church in NC,* p. 283

14. From a letter to a Mr. Goetten in Germany dated May 4, 1784, cited by Dr. Velthusen and quoted in Boyd and Krummel, "German Tracts," No. 1, p. 145.

15. The quotations are from a sermon entitled "The Way of Salvation" preached at Morristown, N. J., in 1829 by Albert Barnes, and cited in Hood, *Reformed America,* p. 179. A leader of the New School movement in the Presbyterian Church, Barnes was tried for heresy and became the key figure in the Old School-New School schism. Ahlstrom, *Religious History,* pp. 467-68.

16. Morgan, *Lutheran Church in NC,* p. 283

17. Loveland, *Southern Evangelicals,* p. 77.

    Since the research on this chapter was completed, Syracuse University Press has published a new biography of Finney by Keith J. Hardman, *Charles Gradison Finney, 1792-1875: Revivalist and Reformer.* Syracuse: Syracuse University Press, 1987.

18. *Lutheran Observer,* Vol. VI (New Series), No. 25 (Feb. 8, 1839). A frequent characteristic of the "anxious" was their remorse over their sinful state. Thus, they were often dubbed "mourners".

19. Ahlstrom, *Religious History,* p. 461.

20. *Lutheran Observer,* Vol. I, No. 12 (Jan. 16, 1832), p. 185. The anonymous reporter of these events was probably J. C. Hope who had just returned from a year at Gettysburg Seminary to take up service at St. Stephen's, Bethlehem, Sandy Run and the preaching point that became Ebenezer, Columbia.

    According to Hope's report, his predecessor at Columbia gave up on the field prematurely and there was an extended period during which the little group of Lutherans in Columbia was without a pastor. Hope moved to Columbia in 1832, as he said, "the year of the Baker Revival - which gave a new start to several denominations, the Presbyterians especially. I effected a partial organization of the Lutheran element, and got up a Sunday School with the aid of some of the theological Students of the Presbyterian Seminary here. . . ." Quoted in Voigt, *Ebenezer Lutheran Church,* p. 10.

21. *Ibid.* The author's assumption was almost universally held among Lutheran defenders of revivals. If at a protracted meeting, St. Paul's admonition about doing all things "decently and in order" were heeded, there could be no basis for criticism. Rarely did someone take the approach of Rev. R. B. Weiser who argued for an acceptance of the fact that revivals of religion necessarily and appropriately excite "animal feelings." Persons commissioned to preach to angels need have no fear of exciting "animal feelings" among their hearers, nor need those who are called to preach to devils. But those preaching to human beings should expect such manifestations since human beings possess animal feelings and, in fact, can "only be reached through the avenue of animal feelings." Weiser, "An Essay on Revivals," p. 279.

22. *Ibid.,* p. [271]. The term "experimental" was used to describe that which was part of one's personal experience.

23. *Ibid.,* p. 273.

24. *Ibid.*

25. *Ibid.,* p. 274.

26. *Ibid.,* p. 275.

27. *Ibid.,* p. 284.

28. *Ibid.,* p. 300.

29. *Ibid.,* p. 301.

30. Nichols, *Romanticism in American Theology,* p. 57. Those representing liturgical denominations were understandably shocked by the emotional outbursts associated with revivalism. Nevin, however, came increasingly to recognize that the real problem with revivalism was not liturgical but ecclesiological and sacramental. He first addressed the subject of baptism tangentially in *The Anxious Bench.* "The Baptist bodies, which rejected infant baptism outright, were the largest denominational family in the country, and," Nevin declared, "the baptistic principle prevails more extensively still; for it is very plain that all true sense of the sacramental value of baptism is wanting in large portions of the church, where the ordinance is still retained."

    Neither Calvin nor Luther would have tolerated the conception of baptism which had come to be dominant in American Protestantism and powerful even in the churches which recognized the Reformers as authorities. The basic trouble was defection from the Reformation doctrine of the church and sacraments. [Nevin argued],

> If the sacraments are regarded as in themselves outward rites only, that can have no value or force except as the grace they represent is made to be present by the subjective exercises of the worshipper, it is hard to see on what ground infants, who are still without knowledge or faith, should be admitted to any privilege of the sort. If there be no objective reality in the life of the Church, as something more deep and comprehensive than the life of the individual believer separately taken, infant baptism becomes necessarily an unmeaning contradiction. Nichols, *Romanticism in American Theology*, pp. 237-38.

31. At Mercersberg, Nevin was a colleague of the famed church historian, Philip Schaff, who in 1845 published *Principle of Protestantism*. This work concluded with the argument that the church has experienced three ages; the Petrine characterized by legalism and authority, the Pauline characterized by grace and freedom, and finally a synthesis of the first two in Johannine love, of freedom in law. Thus, Schaff concludes, "Away with human denominations! Down with religious sects! Let our watchword be: One Spirit and one body! One Shepherd and one flock! All conventicles and chapels must perish, that from their ashes may arise the One Church of God, phoenix-like and resplendent with glory, as a bride adorned for her bridegroom." Quoted by Nichols, *Romantism in American Theology*, p. 137.

32. Bernheim, *German Settlements*, p. 354. In the spring of 1830, the aging Miller wrote an account of his ordination and ordained ministry. He notes that while serving as a lay reader at the request of the Whitehaven congregation, his congregation depended on a neighboring Lutheran pastor, presumably Arends, to supply them with the sacraments. The Lutheran pastor urged him to seek ordination from the North Carolina Ministerium, which he did in 1794. ". . . I consented to receive the Ordination from them, not as a Lutheran minister, but as an Episcopalian! And in the letter of Orders that they gave me at the time, they bound me to be subject to the discipline and rules of the Protestant Episcopal Church in the United States of America." Robert Miller, "Early Church," p. [1].

33. The author of a history of one of the congregations served by Bernhardt at the time he affiliated with the North Carolina Synod seems to concur in this conclusion. "In 1800 and 1801 the great religious revival that was sweeping over the United States reached the Fork. During these trying years the Bethel congregation was fortunate in having Pastor Bernhardt provide spiritual leadership." Cruse, *Bethel Church*, p. 5.

34. For a helpful biography, see Surratt, *Schober of Salem*. Until he retired from the active ministry in 1832, Schober failed to win election as an officer of the North Carolina Synod in only one year. During the first decade of his service as a Lutheran pastor, he was usually elected to the posts of secretary and treasurer. In the eleven years following the schism at Lincolnton in 1820, Schober was nine times elected to both the position of president of the synod and treasurer. Morgan, *Lutheran Church in NC*, pp. 383-84.

35. Jacobs, *The Problem*, p. 5. Jacobs cites letters written by Schober in 1814 to the Pennsylvania ministerium urging the preparation of a common liturgy for use by Lutherans in the United States. "And so, this summer, I have sat around a common table, with the representatives of your United Synod and of the General Synod in this very work; which I am glad to say is rapidly approaching completion. When finished, the book will be a permanent memorial of the influence of the Church in the South." The book was the *Common Service Book*.

It should be noted that concern for Christian unity among Protestants in the United States during the nineteenth century did not embrace Roman Catholics. In fact, even

Episcopalians who emphasized the historic episcopate and apostolic succession were likely to be excluded from consideration when Evangelicalism addressed its strong concern for Christian unity.

36.   Surratt, *Schober of Salem*, p. [193].

37.   Clergy of the Moravian and Calvinistic traditions were noted as participants in the services who would be "welcome". Peschau, *Minutes*, p. 11.

        Paul Henkel was not present for this convention, but it should not be assumed he would have opposed this action by the synod. His diary indicates that he found it possible to appreciate and work with Moravian and German Reformed clergy.

38.   [Schober], *Review of a Pamphlet*, p. 30.

39.   Not so early, however, as suggested by a recent publication, which indicates that when Robert Johnstone Miller resigned at White Haven in 1806, "he recommended to the congregation a young Lutheran minister, the Rev. David Henckle [*sic*], whom they accepted." Duncan, *Pictorial History*, p. 103. Since Henkel was born in 1795, he would have been eleven years old when Miller removed to Mary's Grove near Lenoir! This is probably an instance of confusion between the two brothers, David and Philip. Philip was ordained in 1805 and had come into Lincoln County that year to assist Pastor Arends who reportedly had become blind by 1803.

40.   The constitution of 1817 is printed in [Schober], *Luther*, p. 156. "The North Carolina Synod seems to have been the earliest to be affected by rationalism and it had imbibed rather deeply of the spirit of 'unionism'. However, it was also the earliest of the three existing Synods in this period [i.e., 1790-1820] to posit the Augsburg Confession as a confessional standard in its official constitution, and to prescribe the use of Luther's Catechism." Wolf, "Americanization," p. 458.

        R. J. Miller reports that he drafted the synod's constitution of 1803, "the leading features of which were copied from the General Constitution of the Protestant Episcopal Church." Robert Miller, "Early Church," p. [1]. He was throughout his career as a clergyman a friend of what Nevin would later call "the system of the catechism." Miller wrote, "I had a catechism printed at Salisbury, to which I added an explanation of the two Covenants, and the Feasts of the Church, with some religious terms not generally known." Robert Miller, *Introduction*.

41.   David Henkel, *Answer to Moore*, p. 20. Henkel early realized that the Lutheran understanding of the church and sacraments set Lutherans apart from the ecclesiastical environment in which they found themselves on the southern frontier. He could not accept the view that baptism is something we do to show that we are now converted and have faith in Christ.

        When we teach that we are saved by baptism, we understand nothing else, than that Christ saves us; for he has instituted it, and it is the means in his own hands, to effect our regeneration. *Ibid.*, p. 47.

        To say that Baptism is Christ's means of regenerating us is not to deny the role of the Spirit in our salvation. The spirit by baptism as a means operates on the sinner to effect repentance; hence, the remission of sins; this is the design for which we administer it; and if properly applied, and the operation thereof, be not too violently, and incessantly resisted, will produce these blessings. *Ibid.*

42.   *Extract From Transactions*, p. 18.

43.   David Henkel, *Carolinian Herald*, p. 33, footnote. Henkel's understanding of the doctrine of the real presence is discussed at length, pp. 46-65.

44.   Prior to the constitution of 1817 the North Carolina Synod apparently recognized ordained clergy and two ranks of those in preparation for ordination, the catechist and the candidate.

Article VIII of the new constitution, attempting to create "conformity to the Synodal decrees of the Northern States," called for four classifications, catechist and candidate continuing as preparatory stages for ordination, and deacon and pastor being the two ordained categories. Deacons were ordained but were restricted to service in a particular parish. Ordination as pastor conveyed "general authority." [Schober], *Luther*, pp. 154-55.

45. Peschau, *Minutes*, p. 23. While David could hardly have been classified as "uneducated," he lacked formal schooling and was only nineteen years of age.

46. Since David Henkel encountered such frustrating delays in his pursuit of ordination, and the move from three to four ranks of clergy confronted him with still another obstacle in his quest, he may have been the person challenging the four ranks. The synod cited the example of the Pennsylvania Ministerium as justification for retaining the four classifications.

47. *Ibid.*, p. 36. Pechau's translation may be colored by later antagonism between the rival synods. In 1819 Schober was content to say that "this Synod unanimously approved of our present meeting." *Succinct Information*, p. 10.

    Some pastors reportedly stayed away from the convention because of a letter they received from Philip Henkel. The convention declined to excuse the absences of Philip Henkel, Joseph E. Bell, Adam Miller and Jacob Zink. Schober could also editorialize through the minutes as he did in reporting the convention's decision not to excuse the absence of these pastors: their absence, he noted, "has no color of admissible excuse." *Ibid.*, p. 8.

48. *Ibid.*, p. 20. The secretary was Gottlieb Schober.

49. While it seems Philip Henkel knew of the change in date for the 1819 convention, he claimed he did not receive the notice of the change which was dispatched to all pastors of the synod.

50. The April convention was often referred to by later writers as "the Untimely Synod."

51. David Henkel, *Carolinian Herald*, p. 22. Since David Henkel's brother, Philip, was the only ordained pastor present to conduct the ordination service, the validity of the ordination was challenged on the grounds that only one pastor participated in the laying on of hands. David advanced two arguments in support of the validity of his ordination. First, he contended that ordination was the synod's act; Philip was merely executing a decision previously arrived at by the synod. Secondly, he argued that an ordination service conducted by only one pastor was not considered invalid at the time as was proven by the fact that the synod did not require an ordination service for Joseph Bell when it recognized him as an ordained pastor. *Ibid.*, p. 37. In 1820 the synod passed a rule that at least two ordained persons must be present to perform an ordination.

52. Peschau, *Minutes*, p. 40.

53. *Minutes, NC Synod, 1820*, p. 12.

54. *Lutheran Observer*, Vol. VI [new series], No. 39 (May 17, 1839). See also David Henkel, *Carolinian Herald*, p. 39, footnote.

55. The fact that Tennessee Synod pastors did not hesitate to encourage persons to leave North Carolina Synod congregations and create rival Tennessee Synod congregations did nothing to heal the wound created by the split in 1820. The sharing of church buildings by the rival parties often created difficulties and deepened antagonisms. Still, the Lutheran understanding of the nature of the church made it impossible for either body to ignore the claims of Christian unity, so repeated overtures were made for reconciliation.

56. The description of Schober is by Morris, *Fifty Years*, p. 39. He continues, "In dress, appearance and manners, he was a regular backwoodsman, and his disregard of some of the more refined conventionalities of polite society offended the taste of some of his more precise brethren, whilst they were amused with his drollery and wit." In Tennessee Synod

circles, he would be remembered as "fat, jolly, shrewd, cunning, self-important." L. A. Fox, *The Origin*, p. 3.

57. A year later, the opposition which was led by Paul Henkel and his sons, Andrew and David, persuaded the synod to reverse its position.

58. David Henkel, *Carolinian Herald*, p. 7.

59. The contribution of the Henkel Press to the Lutheran church was extensive. In his *Journal* under the date of October 31, 1806, Paul Henkel tells of a trip from New Market, Virginia, to Organ Church to attend the fourth meeting of the newly-organized synod. He took this opportunity to transport and distribute six hundred copies of the Augsburg Confession. A liturgy was prepared under the direction of the Tennessee Synod. A resolution adopted by the synod in 1838 states, "That Revs. A. Henkel, Jacob Killian, and Jacob Stirewalt, be requested to compile a Liturgy for the use of our Church, and present it to the next session of the Synod for examination." The liturgy, composed chiefly of prayers and hymns, was compiled and widely used. The most significant and influential publication was the English translation of the *Book of Concord*. The translations were made by Tennessee Synod pastors; it is reportedly the first translation into English. The first edition is dated 1851, and the second, reviewed and revised by Charles Porterfield Krauth, W. F. Lehmann and other prominent theologians, is dated 1854. Krauth said concerning the work, "It marks a distinct era in the history of our Church in this country." *Lutheran Encyclopaedia*, p. 194.

60. Henkel's rendering of Article VII of the Augsburg Confession. David Henkel, *Carolinian Herald*, p. 12.

61. *Ibid.*, p. 13. An able and mature son of the Tennessee Synod observed that David's written attack on The General Synod was

> sophomoric, wholly unlike anything else he ever published, and time showed he was mistaken as to the nature and work of the General Synod. We wish he had never written it. L. A. Fox, *The Origin*, p. 7.

Nevertheless, David Henkel wrote at a time when even in the political realm, the relation between states rights and federal authority had not been resolved. He had real concerns about the dangers inherent in the centralization of power in organizations, and, true to his convictions, saw to it that the Tennessee Synod had virtually no power over clergy or congregations during his lifetime. In dealing with Adam Miller, Jr., in 1846, the Tennessee Synod began a gradual move to exercise authority over its clergy. The lingering effects of these polity concerns are reflected in the fact that when the vote was taken by North Carolina Lutherans on the merger creating the ELCA in 1987, the North Carolina Synod of the LCA decided the matter by a convention vote. Sister congregations in the state that had gone the route of the Tennessee Synod, the Tennessee Synod Reorganized, the Joint Synod of Ohio and the ALC, voted by congregation on whether or not to endorse the merger.

62. David Henkel, *Carolinian Herald*, p. 2. The question of granting a license to persons to perform certain ministerial functions, rather than ordaining them, provoked extensive debate in the North Carolina Synod as early as 1816. Bernheim, *German Settlements*, pp. 425-29.

63. Bernheim, *German Settlements*, pp. 441-443.

64. Surratt, *Schober of Salem*, pp. 83-100. Cf. Schober's portrayal of the Episcopal church in "an unflattering light" in Corbett, "Miller Letters," p. 504.

65. McCullough, *Lutheran Church in SC*, pp. 186-193; Socrates Henkel, *Tennessee Synod*, pp. 132; Aull, "Godfrey Dreher."

66. *Minutes, NY Synod, 1823*, p. 20.

67. Miller, who worked long and hard to cement relations between Lutherans and

Episcopalians, came to share Bishop Ravenscroft's perspective. He understood the decision of the North Carolina Ministerium to ordain him to the Episcopal priesthood as an acceptance of an obligation to create a joint ecclesiastical body for the state. "Had this been done, I have every reason to believe, that the state and prospects of both the Lutherans and the Episcopalians, would have been in this section of the country far more promising than they are. However, it surely teaches us this useful and important lesson, how vain, if not absurd, the wide-spread delusion of the present day is, 'that the successful attempt of amalgamating the different sects, creeds, order, and worship of all those who call themselves Christians, will, or can produce that union and unity of Faith and practice enjoined by the sure word of God.'" The effort to combine in one household of faith those of the Lutheran and Episcopal traditions left Miller convinced "how impossible it is to attempt, in any degree, a compromise with error, schism, or heresy, without injury to the truth." Miller claimed that from his early break with Methodism he was thoroughly convinced that the apostolic succession "must ever descend and continue unbroken with the Church of God." Robert Miller, "Early Church," p. [1].

68. Hugh George Anderson, quoting from the minutes of the General Synod in Nelson, *Lutherans of North America*, p. 120.

Chapter IV. Slavery, Sectionalism (p. 69)

1. The comment in 1864 of Presbyterian, Robert Livingston Stanton, in his *The Church and the Rebellion*, quoted in Goen, "Scenario for Secession," p. 11.
2. *Ibid.*, p. 13.
3. President Levi Bedenbaugh of the Georgia Synod, quoted in Anderson, *Lutheranism in the Southeast*, p. 32.
4. *Minutes, NC Synod, 1840*, p. 8.
5. *Minutes, TN Synod, 1845*, p. 8. Miller later contended that the words "provided they honorably acquit him" were not a part of the resolution as prepared by the committee, but were added by Deacons P. C. Henkel and J. R. Peterson "who were to reap the benefits of my condemnation." (Rhyne, "Tennessee Synod Reorganized," p. 8.) Henkel and Peterson were not members of the committee that prepared the resolution, and if they caused it to be amended from the floor, the minutes do not reflect that fact. Miller's perspective may have been colored by the fact that the following year Beaverdam Church, the congregation served by Miller that, when polled, mustered the largest number of votes against him, petitioned the synod for the services of Henkel and Peterson. *Minutes, TN Synod, 1846*, p. 7.
6. Morgan, Lutheran Church in NC, pp.384-385.
7. Rhyne, "Tennessee Synod Reorganized," p. 4.
8. *Liturgy,* or *Book Of Forms*, p. 208.
   When pastors of the Tennessee Synod left that body a few years later to create the Holston Synod, they were careful to define in their constitution "the power of Synod over its Ministers." After noting that each minister holding membership in their body was accountable to the synod for "both the doctrines which he may hold or teach, and for his moral conduct," the constitution went on to provide that the "Synod shall have full power, and it shall be its duty, to impeach and try, according to such laws and regulations as it may adopt for this purpose, any Minister connected with it, for heterodoxy and immorality, and upon conviction thereof it shall have power, and it shall be its duty, to reprove, suspend from the exercise of his office, or depose from the Ministry, any Minister so convicted, according to the nature and magnitude of his offence." *Minutes, Holston Synod, 1862,* p.

10. The constitution is printed as an appendix to the minutes.

9. "The rules and principles of church-government are contained in the Holy Scriptures. Therefore, no body of Christians have [*sic*] authority to dispense with or alter, or transact any thing contrary to them. Human traditions, or rules imposed upon the church as necessary to Christian fellowship, which have no foundation in the Scriptures, are condemned by our Savior. Math. 15. v.9.13.14." The foregoing are the opening words of the text which introduces the six articles of the constitution. *Ibid.*, p. [201].

10. *Minutes, TN Synod, 1846*, p. 6. The secretary actually lists Hebron as being in Lincoln County, but the portion of Lincoln County in which Hebron was located was ceded to the newly created Cleaveland County in 1841. (The current spelling, Cleveland, was adopted in 1887.) Catawba County was carved out of Lincoln County the following year. Sherrill, *Annals of Lincoln County*, pp. 30-31.

11. *Minutes, TN Synod, 1846*, p. 7.

12. The following year St. John's, Conover, repudiated the action of its delegate and asked for, and received reinstatement. *Ibid., 1847*, p. 14.

13. The committee consisted of Virginia Pastors Abel J. Brown of Abington, Jacob Killian of Waynesboro, and Jacob Stirewalt of New Market; along with A. W. Abernathy, Esq., of Philadelphia, Dallas; Daniel Seagle of Trinity, Vale; and John Moser of St. Paul's, Monroe County, Tennessee. *Ibid.*, p. 9. Some four hundred petitioners had reportedly registered their concern in support of Miller. Rhyne, "Tennessee Synod Reorganized," p. 12.

14. Morgan, *Lutheran Church in NC*, pp. 384-85.

15. Miller's obituary appears in the minutes for 1871. *Minutes, TN Synod, Reorganized, 1871*, pp. 7-8.

16. For a history of the school, see D. E. Snapp, "Our Seminary At Hickory, N. C.," in Price, *Lutheran Almanac For 1907*, p. 13. For a picture of the building which housed the seminary, see Lynne C. Sparks, "St. Paul's Seminary," in Fulbright, *Heritage of Catawba County*, Vol. I, p. 17. Sparks notes that when it became apparent to Concordia District congregations in North Carolina that the Joint Synod was going to abandon its educational venture in the South, several of the congregations "withdrew from the synod in a huff." *Ibid.*, p. 18.

17. Eisenberg, *Lutheran Church in Virginia*, p. 195.

18. Cox, *Reminiscences*, p. 6.

19. Eisenberg, *Lutheran Church in Virginia*, p. 308.

20. Virginia Collegiate Institute, at the prodding and with the encouragement of the synod of Western Virginia and the Virginia Synod, was transformed into a college and authorized to award degrees early in 1853. The new college began its operation September 1, 1853. (Eisenberg, *First Hundred Years*, p. 76.) By 1860 the South boasted 260 separate institutions of higher learning. Mathis, "Colleges and Universities," p. 248.

21. H. G. Jones, *North Carolina Illustrated*, pp. 191-92.

22. *Catalogue, North Carolina College, 1860*, p. 7.

23. Muhlenberg, *Journals*, Vol. I, p. 58.

24. Bailyn, *Peopling*, p. 118.

25. While *Historical Statistics of the United States* gives the Negro population of the Colonies in 1700 as 28,000, a figure representing eleven per cent of the population, there is good reason to believe that the actual black population was much closer to 20,000 than to 30,000 in 1700. Hofstadter, *America at 1750*, pp. 66-67.

26. *Ibid.*, p. 75.

27. Lefler and Newsome, *North Carolina*, p. 128.

28. Apparently John Phifer with his seven slaves was the German in the Piedmont owning the largest number of slaves. Gehrke, "Negro Slavery," p. 307.

As noted earlier, the Swiss and Palatines who were settled in eastern North Carolina early in the eighteenth century were thoroughly dispersed among non-Germanic settlers in several eastern counties. It is interesting to note that the descendants of these German and German-speaking colonists became indistinguishable from their neighbors relative to slave ownership. In the counties of Craven, Jones and Onslow, 32.7 per cent held slaves in 1790. Of 163 German or German-speaking families living east of Raleigh in 1790, "43.5 per cent held a total of 544 Negroes, an average of 7.7 per family." *Ibid.,* p. 308, footnote.

29. *Ibid.,* p. 308. Michael Braun's holdings are noted in Jo White Linn, "Michael Braun (or Brown)," in Powell, *Dictionary,* p. 215.

30. Farrison, "Negro Population," p. 325. Not all of the blacks in Guilford County were slaves. In 1790 there were twenty-seven free blacks in the County. In the decade 1800-1810 there was a 157.5% increase, and from 1820 to 1830 a 179.8% increase, bringing the total number of free blacks in the County to 582 by the latter date. *Ibid.*

31. For Lutherans in the North Carolina Synod's congregations in South Carolina's Dutch Fork, the dominant characteristics of slavery among the German citizens seems to have been similar. Speaking of Lexington District Germans and their descendants from c. 1820, Scott writes, "Very few had any Negroes, and those but a small number, who worked with the white members of the family, all wearing pretty much the same clothing, which was made up by the white females, and eating the same food, but never at the same table." Scott, *Random Recollections,* p. 94.

32. Gehrke, "Negro Slavery," p. 310. The thesis that slavery among the Germans in the Piedmont was a milder form of slavery than that existing on the large plantations in the Deep South is supported by the fact that slavery among the Germans rarely had to deal with the problem of run-aways. It may also be significant that after the Civil War, a large number of the former slaves not only retained German surnames (e.g., Barnhardt, Clapp, Dry, Fisher, Graeber, Holt, Koontz, Misenheimer, Phifer, Siler and Sizer) but elected to remain in the employ of their former masters. *Ibid.,* p. 311.

33. Boles, *Masters & Slaves,* p. 4.

34. In reflecting on "the deportation of blacks from Africa to America and their enslavement here," Foster R. McCurley, Jr., notes how "idolatrous prejudice against black people in general" contributed to the misreading of the Bible. Classic was the use of the story about Noah's descendants in Genesis 9 and 10." In this story, the Bible reports a curse falling on Canaan because of a transgression of his father, Ham, Canaan being enslaved to his two uncles, Shem and Japheth. "In white racist thinking this story of the enslavement of Canaan was conveniently transferred to the following genealogy of Ham, and in the process the black Cush (Ethiopian) becomes enslaved to the white Semites (Shem). Since early Americans already saw themselves as the new Israel, it was inevitable that the descendants of Cush should be America's slaves." McCurley, "American Myths," p. 228.

35. Boles, "Slaves in Biracial Churches," p. 99.

36. Although blacks were not as numerous in Lutheran congregations as in the Baptist and Methodist congregations that became so dominant in the South in the years following the Great Revival, the following description of antebellum church life is a reminder of the kind of environment in which Lutherans found themselves as they dealt with questions about slavery and black church members.

> From the inception of institutional church life, particularly among the soon-dominant Baptists and Methodists, slaves were active church members. Of course, the percentage of black members varied according to their percentage in the local population, but in every region blacks and

whites worshiped together. Blacks commonly represented twenty to forty percent of the congregation of Baptist churches; often they were the majority. Generally, blacks sat segregated at the rear of the church, in the balcony, or in a lean-to addition to the church. Blacks and whites heard the same sermons, took communion at the same service, were baptized or confirmed together, and were buried in the same cemeteries. Black delegates attended district association and quarterly meetings down to the Civil War. On occasion, when the white members built a new church building, the blacks were given the old building and allowed virtual autonomy over matters in the adjunct church. A white committee would be appointed to supervise the black congregation, which might be called, for example, the Stamping Ground African Baptist Church to distinguish it from the parent, white Stamping Ground Baptist Church. But such supervision appears to have been nominal. The slaves so separated were less the victims of segregation than the beneficiaries of whites' recognition that bondspeople had special needs and special interests best served by their own leaders. In the far more common biracial churches, black deacons and elders sometimes served alongside whites, and it was not unusual, when no white minister was available, for the whole congregation to listen with approval to a black preacher. In fact, sometimes biracial congregations requested certain black preachers. Across the South, especially talented black preachers gained great fame as pulpit orators, and whites agreed that black ministers such as John Jasper and Andrew Marshall had unrivaled power to move a congregation. *Ibid.,* pp. 100-101.

37. Dolmetsch, *German Press,* pp. 45, 47.

38. In 1860 Lutherans had only one congregation in North Carolina in a county where slaves constituted as much as 33.4% of the population, that one congregation being St. Paul's, Wilmington. For an analysis of the State's slave population by county, see Crofts, *Reluctant Confederates,* p. 41.

39. *Minutes of a Special Conference, 1816,* p. [3]. Schober's theme was apparently all too typical of preaching to slaves when they were segregated from the white congregations in which their owners worshiped. "Lunsford Lane, a North Carolinian who was fortunate enough to purchase his freedom in the 1830s, described the sermons he heard as a slave: 'So great was the similarity of the texts that they were always fresh in my memory: "Servants, be obedient to your masters"....."He that knoweth his master's will and doeth it not, shall be beaten with many stripes;" and some others of this class. Similar passages, with but few exceptions, formed the basis of most of these public instructions. The first commandment was to obey our masters, and the second like unto it: labor as faithfully when they or the overseers were not watching, as when they were.'" Clayton, *Close to the Land,* p. 22.

     Infused by a vibrant spiritual heritage and vitalized by more radical Christian tenets, such as the brotherhood of man, Afro-American slaves developed their own brand of religion. In the intimacy of secret 'hushharbors' deep in the woods, with wet blankets hung from branches to muffle the sound, bondsmen sang and shouted to the glory of an all-powerful though benevolent God who would succor them in slavery and deliver them to freedom, in this world as well as the next. *Ibid.*

40. *Minutes of a Special Conference, 1816,* pp. 7-8. The option of providing or permitting a separate facility for the worship of the slaves was followed on occasion but was never a popular one. The Salem Female Missionary Society which early secured permission from

the North Carolina Synod to organize black congregations in Lutheran parishes seems to have had no notable success outside Salem where a black congregation was organized and entered its frame building in 1823. This congregation erected "a spacious brick edifice in 1861." Gehrke, "Negro Slavery," p. 312.

41. *Ibid.*

42. *Ibid.*, pp. 8-9.

43. Godfrey Dreher to Gottlieb Schober, Ms. letter dated July 10, 1816, NC Synod Archives.

44. October 12, 1816, Ms. letter of Godfrey Dreher to NC Synod, October 12, 1816, NC Synod Archives.

45. *Minutes, NC Synod, 1820,* p. 12.

46. *Ibid., 1819,* p. 17.

47. Socrates Henkel, *TN Synod,* p. 47.

48. *Ibid.*, p. 52.

49. Pastors reporting baptisms of blacks in the early years of the synod's life included Nehemiah Bonham, George Easterly, Ambrose Henkel, David Henkel, Philip Henkel, Adam Miller, Jr., Christian Moretz, and Daniel Moser. *Ibid.*, pp. 65, 67, 71. Gehrke, "Negro Slavery," p. 316. In considering the preponderance of black Tennessee Synod Lutherans in North Carolina, it should be remembered that, apart from Bethlehem near Lancaster and the periodic tours of Bonham in Piedmont South Carolina, the synod was not a significant factor in South Carolina Lutheranism until after the Dreher controversy.

50. "The tradition of the squire required the assumption of responsibility for the well-being and the good conduct of his people. The squire who was a slaveholder frequently placed the happiness of his slaves above his own material prosperity. Thomas Dabney, moving from Virginia to Louisiana in the 1830s, refused to put part of his slaves on another plantation because he would no longer be able to attend to the welfare of each bondsman. John A. Quitman, faced with bankruptcy, refused to part with his slaves. 'I would rather,' he declared, 'be reduced to abject penury than to sell one of them.'" Hesseltine, "Four American Traditions," p. 12. Quitman, a native of New York who served as governor of Mexico and later of Mississippi, was the son of a Lutheran pastor. Gonzales, "John Anthony Quitman," p. 1017.

51. A manumission society was formed in North Carolina as early as 1816 by the Quakers which had twenty-eight local chapters and more than a thousand members by 1825. By 1826 the American Colonization Society could boast "at least forty branches." Lefler and Newsome, *North Carolina,* p. 441.

     A member of St. John's, Salisbury, who was a prominent member of the North Carolina legislature, Charles Fisher, presumably was less enthusiastic about deporting blacks than Pastor Reck. In 1828 Fisher published his *Report on the Establishment of Cotton and Woolen Manufacturing* in which he argued that blacks could serve just as effectively as whites in manufacturing. Gehrke, "Negro Slavery," p. 318.

52. A review of Southern expressions of antislavery sentiment after 1830 prompts one to recognize the limited number of white southerners who expressed any objection to slavery.
     Although...antislavery arguments were heard in the South right down to the moment of secession, the number of people who heeded them, much more uttered them, was always minuscule. Degler, *The Other South,* p. 75.

53. Filler, *The Crusade Against Slavery,* p. 22.

54. Stampp, *The Peculiar Institution,* p. 132.

55. *Ibid.*, pp. 132-34. Filler, *Crusade Against Slavery,* p. 60. Accounts of the Turner revolt and the earlier Denmark Vesey plot in Charleston are found in Haynes, *Negro Community,* pp. 149, 156. For Turner's account of the uprising, see Aptheker, *Documentary History,* pp.

122-25. The circulation of Walker's *Appeal* and Garrison's *Liberator* contributed to the fact that state legislatures in the South were soon enacting laws making it a crime to teach a black person, slave or free, to read.

56.   The Postmaster General ruled "that abolition literature might be mailed in the North, but need not be delivered by southern postmasters." Perkins and Van Deusen, *United States of America*, Vol. I, p. 398.

57.   *Minutes, SC Synod, 1835*, pp. ii-iii. The speaker was Stephen Albion Mealy, pastor of the Lutheran Church of the Ascension, Savannah, Georgia, who was serving his first term as President of the Synod.

58.   *Minutes, SC Synod, 1835*, p. 8.

59.   *Ibid., 1836*, p. 20. The Synod's response was not unusual for a Lutheran body in the nineteenth century. "A study of official attitudes of the several Lutheran synods and the General Synod, 1830-1860, shows very clearly that the church as a whole did not formally and authoritatively deliver itself on the subject of slavery nor did it seek to force a consensus of opinion. The very nature of the Lutheran church of that day in America made this impossible. It was not a united organization. In the second place, it had no desire so to do, since it was always questionable, among Lutherans, whether such a subject as slavery had a proper right to the attention of the church, as an ecclesiastical body." Fortenbaugh, "Representative Lutheran Press," p. 151.

60.   Kreider, *New York and New England*, p. 117.

       The attitude of the Franckean Synod reflected the increasing tendency of the abolitionist movement to depict the conflict as the difference between "sin" and "righteousness", or, as Julia Ward Howe would characterize it in 1861, between "the coming of the Lord" and "the grapes of wrath" he would trample. Changing patterns of development in the North and in the South contributed to this increasingly dominant approach to the question. The late David Potter noted some of the factors contributing to this change. "The North shared fully in the world-wide technological change by which the labour of machines was being substituted for the labour of unskilled humans, so that slavery was rendered economically obsolete, and society could, for the first time, afford to treat the use of involuntary labour as a moral and not an economic question. In the North, the powerful emotional drives of evangelical Protestantism, combined with the natural-rights doctrine of the equality of all men, had produced a profound and pervasive belief in the dignity of the human individual." Potter, "National and Sectional Forces," p. 617.

       For a recent study of the role of classic Lutheran Pietism in shaping the abolitionism of the Franckean Synod, see Kuenning, "New York Lutheran Abolitionists," pp. 52-65.

61.   Kreider quotes from the Minutes of the Franckean Synod for 1839. *History of the Un. Lutheran Synod of N.Y.*, I, 117.

62.   *Lutheran Observer*, Vol. IV [n.s.], No. 45 (June 30, 1837).

63.   *Ibid.*, Vol. VI [n.s.], No. 16 (Dec. 7, 1838). Hazelius and many others shared Kurtz' view that "ultraism" was challenging many tried and tested bulwarks of society. As Hazelius observed in an address earlier in 1838, "The era, in which we live, is one of great excitement. Institutions, venerable for their age and supposed usefulness, are overthrown; and a conviction appears to pervade the world that there is a wrong somewhere, and that the happiness of mankind requires that a change should take place." [Hazelius], *Address of the Temperance Society*, p. 5.

64.   J. G. de Roulhac Hamilton, ed., "Benjamin Sherwood Hedrick," *The James Sprunt Historical Publications*, X (1910), p. 14; quoted in Gehrke, "Negro Slavery," p. 319.

65.   Donald G. Mathews, "Abolitionism," in Hill, *Encyclopedia of Religion*, p. 2.

       Understandings of the abolitionist movement in the second half of the nineteenth and first half of the twentieth centuries were significantly influenced by the abolitionists themselves who were eager to chronicle the story of their victory. The picture they endeavored to create was one in which a small and despised minority of insightful persons fostered and gradually produced a broad-based consensus "at the North" that slavery was morally wrong, and this consensus, in turn, insisted upon and eventually secured the elimination of chattel slavery in the South. Friedman, "Historical Topics," p. 178. This "growth of the dissenting minority" motif has, in fact, "become the governing paradigm for modern-day antislavery scholarship." *Ibid.,* p. 180. An alternative interpretation advanced by historians such as Dwight L. Dumond sees the key to expanding abolitionist influence in the movement of the abolitionists into the political arena through the Liberty, Free Soil and Republican parties.

66. A survey of publications by United States Lutherans makes it clear that slavery was not a question about which Lutherans were deeply agitated. "List of Publications," pp. 542-74.

67. Gehrke, "Negro Slavery," p. 324.

68. For Friendship, Taylorsville, see Crouse, *Historical Sketches,* pp. 6, 9, 16-17. For Salem, see "Historical Sketch," p. [1]. Some churches where making provision for blacks in their facility presented particular difficulties may have adopted the practice of separate afternoon services for black worshippers. Laura Dry, a former slave, recalled attending services on Sunday afternoons at St. John's, Concord. Gehrke, "Negro Slavery," p. 316.

The 1837 resolution of the synodical convention calling upon congregations to provide space in their places of worshippers for black persons was a reiteration of the synod's 1814 action. In 1838 the North Carolina Classis of the Reformed Church took similar action. Preslar, *A History of Catawba County,* p. 92.

69. Loveland, *Southern Evangelicals,* p. 227.

70. South Carolina pastors reported confirming 152 blacks. *Minutes, NC Synod, 1845,* p. 21.

71. *Ibid, 1848,* p. 18.

72. Boles, "Slaves in Biracial Churches," p. 99.

73. *Minutes, NC Synod, 1847,* p. 8.

74. *Ibid., 1848,* p. 20. No statistics were listed for Anthony's black congregation except two baptisms, but Linn reported five adult and four infant baptisms and a congregation of twenty-four black communicants. Thus, Linn was apparently the organizer of the Synod's first black congregation.

75. An undated membership list from Union, Salisbury, from this period lists only two black members, both women. Agner, "Record Books," p. 7. Of the twenty-five confirmands at Friendship, Taylorsville, who received their first Communion in April 1855, two were Richard and Molissee, "servants of Wm. J. Lippard." Crouse, *Historical Sketches,* p. 13. A revival at St. John's, Salisbury, in 1857 produced a large number of converts including Thomas Southerly, a black who was duly received into the church by confirmation. He apparently was the only black member of St. John's at the time, but the following year five additional names (all women) were added to the page set apart for recording Southerly's membership. Agner, *Heritage and History,* p. 142.

Southerly was apparently the first black Lutheran to be licensed as a preacher by the North Carolina Synod. Gehrke believed that "Sam Holt of Alamance County, who harangued his fellow-slaves during the War," was possibly "the first and only Negro Lutheran preacher in the State." Gehrke, "Negro Slavery," pp. 315-16. However, as Agner has shown, Southerly was apparently licensed as early as 1869. Agner, *Heritage and History,* p. 160. Holt was apparently licensed in 1872, and was ordained in 1884. [Norman], *Life Sketches,* p. 238.

76. *The Missionary,* Vol II, No. 5 (May, 1849), p. 43. While comparable data is not available for the North Carolina Synod, it seems probable that more than half the Synod's twenty-

nine congregations enjoying the services of a pastor had black members. The total number of black members and the total percentage of black members would no doubt have been considerably less than in the South Carolina Synod where a missionary had been employed to work among black persons as early as 1837. *Minutes, SC Synod, 1838,* p. 38.

77.   *The Missionary,* Vol. II, No. 7 (July, 1849), p. 56.

78.   *Ibid.,* No. 5 (May, 1849), p. 43.

79.   Gerberding, *W. A. Passavant,* pp. 121ff.

80.   *Minutes, NC Synod, 1849,* p. 18.

81.   *The Missionary,* VII. II [n.s.], No 36 (October 1, 1857).

82.   *Ibid.* The United States Supreme Court had handed down its Dred Scott decision in the spring of 1857, a bitter blow to those who hoped to see the federal government take a more pro-abolitionist stance. The famed newspaper editor, Horace Greely, declared the Dred Scott decision was "entitled to just so much moral weight as would be the judgment of a majority of those congregated in any Washington bar room." Quoted in Perkins and Van Deusen, *United States of America,* I, 609.

83.   *The Missionary,* Vol. II [n.s.], No. 46 (Dec. 10, 1857). Abolitionists usually recognized that they had little hope of portraying the Constitution as being supportive of their views. Hence, they usually appealed to the Declaration as reflecting a higher law than the Constitution. A study of the religion of Abraham Lincoln notes that for Lincoln the Declaration had "the force of revelation itself." Wolf, *Almost Chosen People,* p. 91. On the other hand, southerners reflecting the "squire tradition" stressed obedience to the law, "and above all, the law of the constitution. Speculation about a 'higher law' might be an interesting intellectual exercise, but action based on higher law mandates was treason." Hesseltine, "Four American Traditions," p. 13.

84.   *The Missionary,* Vol. II [n.s.], No. 46 (Dec. 10, 1857). Commensalism, or eating together, and endogamy, marriage within one's own group, are the hallmarks of a caste system, wherever it is found. As Bachman points out, caste practices were not confined to the South.

85.   *Ibid.* Bachman had contacts with slave owners who adhered to the "squire tradition." As Hesseltine observes, "The tradition of the squire required the assumption of responsibility for the well-being and the good conduct of his people. The squire who was a slaveholder frequently placed the happiness of his slave above his own material prosperity." Hesseltine, "Four American Traditions," p. 12.

86.   *The Missionary,* Vol. II [n.s.], No. 46 (Dec. 10, 1857).

87.   When the governor of South Carolina refused to grant the petition of a number of folk who sought a pardon for a white man convicted of killing a black boy, the editor of the *Lutheran Observer* took note of that fact, observing, "The laws of South Carolina make no distinction in cases of deliberate murder, whether committed on a black man or a white man; and neither can I." *Lutheran Observer,* Vol. VI [n.s.], No. 16 (Dec. 7, 1838).

88.   *The Missionary,* Vol. II [n.s.], No. 46 (Dec. 19, 1857).

89.   *Ibid.*

It has recently been argued that a concern for the unity of the church not only prompted southerners like Bachman to plead for the removal of the abolitionist debate from ecclesiastical circles but persuaded many northern Lutherans to take a similar stand. Many Lutherans "at the North" stood in the Pietistic tradition with its strong concern for "moral reform." Of these folk the overwhelming majority were undoubtedly supportive of abolition in one degree or another. However, they were so concerned about maintaining the unity of Lutheranism in the United States and enhancing the ecumenical goals of Protestantism in general (a matter which Pietists had always affirmed), that they were willing to allay their antislavery convictions and in most cases to silence them altogether.

Kuenning, "New York Lutheran Abolitionists," p. 64. Kuenning sees Editor Kurtz as the prototype of the northern pietist in this respect.

90. *Ibid.*

91. Kurtz realized that he was treading on "delicate ground; we did not intend to enter upon it when we commenced, and as our policy has ever been not to take sides on this vexed question, we forbear." *Lutheran Observer*, Vol. 11, No. 44 (July 5, 1844).

92. *Minutes, SC Synod, 1843*, p. 47.

93. *Lutheran Observer*, Vol. 11, No. 44 (July 5, 1844).

94. Craven, *Growth of Nationalism*, pp. 33-34. In the midst of the congressional debate on the Wilmot Proviso in 1847, a South Carolina district recommended that all their congressmen vacate their congressional seats and leave Washington if anything like the Wilmot Proviso be passed. The editor of the *Lutheran Observer* labeled such a proposal "Ultraism." *Lutheran Observer*, Vol. 15, No. 14 (Dec. 3, 1847), p. 55.

95. *Minutes, SC Synod, 1847*, pp. 7-8.

96. *Lutheran Observer*, Vol. 15, No. 16 (Dec. 17, 1847).

97. *Minutes, NC Synod, 1848*, p. [8].

98. It was suggested that Salisbury, North Carolina, be the site of the Southern Church Convention. *Lutheran Observer*, Vol. 16, No. 46 (Nov. 17, 1848). However, Concord was chosen instead.

99. *Minutes, SC Synod, 1848*, p. 34-35. *Lutheran Observer*, Vol. 16, No. 49 (Dec. 8, 1848).

100. *Lutheran Observer*, Vol. 17, No. 12 (March 23, 1849).

101. *Minutes, NC Synod, 1849*, p. 19.

102. *Ibid.*, p. 13.

103. *Lutheran Observer*, Vol. 17, No. 25 (June 22, 1849). While the Virginia Synod did not appoint delegates, delegates were named by the Western Virginia Synod, according to J. C. Hope.

104. *Ibid.* The special convention to deal with educational concerns did not materialize until 1853. In that year, the prodding of President Joseph A. Linn, Sr., culminated in the creation of Western Carolina Male Academy, which, six years later, became North Carolina College.

105. *Ibid.*, No. 29 (July 20, 1849), pp. 113-14. "Scrutator" was critical of the South Carolina Synod for failing to carry through on the Southern Church Convention. To his mind, the key issue centered around the seminary and its collegiate institute. He was among those who understood that the South Carolina Synod had invited other southern synods to meet with them to discuss this problem, then decided before the convention to keep the seminary in its Lexington location and to open the collegiate institute at the same place. *Ibid.*, No. 34 (Aug. 24, 1849).

Even as the attempt to have a Southern Church Convention for Lutherans was collapsing, the Mississippi legislature was following the suggestion of John C. Calhoun and launching a movement for a southern political convention, the Nashville convention which held two sessions in 1850. Green, "The Tarpley Letter," p. 224.

When the state of South Carolina scheduled a "State Convention" for early 1851, John C. Hope was among those who successfully sought a seat at the convention. He was reported by Rev. T. S. Boinest to be among those going "in for using every exertion for obtaining the cooperation of the other southern states before going into separate state action." "Report of Gifts," p. 34.

Ten years after the collapse of Hope's dream of a southern church convention, he would, as a member of the South Carolina legislature, seek to protect himself and his colleagues from the kind of disappointment produced both by his call for a Southern Church Convention and by Calhoun's call for a southern political convention.

Resolved, That it is the sense of the Legislature not to take steps for the immediate formation of a Southern Confederacy; but, when any of the neighboring slave States enter upon the proper course, to appoint deputies to meet with others...in convention, to deliberate and agree upon a plan for such formation, South Carolina will be ready to do her part in this gigantic movement.

Hope's resolution is quoted by Schultz, *Nationalism and Sectionalism,* p. 195, footnote.

106. It has been observed that the popular sovereignty approach to a solution was "laudably democratic" but one that "could not possibly work." It resembled a ten-foot plank laid across a chasm ten feet wide: it just bridged the gap, but no one dared walk on it. Lincoln had called attention to popular sovereignty's fatal flaw as far back as 1854. How could the system function, Lincoln asked, without specifying when the settlers would decide for or against slavery? This ambiguity was present when the idea first appeared in the late forties; it remained there when Congress debated the Kansas-Nebraska Act. Catton, *Two Roads to Sumter,* p. 133.

107. *Ibid.,* pp. 119-20.

108. *Ibid.,* p. 115.

109. *Ibid.,* p. 120.

110. The southern code prescribed either a horse-whip or a cane when one must punish an inferior for an insulting remark. *Ibid.,* p. 121.

A physician determined that the blows which sent Sumner "reeling around against the seats, backwards and forwards," were serious but unlikely to end his career in the Senate. Byrd, *The Senate,* p. 210.

111. Catton, *Two Roads to Sumpter,* p. 122.

112. *The Missionary,* Vol. I [n.s.], No. 1 (June 5, 1856).

113. *Lutheran Observer,* Vol. 24, No. 24 (June 6, 1856); No. 23 (May 30, 1856); No. 26 (June 20), 1856).

114. *Ibid.,* No. 42 (Oct. 17, 1856). "Charitas" was convinced that if Brooks "had sold his plantation and negroes, and given the proceeds to the Abolitionists, and had himself espoused the cause of the Republican party, he could not have prejudiced the cause of the South half as much as he has done by this imprudent act."

115. *Ibid.,* No. 35 (Aug 29, 1856).

116. *Ibid.,* Vol. 29, No. 29 (July 19, 1861).

117. *Ibid.,* Vol. 24, No. 35 (Aug. 29, 1856), quoting from an article in the Newberry, S.C., *Mirror* (July 19, 1856).

118. *Ibid.,* Vol. 29, No. 29, (Aug. 29, 1861.

119. The editor of the *South Episcopalian,* in March 1859 quoted in Wallace, *South Carolina,* p. 433.

120. *Ibid.* Professor Thomas E. Dew of the College of William and Mary is usually credited with having provided the South with the "positive good" theory of slavery. As noted earlier, the *Memoir on Slavery* published by Chancellor William Harper of South Carolina in 1837 provides a classic expression of this argument that slavery was the best of all possible worlds for both the slave and the master.

121. Coulter, *Confederate States,* p. 1.

The most prominent Lutheran clergyman in the South, John Bachman, was invited to deliver the invocation at the Secession Convention. *Harpers Weekly,* Vol. V, No. 212 (Jan. 19, 1861), pp. 33-34.

122. *The Daily Plain Dealer,* quoted by Goen, "Scenario for Secession," p. 20.

123. Richardson, *The Secret Service,* p. 106.

124. Lefler and Newsome, *North Carolina,* p. 443.

125. *Ibid.,* p. 446.

126. When Albert Richardson, the *New York Tribune* correspondent, realized in April, 1861, that it was not safe for him to remain in Charleston, he elected to board a midnight train for "North Carolina, whose Rip Van Winkle sleep seemed proof against any convulsion...." Richardson, *The Secret Service,* p. 109.

127. As war-time Governor Zebulon Baird Vance (1830-94) observed in 1866, "...The people of North Carolina, more, perhaps, than those of any of the eleven seceding States, were devoted to the Union. They had always regarded it with sincerest reverence and affection, and they left it slowly and with sorrow." Quoted in Yearns and Barrett, *Civil War Documentary.* p. 22. North Carolina was not alone in its lack of alacrity in embracing secession. "When the Confederacy organized itself in February, 1861, and prepared to fight a defensive war, forty-nine percent of its voting population had just voted for candidates (Bell or Douglas) both of whom had opposed the formation of a Confederacy." Degler, *The Other South,* p. 160. Interestingly, "....only one of the seven states that created the Confederacy in early February permitted the voters to be heard directly on the action of the secession conventions." *Ibid.,* p. 163.

The impotence of North Carolina's traditional political parties is illustrated by William Holden's editorial in the *North Carolina Standard* on April 13, 1861, concerning the contest between incumbent Congressman Lawrence O'B. Branch and his challenger, Henry W. Miller.

Democracy and Whiggism have nothing to do with this contest. The issue is Union or Disunion. Democratic principles and Whig principles will always exist, but the parties that were once organized on those principles have perished. The old Whig party perished in 1852, and the work of destroying the Democratic party was commenced at Charleston in 1860. That work went on, and the party in this State was finished by Governor Ellis and the disunionists during the last Legislature. Two new parties have since been formed - one at Goldsboro by the politicians, and the other all over the state by the people; the former being for disunion, and the latter opposed to it.

Holden's editorial is quoted by Crofts, *Reluctant Confederates,* p. 332.

128. Crouse, *Historical Sketches,* pp. 17-18.

129. As Governor Vance recalled, "But when Fort Sumter was fired upon, immediately followed by Mr. Lincoln's call for 'volunteers to suppress insurrection,' the whole situation changed instantly. The Union men had every prop knocked from under them, and by stress of their own position were plunged into the secession movement." Yearns and Barrett, *Civil War Documentary.* p. 23.

130. Artz' letter to his brother, David, is quoted in its entirety in Gobel, *Glorious Hill,* p. 26.

131. *Ibid.*

132. *Ibid.* The pastor's son, George V. Artz, had already departed for Fort Johnson near Wilmington.

133. The same force that impelled North Carolina to withdraw from the Union had a similar impact on other southern states. "The whole Unionist front in the South, came apart...when Lincoln, after the fall of Fort Sumter on April 14, called for troops to suppress what he called a rebellion." Degler, *The Other South,* p. 166.

President Lincoln's Secretary of State, William H. Seward, apparently did his best to oppose the folly of militaristic Republicans such as Montgomery Blair and his father, Francis P. Blair, Sr., who believed secession a minority coup and expected loyal southerners to sustain the Union cause as soon as federal armies arrived to crush the conspirators. Seward realized that the initiation of hostilities between the federal government and the Confederacy would, under existing conditions, transform nearly the entire South into a hostile armed camp. Crofts, *Reluctant Confederates,*

p. 357. Whether or not reunion would have been achieved through Seward's pacific approach is not clear. It is clear, however, that the president rejected Seward's approach.

134.   "....The fact is that the continuity between nullification in 1832, disunionist efforts in 1850, and secession in 1860-61 is established by more than a common constitutional interpretation of the Constitution. All three movements were linked by the desire to protect the South's 'peculiar institution,' slavery." *Ibid.*, p. 101.

135.   Troeltsch, *Social Teachings,* Vol. I, p. 207.

Chapter V. The Ordeal of War (p. 111)

1.   Quoted in Tapert, *The Brothers' War,* p. x.

2.   *The Southern Lutheran,* Vol. I, No. 7 (28 Sep 61), p. [1]. The author of the letter, "B.W.H.", was from South Carolina.

3.   H. G. Jones, *North Carolina Illustrated,* p. 197.

4.   Woodward and Muhlenfeld, *Private Mary Chesnut,* p. 150.

5.   Tapert, *Brothers' War,* pp. 111-12.

6.   *Ibid.,* p. 45.

7.   A letter from Capt. Wm. Nugent to his wife in Tupelo, Mississippi, quoted in *Ibid.,* p. 175.

8.   Willard, "Charles Lee Coon", p. 427.

9.   *Minutes, NC Synod, 1862,* p. 5.

10.   Shattuck, *Shield and Hiding Place,* p. 57.

11.   Norton, *Struggling for Recognition,* p. 131. It has been suggested that President Davis' negative attitude toward chaplains may relate to his experience with chaplains at West Point and in the Mexican War.

12.   Walker's report dated April 27, 1861, is quoted in Honeywell, *Chaplains,* p. 117.

13.   Norton, *Struggling for Recognition,* p. 132.

14.   Shattuck, *Shield and Hiding Place,* p. 64. A brigadier general was authorized a salary of $301 per month, a captain $130, a first lieutenant ninety dollars and a second lieutenant eighty dollars. Enlisted men received from thirteen to thirty-four dollars per month.

    In 1862 the Confederacy increased the chaplain's salary to eighty dollars instead of fifty dollars but by that time their Union counterparts were receiving $120 per month. *Ibid.,* p. 65, footnote.

15.   Norton, *Struggling for Recognition,* p. 143. London, *Episcopal Church in North Carolina,* pp. 245-46. The Methodists provided the Confederate Army with two hundred chaplains, the Baptists and Presbyterians with one hundred each. Lutherans are among the "other Protestant groups" who furnished approximately fifty additional chaplains. Prof. Honeywell has noted that

> Those Confederate chaplains who have left a statement of their political views in 1861 accepted unanimously the Southern contention and urged the support of the war as a moral and religious duty. Secession was considered an inherent right of any State. Slavery was a local matter, hypocritically attacked by the North from motives of economic rivalry. They blamed Northern preachers for starting the war by their attacks upon slavery and charged them with corrupting the gospel. The operations of Union troops were denounced as invasion and aggressive war, and the men were exhorted to defend rights as sacred as those of 1776. (Honeywell, *Chaplains,* p. 89.)

16.   In addition to salary, the compensation package included rations and stationery. Forage

for a horse was added, but not the horse. A popular story that made the rounds in the military concerned a chaplain who confiscated for his personal use a Virginia farmer's horse. When his action was challenged by an officer, he attempted to justify it by pointing to the action of Jesus Christ who "took an ass from his owner, whereon to ride into Jerusalem." The officer was not impressed with the chaplain's defense, retorting, "You are not Jesus Christ; this is not an ass; you are not on your way to Jerusalem; and the sooner you restore that horse to its owner, the better it will be for you." Norton, *Struggling for Recognition*, p. 134.

That, among army officers, support for the work of the chaplains was not confined to a few illustrious leaders like Gens. Lee and Jackson is illustrated by Chaplain Betts' report of how line officers, during the period when chaplains were paid only fifty dollars per month, collected a fund to purchase a horse for their chaplain. Honeywell, *Chaplains*, p. 127.

Some denominations supplemented the Army's pay of their chaplains. The Presbyterians began to supplement their chaplains' salaries as early as May 1861. Southern Methodists began in September 1863. By February 1864, the Baptist Sunday School and Publications Board was undergirding salaries of needy Baptist chaplains, and a month later the Domestic Board of Missions was also helping. *Ibid.*, p. 160.

17. Norton, *Struggling for Recognition*, p. 161.

18. Shattuck, *Shield and Hiding Place*, p. 66. ". . . the Confederacy seemed determined to demonstrate that religion had no positive contribution to make to the cause of Southern independence." *Ibid.*

19. Shattuck, *Shield and Hiding Place*, p. 46. The Board of Managers of the North Carolina Baptist State Convention reported in 1863 that "they had been trying to persuade pastors to leave their churches for brief tours as missionaries to soldiers, but the 'strange apathy' of the pastors had defeated this crusade." Yearns and Barrett, *Civil War Documentary*, p. [225].

20. [Norman], *Life Sketches*, p. 178. Where clergy simply visited the soldiers for brief periods as "missionaries" rather than chaplains, they usually had to provide for their own food and shelter. "The *Southern Lutheran* said that 'a missionary must be willing to live on parched corn in the winter and on roasting ears in the summer; to sleep on the ground, to walk, ride a kicking mule or mount a baggage wagon; to preach in season and out of season; to encounter hard usage....'" The Feb. 13, 1861, issue of the *Southern Lutheran* quoted in Daniel, "Southern Protestantism, p. 184.

21. De Bord, Hougen and Shumate, *St. Paul's Lutheran Church*, p.   45.

22. General Lee endeavored to provide support for the chaplains' program through his general orders No. 15 issued Feb. 7, 1864:

I. The attention of the army has already been called [in 1862] to the obligation of a proper observance of the Sabbath, but a sense of its importance, not only as a moral and religious duty, but as contributing to the personal health and well-being of the troops, induces the commanding general to repeat the orders on that subject. He has learned with great pleasure that in many brigades convenient houses of worship have been erected, and earnestly desires that every facility consistent with the requirements of discipline shall be afforded the men to assemble themselves together for the purpose of devotion.

II. To this end he directs that none but duties strictly necessary shall be required to be performed on Sunday, and that all labor, both of men and animals, which it is practicable to anticipate or postpone, or the immediate performance of which is not essential to the safety, health, or comfort of the army, shall be suspended on that day.

     III.   Commanding officers will require the usual inspections on Sunday to be held at such time as not to interfere with the attendance of the men on divine service at the customary hour in the morning. They also will give their attention to the maintenance of order and quiet around the places of worship, and prohibit anything that may tend to disturb or interrupt religious exercises." Quoted in Honeywell, op. cit., pp. 131-32. Norton, *Struggling for Recognition,* p. 145.

23. *Ibid,* p. 146. A chaplain recalled that as troops paused on their way to Manassas, he scheduled a worship service. The response was substantial, the gathered assembly covering "...what seemed a solid acre...."

     While they were singing, a shell fell in their midst but did not burst. They moved to a safer spot for the sermon, and within a short time a score of shells exploded in the area they had left. Honeywell, *Chaplains,* p. 128.

24. Norton, *Struggling for Recognition,* p. 147.

25. *Ibid.,* p. 149. Some chaplains also "attempted to establish libraries, with space for reading and writing." Occasionally, one even learns of a chaplain teaching courses in theology and Greek, or providing a basic literacy course for soldiers who could not read or write. *Ibid.,* p. 155.

26. Peter W. Hairston's note in his diary for Nov. 17, 1863. Everard Smith, "Diary of Peter W. Hairston", p. 76.

27. *Ibid.*

28. John B. Godon, *Reminiscences of the Civil War* (New York: 1903), p. 233, quoted in Daniel, "Southern Protestanism," p. 191.

29. Honeywell, *Chaplains,* p. 88.

30. *Minutes, NC Synod, 1863,* p. 10.

31. *Minutes, TN Synod, 1863,* p. 4.

32. *Ibid.,* pp. 7-8. The committee presenting the report consisted of three pastors (Fox, P. C. Henkel, and Henry Goodman) plus a layman (J. F. Plonk of Philadelphia, Dallas).

     When the synod met in October 1864, it was learned that "several of the brethren" had "visited some portion of our army during the past Winter." *Ibid., 1864,* p. 4. The only clergy person listed as serving in the armed forces was licentiate Daniel E. Fox serving with the Thirty-eighth North Carolina Regiment. *Ibid.,* p. [2]. Alfred J. Fox was among those visiting Lutheran soldiers in 1863 and 1864. Junius Fox, *Biography of Alfred J. Fox,* p. 62.

33. De Bord, Hougen and Shumate, *St. Paul's,* p. 46.

34. The Salisbury *Daily Carolina Watchman* for July 1, 1861 and March 3, 1862, cited in Yearns and Barrett, *Civil War Commentary,* pp. 229-30.

35. *Minutes, GSCSA, 1864,* p. 29.

36. *Minutes, TN Synod, 1864b,* p. 3. The offering produced $163 in the inflated currency of 1864.

37. Shattuck, *Shield and Hiding Place,* p. 83.

38. *Ibid.,* p. 84.

39. Norton, *Struggling for Recognition,* p. 149.

40. *Ibid.,* pp. 149-50. A chaplain in Virginia reported forty chapels were built along the Rapidan in the closing months of 1863 and sixty were erected along the Petersburg line in 1864. Honeywell, *Chaplains,* p. 127.

41. Shattuck, *Shield and Hiding Place,* p. 96.

42. *Ibid.,* p. 99.

43. *Ibid.,* p. 100.

44. *Ibid.,* p. 101. Norton sees the climax of revivalism in the western theater taking place at

Dalton, Georgia, where Gen. Joseph E. Johnston's troops went into winter quarters. Norton, *Struggling for Recognition,* p. 153.

45.   Shattuck, *Shield and Hiding Place,* p. 102. Norton does not comment on the general morale of the troops, but is much impressed with the accounts of the Dalton revivals.

        Results at Dalton were "glorious." Thousands were "happily converted" and "prepared for the future that awaited them." Dalton revivals touched officers and enlisted men alike. One chaplain said work there had no parallel. "In the coldest and darkest nights of the winter," he reported, "the crude chapels were crowded and at the call for penitents, hundreds would come down in sorrow and tears." He said Dalton "was the spiritual birthplace of thousands." Norton, *Struggling for Recognition,* p. 153.

        Norton quotes from William Bennet, *A Narrative of the Great Revival.* Philadelphia: Claxton, Remsen and Haffelfinger, 1877.

46.   William A. Clebsch, "Civil War," in Hill, *Encyclopedia of Religion,* p. 175.

47.   "For a while religious faith may actually have strengthened the morale of some Southerners and enabled them to look on military defeats as disguised blessings---means by which God purified a chosen people. Such early optimism, however, did not survive for long. As Confederate defeat became more certain each day, churchmen were forced to acknowledge that the war had to be an expression of God's wrath and his judgment against an unfaithful nation." Shattuck, *Shield and Hiding Place,* p. 12.

        Shattuck's contention that faith "may actually have strengthened the morale of some Southerners" is appropriately cautious. As a noted historian of religion in the South has observed, "The thesis that religion affected the will of Civil war soldiers is unexceptional; but how and why it did so is still a mystery." Donald G. Matthews, review of Shattuck, pp. 419-20.

48.   Scheck went on to observe that "Alternate hopes and fears, successes and reverses, have kept every mind in perpetual excitement, and men have lived in the last twelve months, half a century of ordinary life." *Minutes, NC Synod, 1862,* p. 4.

        Approximately one fourth of all Confederate battle deaths were suffered by North Carolina troops. The first Confederate to die in battle was a North Carolinian at Big Bethel in June 1861. One fifth of all Confederate casualties growing out of the defense of Richmond against the attack of Gen. George B. McClellan in 1962 were provided by the Old North State.

        Later that year, in the bloodiest day of the war, when the armies clashed at Sharpsburg, Maryland, North Carolinians led by General D. H. Hill were in the middle of the maelstrom. In December, 1862, came Fredricksburg, followed in the spring by Chancellorsville; in those battles North Carolinians suffered one third of the casualties. At Gettysburg, as the stirring monument attests, one out of every five who fell - while advancing the farthest - called North Carolina home. Leutze, "Nation in Microcosm," p. 109.

49.   *The Southern Lutheran,* Vol. I, No. 7, [Charleston, S.C.], (Sept. 28, 1861), p. [1], reprinted from the *Southern Presbyterian.*

50.   Woodward, *Origins of the New South,* p. 145.

51.   *Minutes, TN Synod, 1862,* p. 5.

52.   Quoted in De Bord, Hougen and Shumate, *St. Paul's,* p. 42.

53.   Barringer, *The Natural Bent,* p. 52.

54.   A Warrenton, North Carolina, resident reportedly "bought the contents of a store early in the war, and transferred the stock 'to his own cupboards and pantry.' His home remained a Utopia in the midst of want and privation." Massey, *Ersatz in the Confederacy,* p. 21.

55.   *Ibid.,* p. 144.

56. Barringer, *The Natural Bent*, p. 52. Broken stove lids, window sash weights and skillets were melted down to make replacement bells for the churches. However, they aparently were so lacking in melodious quality that they were rarely rung.

57. *Ibid.*, p. 51.

58. Fitzgerald, "Poor Man's Fight," p. 15.

59. Barringer, *The Natural Bent*, p. 47. Yearns and Barrett, *Civil War Documentary*, p. 78.

60. *Minutes, GSCSA, 1864*, p. 4.

61. *Ibid.*, p. 5.

62. Wall, *Davie County*, p. 262; Clayton, *Close to the Land*, p. 90.

63. McPherson, *Ordeal by Fire*, p. 200. "By the spring of 1865 prices had risen to ninety-two times their prewar level." *Ibid.*

64. Crouse, *Historical Sketches*, p. 20.

65. Yearns and Barrett, *Civil War Commentary*, p. 66. In fact, blockade-running became so lucrative that the State of North Carolina got into the business itself, and Governor Vance later recalled that the decision to do so enabled the state to expand its contribution to the war effort by "large quantites of machinery supplies; 60,000 pairs of handcards; 10,000 grain scythes; 200 bbls. blue stone for wheat growers; leather and shoes to 250,000 pairs, 50,000 blankets, gray woolen cloth for at least 250,000 suits of uniforms, 12,000 overcoats (ready-made), 2,000 best Enfield rifles (with 100 rounds of fixed ammunition), 100,000 pounds of bacon, 500 sacks of coffee for hospital use, $50,000 worth of medicines at gold prices, large quantities of lubricating oils, besides minor supplies of various kinds for the charitable institution of the State." *Ibid.*, p. 70. The fall of Fort Fisher on Jan. 16, 1865, led to the surrender of Wilmington five weeks later. "The loss of the mouth of the Cape Fear destroyed the last major contact of the South with the outside world," and placed "the seal of doom" on the Confederacy. *Ibid.*, p. 91.

66. Clayton, *Close to the Land*, p. 90.
    To many of these people the Civil War brought a level of acute suffering that has not been fully recognized. After what seems to have been a gradual but cumulative rise in nonslaveholders' income during the antebellum period, many North Carolinians were suddenly thrown into poverty. They lost their essential farm laborers to the army, and they encountered shortages 'of almost every article of necessity, from a needle to a scythe blade.' Uncontrollable inflation, heavy taxes, and government impressment of food and war materiel made their situation worse. Bad weather and conscription further reduced supplies. Escott and Crow, "The Social Order", p. 377.

67. In 1850 North Carolina had "an average of only 19.3 inhabitants per square mile." In 1860, "the largest twenty-five towns, taken together, contained only one percent of the state's population." *Ibid.*

68. "38 Ministers Have Served St. Luke's Church At Tyro," *The Dispatch Progress Edition.* Spring, 1968.

69. Steffey, *St. John's, Cabarrus County*, p. 32.

70. Harwell and Racine, *The Fiery Trail*, p. 107.

71. *Ibid.*, p. 200.

72. Drake, *Fast and Loose*, p. 111.

73. *Ibid.*, p. 155. Drake was particularly impresssed with Julia Setser, Sarah Teague and Mrs. Bill Estes. Mrs. Estes' husband fought for the Confederacy through the battle of Gettysburg which destroyed his confidence in the South's military leadership. Returning to his home northwest of Morganton, he hid out in the remote areas in the foot of the mountains, where he was joined by other deserters. By the time Drake and his comrades encountered Mrs. Estes and her friends in late October 1864, there were approximately forty deserters in the band that included Estes. *Ibid.*, p. 164.

Drake also was assisted by Rev. and Mrs. Prickett in their mountain fastness near Grandfather Mountain. Prickett was serving in the Piedmont when the war came. His sympathies for the preservation of the Union resulted in his losing all his "worldly possessions," and he and his family were subjected to many "indignities and privations." This Baptist family fled to the mountains where Prickett's two oldest sons were "lyers-out," i.e., persons who hid out in the mountains during the conflict. *Ibid.,* pp. 187-89.

It should not be assumed that the Prickett family's views were typical for Baptists in North Carolina. The *Confederate Baptist* described desertion as "rebellion against God and against Caesar," and declared that "No man who deserts the flag of his Country is fit for membership in a Baptist Church." Quoted in Bardolph, "Confederate Dilemma," p. 81.

74. Tapert, *Brothers' War,* pp. 184-85. Desertion was a problem for Union as well as Confederate forces. In January, 1863, the Union Army was losing "at least 200" soldiers each day through desertion. McPherson, *Ordeal by Fire,* p. 317.

75. For a discussion of the circumstances surrounding Lee's General Order, see Bardolph, "Confederate Dilemma," pp. 67-68. Shortly after the battle at Gettysburg, Lee wrote Gen. John M. Imboden that there was so "much desertion...from this army...principally from the North Carolina troops [that] I fear nothing but the death penalty, uniformly, inexorably administered, will stop it." *Ibid.,* p. 200.

Chaplain Paris is quoted in Yearns and Barrett, *Civil War Documentary,* p. 58.

76. Although he presumably had been home in Piedmont North Carolina for more than a year when he befriended the fugitive Yankee officers, Bill Estes "had not passed a single night in his own house since his return from the army, for spies were continually watching for him, and for hundreds of others who were in a similar predicament." Drake, *Fast and Loose,* p. 159.

77. Escott and Crow, "Social Order," pp. 393-95.

78. A letter from Joseph Huneycutt, quoted in Sharpe, *Stanly County,* p. 184.

79. Morgan, *Lutheran Church in NC,* p. 385.

80. Goen provides the statistics for 1850, "Scenario for Secession", p. 14. The 1860 standing is provided by Woodard based on a membership figure of 3,492 and 38 congregations. John R. Woodard, "North Carolina," in Hill, *Encyclopedia of Religion,* p. 543. Woodward apparently does not include in his count the Lutheran congregations in North Carolina that were affiliated with the Tennessee Synod. A more reliable source indicates that there were forty-two hundred communicants in the North Carolina Synod's forty-two congregations. The Tennessee Synod is credited with fifty-five hundred members in ninety-three congregations. *Lutheran Almanac for 1861,* pp. 32-33. While the Tennessee Synod covered three states, approximately one-third of its strength was in North Carolina. In 1870 the North Carolina Synod was credited with four thousand communicants in thirty-three congregations. *Minutes, GSNA,* p. 16.

81. *The Southern Lutheran,* Vol. 1, No. 9 (12 Oct 61), p. [2].

82. Cox, *Reminiscences,* p. 8.

83. *History of Sinking Springs,* pp. [3-4.]

84. Pastor William Berly of St. Stephen's, Lexington, S. C. *The Evangelical Lutheran,* Vol. 2, No. 56 (Sept. 26, 1867), p. [2]. In Dec. 1866 Berly considered seeking a teaching position to relieve his personal economic plight. In Aug. 1870 he observed, "I have preached for these people 6 years for nothing, begged nearly all the money to build the church [and] hauled with my own wagon and team." "Report of Gifts," p. 34.

85. Shattuck, *Shield and Hiding Place,* p. 43. From 1860 to 1866 the Methodist Church in the South lost thirty percent of its members, and some areas of financial support declined by as much as fifty percent.

86. De Bord, Hougen and Shumate, *St. Paul's,* p. 42.

87.   *The Southern Lutheran,* Vol. I, No. 7, (28 Sep 61) p. [2]. This revival also produced twenty confirmations. Miller noted

> There were some ten or twelve mourners left, who felt unsatisfied with their soul's condition. We left them in the hands of God and the brethren; they were still labouring with them, hoping they too would find Jesus precious to their souls.

Miller was assisted in the revival by Pastor W. Kimball of Luther's Chapel-St. Paul's and by "Bro. Gannon, a Methodist minister of the Davie Circuit."

88.   *The Southern Lutheran,* Vol. I, No. 9 (Oct. 12, 1861), p. [2].

89.   Shattuck, *Shield and Hiding Place,* p. 3.

90.   *Ibid.,* p. 9. In recent decades a number of historians have argued that in seeking an understanding of why the United States was victorious over the Confederate states, one should look beyond military strategies, manpower and supplies to the question of morale. Those attributing a key role in the collapse of the Confederacy to the breakdown of southern morale include Charles G. Sellers who in 1960 argued a sense of guilt on the slavery issue undercut early enthusiasm for secession and the war. Kenneth Stampp in 1968 further developed that same theme. More recently, James Oakes picked up on the Sellers and Stampp theme, and the 1986 publication, *Why the South Lost the Civil War,* relates the downfall of the South to the "religious fatalism" of southern Christianity. Persons who had grown accustomed to living with guilt played a critical role, it is said, in making military reverses acceptable to the general populace. *Ibid.,* p. 10.

91.   Anderson, *Lutheranism in the Southeast,* p. 21. This excellent study was published earlier in paperback form as *A Social History of Lutheranism in the Southeastern States, 1860-1886.* Kannapolis: Bethany Press, 1963. Anderson notes that four synods in the South, North Carolina, South Carolina, Southwestern Virginia and Virginia, represented one seventh of the clergy and one eighth of the communing membership in the General Synod.

92.   *Minutes, NC Synod, 1861,* p. 12. Bittle's moderate approach with regard to the synod's possible future relationship with the General Synod suggests a parallel in the Episcopal Diocese of North Carolina. Despite action by bishops in Louisiana and Georgia who declared that, with the secession of their states from the Union, their dioceses ceased to be members of the national church and its general convention, the bishop of North Carolina insisted that "the secession of the Southern states did not, in itself, cause a dissolution of the relations existing among the dioceses forming the Protestant Episcopal Church in the United States. He granted that the separation produced by the war might justify, or even require, a separate organization for the Church in the South, but he insisted that the mere action of the states could have no effect whatever ipso facto on the unity of the Church...." London, *Episcopal Church,* p. 244.

93.   D. I. Dreher, *A Sermon Preached on June 13, 1861. Day of Humiliation and Prayer as per Appointment of the President of the Confederate States of America.* Salisbury: n.p., 1861, pp. 3-4, 15; quoted in Anderson, *Lutheranism in the Southeast,* p. 31.

94.   President David F. Bittle of Roanoke College, brother of Daniel H. Bittle, first president of North Carolina College, quoted in Anderson, *Lutheranism in the Southeast,* p. 30. Anderson points out that by the end of June, the *Lutheran Observer* had lost all its subscribers in the South and the officers of the South Carolina Synod had announced their plan to launch a church paper for Lutherans living in the South. *Ibid.,* pp. 30-31.

95.   Levi Bedenbaugh, whose presidential report appears in *Minutes, Georgia Synod, 1861,* is quoted by Anderson, *Lutheranism in the Southeast,* p. 32.

96.   *The Southern Lutheran,* Vol. I, No. 7 (28 Sep 61), p. [1]. The convention also endorsed "the proposition of the Synod of South Carolina, to issue a Church paper in Charleston, under the title of the *Southern Lutheran* to be ultimately under the control of the General Synod

South."

97. Haas' Church (St. James, Newton) sent a petiton to the Tennessee Synod in which they admonished "the Synod to avoid all connection with a contemplated General Synod of the Lutheran church in the Confederate States." *Minutes, TN Synod, 1862*, p. 9. Similar petitions were received from St. John's, Conover; St. Paul's, Newton; and Zion, Hickory. New Jerusalem, Lexington, also wrote in to protest against "any union" of the synod with a general body in the South. P. C. Henkel was serving St. James, Newton, and Henry Goodman was the pastor at Zion.

Apparently as a result of these petitions, the synod "excused as commissioners to [the] Convention at Salisbury" Pastors A. J. Fox, E. E. Smyre, and Adam Efird. *Ibid.*, p. 10. President Adam Efird, in his report to synod, had recommended that the commissioners be continued, and the committee on his report noted that fact. However, the convention concluded that his report contained "nothing which demanded the action of Synod." *Ibid.*

While the Tennessee Synod thus withdrew from the consultations that would lead to the creation of the General Synod in the Confederate States of America, the Holston Synod decided the same month to begin participating in the process. Anderson, *Lutheranism in the Southeast*, p. 36.

98. *Minutes, GSCSA, 1863*, pp. [3]-4.

99. De Bord, Hougen and Shumate, *St. Paul's*, p. 43.

100. *Minutes, GSCSA, 1863*, P. 4.

101. The constitution of the General Synod, as quoted in Anderson, *Lutheranism in the Southeast*, p. 75. The constitution did not define the "fundamental doctrines" nor explain how they were taught by the Lutheran church.

102. *Minutes, GSCSA, 1863*, p. 9.

103. *Ibid.*, p. 32.

Chapter VI. Surrender and Its Aftermath (p. 139)

1. Crabtree and Patton, *Secesh Lady*, p. 694. Despite the high number of casualties suffered by North Carolina troops serving with the Army of Virginia, one fifth of the troops surrendered by Lee at Appomattox were from North Carolina. Leutze, "Nation in Microcosm," p. 110.

2. E. Merton Coulter, *The South During Reconstruction, 1865-1877;* Vol. VIII of Stephenson, *History of the South*, p. 1. The Cattons agree with Coulter that, while abolitionism "hastened its demise," slavery, even without the "moral indignation" of the abolitionists, was an institution "headed for extinction." Catton, *Two Roads to Sumter,* p. 69.

3. Blackmun, *Western North Carolina*, p. 356.

4. Sutherland, *Confederate Carpetbaggers*, p. [9].

5. *Ibid.*, p. 5.

6. Woodward and Muhlenfeld, *Private Mary Chestnut*, p. 247.

7. Foster, *Ghosts of the Confederacy*, p. 22.

8. *Ibid.*, p. 24. Foster quotes the Presbyterian body's resolution from *Appleton's Annual Cyclopedia and Register of Important Events*. New York: 1865, p. 706.

9. Quoted in De Bord, *St. Paul's Lutheran Church*, p. 47.

10. *The Lutheran Visitor,* Vol. II, No. 9 (Sept., 1867), p. [260].

11. Letter from B. Sears to Robert C. Winthrop, dated Feb. 8, 1868, quoted in *Peabody Education Fund*, p. 12. In the rare situations where educational programs were in place, tuition in "good primary schools in the South" ran twenty dollars per year for the ten-

month term, a figure beyond the means of the great majority of southern families.

12. Woodward and Muhlenfeld, *Private Mary Chestnut*, p. xxiii.

13. Clay, *North Carolina Atlas*, p. [204].

14. Barringer, *The Natural Bent*, p. 168.

15. *The Lutheran Visitor*, Vol. 1, No. 1 (Jan., 1866), p. 24. The editor was Joseph Irenaeus Miller, who later became a pastor of the Tennessee Synod.

16. The original article appeared in the Boston *Recorder* for March 30, 1866. The response of the *Christian Observer* to the item in the *Recorder* is reprinted by *The Lutheran Visitor*, Vol. I, No. 6 (June 1866), pp. 140.

    As the new state governments in the South attempted to meet the needs created by the long neglect of such things as public works and also gave birth to new programs such as public schools, tax rates increased dramatically for many land owners. This multiplied the foreclosures prompted by failure to pay taxes, again providing an opportunity for the entrepreneur. "In 1869 some twenty-three Wake County plantations in North Carolina containing 7,872 acres were sold for taxes and brought only $7,718." Franklin, *Reconstruction*, p. 145.

17. *The Evangelical Lutheran*, Vol. 2, No. 56 (Sept. 26, 1867), p. [4].

18. Franklin, *Reconstruction*, p. 10.

19. *Minutes, NC Synod, 1866*, p. 6.

20. *Ibid.*, p. 12.

21. *Minutes, TN Synod, 1867*, p. 11. The committee presenting this assessment was composed of Pastors J. R. Peterson and Thomas Crouse, along with Licentiate D. S. Henkel.

22. Unsigned article in "Literary and Miscellaneous," *The Lutheran Visitor*, Vol. II, No. 1 (Jan. 1867), p. 26.

23. *Minutes, GSCSA, 1866*, pp. 6-7. In a recent address on North Carolina and the Civil War, the speaker observed that not only was the state "devastated in economic and emotional terms," but also that "in economic terms, it is arguable that in many measurable commodities North Carolina did not return to the levels of 1860 for forty years and that the state did not achieve true recovery until sometime in the 1940s." Leutze, "Nation in Microcosm," p. 108.

24. *Minutes, NC Synod, 1870*, p. 6.

25. Steffy, *St. John's, Cabarrus County*, pp. 33-34.

26. Powell, *North Carolina*, p. 380.

27. Diary entry for May 16, 1865, in Woodward and Muhlenfeld, *Private Mary Chestnut*, p. 247.

28. Powell, *North Carolina*, p. 385. Delaware, Maryland, Kentucky, and all southern states except Tennessee, rejected the Fourteenth Amendment which incorporated the Civil Rights Act through which Congress made black persons citizens and bestowed on them the civil rights enjoyed by white persons. The amendment penalized any state failing to enfranchise black persons and removed the franchise from many former Confederates, reserving to Congress the privilege of restoring their right to vote and hold office.

29. *Ibid.*, p. 395. As Powell notes, the celebration of July 4 as Independence Day was a popularly-observed holiday in the South before the war. With the loss of southern independence in 1865, many transferred "some portions of the old celebration - such as setting off firecrackers - to Christmas." *Ibid.*, p. 388, footnote.

30. Tapert, *The Brothers' War*, pp. 166-67.

31. Thomas, "Brazil," p. C12. Thomas notes that another factor encouraging emigration to Brazil was "an emperor (Dom Pedro II) who met them with welcoming arms and sat down with them to break cornbread."

    Many immigrants to Brazil were disappointed with life there, and possibly as many as eighty percent eventually made their way back to the United States. *Ibid.* Weaver is no doubt correct in observing that a significant factor in the unhappiness of many southerners who fled to Brazil was the different religious climate.

Apparently the southerners contemplating emigration to Brazil had slight conception of what it would mean to live in a country in which the Catholic Church was the established one. . . . Opponents of southern migration had warned those who considered colonization that only grief could result from their casting their lot in a popish country where their lives and those of their children would feel the heavy influence of a foreign religion.   The colonists were in no mood, however, to heed these warnings. They were resolved to flee federal domination, and Brazil with its vast land spaces and acceptance of slavery seemed the ideal haven. Moreover, the contracts granted by the Brazilian government to colonial leaders specifically guaranteed religious liberty provided the state religion was respected.   It was not until they were actually living in their new homes that the former Confederates came to realize that freedom of religion as understood in Brazil was not the same as that accepted in the United States. Weaver, "Confederate Immigrants," pp. 452-53.

Thomas notes that at Americana, Brazil, approximately seventy miles from Sao Paulo, descendants of a number of the post-Civil War emigrees continue to maintain Old South traditions, including an annual July 4 celebration, in Sao Paulo State. An earlier report on the annual observance at Americana is that provided by Francis B. Kent, "Alabama Accent in Brazil?", *The Charlotte Observer* (June 3, 1965), p. 7D.

32. *The Evangelical Lutheran,* Vol. 2, No. 56 (Sept. 26, 1867), p. [1].

33. *Ibid.* Stevens was a member of the House of Representatives from Pennsylvania and a "radical reconstructionist." Of a similar disposition was Senator Benjamin Franklin Wade of Ohio who prior to the war was "a flaming crusader against slavery." Potter, *Impending Crisis,* p. 230.   Gerritt Smith devoted his considerable wealth to a variety of causes including abolitionism and woman's suffrage, but was also one of the signers of the bail bond for Jefferson Davis in May, 1867. Martin and Gelber, *Dictionary of American History,* p. 571.

34. *The Evangelical Lutheran,* Vol. 2, No. 56 (Sept. 26, 1867), p. [1].

35. *Ibid.* "The South's greatest leaders, such as Lee, Hampton, and Lamar, frowned upon the migration as ill-advised and impractical and upon the emigres as deserters." Coulter, *The South During Reconstruction,* p. 185.

For Mordecai's offence to Haman, see Esther 3:1-11.

36. Sutherland, *Confederate Carpetbaggers,* p. 21.

37. Quoted in *Ibid.,* p. 17.

38. *Ibid.,* p. 6.

39. William A. Clebsch, "Civil War," in Bruce, *Encyclopedia of Religion in the South,* p. 176.

40. Quoted in Richardson, *The Secret Service,* p. 107.

41. "Our Losses and Gains," *The Southern Lutheran,* Vol. I, No. 9 (Oct. 12, 1861), p. [3].

It should be noted that while the war did not immediately produce massive revolts on the part of the slave population in the South, not all black persons were content to remain in their servile condition. When Union forces occupied portions of North Carolina's Outer Banks and the area around New Bern early in the war, black persons began to flee the interior and seek protection behind the Union lines. Mary Barbour remembered that, as a small child, she was carried by her parents from McDowell County to New Bern, the fugitive family traveling the two hundred miles at night and hiding in wooded areas during the day.

By mid-1862, more than ten thousand contrabands had converged on the North Carolina coast. The population of New Bern swelled from roughly 5,400 to 7,500. By the end of the war, almost sixteen thousand freed slaves would live in the vicinity of New Bern. Cecelski, "A Thousand Aspirations," p. 23.

42. Abbott, *Reminiscences,* p. 236.

43. *Ibid.,* p. 237.

44. *Ibid.*

45. *Ibid.* Abbott, a Congregational clergyman, served from 1865 to 1869 as the general secretary of the Union Commission, an organization that sought to foster and coordinate efforts to create schools for the freedmen and "to aid and cooperate with the people of the South, without distinction of race or color, in the improvement of their condition. . . ." *Ibid.,* p. 261.

46. *The Evangelical Lutheran,* Vol. 2, No. 56 (Sept. 26, 1867), p. [2].

47. Franklin, *Reconstruction,* p. 56. Black North Carolinians held conventions in New Bern and Raleigh in 1865 to protest the disabilities under which they labored. *Ibid.,* p. 228.

48. Powell, *North Carolina,* p. 383. Powell notes that with all its advances, the "Black Code" in North Carolina did not guarantee full civil rights to blacks." *Ibid.*

49. Franklin, *Reconstruction,* p. 157.

50. *Minutes, NC Synod, 1866,* p. 24. In Alabama, a Lutheran pastor also expressed an interest in the hiring of German immigrants. The pastor considering this option was John P. Margart of Eufaula. "Report of Gifts," p. 34.

51. Joseph S. Vandiver, "The Changing Realm of King Cotton," in Mack, *The Changing South,* p. 23.

52. Leonard, *Southern Synod,* p. 43.

53. Powell, *North Carolina,* p.383.

54. Friedman, *The Enclosed Garden,* p. [92].

Reconstruction sought to re-make the South into the image of the rest of the nation. That effort failed, not simply because southern whites needed workers and southern blacks needed jobs. Factors involved in the failure of Reconstruction include (1) the split between northern and southern whites in the Republican Party, (2) the "violent and persistent hostility of the majority of white Southerners to the political equality of Negroes of which the Klan's activities were the most visible measure." (3) "White Southerners also resented the interference of the alien North in their political and social life, of which the hostility toward carpetbaggers was but the tip of the iceberg." And (4), ". . . as the settlement of 1877 makes evident, the failure of the Republicans in the South is related to the North's failure of nerve and commitment. Northerners simply abandoned the protection of Negro political rights, which they had once insisted upon and which was the indispensable electoral foundation for a southern biracial party." Degler, *The Other South,* p. 263.

55. H. G. Jones, *North Carolina Illustrated,* p. 265.

56. Woodward and Muhlenfeld, *Private Mary Chestnut,* p. 251.

57. A letter dispatched by President Jeremiah Ingold and Stated Clerk G. W. Welker of the North Carolina Classis of the German Reformed Church, quoted in Leonard, *Southern Synod,* p. 56.

58. *Ibid.,* p. 49.

59. *Minutes, GS, 1866,* p. 7, footnote 4.

Episcopal leadership in North Carolina reflected a spirit similar to that of President Roehm. Bishop Atkinson, of all Episcopal bishops in the South, "was the least embarrassed or trammeled by the results of the war." The presiding bishop of the church in the United States contacted all bishops in the South urging their attendance at the General Convention in June 1865 in the city of Philadelphia, and encouraging them to see to it that their dioceses were represented in the House of Deputies. Even though the senior bishop of the Protestant Episcopal Church in the Confederate States of America urged caution and elected to convene the bishops in the South only after the General Convention in Philadelphia, Bishop Atkinson, with the blessing of his diocese, attended the Philadelphia convention, was cordially received, and played an important role in insuring that certain convention actions were worded so as to make them as unlikely as possible to offend southern sensibilities. London, *The Episcopal Church in North Carolina*, pp. 252-53.

60. In the first session of the North Carolina synodical convention on Thursday, May 3, 1866, Pastor Heilig served notice that he would, later in the convention, present a resolution pertaining to "the resumption of our former relations with the General Synod of the United States." The following morning, Heilig presented his resolution, calling upon the synod to rescind its action of 1862 which dissolved its relationship with the original General Synod. The convention decided to make this issue the first item of business on Saturday morning. "Considerable animation" marked the discussion of Heilig's proposal, discussion which consumed the entire morning and much of the afternoon. Although the motion was defeated, three pastors and three laymen asked that their votes for the motion be recorded. *Minutes, NC Synod, 1866*, pp. 21-22.

61. *Minutes, GS, 1862*, p. 30.

62. *Minutes, GSCSA, 1866*, p. 4. The initial meeting in Salisbury in May 1862 considered itself a convention of the "Evangelical Lutheran Church in the Confederate States of America," but the constituting convention the following year decided to lay claim to the designation "General Synod," the title of the organization now fractured by the Civil War, an organization which the North Carolina Synod had helped to organize in 1820. This 1866 convention in Cabarrus County sought to keep the "General Synod" title, substituting "in North America" for "in the Confederate States of America," and reversing the order in which the words "Evangelical Lutheran" and "General Synod" appear in the above title, so that the new name came out "Evangelical Lutheran General Synod in North America." Since the "other" General Synod had district synods in much of the then United States except for the South, the title chosen at Mt. Pleasant was really more appropriate for the northern general body than the southern. In 1874 President J. F. Campbell of the southern body noted the "'in North America' is too comprehensive and simulating, and I would prefer 'The Evangelical Lutheran General Synod South.'" In 1878 the change proposed earlier by Campbell was adopted.

Actually, neither the title adopted in 1863 or that adopted in 1866 seem to have altered the popular manner of referring to the South's major Lutheran body; it was "the General Synod South." Only the creation of the United Synod of the South in 1886 produced a new popular name to supplant "General Synod South." Monroe, "Southern Lutheranism," p. 21. In the interest of simplicity and to reduce confusion, the text of this study refers to the southern body as the "General Synod South" even in the years before the word "South" was officially a part of its title.

63. *Minutes, GSCSA, 1866*, p. 3.

64. *The Evangelical Lutheran*, Vol. 2, No. 56 (Sept. 26, 1867), p. [2].

The bishop of the Episcopal Diocese of North Carolina, in a sermon on the Fifth Sunday after Easter, 1861, wisely warned his flock of the dangers inherent in "the growth of rancorous, vindictive, malignant feeling and the use of bitter, scornful opprobrious language concerning those once our brethren, now, alas, it would seem our enemies." Bishop Thomas Atkinson, quoted in London, *Episcopal Church*, p. 241.

65. Bernheim reported on the Cabarrus County convention for *The Lutheran Visitor*, Vol. 1,

No. 8 (Aug., 1866), p. 189, as quoted in Monroe, "Southern Lutheranism," p. 22.

66.   *Minutes, GSCSA, 1866,* p. 7.

67.   *Ibid.,* pp. 7-8. The members of this standing committee were all from North Carolina, Pastors D. I. Dreher and G. D. Bernheim plus Mr. Ransom Winecoff.

The fact that several synods "at the North" encouraged their congregations to aid their destitute brothers and sisters in the South, and that many congregations did send relief supplies to congregations in the South undoubtedly contributed to a diminution of hostile feelings among Lutherans, North and South. W. C. Heathcote, *The Lutheran Church and the Civil War,* p. 88, cited in Monroe, "Southern Lutheranism," p. 23.

68.   *Minutes, GSCSA, 1866,* p. 8.

69.   *The Lutheran Visitor,* Vol. I, No. 8 (Aug. 1866), p. 185.

Nevertheless, the memory of the verbal denunciation of Lutherans in the South by the old General Synod made it difficult for southern Lutherans to consider returning to that fold. In 1871 the old General Synod elected Rev. V. F. Bolton of New York a fraternal delegate to the next convention of the General Synod South. Rev. Peter Shickel of Virginia presented Bolton's credentials to the Charleston convention and moved that he be received. The minutes note laconically, "Motion tabled and credentials returned."

Rev. V. F. Bolton was then, on motion, invited to address this Convention, which he respectfully declined. *Minutes, ELGSNA, 1872,* p. 23.

With the creation of the General Council in 1867, Lutherans in the South had a new option to consider as they thought in terms of an umbrella organization, national in scope.

70.   A. R. Rude's comment in a June 3, 1869, editorial is quoted in Eisenberg, *Lutheran Church in Virginia,* p. 225.

71.   *Minutes, GSCSA, 1866,* p. 33.

72.   *Ibid.,* pp. 33-34. As Rev. Paul Monroe pointed out, in insisting on the catholic creeds "and the Augsburg Confession as the exponents of our faith," while removing the "private judgment" clause, the strengthening of the confessionalism of the Lutheran Church in the South was unmistakable.

If the adjective "unaltered" had been placed before Augsburg Confession in that doctrinal statement, a lot of future trouble might have been avoided, and a future strength might have been assured. The strict Tennessee Synod would have had no reason to remain outside. Monroe, "Southern Lutheranism," p. 21.

73.   *Ibid.,* p. 34.

74.   During his pastorate of more than two decades at Salem, Mt. Sidney, Virginia, Beard enjoyed the distinction of bringing into the Lutheran church a young woman, Ida Elizabeth Stover, who later became the mother of a President of the United States of America, Dwight David Eisenhower. Eisenberg, *Lutheran Church in Virginia,* p. 418.

75.   "Church Intelligence," *The Lutheran Visitor,* Vol. II, No. 1 (Jan., 1867), p. 24.

76.   *Ibid.*

77.   *Minutes, NC Synod, 1844,* p. 27.

78.   *Minutes, TN Synod, 1845,* p. 7. Samuel was one of several sons of Solomon Henkel of New Market and a grandson of Rev. Paul Henkel. Other sons of Solomon who, with Samuel, took over the Henkel Press and transformed it into Solomon D. Henkel and Company after the death of their father included Siram P., Solomon D., and Solon P. C. Henkel. Cassell, Finck and Henkel, *Lutheran Church in Virginia,* p. 312.

79.   *Minutes, TN Synod, 1846,* p. 5.

80.   *Ibid.,* p. 6. Two years later, the Tennessee Synod provided its members with information on how to subscribe to *Der Lutheraner* published by the newly created Lutheran Church-Missouri Synod. *Ibid., 1848,* p. 8, footnote.

81. *Minutes, NC Synod, 1851,* p. 14.

82. *The Southern Lutheran,* Vol. I, No. 7 (Sept. 28, 1861), p. 3.

83. *Minutes, NC Synod, 1862,* p. 14.

84. *Minutes, TN Synod, 1862,* pp. 6, 10.

85. *Minutes, TN Synod, 1864b,* p. 3.

86. Undated clipping from *The Southern Lutheran* providing the minutes of the convention which began on May 15, 1862, in Salisbury.

In January 1862, the South Carolina Synod created a publication committee to have responsibility for *The Southern Lutheran.* Early editorial responsibilities were accepted by Pastors Nicodemus Aldrich, John Bachman, and William Spencer Bowman, all of whom were serving churches in Charleston where the paper was published initially. With the bombardment of Charleston by Federal troops, the printing shop that had produced *The Southern Lutheran* was destroyed. As a result, the production of the paper was moved in 1863 to Columbia, South Carolina, where Rev. Anders R. Rude served as editor.

The paid circulation of *The Southern Lutheran* reached 1,000 by the fall of 1862 and peaked at almost 1,500 in the spring of 1864. Approximately 1,400 copies were mailed without charge each week to men in the Confederate armed forces. Anderson, *Lutheranism in the Southeast,* p. 84.

87. *Minutes, GSCSA, 1864,* p. 21.

88. *Ibid.,* pp. 18-19. When the General Synod South met at Newberry, South Carolina, years later, President Samuel Rothrock reported that Rev. A. R. Rude had declined his election to an editorial post on *The Evangelical Lutheran.* To keep the General Synod South appropriately represented in the paper's editorial department, Rothrock named Rev. D. I. Dreher of St. James, Concord, to fill the post of associate editor. *Minutes, ELGSNA, 1868,* p. 7. The convention was apparently well satisfied with Rothrock's choice of an associate editor.

89. *The Lutheran Visitor,* Vol. 2, No. 3 (March 1867), p. 87. Apparently the Tennessee Synod decided to let its appreciation for the paper's growing confessionalism outweigh its antipathy toward its revivalistic tenor. The Tennessee Synod at its September convention commended the paper to its constituency. *Minutes, TN Synod, 1867,* p. 16.

90. *The Lutheran Visitor,* Vol. 2, No. 3 (March 1867), p. 88.

91. The editor of *The Lutheran Visitor* quotes this item from the April 17 issue of the *Observer. The Lutheran Visitor,* Vol. III, No. 5 (May 1868), p. 156.

And why would the editors of the *Observer* suggest that southern papers failed to support revivals? Perhaps it is "because we have become Symbolical" (i.e., confessional). Or is it that Lutherans in the South with the *The Book of Worship* appear to General Synod folk to be too liturgical? He insists that "one of the trio" editing the *Observer* has "a liturgical service" in his congregation which is "as extensive if not more so" than that contained in *The Book of Worship.* Miller suspects the fact that all the elements of liturgy and confession are brought together in *The Book of Worship* makes it appear more formidable to those in the old General Synod tradition than when the elements are published separately. *Ibid.,* p. 157.

92. Anderson, *Lutheranism in the Southeast,* p. 225. Anderson provides a detailed analysis of the maneuvering surrounding the publication of a church paper by the General Synod South. *Ibid.,* pp. 224-29.

93. S. Henkel, *Tennessee Synod,* pp. 8-9.

94. *Minutes, NC Synod, 1869,* p. 13. It was at this convention of the General Synod South that Pastors A. R. Rude and J. I. Miller submitted a proposal to the body proposing to publish a paper as its official organ.

95. The students were McCullough (R.J.?), Hungerpeler, and Jefferson A. Sligh. Hungerpeler

was killed in 1862, McCullough on May 12, 1864, at Spottsylvania Court House, Virginia. Sligh left the army in 1862 or 1863 to take up teaching. In 1863 he was licensed by the South Carolina Synod and began serving Grace, Prosperity. [McCullough], *Lutheran Church in SC,* pp. 900-01.

96.   *Minutes, GSCSA, 1866,* p. 11.

97.   *Minutes, NC Synod, 1867,* p. 13., as cited in Agner, ms., ch. 6, p. 14. It should be noted, however, that by 1868 there was talk in the North Carolina Synod of creating a seminary "in our bounds." *Ibid., 1868,* p. 12.

98.   The General Synod South was then operating under the title Evangelical Lutheran General Synod in North America. Samuel Rothrock of North Carolina was serving as president. *The Evangelical Lutheran,* Vol. 2, No. 56 (Sept. 26, 1867), p. [2].

99.   *The Evangelical Lutheran,* Vol. 2, No. 56 (Sept. 26, 1867), p. [2].

100.   *Ibid.*

In reporting on the action of the Virginia Synod,, Editor J. I. Miller noted that "The committee on President's Report recommended that the Sabbath nearest to the 31st of the ensuing October, be observed as the 350th anniversary of the Reformation inaugurated by Martin Luther, by all our Congregations, in commemoration of that event; and that services incident thereto be conducted by every Pastor, and that contributions be solicited as a thank offering to Almighty God, for his great mercy in thus restoring to us a pure Gospel; and that the funds so received, be applied to the advancement of our Educational interest. The Resolutions were unanimously adopted." *The Lutheran Visitor,* Vol. II, No. 10 (Oct., 1867), pp. 297-98.

Editor Miller, who later united with the Tennessee Synod, noted that "To preach the doctrines of the Lutheran church does not involve the necessity of saying much, or even anything, personally, about Luther; but it requires everything to be said about Jesus Christ that is revealed in the word." *Ibid.,* p. 298.

101.   Steffey, *Brief History of St. John's,* pp. 34-35.

102.   *Minutes, NC Synod, 1868,* p. 7.

103.   *Ibid.,* pp. 12-13.

104.   *Ibid.,* p. 15.

105.   *The Lutheran Visitor,* Vol. III, No. 6 (June, 1868), p. 185.

106.   *Minutes, NC Synod, 1889,* p. 6. It may be that President Bickle's recommendation and the convention's response were shaped in part by a desire to influence the choice of a site for the seminary of the General Synod South.

107.   *Ibid.,* p. 17.

108.   Cassell, Finck and Henkel, *Lutheran Church in Virginia and East Tennessee,* p. 126.

109.   Eisenberg, *Lutheran Church in Virginia,* p. 234.

110.   *Minutes, TN Synod, 1871,* p. 5.

111.   Actually, the last convention of the Concordia Synod was held at the end of August, 1876, but, true to its Tennessee Synod heritage, the Concordia Synod submitted the question of uniting with the Joint Synod of Ohio to a vote of each of its congregations. The congregations voted unanimously in favor of the merger. Golladay, *History of Concordia District,* pp. 30-31.

112.   *Minutes, ELGSNA, 1867,* p. 13. Dr. Fox' son later observed that if the entire General Synod South had "stood to the doctrinal platform and agreement of their committee" that met with Dr. Fox, "the union of that Synod with the Tennessee Synod would have been the satisfactory result." Junius Fox, *Biography of Rev. Alfred J. Fox,* p. 64.

113.   *The Evangelical Lutheran,* Vol. 2, No. 56 (Sept. 26, 1867). With the geographic spread of the Tennessee Synod, it was not unusual for synodical conventions to be poorly attended when they were held in South Carolina or Virginia.

Suppose the session to be in Virginia. The brethren in North Carolina must travel a journey of 300 or 500 miles, and those in South Carolina of 400 or 600 miles, in order to enjoy the luxury of a few days of fraternal association, and to perform the important service of devising the best things for Zion. Those were indeed laborious, tedious, wearisome trips on horseback, the only possible mode of travel in those days, over dangerous streams, and lofty mountains. They necessitated an absence from home and church work for at least a period of thirty days, and an expenditure of about thirty dollars. J. Fox, *Biography of Rev. Alfred J. Fox*, p. 56.

114. *Minutes, NC Synod, 1868*, p. 8.

115. *Minutes, TN Synod, 1868*, pp. 3-4.

116. *Minutes, NC Synod, 1858*, pp. 10-11.

117. Other important schools established in the same period elected not to serve young women: Wake Forest (Baptist), Davidson (Presbyterian), and Duke (Methodist). H. G. Jones, *North Carolina Illustrated*, p. 191.

118. *Catalogue of North Carolina College, 1860*. It was noted the academic year would begin for Mt. Pleasant Female Seminary on "the last Wednesday in September" and run for 42 weeks. *Ibid.* In its later years, this school for women was called Mont Amoena Female Seminary.

119. *The Evangelical Lutheran*, Vol. 2, No. 56 (Sept. 26, 1867), p. [4]. With regard to costs, the following "terms" were reported for each of the five month sessions:

Boarding, Washing, Fuel and Lights	$75.
Elementary branches	15
Higher English branches	20
Collegiate course	25
Music	25
Drawing, Painting and Modern languages, branches, for day scholars	10

Payable, one-half in advance, the other half in the middle of the Session.

For a summary of Bernheim's career, see Robert W. Delp, "Gotthardt Dellman Bernheim," in Powell, *Dictionary*, Vol. 1, pp. 143-44. Bernheim's educational work included heading Mt. Pleasant Female Seminary; St. Paul's Female Seminary in Wilmington; North Carolina College at Mt. Pleasant where he served briefly as president; and Elizabeth College in Charlotte where he served as dean.

120. *Minutes, NC Synod, 1868*, p. 25. The persons initially selected by the synod to serve on the Board of Trustees for Mt. Pleasant Female Seminary were Pastors Louis A. Bikle and Levi C. Groseclose, along with Laymen Dr. D. L. Henderson, Capt. J. A. Fisher, J. J. Meisenheimer, Alexander Foil and L. G. Heilig.

121. The precise causes of "the bitter dissentions and unchristian alienations" are not specified in the special letter "To The Churches" which the convention had prepared and published in the minutes. *Minutes, NC Synod, 1866*, p. 27.

122. *Minutes, NC Synod, 1868*, p. 7.

123. *Minutes, TN Synod, 1868*, p. 11. Because of his extensive medical practice in Randolph County, Rev. Michael Leonard Fox, M.D., apparently accepted a call only to Melanchthon, Liberty. In 1868 Fox was the synod's only pastor listed as serving but one congregation, but during his twenty-one-year ministry at Melanchthon he served for extended periods as stated supply at Coble's, Julian, and Mt. Pleasant, Burlington, as well. For the fourteen clergy whose parochial reports appear in the 1868 minutes of synod, the average number of congregations served in their parish was 4.2, Rev. Alfred J. Fox, M.D., of Lincolnton leading the way with nine congregations. It is little wonder that pastors concerned for the effectivness of their ministry would find it difficult to resist calls to

parishes in synods where they would be expected to serve fewer congregations.

124. Not all of the "losses" or "gains" from clergy movement produced long term results. For example, Heydenreich came south to serve on the staff of Mrs. Ransom's Female Seminary in Wilmington and, for a time, supplied St. Paul's, but in 1869 was transferred to the Maryland Synod. Pastor Julian's move to New York produced a relatively brief ministry in New York and New Jersey, followed by a return to the North Carolina Synod in December 1873.

125. An historian of the congregation could find no record of any protracted meetings being held at St. John's after the departure of Pastor Grosclose in 1872. Steffy, *Brief History of St. John's*, p. 35.

126. "Church Intelligence," *The Lutheran Visitor*, Vol. II, No. 1 (Jan., 1867), p. [23].

127. *Minutes, NC Synod, 1875*, p. [9].

Chapter VII. From Servant to Leader (p. 177)

1.   *Minutes, ELGSNA, 1870*, p. 3.

2.   Eisenberg, *Lutheran Church in Virginia*, p. 338. Rude declined his initial election, but accepted his 1870 election and tutored two students during the two years the seminary was located in Columbia.

3.   *Minutes, ELGSNA, 1872*, p. 8.

4.   *Ibid., 1872*, p. 8.

5.   *Minutes, NC Synod, 1873*, p. 25.

6.   *Ibid., 1884*, pp. 15, 22.

7.   *Ibid., 1870*, pp. 10-11.

8.   A fourth general body which, like the General Council, represented confessionally conservative Lutheranism, was organized in the summer of 1872. This body designated The Evangelical Lutheran Synodical Conference of North America, included in its membership the synods of Minnesota, Missouri, Ohio, Illinois, Wisconsin and the Norwegian Synod. Lueker, *Lutheran Cyclopedia*, pp. 1030-31. The Tennessee Synod was involved in an exchange of fraternal delegates with the Lutheran Church-Missouri Synod before the Civil War. *Minutes, TN Synod, 1860*, p. 18.

9.   *Minutes, NC Synod, 1870*, p. 11.

10.   *Minutes, TN Synod, 1870*, p. 9.

11.   *Ibid., 1868*, p. 4.

12.   *Ibid., 1870*, p. 13.

13.   *Minutes, NC Synod, 1871*, p. 5.

14.   *Minutes, TN Synod, 1871*, p. 7.

15.   For example, on "Justification" the Basis stated, "Man is justified by faith alone in the merits of Christ. Good works are the legitimate and necessary fruits of justification." *Minutes, NC Synod, 1871*, p. 16.

16.   *Minutes, TN Synod, 1871*, p. 8.

17.   *Minutes, NC Synod, 1872*, pp. 5-6.

18.   While Organ retained its affiliation with the North Carolina Synod, in the early years it "had a noisy minority of determined Henkelites." In 1828 the Henkel party "went to law over the dispute" in a case pursued all the way to the North Carolina Supreme Court. Hammer, "Late German Documents," p.14. See also Hammer's "Organ Church."

19.   *Ibid.*, p. 27.

20.   *Ibid.*

21.   Henkel, *Tennessee Synod*, p. 195. The Tennessee Synod was also engaged in conversations

about union with its daughter, the Holston Synod. The Holston Synod had expressed an interest in uniting with the Tennessee Synod provided the new synod thus created would, in turn, unite with the recently created General Council. Such developments would necessitate the withdrawal of the Holston Synod from the United Synod South. *Ibid.,* p. 193.

22. *Minutes, NC Synod, 1873,* p. 7.

23. *Ibid.,* p. 14.

24. Lefler and Newsome, *North Carolina,* pp. 501-502.

25. *Minutes, NC Synod, 1877,* p. 24.   The South Carolina pastor receiving President Bikle's "congratulations" was William Spencer Bowman who later accepted the call of St. Mark's, Charlotte.

26. S. Henkel, *History of the Tennessee Synod,* p. 198. *Minutes, NC Synod, 1874,* pp. 12-13. The North Carolina Synod asked its president, Samuel Rothrock, and pastors David Melanchthon Henkel of St. John's, Concord, and Jacob Grabenstein Neiffer of St. John's, Salisbury, to serve as its representatives.

27. *Minutes, ELGSNA, 1874,* pp. 20-21. Dr. John G. Frey of Reading, Pennsylvania, attended the Savannah convention as the representative of the General Council and explained to the convention the intent of the General Council's proposal. *Ibid.,* pp. 8-9.

28. Jacobs, *First Free Lutheran Diet in America,* p. 10.

29. *Minutes, ELGSNA, 1876,* p. 19.

30. *Ibid.,* p. 28.

31. *Minutes, NC Synod, 1880,* pp. 21-22.

32. *Ibid., 1883,* pp. 19-20.

33. *Ibid.,* p. 20.

34. *Ibid., 1888,* p. 6.

35. *Ibid., 1889,* p. 15.

36. *Ibid., 1902,* p. 13.

37. Anderson, *North Carolina Synod,* p. 14-15.

38. It has been claimed that, of the black Lutheran pastors serving in North Carolina, only W. Philo Phifer who, as a candidate for ordination, transferred to the North Carolina Synod from the Maryland Synod, could read and write.   The Missouri Synod missionary who came to work with the former North Carolina Synod pastors said, "None of these men, not even the president, was able to recite from memory the text of Luther's Small Catechism." Bakke, *Illustrated Historical Sketch,* p. 49.

    The Rev. F. W. E. Peschau reported that Phifer had been baptized by Rev. D. J. Koontz and that Phifer was a graduate of Howard University, which perhaps accounts for the fact that he came to the North Carolina Synod from the Maryland Synod. [F. W. E.] P[eschau], "Rev. David J. Koontz," in Jensson, *American Lutheran Biographies,* p. 416. Phifer was elected secretary of the Alpha Synod when it was formed.

39. *Lutheran Visitor,* Aug. 31, 1882, p. 4.

40. Anderson, *North Carolina Synod,* p. 15.

41. *Minutes, NC Synod, 1886,* p. 9.

42. *Ibid., 1889,* p. 43.

43. "Though the Alpha Synod . . . was organized in North Carolina in 1889, white southern Lutherans did not commit themselves to white denominationalism in the manner of Southern Methodists, Baptists and Presbyterians . . . , nor did Episcopalians." Bailey, "Racial Separations," p. 467. Bailey points out that the Methodists, Presbyterians and Baptists increasingly capitulated to forces intent on driving the black and white members of their traditions into entirely distinct ecclesiastical bodies, both at the local and other levels.

44. Anderson, *North Carolina Synod,* p. 16.

45. Bakke's remarkable missionary work was not confined to North Carolina. When in 1915 Rosa Young was desperate for the financial assistance needed to continue the operation of her Rosebud School in Alabama, she wrote to Booker T. Washington for the name of some potential benefactor in the North. "He advised her to contact the Board of Colored Missions of the Lutheran Church, which he felt was doing more for blacks in the South than any other denomination. Missionary N. J. Bakke of the German-speaking Evangelical Lutheran Synodical Conference, based in St. Louis, arrived in 1916, took over the Rosebud school, and began an aggressive program of establishing schools and churches throughout the 'black belt.' White Lutherans in the upper Midwest, ensconced in their German cultural enclaves, viewed the mission work in Alabama as a 'foreign' field but persisted sufficiently to establish the Lutheran presence. Today there are fourth-generation black Lutherans, a reminder that a religious history of Afro-Americans should not exclude those who belong to predominantly white denominations." Sernett, *Afro-American Religious History,* p. [320].

46. Lash, "Black Lutherans In Rowan County," p. 76.

47. *Minutes, NC Synod, 1870,* p. 29.

48. *Ibid., 1902 Special,* pp. 68-69.

49. Agner, *The Heritage and History,* pp. 164-65. Among the issues addressed by the representatives of the two synods were "the election of a board of editors and ... the selection of a place of publication." Fox, *Biography of Rev. Alfred J. Fox,* pp. 62-63.

50. The synod accepted it as "our duty, as far as possible, to encourage its circulation among the people of our congregations...." S. Henkel, *History of the Tennessee Synod,* p. 197.

  In 1875 the subscription rate for *Our Church Paper* was $2.00 per year. The three editors were W. E. Hubbert of Mt. Pleasant, North Carolina, L. A. Fox of Waynesboro, Virginia, and S. Henkel of New Market, Virginia. *Minutes, TN Synod, 1875,* p. 17 (inside back cover).

51. Crouse, *Historical Sketches,* p. 37.

52. *Minutes, NC Synod, 1884,* p. 15, 20.

53. *Ibid.,* pp. 25-26.

54. *Ibid., 1886,* p. 6.

55. *Ibid.,* p. 9.

56. Wight, *Robert Anderson Yoder,* p. 84.

57. Cox, *Reminiscenses,* p. 13.

58. Wight, *Robert Anderson Yoder,* p. 87, quoting from *Lutheran Church Visitor,* Apr. 28, 1910.

59. Crouse, *Historical Sketches,* p. 36.

60. Wight, *Robert Anderson Yoder,* p. 85-86.

61. Jones, *North Carolina Illustrated,* p. 265.

62. Glatfelter, *Pastors and People,* vol. ii, 179. Pellens, "The Relation Between the Lutheran Church in N. C. and the Lutheran Churches in Niedersachsen," p. IXX [XIX].

63. Christopher L. Dolmetsch, "German Printing Among North Carolina Moravians," *Moravian Music Journal,* Vol. 29, No. 4 (Winter, 1984), p. 93.

64. Dolmetsch, *The German Press,* p. 67.

65. *Ibid.,* p. 68. Henkel's hymnal did not include musical notations. *Ibid.,* p. 74.

66. Bill C. Malone, "Religious Music of the Protestant South," in Hill, *Encyclopedia,* p. 518.

67. Many song books and hymnals employing the shape-note methodology appeared in the mid-nineteenth century. Among the better known were *Southern Harmony* (1835), *Hesperian Harp* (1848), *Social Harp* (1855), and *Christian Harmony* (1866). The most famous, primarily because of its amazing endurance, is Benjamin F. White's and E. J.

King's *Sacred Harp* (1844). Unlike most of the other books that moved rather quickly toward the acceptance of the seven-note 'do-re-mi' style [which first gained significant acceptance with the publication of *The Christian Minstrel* in 1846], *Sacred Harp* adhered to the use of the four-note style of solmization ('fa-sol-la-mi'). *Ibid.*, pp. 518-19.

Benjamin White was a newspaper editor in Harris County, Georgia, "and a leading teacher in singing schools in the region...." Thorp, *Southern Reader*, p. 609. While rarely found in Lutheran homes, *Sacred Harp* continues in print and is "still revered by thousands of Southerners as second only to the Bible."

68.   The increasing use of music and the other elements in worship to encourage persons to make "a decision for Christ" tended "to silence the congregation in sung praise, the sole remaining corporate liturgy of the Puritan tradition." Nichols, *Romanticism*, pp. 283-84. Nichols notes that around 1850 "there was widespread comment . . . on the prevailing disuse of congregational singing."

The "Sacred Harp" tradition has been preserved and persons interested in the distinctive qualities of this earlier form of church music can hear notable performances of works in this tradition by the Norumbega Harmony under the direction of Dr. Stephen A. Marini of Wellesley College.

69.   Morgan, *Lutheran Church in NC*, p. 119. A full-page advertisement for Mt. Pleasant Seminary and its programs appears in *Minutes, NC Synod, 1872*, p. [29]. "...when the Amite Female Academy was burned by Federal troops thirteen pianos were destroyed. They had been hauled through the wilderness to the academy in Liberty, Mississippi, with great cost and effort." Thorp, *Southern Reader*, p. 608.

70.   Cox, *Reminiscences*, p. 12.

71.   *Minutes, NC Synod, 1813*, p. 9.

72.   Schober's letter is quoted in Jacobs, *The Problem*, p. 4.

73.   Anderson, *North Carolina Synod*, p. 17.

74.   *Minutes, NC Synod, 1873*, pp. 14-16.

75.   Pastor Dosh was serving St. John's, Charleston, South Carolina, at the time of his appointment to this committee. However, by the time of the next convention, he had accepted the call of St. John's, Salisbury, and transfered to the North Carolina Synod which did not hold membership in the General Synod South. Nevertheless, Dosh went to the 1876 convention of the General Synod South held in Staunton, Virginia, in May, and he was welcomed as an advisory member of the convention. *Minutes, ELGSNA, 1876*, p. 3.

76.   *Service Book and Hymnal*, p. vii.

77.   Agner, Manuscript II, p. 1.

78.   *Minutes, NC Synod, 1892*, p. 13.

79.   Agner, Manuscript.

80.   Phillips, *Lutheran Chapel*, p. 9. The convention of the Tennessee Synod, meeting at Cedar Grove, Lexington, South Carolina, took the unusual action of singling out the choir of the congregation for its contribution to the convention. "Resolved, That the thanks of this Synod are due and are hereby rendered to the Choir of this Church for their very acceptable and pleasing performances in leading Divine worship, during the present meeting." *Minutes, Tennessee Synod, 1867*, p. 17.

81.   *The Lutheran Visitor*, Vol. II, No. 1 (Jan., 1867), p.[33].

82.   *Minutes, NC Synod, 1871*, p. [35]. The same page carries an advertisement for a Wilmington competitor, P. Heinsberger, a "dealer in Pianos, Organs, Melodeons, Guitars, Violins, Albums, &c." Stieff's full-page advertisement appears on the back cover of the minutes.

83.   Crouse, *Historical Sketches*, p. 15.

84. "Historical Sketch," Salem, Lincolnton, p. 3.

85. Wight, *Robert Anderson Yoder*, p. 83.

86. Anderson, *North Carolina Synod*, p. 16.

87. *Minutes, NC Synod, 1871*, p. 22.

88. Eisenberg, *The Lutheran Church in Virginia*, p. 308.

89. The young missionary was the son of Rev. Joel W. Swartz who was ordained by the Virginia Conference of the Tennessee Synod in 1855.

90. Morgan, *Lutheran Church in NC*, p. 131.

91. *Ibid.*, p. 141.

92. *Ibid.*, p. 141.

93. *Ibid.*, p. 142.

94. *Minutes, NC Synod, 1897*, p. 30.

95. *Ibid., 1812*, p. 9. A Moravian record for Feb. 7, 1813, notes that Schober was serving Bethlehem and Beaver Dam (Nazareth) churches in Forsyth County every four weeks, "and on the other Sundays free school is held there, and the young people are instructed in reading and singing; adults also attend." Quoted in [Norman,] Life Sketches, p. 186.

96. *Minutes, NC Synod, 1816*, p. 7.

97. *Ibid., 1827*, p. 16. A tradition at Union credits Daniel Jenkins with having served the congregation briefly in 1823. Since Daniel was not licensed until 1834, it may be that the ministry in question was performed by William Jenkins who came to North Carolina from Maryland and was licensed in 1824 at Union before heading west to his missionary labors near Shelbyville, Tennessee. He conducted his first service there in October 1824. [Norman,] *Life Sketches*, p. 99.

98. Young Rev. John Reck was apparently an enthusiastic developer of Sunday Schools. In 1830 he served four congregations but they sponsored eight Sunday Schools. Reck was also an enthusiastic supporter of the American Tract Society and looked to them for instructional materials for his schools. It was reported to the North Carolina Synod that some of its Sunday Schools were using materials provided by the American Tract Society. *Minutes, NC Synod, 1830*, p. 16.

99. The four, Pastors Sherer, Graeber, Strobel and Crim, had ten schools with 450 students. *Ibid., 1840*, p. 13. In 1843, six North Carolina Synod pastors presented parochial reports. Only two, Graeber, who served Organ and St. John's, Concord, and Wm. G. Harter, who served Cold Water and St. James, Concord, reported Sunday Schools. *Ibid., 1843*, p. 5.

100. Hood, *Reformed America*, pp. 186-87. In 1826 the American Sunday School Union reported the conversion of 468 teachers and 532 scholars. Two years later the conversion count was 1,269 teachers and 909 scholars. *Ibid.*, p. 187.

101. Quoted in Anderson, *Lutheranism in the Southeastern States*, p. 126. As Anderson points out, the North Carolina Synod encouraged pastors to return to the use of baptismal and confirmation certificates, a practice that had fallen into disuse in an enviroment where a datable conversion experience and one's decison to accept Jesus as Lord were esteemed more highly than rites of the Church.

Anderson's chapter VI, "Laymen to the Front," provides an excellent survey of the developments prior to 1886.

102. From a report of the synod's Sunday School Executive Committee, quoted in Eisenberg, *Lutheran Church in Virginia*, p. 300.

103. *Minutes, NC Synod, 1875*, pp. 12-13.

104. *Ibid.*, p. 34-35.

105. *Ibid.*, p. 17.

106. *Ibid., 1885*, p. 19.

107. *Ibid., 1902*, p. 43.

108. *Ibid., 1889 (August)*, p. 68.
109. *Ibid., 1898*, p. 39.
110. *Ibid.*, p. 33.
111. *Ibid., 1896*, p. 38.
112. Polycarp C. Henkel and Jonathan Moser were the Tennessee Synod pastors. Andrew Rader was a pastor of the Holston Synod, a body whose creation out of Tennessee Synod congregations in 1860 meant that the Tennessee Synod no longer had congregations in the state from which it took its name. Henkel, Moser and Rader organized the conference after conferring with representatives of the Norwegian Synod and the German Missouri Synod. Eckhardt, *The English District,* p. 11. The original conference became The General English Lutheran Conference of Missouri in 1888, but by 1891 preferred to be called "The English Ev. Lutheran Synod of Missouri and Other States." *Ibid.,* p. 30.

Chapter VIII. Toward Union (p. 221)

1. Grantham, *Southern Progressivism*, ch. 8. Link, *Paradox of Southern Progressivism*, ch. 2-3.
2. Wight, "Robert Anderson Yoder".
3. *Ibid., 1905*, p. 12.
4. *Ibid., 1916*, p. 44.
5. Wight, "Robert Anderson Yoder," p. 112.
6. *Ibid.,* p. 113.
7. *Ibid.,* p. 110.
8. *Minutes, NC Synod, 1904*, p. 20.
9. *Rowan County Lutheran,* Dec. 1908, p. 2.
10. *Ibid.,* Dec. 1908.
11. Morgan, *Lutheran Church in NC,* p. 147.
12. *Ibid.,* p. 148.
13. *Minutes, NC Synod, 1912*, p. 15.
14. Agner, draft, p. 3.
15. Agner, Manuscript, p. 5.
16. *Minutes, NC Synod, 1915*, p. 47.
17. Morgan, *Lutheran Church in NC,* p. 153.
18. *Minutes, ULCA, 1920*, p. 77.
19. *Minutes, TN Synod, 1919*, p. 74.
20. Morgan, *Lutheran Church in NC,* p. 153.
21. Crouse, *Historical Sketches,* pp. 37-38.
22. *Ibid.,* p. 38.
23. *Catawba Lutheran,* Mar. 1907, p. 2.
24. *Minutes, NC Synod, 1908*, p. 48.
25. Agner, manuscript, Brotherhood chap., p. 7.
26. *Minutes, NC Synod, 1902*, p. 34.
27. *Ibid., 1920*, p. 63.
28. *Ibid., 1905*, pp. 36-37.
29. Morgan, *Lutheran Church in NC,* p. 111.
30. *Minutes, NC Synod, 1914*, p. 40.
31. Agner, *History and Heritage,* ch. 7, p. 32, quoting *Salisbury Evening Post,* Nov. 7, 1917.
32. Anderson, *NC Synod,* pp. 28-29.
33. Morgan, *Lutheran Church in NC,* p. 96.

Chapter IX. Reunited under ULCA (p. 243)

1.   Morgan, *Lutheran Church NC,* p. 104.
2.   *Ibid.,* p. 97.
3.   Brown, *Lutheran Church in NC,* p. 8.
4.   *Ibid.,* p. 9.
5.   *Minutes, NC Synod, 1935,* p. 106.
6.   Mauney, *NC Lutheran Men,* p. 43.
7.   *Minutes, NC Synod, 1933,* pp. 26-27.
8.   *Ibid.,* p. 31.
9.   *Ibid.,* pp. 60-61.
10.   *Minutes, NC Synod, 1935,* p. 59.
11.   *Ibid.,* pp. 60-61.
12.   *NC Lutheran,* Sept. 1951, pp. 1, 3.
13.   *Minutes, NC Synod, 1935,* pp. 27-28.
14.   Morgan, *Lutheran Church in NC,* p. 98.
15.   *Minutes, NC Synod, 1933,* p. 33.
16.   *Ibid., 1935,* p. 110.
17.   *Ibid., 1933,* p. 56.
18.   *Ibid.,* p. 92.
19.   *Ibid., 1935,* p. 108.
20.   Agner, Manuscript, II, p. 12C.
21.   LCW, *Sisters in Mission,* p. 47.
22.   Brown, *Lutheran Church in NC,* pp. 42-43.
23.   *Ibid.,* p. 41.
24.   Mauney, *NC Lutheran Men,* p. 39.
25.   Morgan, *Lutheran Church in NC,* p. 155.
26.   *NC Lutheran,* June 1945, p. 1.
27.   Brown, *Lutheran Church in NC,* p. 53.
28.   *NC Lutheran,* Dec. 1924, p. 1.
29.   Brown, *Lutheran Church in NC,* p. 56.
30.   *Ibid,,* p. 63.
31.   *Minutes, NC Synod, 1954,* p. 152.
32.   *NC Lutheran,* Mar. 1930, p. 3.
33.   *Minutes, NC Synod, 1933,* p. 88.
34.   *Ibid.,* pp. 20-21.
35.   *Ibid.,* p. 26.
36.   *NC Lutheran,* Feb. 1943, p. 1.
37.   *Ibid.,* May 1953. p. 2.
38.   *Ibid.,* May 1958, p. 2.
39.   *LLM Newsletter,* May/June 1986, p. [5].
40.   Brown, *Lutheran Church in NC,* p. 11.
41.   *NC Lutheran,* May 1962, p. 1.
42.   *Minutes, NC Synod, 1963,* pp. 187-89.

Chapter X.   LCA in North Carolina (p. 281)

1.   *Minutes, NC Synod, 1971,* p. 150.
2.   *Ibid., 1985,* p. 256.

3. *NC Lutheran*, Oct. 1981, p. 1.
4. *Ibid.*, Oct. 1987, p. 4.
5. *Minutes, NC Synod, 1967*, p. 147.
6. *Ibid., 1977*, pp. 147-48.
7. *Ibid., 1963*, p. 75.
8. *Ibid., 1964*, p. 178.
9. *NC Lutheran*, Dec. 1981, p. 1.
10. Iddings interview, 1986.
11. LCA Constitution, By-Laws, Section II-Ministers, Item 2
12. *Minutes, NC Synod, 1966*, p. 185.
13. *Ibid., 1969*, p. 74.
14. *Ibid., 1976*, pp. 62-63.
15. *Ibid., 1977*, p. 60.
16. *NC Lutheran*, June 13, 1973, p. 1.
17. *Minutes, NC Synod, 1980*, p. 165.
18. *NC Lutheran*, Sept. 7, 1978, p. 2.
19. Agner, Manuscript, II, p. 22.
20. *Minutes, NC Synod, 1986*, p. 87.
21. *Ibid., 1982*, p. 278.
22. *Ibid., 1964*, p. 125.
23. *Ibid., 1967*, p. 129.
24. *Ibid.*, p. 142.
25. *NC Lutheran*, Nov. 3, 1971, p. 1.
26. Norris and Boatmon, *Fair Star*, p. 107.
27. *Minutes, NC Synod, 1964*, pp. 151.
28. *Ibid., 1965*, pp. 148-49.
29. *Ibid., 1979*, p. 254.
30. *Ibid., 1964*, pp. 269-70.
31. *NC Lutheran*, May 1964, p. 1.
32. *Minutes, NC Synod, 1969*, p. 75.
33. *Ibid., 1965*, p. 138.
34. Gilbert, *Commitment to Unity*, p. xi.

Chapter XI. ELCA in North Carolina (p. 321)

1. *Minutes, NC Synod, 1988*, p. 103.
2. *Ibid.*, p. 162.
3. *Ibid.*, 1990, p. 222.
4. *NC Lutheran*, May 22, 1991, p. 26A.
5. *Minutes, NC Synod, 1990*, p. 228.
6. Bernheim and Cox, *North Carolina*, pp. 28-29.
7. *Ibid.*, p. 32.
8. Although the North Carolina Synod was organized after the Ministerium of Pennsylvania and the Ministerium of New York, neither of those first two synods survives (as does North Carolina) in its original geographic form.   ✝

BIBLIOGRAPHY

Abbott, Lymon, *Reminiscences*. Boston: Houghton Mifflin Co., 1915.

Adams, James Truslow, ed., *Dictionary of American History*. New York: Charles Scribner's Sons, 1940.

Agner, Martha Withers, ed. *The Heritage and History of St. John's Evangelical Lutheran Church, Salisbury, North Carolina through 1983*. Salisbury: St. John's Evangelical Lutheran Church, 1988, Vol. I.

Agner, Martha Withers, Manuscript, *The Heritage and History of St. John's Evangelical Lutheran Church, Salisbury, North Carolina*, Vol. II.

Agner, Martha Withers, transcriber. "Record Books, Union Lutheran Church, Rowan County, N. Carolina, 1850-1937." Mimeographed, 1975.

Ahlstron, Sydney E., *A Religious History of the American People*. New Haven: Yale University Press, 1972; 2nd printing, 1973.

Allbeck, Willard D., *A Century of Lutherans in Ohio*. Yellow Springs: The Antioch Press, 1966.

Anderson, Hugh George, *The North Carolina Synod Through 175 Years (1803-1978)*. N.p.: n.p., 1978.

Anderson, Hugh George, "The First Lutheran Synodical Organization in North Carolina," *The Lutheran Quarterly*, Vol. XXIV, No. 3 (August, 1972), pp. 280-85.

Anderson, Hugh George, *Lutheranism in the Southeastern States, 1860-1886: A Social History*. The Hague: Mouton, 1969.

Anderson, Hugh George, ed., *Foundations of Lutheranism in North Carolina*. N.p.: n.p., 1973.

Aptheker, Herbert, ed., *A Documentary History of the Negro People in the United States*. New York: The Citadel Press, 1951.

Aull, James Stroud, "Godfrey Dreher and the South Carolina Synod." Typed B.D. thesis, Lutheran Theological Southern Seminary, 1960.

Bachman, John, *A Sermon on the Doctrines and Discipline of the Evangelical Lutheran Church, Preached at Charleston, S. C., November 12th, 1837, by Appointment of the Synod of South-Carolina and Adjacent States*. Charleston: J. S. Burges, 1837.

Bailey, Kenneth K., "The Post-Civil War Racial Separations in Southern Protestantism: Another Look," *Church History*, Vol. 46, No. 4 (December 1977).

Bailyn, Bernard, *The Peopling of British North America*. New York: Alfred A. Knopf, 1986.

Bailyn, Bernard, *Voyagers to the West*. New York: Alfred A. Knopf, 1986.

Bakke, N[ils] J[ules], *Illustrated Historical Sketch of Our Colored Mission*. St. Louis: Concordia Publishing House, 1914.

Baltzell, E. Digby, *Puritan Boston and Quaker Philadelphia: Two Protestant Ethics and the Spirit of Class Authority and Leadership*. New York: The Free Press, 1979.

Bardolph, Richard, "Confederate Dilemma: North Carolina Troops and the Deserter Problem," Part I & II, *The North Carolina Historical Review*, Vol. LXVI, No. 1 (Jan., 1989), pp. 61-86, No. 2 (April, 1989), pp. [179]-210.

Barringer, Paul B., *The Natural Bent*. The Memoirs of Dr. Paul B. Barringer. Chapel Hill: The University of North Carolina Press, 1949.

Baur, R. H., "Paul Henkel and the Revivals," *Concordia Historical Institute Quarterly,* Vol. 63, No. 3 (Fall, 1990), pp. [113]-122.

Bernheim, G[otthardt] D[ellman], *History of the German Settlements and of the Lutheran Church in North and South Carolina, From the Earliest Period of the Colonization of the Dutch, German and Swiss Settlers to the Close of the First Half of the Present Century.* Philadelphia: The Lutheran Book Store, 1872.

Bernheim, G[otthardt] D[ellman], and Cox, George H., *The History of the Evangelical Lutheran Synod and Ministerium of North Carolina, In Commemoration of the Completion of the First Century of Its Existence.* Philadelphia: Lutheran Publication Society, 1902.

Blackmun, Ora. *Western North Carolina: Its Mountains and Its People to 1880.* Boone: Appalachian Consortium Press, 1977.

Boles, John B, ed., *Masters & Slaves in the House of the Lord: Race and Religion in the American South, 1740-1870.* Lexington: The University Press of Kentucky, 1988.

Boles, John B., "Slaves in Biracial Protestant Churches," *Varieties of Southern Religious Experience,* Samuel S. Hill, ed., Baton Rouge: Louisiana State University Press, 1988.

[Boltzius, Johann Martin, and Gronau, Israel Christian]. *Detailed Reports on the Salzburger Emigrants who Settled in America...Edited by Samuel Urlsberger.* George Fenwick Jones, ed.; Don Savelle, tr. Athens: The University of Georgia Press, 1988, Vol. 9.

The Book of Concord. The Confessions of the Evangelical Lutheran Church. Theodore G. Tappert, ed. Philadelphia: Fortress Press, 1959.

Bost, Raymond M., "The Reverend John Bachman and the Development of Southern Lutheranism." Yale University Ph.D. dissertation, 1963.

Bostian, Frank K.; Cruse, Bernard W., et al., *Dutch Buffalo Creek Meeting House, 1745-1806; Bethel Bear Creek United Church of Christ, 1806-1974.* Mount Pleasant: Bethel Bear Creek United Church of Christ, 1974.

Boyd, William K., and Krummel, Charles A., "German Tracts Concerning the Lutheran Church in North Carolina During the Eighteenth Century," *The North Carolina Historical Review,* Vol. VII, No. 1 (Jan., 1930), pp. 79-147; No. 2 (April, 1930), pp. 225-82.

Brawley, James S., "Wood Grove of Top Interest to Historians," *Salisbury Post,* (March 7, 1954).

Brawley, Martha S., *History of Cold Water Lutheran Church.* N.p.: n.p., 1982.

Brown, Bachman S., et. al., *History of the Lutheran Church in North Carolina, 1953-1963 Supplement.* Columbia, S.C.: The State Printing Company, 1965.

Brown, Marvin A., et al., *Our Enduring Past: A Survey of 235 Years of Life and Architecture in Lincoln County, North Carolina.* Charlotte: The Delmar Co., 1986.

Bruce, Dickson D., Jr., "Brush Arbor," *Encyclopedia of Religion in the South.* Samuel S. Hill, ed. Macon: Mercer University Press, 1984, pp. 118-119.

Busby, L[evi] E., *Life-Sketch of Rev. Charles A. Rose.* Salisbury: Smith & Irvin, [c. 1900], p. 24.

Byrd, Robert C., *The Senate, 1789-1989: Addresses on the History of the United States Senate.* Washington: U. S. Government Printing Office, 1988.

Calhoon, Robert M., *Religion and the American Revolution in North Carolina.* Raleigh: North Carolina Department of Cultural Resources, Division of Archives and History, 1976.

Cassell, C. W, Finck, W. J., and Henkel, Elon O., eds., *History of The Lutheran Church in Virginia and East Tennessee.* Strasburg: Shenandoah Publishing House, Inc., 1930.

Catalogue of the Officers and Students of North Carolina College, at Mount Pleasant, N. C., for the First Collegiate Year, Ending July 18, 1860. Chartered, January, 1859. Salisbury:

Carolina Watchman Office, 1860.

Catawba Lutheran. Mar. 1907.

Catton, William and Bruce, *Two Roads to Sumter.* New York: McGraw-Hill Book Company, Inc., 1963.

Cecelski, David, "A Thousand Aspirations," *Southern Exposure,* Vol. xviii, No. 1 (Spring, 1990), pp. 22-25.

Census of Religious Bodies, 1926. Lutherans: Statistics, History, Doctrine and Organization. Washington: United States Government Printing Office, 1929.

Cheshire, Joseph Blount, Jr., Undated and untitled pamphlet at library of University of North Carolina. Reprint of a series of articles which apparently appeared in a church paper in October 1885.

Clark, Elmer T., *Methodism in Western North Carolina.* N.p.: Western North Carolina Conference, The Methodist Church, 1966.

Clay, James W., Orr, Douglas M., Jr., and Stuart, Alfred W., eds., *North Carolina Atlas: Portrait of a Changing Southern State.* Chapel Hill: The University of North Carolina Press, 1975.

Clayton, Thomas H., *Close to the Land: The Way We Lived in North Carolina , 1820-1870.* Chapel Hill: The University of North Carolina Press, 1983.

Cline, Ned, "Church Historians Still Pursue Full Story of Adolph Nussman." Salisbury, N. C.: *The Salisbury Post,* December 5, 1965.

Cobb, Sanford H., *The Palatine or German Immigration to New York and Pennsylvania.* Wilkes-Barre: Wyoming Historical and Genealogical Society, 1897.

Corbett, D. L., ed., "The Robert J. Miller Letters, 1813-1831," *The North Carolina Historical Review,* Vol. XXV, No. 4 (Oct., 1948).

Coulter, E. Merton, *The Confederate States of America, 1861-1865.* [Baton Rouge]: Louisiana State University Press, 1950.

Cox, Geo[rge] H., *Reminisences* [sic] *of the Founders of the Evangelical Lutheran Holston Synod.* Spencer, N. C.: The Spencer Crescent Print., [1915?].

Crabtree, Beth G., and James W. Patton, eds., *"Journal of a Secesh Lady": The Diary of Catherine Ann Devereux Edmonston, 1860-1866.* Raleigh: Division of Archives and History, Department of Cultural Resources, 1979.

Craven, Avery O., *The Growth of Southern Nationalism, 1848-1861:* Vol. VI, *A History of the South,* Wendell Holmes Stephenson and E. Merton Coulter, eds. Baton Rouge: Louisiana State University Press, 1953; 3rd printing, 1962.

Crofts, Daniel W., *Reluctant Confederates: Upper South Unionists in the Secession Crisis.* Chapel Hill: The University of North Carolina Press, 1989.

Crouse, A. L., *Historical Sketches of Alexander County, North Carolina, Friendship Lutheran, Hopewell Reformed, and Charity Baptist Churches, and of the Bowman and Fry Families.* [Taylorsville ?]: [A. L. Crouse ?], 1905.

Crow, Jeffrey J., "The Whiskey Rebellion in North Carolina," *The North Carolina Historical Review,* Vol. LXVI, No. 1 (Jan., 1989).

Cruse, Guy C. *A History of Bethel Evangelical Lutheran Church, White Rock, South Carolina.* Columbia: Farrell Printing Co., 1962.

Daniel, W. Harrison, "Southern Protestantism and Army Missions in the Confederacy," *Mississippi Quarterly,* Vol. 17 (1964), pp. [179]-191.

De Bord, Martha B.; Hougen, John B; and Shumate, Lottie T., *St. Paul's Lutheran Church, 1776-1976.* Radford: Commonwealth Press, Inc., 1976.

Degler, Carl N., *The Other South: Dissenters in the Nineteenth Century.* Boston: Northeastern University Press, 1982.

DeMoulin-Eckart, Richard, *Geschichte Der Deutchen Universitaten.* Hildesheim: Georg Olms Verlag, p. 275.

Dolmetsch, Christopher L., *The German Press of the Shenandoah Valley.* Columbia: Camden House, 1984.

Dolmetsch, Christopher L., "German Printing Among North Carolina Moravians," *Moravian Music Journal,* Vol. 29, No. 4 (Winter, 1984).

Drake, J. Madison, *Fast and Loose in Dixie.* An Unprejudiced Narrative of Personal Experience as a Prisoner of War at Libby, Macon, Savannah, and Charleston, With an Account of a Desperate Leap from a Moving Train of Cars, A Weary Tramp of Forty-five Days through Swamps and Mountains, Places and People Visited, Etc., Etc. New York: The Authors' Publishing Co., 1880.

Dreher, Godfrey, *A Fair and Candid Statement of Plain Matters of Fact with accompanying Remarks in reference to Difficulties which existed and still exist between the Lutheran Synod of So. Car. and Godfrey Dreher.* Columbia: I. C. Morgan, 1842. A typed copy prepared by T. H. Weeks in 1932 is to be found in the Lineberger Memorial Library at Lutheran Theological Southern Seminary.

Duncan, Norvin C., *Pictorial History of the Episcopal Church in North Carolina, 1701-1964.* Asheville: n. p., c. 1964.

Durden, Robert F., "North Carolina in the New South," *The North Carolina Experience: An Interpretive and Documentary History,* Lindley S. Butler and Alan D, Watson, eds. Chapel Hill: The University of North Carolina Press, 1984.

Eaton, Clement, *A History of the Southern Confederacy.* New York: Collier Books, 1954; Collier Books Edition, 1961.

Eckhardt, H. P., *The English District: A Historical Sketch.* N.p.: The English District of the Synod of Missouri, Ohio, and Other States, 1946.

Eisenberg, William Edward, *The First Hundred Years: Roanoke College, 1842-1942.* Salem: The Trustees of Roanoke College, 1942.

Eisenberg, William Edward, *The Lutheran Church in Virginia, 1717-1962, including an Account of the Lutheran Church in East Tennessee.* Roanoke: The Trustees of the Virginia Synod, Lutheran Church in America, 1967.

Escott, Paul D., and Crow, Jeffrey J., "The Social Order and Violent Disorder: An Analysis of North Carolina in the Revolution and the Civil War," *The Journal of Southern History,* Vol. LII, No. 3 (Aug., 1986).

The Evangelical Lutheran, Vol. 2, No. 56 (Sept. 26, 1867), p. [2].

Extract *From the Transactions of the German and English Lutheran Synod for North Carolina and Adjacent States; in the Year of Our Lord 1820.* Raleigh: Lucas & Harvey, 1820.

Extracts from the Minutes of the Synod of the Evangelical Lutheran Church, in the State of New-York, and Adjacent Parts, Convened at Livingston, Columbia County, N.Y., Aug.-Sept. 1823. New-York: E. Conrad, 1823.

Farrison, William Edward, "The Negro Population of Guilford County, North Carolina, Before the Civil War," *The North Carolina Historical Review,* Vol. XXI, No. 4 (Oct., 1944), pp. 319-29.

Faust, Albert Bernard, *The German Element In The United States With Special Reference To Its Political, Moral, Social, And Educational Influence.* New York: The Steuben Society of America, 1909; reprinted, 1927, 2 vols.

Filler, Louis, *The Crusade Against Slavery, 1830-1860.* New York: Harper & Brothers, 1960.

Finck, William J., ed. and tr., "A Chronological Life of Paul Henkel from Journals, Letters,

Minutes of Synod, Etc." Typescript, 1935-37; reprinted, 1957.

Flohr, G[eorge] D[aniel], *Sermons and Essays, In Two Parts.* The First Containing Popular and Evangelic Sermons, By the Late Rev. G. D. Flohr, of Wythe Co. Virginia, Translated from the Original, By Several Ministers of the Evangelical Lutheran Church. The Second Containing Sermons and Essays, For the Most Part, By Living Ministers. Baltimore: John Murphy, 1840.

Fisher, Ben C., "Christian Higher Education," *Encyclopedia of Religion in the South,* Samuel S. Hill, ed. Macon: Mercer University Press, 1984, pp. 217-21.

Fisher, Roscoe Brown, ed., *Michael Brown (Braun) of the Old Stone House, His Influence and Descendants.* Charlotte: Delmar Publishers & Printers, 1975; 2nd ed., 1977.

Fitzgerald, Michael W., "Poor Man's Fight," *Southern Exposure,* Vol. XVIII, No. 1 (Spring, 1990), pp. 14-17.

Fortenbaugh, Robert, "The Representative Lutheran Periodical Press and Slavery, 1831-1860," *The Lutheran Church Quarterly,* Vol. VIII, No. 2 (April, 1935), pp. 151-72.

Forty-Seventh Annual Catalogue of North Carolina College, Mount Pleasant, N.C., Together With A History of the Institution From Its Founding. 1900-1901. Newberry: Lutheran Publication Board, 1901.

Foster, Gaines M., *Ghosts of the Confederacy: Defeat, the Lost Cause, and the Emergence of the New South. 1865 to 1913.* New York: Oxford University Press, 1987.

Fox, Junius B., *Biography of Rev. Alfred J. Fox, M.D., Evangelical Lutheran Minister of the Tennessee Synod, and Physician.* Philadelphia: Lutheran Publication Society, 1885.

Fox, L. A., *The Origin of the Tennessee Synod.* An Address Delivered At its Centennial Celebration In Lincolnton, N. C., October 14, 1920. n.p.: n.p., c. 1920.

Franklin, John Hope, *Reconstruction: After the Civil War.* Chicago: The University of Chicago Press, 1961.

Freeze, Gary, Manuscript, History of Catawba County, N.C.

Friedman, Jean E. *The Enclosed Garden: Women and Community in the Evangelical South, 1830-1900.* Chapel Hill: The Univeristy of North Carolina Press, 1985.

Friedman, Lawrence J., "'Historical Topics Sometimes Run Dry': The State of Abolitionist Studies," *The Historian,* Vol. XLIII, No. 2 (Feb., 1981), pp. 177-94.

Fulbright, Lucille M., ed., *The Heritage of Catawba County, North Carolina.* Winston-Salem: Hunter Publishing Co., 1986.

Gehrke, William Herman, "Negro Slavery among the Germans in North Carolina," *The North Carolina Historical Review,* Vol. XIV, No. 4 (Oct., 1937), pp. 307-24.

Gerberding, G. H., *Life and Letters of W. A. Passavant, D. D.* Greenville, Pa.: The Young Lutheran Co., 1906.

Gilbert, W. Kent, *Commitment to Unity: A History of the Lutheran Church in America.* Philadelphia: Fortress Press, 1988.

Glatfelter, Charles H. *Pastors and People: German Lutheran and Reformed Churches in the Pennsylvania Field, 1717-1793.* Breinigsville: The Pennsylvania German Society, 1980-81. 2 vols.

Gobel, A. Roger, and Matthews, Donald N. and Elaine C., *On the Glorious Hill: A Short History in Word and Picture of the Lutheran Theological Seminary at Gettysburg.* n.p.: Lutheran Theological Seminary, c. 1976.

Golladay, R. E., *History of Concordia District of the Evangelical Lutheran Joint Synod of Ohio and Other States, 1877-1902,* published in *Proceedings of the Twenty-sixth Annual Convention of the Concordia English District of the Evangelical Lutheran Joint Synod of Ohio and Other States.* Powell's Fort, Va., Mt. Zion Church, September 17, 1902. Columbus: Lutheran Book Concern, 1902.

Goen, Clarence C., "Scenario for Secession: Denominational Schisms and the Coming of the Civil War," *Varieties of Southern Religious Experience,* Samuel S. Hill, ed. Baton Rouge: Louisiana State University Press, 1988.

Gonzales, John Edmond, "John Anthony Quitman," *The Encyclopedia of Southern History,* David C. Roller and Robert W. Twyman, eds. Baton Rouge: Louisana State University Press, 1979.

Grantham, Dewey W., *Southern Progressivism: The Reconciliation of Progress and Tradition.* Knoxville: University of Tennessee Press, 1983.

Green, Fletcher M., "The Tarpley Letter," *Dictionary of American History,* James Truslow Adams, ed. New York: Charles Scribner's Sons, 1940; 2nd ed. rev., 1951, Vol. V, p. 224.

Hahn, George Franklin, *Eastern Cabarrus History,* Concord: George Franklin Hahn, 1986.

Hair, William I., "Lynching," *Encyclopedia of Southern Culture,* Charles Reagan Wilson & William Ferris, eds. Chapel Hill: The University of North Carolina Press, 1989, pp. 174-76.

Hamilton, J. Taylor, and Kenneth G., *History of the Moravian Church: The Renewed Unitas Fratrum, 1722-1957.* Bethlehem: Interprovincial Board of Christian Education, Moravian Church in America, 1967.

Hammer, Carl, Jr., "Late German Documents from Organ Church," *The American-German Review* (Apr. 1951).

Hammer, Carl, Jr., "Organ Church and the Broken Key," *The American-German Review* (June-Aug. 1947).

Hammer, Carl, Jr., *Rhinelanders on the Yadkin, The Story of the Pennsylvania Germans in Rowan and Cabarrus.* Salisbury: Rowan Printing Co., 1943.

Hardman, Keith J., *Charles Grandison Finney, 1792-1875: Revivalist and Reformer.* Syracuse: Syracuse University Press, 1987.

Harpers Weekly, Vol. V, No. 212 (Jan. 19, 1861).

Harwell, Richard and Racine, Philip N., eds., *The Fiery Trail: A Union Officer's Account of Sherman's Last Campaigns.* Knoxville: The University of Tennessee Press, 1986.

Haynes. Leonard L., Jr., *The Negro Community Within American Protestantism, 1619-1844.* Boston: The Christopher Publishing House, 1953.

[Hazelius, Ernest Lewis], *Address of the Temperance Society of South Carolina to the Citizens of the State.* With an Appendix. Columbia: The Telescope Office, 1838.

Henkel, David, *Answer to Mr. Joseph Moore, the Methodist: with a Few Fragments on the Doctrine of Justification.* New Market: S. G. Henkel, 1825.

Henkel, David, *Carolinian Herald of Liberty, Religious & Political, Or a Testimony Against Attempted Measures Which in Their Nature Are Calculated to Lead to the Establishment of Popery Among Protestants.* Salisbury: Krider & Bingham, 1821.

Henkel, Socrates, *History of the Evangelical Lutheran Tennessee Synod, Embracing an Account of the Causes Which Gave Rise to Its Organization; Its Organization and Name; Its Position and Confessional Basis; Objects of Its Organization; Work, Development, and Various Sessions; Its Policy; and Its Future.* New Market: Henkel & Co., 1890.

Hesseltine, William Best, "Four American Traditions," *The Journal of Southern History,* Vol. XXVII, No. 1 (Feb., 1961), pp. 3-32.

Hill, Samuel S., ed., *Encyclopedia of Religion in the South.* [Macon]: Mercer University Press, 1984.

Hill, Samuel S., ed., *Varieties of Southern Religious Experience,* Baton Rouge: Louisiana State University Press, 1988.

"Historical Sketch," Salem Lutheran Church, Lincolnton, 1986. Archives, N. C. Synod.

A History of Sinking Springs Lutheran Church. N.p.: n.p., c. 1965.

Hofstadter, Richard, *America at 1750: A Social Portrait*. New York: Alfred A. Knopf, 1971.

Holborn, Hajo, *A History of Modern Germany: The Reformation*. Princeton: Princeton University Press, 1959.

Holborn, Hajo, *A History of Modern Germany: 1648-1840*. Princeton: Princeton University Press, 1964.

Holloman, Charles R., "Early Settlers in Neuse River Country, 1700 to 1720," *The North Carolina Genealogical Society Journal*, Vol. I, No. 2 (April, 1975), pp. 50-61.

Holston Synod, *Minutes, Evangelical Lutheran Holston Synod*, 1862.

Home News: Ministry for Older Adults (December, 1987); publication of Lutheran Services for the Aging, Salisbury, N.C.

Honeywell, Roy J., *Chaplains of the United States Army*. Washington: Department of the Army, Office of the Chief of Chaplains, 1958.

Hood, Fred J., *Reformed America: The Middle and South States, 1783-1837*. University: The University of Alabama, 1980.

Hook, Wade F[ranklin], "Religious Regionalism: The Case of Lutherans in the South," *Review of Religious Research*, Vol. 27, No. 1 (Sept., 1985), pp. 77-85.

Iddings, J. White, Interview. 1986.

Jacobs, H[enry] E[yster], ed., *First Free Lutheran Diet in America*. Philadelphia, December 27-28, 1877. The Essays, Debates, and Proceedings. Philadelphia: J. Frederick Smith, 1878.

Jacobs, H[enry] E[yster], *The Problem of the Lutheran Church the South*. Hickory: A. L. Crouse, 1902.

Jacobs, Henry Eyster, and Haas, John A. W., *The Lutheran Cyclopedia*. New York: Charles Scribner's Sons, 1899.

Jensson, J. C., *American Lutheran Biographies; or, Historical Notices of Over Three Hundred Fifty Leading Men of the American Lutheran Church, from Its Establishment to the Year 1890*. Milwaukee: Rev. J. C. Jensson, 1890.

Jones, George Fenwick, ed., *Detailed Reports on the Salzburger Emigrants Who Settled in America...Edited by Samuel Urslberger*. Athens: The University of Georgia Press, 1988.

Jones, H. G., *North Carolina Illustrated, 1524-1984*. Chapel Hill: The University of North Carolina Press, 1983.

Jones, Maldwyn Allen, *American Immigration*. Chicago: The University of Chicago Press, 1960; 4th printing, 1965.

Junkin, William Sumner, and Junkin, Minnie Wyatt, eds., *Henckel Family Geneaology*. Spokane, WA: Henckel Family Association, 1964.

Keever, Homer M., "A Lutheran Preacher's Account of the 1801-1802 Revival in North Carolina," *Methodist History*, Vol. VII, No. 1 (October, 1968), pp. 38-55.

Kirkland, James H., "Higher Education in the South," *The South in the Building of the Nation;* vol. X, *History of the Social Life of the South*, Samuel Chiles Mitchell, ed. Richmond: The Southern Historical Publication Society, 1909, pp. 219-37.

Knittle, Walter Allen, *Early Eighteenth Century Palatine Emigration, A British Government Redemptioner Project to Manufacture Naval Stores*. Philadelphia: Dorrance & Co., 1937.

Kornegay, Charles D., compiler, *Kornegay History, 1710-1986*. n.p.: Kornegay Printing Co., c. 1986.

Kreider, Harry Julius, *History of the United Lutheran Synod of New York and New England*. Philadelphia: Muhlenberg Press, 1954, Vol. I.

Kuenning, Paul P., "New York Lutheran Abolitionists: Seeking a Solution to a Historical

Enigma," *Church History,* Vol. 58, No. 1 (March, 1989), pp. 52-65.

Lash, Wiley Immanuel, "Black Lutherans In Rowan County," *Concordia Historical Institute Quarterly,* Vol. 61, No. 2 (Summer, 1988), pp. 74-78.

LCA Yearbook, 1987, Reuben T. Swanson, ed. [Philadelphia]: Board of Publication, Lutheran Church in America, 1987.

Lefler, Hugh Talmage, and Newsome, Albert Ray, *North Carolina: The History of a Southern State.* Chapel Hill: The University of North Carolina Press, 1954; 3rd ed., 1973.

Lemmon, Sarah McCulloh, "The Genesis of the Protestant Episcopal Diocese of North Carolina, 1701-1823," *The North Carolina Historical Review,* Vol. XXVIII, No. 4 (Oct., 1951), pp. 426-62.

Leonard, Jacob Calvin, *The Southern Synod of the Evangelical and Reformed Church.* Lexington: J. C. Leonard, 1940.

Leutze, James R., "North Carolina: The Nation in Microcosm," *Carolina Comments,* Vol. XXXVIII, No. 4 (July, 1990).

Link, William A., *The Paradox of Southern Progressivism.* Chapel Hill: University of North Carolina Press, 1992.

Linn, Charles Adolphus, "The Georgia Colony of Salzburgers." Typed Ph. D. dissertation, Hartford Theological Seminary, 1931.

Linn, Charles Adolphus, *Two Hundred Years of the Grace of God.* Savannah: The Church of the Ascension, 1941.

"List of Publications by Lutherans in the United States," *The Evangelical Review,* Vol. XII (1860-61), pp. 542-74.

Liturgy, or Book Of Forms, For The Use of the Evangelical Lutheran Church. Compiled and Published By Order of the Evang. Lutheran Tennessee Synod: To Which Is Added the Constitution of Said Synod. New Market: Solomon Henkel, 1843.

LLM Newsletter, May/June 1986, p. [5].

London, Lawrence Foushee, and Lemmon, Sarah McCulloh, eds., *The Episcopal Church in North Carolina, 1701-1959.* Raleigh: The Episcopal Diocese of North Carolina, 1987.

Loveland, Anne C., *Southern Evangelicals and the Social Order, 1800-1860.* Baton Rouge: Louisiana State University Press, 1980.

Lueker, Erwin L., ed., *Lutheran Cyclopedia.* Saint Louis: Concordia Publishing House, 1954.

The Lutheran Almanac for 1861. Baltimore: T. Newton Kurtz, 1861. 2nd ed.

Lutheran Church Women of North Carolina, *Sisters in Mission* (History of Lutheran Women's Work in North Carolina, 1885-1987). [Albemarle: Press Printing Co., 1987]

Lutheran Encyclopedia. New York: Christian Literature Co., 1899, Vol. I.

The *Lutheran Magazine,* Vol. II, No. 1 (Feb. 1828)

Lutz, W. A., *Fifty Years in the Ministry.* n.p: n.p., n.d.

Mack, Raymond W., *The Changing South.* n.p.: Aldine Publishing Co., 1970.

Malone, Bill C., "Religious Music of the Protestant South," *Encyclopedia of Religion in the South,* Samuel S. Hill, ed., pp. 517-26.

Marcum, John P. and Williams, Max W. "Population," *Encyclopedia of Southern Culture.* Charles Reagan Wilson and William Ferris, eds. Chapel Hill: The University of North Carolina Press, 1989, pp. 555-57.

Martin, Michael and Gelber, Leonard, *Dictionary of American History.* Ames: Littlefield, Adams & Co., 1956.

Marty, Martin E., *The Irony of It All;* vol. 1 of *Modern American Religion,* Chicago: The University of Chicago Press, 1986.

Massey, Mary Elizabeth, *Ersatz in the Confederacy.* Columbia: University of South Carolina

Press, 1952.

Mathis, Ray, "Colleges and Universities," *The Encyclopedia of Southern History.* David C. Roller and Robert W. Twyman, eds. Baton Rouge: Louisiana State University Press, 1979, pp. 248-50.

Matthews, Donald G., review of Gardiner H. Shattuck, Jr., *A Shield And Hiding Place: The Religious Life of the Civil War Armies,* published in *Church History,* vol. 59, no. 3 (Sept., 1990), pp. 419-20.

Matthews, Donald G., "The Second Great Awakening as an Organizing Process, 1780-1830," *Religion in American History: Interpretive Essays,* John M. Mulder and John F. Wilson, eds. Englewood Cliffs: Prentice-Hall, Inc., 1978.

[Mauney, Aubrey, ed.,] *History of the North Carolina Lutheran Men 1922-1972, With Supplement to 1977.* N.p., n.p., [1977].

McCullough, Paul G., ed., *A History of the Lutheran Church in South Carolina.* [Columbia:] The South Carolina Synod of the Lutheran Church in America, 1971.

McCurley, Foster R., Jr., "American Myths and the Bible," *Word and World,* Vol. VIII, No. 3 (Summer, 1988), pp. 226-33.

McPherson, James M. *Ordeal by Fire:* Vol. II, *The Civil War.* New York: Alfred A. Knopf, 1982.

Mead, Frank S., *Handbook of Denominations in the United States.* New York: Abingdon Press, 1975, 6th ed.

Meining, D. W. *The Shaping of America: A Geographical Perspective on 500 Years of History.* Vol. I, *Atlantic America, 1492-1800.* New Haven: Yale University Press, 1986.

Miller, Randall M. "Germans," *Encyclopedia of Southern Culture.* Charles Reagan Wilson and William Ferris, eds. Chapel Hill: The University of North Carolina Press, 1989, pp. 429-31.

Miller, Robert Johnston[e], *An Introduction to the Knowledge of the Christian Religion.* Published for the Use of the Protestant Episcopal Church of Whitehaven Parish. Salisbury: Printed, by John M. Slump, at Michael Brown's Printing Office, 1799.

Miller, Robert Johnstone, "Early Church in North Carolina," *The Church Messenger,* Vol. I, No. 11 (Oct. 15, 1879), p. [1]; an article written as a report in April, 1830.

Miller, Robert J[ohnstone], to Gottlieb Schober, July 17, 1816. Early Synod Documents, North Carolina Synod Archives, Salisbury, North Carolina.

"Minute Book, South Carolina Synod," Vol. II.

Minutes, Evangelical Lutheran Synod of South Carolina and Adjacent States, 1834, 1835.

Minutes, GS. Proceedings of the Convention of the The General Synod of the Evangelical Lutheran Church in the United States.

Minutes, North Carolina Synod. (See, *Succinct Information*)

Minutes of A Special Conference of the Lutheran Church. Held at St. Michael's Church in Lexington District, S.C. On the 29th of April, 1816. Columbia: Thomas W. Lorrain, 1816.

Minutes, GS. Proceedings of the Convention of the General Synod of the Evangelical Lutheran Church in the United States.

Minutes of the Evan. Lutheran Tenn. Synod, Reorganized; During Its Eleventh Session. With An Address On the State of the Church, By C. L. Hunt, Pastor of the E. L. Church. 1871. Hickory Tavern, N.C.; Carolina Eagle Office, 1872.

Minutes of the Second Annual Meeting of the Evangelicqal Lutheran Holston Synod, held in Miller's Church, Knox Co., Tenn., October 23-26, 1862. Greeneville, TN: Joe. M. Robertson, Job-Printer, 1862.

Minutes of the Second Convention of the General Synod of the Evangelical Lutheran Church, in the Confederate States of America, Held at Organ Church, Rowan Co., N.C., May 12-17, 1864. Savannah: Power Press of George N. Nichols, 1864.

Minutes of the Sixth Convention of the Evangelical Lutheran General Synod in North America, Convened in Winchester, Virginia, Thursday, June 9th, 1870. Wytheville: D. A. St. Clair, Printer, 1870.

Minutes of the Thirty-sixth Annual Meeting of the Evangelical Lutheran Tennessee Synod, Held in Melanchton's [sic] *Church, Randolph County, North Carolina, October 25-30, 1856.* Salisbury: The Herald Office, 1856. Published under various titles and at various places. Cited as *Minutes, TN Synod,* with the appropriate year.

Mitchell, Samuel Chiles, ed., *History of the Social Life of the South;* Vol. X of *The South in the Building of the Nation.* Richmond: The Southern Historical Publication Society, 1909.

Moltmann, Guenter, ed. *Germans to America: 300 Years of Immigration, 1683 to 1983.* Stuttgart: Institute for Foreign Cultural Relations, 1982.

Monroe, Paul E., Jr., "A History of Southern Lutheranism: The General Synod South and United Synod," an S.T.M. thesis presented to Hamma Divinity School, [1953].

Moose, John B., *Adolph Nussmann, Pioneer Lutheran Preacher in North Carolina.* Undated reprint of article appearing in the Oct., 1940, issue of *The Lutheran Church Quarterly.*

Morgan, Jacob L., Brown, Bachman S., Jr., and Hall, John, eds., *History of the Lutheran Church in North Carolina, 1803-1953.* [Salisbury]: United Evangelical Lutheran Synod of North Carolina, 1953.

Morris, John G. *Fifty Years in the Lutheran Ministry.* Baltimore: James Young, 1878.

Muhlenberg, Henry Melchior, *The Journals of Henry Melchior Muhlenberg,* Theodore G. Tappert and John W. Doberstein, trs. Philadelphia: The Muhlenberg Press, 1942; reprinted ed., Philadelphia: Lutheran Historical Society of Eastern Pennsylvania, 1982. 3 vols.

Nelson, E. Clifford, ed., *The Lutherans of North America.* Philadelphia: Fortress Press, 1975.

New York Synod, *Minutes, New York Synod, 1823.*

Nichols, James Hastings, *Romanticism in American Theology: Nevin and Schaff at Mercersburg.* [Chicago]: The University of Chicago Press, 1961.

[Norman, Clarence E., et. al.], *Life Sketches of Lutheran Ministers, North Carolina and Tennessee Synods, 1773-1965.* Columbia, S. C.: The State Printing Company, 1966.

Norris, Jeff L., and Boatmon, Ellis G., *Fair Star: A Centennial History of Lenoir-Rhyne College.* Virginia Beach: Donning Company/Publishers, 1990.

North Carolina Colonial Records, Vol. 8.

North Carolina Lutheran. 1923-1993.

North Carolina Synod, *Minutes of the Evangelical Lutheran Synod of North Carolina,* 1812-1919.

North Carolina Synod, *Proceedings of North Carolina Synod of the Lutheran Church in America,* 1963-87.

North Carolina Synod, *Proceedings of North Carolina Synod of the Evangelical Lutheran Church in America,* 1988-92.

North Carolina Synod, *Proceedings of United Evangelical Lutheran Synod of North Carolina,* 1921-62.

North Carolina Synod Committee on Historical Work, "God's People in a New Land: Celebrating 200 Years of Lutheran Ministry in North Carolina." Slide presentation, 1973.

Norton, Herman A., *Struggling for Recognition, 1791-1865.* Washington: Office of the Chief of Chaplains, Department of the Army, 1977, Vol. II of *The United States Army Chaplaincy,* a five-volume study.

Peabody Education Fund: Proceedings of the Trustees at their Nineteenth Meeting, Held at Washington, 2 February, 1881. Cambridge: University Press, John Wilson and Son, 1881.

Pellens, Eberhard Friedrich Wilhelm Georg Otto, "The Relation Between the Lutheran

Church in North Carolina and the Lutheran Churches in Niedersachsen." Typed B.D. thesis, Lutheran Theological Southern Seminary, 1952.

Perkins, Dexter and Van Deusen, Glyndon G., *The United States of America: A History.* New York: The Macmillan Co., 1962, 2 vols.

Peschau, F. W. E., tr. *Minutes of the Evangelical Lutheran Synod of North Carolina.* From 1803-1826, Twenty-three Conventions. Translated from the German Protocol. Newberry: Aull & Houseal, 1894.

Phillips, Donald M., *History of Lutheran Chapel Church Since 1780.* Marceline: Walsworth Publishing Co., [c. 1984].

Potter, David M., *The Impending Crisis, 1848-1861.* Don E. Fehrenbacher, ed. New York: Harper & Row, 1976.

Potter, D[avid] M., "National and Sectional Forces in the United States," *The New Cambridge Modern History,* Vol. X: *The Zenith of European Power, 1830-70.* J. P. T. Bury, ed. Cambridge: The University Press, 1960, pp. 603-30.

Powell, William S., ed., *Dictionary of North Carolina Biography.* Chapel Hill: University of North Carolina Press, Vol. I, 1979; Vol. II, 1986; Vol. III, 1988; Vol. IV, 1990.

Powell, William S., *North Carolina Through Four Centuries.* Chapel Hill: The University of North Carolina Press, 1989.

Preslar, Charles A., Jr., ed., *A History of Catawba County.* [Newton]: Catawba County Historical Association, Inc., 1954.

Price, W. H., ed., *Evangelical Lutheran Almanac For 1907.* Columbus: Lutheran Cook Concern, 1907.

Principal Transactions of the Synod of the Lutheran Ministry in North Carolina from 1811 to 1812. New Market: Ambrose Henkel & Co., 1812.

"Report of Gifts to the Library by Members of the Society During the Past Year," *The University South Caroliniana Society.* Fifty-third Annual Meeting. [Columbia]: n.p., 1989.

Rhyne, William R., Sr., "The Evangelical Lutheran Tennessee Synod Reorganized, 1848-1884." B.D. thesis, Lutheran Theological Southern Seminary, 1968.

Richardson, Albert D., *The Secret Service, the Field, the Dungeon, and the Escape.* Hartford: American Publishing Co., 1865.

Roeber, A. G., *Palatines, Liberty, and Property: German Lutherans in Colonial British America.* Baltimore: Johns Hopkins University Press, 1993.

Roller, David C., and Twyman, Robert W., eds., *The Encyclopedia of Southern History.* Baton Rouge: Louisiana State University Press, 1979.

Rowan County Lutheran, Vol. 1, No. 1-2.

[Schober, Gottlieb], *Luther, or A Comprehensive Account of the Rise and Progress of the Blessed Reformation of the Christian Church.* Baltimore: Schaeffer & Maund, 1818.

[Schober, Gottlieb], *Review of a Pamphlet, Issued from the Press of the Western Carolinian, in Salisbury, N.C., Written by David Henkel, arrogating to himself in said pamphlet, the title of Bishop,* etc. Salisbury: Bingham & White, 1821.

Schultz, Harold S. *Nationalism and Sectionalism in South Carolina, 1860: A Study of the Movement for Southern Independence.* Durham: Duke University Press, 1950.

Scott, Edwin J., *Random Recollections of a Long Life.* Columbia: Charles A Calvo, Jr., 1884

Sernett, Milton J., ed., *Afro-American Religious History: A Documentary Witness.* Durham: Duke University Press, 1985.

Service Book and Hymnal of the Lutheran Church in America, Music Edition. Minneapolis, Minn.: Augsburg Publishing House, 1958.

Sharpe, Ivey Lawrence, *Stanly County USA; The Story of an Era and an Area, (1841-1972).*

Greensboro: Piedmont Press, 1972.

Shattuck, Gardiner H., Jr. *A Shield and Hiding Place: The Religious Life of the Civil War Armies.* Macon: Mercer University Press, 1987.

Sheftall, John McKay, *Germans in the Southeastern United States of America: An Historic Overview.* Bonn: Consulate General of the Federal Republic of Germany, Atlanta, c. 1981.

Sherrill, William L., *Annals of Lincoln County, North Carolina.* Charlotte: The Observer Printing House, Inc., 1937; reprinted, Baltimore: Regional Publishing House, 1972.

Smith, Elwyn Allen, *The Presbyterian Ministry in American Culture: a Study in Changing Concepts, 1700-1900.* Philadelphia:The Westminster Press, 1957.

Smith, Everard H. "The Civil War Diary of Peter W. Hairston, Volunteer Aide to Major General Jubal A. Early, November 7-December 4, 1863," *The North Carolina Historical North Carolina Historical Review,* Vol. LXVII, No. 1 (Jan., 1990), pp. 59-86.

Soelle, George, "Diary of the Rev. George Soelle, March 23, 1771-April 12, 1773," a typescript translation by Kenneth G. Hamilton which, along with the original diary, is in The Moravian Archives, Winston-Salem, N. C.

Solberg, Richard W., *Lutheran Higher Education in North America.* Minneapolis: Augsburg Publishing House, 1985.

South Carolina Synod, *Minutes, Evangelical Lutheran Synod of South Carolina and Adjacent States,* 1834-1838.

The Southern Lutheran, published in Charleston, South Carolina, 1861 ff.

Stampp, Kenneth M., *The Peculiar Institution: Slavery in the Ante-Bellum South.* New York: Alfred A. Knopf, 1956; 2nd printing, 1961.

Steffey, Sidney D. *A Brief History of St. John's Evangelical Lutheran Church of Cabarrus County, N. C., From Its Earliest Settlement to the Present Time.* Concord: The Times Steam Book and Job Presses, 1899.

Stephenson, Wendell Holmes, and Coulter, E. Merton, eds., *A History of the South.* Baton Rouge: Louisiana State University Press, 1953.

Strobel, P[hilip] A., *The Salzburgers and Their Descendants: Being the History of a Colony of German (Lutheran) Protestants, Who Emigrated to Georgia in 1734, and Settled at Ebenezer, Twenty-five Miles above the City of Savannah.* Baltimore: T. Newton Kurtz, 1855.

Succinct Information of the Transactions of the German and English Lutheran Synod, for North Carolina and Adjacent States: Begun and Held at Buffaloe Creek Church, Cabarras [sic] *County. on the Second Sunday after Easter, April 25th, A. D. 1819.* Baltimore: Schaeffer & Maund, 1819.

Surratt, Jerry L., *Gottlieb Schober of Salem: Discipleship and Ecumenical Vision in an Early Moravian Town.* Macon: Mercer University Press, 1983.

Sutherland, Daniel E., *The Confederate Carpetbaggers.* Baton Rouge: Louisiana State University Press, 1988.

Tait, Adam, ed., *1976 Bulletin Alamanac: A Source of Information about Greater Philadelphia.* Philadelphia: Bulletin Company, 1976.

Tapert, Annette, ed., *The Brothers' War.* Civil War Letters to Their Loved Ones from the Blue and Gray. [New York]: Times Books, 1988.

Tappert, Theodore G., *History of the Lutheran Theological Seminary at Philadelphia, 1864-1964.* Philadelphia: Lutheran Theological Seminary, 1964.

Tennessee Synod, *Minutes, Evangelical Lutheran Tennessee Synod,* 1845-1919.

Tennessee Synod, Reorganized, *Minutes of the Evan. Lutheran Tenn. Synod, Reorganized,* 1871.

"38 Ministers Have Served St. Luke's Church At Tyro," *The Dispatch Progress Edition.*

Spring, 1968.

Thomas, William, "BRAZIL, HO! Descendants Singing Dixie," *Winston-Salem Journal* (July 1, 1990), p. C12.

Thompson, James J.,   *The Church, the South and the Future.* Westminster: Christian Classics, Inc., 1988.

Thorp, Willard, *A Southern Reader.* New York: Alfred A. Knopf, 1955.

Todd, Vincent H., ed., *Christoph Von Graffenried's Account of the Founding of New Bern.* Raleigh: North Carolina Historical Commission, 1920.

Troeltsch, Ernst, *The Social Teachings of the Christian Churches,* Olive Wyon, tr. London: George Allen & Unwin, Ltd., 1931; 4th printing, 1956, 2 vols.

Voigt, Gilbert P., *A History of Ebenezer Lutheran Church, Columbia, S. C.* Columbia, n.p., 1930.

Wall, Bennett H., "Charles Pettigrew, First Bishop-Elect of the North Carolina Episcopal Church," *The North Carolina Historical Review,* Vol. XXVIII, No. 1 (Jan. 1951)

Wall, James W., *History of Davie County in the Forks of the Yadkin.* Spartanburg: The Reprint Co., 1st ed., 1969; rev. ed., 1985.

Wallace, David Duncan, *South Carolina, A Short History, 1520-1948.* Chapel Hill: The University of North Carolina Press, 1951.

Weaver, Blanche Henry Clark, "Confederate Immigrants and Evangelical Churches in Brazil," *Journal of Southern History,* Vol. XVIII, No. 4 (Nov., 1952), pp. [446]-468.

Weis, Frederick Lewis, *The Colonial Clergy of Virginia, North Carolina and South Carolina.* Boston: The Society of the Descendants of the Colonial Clergy, 1955; reprinted, Baltimore: Genealogical Publishing Co., Inc., 1976).

Weiser, R. B., "An Essay on Revivals." *Sermons and Essays, In Two Parts.* The First Containing Popular and Evangelic Sermons, By the Late Rev. G[eorge] D[aniel] Flohr, of Wythe Co. Virginia, Translated from the Original, By Several Ministers of the Evangelical Lutheran Church. The Second Containing Sermons and Essays, For the Most Part, By Living Ministers. Baltimore: John Murphy, 1840.

Weisberger, Bernard A., *They Gathered At The River.* The Story of the Great Revivalists and their Impact upon Religion in America. Boston: Little, Brown and Company, 1958.

Wentz, Abdel Ross, "The Salt That Kept Its Savor," *The Lutheran Church Quarterly,* Vol. VIII, No. 1 (Jan., 1935).

Wight, Willard Eugene, "Robert Anderson Yoder, 1853-1911: A Social Biography." An M.A. thesis accepted by the faculty of Emory University, 1949.

Willard, George-Anne, "Charles Lee Coon," *Dictionary of North Carolina Biography,* William S. Powell, ed., Chapel Hill: University of North Carolina Press (1979ff.), Vol. 1, pp. 427-29.

Williams, Deward C., *The Blackwelders and Allied Families of North Carolina and Illinois.* Mt. Carmel, Ill.: n. p., c. 1960, 2 vols.

Williamson, Hugh, *The History of North Carolina.* Philadelphia: Thomas Dobson, 1812, 2 vols.

Wilson, Charles Reagan, "Jim Crow," *Encyclopedia of Southern Culture,* Charles Reagan Wilson & William Ferris, eds. Chapel Hill: The University of North Carolina Press, 1989, pp. 213-14.

Wolf, Richard Charles, "The Americanization of the German Lutherans." Yale University Ph.D. dissertation, 1947.

Wolf, William J., *The Almost Chosen People: A Study of the Religion of Abraham Lincoln.* Garden City: Doubleday & Co., Inc., 1959.

Woodward, C. Vann, *Origins of the New South, 1877-1913,* Vol. IX of *A History of the*

South, Wendell Holmes Stephenson and E. Merton Coulter, eds.,[Baton Rouge]: Louisiana State University Press, 1951, 1971.

Woodward, C. Vann, and Muhlenfeld, Elisabeth, *The Private Mary Chestnut: The Unpublished Civil War Diaries.* New York: Oxford University Press, 1984.

The Yadkin and Catawba Journal, Apr. 28, 1829.

Yearns, W. Buck, and Barrett, John G., eds., *North Carolina Civil War Documentary.* Chapel Hill: The University of North Carolina Press, 1980; 2nd printing, 1986.

Yoder, Fred Roy, *History of the Yoder Family in North Carolina.* Ann Arbor: Edwards Brothers, 1970.

Yoder, R[obert] A[nderson], *The Situation in North Carolina.* Newton: Enterprise Job Office, 1894. ✞

INDEX

Note: All ordained clergy are indexed as "Rev.", regardless of advanced degrees or titles acquired earlier or later in life to avoid multiple listings such as "Candidate", "Ordinand", "Pastor", "Dr.", "Prof.", "Bishop", etc.

A Mighty Fortress, Charlotte, NC 293, 326
Abbeville Banner 147
Abbeville, SC 147
Aberly, W. F. 233
Abiding Savior, Durham, NC 321, 326
Abolition of slavery 83-89, 92, 96, 101, 104, 107, 131, 144, 147, 149, 160
Abortion 315
Absolutism 2
Abstinence 86
Acquired Immune Deficiency Syndrome (AIDS) 329
ACT 316
Act in Crisis Today 316
Adderholdt, Clarence Cecil, Rev. 253
Adelphos 142
Administrative assistants 290, 314-316, 314
Administrative office building 305
Adoption services 312
Adult literacy 298
Advent, Charlotte, NC 283, 293
Advent, Spindale, NC 250
Advertisements 248
Advisory Board of Missions 196
Africa 84, 92, 258
African Methodist Episcopal Zion Church 288
Agape Camping, Conference and Retreat Center 308
Agner, Terry W., Rev. 282, 283
Ahoskie, NC 328
Aid to black ministerial students 271
AIDS, AIDS education 315, 329
Air Force chaplaincy 253
Akard, Martha 228, 229
Alabama 62, 119

Alamance County, NC 23, 27, 30, 36, 37, 326
Alamance, NC 23
Albemarle Lutheran Home 299
Albemarle sound 112
Albemarle, NC 196, 209, 247, 248, 257, 283, 310
ALC 294, 321, 322, 323, 327
Alcohol and drug statement 291
Alcoholic beverage advertising 315
Alcoholics Anonymous 291
Alcoholism 269, 291
Aldrich, Nicodemus, Rev. 133-135, 139, 147, 161-164, 166, 170, 172, 183, 185, 205
Alien and Sedition Acts 95
Allen, Robert E., Rev. 298
Allran, Albert M. 306
Alpha Synod 190, 192, 271, 314
Alsace 2
Alsace, Berks County, PA 25
Alva, Duke of 1
Amazon Republic 147
Ambulant residents 271
AME Zion 324
Amelia, SC 20, 26
Amendments to the constitution and bylaws 290
American Colonization Society 130
American Evangelical Lutheran Church 275
American Indian 315
American Lutheran Church 270, 271, 276, 286, 293, 315, 317, 321
American Lutheran Church Women 300, 322
American missions 274, 285, 288
American Revolution 1, 21, 30, 31, 49, 79
American Tories 31

Amity, Cleveland, NC 196
Amnesty for Vietnam exiles 315
Anaheim, CA 326
Anderson, Albert B., Dr. 306
Anderson, Dennis A., Rev. 327
Anderson, Hugh George, Rev. 205,
        303, 306, 307, 317
Anderson, R., Gen. 152
Anglican 286
Anne, Queen 8
Anspach, Rev. 129
Anthony, Jacob Brown, Rev. 70, 89,
        127, 128, 129, 172
Anti-revival 39, 56, 163
Anti-slavery 84, 87, 88, 96, 99, 104, 105
Antietam, VA 113, 121
Antioch, Dallas, NC 70
Anton, Leopold of Firmian 7
Anxious Bench (Seat), The 51, 54-56
Aoyama Gakuin, Tokyo, Japan 226
Aoyama, Hikoshiro, Rev. 226
Apostles' and Nicene creeds 192
Appomattox County, VA 139
Appomattox Court House 77
Appomattox, VA 119
Apportionment 271-273, 289, 316
Arabs 77
Archbishop of Austria, Leopold of
        Firmian 7
Archives 238, 246, 281, 322
Arden, NC 268, 328
Area Mission Week 251
Arends, Johann Gottfried, Rev. 29-35,
        40, 46, 56, 80
Arends, Joseph Gottfried, Rev. 56
Arey, Benjamin, Rev. 70, 90, 97, 121,
        202
Arey, Charles 121
Arey, Luther 121
Arey, Theophilus 121
Armistice 236
Army Chaplain's Fund 117
Army Mission 117
Army of Northern VA 127
Army of Tennessee 120
Army of the United States 113
Army of VA 120
Army revivals 119
Arndt, G. Dewey 263
Arndt, Harry M. 263

Arndt, John [James Allen], Arndt 54
Arndt, John, [Arends], Johann
        Gotfried, Rev. 24
Arne, Esther 326
Arne, Harry O. 303, 326, 327
ARP Church, Mooresville, NC 229
Artz, William A., Rev. 48, 70, 106, 160
Asaph 14
Asbestos in the old building 322
Ascension, Shelby, NC 244, 302
Ascension, Wilson, NC 252
Asheville, NC 256, 268, 312, 329
Ashton, Faith 323, 326
Asia 92
Assembly Grounds Committee 268
Assembly of Negroes 81
Assistance for disabled ministers 226
Assistant in the LCA president's office
        307
Assistant to the president 245, 290
Associate director of evangelism 283
Associate in youth ministry 300
Associate Reformed Presbyterian
        Church 255
Associates in ministry 322
Associates of Dr. Bray 79
Association of Evangelical Lutheran
        Churches 317, 321
Association of Missionaries in
        Malaysia and Singapore 295
Athens, GA 172
Atlanta, GA 121, 145, 238, 253, 268,
        293, 301, 323, 327
Atonement, Wilkesboro, NC 251, 259
Audio-visual library 282
Augsburg 18
    League of 6
    War of the League of 2, 3
Augsburg Confession 28, 45, 46, 56,
        58, 62, 63, 134, 135, 157-160,
        164, 169, 181, 182, 187, 188,
        189, 202, 218, 235, 330, 331
Augsburg, Germany 18
Augsburg, Winston-Salem, NC 196,
        207-209, 222, 228, 239, 244,
        245, 255-257, 260, 262, 263,
        274, 286, 299, 304
Augusta, GA 22, 26
Augusta, Princess of Saxe-Gotha 28
Augustana Lutheran Church 275

Augustus Lutheran Church, Trappe,
    PA 15
Austin, TX 76
Austria 1, 7, 8, 17, 18
    Archbishop of 17
    Christian faith in 7
Auxiliary organizations 205

Babel 86
Bachman, John, Rev. 91-94, 97, 124,
    134, 162
Back Creek 39
Bakke, Nils Jules, Rev. 78, 192
Baltimore, MD 32, 59, 60, 62, 160,
    194, 204, 217, 251
BAM 292
Bansemer, C. F., Rev. 211, 212
Baptism 56, 58, 83, 159, 210
Baptist 37, 39, 48, 52, 55, 56, 69, 84,
    115 , 128, 172, 199, 229
Baptists of Wake Forest, NC 288
Baptized membership 196
Barber Junction, NC 257, 300
Barger, Glenn Leroy, Rev. 253
Barger, John L. 326
Barnwell County, SC 20
Barrier, J. D. 233
Barrier, Mathias 75
Barrier, W. A., Capt. (Prof.) 212, 214
Barringer, John Daniel, Rev. 253
Barringer, John Paul 31
Barringer, Paul B. 122
Basis of Union 183, 186
Bauer, Mary 258
Baugher, Rev. 129
Baumgartner, Hugh E., Rev. 292
Bavarians 13
Beam, John T.,Jr. 290
Beam, Keith Junious, Rev. 253
Bear Poplar, NC 206
Beard
    Unknown family 32
Beard, Christian, Rev. 158, 159
Beard, Robert Quincy, Rev. 310, 328
Beatty, Paul B., Mrs. 255
Beaty, Kay 326
Beck, Alfred Riley, Rev. 179, 223, 225,
    248
Beck, William 215

Beck's, Lexington, NC 32, 35, 47, 72,
    73, 142, 168
Begley, Michael J., Roman Catholic
    Bishop 287
Bell, Charles Krauth, Rev. 223
Bell, Joseph E., Rev. 61, 75
Bell, Omar 326
Belmont Abbey, Roman Catholic
    College, Belmont, NC 287
Belmont, NC 287, 288, 300, 307
Beloit, Kansas 281
Beneficiary aid to students 194
Benevolence 272-274, 287, 290, 329
Bergman, John Ernest 34
Berks County, PA 25
Bernhardt, Christian Eberhard, Rev.
    34, 56, 57
Bernheim, Charles Herman, Rev. 172,
    179, 184, 185, 203
Bernheim, Elizabeth Clayton 171
Bernheim, Gotthard Dellman, Rev. 64,
    118, 127, 133, 154-156, 163,
    164, 167, 171, 177, 191, 211
Bessemer City, NC 230
Beth Eden, Newton, NC 70, 244, 248,
    262, 264, 266, 300
Beth Eden, Stoney Man, VA 246
Bethabara, NC 23
Bethany, Boone, NC 323
Bethany, Hickory, NC 225, 268, 284,
    310
Bethany, Kannapolis, NC 253, 259
Bethel, Franklin, NC 207
Bethel, Lexington, SC 82
Bethel, Lincolnton, NC 35, 47
Bethel, Manasses, VA 246
Bethel, Orkney Springs, VA 246
Bethel, Rowan County, NC 70, 178,
    207, 281
Bethel, SC 81
Bethel, Stanly County, NC 71, 178
Bethlehem church, Newberry District,
    SC 51
Bethlehem, Augusta County, VA 73,
    180
Bethlehem, Hickory, NC 224, 304, 326
Bethlehem, Irmo, SC 246
Bethlehem, Pomaria, SC 51
Bethphage, Lincolnton, NC 70
Bible study 52, 260, 266, 292

Bible Study and Witness programs 294
Bible, Tract, and Missionary Societies 103
Bicentennial of the first NC Lutheran synod 330
Bicycle 198
Big Bethel, VA 111
Bikle, Louis Albert, Rev. 139, 145, 167, 170, 177, 187, 189, 195, 211, 212, 215
Bikle, Philip Melanchthon 172
Bishop 283
Bishop of London 28, 79
Bissinger, F. A., Mrs. 228, 255
Bittle, Daniel Howard, Mrs. 171
Bittle, Daniel Howard, Rev. 76, 131, 132, 171, 212
Bittle, David Frederick, Rev. 169
Bittle, Susan Biglow 171, 200
Black congregations 83, 89
Black Lutherans 83, 88, 191, 315
Black Mountain, NC 266
Blackberry wine 129
Blacks 76-79, 82-84, 88-90, 149, 150, 191, 221, 243, 314
Blacks seeking ordination 191
Blackwelder, L. E., Mrs. 255, 256
Blackwelder, Leroy Emerson, Rev. 270
Blackwelder, Rev. 129
Bleeding Kansas 99
Blockade of southern ports 122
Blockade-running 124
Blountville, TN 74
Blue Ridge Assembly Grounds 266
Blue Spring, Greene County, TN 50
Bluefield, West Virginia 224
Blume, Harry W. 326
Board for Congregational Life 317
Board for Higher Education and Schools 317
Board for Home Missions and Church Extension of the United Syn 225
Board of American Missions 244-246, 250, 277, 292
Board of Church Extension 196
Board of Domestic Missions 115
Board of Educational Institutions 267
Board of English Missions of The English Missouri Synod 217

Board of Foreign Missions 232, 244
Board of Higher Education 268
Board of Home Missions and Church Extension 232
Board of Missions of the United Synod South 207, 208
Board of Pensions 284
Board of Publication 284
Board of Social Ministry 284, 294, 309
Board of Social Missions 281, 283, 313
Board of Trade 77
Board of World Missions 284
Bodie, B. T. 268
Bodie, Earl K., Mrs. 259
Bodie, Earl Kennan, Rev. 240
Boger, William Jennings, Mrs. 229
Boger, William Jennings, Rev. 223, 229
Boggs, James Russell, Rev. 253
Boggs, William Gilmer, Rev. 253
Bohr, Christine L., Rev. 297
Boinest, Thadeus Street, Rev. 118, 156
Bolick, Leonard H., Rev. 283, 322, 323
Boliek, Luther G. 263, 284
Boliek, Wynne C., Rev. 251
Bolles, Edwin Abriel, Rev. 154
Bolzius, John Martin 18
Bond-servants 141
Bonham, Brigadier-General 111
Book of Common Prayer 17, 287
Book of Concord 218, 331
Book of Worship 159, 160, 199, 200, 202, 203, 204, 227
Bookout, Joe 290
Books of worship 63
Boone, NC 256, 294
Boozer, Virgil Young, Mrs. 228
Boozer, Virgil Young, Rev. 222, 223
Bost, Clarence 270
Bost, Clarence, Mrs. 270
Bost, Raymond Morris, Rev. 284, 305, 306
Bostian, Jacob's slaves 88
Boston, Massachusetts 51, 77, 84, 143
Botetourt County, VA 206
Bowers, Edgar, Prof. 211
Bowers, Mary Lou 228, 229
Bowles, John D., Rev. 172, 177, 186
Bowman, Elbert 303
Boy Scout(s) 265, 300
Boy's Work program 265

Boys' home 270
Branham, Mack C., Jr., Rev. 307, 327
Braun, Michael 78, 199
Bray, Thomas, Rev. 79
Brazil 147
Breckenridge, John 95
Bremen, Germany 32
Brick Church, German Reformed 88
Brick Church, Guilford County, NC
    27, 49, 82
Brink, Carl A., Rev. 253
Bristol 77
Bristol, Rhode Island 77
Britain 9, 76
British Board of Trade 8
British Government 9, 14
British North America 1, 3, 76
Brittain, Bill D. 311, 312, 328, 329
Broad River 26
Broad River, SC 57
Brokhoff, Wendy 260
Brooks, Preston, Congressman 100,
    101, 160
Brotherhood 232, 263-265, 270, 313
Broughton State Hospital, Morganton,
    NC 253
Brown, Abel Jacob, Rev. 72, 74
Brown, John's raid 102
Brown University 142
Brown vs. Board of Education 271
Brown, A. M., Mrs. 207
Brown, Abel J., Rev. 179
Brown, Bachman Samuel, Rev. 177,
    190, 236
Brown, Bachman Storch, Jr. 270, 277,
    284, 290, 317
Brown, Chrisenberry Alexander, Rev.
    222, 237
Brown, Governor of GA 126
Brown, R. A., Mrs. 207
Brown, Rev. 129
Brown, Ruth 230
Brown, W. R., Mrs. 206
Bube, Christoph 25
Buchanan, James, President 105
Buehler's, Sullivan County, TN 50, 73
Buelow, Joachim 30
Buffalo Creek church (See Dutch
    Buffalo) 61

Buffalo Creek church (See Dutch
    Buffalo) [St. John's,
    Cabarrus] 60
Building for Living 328
Bulwinkle, A. L., Representative 275
Bummers 125
Burk, Carol, Sister 322, 323
Burke County, NC 126
Burlington, NC 23, 192, 196, 231, 240,
    310
Burnsville, NC 302
Burt, Daphne L., Rev. 323
Butler, Andrew P., Senator 99, 100
Butner, NC 301, 302
Butt, James, Rev. 253

Cabarrus County, NC 23, 27, 30, 31,
    34, 78, 98, 106, 154, 224
Caldwell County, NC 80, 126, 128
Calhoun, John C. 84, 104
Call of the ordained ministry 325
Calvary, Concord, NC 224, 304, 326
Calvary, Morganton, NC 250, 270
Calvary, Spencer, NC 223
Calvin, John 7
Calvinist 3, 5, 36, 48, 50, 55, 60, 200
Cambodia 315
Camden, SC 22, 28, 31
Camp Agape 308, 328
Camp Butner, NC 294
Camp Committee 308
Camp Lejeune, NC 265
Camp meeting 37-39, 48, 49, 51, 52, 56
Campbell, Richard R., Rev. 283
Campbell, W. G., Mrs. 206
Camping and Conference Ministry
    Appeal 308
CAMPUS 294
Campus ministry 288, 294
Campus Ministry campaign 316
Canada 92, 266
Candidates 34, 35, 40, 59, 60, 63, 143,
    172, 178, 191, 193, 215, 244,
    285
Cane Creek Presbyterian Church 36
Cane Ridge, Kentucky 36
Cantors 298
Cape Fear facility 308
Cape Fear River, NC 5, 77, 308
Capital funds campaign 294, 316

Capital punishment 315
Capital University, Columbus, Ohio 76
Capps, Bismarck 234, 262, 263
Caravaners 261
Care of NC Elderly Right Now 310
Caribbean islands 77
Carlson, Oscar W., Rev. 251
Carmina Ecclesiae 201
Carolina Freight Carriers Corp.,
    Cherryville, NC 253
Carolina Summer School for Church
    Workers 266
Carolina Watchman 104
Carolinas Evangelism Conference 293,
    325
Carr, Betty 299
Carribean Synod 323
Caruthers, Eli W., Rev. Presbyterian
    88
Casey, VA 282
Castor, David Larry, Rev. 308, 328
Catawba College, Salisbury, NC 294
Catawba County, NC 23, 26, 30, 169,
    195, 221, 311
Catawba Lutheran 225, 248
Catawba River 23, 24
Catechism 164
Catechism for Little Children 235
Catechist 35, 59, 60, 63
Catechization 58, 191, 205
Catechize 191
Catholic(s) 2, 3, 6, 7, 324
Catholic-Lutheran relations 287
Cauble, Frank 260
Cavins, Aden, Lt. Col. 126
Cedar Grove, Leesville, SC 142, 180,
    246
Cedar Grove, Vale, NC 197
Center for Theology 323
Center Grove, Kannapolis, NC 195,
    207, 208, 245, 262, 283
Central District 288
Central PA Synod 172
Certified or non-certified lay
    professional 305
Chancellorsville, VA 127
Chapel Hill, NC 284, 313, 323
Chaplains 113-118, 127, 172, 253
Chapman, George M. 305
Charges of ministerial heterodoxy 193

Charles II, King of England 2
Charles Town, SC 15, 24
Charles, Duke of Lorraine 2
Charleston Presbytery, SC 26
Charleston, SC 5, 19, 20, 22, 25, 26, 28,
    29, 31, 32, 76, 79, 84, 91, 98,
    101, 103, 118, 126, 145, 156,
    171, 177, 181, 317
Charleston, West Virginia 294
Charlotte Area Evangelism Mission
    251
Charlotte Sophia of
    Mecklenburg-Strelitz 28
Charlotte, NC 20, 163, 170, 171, 178,
    192, 213, 214, 228, 230, 233,
    236, 238, 239, 247, 251, 276,
    282, 284, 286, 293, 294, 302,
    310, 312, 314, 323
Chattanooga, TN 127
Chattel slavery 69, 76, 87
Cherryville, NC 35, 253, 284, 328
Chesky, James A. 283, 322, 323
Chestnut Hill (Salisbury), NC) 196
Chestnut, Mary 112, 142, 146, 152
Chicago, IL 283, 314, 321
Chickamauga, VA 120
Chiga, Toransuke, Rev. 226
Child abuse 329
Child care 269
Children of the Church 258, 259
Children's Foreign Missionary Society
    of the Lutheran Church 208
Children's Helper 208
Children's home(s) 236, 270, 273, 329
Children's Home of the South 314
Children's Missionary Society 208
Children's Work 258, 259
Childs, James M., Jr., Rev. 327
Chilstrom, E. Corinne, Rev. 325
Chilstrom, Herbert W., Rev. 325
China 257
China Grove, NC 35, 182, 206, 230,
    284
Chisholm, Robert G., Attorney 118,
    162
Choir members 298
Choral Music 200
Chou, David 314
Chrismons for Christmas trees 299
Christ the King, Cary, NC 293

Christ the King, Whiteville, NC 287, 293

Christ, Charlotte, NC 251, 303, 304

Christ, Durham, NC 252

Christ, East Spencer, NC 195, 243, 255

Christ, Greensboro, NC 252, 321

Christ, Jonesville, NC 293

Christ, Stanley, NC 70, 234

Christ, Winston-Salem, NC 244, 252, 281

Christian Education, M. A. Degree 245

Christian Youth Caravan 302

Christiana, Rowan County, NC 195, 222, 255

Christmas, Clyde J., Rev. 328

Christus Victor, Durham, NC 293, 323, 326

Christus Victor, Fayetteville, NC 293

Church discipline 193

Church Extension Fund 196

Church of Christ in Japan 226

Church of England 17, 28

Church of North India 325

Church of the Saviour, Newland, NC 321

Church Publications 194

Church Women United in NC 299

Cincinnati, Ohio 262

Civil liberties 95

Civil Rights bill 147

Clapp, Nathan, Rev. 191, 192

Clare, R. H. 275

Classis of NC 153

Clergy delegates 289

Cleveland County, NC 262

Cleveland, Ohio 257

Cleveland, Ohio, newspaper 103

Cline, Constance 228-230, 256

Cline, John A., Mrs. 207

Cline, M. L. 169

Cline, Mary 230

Cline, Ray A. 260, 261, 303

Cline, Robert Henry, Rev. 223

Cline, William Pinckney, Rev. 190, 215, 237

Clingman, Thomas L. 105

Coastal District 288

Cobb, John William, Rev. 261, 304

Cobb, Rachel 288, 299

Coble, Julian, NC 47

Coble, Michael M., Licensee 191

Coble, Wade 310

Coble's, Guilford County, NC 180

Coggins, Roscoe R. 265

Cold Harbor 127

Cold Water, Concord, NC 25, 35, 194

College Benefit Association 213

College for women 171

College of William and Mary 87

Cologne 2

Colonization society 84

Colony of GA 18
   Near the Savannah River 8

Colored Congregation 89

Colored population 93

Colton's Piano Fortes 204

Columbia School of Theology for Christian Laity 268

Columbia, SC 20, 103, 118, 126, 145, 179, 236, 268, 306, 322

Columbus, Ohio 74, 317, 321, 327

Commercialism in the church 299

Commission for a New Lutheran Church 322

Commission on Basis and Constitution 240

Commission on Church Papers 284

Commission on Evangelism 293

Commission on Negro Work 271

Commission on Organizational Structure 247

Commission on Study of Nature and Function of the Congregation 284

Commission on the Formation of a New Lutheran Church 317

Committee of Correspondence 151

Committee on American Missions 292

Committee on Brotherhoods 233, 261

Committee on Christian Education 300

Committee on Church Institutions and Education 211

Committee on Church Music 254

Committee on Ecumenical Affairs 288

Committee on Ecumenism 324

Committee on Foreign Emigration 151

Committee on Inclusive Ministry 314

Committee on Letters 182

Committee on Letters and Petitions 187

Committee on Missions 190
Committee on Music and Worship 281
Committee on Operational Activities
      275
Committee on Petitions 70
Committee on Reference and Council
      318
Committee on Social Missions 270
Committee on Stewardship 245
Committee on the President's Report
      163, 167, 224
Committee on the State of the Church
      155, 156, 214, 252, 254, 273
Committee on Work Among the
      Freedmen 191
Committee on Worship 298
Common Service Book 203, 227, 254
Commonwealth of PA 20
Communion 145, 156, 197, 227, 254
Community in Christ, Huntersville, NC
      293
Community literacy councils 299
Companion Church Program 325
Compromise of 1850 99, 104
CONCERN 310, 316
Concord, NC 23-25, 27, 30, 34, 35, 75,
      98, 99, 122, 123, 133, 134, 155,
      156, 171, 178, 191, 192, 201,
      202, 206, 207, 228, 230, 265,
      308
Concordia College 180, 197, 212, 213,
      215, 216, 217, 221
Concordia High School 215
Concordia Synod 168, 169
Concordia, China Grove, NC 195
Conder, Irenaeus, Rev. 179, 182
Cone, William Henry, Rev. 177, 185
Confederate chaplains 113
Confederate Secretary of War 103
Confederate States Bible Society 154
Conference 54, 217
Conference and Camping Ministry
      Appeal 316
Conference of Bishops 317
Confessional 157-159, 164
Confessional basis 189
Confessional Lutheranism 216
Confessional service 254
Confessionalism 65, 157-159, 164
Confirmation class 210

Confirmation of slaves 83
Congregational Brotherhoods 262
Congregational singing 203
Congregational standing 203
Congregational worship 254
Congregationalism 48, 96
Congregations without regularly-called
      pastors 296
Congress 95, 99, 100, 146, 147, 149-151
Conover, NC 190, 215-217, 221, 270,
      309
Conrad, Alexander, Col. 183
Conrad, Flavius Leslie, Rev. 225, 243,
      245, 246, 271, 275, 276
Conrad, Henry H. 215
Conrad, Katherine O. 299, 317, 322,
      323
Conrad, Paul L., Rev. 291
Conrad, R. L., Mrs. 258
Conserve gasoline and tires 275
Consistory of Hanover 28, 29, 31
Constituting convention 244, 257, 266,
      275, 317, 321
Constitution and by-laws 240, 247,
      262, 275
Constitution and by-laws, Revised 247
Constitution of the NC Synod 290
Constitution of the TN Synod 74
Constitution of the United States 102,
      104, 146
Contact chaplain 294
Contact pastor for servicemen 294
Continuing education for ministers 285
Contributions to Catholic-Lutheran
      relations 287
Convention banquet 289
Convention Center, Durham, NC 284
Convention dates 289
Convention delegates 289
Convention facilities 314
Convention practices 289
Convention sites 47, 289
Conversions 36, 48, 49, 51, 79, 172
Converts 172
Convo 302
Cook, C. A., Dr. 233
Cook, James P. 232
Cook, John M., Mrs. 228, 229, 255,
      256
Cook, Jonas 213, 216

Coon, David A. 113
Cooper, David F., Rev. 248, 260
Cooper, Edgar Claudius, Rev. 253
Cooper, Ernest Karl, Rev. 250
Cooper, George Herman, Rev. 253
Cooper, W. L., Prof. 233
Cooperstown, New York 75
Copeland, Maria-Alma, Rev. 322, 323
Cornwallis, Lord 49
Corporal punishment 315
Costner, Adam 60
Costner, Ambrose 169, 183, 189, 215
Costner, T. F. 232
Coupee, Francis 199
Court of George II 1
Court of the King in England 33
Covenant arrangement 273
Covenant Plan 273, 274
Cox, Clarence Brown, Rev. 209
Cox, George Henry, Rev. 177, 196,
        198, 201, 222
Cram, Erin 326
Craven County, NC 15, 16, 77
Credal orthodoxy 3
Crescent View Retirement Community
        328
Crigler, J. F., Mrs. 255, 256, 258
Crim, Jacob, Rev. 97, 127
Crim's Creek (now St. John's),
        Pomaria, SC 25
Cromer, George B. 232
Cromer, Voigt Rhodes, Rev. 243-245,
        267, 274-276, 284, 305, 306,
        313
Cronk, E. C., Mrs. 238
Cronk, E. C., Rev. 232, 238
Cross and Crown, Matthews, NC 293
Cross of Christ, Concord, NC 195
Crouse, Andrew Leonhardt, Rev. 179,
        194, 195, 198, 204, 205, 210,
        215, 217, 234, 235
Crumley, James R., Rev. 283, 287, 318
Cuban oppression, Statement
        condemning 216
Cubans 216
Cullowhee, NC 294
Culp, Sue 260, 261
Currie, D. F., Mrs. 308

Dallas Academy, Gastonia, NC 215

Dallas, NC 126, 190, 228, 229, 231,
        234, 301, 315
Dallmann, William, Rev. 217
Dalton, GA 120
Dan River 22
Daniel's, Lincolnton, NC 25, 47, 71-73,
        112, 180
Das Neu-eingerichtete Gesang-Buch 200
Dau, W. H. T., Rev. 217
Daubenspeck, Wayne Martel, Rev. 253
Davidson College 236
Davidson County, NC 23, 27, 30, 32,
        34, 87, 245
Davidson, NC 196
Davie County, NC 23, 32, 37, 196
Davie Mission 196
Davis, Jefferson, President 84, 113,
        114, 152
Davis, John B., Mrs. 207
Davis, John B., Rev. 172, 211
de Graffenried, Christopher, Baron 4,
        5, 14-16, 18
Deal, Claude Victor, Sr., Rev. 253,
        265, 274
Deal, Jack Donald, Rev. 315
Deal, James Francis, Rev. 238
Deans and districts 290
Deaton, Willis Alexander, Rev. 179,
        223, 225, 227, 240
Declaration of Independence 91, 92,
        107
Deists 53
Delaware River 20
Demetrios I, Patriarch of Eastern
        Orthodoxy 287
Democrats 102, 104, 105, 150
Denominational lines 52
Department of News and Information
        291
Depression 263, 272
DeRosset, Armand L. 148
Derrick, Clarence Kesler, Rev. 253
Deserters, Desertion 113, 126, 127,
        128, 269
Detroit, MI 276
Development Fund campaign 267
Devotionalism 3
Dew, Thomas Roderick 87
Diapers 298
Dickens, Charles 148

Diehl, Rev. 129
Diet 188
Dinglehoff, J. H. 261
Diocese of East Carolina 287
Director of evangelism 245, 251
Director of minority ministries 314
Director of multicultural ministries 322
Director of outdoor ministries 308
Director of Scouting 265
Disabled Ministers Fund 226
Disabled pastors 177
Discipline 3, 135
Displaced Germans 48
Distribution of benevolent
        contributions 290
District brotherhoods 262
District functions and workshops 285
District Luther League of Western NC
        231
District membership for pastors 297
District synod(s) 59, 134, 135, 166, 169,
        181, 239
Disturbed children 269
Diversity in color and language 323
Division for Mission in North America
        284, 295, 314
Division for Parish Services 284
Division for World Mission and
        Ecumenism 295
Division of Parish Education 266
Dobbs, Arthur, Governor (NC) 24, 32,
        77
Doctrine of Salvation 81
Doctrines of the Church 330
Donoghue, John F., Most Rev.,
        Roman Catholic 288, 324
Dosh, Thomas William Luther, Rev.
        154, 163, 169, 203
Double apportionment 274
Douglas, Stephen A., Senator 99
Dover, England 18
Dred Scott decision of the Supreme
        Court 102
Dreher, Gottfried, Rev. 57, 64, 81
Dreher, Daniel Isaiah, Rev. 117, 127,
        133, 162, 212
Duelling 130
Dues plan of financing 265
Duke Charles of Lorraine 2
Duke Divinity School 288

Duke of Alva 1
Duke University Medical Center 282,
        294
Duls, Jacob 154
Duncan, Richard, Rev. 253
Dunkers 200
Dupert, Pastor (Reformed Church) 26
Duplex envelope system 238
Durham (NC) Convention Center 289
Durham convention 289
Durham, NC 196, 289, 294, 295, 317,
        325
Dutch Buffalo Creek (St. John's,
        Concord) (See also Buffalo
        Creek) 30, 31
Dutch country 21
Dutch Fork of SC 24
Dutch Pine Meeting House (Union,
        Salisbury) 78
Dutch Reformed 48
Dutch War of 1672 2
Dutchman's Creek (Reformation),
        Davie County 25, 32, 37
Dyer, Charles A. 265

Early, Jubal Anderson, Gen. 116
Easter 254
Easterly, George, Rev. 73
Eastern and Western NC Episcopal
        dioceses 287
Eastern Conference 191, 247
Eastern district 263, 288
Eastern District of the American
        Lutheran Church 270, 308
Eastern PA Synod 172
Easy Instructor 200
Ebenezer, Catawba, NC 197
Ebenezer, Columbia, SC 19, 202
Ebenezer, Greensboro, NC 323
Ebenezer, Rowan County, NC 141,
        178, 304
Ebenezer, Savannah, GA 19, 30, 34
Ebenezer's hospital 19
Eckard, Albert D. 270
Eckard, Albert D., Mrs. 270
Eckard, Glenn Stine, Rev. 253
Eckard, Ralph E., Rev. 284
Ecology 315
Ecumenical activities 288

Ecumenical conference for theological discussion 288
Ecumenical Institute 288
Ecumenical Relations 285, 314
Ecumenism 285, 330, 331
Eddleman, J. M. 185
Edge, P. M. 261
Edgecombe County, NC 77, 111
Edict of Nantes 2
Edmonston, Kate 139
Education and Missionary Society 118, 206
Education for the ministry 288
Education of young women 200
Educational Institutions 74, 157, 216
Edwards, Jonathan, Rev. 55
Edwards, Ted Elkain, Rev. 253
Effingham County, GA 19
Efird Hall Administration Building 268
Efird, Adam, Rev. 72, 121, 129, 141, 161
Efird, Frank Kimball, Rev. 274, 284
Efird, Ida Brown 230
Efird, J. K., Mrs. 229
Efird, J. S., Mrs. 248
ELCA 323-329
ELCA Council 317
ELCA pastor 323
ELCA structure 323
ELCA synods 323
ELCA Transition Team 318
Elderly and handicapped, Complex for 310
Election of officers 318
Elector of Hanover 28
Elector of the Palatinate 5
Electric lights 227, 235
Electronic organ 257
Eleventh Congressional District 275
Eliminate masculine nouns or pronouns 290
Eliminate Protestantism 6
Eliminate racism 314
Elizabeth College 214, 215, 238
Elkin, NC 196
Elliot, John 152
Ellis, John W., Governor 105
Elon College 236
Emancipation 84, 101, 146, 152

Emancipation Proclamation 89, 149
Emergency appeal 273
Emergency shelter care program 311
Emmanuel (no location given), NC 230
Emmanuel, Greene County, TN 50
Emmanuel, High Point, NC 228, 244, 245, 256, 258, 260, 263, 264
Emmanuel, Lincolnton, NC 35, 47, 198, 224, 225, 234, 240, 245, 256, 260, 262
Emmanuel, Mt. Hermon, SC 246
Emmanuel, New Market, VA 73, 142, 180, 224, 246
Emmanuel, Rockwell, NC 196
Emmanuel, Sullivan County, TN 73
Encounter Retreats 313
Endowment fund 211
England 3, 8, 9, 14, 17, 18, 28, 29, 31, 33, 77, 125, 148, 287
England's Society de Propaganda Christi Cognitione 18
English Lutheran Conference of MO 217
English MO Synod 217
Enochville, NC 223
Envelopes 225, 232, 237, 273
Environmental Task Force 314
Epiphany, Winston-Salem, NC 252, 299, 322, 323
Episcopal 35, 46, 48, 56, 64, 65, 114, 121, 128, 152, 171, 199, 286, 287, 288, 305, 324, 330
Episcopalians and Lutherans 286
Equal employment regardless of race or sex 314
Equal Rights Amendment 315
Erickson, Christina 258
Estes, Bill 128
Estey's Cottage Organs 204
Estill, Robert W., Episcopal Bishop 287
Europe 5, 7, 13, 17, 18, 20, 41, 89, 112, 148, 199
Europe's Protestant and Roman Catholic forces 18
Europeans displaced by World War II 270
Evangelical Lutheran 147
Evangelical Lutheran Church 189

Evangelical Lutheran Church in
    America 317
Evangelical Lutheran Church in the
    Confederate States of Ameri
    118, 161
Evangelical Lutheran Church South
    189
Evangelical Lutheran Concordia Synod
    of VA 168
Evangelical Lutheran General Synod in
    North America 157, 189
Evangelical Lutheran Holston Synod
    74
Evangelical Lutheran Synod of MO
    215
Evangelical Lutheran Synod of Ohio
    215
Evangelical Lutheran Synod of
    Southwestern VA 206
Evangelical Lutheran Synod of
    Western VA 70, 132
Evangelical Lutheran TN Synod,
    Reorganized 74
Evangelical Lutheran, The 163-166
Evangelical Outreach Program 293
Evangelical Theological Seminary,
    Columbus, Ohio 327
Evangelicalism 48, 50, 52, 55
Evangelism 79, 90, 245, 251, 260, 264,
    288, 290, 293
Every Member Canvas 273
Evicted Reformed pastors 3
Ewell, Gen. 116
Examination and ordination 30, 269
Examination of candidates 191
Examining committee 276
Exchange of letters between LCA
    Bishop James Crumley and
    Pope 287
Exchange of representatives 170
Exchange of worship leadership 286
Executive Board 233, 234, 244, 277,
    282, 289, 290, 297, 308, 311,
    313, 314, 316, 317
Executive Committee 194, 196, 207,
    209, 222, 223, 226, 230, 232,
    234, 245, 248, 260, 261, 264,
    268, 271, 274, 276, 301, 310,
    311

Executive Committee on Army
    Missions 118
Executive Committee on Home
    Missions 195
Executive Committee on Missions of
    the Ministerium of Pennsylv
    145
Executive Council 277, 290
Executive Council of the Lutheran
    Church in America 277
Expanded role of the laity 209
Expansion Fund of Southern Seminary
    267
Experimental Christianity 52
Extended payment plans 147
Ezra 53

Faggart, Brady Young, Jr., Rev. 261,
    281, 282, 284, 306, 307
Faggart, Harry E., Jr. 303
Faggart, Max 303
Fairfax, VA 111
Faith, Conover, NC 251, 303
Faith, Rowan County, NC 196, 222,
    228, 283, 322
Fall Training Events 294
Family Aid Program in Catawba
    County 311
Family counseling center 312
Family ministry 312
Family of Faith, Harrisburg, NC 321
Family services 311
Family worker 312
Fayetteville, NC 326
Featherstone, Rudolph R., Rev. 327
Federal Compact 85
Federal Penitentiary, Atlanta, GA 253
Federal tariff laws 104
Federal troops 187
Federal Whigs 104
Federalist-dominated Congress 95
Federalists 95
Federation of synods 276
Female education 170
Female seminaries 200
Female Seminary 171
Ferries 23
Fesperman, Harry B. 303
Ficken, Carl, Rev. 327
Field missionary of the synod 243

Field secretaries 232

Fifty-second Regiment, VA Volunteers 116

Fillmore, Millard 105

Final settlement with the pastor 237

Finances 216, 237, 316, 329

Financial aid 311

Financing of mission churches 292

Financing of parsonages and church sites 292

Finney, Charles Grandison 50-52, 54, 55, 56

Finnish Evangelical Lutheran Church (Suomi Synod) 275

First and Second NC Union Volunteers 127

First black woman to be ordained in the LCA 314

First Church, Greensboro, NC 223

First female assistant to the bishop 322

First full-time president of the synod 243

First German settlement 4

First Lutheran Church, Pittsburgh, PA 89

First ordained Lutheran pastor 4, 25, 26

First permanent German settlement in the Southeast 16

First water powered mill in GA 19

First woman editor of the NC Lutheran 291

First woman pastor 297

First, Albemarle, NC 178, 195, 214, 222, 228, 244, 245, 248, 256, 260-262, 264, 294, 326

First, Greensboro, NC 244, 251, 259, 261, 264, 273, 277, 284, 304, 306, 317, 324, 325, 326

First, Lexington, NC 223

Fisher, Amy Louise 256

Fisher, C. P., Jr., Mrs. 259

Fisher, Carl Melchoir, Rev. 295

Fisher, Charles Lee Thornton, Rev. 212, 213

Fisher, Frederick 78

Fisher, Herman 260

Fisher, J. A., Capt. 183

Fisher, J. E. 274

Fisher, J. H. C., Mrs. 206, 256

Fisher, J. S., Mrs. 212

Fisher, James Henry Cornelius, Rev. 235

Fisher, James L. 263

Fisher, Joshia S., Mrs., (Laura Plunkett) 206, 207

Fisher, Ray R., Mrs. 255

Fisher, Roscoe Brown, Rev. 248

Fisher, Roy Linn, Rev. 253

Fisher, Ruth 299

Fisher's Hill, VA 210

Five hundredth anniversary of Luther's birth 287

Fleming, David C. 303

Florida 306

Florida Conference of the Methodist Episcopal Church 172

Florida Synod 266, 323, 327

Foraging 125

Force Bill 95

Ford, Judy 260, 261

Foreign missions 274

Foreign missions of the Presbyterian Church, U.S.A. 232

Forestville, VA 240

Formalism in worship 202

Formation of a New Lutheran Church 317

Formula for assigning congregational apportionments 316

Formula of Government 203

Forsyth County, NC 23, 30, 32, 196

Forsyth Mission 195

Fort Delaware, MD 116

Fort Pitt 23

Fort Run, VA 25

Fort Sumter, SC 69, 103, 106

Fort Wayne, IN 153, 181

Forum for Theological Discussions 323

Forward Together Campaign 306, 316

Foster care 269, 311, 312

Four day meetings 51

Four hundredth anniversary of the Reformation 227, 239

Fourteenth Amendment 146

Fox, Alfred J., Rev. 72, 117, 141, 161, 168, 169, 179, 183, 186, 189, 194

Fox, Luther Augustine, Rev. 179

France 1, 2, 5, 77, 200
France's King Louis XIV 2
Franciscan order 29
Franck (Francke) 16
Francke, August Hermann, Rev. 32, 54
Francke, Gotthilf August 1, 18
Franckean Synod, New York 86, 172
Frankenberg, Hessen, Germany 15
Franklin, Benjamin 23, 92
Franzen, David M., Rev. 295, 325
Frederick "the Pious" 6
Frederick III, Elector of the Palatinate
    5
Fredericksburg, VA 123
Fredericktown, Dav. County, NC 71
Free Conference of Pastors 238
Free Lutheran Diet 188
Free soilers 99
Free States 92, 102
Free university 324
Free-will giving, offerings 257, 273, 299
Freedmen 149, 151, 152, 191
Freedmen's Bureau 152
Fremont, John C., Presidential
    Candidate 93, 102, 105
Fremont, NB 281
French 2, 6, 8, 21, 200
French and Indian War 78
French Calvinists 13
Frequency of communion 298
Frey, Dr. (Rev.) 187
Friar of Wittenberg 28
Friedens, Gibsonville, NC 24, 32, 35-
    37, 49, 71, 80, 140, 178, 230,
    255
Friedrichs, John George, Rev. 25
Friends of the College 213
Friendship and brotherly love 156
Friendship Church, Alexander County
    106
Friendship Press 258
Friendship, Taylorsville, NC 47, 88,
    106, 124, 194, 198, 204, 234,
    235, 303
Fritz, M. Allen 263
Fritz, Robert Douglas, Rev. 251, 290
Fritz, Robert Lindsay, Rev. 215, 232
Fritz, William 215
Frock, Frances 312
Frontier revival 48

Fry, Franklin Clark, Rev. 276, 277,
    294
Frye, Glenn R. 284
Frye, H. D. 263
Fry, H. D., Jr. 323
Frye, Michael W. 300, 301
Fulenwider, Edward, Rev. 223
Fulmer, Verley Lorenzo, Rev. 225, 227
Fund for Progress 305, 316
Fund-raising 290
Fundamentalist methods of political
    action 315
Funk, Joseph 200

Garden of Rome 63
Garrison, William Lloyd 84
Gary, IN 314
Gas rationing, War-time 255
Gaston College for Girls and Young
    Women 215
Gaston County, NC 30, 180, 260, 262
Gaston District Brotherhood 234, 262
Gastonia, NC 234, 247, 275, 291, 322
Geistliche Lieder 200
Gem, boy named 80
General Assembly of the Presbyterian
    Church 59, 114
General Assembly of the State of NC
    103, 104, 295
General Board, National Council of
    Churches 288
General Council 164, 181, 182, 184,
    187, 188, 202, 203, 239
General Council of the Lutheran
    Church in North America
    181
General Government 106
General Order No. 4 127
General Secretary of Young People's
    Work 230
General Synod 59, 62-65, 75, 86, 94,
    97, 98, 118, 131-135, 153, 154,
    155, 156, 158, 163, 165, 166,
    167, 179-182, 188, 189, 191,
    194, 202, 203, 207, 238, 239
General Synod at Fort Wayne, IN 153
General Synod in North America 159
General Synod in PA 131
General Synod in the Confederate
    States of America 124, 132

General Synod in the South 64

General Synod in the United States
132, 133, 153, 154

General Synod North 159, 181, 191,
201

General Synod of the Evangelical
Lutheran Church 154

General Synod of the Evangelical
Lutheran Church in the
Confed 118, 134

General Synod of the United States
132-134, 153, 155

General Synod South 69, 132, 134, 135,
155, 156-160, 162-167, 169,
170, 178, 179, 181-184, 187,
188, 189, 191, 194, 200-204

General Tract Agency of Raleigh 118

George II, Court of 1

George III, King of England 28, 30, 31

George, John J. 238

Georgia 13, 17-19, 22, 24, 26, 30, 33,
34, 49, 57, 119, 120, 123, 126,
133, 172

Georgia Synod 132

Georgia-Alabama 257, 266-268

Gerhardt
William, Rev. 70, 75

Gerhardt, William, Rev. 212

German 4, 5, 16, 26, 40, 46, 48, 59, 129,
200

German and Swiss Reformed clergy 26

German churches in NC 26

German Coast 5

German colonists 5, 16

German community in Davidson
County 87

German community in the Piedmont
31

German community on the Savannah
River in GA 7

German Fusilier Company 31

German iron workers 5

German language 37, 55, 62

German Palatinate 2

German Parish of St. George in
Germanna 17

German Pietism 18, 52

German press 80

German Reformed Church 5, 24, 46,
153

German Reformed seminary at
Mercersburg, PA 88

German Reformed theological
seminary 55

German Reformed's Brick Church and
Mt. Hope 88

German settlement(s) 4, 8, 17, 21, 23

German settlement on Dutch Buffalo
Creek in Cabarrus County 31

German settlement on the New River in
southwestern VA 34

German settlers 14-16, 21, 23-27

German slaveholders 78, 79

German-language congregations in SC
20

Germanna 5, 17

Germans at New Bern 15

Germans in Craven County 16

Germans in Rowan 27

Germans in SC 31

Germans in the piedmont 78

Germantown, Fauquier County, VA 5

Germantown, PA 199

Germany 1, 2, 6, 17, 25, 26, 32, 34, 151,
200

Germany's Brandenburg 77

Gesungtau, Robert, Rev. 325

Gettysburg College 75

Gettysburg Theological Seminary 75,
89, 96, 181

Gettysburg, PA 96, 181

Gettysburg, VA 112, 113, 127

Gibsonville, NC 23, 88

Giessen University 3

Giessendanner, John Ulrich, the Elder
26

Gilbert, David McConaughy, Rev.
154, 178

Girl Scouts 300

Glass, Joseph Dinson, Jr., Rev. 302

Global Mission 295, 324, 325

Gloria Dei, Salisbury, NC 252, 297

God's People, One in Witness 324

Goen, Clarence C. 69

Goeres, Richard J., Rev. 283, 322

Goetten, Gabriel Wilhelm 33

Golden Rule 85

Goldsboro, NC 196

Good Shepherd, Brevard, NC 250, 286

Good Shepherd, Charlotte, NC 252, 321

Good Shepherd, Goldsboro, NC 250, 263, 282

Good Shepherd, Hickory, NC 251

Good Shepherd, Mt. Holly, NC 196, 224, 229, 230, 247

Good Shepherd, Raleigh, NC 293, 326

Goodman, Henry, Rev. 71, 72, 117, 118

Goodman, J. A. B. 271

Goodman, Reuben Alonzo, Rev. 235

Gorai, Dinesh Cnandra, Bishop (India) 325

Gordon, John B., Gen. 116

Gossman, Joseph, Most Rev. (Catholic) 324

Gottingen, Germany 29

Grace Episcopal Church, Whiteville, NC 287

Grace, Bessemer City, NC 224

Grace, Concord, NC 192

Grace, Gilbert, SC 246

Grace, Hendersonville, NC 225, 270, 286, 287, 291

Grace, Liberty, NC 224

Grace, Newton, NC 35, 47, 130, 133, 170, 205, 208

Grace, Raleigh, NC 321, 322

Grace, Salisbury, NC 195, 207

Grace, Stoney Man, VA 246

Grace, Thomasville, NC 223, 255, 299, 303, 304

Graeber, A. F. 118

Graeber, E. B. 263

Graeber, Henry, Rev. 48, 70

Graeber, R. W. 262

Graf, Richard Byron, Jr., Rev. 302

Graffenried (de), Christopher, Baron 4, 5, 14-16, 18

Grandfather Mountain 128

Granite Falls, NC 225

Grant, Ulysses S., Gen. 77, 139

Grape wine 129

Gravelton, MO 217

Graves, T. A., Rev. 269

Great Awakening 48, 55, 69

Great Merger 239

Great Revival 37, 38, 80, 120

Great Wagon Road 22

Greene County, TN 74

Greensboro Female College 171

Greensboro, NC 192, 196, 213, 223, 282, 284, 294, 303, 312, 314

Greenville, NC 294

Greever, Walton A., Rev. 274

Greever, Walton H., Rev. 232, 237

Gronau, Israel Christian 18, 19

Groseclose, Levi C., Rev. 70, 170-172, 183, 205

Group homes 311

Guidance center 269

Guilford College 236

Guilford County, NC 23, 27, 30, 32, 35, 37, 78, 88, 105, 191

Haas, Harold, Rev. 276, 286

Haas, J. A. W. 235

Haas', Newton 72

Habakkuk 53

Hagerstown, MD 62, 106

Haiti, Haitians 148, 312

Hakata, Japan 226

Halifax County, NC 139

Hall, James, Dr. 39

Hall, John, Rev. 238, 274

Hall, Julia, Mrs. 258

Hall, William Edward, Rev. 253

Halle, Germany 18

Halle, University of 1

Hallman, Samuel Thomas, Rev. 177, 195

Haltiwanger, William Darr, Rev. 227

Haman 148

Hamburg, Germany 25, 283

Hamilton, Elsie 291, 324

Hamm, Luther Boyd, Rev. 251, 274

Hamma Divinity School, Springfield, Ohio 283, 327

Hampton, SC 147

Hancher, James Kniceley, Rev. 72, 201

Hanover, Germany 25, 28, 29, 31, 33

Hapsburg 7

Hard Labor Creek, SC 20

Harmonia Sacra, Being A Collection of Church Music, The 204

Harms, J. Henry, Rev. 232

Harms, Paul, Rev. 327

Harper, William, Chancellor 87

Harper's Ferry 102

Harrisburg, PA 252, 274
Harry, John's Hotel 46
Harter, W. G., Rev. 70
Hartford (Connecticut) Seminary 245
Hartwick College 75
Hartwick Synod, New York 86, 172
Hartwick, New York 96
Hascoosea 139
Hass, John 72
Haven, Salisbury, NC 196, 240, 243,
        244, 256, 300, 303, 304
Haw River, NC 23, 29
Hawkins, Elijah, Rev. 70, 122, 130, 133
Hayes, Rutherford B. 186
Hazelius, Ernest Lewis, Rev. 86, 97
Hebron Church, Madison County, VA
        17
Hebron parish 15
Hebron, Cleveland County 72
Hedrick, Benjamin Sherwood 87, 105
Heidelberg Catechism 6
Heidelberg Community, NC 25
Heidelberg Evangelical Lutheran
        Church, (Reformation,
        Mocksville, NC) 25
Heilig, Charles S. 277, 282
Heilig, George Michael 79
Heilig, J. S., Mrs. 207
Heilig, James D. 209, 240, 282
Heilig, John Samuel, Rev. 153, 172
Heilig's Mills, NC 206
Helmstaedt Catechism 31
Helmstaedt Society 31, 32
Helmstaedt, Germany 31-33
Helper, Hinton Rowan 105
Henckel, Anthony Jacob 3, 4
Hendersonville Mission 225
Hendersonville, NC 266, 268, 286, 288,
        291
Hendrickson, Roy 311
Henkel, Ambrose, Rev. 72, 73, 80
Henkel, David Melanchthon, Rev. 46,
        58-65, 83, 172
Henkel, Paul, Rev. 4, 35, 37-40, 46, 56,
        58, 59, 63, 80, 200, 202, 235
Henkel, Philip, Rev. 35, 37, 39, 40, 46,
        56, 59-61, 75, 80, 83
Henkel, Polycarp Cyprian, Rev. 73,
        106, 169, 189, 215
Henkel, Samuel Godfrey, Rev. 160

Henkel, Socrates, Rev. 168, 179
Henkel descendants 4
Henkel Press 62, 199
Henkelites 185
Henkels 46, 62, 64
Henry River 23, 29
Herb, Donald Warren, Rev. 253
Herion, Elizabeth 260, 271
Herion, John C., Dr. 270
Herman, F. L. 169
Herman, Henry 265, 309
Herman, S. W., Rev. 252
Herring, Ronald 311
Hessians 13
Heterodoxy 193
Hewitt, Marc 326
Heydenreich, Louis W., Rev. 172
Hickory Lutheran Home 301, 309
Hickory, NC 35, 190, 198, 213, 215,
        216, 221, 231, 235, 253, 257,
        263, 265, 270, 274, 284, 286,
        301, 305, 306, 309, 310, 314
High Germans 16
High Germans of the Church of
        England 16
High Point church building 228
High Point, NC 223, 243, 300
Highland Academy 215
Highland College 215-217
Hill, Ambrose Powell, Gen. 116
Hill, NC 294
Hillsborough, NC 22, 23
Himes, John R., Rev. 253
Hinz, Richard T., Rev. 285, 286, 324
Hispanic 315
Hite (Heydt), Joist (Hans Jost) 21
HIV 329
Hoffman, Jonas 215
Hoke, R. F., Gen. 127
Hoke's brigade 127
Holden, Beale M., Rev. 146
Holden, William Woods 105, 146
Holland 3, 17, 18, 29, 77
Holland Memorial Scholarship Fund
        228
Holland, R. C., Mrs. (Mary
        McClanahan) 216
Holland, Robert C., Rev. 177, 222
Holly Grove Academy 215
Holly Grove, Lexington, NC 180, 197

Holmes, Oliver Wendell, Jr. 111
Holscher, Paul 265
Holston River, TN 74
Holston Synod 74, 129, 168-170, 198, 201, 217
Holt, Samuel, Rev. 191, 192
Holy Comforter, Belmont, NC 225
Holy Communion 58, 197, 295
Holy Communion, Banner Elk, NC 70
Holy Communion, Dallas, NC 197, 229-231, 234, 262
Holy Cross, Lincolnton, NC 252, 283
Holy Cross, Mocksville, NC 252
Holy Trinity, Chapel Hill, NC 250
Holy Trinity, Charlotte, NC 224, 259, 283
Holy Trinity, Gastonia, NC 197, 234, 256, 262-264, 302, 324, 326
Holy Trinity, Hickory, NC 180, 196, 224, 229-231, 244, 245, 255, 256, 260, 262-264, 275, 283, 299, 303, 304
Holy Trinity, Mt. Pleasant, NC 141, 178, 191, 207-209, 228, 256, 260, 262, 264, 270
Holy Trinity, Pelion, SC 246
Holy Trinity, Raleigh, NC 224, 243, 263, 284, 288, 299, 311, 326
Holy Trinity, Reidsville, NC 251
Home and foreign missions 195, 207, 229
Home for the Aged 310
Home Mission Foundation 264, 292, 293, 304, 325
Home Mission Foundation of the UELSNC 264
Home missionary 196
Home missions 141, 195, 206, 281
Homestead Act 149
Honduras 147
Hooker, W. P. 263
Hoover, D. R., Rev. 189
Hope, John C., Rev. 97-99
Hoquiom, Washington 302
Horn, Edwin Trail 232
Hotel Concord (NC) 277
House of Delegates of the council 288
House of Hanover 31
House of Representatives 102
Houser, Donald, Rev. 292

Houser, Judy Ford 284
Howard, General 126
Hubbert, W. E., Mrs. (Virginia Ribble) 212
Hubbert, William E., Rev. 172
Huddle, David K., Rev. 318
Hudson River, Lands on 9
Hudson, NC 256
Huffman, J. R. 88
Huguenot 2, 13, 79
Humanitarianism 187
Hungarians 270
Hunger Coalition projects 314
Hunton, W. L., Rev. 238
Hymn book 199, 202, 203, 254

Iddings, John White, Rev. 294, 295
IL 57, 87, 99, 132, 172, 314
Immaculate Conception Roman Catholic, Hendersonville, NC 286
Immanuel College, Concord, NC 192
Immanuel, Rockwell, NC 283
In-home family services 312
Incarnation, Charlotte, NC 252, 303
Inclusive Ministry Committee 315
Independent Living section 310, 328
Independent Lutheran congregations 64
India 18, 89, 206, 258
Indian 5, 14, 15, 18, 21, 22, 23, 314, 315
Indiana 57, 87, 153
Individual communion cups 227
Indochinese 312
Infantile paralysis 255
Influenza epidemic 236
Ingle, Sarah 299
Inner-city ghettos 316
Institutional chaplaincies 296
Institutions 211, 235, 305, 318, 327
Interchurch associations 308
Interdenominational Church Women United in NC 299
Interdenominational ventures 208, 210
Intermediate care 310
International adoption agency 312
International missions 295
Internship involving Lutheran congregations and the Indian com 314

Interpersonal and Self Growth 301
Intonation 254
Intoxicating liquors 236
Iowa 306
Iredell County, NC 37, 38, 78, 281
Irish Settlement (Lutheran Chapel) 32
Iron deposits 5
Isaac 141
Isenhour, Harry E. 247, 262, 265, 274
Islamic conquest of North Africa and
        Spain 77
Isler 16
Istanbul, Turkey 287
Italy 200

Jackson, Andrew, Gen. 95, 119
Jackson, Thomas Jonathon
        "Stonewall", General 114
Jacksonville University in Florida 306
Jacobs, Henry Eyster, Rev. 232
James II, King of England 2
James River, VA 23, 119
Jamestown, VA 13
Janzen, Christen 14
Japan 207, 226, 228, 230, 258, 300
Japan Home for Women Missionaries
        229
Japan Lutheran Church 226
JCLU 275, 276
Jeffcoat, Cora Pearl 256, 258
Jeffcoat, Dorothy 323
Jefferson, Thomas 95
Jeffersonian Republicans 95
John Brown's raid 102
John Harry's hotel 46
John Paul II, Pope 287
Johnson County, NC 126
Johnson, Andrew 145, 146, 152
Johnson, Christopher 326
Johnson, David Frontis, Rev. 246
Johnson, Robert, Governor of SC 5
Johnston's Army 126
Joint Commission on Lutheran Unity
        275
Joint Commission on Union 239
Joint synod 169, 184, 185
Joint Synod of Ohio 74, 168, 197, 218,
        321
Jones County, NC 16
Jones, Bevel, III, Rev., Methodist 288

Jones, Tammy 302, 326
Jorgenson, Wallace 284
Joy, Weddington, NC 325
Jubilee of the Reformation 167
Julian, William Alexander, Rev. 139,
        172
Julius Charles University of Helmstaedt
        31
Junior High Leadership School 302
Junior Luther Leagues 231
Justice and social change 288, 314

Kadell, Tom 284
Kahl, George Calvin, Rev. 253
Kannapolis, NC 196, 223, 265, 277,
        284, 302
Kansas 99, 100, 281
Kansas and Adjacent States Synod 281
Kansas City action 303
Kansas City, Kansas 303
Kansas-Nebraska Act 99, 102, 104
Kant, Immanual 33
Kanuga Lake near Hendersonville, NC
        266
Karatsu, Japan 226
Kearney, Elizabeth K., Rev. 323
Keck, Albert Henry, Jr., Rev. 276, 284
Keck, George 260, 261
Keicher, Conrad 83
Keisler, James Albert, Jr., Rev. 251
Kennedy, Wilton, Rev. 116
Kennesaw Mountain 127
Kentucky 90, 95
Kentucky Synod 131, 153
Kepley, Peter 215
Kester, Moses Lee, Rev. 253
Ketner, Glenn E. 305
Kilimanjaro Christian Medical Center
        299
Killian, Jacob, Rev. 71, 72, 182
Kimball Memorial, Kannapolis, NC
        224, 253, 262, 270, 284, 290,
        313, 317
Kimball, Whitson, Rev. 130, 177, 182,
        195, 205
Kimmel, J. W., Rev. 196
Kinard, M. M., Rev. 222, 225, 232, 238
King Charles II of England 2
King of Glory, Clemmons, NC 293
King, Carl Stanley, Rev. 253

King, Mary Elizabeth 299
Kings Mountain, NC 234, 240, 251,
    265
Kinney, James William, Rev. 253
Kinney, W. L. 263
Kinsey, John 16
Kinston, NC 112, 127
Kiomboi Hospital in Tanzania 299
Klumac Road 246
Kluttz, W. A. 303
Knabe Pianos 204
Know-nothing Party 105
Kobe, Japan 226
Koch, W. W. 232
Kocherthal, Joshua 8, 18
Kohn, Ernest Houseal, Mrs. (Catherine
    Ehrhardt) 229, 247
Kohn, Ernest Houseal, Rev. 179, 239,
    240
Koiner, Junius S., Rev. 179, 235
Koiner's, Augusta County, VA 50, 73
Konnarock, VA 256
Koonce 16
Koontz, David James, Rev. 191, 192,
    198
Kopp, Henry 80
Korean Conflict 253
Kornegay 16
Krause, Harold 263
Krauth, Charles Porterfield, Rev. 187
Krauth, Rev. 129
Ku Klux Klan 151
Kuegele, Frederick, Rev. 217
Kumamoto, Japan 226
Kupke, Harold G., Rev. 286
Kure Beach Lutheran Retreat Center
    307, 308, 328
Kure Beach, NC 307, 308
Kure Memorial, Kure Beach, NC 251,
    259
Kurtz, Benjamin, Rev. 54, 55, 86, 96,
    100, 160
Kurume, Japan 226

Lackey, Jacob L., Mrs. 259
Ladies Aid Societies 257
Lae District Lutheran Synod of Papua,
    New Guinea 325
Lamb Award 265
Lamplighters 258

Lancaster County, PA 21
Lancaster, PA 22, 25, 26, 51, 131,
    227
Lancaster, SC 132
Landis, NC 223
Laotians 326
LARC 286-288
LARCUM 288
Larson, Arthur, Dr. 288
Latin 200
Latin and Anglo America 77
Latin language 330
Latvians 270
Lau's, Guilford County, NC 47, 49,
    140
Law, John 5, 18
Lawrence County, PA 90, 91
Lawson, John 14, 15
Lay assistants 254
Lay delegates 193, 322
Lay leaders 210, 293
Lay professionals 305
Laymen's Evening 233
Laymen's Missionary Movement 231,
    232, 233, 237
Layrle, Christopher 28, 29, 31
Lazareth, William, Rev. 294
LCA 247, 257, 275-277, 282-285, 287,
    293, 294, 295, 297-300, 303,
    305, 308, 313, 314, 316-318,
    321, 326
LCA action in Atlanta 301
LCA Board of American Missions 277
LCA Board of Social Ministry 294, 309
LCA Board of Social Missions 313
LCA Commission on Evangelism 293
LCA Commission on Youth Activities
    300
LCA Commission on Youth Ministry
    302
LCA constitution 295
LCA Department of News and
    Information 291
LCA Division for Mission in North
    America 295, 314
LCA Executive Council 277, 290
LCA fund-raising 310
LCA league 301
LCA merger 298, 308
LCA mission in Whiteville 287
LCA planning services 290
LCA polity 276

LCA structure 276
LCA study of function and structure 290
LCM 300
LCW 257, 300, 311
Leadership training 266, 303
League Calendar 261
League of Augsburg 6
Leagueing in NC 261
Lebanon, Cleveland, NC 196
Lebanon, Lexington, NC 197
Lee, Robert E., Gen. 77, 116, 127, 139
Lee-Harnett Mental Health Center 312
Leesville, SC 100
Leibnitz (von), Gottfried Wilhelm 33
Lenoir College 197, 213, 215, 217, 221, 230, 232, 235, 236, 239, 267
Lenoir Rhyne College 245, 251, 252, 254, 255-257, 259, 260, 262, 265, 266, 267, 272, 273, 275, 283, 284, 289, 290, 294, 297, 301, 302, 304, 305, 306, 313, 316
Lenoir, NC 225, 312
Lenoir, Walter W. 215
Lenoir-Rhyne College 286, 288, 295, 302, 306, 316-318, 322-324, 326, 327, 329, 330
Lenski, Gerhard, Rev. 284
Lenten/Easter Preaching Workshop 294
Lentz, Betty Scott 260
Lentz, John J. 263
Leslie, E. W., Rev. 269
Lewisville, NC 35
Lexington District, SC 81, 98
Lexington mission 195
Lexington, NC 23, 27, 35, 195, 196, 215, 223, 247
Lexington, SC 51, 97, 165
LFS 312, 329
Liberty, NC 23
Licensed to preach 191
Light Brigade 258, 266
"Like Falling in Love" 325
LINC 261
Lincoln, Abraham 89, 102, 103, 105, 106, 134, 145, 152, 154
Lincoln County, NC 23, 30, 37, 40, 47, 59, 71, 78, 80, 186, 194, 260, 262
Lincoln Courier 215

Lincoln, NC 215
Lincolnton convention 62
Lincolnton, NC 25, 35, 41, 45, 46, 47, 56, 61, 62, 178, 237, 265, 267, 283, 302
Lineberger Dining Hall 268, 307
Lineberger Foundation 307
Lineberger, Abel C. 307
Lineberger, E. R. 260
Lineberger, E. R., Mrs. 248, 255
Lineberger, Ernest Robinson, Jr., Rev. 253
Lineberger, J. Harold 307
Lineberger, Martha J. 307
Linn, C. A., Dr. 268
Linn, J. Adolphus, Rev. 212
Linn, Joseph A., Rev. 177, 205, 206, 213
Linn, Joseph A., Sr., Rev. 89, 98, 128, 133
Linn, Joseph Alexander, Rev. 161
Linn, Josephus Adolphus, Mrs. 228
Linn, Josephus Adolphus, Rev. 236
Linn, Justin Arthur, Rev. 253
Linn, Mabel 300
Lintner, George A., Rev. 54
Lippard, Albert Wike, Rev. 253, 270
Lippard, Carl Orestes, Mrs. 256
Lippard, Carl Orestes, Rev. 256
Lippard, Chephas Kelly, Rev. 207
Liquor by the drink 315
Litaker, Betty Jo 304
Litaker, Carl 260
Lithia Springs, NC 237
Lithuania 17
Little JCLU 275
Little Lights 258
Little, Marcus Lafayette, Rev. 215
Little, Richard C., Rev. 283
Little, W. Harold 265
Little, William Herbert, Rev. 270
Liturgical worship 202
Liturgy 201, 202
Liverpool 77
Living Saviour, Charlotte, NC 293
Living Waters, Cherokee, NC 325
Living Word, Laurinburg, NC 293
Livingston, Robert 9
LL-LLA 301
LLA 261
LMIM 326, 327
Loan & Gift Fund 263, 264, 303, 304

Lockard, Linda 260
Lodge(s) 239, 308
Log chapels 119
Lohr, Luther Lindsay, Rev. 215, 223
London 8, 33, 77
London, Connecticut 77
London, England 29, 31
Long Range Planning 312
Long, G. E., Rev. 198
Long, Simon Peter 232
Lord of Life, Garner, NC 293
Lord's Supper 28, 35, 36, 39, 48, 58, 60,
    82, 83, 125, 129, 135, 159, 190
Lords of Trade 8
Lords Proprietors of Carolina 5
Lorraine 2
Louis VI, Elector for the Palatinate 6
Louis XIV, King of France 2, 3, 4
Louisiana 5, 18, 62
Louisiana, Governor of 5
Louisiana settlers of the German Coast
    5
Louvois, Louis XIV's Minister of War
    2
Love of God in Christ Jesus 27
Low's, Liberty, NC 25, 27, 29
Lowman Home 260, 270, 272, 273, 309
Lowman Home for the Aged and
    Helpless 237, 269, 309
Lowman, Malissa, Mrs. 237
LSA 310, 328
Ludwig, Karl 6
Ludwig, David J., Rev. 323
Ludwig, Prof. 212
Luft, John G. 25
Lumberton, NC 248, 322
Lundeen, Malvin H., Rev. 277
Luther College in Iowa 306, 307
Luther Court 328
Luther League 208, 209, 230, 231, 258,
    260, 261, 266, 300, 301
Luther League Convention Stes 262
Luther League in America 259-261,
    301
Luther League of the United
    Evangelical Lutheran Synod
    of North Carolina 231
Luther League Penny Parade 271, 307
Luther League Presidents 260
Luther League Review 208
Luther Manor 310

Luther Memorial Building 196
Luther Northwestern Seminary 322
Luther, Martin, Dr. 7, 28, 46, 54, 58,
    83, 133, 166, 201, 240, 287,
    327
Luther's Chapel, Rowan, NC 71
Luther's Small Catechism 192, 235
Luther's, Richfield, NC 47, 128
Lutheran and Reformed 6, 24
Lutheran assembly ground 268
Lutheran Book of Worship 287, 298
Lutheran Brotherhood 232, 233
Lutheran Brotherhood Movement 233
Lutheran Brotherhood of America 233
Lutheran Brotherhood of The United
    Lutheran Church in America
    234
Lutheran Chapel, China Grove, NC
    35, 71, 130, 178, 181, 185, 204,
    207, 222, 227, 228, 237
Lutheran Chapel, Gastonia, NC 47,
    180, 229, 234, 244, 263, 304
Lutheran Children's Home of the
    South 260, 269, 311
Lutheran Church - MO Synod 192,
    218, 221, 285, 300, 315, 323
Lutheran Church - NC Synod 276
Lutheran Church in America 182, 247,
    275, 276, 277, 281, 285, 295,
    303, 317
Lutheran church in every county 250
Lutheran Church in Malaysia and
    Singapore 295
Lutheran Church in North America
    181
Lutheran church in NC 33, 40
Lutheran Church in the Confederate
    States 69, 135
Lutheran church in VA 15
Lutheran Church literature 132
Lutheran Church Men 265, 266, 303,
    304
Lutheran church paper 56, 86, 161
Lutheran church papers in the South
    164
Lutheran Church South 132
Lutheran Church Visitor 225, 232
Lutheran Church Women 257, 298,
    322
Lutheran colleges 75, 238
Lutheran confessional writings 58
Lutheran confessionalism 64

Lutheran Council of Great Britain 322
Lutheran Family Services 314, 315,
        323, 328, 330
Lutheran Female College at Charlotte
        214
Lutheran Home(s) 253, 257, 309, 310,
        311, 316, 317
Lutheran hospital 311
Lutheran Immigration Refugee Service
        315
Lutheran Laymen's Movement 231,
        232, 294
Lutheran Men 303, 303, 326
Lutheran Ministerium of NC 35, 56,
        65, 330
Lutheran Nursing Homes 310, 328
Lutheran Observer 55, 56, 75, 86, 96,
        97, 98-101, 132, 160, 163, 164,
        194, 210
Lutheran Orphan Home of the South
        at Salem, VA 216, 236, 269
Lutheran Outdoor Ministries 308, 328
Lutheran Pastoral Association of
        Catawba County 225
Lutheran publication 225
Lutheran Resettlement Committee of
        NC 270
Lutheran Retirement Ministries 328
Lutheran Reunion 190
Lutheran revivalism 64
Lutheran Scout Camporee at
        Lutheridge 265
Lutheran Seaman's Mission in
        Wilmington, NC 196
Lutheran Services for the Aging 310,
        328
Lutheran social ministry organizations
        312
Lutheran Standard 160
Lutheran State Sunday School
        Association 266
Lutheran Synod Drive 321
Lutheran Theological Center in Atlanta
        327
Lutheran Theological Seminary,
        Philadelphia, PA 232, 306
Lutheran Theological Southern
        Seminary 194, 243
Lutheran Visitor 142, 156-158,
        162-164, 191, 194, 201, 204,
        210, 225

Lutheran Women's Missionary League
        300
Lutheran World Action 257, 273, 274
Lutheran World Federation 322
Lutheran World Relief 288, 314, 315
Lutheran Youth 302, 326
Lutheran, Anglican and Roman
        Catholic 286
Lutheran, The 226, 273, 284, 291, 324
Lutheran-Catholic 324
Lutheran-Episcopal 324
Lutheran-Episcopal merger 64
Lutheran/Catholic Dialogue
        Commission 287
Lutheran/Episcopal arrangements 287
Lutheran/Orthodox Dialogue
        Commission 284
Lutheranism vs. Rationalism 227
Lutherans and Roman Catholics 287
Lutherhaus 310
Lutheridge 257, 260, 262, 265, 266,
        268, 273, 282, 294, 301, 307,
        308, 312, 327, 328
Lutherische Kirchenzeitung 160
Lutherock, near Newland, NC 321,
        327, 328
Lutz, Elmer 303
Lutz, Paul E. 284, 317
Lutz, William Alonzo, Rev. 177, 191,
        195, 196, 211, 216
Ly, Boua Sy 326
Ly, Nhia 326
Lyerly, John Wilford, Rev. 266, 277,
        281, 282
LYNC 302
Lynchburg, VA 115, 139

Macedonia, Burlington, NC 141, 178,
        208, 209, 222, 228, 230, 240,
        244, 256, 260, 262, 270, 274,
        284, 298, 302, 305, 310, 324
Madison, James 95
Madison County, VA 17
Magdeburg Concert 2
Magill, John, Rev. 116
Maiden, NC 205, 305
Mail ballots 255
Mailroom and printroom 322
Mainz 2
Malaysia 295
Management of the call 297
Marburg Hymnal 199

Marburg, Germany 28
Marburger Gesang-Buch, Das kleine Davidische Psalterspiel 200
Marion, S. J. 263
Markert, Ludwig, Rev. 57
Markets for slaves 77
Marriage and family enrichment 312
Marshall, Thomas F. 90
Marshall, Robert J., Rev. 284
Martin, James 26
Martin Luther Scholarship Endowment 327
Martin, David, Rev. 282, 283
Martin, Ed 303
Martin, Rev. 129
MD & VA Synod 75
MD Synod 131, 153, 172, 191, 192
MD, Western 22
Mason-Dixon Line 84, 87
Mass Lutheran Evangelism Rallies 251
Massachusetts 99, 100
Master Plan for Theological Education 285
Matins 254
Matthews, NC 35
Mauney, Aubrey W. 263, 265
Mauney, Aubrey, Mrs. 255
Mauney, David 215
Mauney, John David, Rev. 227
Mauney, Luther 260
Mauney, Marshall Frantz, Rev. 303
Mauney, W. K. 263
Mauney, William K. 234
McAllister, George F., Prof. 232, 233, 235, 238-240, 267
McAllister, H. C. 195
McClanahan, G. W., Mrs. 229, 255
McClanahan, George Walker, Rev. 216
McClanahan, William S., Rev. 216
McCombs, Charles Augustus, Rev. 253
McCombs, R. Earl, Rev. 253
McCorkle, Samuel E., Dr. 38
McCormick Seminary, Chicago, IL 226
McCullough, Henry Antine, Rev. 235, 238
McDaniel, Michael Conway Dixon, Rev. 283-288, 298, 302, 317, 322, 323-325
McDuffie, George 95, 96

McGaheysville, Rockingham, VA 246
McGaheysville, VA 25
McGinnis, W. W. 72
McKnight, Harold F. 303
McLamb, Marsha 324
McMahan, Anna 302
Mealy, Stephen, Rev. 64
Mecklenburg County, NC 27, 30, 78, 262, 311
Media center 322
Media evangelism 294
Medicaid 315
Medical missionary to a foreign field 252
Meetze, J. Yost, Rev. 82
Meetze's, Lexington County, SC 180
Melanchthon, Randolph County 73
Melchor, Christopher 98, 133
Melodeons 204
Memphis, TN 294
Men's Auxiliary 231, 303
Men's Auxiliary Convention Sites 304
Men's auxiliary in NC 303
Men's Bible Class 235
Men's organization 261, 304
Men's Organization Convention Sites 264
Men's Organization Presidents 263
Men's Work 261
Menees, Mark W., Rev. 283, 322, 323
Mengert, John H., Rev. 172
Mennonite 200
Mercersburg, PA 55, 88
Meredith College 236
Merger 64, 239, 239, 240, 256, 261, 264, 266, 269, 276, 275, 317, 321, 323, 328
Messiah of the Mountains, Burnsville, NC 293
Messiah, Burlington,, NC 252
Messiah, Hickory, NC 251, 259
Messiah, Salisbury, NC 250, 281
Methodist 36, 37, 48, 49, 52, 54, 55, 56, 69, 96, 105, 128, 152, 171, 172, 199, 200, 226, 323
Metropolitan New York 315
Meuser, Frederick W, III, Rev. 327
Mexican War 104
Mexico 147
Miami Beach, Florida 288
Miami, Florida 294

Micawber, Wilkens, the "grand procrastinator" 148
Michael Peeler Memorial Room 274
Michael Peeler Professorship 307
Michael Peeler Trust Fund 305, 307, 317, 325, 329, 330
Michael, Don Malcolm, Rev. 253
Michaux, F. A. 78
Michel, Franz Louis 14, 16
Michel, Louis 4, 5
Middle Conference of the Pittsburgh Synod 90, 91
Midland College 281
Migrants 316
Military chaplaincies 296
Military system 235
Millennium 36
Miller 16
Miller, Adam, Jr., Rev. 70, 71-73
Miller, B. B. 236
Miller, Bachman 208
Miller, Calvin Luther, Rev. 225
Miller, Charles B., Rev. 177, 190, 196
Miller, David Leander, Rev. 227
Miller, Earlean, Rev. 314
Miller, G. C. 303
Miller, Henderson Neiffer, Rev. 212
Miller, Henry, Candidate 168
Miller, John (Joseph) I., Rev. 163, 164, 188, 204
Miller, Joseph Iranaeus, Rev. 154, 156, 158, 162
Miller, M. M., Rev. 130
Miller, Paul Leopold, Rev. 240
Miller, Robert Johnson, Rev. 34, 38, 40, 46, 56, 64, 65, 80, 81, 83
Miller, Thomas W., Rev. 141
Miller's, Hickory, NC 70, 321
Milwaukee, Wisconsin 315
Minimum assignments 274
Minister for leadership 283
Minister for parish life 283
Minister's wife who works outside the home 296
Ministerial candidates 215
Ministerial confidences 295
Ministerial education 206, 216
Ministerial Pension and Relief Campaign 252
Ministerial Pension Fund 272
Ministerial Pensions 272
Ministerial skills 296

Ministerium of PA 35, 41, 62
Ministerium of the Lutheran Church in NC 34
Minneapolis, Minnesota 257
Minnesota 306
Minorities 7, 294, 314-316, 329
Minutes, NC Synod, 113
Misenheimer, David, Rev. 293, 300
Misenheimer, Ernest Luther, Jr., Rev. 245, 246, 273, 281-284, 293, 294, 316, 318
Misenheimer, Stephen 284
Mission Board of the German MO Synod 217
Mission churches 263, 264, 292
Mission Committee 271
Mission congregations 260, 264, 291, 292
Mission developer 281, 314
Mission Hall at Lutheridge 257
Mission profile 316
Mission school in Tanzania 299
Missionaries 324
Missionary for the State at large 195
Missionary Ridge, VA 120
Missionary to Malaysia 295
Mississippi 114
Mississippi River 5
Mississippi Synod 267, 268
Missouri 62, 99, 217, 222
Missouri Synod 192, 217, 271, 285, 286, 295, 323, 324
Mitcham, Jane P. 323
Mitchell, Carveth P., Rev. 284, 310
Mite Box 207
Mittelnkirchen bei Stade, Germany 25
Mocksville, NC 124, 196
Model constitutions 262
Moller, Mary Ann 302
Momodani, Osaka, Japan 226
Monroe Auditorium, Lenoir Rhyne College 257
Monroe, NC 229
Monroe, Paul E. 263
Monroe, Pleasant Edgar, Rev. 252, 266, 267
Mont Amoena Female Seminary 200, 208, 213, 214
Mont Amoena Seminary 235, 236, 239, 267
Montagnards 312
Montgomery County, NC 78

Montgomery, Alabama 103
Moore General Hospital, Oteen, NC 294
Mooresville Mission 196
Mooresville, NC 196, 223, 255, 272
Moose, Donald W. 322, 323
Moose, John Baxter, Rev. 224
Moravian 23-25, 27, 28, 37, 46, 57, 171, 330
Mordecai 148
Moretz, Christian, Rev. 182
Moretz, J. A., Mrs. 255
Moretz, Joe 260
Moretz, O. Leonard 284
Morgan, Carroll Irving, Rev. 225, 227
Morgan, Gladys 252
Morgan, Jacob Levi, Mrs. 255, 256
Morgan, Jacob Levi, Rev. 222-224, 233, 234, 238, 240, 243, 244, 247, 249, 252, 272
Morgan, Paul Lowman, Rev. 277, 316
Morning Star, Matthews, NC 35, 47
Morning Star, Orkney Springs, VA 246
Morning Star, Stoney Man, VA 246
Morphine 123
Morris, Rev. 129
Moser, Adam David Luther, Rev. 172
Moser, J. M. 233
Moser, Jacob, Rev. 64
Moser, Jason Chrysostom, Rev. 179, 190, 223
Moser, John Franklin, Rev. 179
Moser, Timothy, Rev. 129, 133, 169, 183
Moses 53
Mosheim (von), Johann Lorenz 33
"Mother's Parting Words to her Soldier Boy, A" 118
Mt. Calvary, Claremont, NC 197, 263
Mt. Calvary, Page County, VA 180, 246
Mt. Carmel, Cabarrus County, North Carolina 128
Mt. Gilead, Mt. Pleasant, NC 197
Mt. Hebron, Hildebran, NC 224
Mt. Hermon, Concord, NC 195
Mt. Hermon, Statesville, NC 197
Mt. Holly, NC 229, 240
Mt. Hope Church, German Reformed 88
Mt. Horeb, Chapin, SC 224, 246

Mt. Moriah, China Grove, NC 47, 224, 244, 255, 256, 258, 300, 301
Mt. Nebo, VA 246
Mt. Olive, Hickory, NC 197, 283, 323
Mt. Olive, Mt. Pleasant, NC 195
Mt. Pisgah, Hickory, NC 70, 321
Mt. Pleasant Collegiate Institute 232, 235, 248
Mt. Pleasant Female Academy 212
Mt. Pleasant Female Seminary 170, 171, 200
Mt. Pleasant, Boone, NC 70
Mt. Pleasant, NC 23, 32, 75, 76, 106, 167, 170, 171, 178, 183, 186, 191, 194, 200, 206, 209, 211, 212, 214, 228, 235, 271, 283
Mt. Pleasant, SC 236
Mt. Tabor, West Columbia, SC 180, 224, 246
Mt. Zion ALC Church 309
Mt. Zion, Conover, NC 197, 321
Mt. Zion, New Market, VA 246
Mt. Zion, Richfield, NC 196
Mountain Island Cotton Factory in Gaston County, North Carolina 142
Mountain Island, NC 142
Mountainside, Robbinsville, NC 321
Movement of ministers 296
MPCI (Mount Pleasant Collegiate Institute) 235, 236, 266, 267
Mueller (Miller), Adam 21
Muenster in Westphalia, Germany 29
Muhlenberg 41, Henry Melchoir 1, 19, 25, 33, 76, 79
Muhlenberg College 306
Mull, Mary 23
Multicultural Advisory Committee 326
Murdock Center for Retarded Children at Butner, NC 301, 302
Murray, Waldo Emerson, Rev. 227
Music 200
Music and worship 288
Music editions of worship books 227
Musical Advocate and Singer's Friend 204
Musical instruments 204
Musical settings 254
Muskets to the worship service 129
Myers, Haley 215

Naboth's vineyard 2
Nagasaki, Japan 226
Namibia struggle for independence 315
Nantes, Edict of 2
Nashville convention of 1850 104
Nassau-Siegen, Germany 5, 16
National Association of Social Workers
        328
National auxiliary 298
National brotherhood 264
National Chaplains' Association 253
National church paper 132
National Council of Churches of Christ
        in the USA 288
National executive committee 261
National LCW organization 299
National league 260
National Lutheran Brotherhood 233
National Lutheran Campus Ministry
        294
National Lutheran Church Men 265
National Lutheran Committee on
        Scouting 265
National Lutheran Council 270, 294
National merger 239
National women's organization 255
Native Japanese worker 208
Nativity, Arden, NC 286, 293, 328
Navy chaplains 253
Nazareth, Forsyth County 32, 35, 195
NCLLU 301
NCLM 304
Neandris Harfenspiel 200
Necrologist 281
Negroes 36, 78, 81, 149, 151, 313
Negroes, Ministry among 271
Nehemiah 53
Neiffer, Jacob Grabenstein, Rev. 145,
        172
Nelson, George W., Rev. 231, 240
Nestle infant formula 315
Netherlands 18
Neuse River (Valley) 5, 15
Nevin, John Williamson, Rev. 55
New Bern, NC 14-17, 112, 127, 196
New Bethel, Concord, NC 128
New Bethel, Richfield, NC 47, 128
New Brookland, SC 229
New Covenant, Archdale, NC 252
New England Puritanism 52
New Garden Boarding School
        (Guilford College) 171

New Guinea 325
New Hanover County, NC 77
New Jersey 126
New Jerusalem, Hickory, NC 224, 303
New Jerusalem, Lexington, NC 70
New Market, VA 62, 194, 199
New Orleans, LA 5
New River settlement 34
New River, VA 21, 34
New Testament in the Greek language
        330
New Windsor, GA 26
New Windsor, SC 20
New York 9, 14, 54, 77, 172
New York City, NY 51, 148, 239, 276,
        305, 307, 315, 321
New York Ministerium 59, 62
New York, Governor of 9
Newberry College 212, 232, 327
Newberry, SC 164, 167, 180
Newburgh, New York 8
Newhall, Horatio 112
Newland, NC 287, 327
Newlanders 5
Newport, Rhode Island 77
News bureau director 281
Newsletters 261
Newton, NC 35, 71, 190, 225, 229, 245
Nicene creed 192
Nicolai, Conan 32
Nominating Committee 317
Non-Lutheran participation 310
Norfolk, VA 283
Norris, Catherine B. 299, 304
Norris, Jeff L. 248, 260, 284
Norris, Jefferson Leander, Rev. 270,
        271, 291, 309
North Africa 77
NC and SC synods 293
NC Classis 153
North Carolina College 76, 131, 167,
        171, 191, 211-214, 235, 238,
        243
NC Conference 224, 225, 227, 230, 235,
        238
NC Council of Churches 247, 257, 281,
        288
NC Episcopal diocese 64, 286, 287
NC Family Services 314
NC leaguers 261
NC LMIM 326

NC Luther League Unit 300, 301
North Carolina Lutheran 248, 261,
        268, 273, 274, 291, 298, 313,
        324
NC Lutheran Brotherhood 233, 261
NC Lutheran Church Women 299
NC Lutheran Homes 253, 260, 270,
        310
NC Lutheran Men 303, 308
NC Lutheran Men in Mission 326
NC men's organization 265
NC Ministerium 41, 56, 57
North Carolina Standard 146
NC State mental institution 253
NC State Prison System 253
NC Synod Convention Sites 49, 71,
        128, 140, 178, 222
NC Synod of the ELCA 317
NC Synod of the LCA 318
NC Synod of the Lutheran Church in
        America 275
NC Synod Presidents 48, 70, 127, 139,
        177
NC Synod WHFM 206, 207
NC Synod's Central Conference 128
NC Synod's Executive Board 285, 307
NC Synod's pastors in SC 82
NC's congressional delegation 103
NC's General Assembly 104
NC's German Reformed community
        153
NC's Germans 27
NC-TN merger 255
Northampton, PA 21, 55
Northern Church papers 164
Northern Conference of the NC Synod
        236
Northern district 263, 288
Northern General Synod 154, 157, 188
Northern States 92
Northwestern District 288
Nuclear armaments 315
Nugent, William, Capt. 146
Nullification 95, 104
Number of consecutive terms 290
Nussmann, Adolph, Rev. 29-34, 49, 57

Oakview Hall at Lenoir College,
        Hickory, NC 230
Oath-bound secret societies 239
Observer, (Lutheran) (See *Lutheran
        Observer*) 164

Oceanfront facility 307
Odom, John G. 270, 309
Off-campus child-care 311
Office of Defense Transportation 275
Offman, David Isaiah, Rev. 223
Oglethorpe's colony in GA 18
Ohio 4, 57, 87, 95, 327
Ohio District 322
Ohio Synod 62
Okazaki, Japan 226
Old General Synod 159
Old Testament 93
Oldest German Reformed congregation
        in America 5
Oldest Lutheran synod 331
Omaha Mid-America Pan Lutheran
        Conference on Evangelism
        293
On leave from a call 297
One hundredth, and final, convention
        of the TN Synod 240
Only ordained colored Lutheran
        minister 191
Opossum Town just south of Salem,
        NC 35
Orange County, NC 23, 27, 30, 77
Orangeburg, SC 20, 26
Ordained colored Lutheran minister
        191
Ordained fifty years or more 288
Ordained its first woman pastor 297
Ordinance of Nullification 95, 104
Ordinaries 22
Ordination approval process 325
Ordination of foreign ministers 226
Ordination of seminary graduates 325
Ordination vows 197
Ores and minerals 5
Organ Lutheran Church, (see also Zion
        Evangelical Lutheran
        Church), Rowan Co., NC 24,
        30, 32, 40, 47, 49, 57, 71, 118,
        128, 162, 178, 184, 204, 206,
        207, 228, 244, 298
Orphan home 216, 237
Orthodoxy, Credal 3
Osborn, Thomas Ward 126
Our Church Paper 194, 225
Our Father, Greensboro, NC 252
Our Redeemer, Greenville, NC 252
Our Saviour, Dallas, NC 252
Our Saviour, Jacksonville, NC 251

Our Saviour, Southern Pines, NC 252
Our Saviour, Welcome, NC 293
Outdoor ministries 290
Outreach Appeal 306
Ovens Auditorium, Charlotte, NC 251, 293
Oxford University 322
Oxford, NC 22
Oxner, Jason Witherspoon, Rev. 253

Pacific (Presbyterian) Seminary, California 226
Pacific Lutheran University 322
Page County, VA 21
Page, George 303
Palatinate 1-3, 6-8, 14, 17
Palatinate, Elector of the 5
Palmer, Renee 314
Pamlico sound, NC 15, 112
Pannell, Martin C. 303
Papua synod 325
Paris, John, Rev. 127
Paris, Royal court of 4
Parish and Church School Board 259
Parish and Church School Board of the ULCA 258
Parish education 288
Parish Education Committee 259
Parish paper 195
Parish Renewal 298
Parish visitation 294
Parish worker 245
Park, Fred L. 328
Park, Karl Monroe, Rev. 286, 291
Parker, Emmanuel P., Rev. 195
Parlor and Church Organs 204
Parochial reports 315
Parochial schools 192, 214
Parsonage(s) 198, 253
Parsonages and church sites 292
Participation by lay delegates 289
Passavant, William A., Rev. 89, 100, 129
Pastor's classes 251
Pastor's house 199
Pastor's Institute 268
Pastor's salary 193, 198, 237
Pastor/Evangelist 294
Pastoral assignments 194
Pastoral counseling 296
Pastoral credentials 24
Pastoral Districts 193

Pastoral duties 73
Pastoral functions 116
Pastoral Letter 157, 158
Pastoral ministry 276
Pastoral preparation 325
Pastoral supervision 209
Pastoral visitation 197
Pastors for small congregations 296
Pastors on Leave from Call 297
Patterson Memorial Fund 257, 299, 326
Patterson, George R., Mrs. 255
Patterson, I. Frank 195, 209, 257
Patterson, Maria 257
Patterson, R. L., Mrs. 228
Patterson, Robert Leonidas, Rev. 232
Paul, Apostle 81, 93
Peabody Education Fund 142
Peace of Ryswick 6
Peace of Westphalia 6
Peace, Gibsonville, NC 196
Peace, Greensboro, NC 293
Pectoral cross 281
Peculiar institution 89, 101, 102, 149
Pedagogical approach 254
Peeler, Eva 261
Peeler, John Michael 274, 294
Peery, John Carnahan, Rev. 225, 267
Peery, Robert N., Jr. 300, 301
Peery, Rufus Benton, Rev. 207
Penn, William 17, 20-22
PA College at Gettysburg 75
PA Ministerium 59, 60, 62, 181, 201
PA Seminary 75
PA Synod's Executive Committee on Missions 145
Pension payments 252
Pentecost 53, 254
Pericope 201
Perkiomen Creek, PA 21
Perry, Frank Caston, Rev. 253, 313
Perry, Richard J., Jr., Rev. 284, 314, 315
Persians 148
Persons of color 314, 329
Peschau, Ferdinand William Elias, Rev. 177, 190, 196, 198
Peterson, Jesse Reuben, Rev. 118, 129, 161, 169, 179
Petrea, Brunner Eugene, Rev. 248
Petrea, Hugh C. 248
Phanuel's, Rowan County, NC 50

Pharr, William, Father 286
Phebe Hospital in Monrovia, Liberia
    298
Phifer, Esther 78
Phifer, W. Philo, Rev. 192
Philadelphia Seminary 232
Philadelphia, Dallas, NC 25, 47, 183
Philadelphia, Granite Falls, NC 141,
    245
Philadelphia, Lincoln County, NC 50
Philadelphia, PA 15, 20-22, 94, 181,
    188, 238, 239, 247, 317
Philemon 81
Phillippi, Alexander, Rev. 115
Phillips, Bryan 326
Pickett, George C., Gen. 127
Pietism 3, 4, 18, 32, 33, 51, 52, 57, 58,
    89, 94, 121, 155, 156, 193
Pifer, J. S., Col. 154
Pilgrim, Davidson County, NC 25, 27,
    39, 47, 49, 72, 73, 178, 180,
    183, 222
Pine (Union) Church 29, 32, 41
Pipe organ 204
Pitts, Oscar 268
Pittsburgh Synod 90
Pittsburgh, PA 131, 160
Plan Entwurf 59
Plan of Union 57
Pless, John Albert, Rev. 270, 309, 310
Plexico, Thurman Claude, Rev. 281,
    302
Pluetschau
    Heinrich 89
Pohlman, Rev. 129
Polish refugee resettlement 315
Political action 315
Polity and Practice 192, 247, 288
Polity, church 72, 96, 119, 135, 192,
    247, 276, 277, 288
Pollock, Thomas 15
Polvagt, C. W. 232
Pomaria, SC 25
Pope John Paul II 287
Port Royal, SC 13
Portsmouth, New Hampshire 77
Portuguese 77
Potomac River, VA 124
Poverty and social injustice 313
Powder Springs, Orkney Springs, VA
    246
Powell, Eugene Rev. 314

Powlas Scholarship, Maud and Annie
    257
Powlas, Annie 228, 257, 258
Powlas, Maud 228, 257, 300
Powles, L. C., Mrs. 256
Practical English Seminary 74
Preaching-Teaching Missions 251
Predestination 217, 222
Predominantly black denominations
    314
Preparatory department(s) 211, 236
Preparatory or fitting schools 238
Preparing and examining candidates
    297
Presbyterian 37, 39, 69, 88, 114, 141,
    232
Presbyterian church 38, 59
Presbyterian clergy 60
Presbyterian ministers 36
Presbyterianism 48
Prescribed forms of religious worship
    203
President emeritus 244
President's Conference 261
President's home 268
President's Task Force on Justice and
    Social Change 313
Presidential Assistant 273
Presidents of the Synods 185
Primary language other than English
    314, 315, 329
Prince of Peace, Greensboro, NC 283,
    314
Prince of Peace, Kinston, NC 251
Prince of Peace, Salisbury, NC 251
Priority Program on Justice and Social
    Change 313
Prison ministry 312
Proclamation to the People of SC 95
Program budget 316
Progressivism 221
Prohibit the disclosure of confidential
    communications 295
Prohibition 243
Project Equality 314
Proselytizing 27
Prosperity, Concord, NC 207
Protective tariff 95, 103
Protestant and Roman Catholic
    understandings 7
Protestant Episcopal church 114
Protestant persecution 7

Protestant Reformation 3, 17, 26
Protestant-Catholic distinctions 6
Protestantism 2, 69, 158
    Cleanse of all traces 7
    Eliminate 6
Protestantism in France 2
Protestants 3, 7, 13, 17, 18
    Expulsion of 18
    Persecution of 6
Protestants and Roman Catholics 7
Protracted meeting(s) 51, 52, 54, 130,
        144, 164, 172, 205, 210
Providence, RI 77
Provisional Congress 113
Provisional Constitution of the
        Confederate States of
        America 107
Provisional governor of NC 146
Prussia 3, 57
Public education 187
Public relations 245
Publication disagreements 194
Puerto Rico 258
Pugh, Clarence L. 326
Pulpit and altar fellowship 190
Puritan Protestantism 48
Purry, Jean-Pierre 5
Purrysburg, SC 5, 17, 19, 20

Quadri-Centennial Reformation
        Service 227
Queen Anne 8
Queen Louise Home, Virgin Islands
        258
Quorum 289

Rabies Carolina 9
Race Relations Statement of the LCA
        Board of Social Missions 313
Racial injustice 221
Racial prejudice 187, 313
Racially segregated society 313
Rader, Daniel 72
Rader's Church, Timberville, VA 167,
        224, 246
Rader's, Fort Run, VA 25
Rader's, Rockingham County, VA 73,
        180
Radloff, Mark P., Rev. 327, 328
Rahn, Sheppard Seneca, Rev. 212
Railroads 143
Raleigh Diocese, (Catholic) 324

Raleigh, NC 105, 106, 118, 131, 196,
        224, 243, 251, 294, 312, 314,
        328
Ramm, Pater 16
Randolph County, NC 128
Rapidan River, VA 17, 120
Rappahannock 5
Rappahannock River, VA 120
Rationalism 32, 33, 57
Ravenscroft, John Stark, Rev.,
        (Episcopal) 65
Reading, PA 25, 181
Reaffirmation of faith 251
Receive clergy by transfer 194
Reck, Abraham, Rev. 54
Reck, John B., Rev. 84, 209
Reconciliation, Wilmington, NC 293
Reconstruction 146, 150, 152, 157, 172,
        177, 186, 187
Recording secretary 272
Recreation 260, 266
Recruiting full-time Christian workers
        303
Recycling 329
Red River church 36
Redeemer, Atlanta, GA 268
Redeemer, Charlotte, NC 251
Redeemer, Gastonia, NC 293
Redeemer, Kannapolis, NC 250
Redeemer, Newberry, SC 206
Reformation 5, 6, 33, 34, 37, 50, 92,
        158, 166, 217, 227, 254
Reformation anniversary observance
        240
Reformation, Mocksville, NC 25
Reformation, Taylorsville, NC 250
Reformed 3, 6, 14, 16, 17, 24-27, 31,
        48, 55, 57, 62, 197
Reformed Church, Guilford County,
        NC 47
Refugee problem in England 9
Refugee resettlement services 312
Region IX 317, 323
Regional director 246
Rehder, J. H. 223
Reinartz, F. Eppling, Rev. 251, 268,
        306
Reisz, H. Frederick, Jr., Rev. 327
Reitzel, C. E., Dr. 233
Relations between Lutherans and
        Roman Catholics 287
Religious ecstasy 120

Religious education 245
Religious journal 194
Repass, S. A., Rev. 203
Repentence of drinkers 236
Representative principle 308
Republic of Texas 104
Republican Party 102, 104, 105, 186
Research Triangle Area 310
Resettlement service 315
Respect for the Sabbath 130
Resurrection, Greensboro, NC 293
Resurrection, Kings Mountain, NC
    251
Resurrection, Rocky Mount, NC 321
Retarded youth 302
Retired ministers 277
Revivalism 39, 51-53, 55, 56, 58, 64,
        119, 120, 130, 160, 164, 210
Revivals 49, 50, 52-58, 119-121, 163,
        164, 210
Revolutionary War 125
Revolving loan fund 263
Reynolds, Rev. 129
Rhein 16
Rhenish Palatinate 2
    Elector of the 6
Rhine River 1, 17
Rhine valley 1, 2
Rhineland 2, 9
    Devastation 3
Rhoads, Harold Emmett, Rev. 253
Rhodes, George Heilig, Rev. 248, 250
Rhodes, John M. 215
Rhodhiss, NC 245
Rhyne, Avery R. 262
Rhyne, Classroom Building 306
Rhyne, Daniel Efird 237, 267
Rhyne, George L., Rev. 323
Rhyne, Richard W., Rev. 282, 283,
        314, 315
Rhyne, S. White 230, 231
Ribault, Jean 13
Richmond, VA 118, 177, 189
Ricks, Edwin 260, 261
Ridenhour, Joe C. 284
Rintelmann, Christopher 28, 29, 31
Riser, Y. Von A., Mrs. 229
Ritchie, Clarence Ross, Rev. 253
Ritchie, George E. 185
Ritchie, Paul 263, 303
Roanoke College in VA 75
Roanoke Valley, VA 311

Robbinsville, NC 287
Roberts, John M. 215
Robertson, George Gaston, Rev. 253
Robinson River 17
Robinson, Harry Hoover, Jr., Rev. 302
Robinson, O. B. 262
Rock Hill, SC 126
Rockingham County, NC 78
Rockwell, NC 228, 295
Rocky Mount, NC 265
Roeber, A. G., Professor 3
Roedel, William D. 201
Roehm, J. C., Rev. 153
Rohrbaugh, T. C. 269
Role of the Laity 205, 325
Role of the pastor 297
Roman Catholic 7, 8, 29, 58, 60, 79,
        286-288, 324
Rome, Italy 63, 287
Romoser, G. A., Rev. 217
Roof, Walter James, Rev. 227
Rosaries 7
Roschen, Arnold 32-34
Rose, Charles Alexander, Rev. 177
Rothrock, Lewis Hazelius 212
Rothrock, Samuel, Rev. 70, 97, 115,
        139, 166, 177, 184, 185, 189,
        194, 195, 203
Rotterdam, Netherlands 18
Roundheads 120
Rowan Bible Society 118
Rowan County Lutheran Pastors'
        Association 227
Rowan County Minister's Association
    224
Rowan County, NC 23, 25, 26, 27-32,
        37-39, 46, 56, 77, 78, 80, 98,
        105, 115, 204, 223, 243, 260,
        268
Rowan County's *Carolina Watchman*
    84
Rude, Anders Rudolph, Rev. 118, 154,
        163, 169, 179, 202
Rudisill, A. P., Mrs. 229, 255
Rudisill, Barbara Yount, Mrs. 259
Rudisill, Fred H. 265
Rudisill, Michael 72
Rudisill, Phillip 78
Rueckert, J. F. 204
Runcie, Robert, Anglican Bishop 287
Rural Hall, NC 35, 268
Ryswick, Peace of 6

Sabbath, Respect for 130
Sabine Cross Roads 127
Sacrament of the Altar 28
Sacraments 58
Sacred Harp 200
Sacred Heart College 300
Sacred Heart Roman Catholic,
        Brevard, NC 286
Safrit, Catherine 299
Safrit, Gary Lee, Rev. 302
Safrit, Roy S. 263
Saga City, Japan 226
Saga Prefecture, Japan 226
St. Andrew's, Columbia, SC 246
St. Andrew's, Concord, NC 196, 209
St. Andrew's, Hickory, NC 180, 197,
        229, 230, 244, 255, 256, 260,
        261, 263-266, 276, 299, 300,
        304, 310, 312, 322, 326
St. Andrew's, Mt. Airy, NC 282, 293
St. Andrew's, New Bern, NC 250
St. Ann's Church
    Augsburg, Germany 18
St. David's, Kannapolis, NC 250, 297
St. David's, Tom's Brook, VA 246
St. Enoch, Rowan County, NC 47, 71,
        178, 196, 203, 207, 228, 243
St. Jacob's, Chapin, SC 224, 246
St. Jacob's, Edinburg, VA 246
St. Jacob's, Lexington County, SC 180
St. Jacob's, Rockingham, VA 246
St. James Episcopal, Hendersonville,
        NC 286
St. James, Concord, NC 70, 71, 117,
        131, 133, 162, 178, 203, 206,
        207, 209, 222, 228, 230, 233,
        238, 244, 245, 255, 256,
        262-264, 277, 281, 284, 298,
        299, 302, 304
St. James, Fayetteville, NC 250, 283,
        303, 308, 326
St. James, Greene County, TN 50, 73
St. James, Leesville, SC 246
St. James, Lexington County, SC 180
St. James, Newton, NC 141, 180, 205,
        229, 300
St. James, Rockwell, NC 223, 244, 256,
        259, 283
St. James, Shenandoah, VA 246
St. John's Reformed Church, SC 26
St. John's, Asheboro, NC 250

St. John's, Cabarrus County, NC 24,
        34, 47, 49, 71, 98, 125, 128,
        133, 154, 166, 172, 178, 185,
        192, 199, 205, 207, 208, 222,
        228, 244, 260-262, 289, 303,
        304
St. John's, Catawba County, NC 47,
        50, 73, 130
St. John's, Charleston, SC 25, 89, 134
St. John's, Cherryville, NC 196, 234,
        244, 258-261, 303, 304, 326
St. John's, Conover, NC 72, 117, 209
St. John's, Hudson, NC 225, 245
St. John's, Lenoir, NC 197, 248
St. John's, Lexington County, SC 130,
        180
St. John's, Lincoln County, NC 50
St. John's, Pelion, SC 246
St. John's, Pomaria, SC 25, 246
St. John's, Salisbury, NC 24, 47, 49,
        84, 140, 145, 154, 178, 204,
        207-209, 213, 222, 225, 227,
        228, 232-236, 238-240, 244,
        247, 248, 252, 254, 255, 256,
        259-264, 271, 273, 274, 276,
        281-284, 289, 290, 298, 305,
        318
St. John's, Statesville, NC 197,
        229-231, 256, 259, 260, 262,
        304
St. John's, Taylorsville, NC 225
St. John's, Timberville, VA 246
St. John's, Wythe County, VA 49, 132
St. John-in-the-Wilderness Episcopal,
        Flat Rock, NC 286
St. Luke's, Bear Poplar, NC 206, 208
St. Luke's, Charlotte, NC 298, 304
St. Luke's, Conover, NC 197, 291
St. Luke's, Davidson County 32
St. Luke's, Lexington, NC 35, 125,
        270, 309
St. Luke's, Lincolnton, NC 35, 47, 245
St. Luke's, Manasses, VA 246
St. Luke's, Monroe, NC 197
St. Luke's, Mt. Ulla, NC 141
St. Luke's, Rowan County, NC 28
St. Luke's, Shallotte, NC 325
St. Luke's, Shenandoah, VA 246
St. Luke's, Summerville, SC 245
St. Luke's, Taylorsville, NC 197, 321
St. Luke's, Tyro, NC 198

St. Mark's, Asheville, NC 268, 295, 326
St. Mark's, Blowing Rock, NC 256
St. Mark's, Charlotte, NC 70, 115, 117, 128, 133, 154, 192, 206, 207, 209, 222, 228, 230, 232, 234, 244, 251, 255, 256, 258, 260, 262, 264, 275, 293, 299, 303, 304, 310, 325
St. Mark's, Cherryville, NC 35, 47
St. Mark's, China Grove, NC 193, 196, 208, 222, 227, 228, 230, 234, 240, 256, 259, 262, 268, 281, 282, 298, 304
St. Mark's, Claremont, NC 197, 321
St. Mark's, Gaston County, NC 130
St. Mark's, Lumberton, NC 251, 259
St. Mark's, Mooresville, NC 223, 228, 255, 256, 270, 283
St. Mark's, Salisbury, NC 195, 323
St. Martin's, Albemarle, NC 47
St. Martin's, Concord, NC 47
St. Martin's, Maiden, NC 197
St. Mary's (college) in Raleigh 171
St. Mary's, Forestville, VA 246
St. Mary's, Mt. Jackson, VA 224
St. Mary's, Shenandoah, VA 180
St. Matthew's, Caldwell County, NC 225, 245
St. Matthew's, Charleston, SC 283
St. Matthew's, Kings Mountain, NC 196, 224, 230, 234, 244, 255, 261-265
St. Matthew's, Rowan County, NC 70, 71, 128, 130, 133, 244
St. Matthew's, Shenandoah County, VA 180
St. Matthew's, Tom's Brook, VA 180, 246
St. Matthew's, Wilmington, NC 196, 317
St. Michael's, High Point, NC 293
St. Michael's, Iredell County, NC 71, 128, 178, 203, 231
St. Michael's, SC 81
St. Paul's Seminary 74
St. Paul's, Alamance County, NC 25, 71, 75
St. Paul's, Asheville, NC 209
St. Paul's, Burlington, NC 300
St. Paul's, Catawba County, NC 25, 26, 47, 71, 72, 97, 321

St. Paul's, Crouse, NC 197
St. Paul's, Dallas, NC 197
St. Paul's, Durham, NC 258, 288, 294, 302
St. Paul's, Gilbert, SC 246
St. Paul's, Hamlet, NC 250
St. Paul's, Hickory, NC 197, 321
St. Paul's, Iredell County, NC 70, 71, 291
St. Paul's, Lexington County, SC 180, 224
St. Paul's, Lincoln County, NC 49, 50
St. Paul's, Orange County, NC 71
St. Paul's, Orkney Springs, VA 246
St. Paul's, Page County, VA 224
St. Paul's, Pomaria, SC 30, 82
St. Paul's, Rockingham, VA 246
St. Paul's, Salisbury, NC 47, 185, 178, 204, 207, 222, 234, 244, 264, 275, 298, 299, 304
St. Paul's, Shenandoah, VA 246
St. Paul's, Startown, NC 224
St. Paul's, Taylorsville, NC 198
St. Paul's, Timberville, VA 246
St. Paul's, Wilmington, NC 70, 128, 131, 172, 178, 196, 198, 207, 214, 222, 223, 228, 232, 244, 254, 256, 262
St. Paul's, Wythe County, VA 49
St. Peter's, Catawba County, NC 130, 180
St. Peter's, Chapin, SC 246
St. Peter's, Lexington County, SC 73, 180, 224, 246
St. Peter's, Rowan County, NC 47, 178, 207, 230
St. Peter's, Shenandoah, VA 224, 246
St. Peter's, Southport, NC 293
St. Peter's, Wythe County, VA 71
St. Philip's, Raleigh, NC 293
St. Stephen's, Cabarrus County, NC 47, 71, 178
St. Stephen's, Hickory, NC 47, 231, 263, 270, 304, 309
St. Stephen's, Lenoir, NC 224, 248
St. Stephen's, Lexington, SC 51
St. Stephen's, Tom's Brook, VA 246
St. Thomas, Chapin, SC 246
St. Thomas, Charlotte, NC 252, 303
St. Thomas, Lexington County, SC 224
St. Timothy, Havelock, NC 252

St. Timothy, Hickory, NC 197, 259
Salaries of pastors 198, 252
Salem Boarding School 171
Salem College 236
Salem seminary 180
Salem, Catawba County 73
Salem, Edinburg, VA 246
Salem, Lincoln County, NC 35, 47, 50,
        72, 73, 88, 142, 169, 183, 205
Salem, MA 77
Salem, NC 23-25, 27, 35, 46, 57, 228
Salem, Rowan County, NC 70, 140,
        231, 222, 304
Salem, Taylorsville, NC 198
Salem, VA 179, 216, 236, 269, 311, 312
Sales tax on food 329
Salisbury District 78
Salisbury, NC 22-24, 32, 34, 35, 40, 41,
        104, 105, 131, 132, 133, 171,
        194, 199, 209, 213, 214, 231,
        232, 236-240, 244, 247, 251,
        257, 260, 262, 263, 265, 274,
        282, 289, 294, 303, 307, 310,
        312, 323, 327
Salkehatchie River 20
Saluda River, SC 26, 57
Salvation 3, 50, 182, 188, 222
Salzburgers 8, 18, 19, 24, 30, 33
Sammlung von erbaulichen Gesaengen,
        zum Gebrauch bey dem oeffe
        199
San Antonio, TX 326
Sanders, B. Sidney, Most Rev.,
        Episcopal 287
Sandy Creek, Davidson County, NC
        71, 178
Sanford, NC 308, 312
Santmiers, George 269
Sarah, girl named 80
Sardis, Hickory, NC 141
Sassafras tree 123
Sasse, Bernhard H. 200
Sauer, Kenneth, Rev. 317
Saur, Christopher 199, 200
Savannah River 5, 8, 17, 19, 26
Savannah, GA 5, 19, 30, 145, 187, 189,
        250, 283
Saxe-Gotha, SC 20
Saxons 13
Scandinavian(s) 196, 224
Scattered Lutherans 195

Schaeffer, George Francis, Rev. 171,
        211, 212
Schaeffer, Harry Brent, Rev. 240, 261,
        267
Schaff, Philip 48
Schaidt, J. G., Rev. 211
Scheck, J. D., Rev. 70, 98, 205
Scheck, John Daniel, Rev. 121, 127,
        129, 172
Scherer, Jacob, Rev. 48, 70
Scherer, Melanchthon Gideon
        Groseclose, Rev. 208, 211,
        240
Scherer, Simeon, Rev. 70, 183, 205
Schickel, Peter, Rev. 141
Schlump, John Martin 199
Schmucker, Beale M., Rev. 145, 187
Schmucker, George, Rev. 168
Schmucker, J. G., Rev. 54
Schmucker, Samuel Simon 89, 181
Schnapp, Lawrence 78
Schober, Gottlieb, Rev. 45, 46, 48, 57,
        58, 59, 60, 62-65, 81, 202, 209
Schoepf, Albin F., Brig. Gen. 116
Schofield, Union general 152
Scholarship grants 299
Schramm, John 300
Schramm, Mary 300
Schriber, Robert T., Father, Episcopal
        287
Schroder, Henry Andrew, Rev. 294
Schulze, John Christian, Rev. 15
Schuylkill River 20
Schwarmer 47
Schwartz, John G. 97
Schwarzach 8
Scotch Irish 21, 23
Scouting 265, 303
Seaford, P. A. 98
Seagle, Inez 256
Seagle, Mabel 260
Sears, Barnas 142
Seattle, Washington 283
Second career students 327
Second Creek in Rowan County 27-30
Second Great Awakening 37, 40, 48,
        56, 87, 119, 210
Secret lodges & societies 151, 239
Secretary of Christian education 245,
        281, 290
Secretary of the synod 281
Secretary of the ULCA 251

Sectionalism 94, 107, 164
Secularism 296
Segregation 221
Seip, Rev. 129
Seitz, Myra 300
Self-administration of the Lord's
        Supper 190
Selling of goods or services in the name
        of the church 299
Seminary Board of Trustees 267
Seminary endowment 307
Senate gallery 100
Senecker, James E., Rev. 168
Separate black congregations 83
Service Book and Hymnal 254, 298
Service flag 274
Sesquicentennial convention at St.
        John's, Salisbury 273
Setzer, Charles Peter, Mrs. 302
Setzer, Charles Peter, Rev. 302
Setzer, Henry 215
Seventh Jubilee 166
Shalom Conference 300
Shaner, Martin Luther, Rev. 253
Sharon, Gibsonville, NC 196, 230
Sharon, Statesville, NC 70
Sharpsburg, VA 115
Sheets, Jacob 16, 298
Shelby, NC 326
Shelby, Robert Fitzhugh, Jr., Rev. 271
Shelfer 16
Shell, Ephriam 72
Shell, Austin Focht, Rev. 205, 284
Shenandoah Valley, VA 21, 22, 200
Shenk, Elonzo Ashby, Rev. 261
Shepherd of the Hills, Sylva, NC 293
Shepherd of the Sea, Atlantic Beach,
        NC 293
Shepherds Cross Roads, Mooresville,
        Iredell Co., North Carolin 38
Sheppard, J. D., Mrs. 259
Sherer, Daniel, Rev. 83
Sherman, William Tecumseh, Gen.
        125, 126, 129
Shiloh, Forsyth County 32, 35
Shiloh, Hickory, NC 197
Shimpoch, John, Col. 133
Shirey, Ella Belle 206, 208, 256
Shirey, John Daniel, Mrs. 207, 208
Shirey, John Daniel, Rev. 208, 211
Shirey, Julia 207

Shoffner, Robert A., Rev. 283, 300,
        301
Shuford, George Washington, Rev.
        291
Sieg, Paul, Mrs. 269
Sieg, Paul, Rev. 269
Sifford, Paul A., Dr. 183
Sigman, Walter Augustus, Rev. 253
Sigmon, Jane 245
Simons, John 16
Singers Glen, VA 200
Sink, Olin W., Mrs. 259
Sink, Voigt Mock, Rev. 253
Sinking Spring, Greene County, TN 50
Sinking Springs congregation 129
Sipe, Vernon O. 270
Sipe, Vernon O., Mrs. 270
Sipes Orchard Home for Boys, near
        Conover, NC 270, 308, 309
Skilled care 310
Skills required of the parish pastor 296
Slavery 76, 78, 79, 86, 87, 90, 91, 93,
        94, 96, 99, 101-105, 107, 141,
        147
Sloop, Leon E. 261
Slough, Lillian 207
Small Catechism 192, 197, 201
Small pox 123
Smeltzer, J. P., Rev. 118
Smeltzer, Josiah Pierce, Rev. 118, 154,
        165, 179, 203
Smith, Gerritt 147
Smith, J. Roun 232
Smith, Jasper J., Rev. 253
Smith, John M., Rev. 129, 141, 170,
        179, 183, 184, 186, 215
Smith, L. L., Prof. 230
Smith, Marcus C. 282, 327
Smithdeal, John L., Rev. 129, 172
Smyre, Fred R. 263
Snider, Arnold H. 233
Snyder, Nancy 326
Social ministry 251, 269, 270, 282, 288,
        308, 315, 328, 329
Social Ministry Committee 271, 294,
        311, 313, 314, 329
Social Ministry Organizations Board
        317
Social statements 329
Society for the Promotion of Christian
        Knowledge 18

Society for the Propagation of the
      Gospel in Foreign Parts 17,
      29
Society of Friends 171
Soelle, George 25, 27
"Soldier's Prayer, A" 121
Soli Deo Gloria 298
Solid gold cross 281
Solomon's Church, Greene County,
      TN 47, 50, 73
Solomon's, Shenandoah County, VA
      73, 180, 224, 246
South African investments 316
South Bend, IN 265
South Carolina 1, 5, 13, 19, 20, 22, 24,
      25, 26-28, 30, 31, 55, 57, 61,
      64, 76, 77, 80-82, 90, 95, 96,
      98, 99-105, 125, 126, 131, 133,
      146, 154, 165, 169, 172, 187,
      194, 206, 215, 224, 229, 236,
      237, 240, 251, 257, 327
SC Conference of the TN Synod 229
South Carolina Gazette 20
SC Synod 64, 75, 85, 86, 89, 91, 96-99,
      117, 118, 134, 161, 165, 180,
      206, 212, 237, 245, 246, 251,
      266-268, 270, 275, 307, 323,
      325, 327, 328
SC Synod's Seminary, Lexington, SC
      75
South's "peculiar institution" 80
Southampton County, VA 84
Southeastern District 285
Southeastern District of the ALC 318
Southeastern Synod 307, 323, 327
Southern Baptist Convention 115
Southern Church Convention 97-99
Southern church paper 97, 98, 118
Southern Conference 223, 247
Southern District 288
Southern General Synod 182
Southern Lutheran, The 119, 121, 125,
      161, 162
Southern Seminary 75, 86, 245, 267,
      272, 273, 283, 284, 304, 306,
      314, 316, 320, 325, 329
Southwest VA Synod 206
Southwestern District 288
Southwestern VA 23, 31, 34, 70
Southwestern VA Synod 122, 130, 141,
      172, 206

Sox, Enoch Jefferson, Rev. 223, 225,
      227
Sox, Irene 260
Sox, Rosa 261
Sox, Samuel, Mrs. 259
Spain 3, 77, Crown of 3
Spanish Succession, War of 3, 4, 6
SPCK, (Society for the Promotion of
      Christian Knowledge) 18
Speagle, Frederick Martin Luther, Rev.
      227
Special Conference 81, 82
Speer, Robert E. 232
Spencer, NC 196
Spener, Philip, Rev. 32, 54
Spiritual welfare of the slaves 79
Spotswood, Alexander, Lieutenant-
      Governor of VA 5, 17
Spotsylvania County, VA 17
Spracher, Levi Bittle, Rev. 238
Springfield, OH 76, 264, 327
Stackel, VA 299
Stamey, Mary 302
Standard Leagues 261
Stanger, John 34
Stanger, Unknown first name 34
Stanly County, NC 27, 30, 128
Starr, Charles Marion, Rev. 290
Starr, Gail A. 317
Starrtown, NC 205
State Board of Education 236, 267
State Board of Health 271
State brotherhood 262, 264
State juvenile justice system 311
State Luther League of NC 231
State men's organization 265
State Missionary 196
State Normal College 236
State Rights Whigs 104
State sales tax on food 315
Statement of mission 316
Statesville, NC 229, 247, 323
Statistician 281
Statutory law 295
Staunton, VA 162, 163, 169, 204
Steck, Charles F., Jr., Rev. 253
Steck, Charles F., Rev. 253
Steere, Amos 112
Steffy, Sidney D., Rev. 125
Stelling, Thomas Osborne, Rev. 253
Stephenson, James, Rev. 294
Stevens, Thaddeus 147

Stewardship 245, 288, 290, 299, 331
Stewardship Committee 273, 314
Stewardship Sector Project School 251
Stewart the Steward 259
Stickley, Vastine Rinker, Rev. 177
Stieff, Charles M. 204
Stiemke, Frederick A., Rev. 295
Stirewalt 4
Stirewalt, Arthur Julius, Rev. 207, 232
Stirewalt, Catharine, Sister 256, 260
Stirewalt, Jerome Paul, Rev. 179, 223
Stirewalt, John N., Rev. 179
Stirewalt, John, Capt. 204
Stirewalt, Martin Luther, Jr., Rev. 271
Stirewalt, Martin Luther, Rev. 232,
        240
Stirewalt, Martin Luther, Sr., Rev. 252
Stockman, J. Edgar, Rev. 253
Stoever, John Caspar 15
Stoever, John Caspar, Jr. 15
Stoever, John Caspar, Sr. 15-17, 25
Stoever, Mary Magdalena, Mrs. 15
Stokes County, NC 22, 23, 27, 30, 78
Stoneman, George F., Gen. 125
Storch, Carl August Gottlieb, Rev. 32,
        33, 35, 38, 40, 46, 48, 56, 58-
        60, 80, 81
Stork, Rev. 129
Stout, Paul, Mrs., (Kathleen) 255, 299
Strategy for the Seventies 306
Strength for Mission 316
Strobel, E. M., Mrs. 212
Strobel, Philip A., Rev. 89, 901 97, 129,
        172, 212
Strobel, W. D., Rev. 129
Stroup, Herbert Wilson, Jr., Rev. 253
Stryker, T. L. 263
Student ministries 294
Student Volunteer Movement 232
Stump, Joseph 235
Stuttgart, Germany 34
Subscriptions 248, 273
Subscriptions for the pastor's salary
        237
Sugg, L. L. 215
Sullivan, Clara 257
Summer camp 243
Summer School for Church Workers
        266, 268
Summer, Cathy 326
Summit Rule 190

Sumner, Charles, Senator 99-101, 150,
        160
Superintendent of home missions 246
Supreme Court's Dred Scott decision
        102
Surratt 64
Surry County, NC 78
Suther, Samuel, Rev. (German
        Reformed) 27-29
Swabians 13
Swartz, William P. 206
Sweden 3, 17, 77
Swicegood, Dermont Fritz, Rev. 309
Swing, Stafford Leroy, Rev. 248
Swiss 4, 5, 9, 13, 14
Swiss Reformed 26
Switzerland 14
Symbolical Books 182
Symbols of our Church 202
Synod Assembly 321
Synod congregational roster 275
Synod Convention Sites 244
Synod Council 318, 321, 322, 330
Synod Endowment Fund 330
Synod headquarters manager 281
Synod Mission Profile 312, 316
Synod of SC 166
Synod of Southwest VA 70, 133
Synod of Texas 153
Synod of the German Reformed
        Church 153
Synod of Western VA 132, 133, 163
Synod Presidents, Prior to division 46
Synod staff 290
Synod Sunday 289
Synod's apportionment 273
Synod's Committee on the State of the
        Church 252
Synod's Executive Board 300
Synod's history 247
Synod's mission 250
Synod's rules of procedure 277
Synod's synodical headquarters
        building 274
Synod-LCA relationship 275
Synodical Alignments 70, 131, 152,
        216, 238, 246, 283, 323
Synodical auxiliary 257-259, 277, 298
Synodical brotherhood 234, 263, 264
Synodical budget 273
Synodical Christian education secretary
        307

Synodical constituting convention 276
Synodical constitution 277
Synodical convention 248, 317
Synodical Executive Committee 248,
        264
Synodical field secretary 222
Synodical headquarters in Salisbury,
        NC 245, 246, 257, 282, 299,
        321
Synodical institutions 247, 273
Synodical Lay Leadership 304
Synodical lines 252
Synodical Lutheran Church Women
        Presidents 299
Synodical Mission Committee 250
Synodical missionary 222-224
Synodical missionary posts 249
Synodical multimedia center 322
Synodical paper 248, 291
Synodical publication 247, 291, 324
Synodical representatives 288
Synodical secretary 281
Synodical secretary of Christian
        education 302
Synodical staff 246, 283
Synodical Women's Missionary Society
        248
Synodical women's organization 323
Synodical Youth Committee 300, 301
Synodwide appeals for gifts 316

Takimoto, Kockichiro, Rev. 226
Tanzania 299
Tariff laws 95, 104
Task Force on Communications 324
Task Force on Family Living 314
Task Force on Justice and Social
        Change 271, 313, 314
Taverns 22
Taxes 2
Teacher education workshop on human
        relations 314
Temperance 236
Temporary places of worship 292
Ten Commandments 192, 201
Ten Imperial towns 2
TN Luther League 231
Tennessee Synod 46, 47, 59, 61, 62, 64,
        65, 70, 72-76, 83, 88, 91, 117, 118,
        121, 129, 133, 134, 141, 144, 160,
        161, 167-170, 172, 181, 182-191,
        194, 196-199, 202, 203, 205-207

Tennessee Synod, Continued
        210, 212-218, 221, 222, 223-227,
        229-231, 234, 235, 236-240, 243,
        245, 246, 249, 254, 261, 321
TN Synod college 217
TN Synod congregations 217
TN Synod Convention Sites 50, 73,
        142, 180, 224
TN Synod Presidents 72, 129, 141, 179,
        223
TN Synod, Reorganized 74, 160, 169,
        321
TN Synod's professor of theology 217
Tenure of synodical officers 277
Tenure of the editor 291
Terrorism 2
Terry, Roger Harold, Jr., Mrs. 298,
        324
Terry, Roger Harold, Jr., Rev. 298,
        324
Texas 153, 171
Texas Lutheran College 327
Texas Synod 131, 153
Texas, Republic of 104
Thanksgiving 254
Thanksgiving Clothing Drive 315
Theological Conference for Women
        300
Theological seminary 74, 96, 97, 157,
        159, 165-167, 178, 179, 185
Theological study 50
Theus, Christian, Rev. 26
Thirty Years' War 1, 2, 6, 7
Thomas, Eloise D. 317
Thomasius, Christian 33
Thomasville, NC 223
Thompson, Robert, Mrs. 302
Thornburg, J. Lewis, Mrs. 258, 259
Thornburg, J. Lewis, Rev. 265, 268,
        307
Thyatira Presbyterian Church, Rowan
        County, NC 39
Timberville, VA 167
Timbuktu 77
Torchbearers 258
Tories 30, 31
Townsand, Mother 235
Trailer sites 308
Trainer, John E., Dr. 306
Transition Team 318
Trapier, First name unknown 152
Travel restrictions 266

Travis, Joseph 84
Treasurer 272, 290
Treasurer's Report 292
Treaty of Westphalia 7
Trent River 16
Tretheway, Jack Evans, Rev. 253
Trexler, E. R., Mrs. 255, 256, 258
Trexler, Edgar R., Jr., Rev. 284, 317
Trexler, Zeb B. 263, 265
Trinity College 236
Trinity Oaks 328
Trinity Seminary in Columbus, Ohio
        321, 327, 329
Trinity, Cabarrus County, NC 140,
        153, 207
Trinity, Lancaster, PA 25
Trinity, Landis, NC 223, 243
Trinity, Lincoln County 73
Trinity, Manasses, VA 246
Trinity, Reading, PA 25
Trinity, Rockingham, VA 246
Trinity, Rocky Mount, NC 260, 261,
        304
Trinity, Sanford, NC 250, 263
Trinity, Vale, NC 47, 71
Troutman, Cheryl L. 314
Troutman, Elmer 260
Troutman, Evelyn 260
Troutman, M. F. P. 231
Troutman, Robert Love, Rev. 281,
        307, 328
Tryon, Governor 29
Tulsa University, Oklahoma 281
Tulsa, Oklahoma 281
Tunes, Book of 227
Turner, D. McNeill, Dr. 147, 148
Turner, J. H., Rev. 211
Turner, Nat 84, 149
Tuscarora War 15
Twenty-eighth NC Regiment 116
Twenty-ninth VA Regiment 115
Twin Lakes Center 310
Tyson, Bryan 143

U. S. Office of Defense Transportation
        266
ULCA 231, 233, 239, 240, 243-247,
        250, 251, 252, 257, 259, 260,
        262, 265, 267, 273-275, 281
ULCA Board of American Missions
        245, 246
ULCA Board of Higher Education 268

ULCA Board of Parish Education 249
ULCA Board of Social Missions 281,
        283
ULCA Brotherhood 262, 265
ULCA Commission on Organizational
        Structure 247
ULCA Division of Parish Education
        266
ULCA Foreign Mission Board 252
ULCA merger 245
ULCM 265, 266
ULCW 257
Ulrich, John 26
Ultraism 86
Unaltered Augsburg Confession 181,
        187, 188
Union armies 154
Union blockade 123
Union Theological Seminary 245
Union, Rowan County, NC 34, 35, 47,
        49, 71, 178, 207, 209, 222, 238,
        248
Unit literacy coordinator 299
United Lutheran Brotherhood 234
United Lutheran Church Men of the
        Lutheran Synod of North
        Caro 265
United Lutheran Church Women 257
United Methodist Church in Western
        NC 288
United Synod 216, 225
United Synod Board of Home Missions
        225
United Synod of the South 203, 227
United Synod South 213, 214, 218,
        222, 225, 228, 229, 232,
        236-239
University Lutheran Church,
        Cambridge, Massachusetts
        327
University of Chicago 283
University of Gottingen 25, 29, 33
University of Halle 1, 33
University of Hamburg in Germany
        283
University of Helmstaedt 33
University of NC 105, 236, 252
University of NC at Chapel Hill 76
University of NC at Chapel Hill, NC
        76, 283
University of Oklahoma 306
University of SC 245

University of Tuebingen 34
Unpaid pledges 271
Upper Peaked Mountain,
        McGaheysville, VA 25
Urlsperger, Samuel, Rev. 18
Ursinus 6
Utica, New York 51

Vacation Church School 300
Vade Mecum near Rural Hall, NC 268
Vanderbilt University 323
Velthusen, Johann Caspar, Rev. 29,
        31-34, 40
Venezuela 147
Vesey, Denmark 149
Vespers 254, 266
Vice pastor 277
Vicksburg, VA 124, 146
Vietnam War 253
Viola, Alex, Rev. 286
Violence 315, 329
VA Collegiate Institute at Salem
VA Conference 168, 246
VA Conference of the TN Synod 167,
        169
VA Resolutions 95
VA Synod 98, 117, 131, 157-159, 163,
        166, 187, 246, 267, 309, 323,
        328
VA Synod Sunday School 210
Visitor 142, 204
Voelkert, Barbara 300
Volunteer reading aides 299
von Leibnitz, Gottfried Wilhelm 33
von Mosheim, Johann Lorenz 33
von Wolff, Christian Freiherr 33
Voting Rights Act 315

Wachovia, Carolina settlement 25
Wainwright, Goeffrey, Rev. 288
Wakayama, Japan 226
Wake Advancement Center 312
Wake County Citizens for Improved
        Youth Services 311
Wake County, NC 311, 312
Wake Forest College 236, 306
Walker, David 84
Walker, Leroy Pope, Confederate
        Secretary of War 103, 113
Walker, Robert Glenn, Rev. 254, 294
Waller, John L., Rev. 90
Wannemacher, John Henry, Rev. 225

War Between the States 200
War Committee on Conventions 275
War of Spanish Succession 4
War of the League of Augsburg 2, 3
War of the Spanish Succession 3, 6
War with Mexico 96
War-time gas rationing 255
War-time service centers in NC 260
War-time travel restrictions 266
Wartime conventions 274
Wartime draft 236
Wasa, Tsunenari, Rev. 226
Washington, D. C. 146, 231, 253, 293,
        324
Watauga County, NC 235, 256, 258
Waterman (Wortman?) 25
Webb, Carl 303
Webb, J. Kenneth, Rev. 270, 309
Week of Prayer 207, 256
Weekday Church School 300
Weekly communion 298
Weidner (Whitener), Henry 23
Weinhauer, William G., Episcopal
        Bishop 286-288
Weiser, R. B., Rev. 52-55
WELCA 325, 326
Welker, George William, Dr., German
        Reformed 88
Wentworth Street Church, Charleston,
        SC 156
Wertz, J. Q., Mrs. 206, 208
Wertz, John E., Rev. 291
Wesleyan Methodist church 105
Wessinger, Bernice Justus, Rev. 223
Wessinger, Elmore Lafayette, Rev. 223
West Columbia, SC 303
West PA Synod 75
West TN Synod 97
West Virginia 224
Western Carolina Male Academy 75,
        170
Western Conference 186, 247
Western Diocese of NC, Episcopal
        Church 288
Western District Brotherhood 263
Western District Synod in Ohio 160
Western NC Conference of the United
        Methodist Chur 288
Western Seminary at Fremont,
        Nebraska 281
Western VA Synod 97, 115, 131
Westphalia, Peace of 6

Westphalia, Treaty of 7
Wetzel, Henry, Rev. 168
Wetzel, Luther, Candidate 168
Whig Party 104
Whisnant, Clarence L. 268
White Haven 61
White House 150
White Oak Run 17
White Rock, Lexington, SC 82, 237, 269
White, J. Campbell 232
Whitefield, George 19
Whiteville Episcopalians 287
Whiteville Lutherans 287
Whittecar, George Richard, Rev. 277, 281, 282, 284, 288, 296, 311, 313
Whittecar, Ruth 261
Whitteker, J. E., Rev. 227
Wike, Polycarp Cyprian, Rev. 179
Wilds, Bruce E. 269
William, John, Elector 6
William III, King of England 8
Williams, F. Wayne, Rev. 328
Wilmington, DE 51
Wilmington, NC 123, 124, 131, 152, 177, 192, 196, 204, 228, 237, 245, 294, 301, 310, 312, 329
Wilmot, David 96
Wilmot Proviso 96
Winchester, VA 22, 54, 178, 181
Wine, blackberry 129
Wine, grape 129
Winecoff, Ransom 133
Winnsboro, SC 126
Winston, NC 196, 213
Winston-Salem, NC 23, 192, 196, 207-209, 213, 222, 230, 247, 285, 294, 301, 317, 323, 328
Winter, Margaret 322, 323
Wisconsin 253
Wise, Curtis 260
Wise, Walter Daniel, Rev. 227
Wittenberg College, Springfield, Ohio 76
Wittenberg, Germany 28
Wittenberg, Granite Quarry, NC 196
WMS 229, 256
Wobler, David A., Rev. 318
Wolf, S. A., Prof. 215
Wolfe, Lester, Rev. 285
Wolff (von), Christian Freiherr 33

Woman's Home and Foreign Missionary Society 206, 228, 229
Woman's Memorial, (Later Emmanual), High Point, NC 223, 228
Woman's Missionary Conference for the Southern Lutheran Church 228
Woman's Missionary Society 233
Women in Action for Mission, (Catholic) 300
Women in the Lutheran church in America 214
Women missionaries 257
Women seminarians 306
Women's dormitory 305
Women's Missionary Society 206, 229, 248, 257, 266
Women's Missionary Society Convention Sites 228
Women's Missionary Society of the Evangelical Lutheran TN Synod 229
Women's Missionary Society of the SC Synod 206
Women's Missionary Society of the ULCA 229, 252
Women's Missionary Society Presidents 228, 229
Women's Organization Convention Sites 256
Women's Organization Presidents 255
Women's synodical auxiliary 258
Woodland, NC 328
World Child, Inc. 312
World Hunger 315
World missions 252, 288
World War I 237
World War II 274, 294
World-Wide Communion Sunday 254
Worship 199, 227, 297
Worship and Music Committee 289
Worship leader 254
Worship practices 254
Worshippers expelled 6
Worth, Daniel, Rev., Wesleyan Methodist 105
Wortmann, Heinrich Burchard Gabriel "Wartmann" 25, 26
Wortmann, Laurentz 26
Wuerttemberg, Germany 34

Wyatt, Henry Lawson 111
Wythe County Court House, VA 34
Wytheville Female College in VA 201
Wytheville, VA 132, 201

Yadkin River 22, 23, 27, 40
Yadkin Valley 23
Yeager, Marie 230
Yoder, Conrad 24
Yoder, Classroom Building 306
Yoder, Harold Monroe, Rev. 254
Yoder, J. Larry, Rev. 317, 323
Yoder, M. C., Mrs. 255
Yoder, Robert Anderson, Rev. 179,
        197, 198, 199, 205, 215, 221,
        222, 224, 225
York, PA 21, 22
Yorktown, New York 49
Yost, John Louis, Rev. 267, 268
Yost, John Louis, Jr., Rev. 275, 276,
        284, 317
Young People's Federation 230
Young People's Missionary Societies
        230, 231, 233
Young Women's group 208
Yount, Joshua Alonzo, Rev. 227
Yount, Peter 215
Yount, Walter Nicholas, Rev. 304, 308
Youth activities 245, 300
Youth and Child Work 229
Youth Commission 284
Youth Committee 300, 301
Youth Convo 302
Youth ministry 288, 290, 300-302
Youth Ministry Committee 302
Youth Ministry Consultation Teams
        302
Youth Ministry in Action 302
Youth Ministry program 302
Youth Rally 302, 325

Ziegenbalg, Bartholomaeus 89
Zion Evangelical Lutheran Church, see
        also Organ Lutheran Church,
        Rowan County, NC 160, 201,
        204
Zion, Blountville, TN 74
Zion, Botetourt County, VA 49
Zion, Catawba County 35, 47, 73, 229,
        230
Zion, Edinburg, VA 246
Zion, Lexington, SC 73, 82, 180, 246

Zion, Manasses, VA 246
Zion, Shenandoah County, VA 73
Zion, Sullivan County, TN 50
Zion, Wythe County, VA 71
Zouberbuehler, Bartholomew 26
Zouberbuehler, Bartholomew, Jr. 26
Zubly, John Joachim 26
Zubly (Zubli), David 26
Zwingli, Huldrych 28

NOTES

NOTES